Ethnicity and Human Rights in Canada

A Human Rights Perspective on Ethnicity, Racism, and Systemic Inequality

Third Edition

Evelyn Kallen

OXFORD
UNIVERSITY PRESS
70 Wynford Drive, Don Mills, Ontario M3C 1J9
www.oup.com/ca

Oxford University Press is a department of the University of Oxford.
It furthers the University's objective of excellence in research, scholarship,
and education by publishing worldwide in

Oxford New York
Auckland Bangkok Buenos Aires Cape Town Chennai
Dar es Salaam Delhi Hong Kong Istanbul Karachi Kolkata
Kuala Lumpur Madrid Melbourne Mexico City Mumbai Nairobi
São Paulo Shanghai Taipei Tokyo Toronto

Oxford is a trade mark of Oxford University Press
in the UK and in certain other countries

Published in Canada
by Oxford University Press

First published 2003

National Library of Canada Cataloguing in Publication

Kallen, Evelyn, 1929–
Ethnicity and human rights in Canada : a human rights perspective
on ethnicity / Evelyn Kallen. — 3rd ed.

Includes bibliographical references and index.

ISBN 0-19-541742-9

1. Human rights—Canada.
2. Minorities—Legal Status, laws, etc.—Canada
I. Title

JC599.C3K34 2003 323.1'71 C2002-906145-8

Cover Design: Brett J. Miller

1 2 3 4 - 06 05 04 03
This book is printed on permanent (acid-free) paper ♾.
Printed in Canada

CONTENTS

TABLES

BOXES

ACKNOWLEDGMENTS

I wish to express my gratitude to Megan Mueller of Oxford University Press, whose helpful suggestions and unflagging support of my work greatly encouraged my efforts throughout the process of drafting this third edition of *Ethnicity and Human Rights in Canada*. I also wish to thank the anonymous reviewers whose insightful suggestions both at the proposal stage for the book and on the original draft helped me to clarify and to enhance my analysis. My research assistant at York University, Peter Dawson, provided me with a wealth of relevant material with which to update the book and its theoretical underpinnings. Thank you, Peter, for your research efforts, and for your continuing support.

I must also express my appreciation to my husband David and to my stepdaughter Joanna for their loving support and understanding. There were times when I couldn't blame my husband for wondering if I was wedded to my computer . . . no competition, David.

Finally, I wish to express my thanks to the thousands of students who helped me to develop and refine the theoretical framework for the three editions of this book, as well as to deepen my understanding of the human rights issues facing racial and ethnic minorities in Canada. I thank all of you.

Evelyn Kallen

PREFACE

In previous editions of this book, I have tried to provide an understanding, from a social scientific perspective, of the ways in which members of distinctive ethnic communities, intentionally or unintentionally, create barriers to caring relationships with members of different ethnic communities. My concern stems from an abiding commitment to universal human rights principles, principles built on the cardinal premise that all human beings, as members of humankind, share the same fundamental human rights and freedoms. This being so, how then, can we explain the dogged persistence of interethnic antagonisms as we move into the second year of the twenty-first century? And how can we explain the increasingly violent forms of terrorism and ethnic cleansing in which racism now expresses itself throughout the globe? Most importantly, what can we do about it? How can we ensure that the fundamental rights and freedoms of all human beings and the collective cultural rights of all ethnic communities are equally recognized and protected?

Each time that I have considered writing a new edition of this book, what has come to mind is a question I am continually asked by others who share my concern for human rights issues. Why, I am asked, have I continued to focus my attention on infractions of human rights in democratic societies—such as Canada—rather than on the more glaring human rights abuses in non-democratic societies, where human rights violations are routinely carried out by both governments and citizens with relative impunity? Notwithstanding the legitimacy of this concern, which currently occupies the attention of increasing numbers of human rights activists and legal scholars, the problem this question raises for me is its implication that human rights violations in democratic societies pale by comparison with such violations elsewhere and that our time would better be spent in addressing the more urgent situations demanding international action. My own position here is that if all human rights scholars and activists shifted their attention away from democratic societies, what could very well happen is that we neglect to 'clean up our own back yards'. It is relatively easy for people living in democratic contexts today to understand the occurrence of human rights abuses when they occur in politically repressive regimes where the right to dissent is virtually non-existent and glaring human rights violations are rampant. But how do we explain the continuing occurrence of violations of human rights in democratic societies like Canada where laws and social policies are predicated on human rights principles of justice and equity for all citizens?

Despite vastly increased legal protection for human rights across Canada in the post-Charter decades, and, perhaps, as a backlash against increased recognition and protection of the human rights of racial and ethnic minorities in this country, racism continues to ravage the multicultural fabric of Canadian society. This unsettling observation persuaded the author that the human rights message of the predecessors of this book needed to be forcefully restated and explicitly updated.

From a human rights perspective, the challenge for humankind posed by ethnocultural diversity is, first, to recognize and celebrate the *affinities* among all human beings as members of the same human species and, second, to foster a global climate of respect and tolerance for ethnocultural differences, in order to enable human beings, as such, to interact amicably across group boundaries.

In order to protect both the individual human rights of all persons as members of humankind, and the collective, cultural rights of all ethnocultural communities as distinct communities, international human rights instruments have been developed by the United Nations to serve as moral guidelines for human rights legislation within states. Following international guidelines, Canada has enacted human rights statutes in virtually every jurisdiction across the country. At the time of writing the original version of this book, the Canadian Charter of Rights and Freedoms (Constitution Act, 1982) had not yet been enacted. In the following two decades, under the national, constitutional standard provided by the Charter, protection for human rights under statutory codes across Canada has been expanded and strengthened. Yet, racism continues to flourish and thus to debase the very essence of human rights in Canada.

In this book, as in its predecessors, my primary focus is on group-based racial and ethnic inequalities in Canada. My conceptual framework incorporates international human rights principles in a social scientific analysis that provides, first, an understanding of the way in which human rights *violations* lead to the *social construction* of group-level racial/ethnic inequalities. Second, my analysis shows how members of Canadian racial/ethnic minorities can use *international human rights principles,* incorporated into Canada's system of legal protections for human rights, to gain *redress* against past human rights violations. Third, my analysis provides a prospectus for the future in which newer and stronger measures adopted by governments to reduce group-level racial and ethnic inequalities can enable Canada to move forward towards a goal of equity and justice for all.

Outline of Chapters

In the Introduction, I draw on the provisions of international human rights instruments in order to develop a comprehensive, human rights–oriented conceptual framework for the analysis of ethnicity and human rights in Canada. In Chapter 1, I critically assess the pseudo-biological concept of 'pure race', and I show how scientific evidence demonstrates, beyond doubt, that it is in the *unity* of the human species—over and above arbitrary racial divisions—that the biological roots of human rights are grounded. I then examine the way in which the *socially constructed* concept of race and ethnicity are used by dominant authorities to legitimate ideologies and practices of racism. In Chapter 2, I begin by defining the conceptual foundations of racism. My analysis then demonstrates the ways in which racist ideologies are employed by dominant authorities to justify human rights violations of members of racial/ethnic minorities. In Chapter 3, I begin my analysis by delineating the key dimensions of power—political, economic, and social—behind systems of structured inequality. The analysis to follow demonstrates how human rights violations, predicated on unequal power relations between dominant and subordinate populations, lead to the development of systems of social stratification and to the *social construction* of ethnic and other minorities. In Chapter 4, my analysis focuses on the vertical Canadian mosaic, Canada's ethnic stratification system. Here, my analysis reveals the crucial part played by violations of ethnic minority rights in creating and sustaining Canada's hierarchy of racial/ethnic inequality. In Chapter 5, I delineate the key variables affecting patterns of intraethnic and interethnic relations. Here, I show how ethnocentric and racist boundary-maintaining mechanisms employed by both minority and majority groups impact upon and reinforce dominant/subordinate ethnic relationships. In Chapter 6, my analysis reveals the disparity between Canadian democratic models of ethnic integration—designed to obtain justice and equity for all citizens as part of mainstream society—and the glaring reality of Canada's institutionalized racial/ethnic hierarchy. The analysis shows how racist public policies violate minority rights and thereby impede the processes of ethnic integration of immigrant and aboriginal racial/ethnic minorities into the mainstream Canadian culture. In Chapter 7, I begin my analysis by providing a conceptual framework for understanding the evolution of ethnic minority protest in Canada. I then explore the directions and the prospects for success of current minority rights movements among aboriginal peoples, immigrant racial and ethnic minorities, and the Franco-Quebecois. In Chapters 8 and 9, my analysis begins with a brief history of the development of the legal framework of (statutory and constitutional) human rights protection in Canada. In Chapter 8, the analysis focuses on current minority rights claims, put forward in cases of alleged racial/ethnic discrimination brought before statutory human rights commissions, tribunals, and courts. In Chapter 9, my analysis focuses on current minority rights claims, put forward in cases of alleged *legal* discrimination, brought before Constitutional courts and tribunals. In conclusion, I offer a prospectus for the future that outlines suggestions for human rights–oriented changes in law, public policy, and public practice. It could propel Canada towards a goal of justice and equity for all racial and ethnic groups across this country.

Caveat

This book addresses human rights issues from a social scientific, rather than a legal perspective. The concept of 'rights' is employed throughout this book to refer to 'just' or 'justifiable' claims for specified kinds of treatment made by or on behalf of individuals or social groups against other individuals, social groups, or the state.

This concept should not be confused with the legal concept of rights, that is, rights recognized as such in law.

E.K.
2003

Conceptualizing the Human Rights Approach: Guidelines from International Human Rights Instruments

Introduction

The theoretical framework of this book adopts a human rights approach to the social scientific analysis of issues of social inequality and social injustice confronting minorities in Canada, and throughout the globe.[1] In my view, the primary contribution of a human rights-oriented theoretical design is that this conceptual framework is rooted in the internationally recognized and endorsed human rights principles of *social equality* and *social justice* enshrined in the provisions of the International Bill of Human Rights (IBHR; United Nations 1978, 1988) and related covenants. These international human rights principles are advocated by United Nations authoritative bodies as *moral guidelines*, the universal human rights standards, to which all systems of justice should conform. As currently endorsed by the United Nations, fundamental human rights represent universally agreed-upon ideals for systems of justice throughout the globe.

What this means, with regard to furthering the social scientific understanding of social inequality and social injustice, is that issues of group-level inequality and injustice confronting virtually all minorities throughout the globe can be conceptualized and studied within the same overarching interpretive framework. Whether the social construction of minority status derives from attributes of race, religion, language, gender, sexual orientation age, or any other unjustly invalidated human or cultural characteristic, the human rights violations experienced by members of these subordinate populations can be addressed, and hopefully *redressed*, under the rubric of social equality and social justice endorsed in international human rights principles.

The latter point highlights another important consideration that influenced my decision to develop a human rights–oriented framework for the analysis of issues of social inequality and social injustice confronting minority groups. The current international human rights system provides members of minority groups with an internationally recognized basis for making human rights claims for equitable treatment. For minority populations, by definition, lacking the power to vastly change their disadvantaged status, the human rights approach provides a positive avenue through which to seek redress against past human rights violations and through which to seek new protections for their fundamental human rights in law and public policy.

The International Human Rights System

From a human rights perspective, international **human rights principles** set down in the provisions of various international human rights treaties and covenants are *prior to law:* essentially, they serve to challenge states to revise laws in ways that offer guaranteed protections for the rights of citizens, especially members of minority groups, against abuses of state power. However, human rights are not absolute: like democratic conceptions of citizenship, human rights principles link rights and responsibilities. There is always the question of the conflicts and paradoxes that beset democratic societies, not the least of which is 'the freedom of each versus the welfare of all'.

The human rights perspective that I adopt in this book accepts the key human rights principles advanced by the Charter of the United Nations, and endorsed in the provisions of current international human rights instruments as universal moral guidelines for human relations. Put another way, this book accepts the principles of the International Bill of Human Rights (United Nations 1978, 1988) and related UN covenants as human rights ideals, the universal human rights standards, to which all systems of justice should conform. This is not to say that these principles are absolute or that they leave nothing further to be desired. Indeed, international human rights principles are continuously evolving as nations and concerned citizens within nations reconsider them and develop ever newer covenants to more explicitly protect the human rights of persons and groups throughout the globe. What I am accepting, on a practical level, as universal human rights ideals, are the currently agreed-upon human rights principles endorsed and promoted by the United Nations.

Taking these principles as the international guidelines for systems of justice, this book will examine how powerful authorities within states endorsing these international standards can continue to *justify injustice* by supporting existing laws, social policies, and practices that violate the human rights of racial and ethnic minorities and thereby perpetuate group-level inequality and injustice within their societies.

The Development of International Human Rights Covenants

The various human rights covenants in which international principles of human rights are put forward were developed soon after the Second World War, in response to the world's outrage when the full account of Nazi atrocities—enslavement, torture, genocide—became public knowledge. These resolutions represent the attempt by the world's nations to prevent such *crimes against humanity* from ever happening again.

On 9 December 1948, the United Nations General Assembly approved the Convention on the Prevention and Punishment of the Crime of Genocide. On the very next day, 10 December 1948, the United Nations General Assembly adopted and proclaimed the Universal Declaration of Human Rights (UDHR), a declaration that represents a statement of principles or moral guidelines for the recognition and protection of fundamental human rights throughout the globe.

Articles 1 and 2 of the UDHR set out the three cardinal principles of human rights—**freedom, equality, and dignity**—as rights and freedoms everyone is entitled to without distinction of any kind. The 28 articles that follow identify particular rights and freedoms exemplifying the three central principles.

Since its proclamation, the Universal Declaration has had international impact, influencing national constitutions and laws, as well as later, more specific international declarations that build upon its central principles. The UDHR has become one of the most important statements of the twentieth century: the declaration has been called the Magna Carta of humanity. Yet, the primary author of the original draft of the declaration, a Canadian legal scholar, the late John Peters Humphrey, was not acknowledged as its author nor honoured by the Canadian government for his lifetime devotion to human rights, until the very last years of his life. It may therefore be appropriate, at this juncture, to present a profile of this remarkable human being—the father of the current international human rights system (see Box I-1).

The Articles in the Universal Declaration of Human Rights

In 30 articles, the Universal Declaration clearly states the fundamental rights of all human beings.

BOX I-1:PROFILE

John Humphrey and the Universal Declaration of Human Rights

On 10 December 1998, the day marking the 50th anniversary of the Universal Declaration of Human Rights—adopted by the United Nations on 10 December 1948—the CBC aired a documentary on the history of the drafting of the declaration and on the life of its primary author, Professor John Humphrey.

The documentary revealed that for 40 years it was assumed that the first draft of the UDHR was written by a French jurist. But, in fact, the declaration first started taking shape from the pen of a Canadian, the late John Peters Humphrey. Born in New Brunswick, educated at McGill, John Humphrey went on to become the Father of the modern human rights system.

On the program, Nelson Mandela remarked that John Humphrey was one of those rare men and women who make the world a theatre of their operations. Humphrey had always claimed that he wrote the first draft of the Universal Declaration of Human Rights. But until the last years of his life, hardly anyone believed him. For a long time, John Humphrey wasn't even honoured by his own government.

John Hobbins, the author of four volumes of monographs, based on the diaries of John Humphrey, points out that the Canadian government did nothing about this travesty until they became interested in celebrating the 50th anniversary of the UDHR. John Hobbins is a McGill University historian who became John Humphrey's literary executor, and friend. He has given much thought to the question of why one of the founders of the modern human rights system remains so little known and appreciated. He suggests that in order to be heard of you have to be popular with your government, and that John Humphrey spent a good 50 years at odds with the Canadian government. For, what may come as a surprise to Canadians in the 21st-century climate of support for human rights, the Canadian government was, from the very beginning, quite opposed to the Universal Declaration of Human Rights and equally opposed to the whole UN human rights system that John Humphrey strongly supported.

John Humphrey lived on the 'edge of greatness', as John Hobbins puts it, often in the shadow of greater characters, but also often the architect who put high ideals into practice. John Humphrey's life is the story of how human rights have emerged from obscurity to prominence.

Hobbins recounts that John Humphrey was born in Hampton, NB, in 1905. Humphrey did not have an easy childhood, and his experience in his early years had a profound influence upon him for the rest of his life. His father died before Humphrey's first birthday. He was an orphan at age of 11 when his mother died. At the age of 6 he had a serious accident, playing with fire. It took a year for doctors to decide, but finally they amputated his left arm. Humphrey, however, never looked on it as a handicap. He once remarked that he could even tie a bow tie. Nevertheless, according to Hobbins, school children teased him unmercifully because of his disability; they called him the one-armed Doukhobor. Not surprisingly, Humphrey developed a bad temper and he got into a number of fights with these children, all of which he lost because of his disability. The school authorities considered he had a chip on his shoulder so they exercised corporal punishment with some frequency. But, from this, Humphrey concluded that society can exercise a tyranny on the individual and fighting doesn't help, because fighting doesn't necessarily mean the right side wins. So he came to believe, from an early age, that you have to protect the individual from society, and from its government. So was born his lifetime interest in fundamental human rights.

John Humphrey arrived in Montreal in the 1920s with a potential or incipient social conscience that had not yet been stirred. Ronald St. John Macdonald knew Humphrey for 30 years. Macdonald is a professor of international law and a judge of the European Court of Human Rights. He recalls that when the young Humphrey was orphaned, his guardians set him on a track to become a banker. They supported him during four years at McGill University studying commerce. But, Macdonald recalls, Humphrey hated it. Humphrey was told that the only way to advance in Montreal's business community was to become a great man's secretary or a lawyer. Humphrey decided on the latter. He entered the McGill law program, and graduated second in his class. In all, John Humphrey earned four degrees at McGill and later became a professor and dean of law.

Humphrey was studying at McGill at a time when some very active and articulate people were there: Frank Scott, Eugene Forsey, King Gordon, Leonard Marsh, and David Lewis. All these people were in the language of the day 'on the left'; active members of the League for Social Reconstruction, they were in on the Regina Manifesto. According to Hobbins, this group was the intellectual precursor to the CCF. It was during this period that Humphrey converted from his innate NB conservatism to socialism. Macdonald asserts that an additional, very strong influence on his thinking was the Great Depression of 1929. The poverty was appalling. There was no social net, as we know it today. Humphrey was horrified by what he saw, and it awoke in him a recognition of the importance of economic and social rights. According to Macdonald, Humphrey could make the link between economic, social and cultural rights on the one side and the more traditional civil-political rights, almost automatically. It became part of his outlook.

Humphrey went into private law practice for a few years before joining the McGill faculty. At the end of the Second World War, a former free-France diplomat Humphrey had befriended asked him to come to New York to be the first director of the Human Rights Division in the United Nations. This was a pioneering move. No international organization had ever had a human rights program. But with the atrocities of war fresh in their minds, the founders of the United Nations agreed that the new world body should have an international Bill of Rights; and as historian John Hobbins explains, Humphrey was to be the bureaucrat at the service of diplomats on the Human Rights Commission. In 1946, Humphrey was asked to set up the UN's Division for Human Rights, of which he became the Director. In 1947, the Commission suggested that Professor Humphrey should prepare the first draft of an international declaration of human rights. He prepared a 400-page background paper for the proposed Universal Declaration and wrote its first draft in 1947. According to Hobbins, Humphrey wrote about 6 handwritten drafts of the declaration, based on documentation the secretariat had received on the provisions of other declarations of human rights.

Humphrey later declared publicly that he put several provisions in his draft that were not accepted. For example, one article in the draft was based on the League of Nations declaration which called for the protection of minorities. Humphrey alleged that this article was left out of the final version because, he asserted, most governments are more interested in assimilating their minorities than in protecting them.

According to Hobbins, Humphrey did decide, for the most part, what he would put in and what he would take out of the draft declaration. In Humphrey's view, the most important decision was to include economic and social rights. He pointed out that, in 1948, economic and social rights were considered 'pure socialism'. Some of the great powers, including the United States, Great Britain and France had expressed concern about this. But they were not able to have the provision removed.

Humphrey had originally penned 48 articles for the declaration of human rights. This initial draft was handed over to a French jurist, René Cassin, who made some additions and changes. Then, the diplomats on the Human Rights Commission went through 187 meetings and 1400 resolutions before agreeing on the precise wording of 30 articles. This agreed-upon declaration was put to a vote in late 1948.

It was in the voting process that John Humphrey got the shock of his life from his own country. Canada could hardly have been more negative. There were no votes against the declaration, but there were several abstentions, and Canada was one of these. However, three days later, Canada reluctantly changed its position and voted for the declaration in plenary.

Humphrey believed that Canada reversed its initial abstention more because of embarrassment over the company it was keeping—the Soviet Bloc and South Africa—than because of its enthusiasm for the declaration. But why had Canada abstained in the first place? At the time, External Affairs Minister Mike Pearson explained that it was because some provisions were vague and that the declaration might intrude in areas of provincial jurisdiction. This was the explanation that was accepted for 50 years. But only a few weeks before the 50th anniversary of the UDHR, a different version came to light.

Professor William Schabas, a law professor at the University of Quebec at Montreal, had, like many others, mistrusted the 'official' explanation of why Canada had initially abstained in the voting on the declaration. Professor Schabas sifted through old documents at the national archives in Ottawa and found old telegrams and memos about the Universal Declaration, some penciled by Prime Minister St-Laurent himself. On the basis of this newly uncovered evidence, he contended that Canada had abstained essentially because the Cabinet, going right up to Prime Minister St-Laurent at the time, was very uncomfortable with the protections for human rights set out in the Universal Declaration of Human Rights. They were bitterly opposed to the inclusion of economic and social rights in the Universal Declaration. The Canadians, he claims, also were uncomfortable with the fact that the communists might invoke the Universal Declaration and that the Jehovah Witnesses might invoke freedom of religion. They were especially concerned about the Japanese-Canadians. The Canadian government had just renewed the oppressive measures depriving Canadian-born citizens of Japanese origin of the right to vote; these measures had been renewed in March of 1948. According to Professor Schabas, the official explanation Canadians put out in 1948 about why they had abstained was essentially a cover-up for their discomfort with the declaration itself, and, in particular, with its provisions for economic and social rights.

Ironically, the inclusion of economic and social rights is now widely acknowledged to represent one of the major accomplishments and achievements of the Universal Declaration because it makes a link to the past, which was the civil and political rights tradition that grew out of the French and American revolutions, and a more modern view that holds that fundamental rights like freedom of speech and freedom of assembly go hand-in-hand with the right to a job, the right to medicare and other social and economic rights.

Viewed in retrospect, the act of adopting the Universal Declaration can be seen as part and parcel of the politics of the day. The United States felt it could utilize the declaration as a propaganda weapon against its communist enemies. And the Soviets wanted to use it to criticize racism and poverty in the United States. Many nations allegedly voted for the declaration with no intention of respecting it. But John Humphrey and Eleanor Roosevelt, the widow of the former US President, and then chairman of the UN Human Rights Committee, had higher hopes for the declaration. When the declaration was passed, Mrs Roosevelt proclaimed that the declaration was predicated on mankind's desire for peace. She asserted that the impetus behind the drafting of the declaration came from the realization by the nations of the world that it was the flagrant violation of human rights by Nazi and Fascist countries which had sown the seeds of the

Second World War and which, in turn, had spawned the atrocities of the Holocaust. The Universal Declaration of Human Rights, she announced, could well become the international Magna Carta of all human beings throughout the globe.

Despite the lofty rhetoric of the time, Professor Ronald Macdonald has expressed doubt that most nations really understood the significance of adopting the Universal Declaration. He asserts that it was quite clear at the time that the Universal Declaration was not to be regarded as binding, positive international law. But what was not anticipated was that it quickly acquired a life of its own. And today, most authorities agree that the general principles of the Universal Declaration of Human Rights have become part of customary international law, which means that they are binding on all states of the world. The UDHR has become one of the most important statements of the 20th century. As Eleanor Roosevelt predicted, the declaration has been called the Magna Carta of humanity. And it has inspired, and continues to inspire, human rights activists across the country and around the world.

While the crafting and adoption of the Universal Declaration was probably the crowning achievement of John Humphrey's life, it was not the only one. For 20 years he kept the human rights cause alive at the United Nations, fending off attacks from member states, the hostility of some Secretaries-General, and the communist witch hunts of United States Senator Joe McCarthy. He oversaw the implementation of 67 international conventions. He built up the work and stature of the Human Rights Commission. He set up international mechanisms for human rights work.

In 1966 John Humphrey retired from the UN. He returned to teaching international law at McGill University. From this time on, he devoted himself to human rights teaching and advocacy. According to Macdonald, John Humphrey was pugnacious; he had an ironlike will and he used it in his continual struggle for what he believed in—the recognition and protection of fundamental human rights. He was the founding president of the Canadian Section of the International Commission of Jurists. He served on Royal Commissions, help set up the Canadian Chapter of Amnesty International and the Canadian Foundation for Human Rights, and continued teaching at McGill. But one thing troubled and depressed him. Someone else was getting the credit for his work.

In 1968, René Cassin had won the Nobel Peace Prize, in part because his friends and his government, more than Cassin himself, promoted the Frenchman as the author of the first draft of the Universal Declaration. In fact, he had only slightly reworked the draft done by John Humphrey.

After leaving the UN, Humphrey had written and spoken about his role in the process. But, as John Hobbins explains, there was some feeling in official circles and in academia that Humphrey was exaggerating his own importance. They believed Cassin wrote the declaration. At the time, Humphrey didn't know that his initial drafts of the declaration existed, that they had survived the test of time. He had given a whole stack of his papers to McGill when he retired, and these drafts were later found among them. But Humphrey was unaware of that when the debate about authorship of the declaration was taking place.

The debate was finally settled in 1988. In June of 1988, Hobbins was asked to be acting law librarian at McGill. During his first week on the job, John Humphrey came to the library and asked the staff to find his notes on Roman law. One of the staff looked in the filing cabinet in Hobbins' new office because she said there was a file labeled Humphrey. Although the lecture notes were not there, the staff member came across an old paper which she told Hobbins, was considered to be the first draft of the Universal Declaration of Human Rights. With this discovery in hand, Hobbins began preparing an article on the real authorship of the first draft of the Universal Declaration. Then word got to France. Friends of René Cassin and officials close to the government of the day were less than pleased that the reputation of their national Nobel Prize winner might be diminished by a Canadian. According to

Hobbins, at this point, the French delegation to UNESCO had approached the Canadian embassy and suggested that an institution of McGill's reputation should not put that reputation on the line for the ramblings of a 'paranoid imbecile'. They suggested stopping the publication of Hobbins' article. Hobbins then began receiving threatening calls, and, in order to safeguard his documents, he moved all of the documents out of the law library, where they were not safe, to the McGill University archives. Hobbins eventually published four volumes of monographs, based on the diaries of John Humphrey.*

John Humphrey died in 1995 at the age of 90. He had taught at McGill up until the previous year, and had authored numerous articles and several books. He received 13 honorary degrees and, in 1974, was named an Officer of the Order of Canada.

After his death, memorials to John Humphrey began to appear as Canadians came to recognize his achievements. In his honour, the International Centre for Human Rights and Democratic Development established the $25,000 John Humphrey Freedom Award, which is presented each year. And Canada Post issued a stamp in his honour in October 1998 (Copyright 1998–99 New Brunswick Human Rights Commission).

* A.J. Hobbins, ed., *On the Edge of Greatness: The Diaries of John Humphrey, First Director of the United Nations Division of Human Rights* (Fontanus Monograph Series). Montreal: McGill University Libraries, 1994.

SOURCE: Documentary aired on CBC Radio's *This Morning*, 10 December 1998. Transcript available from CBC.

These include the right to life; protection from slavery and torture; freedom of thought, opinion, and religion; the right to work and to education; the right to marry and form a family; and the right to participate in the social, political, and cultural life of one's society.

The Declaration contains three areas of rights: civil and political rights; economic, cultural, and social rights; and rights and responsibilities linking the individual and the society.

Civil and political rights—set out in Articles 2 to 21 of the Declaration—are derived from Western democratic traditions and a political philosophy of 'liberal individualism'. These rights are often described in a negative form ('freedom from') rather than a positive form ('rights to'). They attempt to safeguard the individual, alone and in association with others, against the misuse of political authority.

Economic, cultural, and social rights—set out in Articles 22 to 28 of the Declaration—find their origins in the socialist traditions of early nineteenth-century France and subsequent revolutionary struggles. These rights require state intervention to ensure citizens are able to participate fully in society, such as the right to work and to education. They are 'positive' rather than 'negative' rights.

Articles 29 and 30 of the UDHR introduce the principle of the duty and the responsibility of the individual to others in the community. They lay out the rights, obligations, and duties of the individual in her/his relationship to the community and the expectations of reciprocity that is the cornerstone of comprehending the interdependence of rights of the individual and the community. Articles 29 and 30 of the UDHR emphasize that individual rights can only be developed fully in community with others. They emphasize the essential reciprocity of human rights and fundamental freedoms on the one hand and of human duties and responsibilities to others in the community, on the other. Just as each individual owes duties to the community, and indeed only in the community is the free and full development of the personality of the individual possible, the community has an obligation to recognize its duty towards the individual and to ensure that the individual has the opportunity to learn of her/his rights and duties.

The Influence of the UDHR on the Content of International Human Rights Provisions

The bulk of the declarations advanced in current international human rights instruments have their roots in the UDHR. Building on the three guiding principles of the Universal Declaration—freedom, equality, and dignity—they address a common, threefold theme: the right of every human being to participate in the shaping of decisions affecting one's own life and that of one's society (freedom to decide/political rights); reasonable access to the economic resources that make that participation possible (equality of opportunity/economic rights); and affirmation of the essential human worth and dignity of every person, regardless of individual qualities and/or group membership (dignity of person/social rights).

Clearly, the single most basic human right is the right to life. The fundamental principle behind the human right to life requires that every human being have access to the economic resources that maintain life. For without adequate economic maintenance—work, food, shelter, and clothing—the other rights and freedoms are virtually meaningless.

Under current international human rights instruments, the human right to economic maintenance includes not only the right to the minimal, life-maintaining essentials (which were even provided to 'chattel', under slavery) but also, the right to an adequate standard of living, and to the kinds of public services, such as medical and health care, social services, and especially, education—which afford the basic supports for a decent living standard in modern society.

Freedom to decide and to determine one's own destiny is another fundamental human rights principle. Indeed, the right to self-determination of all individuals—regardless of their race or class—was one of the earliest of the fundamental human rights to gain universal recognition, for it provided the cornerstone of the early movement to abolish slavery. The exercise of this right requires access to political power, hence, within the context of the political process, it translates into the right to the franchise. But beyond the political process, this right extends into decision-making in all life spheres: home and family, work, school, church, club, and choice of lifestyle.

The right to human dignity is another fundamental human rights principle. It embodies the right of each individual to be held worthy, and to feel worthy; to be held in esteem and accorded respect by others, and to experience a personal sense of self-esteem and self-respect.

Many of the invalidating labels commonly used in identifying members of racial and ethnic minorities can be seen to violate minority members' fundamental right to human dignity and personal respect. For example, the derogatory epithet 'nigger' referring to blacks; 'kike' referring to Jews; 'chink' referring to Chinese—all of these negative epithets disrespect and deny the very humanity of their bearers.

Freedom to decide is essential to the enhancement of dignity. Although it is likely that slaves could receive adequate amounts of food, clothing, and shelter, it is unlikely that they would ever acquire an adequate amount of respect for their own unique human personalities. One's sense of self-worth and dignity requires some control over one's own destiny. To be held worthy, and to feel worthy, each human being should be free to determine their own life in their own way. Each person should be free to decide whether and whom to marry, whether and how to worship, whether and what to read, write, watch, hear, see, or say.

Justifiable Restrictions on Human Rights

Under current UN human rights covenants, the three pivotal human rights principles—freedom to decide, equality of opportunity, and dignity of person—are held to be *inalienable*: these fundamental human rights are held to be rights that belong to every human being, solely by virtue of his or her *humanity*. This is the precise sense in which they are said to be universal (Murumba 1998). What this means is that these fundamental human rights can be claimed equally by all human beings, regardless of demonstrated or assumed differences among individual persons in their talents, abilities, skills, and resources, and regardless of their membership in different human groups. As moral principles, fundamental rights can be said to be inalienable, individual rights, but they are not absolute: in the exercise of his or her fundamental rights, each human being must not violate, indeed must respect, the fundamental human rights of others. Human rights, then, are not unconditional: they are conditional on the exercise of social responsibilities or duties to others.

The fundamental principles of the interdependence of the individual and community and of the reciprocity of rights and duties, provide the underpinnings for the moral justification of necessary *restrictions* on individual human rights.

From a human rights approach, restriction or denial of the exercise of the fundamental human rights to freedom, equality, and dignity of any human being can be justified only in instances where violations of the human rights of others can be fully substantiated. In such cases, restrictions justifiably may be imposed on the violator's exercise of human rights, but only to the extent necessary to prevent further violations of the rights of others. Suppose, for example, that my greatest joy comes from the thrill I feel in racing my souped-up sports car. Should my individual freedom, then, include the right to drive my car at 100 kilometres an hour down the busy main street of the city during the Christmas shopping rush? My freedom to drive in this manner immediately clashes with the freedoms of others—shoppers, pedestrians, other motorists—who wish to enjoy the holiday season's many attractions in safety. If I exercise my freedom to speed down Main Street, their freedom will be severely restricted. Obviously, our freedoms cannot coexist. One must give way to the other (Borovoy 1988).

Everyday life provides us with endless examples of rights in conflict. For instance: Does the freedom of the individual include the freedom to kill, maim, rape, and assault? The assailant and the victim cannot both have absolute freedom of choice. Thus, we must face the fundamental paradox. The existence of freedom demands the imposition of restrictions. In order to accomplish this task, democratic societies have developed systems of justice—laws, law enforcement agencies, courts, and so forth. However, the critical question remains concerning the kind and the extent of restrictions or laws we should have. To put it even more specifically, what restrictions are appropriate in a democracy where the object is to promote the greatest possible freedom of the individual and, at the same time, to promote the greatest good of the society as a whole?

The renowned nineteenth-century philosopher on liberty, John Stuart Mill, attempted to grapple with this problem. Mill contended that the only purpose for which power can rightfully be exercised over any member of a civilized community, against his will, is to prevent harm to others.

In some of the foregoing examples, the restrictions we enact enjoy a virtually universal consensus. In order to prevent physical harm to others, we prohibit the individual from engaging in physical attacks upon other people. In order to prevent economic harm to others, we outlaw theft, robbery, forgery, etc. These kinds of examples form the basis of our criminal law.

During the twentieth century, however, democratic societies, such as Canada, have gone much further. In order to prevent the harm caused to industrial workers by the conditions of modern industry, we have imposed restrictions upon the conduct of individuals engaged in business activity. We have required employers to install safety equipment, pay minimum wages, observe maximum hours, and bargain collectively with unions. Employers lost the freedom to determine unilaterally the conditions of work for their employees. In order to prevent the harm caused by racial discrimination, we have imposed restrictions upon the selection of employees by employers and tenants by landlords. Employers and landlords lost their freedom to base their selections on considerations of race, creed, and colour. Indeed, the entire apparatus of the modern democratic state represents a series of intrusions upon the freedoms of some sectors of society in order to promote the welfare of other sectors of society, and to promote the welfare of the society as a whole.

The crucial question at any given time is which freedoms to be exercised by which persons in which situations are to be given more weight. Is the harm inflicted in the absence of restrictions greater than the harm inflicted through the adoption of restrictions? Put another way, which decision would lead to the greater good . . . which would more likely achieve the democratic aims of peace and order, security and safety, and harmonious relations between all individuals and groups in the society?

This question brings us to the relationship between freedom and equality. The restrictions that a democracy imposes upon its citizens must reflect an *equal consideration* for everyone affected. On the moral and social scales, we all weigh the same. Since one person's freedom may be another's restriction, administrators of justice cannot help assessing the relative importance of the interests in conflict. Thus, while it is impossible to avoid restrictions that may benefit some and burden others, democratic societies believe in the principle of equal consideration. Even if people are sometimes subject to differential treatment, they must receive equal consideration through equivalent treatment.

The right to equality principle is probably one of the most misunderstood (and variously interpreted) of all tenets of fundamental human rights. In its application in diverse societal contexts, *EQUALITY* represents a continuum of concepts. In various contexts it can mean equality of opportunity, freedom from discrimination, equal treatment, equal benefit, equal status and equality of results (Canada, Department of Justice 2000).

Formal equality prescribes identical treatment of all individuals regardless of their actual circumstances. **Substantive equality** requires that differences among social groups be acknowledged and accommodated in laws, policies, and practices to avoid adverse impacts on individual members of the group. A substantive approach to equality evaluates the fairness of apparently neutral laws, policies, and programs in light of the larger social context of inequality, and emphasizes the importance of equal outcomes that sometimes requires equal, standard treatment and sometimes different but equivalent treatment (ibid.).

The right to equality essentially represents equality/equity of opportunity and results. Equality does not necessarily mean sameness. What it does imply, from a human rights view, is equal consideration for all. Equal consideration in some instances, may be appropriately expressed in equal (standard or same) treatment, but in other instances, equivalent (special) compensatory treatment may be required.

In those instances where standard (same) treatment of members of different populations affords true equality of opportunity, application of the principle of equal treatment is required. Qualified members of racial and ethnic minorities must be afforded the same opportunities as equally qualified majority members to enter the professional fields of their choice, to obtain jobs for which they are suitably skilled, to obtain deserved promotions and so forth.

Alternatively, in those instances where standard treatment denies true equality of opportunity, application of the principle of equivalent treatment is required.

For example: equal consideration for the educational opportunities of the wheelchair-bound, as well as for the ambulatory members of society, would be expressed architecturally, where educational facilities are equipped with ramps and handrails as well as with stairs. In this particular example, the provision of equal (standard) treatment for all, in the form of access to the facility by open stairways only, would not provide equal opportunity for mobility-impaired persons. Access to the facility for persons disabled with unstable gait and for the wheelchair-bound would be seriously impeded, if not entirely prevented. This is but one example of the multitude of documented instances, where, in order to offset the handicapping effects of a disability, special, compensatory measures (for example, architectural adaptations to buildings) must be provided. In these cases, equivalent, rather than equal (standard) treatment is required.

Twin Principles of Human Rights: Human Unity and Cultural Diversity

Fundamental **individual human rights** are rooted in the distinctive biological attributes shared by all members of humankind as a single species (*homo sapiens*). Recognition of the essential biological oneness of humankind provides the scientific basis for the universal principle of fundamental individual human rights. For fundamental human rights are rights based solely on one's *humanity* (Murumba 1998). They are bestowed on every human being simply by virtue of belonging to the human species. A primary assumption, then, behind international human rights covenants is that of the fundamental unity and kinship among all members of humankind.

Yet, every human being is born not only into the human species, but also into a particular human population and ethnocultural community. The diversity of the ethnocultures developed by different ethnic groups within humankind is the feature of humankind that provides the basis for **collective cultural rights**. Like human unity, cultural diversity is recognized under international human rights covenants as a characteristic feature of humankind. *Collective* human rights represent the principle of cultural diversity, the differentness of the unique cultures or blueprints for living developed by the various ethnic populations of humankind. Taken together, individual and collective human rights represent the twin global principles of **human unity and cultural diversity**.

Although the key principles of the *universality* of individual and collective cultural rights are central tenets of current international human rights instruments, they have long been the subject of both political and scholarly controversy, and, even today, they are not without their critics. Accordingly, before I proceed to elaborate on the internationally endorsed concepts of cultural diversity and collective cultural rights, I will digress briefly, in order to highlight the main arguments in this continuing debate.

The Debate over the Universality of Human Rights in International, Cross-Cultural Application

The twentieth-century creation by the United Nations of an international system of protection for the **universality of human rights** has not been without its critics. The universality of human rights in a world of widely varying cultures has been a controversial theme in international politics and law since the Universal Declaration of Human Rights was adopted in 1948. It has spawned a vigorous scholarly debate over the question of the normative and conceptual universality of human rights. This controversy has deep, historical roots in the age-old tension between 'social cohesion and individual liberty' (in Bertrand Russell's words). Today, in its contemporary version, it is expressed in the lively debate between libertarians and liberal individualists such as Nozick (1974). Rawls (1971) and Dworkin (1977), on the one hand, and communitarians such as Taylor (1995) and Sandel (1992) on the other (Murumba 1998: 208).

Murumba (1998) offers a penetrating analysis and critique of both sides of this debate. He exposes the flaws in the thesis of incompatibility between individual rights and collective cultural and national rights posited by proponents of both positions. He proposes a new 'symbiotic model' for the twenty-first century in which culture and human rights are mutually reinforcing rather than mutually exclusive (Murumba 1998: 209).

Murumba begins by pointing out the problems in the 'heterogeneity thesis', which he calls the 'incompatibility thesis'. This is the thesis that the universality of human rights is incompatible with the heterogeneous character of the world community. Of particular importance to this thesis is the alleged incompatibility of Western (presumably 'individualistic') and non-Western (presumably 'communitarian') societies and cultures. The incompatibility thesis, Murumba argues, consists of three propositions: 1) No concept is valid outside if its cultural context; 2) The cultural context for the human rights concept is the Western one; therefore, 3) The human rights concept has no validity in non-Western cultures. After critically examining three sets of arguments based on this thesis, Murumba concludes that the major flaw in the thesis lies not in the contextual boundedness of concepts, but in the premise of the Western particularity of human rights. The most basic problem with this thesis, Murumba argues, is a conceptual one. International human rights, he points out, are rights that belong to every human being by virtue of his or her humanity; this is the precise sense in which they are said to be universal. To suggest that human rights is simply a twentieth-century name for the historical concept of natural rights is to overlook the crucial fact that so-called natural rights were not rights held solely by virtue of one's humanity. Indeed, race, gender, and nationality were also relevant criteria. Natural rights, in reality, were the rights of dominant Westerners—Euro-Whites and men. Some 80 per cent of all human beings were excluded. Murumba argues that the concept of human, as distinct from natural, rights is a distinctly twentieth-century invention. Rights that human beings have purely by virtue of their humanity would have been unthinkable before the twentieth century. While Western culture must be credited with the articulation of a central component of rights, as claims upon society, the normative content of rights has older and more diverse roots. Human rights are claims against society, but claims against society are not human rights unless they are predicated upon one's humanity. Rights predicated on any other attribute, such as race, class, or gender, are not human rights.

The second premise on which the incompatibility thesis rests is that of the conflict between the communitarian concept of culture and human rights. Murumba explains that the liberal individualist vision of society is of a collectivity created by independent individuals as 'unencumbered selves' who come together to form a society in order to gain benefits through common action that they could not secure individually. Both the contractual and the utilitarian versions of this vision entail that society has no interests above or beyond those of its constituent 'unencumbered selves'. In direct contrast to this atomistic, liberal individualist vision, the distinctive feature of the communitarian vision is that it reverses the priority between individual and society. In the communitarian vision, the community or society comes first, the individual second. Its organizing principle is that of a 'people'—not a loose coalition of 'unencumbered selves', but a closely knit community of 'situated selves'; individuals are born into and become an integral part of a complex web of social entanglements. The rights of individuals in the communitarian vision of society are derived from and contingent upon the nature of the society, but the society always comes before the individual.

Murumba suggests that the principal communitarian charge against liberal individualism today is that its atomistic conceptions of both personhood (the 'unencumbered self') and society (collection of individuals) are false. In the words of Charles Taylor, 'the free individual of the West is only what he is by virtue of the whole society and civilization which brought him to be and which nourishes him' (quoted in Murumba 1998: 228). However, Murumba argues, this line of criticism can be easily deployed against communitarianism itself. It is possible to demonstrate that individuals are not wholly 'situated selves', and that community, culture, and society cannot capture the uniqueness of the human person, without remainder.

Murumba concludes his analysis of the libertarian/communitarian debate by arguing that while their rival images of individuals and society compete with one another, they cannot live without each other. This, he contends, is because they both have roots deep in the human psyche, in the motivational duality of individualistic drives and communitarian drives. He then proceeds to defend a concept of human rights that reflects this fundamental duality.

To begin, Murumba emphasizes the primacy of human rights over particular cultural and social arrangements. Since human rights are rights that all human beings have solely by virtue of their humanity, they must *ipso facto* transcend all other particularities. Since 1945, Murumba points out, acting on international principles of human rights, the international community has proclaimed, over protestations of sovereignty, that a state's mistreatment of its own nationals is a legitimate concern of the rest of the world. But it is not only states that can violate the human rights of their members: cultures and communities also can be instruments of human rights violations. Particular cultural practices or forms may conflict with fundamental human rights. Human rights claims are claims of individuals against society, whether that society is organized along state, ethnic, or cultural lines. Indefensible cultural practices, allowed, or even prescribed by culture—such as female circumcision, racial discrimination, or the execution of minors—constitute human rights violations and cannot be immune to censure from the international community. In such cases of *bona fide* conflict between individual and culture, the primacy of human rights must prevail.

But this possibility of conflict, Murumba contends, must not obscure the fact that the greater part of the relationship between culture and human rights is positive, even symbiotic. Murumba proposes that there is a human rights dimension of culture (human rights in the service of culture) and a corresponding cultural dimension of human rights (culture in the service of human rights). The human rights dimension of culture is demonstrated in the fact that one's cultural rights are a category of human rights protected under international human rights instruments such as Article 27 of the ICCPR (International Covenant on Civil and Political Rights) and Article 15 of the ICESCR (International Covenant on Economic, Social and Cultural Rights). Murumba argues further that an even more important consideration is the now widely acknowledged fact—at the heart of multiculturalism—that culture plays a crucial role in shaping personality and identity. Put another way, one's personhood is not developed in a cultural vacuum; each individual's personhood is shaped by the cultural particularities of his or her socialization. The cultural dimension of human rights emerges in the distinctive cultural conceptions of what it means to be human. This brings us back to the earlier discussion of the tension between competing visions of humanity—Western/liberal/individualistic and non-Western/communitarian visions. Murumba points out that it was these competing visions of 'true humanity' that haunted international human rights norms from their inception. The ensuing dispute between the 'West and the rest' was responsible for the creation of two separate covenants—the ICCPR and the ICESCR—reflecting the Western and non-Western conceptions of human rights, respectively.

What is emerging as we usher in the twenty-first century, Murumba suggests, is an abandonment of the chauvinistic paradigm that papers over the inadequacies in both competing conceptions and conceals their complementarity. Just as the Western conception of human rights suffers from too much individualism and atomism, and not enough community, the non-Western approach suffers from too much communitarianism and not enough individualism. A cross-cultural approach, incorporating both conceptions, would reveal that they are indispensable components of the same notion—what it means to be human. This approach would thus provide a richer and more accurate conception of human rights. Murumba argues that a cross-culturally enriched concept of human rights has another advantage: it facilitates a nuanced but principled approach to human rights problems, instead of a one-size-fits-all prescription. A nuanced approach may tell us, for instance, that the public-private distinction may be a problem to women's rights in the West, but a necessary condition for their protection in non-Western countries (Murumba 1998: 239).

In closing, Murumba draws attention to the fact that human rights themselves are, in the last analysis, a cross-cultural invention. Without cultures, which shape and define the very personhood for which human rights were invented, there would be no human rights. However, he contends, for cultures to operate effectively in the multicultural, global environment of the twenty-first century, they must become more flexible, for culturally shaped personality and identity will need to be open to the possibility of multiple allegiances. Put another way, he says, in the twenty-first century 'we shall need to wear our cultures lightly' (Murumba 1998: 240).

The United Nations: Attempts to Gain Universal Acceptance for the Implementation of Human Rights in Different Sociocultural Contexts

As indicated in the foregoing discussion, the universality of human rights in a world of widely varying cultures has been a controversial theme in international politics and law since the Universal Declaration of Human Rights was adopted in 1948. The conception of the universality of humanity and of human rights currently built into virtually all international human rights documents had its core articulation in the Charter of the United Nations. The UN Charter, which serves as the written constitution of the international community, was drawn up for the purpose of promoting international cooperation in the realization of human rights and fundamental freedoms for all members of humankind, without distinction of any kind. The 1948 Universal Declaration of Human Rights could do no other than follow and reinforce the universalist viewpoint of the Charter. This essential character of the Declaration was reaffirmed by the adoption of the term 'universal', rather than 'international' in its title (Espiell 1998).

The Declaration proclaims equal rights for all members of the human family, taking into account their respective identities and differences. The cornerstone of the Declaration is to proclaim the essential dignity of all human beings, and an integral part of human dignity is each person's right to difference. The universalistic objective of the Declaration is to unite all individuals, over and above their identity differences; to combine unity and diversity in the name of equal dignity, the crux of humanity (Espiell 1998).

In the 50 years since its adoption, the Declaration has reached a general level of international acceptance, well beyond the expectations of its original adopters. It was thus thanks to the Declaration that the universality of human rights became a generally accepted axiom. While the universality of human rights in a global context of cultural diversity has continued to spark debate in the realms of international politics and law, in recent years, only a few isolated voices in one particular region of the world have questioned the universal character and international force of the Declaration (Espiell 1998).

This group of non-Western nations sees the UDHR conception of universal human rights as part of the ideological patrimony of Western civilization. They argue that the principles enshrined in the UDHR reflect Western values, and not their own. They claim that the West is interfering in their internal affairs by imposing their definition of human rights upon them, and that this hinders their trade and competitiveness. They argue that because of their countries' social and cultural differences from the West, they should not be held to Western standards. This attempt to undermine the internationally enshrined notion of the universality of human rights is attributed to such countries as China, Colombia, Cuba, Indonesia, Iran, Iraq, Libya, Malaysia, Mexico, Myanmar, Pakistan, Singapore, Syria, Vietnam, and Yemen. But the strongest advocates of this position are the Asian states experiencing the most dynamic economic growth (Cerna 1994).

This debate occupied centre stage at the second UN World Conference on Human Rights held in June 1993 in Vienna, Austria. The Western states, fearing the erosion of the notion of universality of human rights, undertook steps toward 'damage control' to ensure that the Conference issued a strong endorsement of the universality principle and clearly rejected the idea that human rights can be measured differently in some countries (Cerna 1994). The most significant success of this World Conference was the achievement of consensus on the reaffirmation of universality of human rights, 45 years after the adoption of the UDHR. The Vienna Declaration and the regional declarations reiterated that all human rights—civil and political, as well as economic, social, and cultural—should be implemented simultaneously, and that neither set of rights should take precedence over the other.

The challenge to the concept of universality of human rights, coming primarily from Asia, had to do with 'private' rights. It is these provisions of the UDHR that have not become universally accepted. The private sphere deals with issues such as religion, culture, the status of women, the right to marry, to divorce, and to remarry, the protection of children, the question of choice as regards family planning, and the like. These rights have traditionally been covered by religious law, and in some countries, they still are (Cerna 1994). This tension between the universality of rights in the private sphere and the competing religious and/or traditional law means that some societies are unwilling to assume international human rights obligations in the private sphere.

Cerna (1994), in commenting on this seeming impasse, concludes that achieving universal acceptance of international human rights norms is a process, and different norms occupy different places on the continuum. Although the international community may censure countries for practices based on norms that violate human rights, it cannot impose international human rights norms to replace traditional ones. It is important that the international supervisory bodies come to recognize that change and acceptance of these norms must come from within the countries themselves. It seems clear, as we enter the twenty-first century, that international norms dealing with rights that affect the private sphere of life will take the longest time to achieve universal acceptance.

Later, in this chapter, we will offer a case study that should enable the reader to consider the issues in debate over the universality of human rights (addressed earlier) in the context of modern multicultural democracies. At this juncture, however, we will return to our earlier discussion of cultural diversity and we will elaborate on the meaning of the concepts of cultural diversity and collective cultural rights, as currently articulated and endorsed under international human rights instruments.

Cultural Diversity and Collective Rights

Cultural diversity, as a human rights principle, and as the basis for collective human rights claims, rests on the anthropological conceptualization of culture as ethnoculture. The concept **ethnoculture** refers to the culture developed and maintained by a particular people or ethnic group. Ethnoculture refers to the distinctive ways of viewing and doing things—eating, dressing, speaking, worshiping, loving—shared by members of a particular ethnic community and transmitted by them from one generation to the next; it is the unique design for living of a particular ethnic group. This concept of culture as ethnoculture underscores protections for collective cultural rights endorsed in the provisions of Article 27 of the International Covenant of Civil and Political Rights (United Nations 1978, 1988) and reinforced in the provisions of the Declaration on the Rights of Persons Belonging to National, Ethnic, Religious and Linguistic Minorities (United Nations 1992).

The reader should note that this conceptualization of culture as ethnoculture means that, under the provisions of current international human rights instruments, only *ethnic* communities can make collective rights claims. Because the subcultures of non-ethnic groups or communities (such as gays and lesbians) are not *bona fide* ethnocultures, non-ethnic groups have no legitimate basis, under current international human rights norms, for making *collective rights* claims.

The most important point about culture, from a human rights perspective, is that it is *learned*; it is acquired, for the most part, through the ordinary processes of growing up and participating in the daily life of a particular ethnic community. Insofar as culture is part of the condition of being human, then all individuals must learn to be human. But culture is not learned in the abstract, for no human being is born into a cultural vacuum. Every member of humankind learns to be human by learning the language, religion, values, and customs of a particular culture.

The principle of collective human rights recognizes the collective right of every ethnic community, to practise and to perpetuate the distinctive culture or way of life developed and shared by its members. From a human rights view, just as every individual human being is equally human, every human culture is equally human: no human being or human culture is superior or inferior to any other. Put another way, all human beings and all human cultures are equally valid. Just as all human beings, as members of humankind, must respect the fundamental individual rights of all other human beings, so, also, all human beings, as members of particular human cultures must respect all of the different human cultures shared by other human beings.

Similar parallels can be drawn between individual and collective human rights with regard to the imposition of justifiable restrictions on their exercise in order to prevent human rights violations. In the increasingly multicultural context of modern democratic societies, just as we can justifiably impose restrictions on one human being's exercise of individual rights in order to prevent harm to others, so we can, justifiably, impose restrictions on one population's exercise of cultural rights in order to prevent harm to other human beings. For example, if the traditional cultural practices of a particular community include the stoning to death of a woman who commits adultery or abortion, or the cutting off of the hands of a thief or the burning at the stake of homosexuals, we can, justifiably, impose restrictions to prevent such human rights violations. Freedom of cultural expression, like freedom of speech, is not absolute. All human rights, both individual and collective, are conditional on the cardinal principle of non-violation of the rights of others.

Conflict of Rights: Individual versus Collective (Cultural Group) Rights

A critical question surfaces at this point: Given the increasingly multicultural nature of modern democracies, are there basic conflicts that arise between our commitment to the fundamental rights of freedom, equity, and dignity of each individual citizen and our increasing desire to respect the distinctive customs and lifestyles of minority cultures or religions? As suggested earlier, respect for culture can never be unconditional and condone acts of inhumanity and oppression. However, once we move beyond the incontrovertible cases of patent physical and psychological harm, intercultural moral judgments become problematic. We must be careful not to arbitrarily impose the values of democratic liberalism upon the immensely rich and varied moral universe introduced by multiculturalism.

Earlier in this section of our analysis, we raised the crucial question: Given the increasingly multicultural nature of modern democracies, are there basic conflicts that can arise between our commitment to the fundamental rights of freedom, equity, and dignity of each individual citizen and our increasing desire to respect the distinctive customs and lifestyles of minority cultures or religions? To illustrate the kinds of conflicts that can develop from the tension between individual rights and collective cultural rights, we will offer a case study: This case study should enable the reader to consider the issues in debate over the universality of human rights (addressed earlier) in the context of modern multicultural democracies (see Box I-2).

Group Level Human Rights and Claims: Categorical versus Collective Cultural Rights Claims

As far as it goes, Kymlicka's argument for equity of treatment of women and ethnocultural minorities (outlined in Box I-2) is on firm ground. However, what he fails to address is the conceptual distinction between the nature of group-level rights claims raised by women and other non-ethnic minorities, on the one hand, and by ethnocultural minorities, on the other.

The kinds of group-level rights claims raised by women and other non-ethnic minorities (to which Kymlicka refers) are best conceptualized as **categorical rights** claims. Because categorical rights claims are predicated on perceived violations of fundamental individual rights (freedom, equality, dignity), rather than violations of collective cultural rights, they may be put forward by members of both ethnic and non-ethnic groups. Categorical rights claims may represent claims for redress against past, categorical discrimination on the basis of ethnicity, nationality, race, religion, age, sex, sexual orientation, mental or physical disability, or other grounds. Any member of a specified social group or category who perceives that s/he or his/her group as a whole has experienced violations of the right/s to freedom, equal opportunity, or dignity on the arbitrary basis of (assumed) membership in the group, and has as a result suffered unfair disadvantage can make categorical rights claims.

By way of contrast, under the provisions of current international human rights instruments, *collective cultural rights* claims can only, justifiably, be put forward by representatives of ethnic minorities with distinctive *sui generis* ethnocultures. Subcultures of non-ethnic minorities are neither recognized nor protected. The basic principle behind collective cultural rights is the right of ethnic communities *as such* to legitimately and freely express their cultural distinctiveness. When this right is violated—when members of the community are denied the right to practise and maintain their distinctive religion, language, or customs—then a collective cultural rights claim can legitimately be put forward.

International Human Rights Instruments: Key Provisions of the Special Covenants

Since its proclamation, the Universal Declaration has had international impact, influencing national constitutions and laws, as well as international declarations such as the United Nations Declaration on the Elimination of All Forms of Racial Discrimination (1963) and the International Convention on the Elimination of All Forms of Racial Discrimination (1965). This impact notwithstanding, the UDHR represents only a general statement of ideals: It is morally but not legally binding on member states of the United Nations. Some countries sought a more forceful declaration that would establish binding obligations on the part of member states. As a result, two additional Covenants were drawn up and came into force in 1976. Their provisions, however, apply only to those member states that have decided to ratify them. Less than half of the member states, including the United States, have not ratified either covenant. Canada, however, has ratified both.

BOX I-2: CASE STUDY

Human Rights of Women in a Multicultural Context

Okin (in Okin et al. 1999) points out that a great many practices and conditions that clearly violate international human rights principles—polygamy, forced marriage, female genital mutilation, punishing women for being raped, differential access for men and women to health care and education, unequal rights of ownership, assembly, and political participation, unequal vulnerability to violence—are standard in some parts of the world. This observation, she suggests, raises the following critical questions: Do demands for multiculturalism make these sexist customs more likely to continue and to spread to liberal democracies? Are there fundamental conflicts between our commitment to gender equity and our increasing desire to respect the customs of minority cultures or religions?

Okin contends that some group [*sic*] rights can, in fact, endanger women. She points, for example, to the French government's giving thousands of male immigrants special permission to bring multiple wives into the country, despite French laws against polygamy and the wives' own bitter opposition to the practice. Okin argues that if we agree with a liberal, egalitarian and feminist approach which mandates that women should not be disadvantaged because of their sex, then we should not accept group rights that permit oppressive practices on the grounds that they are fundamental to minority cultures whose existence may otherwise be threatened.

By way of response to Okin's position, Parekh (in Okin et al. 1999) submits that all 'liberals' agree that minority communities should have a right to preserve their cultures, but disagree about the basis and limits of that right. For some, such as Michael Oakeshott and John Gray, they should enjoy the right so long as they meet the basic condition of civility and do not practice murder, incite hatred against outsiders, live as freeriders, etc. Some others such as Chandran Kukathas require that they should also allow their dissenting members the right of exit. Yet others, such as Will Kymlicka, go further and ask minority communities to internally organize themselves along liberal lines. This involves respecting fundamental freedoms, encouraging personal autonomy, practising equality between the sexes, and so on.

Although sympathetic to this last approach, Susan Okin thinks that it is not enough. Many minority and even majority cultures, she argues, are deeply sexist, and perpetuate women's subordination through a variety of practices too subtle for the law to catch, let alone disallow. They also condition their women into taking a low view of themselves and rationalizing and accepting their subordinate status, with the result that their wellbeing is damaged and they grow up without a strong sense of self-respect and self-esteem. In Okin's view, liberal democratic societies should ensure that respect for cultural diversity does not become a shield for sexism, and that self-proclaimed leaders of minority cultures, almost always male, should not be allowed to be their sole spokesmen. She also implies that deeply sexist cultures should not qualify for cultural group rights.

Parekh agrees with Okin that polygamy, clitorectomy, forced or child marriages, callous treatment of rape victims, and suppression of women in general are all evil, not only on liberal but also on any conceivable moral ground. He also agrees that Okin is right to insist that respect for culture can never be unconditional and condone acts of inhumanity and oppression. His disagreements relate to the issues she allegedly ignores and her conclusions. Parekh contends that Okin concentrates on extreme cases, and, by doing so, she ignores the problems involved in judging other cultures. Parekh agrees, for example, that clitorectomy on children is unacceptable, but points out that in some societies adult and sane women (including academics) freely undergo it after the birth of their last child as a way of regulating their sexuality and reminding themselves that from now onwards they are primarily mothers rather than wives. Should we disallow this, he asks? Again, he agrees with Okin that polygamy, meaning a man having multiple wives, is sexist and unacceptable, but, he asks, what about polygamy that allows both sexes the same freedom? It violates no liberal equity principle, for it is based on uncoerced choices of adults, causes no apparent harm, encourages experiments in living, and relates to the realm of privacy with which the liberal democratic state should not interfere. Should it also be disallowed? Here, he points out, the American Civil Liberties Union is divided, and so are 'liberals'. In short, Parekh contends, once we move beyond the incontrovertible cases of patent physical and psychological harm, cross-cultural moral judgments become problematic.

Parekh agrees with Okin that deep inequalities between the sexes are difficult to discern and demonstrate. Beyond a certain point they're even difficult to define. In some societies women are treated as inferior when young, but are revered and even enjoy superiority over men once they reach a certain age, become grandmothers, lead virtuous lives, or display unusual qualities. That is why, he suggests, these societies present the apparent paradox of being sexist and yet are accepting, even welcoming, of women leaders in all walks of life. In short, Parekh contends, given that in many societies women at different stages of life or in different relationships are perceived differently and endowed with different rights, the general concept 'woman' is an oversimplified abstraction that blinds us to cultural complexities.

There is also the further question, Parekh suggests, of how women themselves perceive their situation. If some of them do not share the feminist view, should we assume that they are brainwashed, victims of culturally generated false consciousness, and in need of liberation? To do so uncritically, he argues, denies these women the very equality we espouse. Parekh contends that it is imperative that we find ways of negotiating our moral responses between the two positivist extremes of uncritically accepting their self-understanding and equally uncritically imposing ours on them. In Britain, he points out, several university-educated white liberal women have in recent years converted to Islam because, among other things, they allegedly found its view of women more satisfying. In France and the Netherlands, several Muslim girls freely wore the hijab (customary head scarf), partly to reassure their conservative parents that they would not be corrupted by the public culture of the school, but also to indicate to 'white boys' how they wished to be treated. Wearing the hijab in their case, Parekh suggests, was a highly complex autonomous act intended to use the resources of the Muslim tradition both to change and to preserve it. To see it merely as a symbol of their subordination, as many French feminists did, is to miss the subtle dialect of cultural negotiation.

Parekh agrees with Okin that the way a culture treats women is of considerable importance. However, he insists, a culture encompasses many other customs as well, such as how one should live, relate to one's fellow humans and the natural world, and find meaning in one's life. It also gives its members a sense of collective identity, rootedness, and intergenerational continuity, as well as a ready access to an ongoing community and its vital economic and political resources. He argues therefore that it is a serious mistake to judge any culture solely or even primarily in terms of, and to make its rights dependent on, its treatment of women.

Kymlicka (in Okin et al. 1999) agrees with the basic claim of Okin's paper—that a liberal egalitarian (and feminist) approach to multiculturalism must look carefully at intragroup inequalities, and specifically at gender inequalities, when examining the legitimacy of minority group rights. Justice within ethnocultural groups is as important as justice between ethnocultural groups. Group rights are legitimate, he argues, if they help promote justice between ethnocultural groups, but are illegitimate if they create or exacerbate gender inequalities within the group. Kymlicka emphasizes this point by distinguishing between two kinds of group-level rights.

The first kind of group rights, which Kymlicka calls 'internal restrictions,' consist of ethnocultural group rights against its own members—in particular, the right to restrict individual choice in the name of cultural 'tradition' or cultural 'integrity.' Such collective rights restrict the ability of individuals within the group (particularly women) to question, revise, or abandon traditional cultural roles and practices. Such internal restrictions, Kymlicka argues, are unacceptable in a liberal democracy since they violate the autonomy of individuals, and create injustice within the group.

A second kind of group rights, which Kymlicka calls 'external protections,' refers to rights that are claimed by a minority cultural group against the larger society in order to reduce its vulnerability to the economic or political power of the larger society. Such collective rights can take the form of language rights, guaranteed political representation, funding of ethnic media, land claims, compensation for historical injustice, or the regional devolution of power. Kymlicka contends that all of these collective rights are acceptable in a liberal democracy because they can help to promote justice between ethnocultural groups, by ensuring that members of the minority have the same effective capacity to promote their interests as do members of the majority.

Kymlicka takes issue with Okin's inference that feminists should be deeply skeptical about the very category of cultural group rights. He argues instead that both feminism and multiculturalism are making the same point about the inadequacy of the traditional liberal conception of individual rights. Both feminists and multiculturalists argue that justice cannot be achieved simply by giving these minorities the same set of formal individual rights that the majority possesses. What is needed, they argue, is a form of equity, i.e., equitable but distinctive treatment. In both cases, it is argued that the distinctive needs and interests of women and ethnocultural minorities are simply never addressed through standard, equal treatment and the result is that liberalism has been blind to grave injustices that limit the freedom and harm the selfrespect of women and ethnocultural minorities. Other minorities, Kymlicka points out, including persons with disabilities and gays and lesbians, have made similar arguments about the need for group-specific rights and benefits. All of these movements are challenging the traditional liberal assumption that equality requires identical treatment. They are arguing instead for equity of treatment.

SOURCE: Adapted from Okin, Cohen, Howard, and Nussbaum 1999.

The International Covenant on Economic, Social and Cultural Rights (ICESCR) deals primarily with collective societal rights—defined as rights that are due to all people of a society and that are the responsibility of governments to provide. The second Covenant, the International Covenant on Civil and Political Rights (ICCPR), deals with individual rights—freedoms and responsibilities that all individual citizens must be allowed to exercise.

The International Covenant on Economic, Social and Cultural Rights adopts a collective societal or nation-wide perspective, which puts the onus on governments to provide adequate living conditions for all persons. The Covenant recognizes that all persons have a right to work, to fair wages, to social security, to freedom from hunger, to health and education, and to the formation of and membership in trade unions. While considerable time may be required, especially for developing countries, to implement all of these rights, nations choosing to ratify the Covenant are expected to initiate appropriate legal measures following ratification.

The International Covenant on Civil and Political Rights adopts an individual perspective, which places the onus on nations and judiciaries to protect all individual citizens against cruel, inhuman and degrading treatment. This Covenant recognizes the right of every person to life, liberty, security, and privacy. It prohibits slavery, guarantees the right to a fair trial, and protects against arbitrary arrest or detention. It recognizes freedom of expression, freedom of association, and the rights to peaceful assembly and emigration. These rights and freedoms that guarantee protection to the individual, include protection from abuses by governments. The burden of responsibility to uphold individual freedoms, therefore, lies not with governments but with the judicial system.

Nations that ratify this Covenant are expected to introduce laws that will reflect its provisions. Canada has taken measures to fulfill its commitment by enacting human rights legislation at both provincial and federal levels of jurisdiction and by entrenching a Charter of Rights and Freedoms in the Canadian Constitution (1982).

The Optional Protocol to the ICCPR provides individual citizens with direct recourse to the United Nations (UN). Persons who believe that their rights as specified in the Covenant have been violated can state their case before the UN Human Rights Committee. Such persons must first have exhausted all legal avenues within their own country. To date, Canada is one of only a small number of the nations signing the Covenant which has ratified the Optional Protocol.

In 1978, the UDHR and the two later covenants (ICCPR and ICESCR) were incorporated into the International Bill of Human Rights (United Nations 1978).[2]

The major thrust of international human rights instruments has been to endorse the principle of the global unity of humankind and to afford protection for the fundamental rights and freedoms of individuals. Notwithstanding this observation, there are a number of important provisions that can be seen to endorse the global principle of group diversity and to afford protection for collective cultural rights and for categorical rights.

Collective Cultural Rights

Unique among international instruments (Magnet 1989: 746) is the provision for minority rights found under Article 27 of the ICCPR. This article states that:

> In those states in which ethnic, religious or linguistic minorities exist, persons belonging to such minorities shall not be denied the right, in community with the other members of the group, to enjoy their own culture, to profess and practice their own religion, or to use their own language.

Magnet (1989: ibid.) points out that legal interpretation of this article has shifted from a restrictive stance that limited its application to individual members of historically well-established minorities and imposed only negative obligations (non-interference) on ratifying states, to a broader stance that extends its application to old and new minorities as groups and that imposes affirmative obligations on ratifying states.

The latter interpretation of Article 27 has gained considerable support with the recent adoption by the General Assembly of the United Nations, in plenary, on 18 December 1992, of the Declaration on the Rights of Persons Belonging to National or Ethnic, Religious and Linguistic Minorities. In particular, Articles 4 through 7 of this declaration (reproduced below) specify the obligations on ratifying States to take appropriate measures to protect the collective cultural rights of minorities specified in the Declaration.

Declaration on the Rights of Persons Belonging to National or Ethnic, Religious, and Linguistic Minorities

Article 4

1. States shall take measures where required to ensure that persons belonging to minorities may exercise fully and effectively all their human rights and fundamental freedoms without any discrimination and in full equality before the law.

2. States shall take measures to create favourable conditions to enable persons belonging to minorities to express their characteristics and to develop their culture, language, religion, traditions, and customs, except where specific practices are in violation of national law and contrary to international standards.

3. States should take appropriate measures so that, wherever possible, persons belonging to minorities have adequate opportunities to learn their mother tongue or to have instruction in their mother tongue.

4. States should, where appropriate, take measures in the field of education, in order to encourage knowledge of the history, traditions, language, and culture of the minorities existing within their territory. Persons belonging to minorities should have adequate opportunities to gain knowledge of the society as a whole.

5. States should consider appropriate measures so that persons belonging to minorities may participate fully in the economic progress and development in their country.

Article 5

1. National policies and programs shall be planned and implemented with due regard for the legitimate interests of persons belonging to minorities.

2. Programs of cooperation and assistance among States should be planned and implemented with due regard for the legitimate interests of persons belonging to minorities.

Article 6

States should cooperate on questions relating to persons belonging to minorities, including exchange of information and experiences, in order to promote mutual understanding and confidence.

Article 7

States should cooperate in order to promote respect for the rights set forth in this Declaration.

Collective Right to Self-Determination of Peoples

The collective right of self-determination of peoples is protected under the provisions of Article 1 of both the ICESCR and the ICCPR. This article states:

> All peoples have the right of self-determination. By virtue of that right they freely determine their political status and freely pursue their economic, social and cultural development (IBHR 1978:10).

Until quite recently, legal interpretation of this article has been based on a very narrow concept of 'people' that, in essence, equates 'people' with 'nation'. That is to say, the collective rights of peoples apply only to peoples [ethnic groups] whose cultural/territorial boundaries coincide with or have the potential to coincide with the boundaries of a state unit (Wiberg 1980). Indeed, in its application under international law, the concept of peoples has been interpreted even more narrowly, so as to support the right to self-determination only in cases of non-self-governing territories formerly under colonial rule by overseas states (ibid.). This restrictive interpretation affords no support for the nationhood claims of peoples/nations living inside the territorial boundaries of recognized, sovereign states.

Over the past two decades, however, largely in response to resolute lobbying by organizations and coalitions representing the world's 'internally colonized' aboriginal [indigenous] peoples, there has been increasing support for a broader interpretation of Article 1 among international legal scholars.

A draft proposal for an International Covenant on the Rights of Indigenous Peoples was adopted in Principle by the Third General Assembly of the World Council of Indigenous Peoples in May 1981. This draft proposal incorporated the right to self-determination of peoples (under Article 1) as a cardinal principle of the rights of aboriginal [indigenous] peoples. In response to this and other, parallel, declarations submitted by aboriginal organizations, in 1982, a United Nations working group on indigenous populations was established by the Sub-Commission on Prevention of Discrimination and Protection of Minorities. The Working Group is open to representatives of all indigenous peoples and their communities and organizations. The mandate of the UN Working Group was to produce an international declaration on the rights of indigenous peoples for consideration by the General Assembly (Sanders 1989: 407). A preliminary document, the Draft Universal Declaration on Indigenous Rights, was introduced in August 1988. While this draft recognizes the collective cultural and aboriginal rights of indigenous peoples as well as their 'collective right to autonomy in matters relating to their own internal and local affairs . . .' (Article 23, quoted in Sanders 1989: 429) within the institutional structures of recognized states, it falls short of an explicit recognition of aboriginal peoples as *nations* with an inherent right to self-government. In response, aboriginal representatives have continued to press for unambiguous recognition of the right of self-government of aboriginal nations in the declaration.

The Working Group continued to amend the draft declaration until 1994, putting special emphasis on the second of its two formal tasks, namely, to review national developments pertaining to the promotion and protection of the human rights and fundamental freedoms of indigenous peoples; and to develop international standards concerning the rights of indigenous peoples, taking account of both the similarities and the differences in their situations and aspirations throughout the world. In 1994, the Working Group submitted its amended draft declaration to the Sub-Commission on Prevention of Discrimination and Protection of Minorities. By its resolution 1994–5 of August 26th, 1994, the Sub-Commission adopted the draft declaration and submitted it to the Commission on Human Rights for consideration.

Like its predecessor, the 1994 Draft Declaration recognizes the collective cultural and aboriginal rights of indigenous peoples as well as their collective right to autonomy in matters relating to their own internal and local affairs (Article 31) and it also mandates governments to adopt positive measures to ensure that indigenous peoples can avail themselves of such rights in practice (Article 37). However, the Declaration has not met the demands of aboriginal peoples, for it does not accord unambiguous recognition to the right of self-government of aboriginal nations. The relevant articles of the Declaration are reproduced below.

Draft Declaration on the Rights of Indigenous Peoples (E/CN.4/Sub.2/1994/2/Add.1 [1994])

Article 31

Indigenous peoples, as a specific form of exercising their right to self-determination, have the right to autonomy or self-government in matters relating to their internal and local affairs, including culture, religion, education, information, media, health, housing, employment, social welfare, economic activities, land and resources management, environment and entry by non-members, as well as ways and means for financing these autonomous functions.

Article 37

States shall take effective and appropriate measures, in consultation with the indigenous peoples concerned, to give full effect to the provisions of this Declaration. The rights recognized herein shall be adopted and included in national legislation in such a manner that indigenous peoples can avail themselves of such rights in practice.

Following the World Conference against Racism, Racial Discrimination, Xenophobia, and Related Intolerance (WCAR), held in Durban, South Africa, from August 31st to September 7th, 2001, a Declaration was put forward that gave strong support to the 1994 Draft Declaration on the Rights of Indigenous Peoples (WCAR Declaration). Yet, like the Draft Declaration, it did not meet the nationhood demands of indigenous peoples, including those put forward by Canada's First Nations. Indeed, section 24 of the Declaration asserted that 'the use of the term "indigenous peoples" in the Declaration and Programme of Action of the World Conference against Racism, Racial Discrimination, Xenophobia, and Related Intolerance is in the context of, and without prejudice to the outcome of, ongoing international negotiations on texts that specifically deal with this issue, and cannot be construed as having any implications as to rights under international law'. Thus, nationhood status, as construed in the demands of Canada's First Nations, was not sanctioned. Here, it is important to note that although the WCAR Declaration clearly endorsed the 1994 Draft Declaration on the Rights of Indigenous Peoples, Canada has not yet signed or promoted the Draft Declaration.

Human Rights as Legal Rights

At this point, it is important to distinguish clearly between international human rights principles and public policies or laws enacted by governments. For laws and government policies may violate human rights. As pointed out earlier, human rights principles are international, moral guidelines that are *prior to law*. They represent the global standards to which all laws of all countries should conform. However, as this book will amply demonstrate, laws do not always incorporate human rights principles: while some laws are modelled on human rights guidelines (for example, human rights statutes prohibiting discrimination on specified grounds, such as race or ethnic origin); others violate human rights principles (for example, laws that discriminate against particular populations on specified grounds, such as race or religion). When human rights principles do become incorporated into law, they become **legal rights** that can be invoked by persons or groups who perceive that their human rights have been violated in order to seek redress for the alleged violation.

The Legal Framework of Human Rights in Canada: Implications for Racial and Ethnic Minorities

The importance of human rights instruments, both at the international and the national levels, is that they provide standards upon which those who perceive that their rights have been violated can base claims. In Canada, the legal framework of human rights protection is based on a three-tiered system of standards governing human relations within the state (Binavince 1987).

International human rights instruments (IBHR and related covenants) apply to relations between states and provide the global standards to which all state legislation should conform. In keeping with the principles endorsed by international human rights instruments, Canada has enacted human rights legislation that prohibits discrimination on the grounds of race and ethnicity at all jurisdictional levels—provincial, federal, and constitutional.

Constitutional rules apply to relations between governments within the state and provide the national standard to which all statutory laws should conform. In order to provide a national, constitutionally endorsed standard for human rights legislation throughout the country, Canada has enacted a Charter of Rights and Freedoms in its amended (1982) Constitution. In keeping with the non-discriminatory provisions of Articles 1 and 2 of the UDHR, Canada has enacted the equality rights provisions of section 15 of the Charter under which discrimination on the specified grounds of race and ethnicity is prohibited. Moreover, in keeping with the international principle of collective cultural rights under the provisions of Article 27 of the ICCPR, Canada has enacted section 27 of the Charter affording ethnic minorities constitutional protection for their 'multicultural' rights.

Statutory human rights legislation applies to relations between individuals and organizations within the state and should conform to the guarantees for human rights in the Charter and related constitutional provisions. Since the enactment of the Charter, Canada's provincial and federal human rights laws have been undergoing a process of amendment so as to bring their provisions into conformity with the Charter standard. For example, the constitutional provision for affirmative action under section 15(2) of the Charter has provided the catalyst for parallel, statutory legislation allowing affirmative remedies against the collective, adverse impact of systemic discrimination for disadvantaged racial and ethnic minorities.

Human Rights Legislation and Minority Rights Claims

A legal framework of human rights protection allows those whose rights have been violated to bring forward claims for legal redress and recompense.

When individual members of minorities are discriminated against, and their human rights violated, because of their perceived minority group affiliation, the violation is not an act directed against the individual *per se*. That is to say, the violation is not based on the target individual's unique personal characteristics. Rather, the real target is the minority group with which the individual has been identified. As will be discussed in some detail in Chapter 2, this form of discrimination is *categorical* discrimination—against the minority category as a whole.

What this means for individual members of a particular target group is that offences against the minority community as a whole can be and often are experienced as offences against the individual person. Accordingly, denial of ethnic group autonomy (the group's right to determine its collective destiny) is experienced as a restriction on individual freedom of choice (oppression); denial of group-level equality of opportunity, is experienced as a limitation on individual equality rights (neglect), and an affront to the minority group (group defamation) is experienced as a denial of the individual right to dignity of person (diminution). As will be shown later in this chapter, this melding of individual and community experience reveals the collective dimension of individual rights, and it has important implications for the putting forward of *categorical* rights claims.

As stated earlier, any member of a particular social group or category who perceives that s/he or his/her group as a whole has experienced violations of the right/s to freedom, equal opportunity or dignity on the arbitrary basis of (assumed) membership in the group, and, has as a result suffered unfair disadvantage, can make *categorical rights claims*.

By way of contrast, *collective cultural rights claims* can only, justifiably, be put forward by representatives of ethnic minorities with distinctive ethnocultures. As indicated earlier, the basic principle behind collective cultural rights is the right of ethnic communities *as such* to legitimately and freely express their cultural distinctiveness. When this right is violated—when members of the community are denied the right to practise and maintain their distinctive religion, language, or customs—then a collective cultural rights claim can legitimately be put forward.

The one component of ethnicity that differentiates the kinds of collective rights claims that may be put forward by particular ethnic groups is that of *territoriality*. Internationally, a 'people' whose territorial/ethnocultural boundaries potentially or actually coincide with the geo-political boundaries of a state unit can be conceptualized as a 'nation'. As applied to ethnic groups within the boundaries of a given state unit, this interpretation is more problematic. Nevertheless, there is growing support among legal scholars not only for the view that all ethnic communities can claim collective cultural rights, but also for the argument that all ethnic communities that can demonstrate a continuing, integral association between the people, its ancestral territory, and its distinctive ethnoculture within the boundaries of a given state unit (such as the Franco-Quebecois in Canada) can claim collective national rights (*nationhood* claims).

Territoriality has a unique dimension in connection with the collective claims of aboriginal ethnic groups. From the aboriginal perspective, aboriginal right and title to land derive from occupancy and use (*usufruct*) by their ancestors 'from time immemorial'—as far back as any member of a particular aboriginal group can remember. Moreover, aboriginal rights are seen as derived from a collective form of land occupancy and use; they are collective rights; rights of aboriginal communities, not rights of individuals (Boldt and Long 1985: 17). Those aboriginal peoples whose ancestors never signed land cession treaties with State authorities whereby their aboriginal right and title were deemed, by the State, to be 'extinguished', can make land claims based on *aboriginal rights*. Aboriginal peoples represented by living communities whose members continue to occupy and use their aboriginal lands and whose distinctive culture continues to be, at least in part, land-based, not only can claim aboriginal rights, but also can make *nationhood* claims.[3]

Human Rights as Legal Rights: Individual, Categorical, and Collective Claims

Under statutory human rights legislation at the provincial and federal levels, all Canadians, as individual persons, can put forward claims for redress against perceived violations of their individual human rights by other individuals or by organizations. Additionally, under the Charter and related constitutional provisions, individuals can put forward claims that challenge governments when their laws, policies, or practices do not conform with constitutional guarantees for human rights. Under the equality rights provisions of the Charter, section 15(2) permits members of disadvantaged minorities to put forward categorical rights claims, individually or collectively, against governments, for redress against the adverse impact of systemic discrimination upon the minority as a whole. Parallel legislation has been enacted by federal and provincial governments, allowing categorical rights claims to be put forward under statutory human rights laws.

As groups, ethnic minorities who perceive that their collective right to freely express their distinctive religion, language, or other ethnocultural attributes has been denied, can bring forward claims against governments under the combined provisions of section 15 (equality rights) and section 27 (multicultural rights) of the Charter. These collective rights claims essentially represent claims for recognition and protection of minority ethnocultures.

Collective Ethnic Claims: Cultural, National, and Aboriginal Rights

For purposes of analysis, I propose a threefold division among Canadian ethnic groups, on the basis of the differential nature of their collective claims: founding (English/French), multicultural (immigrant), and aboriginal (Indian, Inuit, and Métis) peoples. While all ethnic groups are able to put forward cultural rights claims, not all ethnic groups can legitimately make national rights claims. Insofar as immigrant/multicultural ethnic groups cannot provide evidence for ancestral/territorial links to a particular geographical area within Canada, they cannot, justifiably, make nationhood claims. The collective, nationhood claims put forward by founding/charter and some aboriginal peoples derive their legitimacy from a demonstrable, continuing link between ethnicity and territoriality.

The constitutionally recognized and historically grounded link between Franco-Quebecois and Quebec—their ancestral homeland, underscores their claim to nationhood. Aboriginal peoples can make two kinds of claims: claims based on **aboriginal rights** and claims based on **national rights**. The latter (nationhood) claims rest on the demonstrable link between particular aboriginal peoples, their traditional aboriginal territories, and their living, land-based ethnocultures.

Human Rights Claims Differentiated in Terms of Goals Sought

A critical distinction between human rights claims alleging violations of individual and/or categorical rights and claims alleging violations of collective rights lies in the goals sought by claimants.

Individual and categorical rights claims are equality-seeking claims. That is to say, the ultimate goal of claimants is to secure equal status of individuals and equality/equity of opportunity and treatment (for example, equal pay for the same work/equal pay for work of equal value). Collective rights claims, alternatively, are predicated on the collective right to be different. The ultimate goal of claimants is 'distinct group survival' (Sanders 1989: 406).

Collective rights claims can be divided into two categories, those based on *special status* and those based on *equivalent status*. Claims based on equivalent status seek a goal of equality/equivalence of group status and the right to equal/equivalent expression of unique ethnocultures (for example, multicultural group status). Claims based on special status seek a goal of distinctive group status and the right to special treatment (for example, founding/charter group status, aboriginal group status).

The human rights framework for the analysis of ethnicity and human rights in Canada, proposed in this introductory chapter, conceptualizes human rights issues in terms of moral principles, violations, and claims. A schematic representation of this framework is found in the typology of human rights, violations, and claims introduced in Table I-1.

Table I-1 suggests that, in Canada, individuals or groups who perceive that they have been subject to human rights violations may put forward the following types of claims:

1. *Individual Rights Claims* can be put forward by individuals who perceive that they have been personally subject to acts of individual or institutional discrimination (for example, Chinese, Sikh, or Inuit applicants denied jobs on the grounds of race, religion, and aboriginal status, respectively, can make complaints for redress [job opportunities]).

2. *Categorical Rights Claims* can be put forward, individually or collectively, by members of minorities who perceive that the minority as a whole has been defamed and/or disadvantaged as a result of past discrimination (for example, aboriginal or black minorities, collectively disadvantaged by a lack of adequate job qualifications as a consequence of deficient educational opportunities in Canada, can make claims for redress [special education and training programs]; Japanese-Canadians, incarcerated in internment camps in Canada during the Second World War, can make claims for redress against group defamation and disadvantage [public apology and monetary reparation from the Canadian government].

3. *Collective Rights Claims*
   a) *Collective cultural rights* claims can be put forward by minorities whose members perceive that the minority as a whole has been subject to cultural discrimination (for example, aboriginal or ethnocultural minorities such as Cree or Ojibway,

Table I-1: A Typology of Human Rights Principles, Violations, and Claims

Principles	Violations	Claims
Fundamental Human Rights		
Individual		individual claims
Right to life	homicide	
Freedom (self-determination)	oppression	
Equal opportunity	neglect	
Dignity of person	diminution	
Group or Category		categorical claims
Right to life	genocide	
Freedom (group autonomy)	group oppression	
Equal opportunity	group inequity	
Group dignity	group defamation	
Collective Cultural Rights		collective claims
Distinctive ethnocultural design for living (language, religion, institutions, customs)	cultural discrimination (deculturation/ cultural genocide)	
Collective National Rights		nationhood claims
Self-determination as a distinctive nation within own ancestral/territorial bounds	national discrimination (denial of nationhood status)	
Collective Aboriginal Rights		aboriginal rights claims
Right and title to aboriginal lands based on collective use and occupancy by aboriginal ethnic group 'from time immemorial'	land entitlement discrimination	

Ukrainian or Jewish) whose distinctive language, religion, customs, or lifestyles have been denigrated, suppressed, or destroyed can make claims for recognition and protection of their distinctive cultural practices.

b) *Collective national rights* (nationhood) claims can be put forward by minority ethnic groups with demonstrable links to an ancestral-territorial base or 'homeland' within Canada, whose members perceive that the minority as a whole has been subject to national discrimination, i.e., denial of their collective right to self-determination as internal nations within their own territorial bounds (for example, Inuit of Nunavut and Franco-Quebecois) [cultural sovereignty and self-government].

c) *Collective aboriginal rights* claims can be put forward by aboriginal ethnic groups (Indian, Inuit, or Métis peoples) whose aboriginal right and title to lands used and

> occupied 'from time immemorial' have not been 'extinguished' through land cession treaties with governments or by other lawfully recognized means [claims for monetary recompense and/or to occupancy and use of designated aboriginal lands].

While the human rights framework elaborated in this introductory chapter will inform the analysis of ethnicity and human rights throughout this book, the reader should note that it will be in the last two chapters, Chapters 8 and 9, that our analysis will focus on the *legal* implications of the human rights framework for the putting forward of minority rights claims.

Concluding Comments

Our examination of internationally endorsed human rights principles advanced in the provisions of the International Bill of Human Rights (United Nations 1978, 1988) and related covenants, confirms that the international human rights system is rooted in the fundamental human rights precepts of social equality and social justice. These international human rights principles are advocated by United Nations authoritative bodies as moral guidelines, the universal human rights standards, to which all systems of justice should conform.

International human rights principles provide an overarching paradigm for social equality and social justice for all of humanity, rooted in the twin foundations of human unity and cultural diversity. The principle of biological unity of humankind emphasizes the oneness of all human beings as members of the same human species and recognizes the close affinities between members of all human populations. The principle of cultural diversity respects the unique contributions to all of humankind made by each cultural community throughout the globe. Together, these cardinal principles underscore the theme of unity in diversity, recognizing and embracing the essential oneness of all humanity, while celebrating the uniqueness of each human being and of each human group.

In light of the current endorsement of these international human rights principles and their incorporation into human rights laws by the bulk of the world's democratic nations, how do we explain continuing violations of human rights in democracies throughout the globe, violations that create and sustain regimes of social *inequality* and social *injustice*? In particular, how do we explain the continuing violations of the fundamental human rights of members of racial and ethnic minorities throughout this country?

In order to answer these questions in the next chapter, we will first provide a social scientific understanding of the key concepts of race, ethnicity, and racism. We will then demonstrate how majority authorities are able to use *socially constructed* concepts of race and ethnicity as tools in racist ideologies employed to *justify injustice* by legitimating discriminatory laws, policies, and social practices that violate the human rights of members of racial and ethnic minorities.

Key Concepts

- aboriginal rights
- categorical rights
- collective cultural rights
- ethnoculture
- formal equality and substantive equality
- freedom, dignity, and equality
- human rights principles
- human unity and human cultural diversity
- individual human rights
- legal rights
- national rights
- universality of human rights

Critical Thinking Questions

1. How can an understanding of international human rights principles benefit members of racial and ethnic minorities?
2. What is the basis of criticism levied against the principle of the *universality* of human rights? How have supporters defended this principle?
3. Can conflicts between individual and collective rights be resolved? Elaborate.
4. What is the difference between categorical and collective rights, and how does this distinction affect the nature of claims that can be raised against human rights violations?
5. What is the difference between human rights principles and human rights legislation? How are these related?

CHAPTER 1

Human Unity and Cultural Diversity: The Janus-faced Underpinnings of Ethnicity, Human Rights, and Racism

Introduction: The Biological Roots of Human Rights

The Introduction presented the key international human rights principles adopted by the United Nations and endorsed by most of the world's democratic nations. It then raised the question: How do we explain continuing violations of human rights in democracies such as Canada that have sanctioned principles of social equity and justice for all? In particular, since this book focuses on ethnicity and human rights in Canada, the question arises: How do we explain the continuing violations of the fundamental human rights of members of racial and ethnic minorities throughout this country?

To answer these questions, I will establish a human rights framework to aid in the social scientific understanding of the key concepts of race, ethnicity, racism, and human rights—concepts that are widely misunderstood. Ethnicity has long been confused with race, and race continues to be erroneously equated with racism. The latter concept implies the restriction or denial of human rights: But on what scientific premises are human rights based?

To understand the nature of the scientific evidence behind the concept of human rights, one must first grasp some of the facts concerning humankind as a biological species. The first thing to stress is the biological unity of humankind today within one human species, that is, *Homo sapiens*. What do we mean here by unity? Our human species is a closed genetic system; that is to say, our species is unable to hybridize with any other. This is because no other species of the genus *Homo* now exists; in fact, none has existed for probably a quarter of a million years. For reproductive purposes, therefore, our species is restricted to its own members. That there is no biological barrier to reproduction between any of the world's peoples is abundantly clear from our history, and from the many crossbred members of the human species.

Mating between members of different human groups has led to the creation of new populations such as the Canadian Métis and American blacks. This process of miscegenation involves a biological overlap of gene pools—introducing through reproduction, genes, perhaps numerous in one population, into another population where they may be rare or even absent. The overall effect, then, is to broaden the spectrum of human variability. It is important to recognize this process not as one of blending characteristics, but as bringing forward new combinations or permutations of genes. Thus, a new gene pool, such as that possessed by Canada's Métis, includes genes characteristic of Canadian Indian peoples as well as those derived from Canada's British and French settlers. The test of whether such miscegenation is viable or not is a simple one: reproductive success. The answer is clear and positive.

We must not lose sight of the fact that, despite there being no convincing biological argument against miscegenation within our species, its occurrence is more likely to be dependent on sociocultural reasons such as religious prohibitions or language barriers. Looking at what is commonly called our Canadian ethnic mosaic, there is a tendency to think in terms of stereotypes, and to misconceive of particular ethnic groups as virtually discrete and homogeneous racial and cultural units. This all-too-human tendency to emphasize and exaggerate observable differences among human populations obscures the range of individual variation within each of these groups. It also deflects attention from the very real affinities and similarities among all groups belonging to the same human species.

One of the contemporary tasks of the physical anthropologist is to demonstrate the biological *affinities* among human populations. Before we undertake this task, some of the common misconceptions and misunderstandings associated with the concept of race need to be clarified. For it is these misunderstandings that have often influenced the prejudicial attitudes and discriminatory practices toward particular human populations that we refer to as racism.

Defining the Term *Race*

The word *race* first occurs in the English language about AD 1500. A study of its etymology shows that it was adopted from the French word *race,* which is connected to the Italian word *razza* and the Spanish word *raza.* Beyond this, its origin is obscure.

The initial English usage of the word was apparently to indicate a class or set of persons (or even plants and animals) possessing some common feature or features, which might be of common descent or origin. In the sixteenth century, the term *race* was used more widely, and could mean the people of a house, or a family, as well as a tribe, nation, or people regarded as being of common stock. It was not until the eighteenth century, however, that the term was used to indicate major divisions of humankind by stressing certain common physical characteristics such as skin colour. While in earlier usage the term had generally been used to mean 'the human race', 'the race of men', or 'the race of mankind', its later meaning grew more narrow, particularly as the voyages of explorers and the journals of travellers revealed more and more physical varieties of humankind.

By the middle of the nineteenth century, English usage of the term had come to include behavioural or temperamental qualities resulting from belonging to a particular people or ethnic origin group. Groups of several tribes or peoples were considered to make up these culturally distinct ethnic stocks or races. This erroneous connecting of physical attributes with behavioural and other cultural traits has persisted into modern times, and, unfortunately, continues to be used in the social construction of pseudo-scientific racist ideologies.

We should remember, of course, that earlier scholars had no knowledge of the science of human genetics that so importantly influences the scientific concept of race today. Beginning with the discoveries of Gregor Mendel (1822–84), Abbott of Brunn, and subsequently elaborated by innumerable other scholars, the science of genetics revolutionized scientific thinking about the relationships among all human populations. Most important, study shifted from the old preoccupation with racial *differences*, to a new interest in the biological *affinities* among human populations.

Evidence from the study of human genetics demonstrates unequivocally that there is no such thing as *pure race*. Rather, racial differences are relative phenomena, indicated by greater or lesser frequencies of particular genes, rather than their absolute presence or absence. Indeed, the study of human genetics indicates that there is a greater range of variation *within* any given human population than exists *between* human groups.

Let us consider, then, evidence based on some commonly used genetic markers, such as the frequencies of certain blood group substances. What kinds of primary racial divisions can be made using this kind of information alone, disregarding the physical appearance of the population samples being tested?

It is clear from these genetic data that primary divisions of humankind are distinguishable from one another. The evidence of physical features, skeletal features, and many genetic markers combine to indicate clearly that there are differences among populations of the same human species that are drawn from the three major, geographical breeding grounds of human populations in Africa, Asia, and Europe. These broad biogeographical divisions (races) are commonly identified as Negroid (black), Mongoloid (yellow), and Caucasoid (white), respectively.

Evolving Races of Humankind

It should be borne in mind, of course, that what are virtually new races of humankind have been evolving as the species has become increasingly mobile. As suggested earlier, what has been happening is an interchange of genetic material through repeated miscegenation. The gene pools originally characteristic of certain human populations have been modified accordingly. This brings not only variation in the frequencies of certain genetic markers, but also variation in external physical features. Such comparatively new populations are numerous on the world scene. The American black is one example. Historic and genetic evidence indicates that the American black is the product mainly of African (black) and European (white) miscegenation. The human geneticist T.E. Reed (1969) has demonstrated this by analysis of frequency data relating to the presence of Duffy blood group antigens in American blacks, African blacks (from the forced migration regions), and American whites. It is clear from his data that there has been a contribution of Duffy positive antigen genes from Caucasian gene pools to the American black gene pool.

In the past these new populations were commonly considered below the levels of fertility, intelligence, and achievement of the two parental stocks. Such racist myths about 'half-breeds' are now clearly held to be scientifically erroneous, and the viability of many of these new races is proof of this.

Race and Intelligence

Can racial differences in intelligence be demonstrated to exist? Obviously, differences between individuals, whatever their racial affinities might be, are going to exist, but what about means for intelligence quotients derived from large population samples of different racial affinities?

Intelligence tests have been conducted on a worldwide basis for many years in an effort to elucidate any connection between race and intelligence. The results seem to point to certain very general conclusions. The culture of the population being studied appears greatly to affect average scores. Tests found useful in one culture are often completely inappropriate in another. A test devised for, say, English Canadians, is unlikely to be as appropriate for testing Canadian Inuit, American blacks, or Australian aborigines. Intelligence tests can never be culture-free; they inevitably reflect the background of experience and skills considered important by the testers. Again, different peoples will approach tests with different degrees of sophistication and will expend different amounts of mental energy and perseverance on them. Social custom may affect motivation in tests, so that in one culture individuals may strive for personal success, while in others they may have been taught to avoid it. Survival may have been facilitated in some communities by a pretense of stupidity in the presence of superiors. Nutritional status and health status will affect test results. It is difficult, if not impossible, then, to weigh the many imponderable variables, and attempts to objectively relate human genetics and intelligence in situations of this kind are clearly premature. They may well remain so.

Today, many social scientists, human geneticists and educators have virtually abandoned the proposition that intelligence, however defined, can be accurately and objectively tested. Such tests as are now administered are usually given with restricted objectives in mind and designed in accordance with the population sample being studied.

The aforementioned problems of objectively measuring intelligence notwithstanding, it is worth noting at this juncture one of the key findings of an extensive review of the evidence on racial differences in intelligence in the United States by Loehlin, Lindzey, and Spuhler (1975). These three social scientists found that: 'The majority of the variation in either patterns or levels of ability lies within US racial-ethnic and socioeconomic groups, not between them. Race and social class are not very powerful predictors of an individual's performance on tests of intellectual abilities' (ibid.: 235). These authors attribute observed differences in the average scores of members of different racial-ethnic groups on intelligence to three factors: 1) the biases and inadequacies of the tests themselves; 2) differences in environmental conditions among the racial-ethnic groups; and 3) genetic differences among the groups (ibid.: 238). They conclude that '[r]egardless of the position taken on the relative importance of these three factors, it seems clear that differences among individuals within racial-ethnic (and socioeconomic) groups greatly exceed in magnitude the average differences between such groups' (ibid.: 239).

A recent report by four Canadian psychologists (Weizmann et al. 1990) indicates strong, continuing support for this position. This report exposes the highly publicized racist theories of Professor Phillipe Rushton (University of Western Ontario), which will be analyzed in some detail later in this chapter. Most significant, a new compendium of articles entitled *Race and I.Q.* edited by the renowned anthropologist Ashley Montagu (1999) debunks the mythology attributing differences in IQ scores to racial differences. What emerges in chapter after chapter is a deep skepticism about the scientific validity of intelligence tests, especially as applied to evaluating innate intelligence, if only because scientists still cannot distinguish between genetic and environmental contributions to the development of the human mind.

The Oneness of Humankind: Biological Roots of Human Rights

The foregoing conclusions about race and intelligence bring us full circle in our discussion of human unity and diversity. Today, there is a general scientific acceptance that all members of contemporary humankind belong to the same biological species, *Homo sapiens*. One important criterion in defining a species is that it has reproductive or genetic unity. Members of a species are interfertile. They can mate with one another without hindrance if given the opportunity. In some cases, of course, geographical barriers or distance may preclude such mating opportunities; thus there are no recorded instances, for example, of Canadian Inuit mating with Australian aborigines or with Kalahari Bushmen. On the other hand, there are numerous examples of interethnic matings within the human species (for instance, between Chinese or Japanese and American blacks or Europeans) that, in biological terms, have resulted in no deleterious effects. We may confidently assert that there is no basic biological or genetical difference between the various populations making up our contemporary species. Differences such as skin, hair, and eye colour have no bearing on human reproductive abilities. Such superficially obvious physical racial characteristics do not display discrete boundaries between populations. The tendency, rather, is for them to grade imperceptibly from one category to another across a continent.

Biological Unity, Cultural Diversity, and Human Rights

It is the essential biological oneness of humankind that provides the scientific underpinnings for the concept of fundamental and universal human rights. For fundamental human rights are rights of *humanity* that accrue to every human being simply by virtue of belonging to the human species. As pointed out in the Introduction, in the very first paragraph of the preamble to the Universal Declaration of Human Rights (UDHR 1948) recognition is given to the 'inherent dignity' and the 'equal and inalienable rights of all members of the human family' as 'the foundations of freedom, justice and peace in the world'. Thus, a primary assumption behind the UDHR is that of the fundamental unity and kinship among all members of humankind.

Like human unity, cultural diversity is recognized under international human rights instruments as a characteristic feature of humankind. However, as this book will demonstrate, ethnocentric biases of different ethnocultural communities can render arbitrary racial-ethnic differences salient and can lead to ethnic antagonisms. When invidious distinctions based on assumed or perceived racial or ethnocultural differences are used to justify the denial of human rights of members of particular human groups, racism rears its ugly head. In order to comprehend the complex social processes through which racism is generated, justified, and perpetuated, attention must be paid to the *social construction* of race and ethnicity within human societies.

Race and Ethnicity as Social Constructs: Demolishing the Myth of Racial Inferiority and Superiority

Scientific evidence on the biological attributes of the world's various racial and ethnic population groups demonstrates beyond doubt that no human population is innately superior or inferior to any other human population (UNESCO 1978). In order to *invalidate* any particular human population, therefore, one must rely on erroneous and negatively prejudiced invalidation myths about the inferiority of that population's human attributes. Myths of racial superiority and inferiority have long been used by those in power to justify unjust and often cruel acts of discrimination against particular racial and ethnic groups.

In order to demonstrate the scientifically erroneous premises behind racist myths and ideologies, it is important to clarify the social scientific meaning of the key concepts of race and ethnicity that are distorted and manipulated in these invalidation myths and ideologies. While there has long been considerable variation among theorists on social scientific definitions of these concepts, there is general agreement today that the concepts must be distinguished from one another and that the concept of race, if it is to be employed at all, should refer only to biological human attributes, and not to cultural attributes (Barker 1981; Rex 1983; Satzewich 1998a; Wilson 1978).

What Is 'Race'?

As employed in this book, the scientific term **race** refers to any arbitrary classification of human populations using biological measures such as observable physical traits and/or genetic indicators (gene frequencies for particular traits). This scientific definition of race is based solely on biological differences between human populations and not on cultural or behavioural differences.

The three most common racial categories today are Caucasoid (white), Mongoloid (yellow), and Negroid (black). Clearly, these categories are not based on cultural criteria—there is no white culture or black culture or yellow culture—but are based solely on race. However, each broad racial category can be subdivided along lines of ethnic origin, national origin, religion, and many other variables. Once we begin to differentiate among various populations within the broad racial categories, we introduce the component of culture. For example, within the 'white' category we find Italians, Irish, Jews, English, Spanish, and many other national, ethnic, and religious groups. Within the 'yellow' category we find such diverse populations as Chinese, Inuit, Japanese, and Vietnamese. Within the 'black' racial category we find a similar range of variation: Jamaican, Nigerian, Afro-American, Trinidadian, and so forth. The diverse populations within the three broad racial categories can be distinguished, at least in part, by cultural differences. Some of these differences pertain to ethnicity.

What Is Ethnicity?

As employed in this book, the social scientific term **ethnicity** refers to any arbitrary classification of human populations based on the biological factor of common ancestry in conjunction with cultural factors such as language or religion. Ethnicity, then, has both biological and cultural dimensions. It refers to one's biological ancestors, their ancestral territory or homeland, and their ancestral culture or ethnoculture. For members of existing ethnic communities, in addition to common ancestry that links members through time, there are the bonds of common kinship and ethnoculture that link living members. What this means, then, is that members of the same ethnic group are linked through time and space by common bonds of kinship and culture.

The root of this notion of ethnicity is the term *ethnic*, which simply refers to a people. Probably the easiest way for the reader to grasp this rather complex idea is to think of one's own family and family background. Can you name the particular people (ethnic group) with which your parents identified themselves? What about your grandparents and great-grandparents, and your ancestors before them? What part of the world would they have identified as their homeland? Where did they come from? What language did they speak amongst themselves? What religion did they practice? How did they dress and what kinds of foods did they eat?

Common ancestry links members of a given ethnic group, however, ethnicity is expressed as well in living ethnic communities whose members maintain distinctive, but ever-changing, ever-adapting ethnocultures. With changing circumstances—modernization, immigration, and so forth—ethnic communities and their distinctive cultures become transformed, even transported, to adapt to changes around them. As long as enough members of a given ethnic group continue to identify with and to maintain even selected aspects of their distinctive culture, however, their common ethnicity is maintained through bonds of kinship and culture.

Ethnicity may be expressed in a wide variety of forms, ranging from denial (disassociation from one's ethnic category), symbolic ethnicity (voluntary psychological identification with selected aspects of the cultural tradition of one's ethnic category), to some degree of commitment to the preservation of aspects of one's cultural heritage and some degree of participation in the living institutions of one's ethnic community.

What Is Culture?

In order to fully comprehend the meaning of ethnocultural diversity, it is important to clarify the concept of *culture* underlying it. In its anthropological sense, culture is synonymous with ethnoculture. Both terms refer to the distinctive ways of viewing and doing things shared by members of a particular ethnic community and transmitted by them from one generation to the next through the process of enculturation (distinctive ethnic socialization). More specifically, the culture/ethnoculture concept refers to the total configuration of patterned and institutionalized ideas, beliefs, values, standards, skills, and behaviours that characterize the distinctive worldview, ancestral heritage, and lifeways of a particular ethnic group. The most important point about culture, from a social scientific perspective, is that it is a learned phenomenon; it is acquired, for the most part, through the ordinary processes of growing up and participating in the daily life of a particular ethnic community.

Anthropologists generally agree that for a cultural lifestyle to be categorized as a culture in the sense of ethnoculture, it must have both a spatial (synchronic) and a historical (diachronic) dimension. When a given cultural lifestyle has been transmitted over at least three generations, it can be regarded as a genuine ethnoculture rather than a subculture (an alternative lifestyle within a given culture).[1] This distinction has important implications for the question of collective cultural rights, since legal precedent reveals that under international human rights instruments, cultural rights accrue only to members of genuine ethnocultures.

Insofar as culture is part of the condition of being human, then all individuals must learn to be human. But culture is not learned in the abstract. No human being is born into a cultural vacuum. Every member of humanity learns to be human by learning the distinctive lifeways—language, religion customs, etc., of a particular culture. Because of the very particularistic nature of learning to be human through distinctive enculturation, human beings identify themselves first as members of their own ethnocultural community and only second as members of the global community of humankind.

Members of ethnic communities committed to the maintenance of their distinctive ethnocultures are constrained to adopt *boundary-maintaining mechanisms*, designed to keep ethnic insiders in, and to keep ethnic outsiders out. Ethnocultural boundaries provide artificial barriers to human intercourse between insiders and outsiders, and, the more ossified the ethnic bounds, the greater the tendency to deny human rights to outsiders on arbitrary racially or culturally defined grounds. This observation may be taken as a starting point when we turn our attention, later in this chapter, to an analysis of the socially constructed roots of racism.

Unequal Power Relationships and the Social Construction of Race and Ethnicity

Within any human society, in any historical era, the **social construction** of the concepts of **race** and **ethnicity** reflect the ideological, political, economic, and cultural biases of the ruling authorities of the society. For those with the power to rule inevitably have the power to define. Populations defined in terms of the social constructs of race and ethnicity are not merely categorized or classified in a statistical sense; they also are evaluated in terms of the values and standards established by majority authorities as the norms for all members of the society. It follows, then, that the social constructs of race and ethnicity are not neutral or scientific classifications. Their social relevance, however, lies not in themselves, but in how they can be manipulated by majority authorities to serve their own vested interests. When social constructs of race and/or ethnicity are used by majority authorities to rationalize differential treatment of populations so-classified, socially created 'race' becomes translated into the social reality of racism.

Troper (1993) has argued that [socially constructed] race was always the key concept used to discriminate against ethnic minorities in Canada. Prior to the changes in immigration laws that opened the doors to 'visible minorities' (defined in terms of skin colour and assumedly related 'racial' attributes), immigrants whose ethnocultural characteristics (religion, language, customs) were perceived to differ in undesirable ways from dominant British-Canadian norms were viewed and treated as 'races'. Considered distinct from and inferior to Canada's two 'founding races' (English and French), they were socially constructed as people of colour on the basis of various combinations of physical, cultural, and behavioural criteria. In recent years, a growing number of theorists have come to refer to this phenomenon as **racialization** (Miles 1989; Satzewich 1998a).

Troper suggests that with the immigration to Canada of many racially visible minorities, the earlier immigrant 'races' have today become 'whitened'. I would also suggest that previously *racialized* ethnic minorities now have become *ethnicized*. Majority authorities in Canada now make clear distinctions between visible minorities (defined in terms of the social construct of race) and ethnocultural minorities (defined in terms of the social construct of ethnicity). Such distinctions can be constructed and deconstructed by those in power to suit their priorities at any given time. Moreover, they can be totally obscured in politically devised ideologies and policies of racism.

Race, Racialization, and Racism: Contested Concepts

The concepts of race, ethnicity, and racism used in this book are informed by a human rights perspective. I have adopted the provisions of current international human rights instruments as my guide to conceptualization of these key ideas. However, it is important for the reader to understand that social scientists are anything but unanimous in their interpretation of these concepts.

Satzewich (1998a: 25–45) provides a provocative review of the current scholarly debates concerning the use and validity of the concepts of race, racism, and racialization by social scientists. He traces the historical shift in meaning of the concept *race*, from lineage to biological reality to social construct. Today, he points out, biologically grounded definitions of race tend to be rejected in favour of those that focus on the socially constructed *label* of race. This, Satzewich states, has led some social scientists to abandon the use of race as an analytic concept. Other social scientists, however, express ambivalence over the political implications of focusing on race as a social construct and abandoning it as an analytic concept. Some suggest that this could lead to a denial of the reality of racism and an undermining of the anti-racist struggle. According to Satzewich, the maxim of W.I.Thomas—that if people define situations as real they are real in their consequences—is often invoked by critics (Driedger 1989; Fleras and Elliot 1995) to justify the continued use of race as an analytic concept.

Satzewich questions the continuing use of race as an analytic concept because the concept has been scientifically discredited. Here, I would have to point out that not all definitions of race have been scientifically discredited. Erroneous notions of 'pure race', 'race determines culture and temperament', and the racist ranking systems of racial superiority and inferiority predicated on these notions certainly have been scientifically discredited. But, the arbitrary classification of human populations on the basis of biological attributes has not.

The next contested concept discussed by Satzewich is that of *racialization*. Satzewich argues that the crucial element in the process of racialization is the 'delineation of group boundaries and identities by reference to physical and/or genetic criteria or by reference to the term race' (1998a: 32). The use of physical criteria is demonstrated in the concept of 'black/white relations'. The use of the term *race* is demonstrated in the concept of 'race relations'. Racialization can derive from self-definition as well as from other-definition, and it is not necessarily racist in implication. Satzewich suggests that to adopt an identity, whether externally imposed or self-defined, that revolves around certain characteristics such as skin colour reflects a process of racialization, but is not necessarily racist. What, then, Satzewich asks, is the difference between racialization and racism?

Like the concept of race, the concept of racism is a contested notion among social scientists. Satzewich looks at a number of different definitions of racism—ranging from the more traditional theories (biological determinism) to the new racism (cultural determinism). He is particularly critical of the concept of 'democratic racism' (Henry et al. 1995), which, he suggests, is a peculiarly Canadian form of racism that reflects an effort to reconcile the conflict between democratic values of justice, equality, and fairness, with maintenance of prejudiced attitudes and discriminatory acts against racial minorities. Satzewich argues that the definition is so broad that virtually any idea that denies, negates, or questions the significance of racism directed against black people is held to be automatically racist. I would add, by contrast, that from a human rights view, the definition is too narrow. While the definition of racial discrimination endorsed by the United Nations is not worded as 'racism', in its broad application, the meaning of racism extends far beyond the notions of race and colour, and includes also descent and national or ethnic origin (International Convention on the Elimination of All Forms of Racial Discrimination 1965).

Satzewich endorses the sociological definition of racism proposed by Miles (1989). In Miles' view, racism refers to ideas that delineate group boundaries by reference to race or to real or alleged biological characteristics, and which attribute groups so racialized with other negatively evaluated characteristics. Unlike the definition of Henry and colleagues, this concept of racism is broad enough to extend to 'white' ethnic minorities, whose members (as Satzewich points out in his critique of the Henry et al. notion of democratic racism) have become racialized at some period of time, by self or other definition.

Racism and Human Rights

Racism, in its most generally endorsed, classic sense, contains both ideological and behavioural assumptions. **Racism** can be defined as a set of beliefs, policies, and/or practices predicated on the erroneous assumption that some human populations are inherently superior to others and that human groups can be ranked in terms of their members' innate (biological) superiority/inferiority. A second erroneous assumption behind racism is that biology determines culture, temperament, and morality. Following from these premises, the diverse populations of humankind are ranked in accordance with the presumed superiority/inferiority of their member's physical, cultural, and behavioural characteristics.

From a human rights view, it is important to distinguish between the ideological and the behavioural dimensions of racism. Racist ideologies do not, in themselves, violate human rights; racist behaviours invariably do. When racist ideologies are used to justify policies or acts of discrimination against members of particular human populations, then racism becomes the instrument for human rights violations.

International Protection for Human Rights: Anti-racist Declarations

The United Nations pronouncements most specifically addressed to the relationship between ethnocultural diversity, racism, and human rights are the Convention on the Prevention and Punishment of the Crime of Genocide (1948) and the International Convention on the Elimination of All Forms of Racial Discrimination (1965). In the latter covenant, racial discrimination is defined, under Article 1, as

> any distinction, exclusion, restriction or preference based on race, colour, descent, or national or ethnic origin which has the purpose of nullifying or impairing the recognition, enjoyment or exercise, on equal footing, of human rights and fundamental freedoms in the political, economic, social, cultural or any other field of public life.

The most extreme form of racial discrimination against a human group is undoubtedly the act of genocide. Article 1 of the United Nations Convention on the Prevention and Punishment of the Crime of Genocide declares genocide, whether committed in time of peace or time of war, to be a crime under international law. In the process of drafting this covenant, genocide was defined as a criminal act directed against national, ethnic, racial, or religious groups of human beings, with the purpose of destroying a human population in whole or part, or of preventing its preservation or development. Phrased succinctly, the crime of genocide refers to discriminatory measures for the extermination of any national, ethnic, racial, or religious group.

Genocide represents racism, carried to its extreme. However, as a prelude to the analysis of racism and human rights in this chapter, it is important to point out that any human being who violates the human rights of another human being on the arbitrary grounds of assumed racial or cultural differences is committing an act of racism.

Invalidation Myths and Ideologies: The Paradigm of Racism

Dominant or majority groups, whose members are overrepresented among the governing authorities in a society, have the power to use invalidation myths and ideologies to rationalize categorical discrimination against less powerful minorities and, thereby, to violate their human rights.

Invalidation myths are falsified statements that allege that identified human populations are innately inferior or invalid (defective) with regard to particular human attributes. **Invalidation ideologies** are unsubstantiated theories that are designed to give credibility to invalidation myths by providing *pseudo-scientific* or *pseudo-religious* 'evidence' for them.

Invalidation ideologies contain both prejudicial and discriminatory assumptions. That is to say, they can be expressed in negatively prejudiced attitudes towards particular populations and in invocation to discriminatory acts against particular populations.

In general, invalidation ideologies—like racism, sexism, and ageism—can be conceptualized as a set of beliefs, policies, and/or practices designed to justify and legitimate invalidation myths by fabricating theories that offer *pseudo-scientific* or *pseudo-religious* evidence for them. Starting from the erroneous assumption that some human populations are innately inferior to others with regard to particular human attributes, a second assumption behind these theories is that human populations can be ranked re: their members' inherent superiority and inferiority. This false assumption regarding a 'natural' hierarchy of human populations provides a platform for discriminatory action against invalidated and inferiorized populations. It affords the rationale for alleged superior populations to claim that they are the 'natural' rulers of society and that they should control the life destinies of alleged inferior populations. In this way, invalidation ideologies provide the justification for categorical discrimination—involving human rights violations—against alleged inferior populations.

The role of invalidation myths and ideologies in legitimizing categorical discrimination against minorities is of critical importance for the understanding of majority/minority relations in Canada, for Canada is a democratic country with an international reputation and a constitutional mandate for the equal protection of the human rights of all its citizens. In order to legitimize the enactment or the continuation of discriminatory laws, policies, and/or practices against any particular minority, majority authorities in Canada must be able to provide a persuasive rationale in order to gain public support for their proposals. However, as has been convincingly argued in the introduction to this chapter, no scientific evidence exists to support any ideology based on notions about the superiority or inferiority of any human population. Majority authorities determined to promote such ideologies must, therefore, rely on invalidation myths that have become deeply imbedded in the public psyche and thus can be counted upon to generate public support.

The invalidation myths and ideologies to be considered in this book underscore racism. We have previously defined racism as follows:

> Racism, in its most general sense, contains both ideological and behavioural assumptions. Racism can be defined as a set of beliefs, policies and/or practices predicated on the erroneous assumption that some human populations are inherently superior to others and that human groups can be ranked in terms of their members' innate (biological) superiority/inferiority. A second erroneous assumption behind racism is that biology determines culture, temperament and morality. Following from these premises, the diverse populations of humankind are ranked in accordance with the presumed superiority/inferiority of their member's physical, cultural and behavioural characteristics.

In the following pages we will illustrate this definition of racism by providing concrete examples of racist myths and ideologies used by dominant powers to deny the human rights of racial and ethnic minorities.

The Socially Constructed Races of Humankind: Mythical Models

Prior to the twentieth century, Euro-Western anthropologists were preoccupied with the process of classification of humankind into various, arbitrary subdivisions or 'races' on the basis of observable biological criteria. Differences between Europeans and visibly different peoples from other parts of the world were assumed, at this time, to be preordained by some Divine Maker. Accordingly, 'races' initially were mistakenly assumed to represent discrete and immutable divisions within humankind (the fallacy of 'racial purity'). A second fallacy, predicated on the first, was that race determined culture. Observable cultural differences were thus mistakenly attributed to innate racial differences among the peoples of the world. These two invalidation myths—the 'pure race' myth and the 'race determines culture' myth—formed the basis of racist invalidation ideologies that were used to justify the subordination of non-white, non-European peoples by Euro-Western powers.

Racism: Early Religious Ideologies

In the era of colonial expansion, Euro-Western governments sent administrators to 'undeveloped' overseas countries in order to ensure that the colonial powers gained access to the valued resources in the area. In order to facilitate their control over the 'savages' residing in the newly administered territories, colonial governments encouraged Christian missionaries from the so-called 'mother' country to undertake the task of civilizing (Christianizing and Westernizing) the aboriginal inhabitants of the administered countries. This civilizing mission was 'justified' by biblical invalidation myths such as the myth of 'manifest destiny' and the 'hamlite rationalization' (Anderson and Frideres 1981: 211–12). Passages in the Christian bible were interpreted so as to lend support for the contention that white peoples are destined to rule the world (manifest destiny) and that non-white peoples are destined to be the servants of white masters (hamlite rationalization).

The manifest destiny postulate included two related ideas, that of the 'white man's burden' and that of 'noblesse oblige'. The white man's burden was the task of civilizing the savages. Noblesse oblige referred to the idea that privilege entails responsibility, that is, the white man, privileged with the power to rule, had the responsibility to care for and to protect the non-white savages under his control. The hamlite rationalization postulate provided an invalidation myth designed to justify the subordinate and even servile position (as slaves) of non-white peoples.

While the idea of manifest destiny has been supported through reference to various passages in biblical texts, the hamlite rationalization refers specifically to the biblical story of Ham. The main points of this myth may be summarized as follows: Ham and his brother came home late one evening and found their father drunk and lying naked on the floor. The room was in disarray and looked as though a wild party had taken place. Ham stood and stared at his father but his brother did not. His brother fetched a blanket and covered his father's body. The story concluded with the decree of God that Ham and all of his descendants should have a mark placed upon them and that they should occupy the status of servants forever. Over the years, the 'mark' has been interpreted as non-white skin, and the 'servants' decree has been used to justify the subordination of non-whites by whites.

Racism: Current Religious Ideologies

Among the many and varied hate groups in North America, some of the most virulent racists are represented in a number of fundamentalist right-wing Christian groups. Generally speaking, these religious groups share with other fundamentalists a rejection of the values of modern society which they perceive as atheistic, secular, materialistic, and immoral. Where they differ is in their explanation for the perceived ills of modern society: They hold that specified 'inferior' groups, in particular, Jews, who are portrayed as synonymous with Satan, are responsible for all of the world's social ills. A prime case in point is that of the Aryan Nations church.

Aryan Nations

Aryan Nations is a paramilitary hate group founded in the mid-1970s. It was formed around the Church of Jesus Christ Christian, one of several hundred churches affiliated with 'Identity', a pseudo-theological hate movement. Identity doctrine maintains that Anglo-Saxons, not Jews, are the biblical 'chosen people', that non-whites are 'mud people' on the level of animals, and that Jews are 'children of Satan'. Anti-Semitism is a basic tenet of the Aryan Nations ideology. Dennis Hilligoss, the group's state coordinator in Oregon, recently said, 'The Jew is like a destroying virus that attacks our racial body to destroy our Aryan culture and purity of our race.'

In 1996, Aryan Nations published a 'Declaration of Independence' for the Aryan race on its website. The declaration claims that the history of the present Zionist Occupied Government of the United States of America (ZOG) is a history of repeated injuries and usurpation, controlled by Jews, and aiming to establish a regime of absolute tyranny not only over the United States, but also over the entire world. In the declaration, the representatives of the Aryan people, in council, appeal to the supreme God 'of our folk' to endorse their declaration that the 'Aryan people in America, are, and of rights ought to be, a free and independent nation; that they are absolved from all allegiance to the United States of America, and that all political connection between them and the Federal government thereof, is and ought to be, totally dissolved; and that as a free and independent nation they have full power to levy war, conclude peace, contract alliances, establish commerce, and to perform all other acts which independent nations may of right do. The declaration concludes, "WE MUST SECURE THE EXISTENCE OF OUR PEOPLE AND A FUTURE FOR WHITE CHILDREN"' (*Aryan Nations*, 2 March 1988).

The aim of the Aryan Nations Church is to establish an all-white, all-Christian, Aryan-governed nation-state in the territory of North America. In Canada, Terry Long, a church leader who operates out of Alberta's Aryan Nations group, holds the position of 'High Aryan Nation Warrior Priest' (*INTERCOM* 9, 2: 4).

Modern Racism: Pseudo-scientific Racist Ideologies

Like religious racism, pseudo-scientific racism is predicated on the twin invalidation myths of racial purity and racial determination of culture. The difference between the two forms of racism is in their grounds of legitimation: *pseudo-religious* ideologies versus *pseudo-scientific* ideologies.

Prior to the publication in 1859 of Charles Darwin's pathbreaking treatise *Origin of Species*, anthropologists and naturalists who classified human beings into racial categories on the basis of observable physical characteristics tended to erroneously equate these biological traits with social and cultural attributes. Moreover, many of those involved in classification also tended to evaluate and rank the different racial categories. Samuel Morton (in *Crania America*, 1839), for example, suggested that the Caucasian race was superior to the Ethiopian race because the Caucasian skull was nine cubic centimetres greater in internal capacity than that of the Ethiopian (Rose 1968: 35).

With the publication of Darwin's theory of biological evolution of species, a new (pseudo-scientific) rationale for ranking of 'races' came into being. Popularized in the phrase 'survival of the fittest,'[2] Darwin's theory of natural selection was erroneously applied by nineteenth-century anthropologists and other 'Social Darwinists' to lend scientific legitimacy to their racist theories.

While Darwin's own concern was largely with the biological evolution of species, early Social Darwinists like Knox (1850), Bagehot (1873), and Kidd (1894) used his theories to link together biological and social evolution of sub-specific groupings, that is, human societies and cultures. Despite the fact that some of these scholars later retracted their earlier racist theories, their thinking, generally, had an important and lasting influence on the development of modern racism as exemplified in the writings of such diverse scholars as Gobineau (1854), Chamberlain (1899), Putnam (1961), Coon (1962, 1965), Collins (1979), and many others.[3]

Historically, one of the most insidious political uses of Social Darwinist invalidation ideologies lay in their provision of a pseudo-scientific basis for colonialism. Indeed, the pejorative connotation that has come to be attached to the term *colonialism* derives from the racist consequences of invalidation ideologies of White Supremacy, used to legitimate the subordination and exploitation of colonized non-white peoples by white colonizers.

Invalidation ideologies of White Supremacy developed by European whites in the grand era of empires and colonial expansion, in which they reigned supreme, depict the white races, variously defined, as the 'fittest', that is, as culturally and biologically superior to all other so-called races. At the bottom of this purported scale are the dark-skinned 'savages'. Their supposed inferior or uncivilized culture and technology is attributed to an assumed evolutionary lag by virtue of which they are deemed biologically incapable of achieving the fullest human and cultural development. Such invalidation ideologies have served to endow the words *primitive* and *native* with a connotation of innate inferiority, and have served, at the same time, to legitimize paternalistic colonial government policies toward aboriginal peoples so-defined.

Similarly, the racist ranking order spelled out in the invalidation ideology of anti-Semitism, an anti-Jewish political movement that surfaced in Germany in 1873, classified the Germans as the elite of the supreme Aryan or Nordic category; all other races were superseded, accordingly. Specifically, the Jews were singled out as an inferior, vile, and depraved Semitic race; their very presence in Germany was considered to present a threat of contamination and degeneration of the 'superior' civilization. The foundation for this ideology was provided in the writings of Houston Stewart Chamberlain (1899), who argued that the Jews were waging a permanent war for the destruction of Aryan civilization, and advocated expelling this alien and noxious element from the body of European society. The ideology of anti-Semitism was used to justify repeated acts of hostility toward and persecution of Jews in the nineteenth century. In the twentieth century Adolph Hitler used it to justify the racist policy of genocide that culminated in the death of millions of Jews during the Second World War. Like the thinking that underscored colonial suppression of the world's 'primitives', the Nazi theory of Aryan apotheosis was an extreme variation of the common invalidation ideology of White Supremacy.

Critique

Let me address two key fallacies behind pseudo-scientific racial myths and the racist ideologies predicated upon them. First, let's look at the fallacy of 'pure', discrete races. This myth is based on the erroneous assumption that there are absolute biological differences between discrete populations, which are responsible for qualitative differences in culture, personality, temperament, morality, etc. Associated with this view is the myth that interbreeding between superior and inferior races interferes with the natural order, corrupts the pure stock of the superior race, and results in degeneration and decay. Interbreeding, the myth holds, will eventuate in a 'race' of subhuman creatures (idiots and monsters). To illustrate the kind of racist propositions that derive from these fallacies, here are a few quotes taken from a pamphlet distributed by a White Power group centred in Australia:

- p. 4 'Choose an Aryan mate of the same or Nordic blood. When like meets like, you get harmony. When breeds mix that do not harmonize, the result is degeneration and decay.'
- p. 6 'MIXED BLOOD IS THE CAUSE OF ALL OUR TROUBLES, SPIRITUAL, PHYSICAL AND ECONOMIC, as we always find that people of bad blood are of low moral standards and practices, and this reacts on the social position and conditions.'
  'We can all see the tragic state of affairs in America, who threw her gates open to all and sundry to solve a labour problem. By this tragic error she sold her birthright.'
  DO NOT LET THIS HAPPEN HERE: UNITE TO KEEP AUSTRALIA WHITE
- p. 16 As the prime example of the dangers of inter-racial breeding, the pamphlet describes the Jews as a mongrelized people, made up of a mixture of races, mostly all bad, including mediterranean, oriental, and negroid strains. The pamphlet goes on to point out a few basic characteristics by which Jews can be readily identified: 'Feet pointed outwards, feet pointed inwards, this is Jew or Jew strain. If one waddles like a duck when walking, this is also Jew or Jew strain. If body is bird-shaped . . . chest out, stomach in and behind out—this is Jew . . . Jewish humour is always sexual perversity. Jews have no creative ability . . . only low cunning. . . . Fish eyes (bulging out)—this is Jew. . . . After a man finishes shaving, one sees a steely bluish tint on his face. This is Jew or Nigger.'

(Source: T. Graham, 'Be True to Your Race', Sydney, Australia, undated)

Pseudo-scientific Racism Today: The Phillipe Rushton Controversy

For some time, during 1989, media attention in Canada was conferred on the newly reported findings of research studies conducted by J. Phillipe Rushton, a psychology professor at the University of Western Ontario. Rushton's findings reportedly revealed an evolutionary hierarchy of races of humankind in which orientals rank highest, closely followed by whites, who far outdistance blacks, ranked at the bottom of the scale.

In 1995, Professor Rushton published his research findings in a highly controversial book *Race, Evolution and Behavior*. The book revealed that Rushton's research was based on the premise that the different races of humankind (oriental, white, and black) can be ranked re: superiority and inferiority on the basis of some 60 biological, behavioural, and sociocultural variables including brain size and intelligence (measured re: IQ tests), penis size and sexual energy and activity; sexual restraint; aggressiveness and criminal behaviour; family stability and law-abidingness. Rushton's propositions in regard to these criteria were: the larger the brain, the more intelligent and advanced the race; the smaller the brain, the less intelligent and the less advanced the race; the larger the penis, the more sexually and criminally aggressive, the more prone to sexually transmitted disease like AIDS, and the less advanced the race; the smaller the penis, the greater the ability to restrain sexual impulses (and thus to control family size and restrict exposure to sexually transmitted disease like AIDS) and the more law-abiding (measured re: criminal statistics) and the more advanced the race. On the basis of these criteria, Rushton claimed that orientals rank highest on the evolutionary scale, whites rank second (close behind), and blacks rank lowest (far behind).

Rushton claims that his findings confirm his Darwinian-based, evolutionary theory which holds that the more recently 'emerged' the race, the more superior its members' attributes, re: the criteria used in his research. Rushton claims that orientals emerged most recently (some 40,000 years ago), whites emerged earlier (some 100,000 years ago), and blacks emerged earliest (some 200,000 years ago).

In light of the scientific observations on race and the social scientific paradigm of racism presented earlier in this chapter, Rushton's theories clearly constitute invalidation ideologies that fall within the parameters of pseudo-scientific racism. Submitted to the scrutiny of academic authorities in his own field (Psychology), Rushton's research findings were found not only to be based on outdated and discredited theories and methodologies but also to be replete with errors of fact and interpretation. Weizmann and associates (1990: 22) comment that 'the repeated acceptance of his work in reputable publications raises some disturbing questions'. These questions go beyond Rushton himself to the performance of those institutions through which science regulates itself.[4]

Summary: Racism as the Debasement of Human Rights

Racist myths and ideologies, and the policies, programs, and practices predicated on them, tend to follow a fallacious, unscientific or pseudo-scientific line of reasoning whereby a human population's distinctive biological endowment is held to determine the equally distinctive culture, personality, mentality, and morality of its members. The logic of the argument that ensues from these erroneous assumptions is that the higher the race in the natural hierarchy of humankind, the more advanced the culture and the more civilized and human the person. The political implication of this line of reasoning is that the highest human race(s) should naturally dominate if not exterminate the lower ones. The human rights' implication is that only 'full' human beings (the highest human races) have inalienable human rights: races defined as less-than-human (the lowest races) can thus, 'justifiably', be denied human rights.

Racism and human rights are diametrically opposed concepts. Every human being, simply by belonging to the human species, has the same, inalienable human rights. Racism debases the very premise of inalienable human rights by violating the human rights of those human beings whom racists define as members of inferior, less-than-human 'races'. The various UN human rights instruments that currently prohibit racial discrimination against any human population represent a modern attempt to combat and eliminate racism in all of its insidious manifestations.

The 'New Racism'

Among the most pernicious expressions of racism in contemporary democratic societies, is a subtle form of ideological deflection that serves to deny the social reality of racism. This '**new racism**' has been conceptualized as an 'ideological gambit' (Baker 1981) employed by majority authorities in a democratic society to maintain the 'status quo' of racial and ethnic inequality in the face of espoused democratic ideals of anti-racism and egalitarianism. More recently, in the Canadian context, Henry et al. (1995) have coined the concept of *democratic racism* to refer to this phenomenon.

In Canada, the constitutional protection for equality rights, under sections 15(1) and (2) of the Charter, is impugned by the systemic inequality of visible minorities. Theorists adopting the perspective of the new racism argue that, in order to maintain the status quo of racial-ethnic inequality in face of an anti-racist/egalitarian national ideology, majority authorities have shifted their ideological stance from a focus on inherent (biological) racial inferiority to a focus on 'natural' cultural difference. This shift, however, does not alter the fundamental premise of 'white racism', that of blaming the victim for social and economic problems perceived as a 'natural' consequence of group differences.

Baker (1981) argues that the new racism is expressed in a language of innocence that disguises its insidious intent by framing its messages in a way that endorses 'folk' values of egalitarianism, social justice, and common sense. Racism, in effect, is ideologically transformed in ways that disavow, diminish, or distract from its actuality in a democratic society. In the context of the British political debate over the issue of immigration of visible minorities, Baker demonstrates that one ideological gambit frequently used is the argument based on 'genuine fears'. The case is presented that we (British) are normally fair and tolerant, but that these good qualities are overstrained. The (folk) ordinary people's fears and resentments concerning immigration are genuine ('there is no smoke without fire'). A tough stand on immigration is not racist; it is not based on irrational fears or racial prejudice. Rather, it is a rational, realistic (common sense) response based on facts about real economic and social problems that may arise from immigration.

The 'genuine fears' idea, Baker suggests, is a 'bridge concept' between the idea of protection of a distinctive national culture or way of life and the avoidance or elimination of a perceived threat to that way of life. The 'genuine fears' idea is used to justify policies taken to remove the perceived threat (repatriation, restrictions on immigration).

In contrast to traditional, pseudo-scientific racism, which posits a hierarchy of human superiority and inferiority based on immutable racial differences, the new racism is expounded in theories of ethnic absolutism based on 'human nature'. This approach posits the existence of 'natural' boundaries between human populations (nations) rooted in immutable cultural differences.

The theory of human nature behind the new racism proposes that human beings have a natural 'instinct' to form a bonded community, a nation, aware of its differences from other nations. Each national community, it is argued, has a natural home and its members share a natural instinct to preserve their common, national identity and to defend their territory (homeland). The language of this theory is race-free; but its covert agenda links together race/ethnicity/culture and nation, based on 'legitimate', 'natural' human instincts.

As Baker so astutely observes, the language of innocence in which the new racism is couched leaves racists free of any imputation of racial superiority/inferiority, or even of dislike or blame against those who pose the threat of 'cultural alienness'. The theory of 'pseudo-biological culturalism' holds that nations are built on human nature. Our biological instincts predispose us to defend our way of life, traditions, and institutions against outsiders, not because they are inferior, but because they are naturally different.

Gilroy (1991) suggests that the 'novelty' of the new racism lies in its capacity to link discourses of patriotism, nationalism, xenophobia, militarism, and sexism (patriarchy is 'natural') to provide a definition of race framed in terms of culture and identity. The theory of ethnic absolutism, Gilroy argues, views nations as culturally homogeneous 'communities of sentiment'. National cultures are seen as fixed, mutually impermeable expressions of ethnic and national identity. The new racism denies that race is a meaningful biological category: instead, race is displayed as a cultural issue.

Gilroy's position is illuminated by some very astute observations put forward by Thompson (2001: 63–4) who emphasizes the importance of seeing race and ethnicity in conjunction, because, he argues, the cultural differences of ethnicity are manipulated as political weapons [techniques of domination] by majority authorities to reinforce their power and control over minorities, insofar as these ethnocultural differences are seen as deviations from the ethnocentric majority norm. Failure to recognize this covert shift from ethnicity to race, Thompson argues, serves to mask racism and its subtle influences.

Gilroy (1991) uses the example of 'black criminality' to illustrate this point. While Gilroy's data are based on the British experience, a parallel case can be made for Canada. Here, I refer the reader to later sections of this chapter dealing with relations between blacks and the police.

Gilroy argues that the new racism endorses the view that law represents the cultural ideals of national unity and equality of citizens in a democratic nation. Identification of racially distinct crimes and criminals is attributed to the economically disadvantaged and politically marginalized status of blacks, which, in turn, is attributed to 'residual ethnic factors' in their inner-city culture ('deviant', single-parent, female-headed families; lack of work ethic, street-gangs bent on revenge against the white oppressor; drug subculture, and so forth). Legality, the ultimate symbol of national culture is held to be threatened by the entry of the 'alien wedge'. Cultural aliens (blacks) are seen as hedonistic (non-productive) and dangerous (criminals). Deviant black culture, it is argued, is expressed in particular forms of crime—drugs, street violence, and robbery ('mugging'), which have resulted in national chaos, a crisis in law and order, and a real threat to the distinctive, national way of life cherished by loyal and law-abiding citizens.

Another form of the new racism is found in sociobiological theories of 'social nationalism' (see, for example, van den Berghe 1978). This school of xenophobia holds that the source of racism, ethnocentrism, and nationalism is genetic. The argument holds that, in the struggle for existence, evolutionary processes have genetically and, therefore, immutably programmed humans to forge powerful in-group bonds ('kin altruism') within one's own genetic community (breeding population) and nation (cultural community characterized by organic social unity). At the same time, it is argued, human nature has been programmed with the opposite instincts of selfishness, hostility, and aggression towards competitive outsiders. The theory holds that xenophobia is an evolutionary trait bred into human beings over millions of years because of its genetic advantage. It is, therefore, 'natural' for nations to isolate themselves behind cultural and genetic barriers.

Baker (1981) observes that, like the 'genuine fears' form of the new racism, the sociobiological form leaves racists free of any imputation of racial superiority or inferiority. The theory appears 'neutral', and, like earlier pseudo-scientific theories of racism, it appears 'scientific', in the context of its time. Baker suggests that this form of the new racism is particularly insidious in its implications for ethnic relations because it has a powerful selling image in contemporary, democratic societies.

In Canada, as in Britain, the professed ideals of egalitarianism and anti-racism have become incorporated into law; thus the contemporary constraints against overtly racist acts or words are formidable. Canada's constitutional commitment to the values of multiculturalism and social harmony provide further constraints against overtly racist commentary. In consequence, the old racism has 'gone into the closet' where it has become transformed, in cultural guise, into the new racism. As in Britain, in Canada, the cultural differences (real or assumed) and the empowerment demands of visible minorities, have been perceived as a threat to national unity and identity and to national values of equal opportunity and justice for all citizens.

Polite Racism: The New Racism in the Mass Media

Fleras (1995) points out that blatant expressions of discrimination or racial slurs are rarely encountered in the mass media today. Overt hostility and discrimination is neither acceptable nor legal in Canada. Various human rights codes and the Charter of Rights and Freedoms prohibit discriminatory behaviour on the basis of race, colour, or national origin. Yet coverage remains that is 'politely' racist. Fleras refers to the work of Effie Ginzberg, who carried out a content analysis of columns and editorials in the *Toronto Sun* between 1978 and 1985. Her study findings reportedly exposed a 'biased, inaccurate, and unbalanced portrayal of visible minorities'. Prejudicial attitudes were directed at racial and aboriginal minorities through circulation of stereotypes, defensive strategies (denial of racism in Canada), biological racism (genetic superiority of whites), scapegoating, and incitement of fear and hatred toward racial out-groups. Fleras, among others, suggests that while such hostility may be muted, yet the accumulative effects may be powerful and long-lasting. Subtle racism can mask as a belief that the majority group is somehow losing out to minorities in jobs or housing or it may appear as criticism of multiracial immigration. Fleras suggests that someone who wants fewer Asians admitted to Canada, and yet does not call them genetically inferior, is engaging in polite racism. Polite forms of prejudice and discrimination continue to fester beneath the surface in the refusal to hire or promote racial minorities for one reason or another. The exclusion of minorities from advertising, for example, is discriminatory in consequence (if not in intent) because it leads to the restriction of employment opportunities. This is not overt discrimination, but can be 'justified' on political, economic, or social grounds.

In the Canadian context, two examples from the nineties come to mind: the controversy over Sikhs wearing turbans; and the escalating opposition to affirmative action measures designed to provide visible minorities with redress against the adverse (disadvantaging) impact of systemic discrimination.

Caveat

Although there is considerable evidence to support the view that the new racism has gained a foothold in Canada today, from a human rights view, I am compelled to introduce a cautionary note. I believe that a careful distinction should be made between legitimate, informed criticism of social policy and racist commentary.

In 1993, Alan Borovoy, general counsel to the Canadian Civil Liberties Association, criticized Ontario's then proposed employment equity law (Bill 79) for attempting to 'right yesterday's wrongs' against minorities by discrimination against majority members (*Toronto Star,* 2 September 1993). He argued that a legitimate plan of compensation for the disadvantaging effects of past discrimination would be to give (hiring) preference to the actual individual who suffered in the past, not to someone else who just happens to share the same minority status. This line of argument is supported by many well-respected scholars who have criticized programs of affirmative action on this ground and on other grounds (see Chapter 8). Can we, in all fairness, label all of these critics as 'new racists'? I think not. Indeed, I hope not.

The Old and the New Racism: Canada 2003

In Canada today, the **old** and the **new racism** flourish side by side. Dyed-in-the-wool bigots (Aryan Nations, Ku Klux Klan, Heritage Front, and other organized racist groups) continue to promote the religious and pseudo-scientific theories behind the established models of racism, while 'polite racists', as well as many self-professed anti-racists, cloak their parallel views in the discourse of culture promoted by exponents of the new racism. Yet, the source of both forms of racist discourse is the same—xenophobia—'an unreasonable fear or hatred of anyone or anything foreign or strange' (Hendrickson 1987: 571).

From a human rights perspective, what appears to distinguish the two forms of xenophobia is this: the established models of racism *racialize* culture (for example, Jews as a vile and depraved 'race'); the new models of racism *culturalize* race (for example, blacks as a dangerous and deviant 'subculture'). But the end result is the same: blaming the victim for the disadvantaging consequences of institutionalized and systemic racism.

Racism and Social Reality in Canada

Over the past four decades, human rights legislation has been enacted and amended so as to provide expanded equal protection for the human rights of all Canadians, regardless of racial-ethnic differences. To this same end, multicultural and anti-racist policies and measures have been

BOX 1-1: SURVEY

Public 'Folk' Attitudes Towards Racial and Ethnic Minorities

A 1995 survey of public attitudes toward ethnic diversity carried out by Decima Research for the Canadian Council for Christians and Jews (CCCJ) revealed that while Canadians support diversity, in principle, the majority believe that all Canadians should share a common way of life and values. The study findings are based on a national telephone survey undertaken among 1200 Canadians, 18 years of age or older. The interviewing for the study was conducted between February 12 and February 19, 1995. A similar study was carried out in 1993. Among the highlights of the study findings are the following:

Perceptions of the Canadian Community

- 74% of Canadians would define the 'ideal' community as one where members observe different religions and come from different racial or ethnic backgrounds, but share a common way of life and values.
- 72% feel that the values of the majority population should take precedence over those of minorities where there arises a conflict in traditions. [1993]
- 77% of Canadians feel that different ethnic groups should try to adapt to the value system and way of life of the majority. [1993]

Barriers to Community

- 50% of respondents feel that the greatest barrier to building a sense of community is the unwillingness of Canadians to accept diversity, while
- 44% feel that it is the reluctance of ethnic groups to integrate. [1993]

Multiculturalism

- 67% of Canadians agree that being a multicultural society is one of the best things about Canada. [1993]
- Only 20% feel that government should provide funding to ethnic minority groups to maintain their unique cultures.
- 76% agree to helping immigrants to integrate into Canadian society and institutions.

Intolerance/Isolationism

- Canadians are equally divided about the ability of the various ethnic groups to get along. [1993]
- 85% see at least some degree of racism as existing in Canada. [1993]
- 49% feel that ethnic minorities are more interested in maintaining their unique ethnic traditions than in learning how to become 'Canadian'. [1993]
- A slight majority feels that current immigration policy allows too many people of different races and cultures into Canada. [1993]

Community Relations

- 41% state that language issues present a substantial barrier to harmonious relations in Canada.
- 31% perceive race or ethnicity to be disruptive forces in terms of Canadian unity.

While these study findings do not reveal direct evidence of overt racism, subtle or polite racism is manifested in a palpable level of covert concern and unwillingness to accept racial and ethnic differences. This subtle, covert racism exemplified in the study findings highlights the continuing reality of the 'new racism' in Canada. The new racism infringes subtly but seriously on the human rights of Canada's racial and ethnic minorities.

SOURCE: *Survey of Public Attitudes Toward Ethnic Diversity*, 1995. CCCJ website.

enacted and implemented. Yet racism—old and new—continues to undermine the democratic goals of fairness, justice, and equity and to maintain the institutionalized inequalities among racial and ethnic groups in Canada.

Racism and Policing

Over the last two decades, a number of reports from commissions of inquiry as well as research reports from studies carried out by social scientists have proven, beyond doubt, that racism towards racialized groups and ethnic minorities is a systemic problem within Canada's police forces (Canadian Race Relations Foundation [CRRF]). Not only are citizens from racialized groups and ethnic minorities subjected to more suspicion by police (and treated accordingly), but they are also given less protection (Jacob 1993; Manitoba Public Inquiry 1991; QHRC 1988; Stenning 1994; Ungerleider 1993). These inquiries and research studies have identified varying manifestations of racism in the police services. An overview of differential police practices includes the following:

- tolerance of racial comments and jokes at the expense of racialized groups among police officers in the workplace
- ostracism of colleagues with origins in a racialized group
- ostracism of colleagues seen as too sympathetic to racialized groups
- perception that racialized groups are more inclined than others to commit crimes
- use of coarse epithets for individuals from racialized groups
- excessive mistrust of racialized groups
- more frequent arrests of individuals from racialized groups
- tendency to use more force than necessary when arresting suspects from racialized groups
- excessive harassment of youths from racialized groups
- remarks about inappropriate behaviour because the individual is black
- bias in favour of citizens from majority groups
- more systemic, more frequent accusations of members of racialized groups
- false or unjustified imprisonment of members of racialized groups
- more frequent objections to bail requests from members of racialized groups
- racial profiling: the practice of routinely stopping members of racialized minorities—particularly black men
- higher frequency of searches without a warrant of racialized groups
- omission of services commonly offered to the public for members of racialized groups

(Source: *CRRF Fact Sheet*, Table 1, p. 5)

Anti-Semitism: Racism against Jews

The *Year 2000 Audit of Anti-Semitic Incidents* was released by the League for Human Rights of B'nai Brith on 20 February 2001 (B'nai Brith, 'Anti-Semitic Incidents Rise in Canada in 2000'). There were 280 reported incidents of anti-Semitic harassment and vandalism in Canada. This represents a 5 per cent increase over the 267 incidents reported across the country in 1999.While the overall total of anti-Semitic incidents in Canada is up, regional patterns showed a tremendous variation. Montreal had a significant rise in anti-Semitic incidents, with 71 reported in 2000—nearly double the 37 reported in 1999. Toronto, however, showed a 7.6 per cent decrease in incidents with 110 reported anti-Semitic occurrences, compared to 119 incidents reported in 1999. The western and eastern provinces showed a slight decline in overt incidents, in spite of evidence of continued hate-group activity in both regions.

Reported acts of anti-Semitic vandalism increased for the second straight year. The number of reported incidents of anti-Semitic vandalism was 88 in 2000, a 42 per cent increase over the 62 incidents reported last year. Vandalism in 2000 included firebombings and arson attacks on synagogues, desecrations at cemeteries, and graffiti sprayed on synagogues, schools, and private residences. Reported acts of harassment of Jewish

Canadians included serious assaults and death threats. Most anti-Semitic incidents for 2000 involved harassment, with a total of 192 reported incidents. Although the overall number of incidents of harassment was down 6 per cent from the 205 reported cases in 1999, there were several serious assaults, particularly in Montreal where victims were punched, kicked, knocked unconscious, and held over the rails at a metro station. Death threats against Jewish leaders and bomb threats at a school, synagogues, the Israeli consulate, and a Holocaust memorial ceremony at the Parliament Buildings in Ottawa were also included. Hate mail, verbal assaults and slurs, and systemic discrimination accounted for the majority of the other incidents of harassment.

In the year 2000, the Middle East Crisis was felt in increased incidences of anti-Semitic violence in Canada. Spokespersons for B'nai Brith Canada contend that it is clear that the rise in incidents for 2000 was the result of the fallout from the increased tension in the Middle East. Data from the first half of the year indicated a decrease in incidents from the number of reported acts of anti-Semitism during the same period in 1999. The second half of the year, however, showed a drastic increase. There were 96 incidents of anti-Semitism reported across Canada in October and November of 2000, immediately following the recent escalation of the *intifada*. This was more than double the 41 reported incidents during the same months in 1999. The incidents of vandalism in October and November (including firebombings of synagogues and Jewish institutions targeted for graffiti) increased by over 200 per cent, from 12 incidents in 1999 to 40 in 2000. There were 5 bomb threats to Jewish or Israel-related organizations, and 4 death threats to lay leaders and staff people of Jewish community groups. During this period, two synagogues in Edmonton were firebombed and their windows were smashed. At one of the synagogues, the police found that a nearby tree had been scorched in an attempt to start the blaze. Three weeks earlier one of the synagogues had a Molotov cocktail thrown through the window. In Ottawa, there was an arson attack at a Jewish memorial chapel, where the door was doused in gasoline and then set ablaze. Anti-Israel demonstrations in Montreal, Toronto, and Ottawa degenerated into anti-Semitism with participants chanting in Arabic 'Kill the Jews', while harassing local Jewish people and blaming them for the situation in the Middle East. Demonstrations across Canada turned from legitimate political protest to Holocaust trivialization, with placards equating the Star of David with the Nazi swastika.

Conclusion: The Self-fulfilling Prophecy of White Racism

While the manifestations of institutionalized racism against blacks and other visible minorities in Canada highlight discrimination on the basis of non-white skin colour, the continuing anti-Semitic tirade of many White Supremacists makes it clear that skin colour is not the only criterion behind racist acts. Assumptions of racial inferiority are imputed to a wide range of minorities whose cultural and/or behavioural characteristics are assumed to deviate from the norms of those who define themselves as white. Once these groups become *racialized by definition*, White Supremacists are able to define themselves exclusively as white. All other racial and ethnic groups become defined as non-whites. The reader should note that it is this *socially constructed*, self-definition of white (and other-definition of non-white) that is employed in the discussion of white racism to follow.

We may summarily define white racism as the adoption of ideologies, policies, and practices predicated on the erroneous assumption that whites are naturally superior to non-whites. Because non-whites are assumed to be innately inferior, and somewhat less than human, their political, economic, and social rights are violated through denial of equal opportunities; and because they are accorded inferior opportunities, they become in fact 'inferior', not as human beings, but in terms of their inferiorized and disadvantaged societal status as stigmatized minorities.

Over time, non-white minorities, in a white racist society, become locked into their inferiorized and subordinate social position. This social fact is then used by whites to justify differential and unequal treatment of non-white minorities by pointing to their inability to get ahead in white society. This vicious cycle of events constitutes the self-fulfilling prophecy of white racism.

The important point here is that the inferior position/minority status of non-whites in a white racist society has nothing to do with their alleged racial inferiority. The disadvantaged social position of non-whites is the virtually inevitable outcome of long-term oppression (denial of political rights), neglect (denial of economic rights), and diminution (denial of social rights/human dignity). Racism is not a function of racial differences *per se*; rather it is a function of the way in which alleged or perceived racial or cultural differences are manipulated by members of one human population so as to deny fundamental human rights to members of other populations. The example of white racism is particularly instructive here, in that it demonstrates the way in which more powerful, self-defined 'white' ethnic groups are able to utilize racist myths and ideologies to their own advantage—to justify their own superior social position in a given society and to rationalize the disabilities to which *racialized* 'non-white' minorities are subject.

But self-defined whites do not have a monopoly on racism. Any member of any social group who denies outsiders equal societal opportunities, human rights, and fundamental freedoms, on the arbitrary basis of racial or ethnic differences, is indulging in racism. Because much of the current evidence on racism in Canada provides documentation of acts of discrimination by whites against visible minorities, there has been a notable increase in public references to white racism. The latter term, while not entirely inappropriate, is nevertheless misleading, because white racism suggests that so-called whites have a virtual monopoly on racism. While this notion is hard to refute in a white/Euro-dominated society like Canada, it is far from the truth of the matter. Racism (like sexism and ageism) is not the prerogative of any particular ethnic group. The cross-national evidence indicates beyond a doubt that it is endemic to humankind (Glaser and Possony 1979: 208–11).

The next chapter analyzes in detail the key multidimensional components of the concept of racism, as expressed in racist ideologies, policies, and practices.

Key Concepts

- ethnicity
- invalidation myths and ideologies
- new racism
- old racism
- race
- racialization
- racism
- social construction of race and ethnicity

Critical Thinking Questions

1. From a human rights perspective, provide a critique of the concepts of 'pure race' and 'human race'.

2. What is the difference between the social scientific concepts of race and ethnicity? Provide examples to illustrate this conceptual distinction.
3. Is the concept of racialization useful in helping us understand the dynamics of racism? Why or why not?
4. From the perspective of a member of one of Canada's racial-ethnic minorities, is there a difference between the old and the new racism?
5. It has been suggested that racism and human rights are diametrically opposed concepts. Explain.

CHAPTER 2

The Anatomy of Racism: Key Concepts behind the Invalidation of Racial-Ethnic Difference

Introduction

In Chapter 1, we saw how the social construction of the concepts of race and ethnicity by dominant authorities provides the underpinnings for *invalidation* ideologies of racism. Fallacious racist ideologies, concocted on the basis of *pseudo*-religious and *pseudo*-scientific evidence to 'prove' that members of invalidated target populations are inherently inferior human beings, are utilized by dominant authorities to *justify* violations of the human rights of racial and ethnic minorities. Such violations are carried out through the enforcement of public policies and practices that categorically discriminate against target minority populations.

In this chapter, I want to elaborate on some of the key concepts behind racism—ethnocentrism, prejudice, stereotype, and discrimination. These concepts also provide the building blocks for the social construction of minority status. Before I begin, I want to emphasize the *categorical* nature of ethnocentrism, prejudice, stereotype, and discrimination, which leads to the social construction of minority status.

The Categorical Predisposition of Racism

Most people think of prejudice and discrimination simply as biased beliefs, feelings, and actions of one individual for or against another individual. This common form of prejudice and discrimination refers to *personal* prejudice and discrimination. But the *categorical* form of prejudice and discrimination can be far more harmful. This form refers to biased beliefs, feelings, and actions of members of one population group for or against members of another population group. In this second form, the real target of prejudice and discrimination is not the individual victim, but the particular population group with which the victim is identified. Let me explain by offering an example.

Let us suppose that I have been told by gossiping friends that my new, next door neighbour is a very sloppy and filthy person who does not take care of her home, which is always untidy and smelly. If I simply accept this gossip, without questioning it, and then I act on it by not visiting my new neighbour and not inviting her to my home, I have carried out an act of personal discrimination based on personal prejudice.

Suppose, however, that I have never heard gossip about my new neighbour, but that I have seen her and I have identified her as a 'Paki'. My preconceived notions about peoples from Pakistan and other areas of Southeast Asia are that 'they' are dirty and smelly and that their homes are overcrowded, messy, and filthy. I then act on these notions by not visiting my new neighbour and do not invite her to my home. In this case, I have carried out an act of categorical discrimination based on categorical prejudice. My actions against my neighbour are not motivated by any feelings or ideas that I have about her as a unique person, but rather, they are motivated by my negative pre-judgments about the particular population ('Pakis') with which I identify her.

I caution the reader, then, to remember that my focus of discussion throughout this book will be on *categorical* ethnocentrism, prejudice, stereotype, and discrimination, which are the concepts that provide the building blocks to the social construction and maintenance of minority status.

Ethnocentrism

The concept of **ethnocentrism** is self-explanatory. It refers to the ubiquitous tendency to view all the peoples and cultures of the world from the central vantage point of one's own particular ethnic group and, consequently, to evaluate and rank all outsiders in terms of one's own particular cultural standards and values. From an ethnocentric perspective, the traditions, customs, beliefs, and practices that make up the culture of one's own ethnic group are exalted as highest and most natural. An inevitable consequence of ethnocentrism is the making of invidious 'we' versus 'they' comparisons. Whether actual or assumed, the greater the differences between the insiders and the outsiders, the lower the evaluation and ranking of outsiders, by insiders.

Ethnocentrism is as old as recorded history. Although commonly attributed to the ancient Hebrews, the idea of a 'chosen people' is neither original with them nor unique to them. Anthropological research has revealed the extent to which preliterate peoples referred to their own ethnic groupings as 'the people'. The English translation for many of the names in common use among aboriginal peoples, Inuit and Dene for example, is 'the people' or 'human beings', distinguishing members of the ethnic group from outsiders.

Inuit mythology depicts the first man to be created by the 'Great Being' as a failure—that is, imperfect—and accordingly to have been cast aside and called Qallunaat. The second man, a perfect human being, was called Innu (the singular of Inuit). The contemporary designation of Euro-Canadians as Qallunaat (whites, Southerners) reveals the persistence of the traditional assumption of Inuit superiority over other peoples.

Ethnocentrism and Social Differentiation

Ethnocentric evaluations of members of one's own ethnic group and of outsiders are based on shared assumptions as to differences among peoples. Not all kinds of differences are, however, accorded the same social significance. Assumed differences among ethnic groups or categories may be physical, cultural, or behavioural. Since the members of an ethnic group presumably share a common ancestry, hereditary physical attributes such as skin and eye colour, hair colour and texture, the shape of the nose, and the thickness of the lips—traits that visibly differentiate human populations on a global scale—often become important social indicators of ethnicity. But their importance lies solely in the purpose they serve, that is, the extent to which they facilitate ethnic labelling. Because they often increase the visibility of categories of people, these physical characteristics enable outsiders to identify persons who share the attributes as being alike by virtue of common ancestry. However, the particular physical traits used as social indicators of ethnicity by outsiders are often not the characteristics used by insiders to define themselves.

Perceived physical differences are only one potential source for ethnic labelling. Many cultural and behavioural traits, such as style of dress, food habits, language, religion, and even certain occupations may be predominantly associated with a particular ethnic group, by outsiders. The parka and mukluks, attire that has traditionally been associated with the Canadian Inuit, are probably more reliable social indicators of ethnicity to outsiders than are the particular physical features of the Inuit. Southern Canadians who have had little or no contact with aboriginal peoples might find it difficult to differentiate between some Indian and Inuit populations, particularly in the regions of the western Arctic and Labrador, were it not for the traditional differences in dress, type of dwelling, and food habits. The unreliability of physical indicators in pinpointing ethnic group membership is well demonstrated in the common use by outsiders of the derogatory term *Paki* in reference to a wide variety of people. In reality, few visible Canadians labelled *Paki* by outsiders come from Pakistan. They originate from a variety of countries—India, Pakistan, Sri Lanka, Fiji, Tanzania, Kenya, Singapore, Guyana, and elsewhere—and they represent an even wider variety of cultural, religious, and linguistic groupings (Buchignani 1977).

Ethnocentrism and Prejudice

Although ethnocentrism and prejudice are closely related concepts, one does not necessarily follow from the other. Ethnocentrism may be expressed, at least theoretically, in a laissez-faire mode of ethnic relations, whereby members of different ethnic communities, committed to different but not highly incompatible values, can coexist symbiotically or even cooperatively, because they are willing to tolerate each other's differences and to accord one another mutual respect. Ethnocentrism turns into prejudice when it leads to intolerance of ethnocultural differences and to the stigmatization of one human population by another. Glaser and Possony (1979: 84–8) make an important behavioural distinction between forms of **enlightened** and **pernicious ethnocentrism.** Enlightened ethnocentrism seeks the self-interest of the in-group, but does so with due regard for the rights and interests of the outgroup. Pernicious ethnocentrism, on the other hand, seeks the self-interest of the in-group at the expense of the rights and interests of outsiders.

The strategies and goals of the Anti-Defamation League (ADL), whose motto is 'Fighting Anti-Semitism, Bigotry and Extremism Since 1913', represents a prime example of enlightened ethnocentrism (ADL website). Although the original goal of the ADL was to combat anti-Semitism, the scope of its activities has extended to combat discrimination against minorities in general. By way of contrast, the agenda of the Skinheads of the Racial Holy War—bent on provoking hatred and violence against Jews, blacks, and all non-whites—represents a prime example of pernicious ethnocentrism:

> [W]e again go back to the basic Laws of Nature, which show that each species or subspecies has its natural enemies, and it is a cold hard fact of life that the most deadly enemies of the White Race are first of all the Jews, and secondarily, all the other mud races who are competing for food and living space on this limited planet. We have but two hard choices: (a) Of either race-mixing and amalgamating with the mud peoples of the world, and thereby dragging down and destroying the White Race, or taking the course that the CHURCH OF THE CREATOR has chosen, namely, (b) to keep our own race pure and expand until we finally inhabit all the good lands of this planet Earth (quoted from the Skinheads of the Racial Holy War website).

Prejudice

In contrast to ethnocentrism, which focuses on the in-group, distinguishing it from outsiders in general, **prejudice** focuses on and is directed toward a specific out-group. Simpson and Yinger (1972: 24) define prejudice as an emotional, rigid attitude, rooted in prejudgment, toward a particular group or category of people.

In this book, my general usage of the terms *ethnic prejudice* and *ethnic discrimination* subsumes the 'racial' referent. However, when prejudice and discrimination are predicated on racial visibility, the racial referent will be employed. *Ethnic prejudice* refers to biased beliefs about and attitudes toward members of particular ethnic communities based on unsubstantiated assumptions about their shared physical, cultural, and/or behavioural characteristics. With specific reference to the concept of racism, ethnic prejudice represents the ideological/affective component, whereas *ethnic discrimination* represents the behavioural/action component.

Probably the most insidious feature of prejudice is that it is based on *unsubstantiated* opinion. Because prejudice is learned through the normal process of enculturation, that is, by the examples, exhortations, and actions of persons whom the growing child trusts and respects, the unsubstantiated assumptions behind the expressions of prejudice remain unquestioned and untested. For example, when Euro-Canadian children are exposed to derogatory anti-Arab or anti-Muslim remarks as part of the family conversation, when media reports of attacks by Arab extremists tar the entire Arab community with the blame for terrorism, when threats and assaults against Arab communities are given sensationalist media coverage, it is not surprising to find that prejudice against Arabs quickly becomes widespread.

Anti-Arab, Anti-Muslim Prejudice: The Aftermath of 11 September 2001

Since the catastrophic terrorist attacks in New York and Washington on 11 September 2001, Arab-Canadian groups say an anti-Arab backlash has ensued: Canadian Arabs have been subjected to assaults, verbal abuse, and ethnic stereotyping (*Toronto Star*, 30 October 2001). Schoolmates reportedly assaulted five students with Arabic-sounding names in Oakville, Ontario. Also in Ontario, police charged a man after a woman was threatened with death over the phone in Niagara Falls. Niagara Region police confirmed that the threats were directly related to the terrorist attacks in the United States and the woman's Islamic religious affiliations. No group or individual has claimed responsibility for the deadly airplane attacks on the World Trade Center and Pentagon, but media commentators and US federal authorities have focused on Saudi terrorist Osama bin Laden as a prime suspect. The Arab community fears it is being 'tarred with the same brush' and blamed for the terrorist attacks.

The Arab-speaking community, which numbers about 300,000 in Canada, has seen Arab people being abused on the street. Spokespersons allege that non-Arabs are trying to portray all Arabs in the world as being responsible. They feel that the media has to share a large part of the blame for the baseless and irresponsible assumptions about the culpability of the entire Arab community. The executive director of the Canadian Arab Federation said employees in the organization's national office in Toronto have received phone calls that were abusive and threatening. 'You will pay for this,' said one caller. The federation said it feared a potential backlash against Arab-Canadians in the workplace and at schools. In Calgary, more than a dozen Muslims have received threatening phone calls at home. The callers reportedly made derogatory remarks such as 'You guys should be thrown out of here; you guys should be blown up.' The Muslim community responded by closing an Islamic grade school to protect 600 children. Police security was also posted at a popular mosque (*Toronto Star*, 30 October 2001).

While there reportedly have been no abusive attacks on Arab-Canadian associations' websites, there have been reports in the United States of anti-Arab and anti-Muslim messages spreading on the Internet. This poses a serious threat to the Arab community across the globe because the World Wide Web is today the most potent force for the international spread of racially motivated hatred and discrimination against identified target populations.

Influences on Prejudice

Research studies show that television can influence children's behaviours and beliefs (*Racial Stereotypes in Children's Programs*). When children watch television shows, they are strongly influenced by images of racial and ethnic minorities (Anderson and Williams 1983; Williams and Morland 1976). Although blacks appear more frequently on television than they once did, they are often depicted negatively as criminals or victims of violent crime.

Similarly, there are few responsible adult black males portrayed on television shows. These factors have a powerful effect on black children. When black people appear less frequently on television, black children feel that individuals of their own race are not important to society. Also, black children cannot easily find role models of their own culture and ethnic group. This could have a negative effect on the child's self-esteem. When the images of visible minorities are negative and when Euro-Canadian values and achievements are apotheosized, ethnic prejudice becomes an integral aspect of the forces shaping Euro-Canadian children (Ashworth 1979).

Another aspect of prejudice that reinforces the unsubstantiated racist prejudgment, even in the face of scientific facts to the contrary, is its emotional or affective underpinnings. Attitudes of prejudice may be expressed in diverse forms, from a relatively unconscious attraction or aversion to members of particular ethnic communities, to a comprehensive ideology of racism, such as a theory of White Supremacy. When the emotional component of ethnic prejudice is strong, unsubstantiated ideas increase in salience and resistance to change. Because of the strength of the emotional component in prejudice in general, confronting the prejudiced person or group with facts that invalidate their racist assumptions is a tactic that is likely to prove ineffective in reducing or eliminating the prejudice (Glaser and Possony 1979: 86). Indeed, this kind of tactic may have the opposite effect.

In the 1930s the results of a psychological study of attitudes toward Jews in Toronto revealed that anti-Jewish prejudice sometimes bordered on hysteria. At that time, the myth of an international Jewish conspiracy for world domination, codified in the so-called 'Protocols of the Elders of Zion', was providing a racist rationale for widespread anti-Semitism in Canada. Betcherman reports that the Protocols were used by anti-Semitic politicians such as Adrien Arcand and Joseph Ménard as 'proof' that Jews were the enemy of the Christian people. Indeed, evidence that the documents were forged did not deter Arcand and Ménard from using them to spread their defamation of Jews through the press, as a 'campaign of national defence' (Betcherman 1975: 22, 49).

Positive and Negative Prejudice: The Two Faces of Racism

By its very nature, any general discussion of the concept of racism tends to emphasize the negative aspects of prejudice, stereotypes, and discrimination. The reader should, therefore, always keep in mind the fact that for each negative notion associated with the out-group, there is a corresponding, positive notion associated with the in-group. For example, negative traits, such as moral and intellectual inferiority, attributed to non-whites by White Supremacists have their positive counterparts in the glorified images of the pure white supreme race, represented by the members of White Supremacist organizations themselves. Racist ideas and images tend, as the foregoing suggests, to be strongly biased in favour of the in-group, and against the out-group. When such images become entrenched as mental *stereotypes*, they become highly resistant to change, and thus they are extremely difficult to eradicate.

Stereotypes

The concept of **stereotype** refers to a rigid, cognitive map or 'picture in one's head' based on unsubstantiated and inaccurate beliefs about members of a given social category (Glaser and Possony 1979: 91). Ethnic stereotypes are associated with the cognitive or ideological component of prejudice. An ethnic stereotype is an overgeneralized, standardized ethnic group image that amplifies selected physical, cultural, and/or behavioural characteristics and disregards others. When ethnic stereotypes are employed by outsiders as a component of ethnic distinction, those ethnic attributes considered the most dissimilar from characteristics ascribed to the in-group are selected for emphasis.

Although ethnic stereotypes are not entirely false—they generally contain a 'kernel of truth' (Mackie 1974)—they invariably represent distorted images or caricatures that exaggerate some group attributes and disregard others. Not only do ethnic group stereotypes ignore the natural range of individual variation within all human populations, but they also overlook the strong, natural affinities in human attributes between populations. Group stereotypes, therefore, are rendered invalid by scientific evidence (see the Introduction) that clearly demonstrates that differences *within* human groups are far greater than differences *between* them. Because ethnic stereotypes frequently highlight and thereby increase the salience of unsubstantiated racial prejudgments, they often reinforce existing prejudices toward the ethnic communities they purport to represent.

The Role of Education in the Eradication of Racial and Ethnic Stereotypes

Research studies (see Ponting and Gibbins 1980 and Ponting 1990, for example) suggest strongly that, contrary to public belief, knowledge *per se* does not induce sympathy or generate a more positive image. Accordingly, public relations campaigns designed to inform the Canadian public about the social realities of the cultures and life conditions of Canada's minorities may have little or no effect on public opinion. Indeed, such campaigns may serve to raise or lower the image of a given minority.

The educational implications of these observations are manifold. They should alert educators to the fruitlessness of textbook-focused teaching designed to correct stereotypes and to reduce prejudice. The teaching of ethnic relations in a vacuum without the active participation of members of living ethnocultures, and by educators who have never had first-hand contact with the peoples about whom they are teaching may have the unanticipated consequence of reinforcing existing prejudices rather than eradicating them. Educational programs designed to reduce ethnic prejudice must be aimed at overcoming the social psychological barriers of 'difference' between members of diverse ethnic communities by promoting interethnic encounters in which their human similarities can be mutually revealed. If such face-to-face interaction is not encouraged, then negative ethnic prejudice and stereotypes fed by biased media images of minorities are likely to take root in the public psyche.

The Problematic Relationship between Prejudice and Discrimination

It is important to distinguish clearly between two key concepts—prejudice and discrimination. *Ethnic* **prejudice** (as defined earlier) refers to biased beliefs about and attitudes toward members of particular ethnic communities based on unsubstantiated assumptions about their shared physical, cultural, and/or behavioural characteristics. *Ethnic* **discrimination** refers to biased acts or practices toward members of particular ethnic communities, which afford categorical advantage or disadvantage on the basis of unsubstantiated assumptions about their shared physical, cultural, and/or behavioural characteristics. Although prejudice and discrimination—as two of the key components of the phenomenon of racism—are related concepts, in any given empirical situation their relationship must be taken as problematic. A racist belief or doctrine represents a form of prejudice; a racist act or practice represents a form of discrimination.

Simpson and Yinger (1972) have argued convincingly that to say that prejudice and discrimination are conceptually distinct phenomena is not to say that they are empirically separate. Prejudice and discrimination, they contend, can be found separately, or together, and each may or may not be among the causal determinants of the other. Probably the most frequent empirical situation is the one in which prejudice and discrimination are found to be mutually reinforcing (1972: 29). In any given instance, the need is to

BOX 2-1: CASE STUDY

Negative Stereotyping of Racial Minorities by the Mass Media

Aboriginal and racially defined immigrant minorities have long accused Canada's mass media of biased coverage, ranging from the unjustified and inadequate to allegations of blatant racism. The media have defended their actions by pointing out headway in a field historically resistant to change.

The media in Canada communicate information (both considered and unintentional) about minorities, including who they are, what they allegedly want, how they propose to achieve their goals, and with what repercussions for Canadian society. How accurate and representative is the coverage of media minority relations? Who makes the decisions, and on what basis? While answers to these questions are, essentially, subjective and subject to diverse interpretation, common themes can be discerned in describing media treatment of visible minorities.

Minorities are portrayed 1) as invisible and irrelevant, 2) in terms of race-role stereotyping, 3) as a social problem, and 4) as tokens for entertainment or decoration.

Minorities as Invisible

Aboriginal and racially defined immigrant minorities have long been ignored by the mass media, except when it has been convenient for them to do otherwise. Whether in advertising, newscasting, or TV and film, minorities are rendered virtually invisible through underrepresentation in programming, staffing and decision-making. Minorities have appeared to be unworthy of coverage unless caught up in situations of conflict or crisis.

The underrepresentation of visible minorities in the media has been documented in numerous studies. A 1984 survey of English-language broadcasting revealed that racial minorities represented 9 per cent of the characters in dramas, 2 per cent of news anchors, 4 per cent of reporters, 5 per cent of the guests on news features, and 6 per cent of music and variety-show participants. Statistics from a 1984–8 national survey on advertising disclosed the presence of racial minorities in 7 per cent of the advertisements, including 3 per cent in alcohol ads and 11 per cent in Ontario government ads. The findings elsewhere were even less positive. A 1987 ACTRA (Alliance of Canadian Cinema, Television and Radio Artists) study found minority actors comprised only 3 per cent of the characters on Canadian stages, less than 3 per cent in commercials, and 5.5 per cent of television performers. A 1990s study on billboard advertising in Montreal subway stations found minorities featured on only one billboard (a promotion by Ontario Tourism featuring the image of a black ballerina repeated ten times) from a total of 163 on display. Another study underscored the invisibility of visible minority women in *Maclean's* magazine over a 30-year period. Most were also restricted to limited roles as well as to a narrow range of goods and services. However, a 1992 study by MediaWatch pointed to some progress, with minorities having 16.6 per cent of the appearances in a select sample of Canadian-produced TV shows.

Visible minorities are certainly not ignored by the media; but it can be shown that their presence or absence is manipulated by media executives to suit their primary interest in capturing audience attention. A prime example is the presence of African-Americans on TV. African-American performers are disproportionately represented on TV programming, particularly during the early evening slots. This finding may be linked to audience studies that show that blacks are the heaviest consumers of prime-time fare.

Yet African-Americans are rarely seen outside the sphere of situation comedies. If they do appear, they are likely to be depicted either as criminals or victims in detective or police shows. Thus, African-Americans may be tolerated as comics or criminals, but are routinely ignored after the 9 p.m. slot—outside of cameo appearances for certain period pieces.

The situation is similar in newscasting: a one-sided image of racial minorities is fostered that defines them as less than human because of a taste for violence and propensity for crisis.

A further problem is the absence of racial minorities in creative positions (such as those of director, producer, editor, or screenwriter). Fewer still are employed in the upper levels of management where key decision-making occurs. The experiences and realities of racial minorities are thus misconstrued or diminished. Largely white, middle-class personnel are unable to comprehend the world from the diverse points of view of Canada's visible minorities, much less to appreciate the intensity of minority concerns.

For women of colour, the situation is compounded. They are doubly jeopardized by white male chauvinist ideologies that devalue women's contributions, misconstrue their experiences, limit their options, and undermine their self-confidence. The magnitude and scope of such insensitivity and inaccuracy suggest that racial stereotyping and discrimination are an endemic component of the mass media.

That the mass media advances a black-and-white view of the world exacts a toll on visible minorities. In psychological terms, media 'white-washing' (especially advertising) intensifies the invisibility of racial minorities in society. Minorities are circumscribed in ways that either deny their existence or devalue their contribution to society, and render irrelevant their aspirations to participate, as fullfledged members.

As noted earlier, those with the power to define others through images and representations are positioned to control and manipulate. The invisibility of racial minorities serves to consolidate the *status quo*, with its prevailing, unequal distribution of power and resources. Thus, the interests of those at the upper echelons of the power structure are protected and furthered. For people of colour, the perpetuation by the media of the white image of Canada, leaves them with feelings of rejection, exclusion, and social marginality. 'Whiteness' is conveyed not only as the norm from which all else deviates but also as a source of privilege not accessible to non-whites.

Minorities as Stereotypes

Aboriginal peoples and visible immigrant minorities have long complained of negative media stereotyping. Historically, racial minorities were presented as caricatures in a manner consistent with prevailing and grotesquely distorted stereotypes. For example, media stereotypes of aboriginal peoples dwelt on themes of 'the noble savage', the 'savage Indian', the 'drunken Native', and the 'subservient squaw'.

Blacks in film and TV roles were typically portrayed in stereotyped ways—as entertainers or sport figures, villains, victims, buffoons, and domestics. Rarely did racial minorities appear with something significant to say or do. Through stereotypes, minorities were put down, put in their place as subservient to whites, or put up as props and adornments for audience gratification. Minorities were obligated to know their place in films, a subservience often conveyed by deferential actions related to serving, smiling, or shuffling. Similarly, Third World women of colour were slotted into the category of background or filler as servant, alternatively as dangerous or evil, with potential to destroy all that is civilized or ordered. In other situations, minority women were deemed to be helplessly in need of paternalistic protection.

Progress toward eliminating mass media stereotyping is proceeding at a sluggish pace. Race-role images continue to be reinforced, perpetuated, and even legitimized through selective media coverage. Identifying a person by racial labels even when irrelevant to the story ('race-tagging') remains an intermittent problem. In advertising, racial minorities are often cast into slots that reflect a 'natural' propinquity for the product in question, for example, quality chambermaid service in hotels and athletics and sporting goods such as high-cut gym shoes. They also are portrayed as famine victims (usually children) in underdeveloped countries. The net effect of this stereotyping is that racial minorities are slotted or labelled as different and inferior, and this invalidating practice precludes their full acceptance as normal and fully contributing members of society.

In an industry geared to image and appeal, there is pressure to enforce the rule of homogeneity and conservatism through racial stereotyping. Images of consumer goods need to be stripped of controversy or negative connotation for fear of lost audiences, hence revenue. Stereotypes serve to 'sanitize' audience perceptions of the world. Majority wariness of minorities is rendered less threatening through exposure to familiar and reassuring images.

Minorities as Social Problem

In general, the media tend to portray aboriginal and racially defined immigrant minorities as representing a 'social problem'. They are characterized as having problems in need of solutions that consume an inordinate amount of political attention or an unduly large portion of national resources. In addition, the media are likely to define racial minorities as troublemakers who 'create problems' by making demands unacceptable to the social, political, or moral order. Time and again, aboriginal peoples in Canada are portrayed as bothersome constituents whose claims for self-determination and inherent right to self-government are contrary to Canada's liberal-democratic tradition. The First Nations are portrayed as a threat to Canada's territorial integrity (the Lubicon blockade in 1988) or national interests (the Innu protest of NATO presence in Labrador); a risk to Canada's social order (the Oka crisis); costly (over $5 billion in federal expenditures); an economic liability (the massive land claims in the North); a crisis for the criminal justice system (disproportionate numbers incarcerated); and a medical concern (suicides and rehabilitation).

Other racial minorities also tend to be depicted as vexatious: they are seen hassling police, stumping immigration authorities, cheating on welfare, or battling among themselves or with their families. Stereotyping visible minorities as troublemakers is conducive to minority scapegoating for an assortment of social or economic ills. It can generate fear and resentment of minorities who do not conform in outlook, appearance, or practice with white Euro-Canadian mainstream norms.

Media dealings with refugees are often couched in terms of illegal entry and associated costs of processing and integration into Canada. Several studies support these examples. In a 1986 content analysis, researchers reviewed the national newspaper coverage of Canada's immigration policy between 1980 and 1985. Items were examined in terms of several persuasion techniques: the positioning and layout of the story, article length and type size, content of headlines and kickers (phrases immediately after the headline), use of newspeak or inflammatory language, use of quotes, statistics, and racial origins. Researcher Michelle Ducharme found that use of these criteria resulted in immigrant portrayals that were both racist and discriminatory—albeit in a subtle, almost subliminal, manner. The use of clichés, stereotypes, and provocative language combined to escalate the negative aspects and perceived costs of immigrants and immigration policy. DuCharme suggested that by emphasizing the problems visible immigrants cause for the system, obvious solutions are suggested: entrance rules have to be made tougher, quotas have to be set, amnesty policies have to be questioned, refugee totals have to be cut, visa card systems need to be reconsidered to curb illegal entry, and marriages of convenience must be refused. These are but a few examples from newspaper articles that suggest that readers may come to believe that Canada has a serious 'immigration problem' and that visible immigrants themselves pose a threat, not only to the system, but also to Canadians as individuals. In other words, visible immigrants are perceived as troublemakers who steal jobs from Canadians, engage in illegal activities such as drugs or smuggling, and offer nothing to Canada in return for its largesse.

Negatively stereotyped media images create a strong psychological barrier between visible minorities and white Euro-Canadian society. The cumulative effect of perpetual negative stereotyping of racial minorities serves to marginalize these minorities as irrelevant or as a threat to society. Depicted as violent and emotionally unstable, with a diminished respect for human life or basic decency, they are socially constructed as the undesirable and dangerous 'other'.

Strategies for Change: Diversifying the Racial Face of Canada

The media in Canada have come under considerable pressure to adapt to the reality of a multiracial/multicultural Canada. A preoccupation with economic incentives and organizational agendas has left the media poorly equipped for managing Canada's diversity. Some progress has been made in the attempt to present a more positive and realistic portrayal of racial minorities and concerns. Reforms within the CBC include sensitivity training for program and production staff, language guidelines to reduce race and role stereotypes, and the monitoring of on-air representations of racial minorities. Rules are in place to deter derogatory representations of individuals on the basis of race, ethnicity, age, gender, religion, or disability. The Broadcasting Act of 1991 has firmly endorsed the concept of 'cultural expression' by expanding airtime for ethnoracial minorities. Additionally, the CRTC has made policy changes to ensure that broadcasters will be evaluated on the basis of employment equity hiring when licences come up for renewal. These initiatives are consistent with the provisions of the Multiculturalism Act, with its expectations that all government departments and Crown agencies improve minority access, equity, and representation.

Some ambiguity remains with respect to policy, which leaves many questions of implementation unanswered. However, various recommendations already have been proposed for attainment of a media reflective of Canada's emergent plurality. Some have suggested government intervention to assure that the objectives of multicultural policy are met at all levels of mass media. Others propose to establish government advisory bodies (such as MediaWatch) to monitor the coverage of racial minorities, as well as to establish codes and standards with 'teeth'. Still others argue for more hiring and promotion of aboriginal and other racial minorities at all levels in the media industry.

In an ostensibly progressive society such as Canada, the media have been sluggish in making a real attempt to mainstream racial and ethnic diversity. Yet, as has been pointed out, some progress has been made in the restructuring of minority/media relations. In the long run, what is needed is a fundamental transformation of the media, which have historically ignored many of the interests of minority-group members. As in any genuine attempt to restructure social systems, the process is closely allied with the struggle for power. Unfortunately, the competition for power in the struggle for scarce resources is taking place in a societal context of group-level racial and ethnic inequality. What is of critical importance, at this juncture, is for both government and media to adopt measures geared specifically towards 'levelling the playing field'.

SOURCE: Adapted from Fleras 1995.

specify the personal and structural conditions under which a given relationship between prejudice and discrimination prevails.

By way of example, let us consider the results of a hypothetical survey on interracial-ethnic friendships that revealed that Euro-Canadian respondents ranked blacks lowest among the various racial-ethnic groups from which one could choose friends. Does this response indicate a high degree of anti-black prejudice, discrimination, or both? Insofar as the response represents an opinion about potential friendships, it represents an attitudinal referent that may be taken as an indicator of prejudice. If, however, the respondent is asked about actual friendships, the response represents a behavioural referent that may be taken as an indicator of discrimination.

The point to be emphasized is that prejudice does not *necessarily or invariably* lead to discrimination. Put simply, the distinction between prejudice and discrimination lies in the difference between what one thinks, feels, and believes, and what one does.

From a human rights viewpoint, a critical distinction between prejudice and discrimination is that prejudice, in and of itself, does *not* violate human rights; discrimination (whether positive or negative) *invariably* violates human rights principles. A person may be highly prejudiced for or against any number of categories of people, but, unless that person *acts on* one of these prejudiced beliefs or feelings, the prejudice, in itself, violates no other person's human rights. On the other hand, if a person performs, acts, or carries out practices that categorically advantage or disadvantage particular categories of people—politically, economically, socially, or culturally, then the discriminatory acts themselves violate the human rights of members of the target population.

For example, if a black woman wants to pursue a career as a constitutional lawyer, it is quite conceivable that she might apply to an elite law school staffed by highly racist and sexist white male professors. However, unless one of these professors discriminates against her on the grounds of race or sex, the racist and/or sexist prejudices and stereotypes held by the professors do not violate her human rights. However, if one of the professors tries to exclude the black female applicant from entering the law school on the grounds of race or sex, or, if the applicant succeeds in becoming a law student and one of the professors makes racist or sexist remarks to her in class, or gives her low grades, or refuses to give her job references on the grounds of race or sex, then the human rights of the black woman are unquestionably violated. She is denied the fundamental human rights to equality of opportunity and dignity of person.

Forms of Ethnic Discrimination

Ethnic discrimination can be manifested in many ways. At the level of the individual, an act of discrimination may stem from conscious, personal prejudice. This form of discrimination is termed **individual discrimination.** For example, an employer who is prejudiced in favour of English Canadians and against French Canadians acts on his or her personal prejudice to exclude equally qualified or more highly qualified French-Canadian applicants for positions with his or her firm. This case provides an example of individual discrimination based on ethnic prejudice.

Often, however, an act of discrimination does not derive from the personal prejudice of the actor, but from the carrying out by the actor of the dictates of others who are prejudiced or of a prejudiced social institution. This form of discrimination is termed **institutional discrimination.** For example, a Jewish high school teacher applies for a position at an exclusive private school. The school principal is not anti-Semitic; indeed, he happens to be married to a Jewish woman. However, the principal refuses to hire the Jewish teacher, despite his excellent credentials, because of a 'gentleman's agreement' between the school board and the students' parents excluding Jewish persons from staff positions. This case provides an example of institutional discrimination based on ethnic prejudice. In this case, the person who performed the discriminatory act was not prejudiced against Jews; however, the discriminator acted in accordance with the prejudiced (anti-Semitic) policy of the (educational) institution.

To illustrate a different point, let us change the foregoing scenario by just one variable. Let us suppose that the school principal in the case *is* prejudiced against Jews. He harbours negative stereotypes of Jews as unscrupulous, money-hungry cheats. (He regards his own Jewish wife as a clear 'exception'.) Moreover, the principal fears that if a Jewish teacher should be hired, the carefully hidden fact that his own wife is Jewish might be discovered, and he might lose his own job. The principal, then, is predisposed to discriminate against Jewish applicants, and his own ethnic prejudice is supported by the anti-Semitic policy of the institution (private school) he represents. This case is an example of *both* individual and institutional discrimination.

Both individual and institutional forms of discrimination can ultimately be attributed to prejudicial attitudes: either the actor is prejudiced, or the actor conforms to the sanctions of a prejudiced reference group. Yet, discrimination can occur even in the absence of conscious prejudice.

Unlike individual and institutional forms of ethnic discrimination, the *structural* or *systemic* form of ethnic discrimination cannot be attributed to prevailing prejudices (except, perhaps, with reference to their historical origins). Established, system-wide policies and practices in a society can have *unintended* yet pervasive discriminatory effects on disadvantaged ethnic minorities, by sustaining long-term, group-level ethnic inequalities.

The concept of **structural** or **systemic discrimination** refers to ethnic-group inequalities that have become rooted in the system-wide operation of society as a long-term consequence of institutional discrimination against particular ethnic minorities.

This is how it happens: When members of ethnic minorities have been categorically denied opportunities to acquire or to use political, economic, educational, and/or social skills and qualifications, as a long-term result, the minority category *as a whole* becomes collectively disadvantaged. The collective, adverse impact of group disadvantage can become compounded through the self-fulfilling prophecy of racism through which minority members come to internalize invalidating, majority-imposed ethnic labels and stereotypes, to blame themselves for their disadvantaged status, and to give up hope of status improvement. Members of ethnic minorities can thus become locked into their increasingly disadvantaged minority status and excluded from large areas of significant political, economic, and social participation.

In the area of equality rights (for example, equality/equivalence of educational and employment opportunities), one way of looking at the difference between institutional and systemic forms of discrimination is this: Institutional discrimination denies equal opportunities for majority and minority group members with *equal qualifications*; systemic discrimination *prevents* minority group members from acquiring or utilizing qualifications that are equal/equivalent to those held by majority members.

To illustrate, let me refer back to an earlier example, that of the black woman who wants to become a constitutional lawyer. Let us suppose that the woman succeeds in obtaining a law degree and then applies for a position with a prestigious law firm. Her credentials are superior to those of a white male applicant for the same position, but the male applicant is hired because the all-white, all-male law firm wants to keep it that way: the firm's policy is white males only. This is an example of institutional discrimination.

Suppose, however, that the black woman applicant had never succeeded in acquiring a law degree because, as a rule, law schools did not admit blacks or women. In this case, the black female applicant clearly would not have the qualifications for the position in the law firm, not because of her race or her sex, but because of the collective adverse impact upon blacks and women of past discrimination, that is, denial of the human right to equality of educational opportunity. In this case, even if the law firm in question removed its racist and sexist hiring policy, the black female applicant could not compete for the position because she would still lack the necessary qualifications.

Forms of Discrimination in the Canadian Context

The most blatant form of racist behaviour, and one that most Canadians today would probably vehemently disclaim, is individual discrimination. Over the years, the various Human Rights Commissions in Canada have handled a host of cases of negative discrimination, but rarely has the discriminator admitted that the act in question was motivated by personal prejudice. In many cases of discrimination against ethnic minorities in the areas of employment and housing, for example, the personnel manager or realtor typically disclaims personal prejudice as the reason for having refused the member of the ethnic minority. In fact, the grounds for the racist action may not have been personal prejudice. An employee may have been carrying out the unwritten policy or 'gentlemen's agreement' of the employer or client against hiring or selling to members of particular ethnic minorities. In such cases, the discriminatory act would be an example of **institutional discrimination**. In both cases (individual and institutional discrimination), the effects of the action would be the same: equal opportunities for societal participation would be arbitrarily denied to members of ethnic minorities whose qualifications are equal to those of the ethnic majority members accorded such opportunities.

The most powerful and pernicious form of institutional discrimination is legislative or legal discrimination. For the most part, overtly racist legislation has been gradually phased out in Canada since the Second World War. As will be detailed in Chapter 6, however, Canadian immigration laws were decidedly racist until the 1960s—at first, overtly excluding particular racial and ethnic groups from immigration to Canada, and then covertly instituting criteria that militated against non-white immigration.

Historically in Canada, racism toward aboriginal peoples has taken the form of paternalistic policies and treatment. The Indian Acts passed by Parliament nearly a century ago provide the chief legal source for paternalism toward Canadian Indians. These Acts, dating from 1876 to the present, continue in practice a policy of wardship initiated by the British to protect a supposedly childlike people considered incapable of managing their own affairs. An additional and even more paternalistic tendency toward protecting Indians against themselves is readily discerned in reading these legal documents (Indian Act—Office Consolidation 1965).

Prior to the Emancipation Act passed by the British Parliament in 1833, racism toward blacks in Canada was overtly expressed in the institution of slavery. As slaves, black men and women were advertised and sold on the open market in much the same manner as cattle or home furnishings. They were evaluated and treated as things rather than as human beings (Winks 1971: 26). The foregoing examples provide only an initial glance at the historical picture of legal forms of institutional racism in Canada. A more detailed analysis of this phenomenon and its contemporary implications will be presented later.

Individual and institutional forms of ethnic discrimination can be ultimately attributed to either overt or covert prejudicial attitudes. If, however, existing prejudices could be suddenly totally eliminated, the structural or systemic inequalities rooted in the daily impersonal (that is, non-intentional) operation of the Canadian social system would continue to exclude substantial numbers of members of some ethnic minorities from full participation in public life. Because of the existing, unequal distribution of opportunities and rewards, blacks, as well as Indians, Inuit, and most members of visible ethnic minorities—victims of the self-fulfilling prophecy of racism—are less likely to possess the qualifications required for skilled jobs or the economic resources necessary for the purchase of a home.

Systemic Discrimination and Affirmative Action Remedies

The crucial human rights issue involved in systemic discrimination is not that of providing equal chances for those with equal qualifications, but prior to this, the question of redressing the unequal access of different ethnic communities to the opportunities to acquire the necessary qualifications, skills, and resources for full participation in the public life of the society.

In such cases, it can be argued that some form of intervention (such as programs of *affirmative action*) is necessary in order to ensure that: 1) members of all racial and ethnic minorities are given an opportunity to acquire the education and training necessary in order for them to compete for jobs, at all levels, on an equitable basis with other Canadians; and 2) members of all racial and ethnic minorities are proportionately represented throughout the ranks of the job market (that is, proportionate to their numbers in the population).

Under the equality rights provisions of section 15 of Canada's constitutional Charter, section 15(1) protects all Canadians against individual and institutional discrimination. Section 15(2), however, allows special measures of redress against the collective, adverse impact of systemic discrimination for disadvantaged Canadians. This subsection was inserted in order to guarantee that programs of affirmative action would be allowed. These programs are designed to provide disadvantaged minorities with some form of remedy for the adverse impact (disadvantaging effects) of systemic discrimination on the minority as a whole. Canada's affirmative action mandate will be discussed in some detail in Chapter 8.

Cultural Discrimination: Subtle Racism by Commission and Omission

Cultural discrimination is a function of ethnic diversity in a socially stratified society. In a hierarchical, multiethnic society, only representatives of ethnic majority group(s) have the power to transform their ethnocentrism into cultural discrimination by imposing their cultural attributes, values, standards, and definitions of reality on all peoples in the society. For it is the normative imperatives of the dominant or majority ethnic group(s) that become sanctioned in law and incorporated into public institutional policies, thereby providing the moral and cultural guidelines for the whole society.

Cultural discrimination occurs when alternative ethnocultural moral imperatives are denied expression in public life. Cultural discrimination is thus built into the majority group(s)' requirement of minority acculturation, since this automatically denies the validity of minority ethnocultural alternatives.

Cultural discrimination may be expressed in the form of individual, institutional, and/or systemic discrimination. At the individual and institutional levels, it may consist of discrimination against members of a particular ethnocultural community on the grounds of language, religion, or any other distinctive *cultural* characteristic. At the systemic level, cultural discrimination may be expressed in the fact that opportunities for participation in society are imbued with the cultural assumptions of the dominant ethnic groups. To the degree that members of all ethnic communities are expected and often required to conform to majority norms and lifeways to fully participate in public life, cultural discrimination is built into the institutional framework of society.

In Canada, cultural discrimination—institutionalized, for example, through the Official Languages Act—reflects Anglo-Canadian dominance outside of Quebec and Franco-Canadian dominance within the province of Quebec. In a multiethnic society such as Canada, where cultural discrimination operates through expectations of cultural conformity to majority norms in public life, those ethnic minorities whose cultural attributes are perceived to deviate most markedly from majority norms are most severely culturally discriminated against. Alternatively, the more an

BOX 2-2: CASE STUDY

Unequal Access: A Canadian Profile of Racial Differences in Education, Employment, and Income

A report released by the Canadian Race Relations Foundation confirms the belief that in Canada, aboriginal and visible minority groups are disadvantaged in the areas of employment and income, and also in levels of educational attainment. The report, *Unequal Access: A Canadian Profile of Racial Differences in Education, Employment and Income*, prepared by the Canadian Council on Social Development (CCSD), combines for the first time, qualitative and quantitative analyses in the area of race relations in Canada. Using a combination of Census data, existing quantitative analyses and focus group discussions, the authors Dr Jean Lock Kunz, Anne Milan and Sylvain Schetagne conclude that notwithstanding the increase in the diversity of the Canadian population, racial discrimination is still very much a part of the workplace environment. While there is evidence that points to increased employment of aboriginals and visible minorities, that increase reportedly is largely at the bottom and middle levels of the labour force pyramid. The higher the level of the pyramid, the less diverse and the 'whiter' it becomes.

The report also concludes that:

- Although Canada's labour force is becoming increasingly diverse, racial minorities still face limits in their access to employment.
- Of all groups, aboriginal peoples are the most disadvantaged in education, employment and income. Even given the same levels of education, 'white' Canadians are more likely than visible minorities and aboriginal peoples to be in the top 20 per cent of the income scale. Specifically, given a university education, white Canadians are three times as likely as aboriginal peoples with the same level of education to find themselves at the top of the income scale.
- The unemployment rate, based on the 1996 Census, among visible minorities was higher than 'non-racialized groups' (Canadian- or foreign-born), and that the rate for aboriginal peoples was highest.
- Many racial minorities and aboriginal peoples have difficulties finding jobs that are fulfilling to them. For recent immigrants, one of the main challenges is to have their foreign-trained credentials recognized.
- *Racism is still persistent at the individual and systemic levels, although overt racism is generally seen as socially unacceptable.*

One element of the qualitative research was conducting a series of focus groups across the country. This method brought forward many anecdotal experiences with racism expressed in practices of systemic discrimination which identify its 'subtle' qualities.

- One participant observes: 'We were four on a shift in a fast food restaurant. On one shift it was me (an aboriginal person) and three white girls. On the other shift it was three white people and an East Indian girl. That girl and I always had to clean the toilets and do the garbage. It was never them, always us.'
- Another participant describes a situation in that there are certain cliques which have the advantage in promotions. 'We have a group of guys at work, they sit around the boss's office and talk

about what they did over the weekend and stuff like that. They are all white and I'm Black. They're not mean to me or anything, but those guys get the promotions.'

The authors of the study conclude that a fundamental obstacle to equity is the difficulty in eradicating the many forms of discrimination that are hard to quantify, especially at the systemic level. In this case, racial discrimination in the workplace is becoming more subtle—often referred to as 'hidden discrimination'.

SOURCE: Excerpted from Kunz et al. 2001.

ethnic minority approximates the language, religion, and cultural institutions of the dominant ethnocultural model, the more the society's public institutions are accessible.

Cultural Discrimination in Education

Nowhere is cultural discrimination more evident than in the 'hidden' cultural curriculum of the Canadian educational system. Whether in its Anglo or Franco manifestation, the Canadian educational institution is a cultural monolith.

Cultural discrimination in Canadian education is manifested in acts of commission and omission. A study of the educational history of children from five ethnic minorities in British Columbia carried out in the 1970s clearly demonstrated that there was a strong tendency for the teacher, the curriculum, and the environment of the classroom to apotheosize the achievements of the dominant ethnic group and to ignore the equally important contributions to Canadian society made by members of ethnic minorities (Ashworth 1979). More than 20 years later, a report on *Racism in Our Schools* released by the Canadian Race Relations Foundation in 2001 revealed that a monocultural curriculum is a continuing barrier to equal educational achievement for visible minority children (CRRF 2001b). Failure to represent Canada's ethnic diversity accurately throughout the educational process violates the human rights of minority ethnic students during every school day of their formative years.

Discrimination of Silence

An important form of institutional and systemic discrimination that persists, despite lip service to anti-racism initiatives on the part of educators, is the **discrimination of silence.** Discrimination *by omission* continues to plague our educational system when educators and other Euro-Canadians in powerful positions say nothing and do nothing about racism in Canada. Case (1977: 37) has suggested that silence can be a form of complicity in an act of violence. The fear of denouncing the racist, the fear of discussing (let alone teaching) ethnic relations, and the fear of engaging in racially mixed encounters constitute expressions of *covert racism* that violate the fundamental principles of human rights. The 'race relations avoidance syndrome' (Hill and Schiff 1988) whereby Canadian teachers, until very recently, chose to avoid any discussion of race despite the increased numbers of members of visible minorities in their classrooms, provides a glaring example of the discrimination of silence.

Subtle forms of cultural discrimination, systemic discrimination, and the discrimination of silence, serve to perpetuate the unequal racial-ethnic *status quo* by allowing racist barriers to interethnic understanding and interaction to remain solidly entrenched. Thus, negative ethnic prejudice, stereotypes, and discrimination continue to flourish and to fuel the fires of racism.

As Glaser and Possony (1979: 95–6) have so astutely pointed out, if all the international human rights conventions were applied literally, all the countries of the world would be found discriminatory. Because of the subtle forms of systemic and cultural discrimination built into the social system as a whole, measures taken in the name of ethnic equality but not tuned to the specific needs and concerns of ethnic communities, and failing to encourage positive face-to-face interaction between members of different ethnic communities may serve to produce new inequalities and human indignities rather than to resolve old ones.

Conclusion

The key concepts that facilitate our understanding of the multifaceted concept of racism—ethnocentrism, prejudice, stereotype, and discrimination—reflect the inability of members of humankind to respect the fundamental human rights and freedoms of peoples they consider inherently different from themselves. This chapter has shown that when invidious distinctions based on assumed or perceived racial or ethnocultural differences are used by members of one community to justify forms of discrimination that serve to violate the human rights of members of another community, racism rears its ugly head. In Chapter 3, we will demonstrate how these same concepts also provide the building blocks for the social construction of racial-ethnic and other minorities. Our analysis will reveal how human rights violations of members of ethnic and other invalidated social groups have produced group-level inequalities in political, economic, and social power across Canada, and have led to the development of Canada's system of social stratification.

Key Concepts

- cultural discrimination
- discrimination
- discrimination of silence
- enlightened and pernicious ethnocentrism
- ethnocentrism
- individual discrimination
- institutional discrimination
- prejudice
- stereotype
- structural or systemic discrimination

Critical Thinking Questions

1. The anthropologist Ruth Benedict made the observation that we all view the world through culturally tinted lenses. What concept, introduced in this chapter, would be most useful in explaining her comment? Elaborate.
2. Glaser and Possony have posited an important behavioural distinction between enlightened and pernicious forms of ethnocentrism. Explain this distinction, using examples to illustrate your argument.
3. It has been argued that prejudice, in and of itself, does not violate human rights. However, discrimination invariably does. Explain.
4. Distinguish between the concepts of institutional and systemic discrimination. Provide examples to illustrate this distinction.
5. From your own experience and observations as a student, provide examples of cultural discrimination that exemplify individual, institutional, and systemic forms of discrimination.

CHAPTER 3

Social Stratification: Human Rights Violations and the Social Construction of Ethnic and Other Minorities

Introduction

In Chapter 2, we looked at the key concepts that facilitate our understanding of the multifaceted concept of racism. In this chapter, we will see how these same concepts—ethnocentrism, prejudice, stereotype, and discrimination—provide the building blocks for the *social construction* of racial-ethnic and other *minorities*.

Our analysis thus far has indicated that one of the major variables affecting both the nature and the outcome of interethnic relations is the relative rank or social status of different ethnic groups within Canadian society. In this chapter, we will examine how racist barriers imposed by majority authorities, barriers that serve to violate minority rights, have produced group-level inequalities in political, economic, and social power across Canada. Our analysis will demonstrate how institutionalized inequalities in power have led to the development of Canada's system of *social stratification,* and, at the same time, have played a major role in the social construction of ethnic and other minorities.

Dimensions of Social Stratification

Systems of social stratification can be based on a wide variety of criteria: race, ethnicity, gender, sexual orientation, age, class, and other factors. Any individual, social, or cultural attribute accorded social significance in a society based on unequal power relations can provide the basis for differential and unequal treatment of less powerful populations by more powerful ones.

Regardless of the criteria used as the basis for social ranking, a society predicated upon unequal power relations can be referred to as a socially stratified society. The concept of **social stratification** refers to the hierarchical structuring of society that ensues from the differential ranking of various social categories with regard to their members' degree of political, economic, and social power.

From a human rights perspective, equal access of all individuals to these three dimensions of power has been conceptualized as political, economic, and social rights, respectively. Insofar as these rights of all members of society are respected, and, taking into account the ubiquitous range of variation in motivation, interests, skills, and abilities among members of every human population, one would expect to find members of all social categories represented, in proportion to their numbers in society, at all ranks (strata) in the hierarchy. Where one finds, instead, differential ranking of various social categories, it may be hypothesized that group-based inequality is the long-term consequence of categorical discrimination—the denial or restriction of the political, economic, and/or social rights of members of particular social categories.

Political, Economic, and Social Power

The concept of **political power** refers to the ability of some people to control the life chances of others. The prime social indicator of political power in a modern industrialized society such as Canada's is the attainment of strategic decision-making positions within major societal institutions. Through the attainment of these high-ranking positions, members of some social categories are able to make the crucial decisions that affect the life chances (opportunities and rewards) of others.

The concept of **economic power** (or privilege) refers to the accumulation and means for accumulation of the valued material and technological goods or resources of society. Social indicators of economic power in Canadian society include wealth, property, income, education, and occupation. Non-Marxian sociologists often refer to this dimension of a stratified system as 'socioeconomic class'. Scholars who favour a Marxian or quasi-Marxian approach to social scientific analysis tend to emphasize one aspect of economic class, namely, economic control. The latter dimension of economic power is seen largely as a function of the ownership of the means of production in a society.

The concept of **social power** (or prestige) refers to the social recognition of honour (dignity) accorded members of society by others on the basis of their particular status, that is, their culturally defined position in society.

Parsons (1953) delineated three sets of social attributes that may be used as bases for prestigious evaluation and status ranking in any society: possessions—impersonal items people own (houses, businesses, patents, and the like); inherent (ascribed) personal attributes (age, gender, race, and ethnicity); acquired personal attributes (specific abilities or skills); and performances—demonstrated proficiency in the performance of particular social roles (the behavioural expectations associated with different status positions). Curtis and Scott (1979) have suggested that in Canadian society, prestige is based largely on widely understood evaluations of statuses based on such criteria as political power, economic control, education, wealth, and income, as well as race, ethnicity, gender, and age. In short, Curtis and Scott argue that prestige is premised on social evaluations of persons on the basis of their multiple achieved and ascribed statuses in society.

What appears to be lacking in all of the foregoing definitions is some way to conceptualize the fact that prestige, *at the level of the social category as a whole*, is a socially constructed phenomenon, derived from a composite of status attributes, but signifying something more than a mere sum of its components. Viewed in terms of concepts of majority/minority relations, social categories that are accorded prestige (majorities) are thereby *superiorized;* those denied prestige are thereby *inferiorized*. The implications of superiorization and inferiorization are to socially construct *superior* and *inferior* categories of people, with majority and minority status, respectively.

From a human rights view, it may be argued that the denial of prestige (social rights/human dignity) has more enduring, disadvantaging effects on minorities than the denial of political and economic rights. For denial of the human right to dignity begets inferiorization, and inferiorized minorities tend to become branded as *inferior by ascription*.

Social Stratification: Intersecting Dimensions of Ethnicity, Gender, and Class

As indicated earlier, systems of social stratification can be based on a wide variety of criteria: race, ethnicity, gender, sexual orientation, age, class, and other factors. In a society predicated on unequal power relations, any human attribute accorded social significance by dominant powers may be subject to arbitrary inferiorization or superiorization, and thus can provide the basis for differential and unequal treatment of particular populations. Members of social categories assumed to share the inferiorized version of the attribute will be unfairly disadvantaged; those assumed to share the superiorized version of the attribute will be unfairly advantaged. In both cases, the dominance and control of the powers-that-be is maintained.

In recent years, social scientists and other scholars have expressed a growing interest in the interlinkages among the various dimensions of social stratification. In particular, there is a growing body of literature that embodies the contemporary search by social analysts to conceptualize the links among relations of inequality based on race, ethnicity, gender, and class.

It is beyond the scope of this book to fully address the many scholarly debates that have informed these efforts to theorize connections among the different variables. However, in order to whet the scholarly appetite of the interested reader, I will offer a preliminary look at some of the central issues in the debate. My digest is derived in large part from Stasiulis (1990).[1] The debates highlight the disagreement among scholars as to which of the variables (if any) assumes priority. Which of these variables—race, ethnicity, gender, or class—logically precedes the others in structuring relations of group-level inequality?

Stasiulis' review of the literature reveals that, on the race versus class question, there are two main opposing positions. The first position holds that social class is logically prior to race. The most extreme version of this view holds that race and ethnic relations are epiphenomena that can be understood solely within the analytic constructs of historical materialism, class, and production relations. More moderate versions of this position vary with respect to the amount of autonomy from class-based social relations they accord the analytic constructs of race and ethnicity.

The opposing view holds that race and ethnicity are logically prior to class. The most extreme version of this view accords full autonomy to the analytic constructs of race and ethnicity and denies any influence of class or economic relations. More moderate versions of this position consider race and ethnic relations to be relatively autonomous forces that are independent of class factors.

A third position, which can be seen to reflect a move away from the determinism and reductionism of both extreme positions on the debate, holds that race and class represent independent but interacting forces that structure relations of inequality. While race and class are held to be separate analytic constructs, this view posits that they interact in a multifaceted way to generate autonomous but interrelated systems of social stratification.

As compared with the substantial literature on race/ethnicity and class, the literature on gender and race/ethnicity is only in its infancy. Stasiulis (1990) contends that the omission of gender in theories dealing with the race versus class question reflects, in part, the immensity of the scholarly challenge posed in the attempt to develop an integrated analytic framework that takes into account two or more social dimensions of stratification, both as separate analytic constructs, and in their complex interaction.

Stasiulis observes that, within the feminist literature, socialist-feminist theories have incorporated the analytic construct of class as a key explanatory variable, but, until recently, they have been silent on race and ethnicity. The attacks on 'white feminism' (feminist writing by white women that ignores or marginalizes race and ethnicity) by women of colour, has sparked the countertheorizing of 'black feminism' (feminist writing by women of colour that incorporates race and ethnicity as key explanatory factors). In the political arena, as well as in theoretical debates, black feminists have criticized the bias within white feminism that prioritizes gender divisions and sexism (or, in socialist feminism, gender and class divisions) over race divisions and racism. Moreover, black feminism challenges the eurocentric premises even of the central concepts within white feminism: analytic constructs such as 'the state', 'reproduction', and 'the family' are all held to embody white racist logics. Stasiulis criticizes the approach of black feminism on two counts. First, she challenges its implicit black/white dichotomy frequently assumed to structure the racist and sexist subordination of women of colour. Second, she challenges its treatment of women of colour as a homogeneous social category, thus avoiding analysis of the mediating role of class on the disadvantaging effects of race and gender.

The linkages between ethnicity and gender (or femininity) have been theorized in two different ways. Gender has become incorporated into the ethnicity literature and ethnicity has become incorporated into feminist analysis. A special issue of *Canadian Ethnic Studies* (vol. 13, no. 1, 1981), which focused on the relationship among ethnicity, femininity, and class, provided an opportunity for scholars with opposing perspectives on the debate to present their views. Some argued that ethnicity, race, and femininity were separate but interacting analytic constructs that combined to doubly or triply disadvantage immigrant women, women of colour, and immigrant women of colour (the double or triple jeopardy thesis).[2] Others argued that race and ethnicity were simply epiphenomena of the fundamental forces of class relations in Canadian society.

In her discussion of the race and class debates, Stasiulis points out that at both the political and analytical levels, the arguments have been weighted in terms of the greater or lesser 'evil' (or, in my way of conceptualizing the issues, greater or lesser human rights violations). Which 'evil' (or area of human rights violations) is the more 'primary'?

My own response to this question is simple: Ask the person who has experienced the human rights violations. In my view, it is not possible, with a human rights framework of analysis, to socially construct a *hierarchy* of 'evil' that can then be used to socially construct a hierarchy of human suffering based on different, majority-imposed, criteria for inferiorization and unequal treatment. From a human rights view, my own position on the debate would clearly favour a perspective that considered each analytic construct (race, gender, class, and so forth) as autonomous, but that also took into account the complexity of interaction between the separate systems of social stratification predicated on the different analytic constructs.

Regardless of the variables singled out for analysis, systems of social stratification share one common denominator: they are built on unequal power relations between members of superiorized and inferiorized social categories in the society. Social scientists have conceptualized intergroup relations based on group-level inequalities in political, economic, and social power as *majority/minority* relations.

Social Stratification and Majority/Minority Relations

Although systems of social stratification may be based on a wide variety of criteria, the concept of majority, or dominant social category, within any system of social stratification, refers to the social category with superordinate social status at a given structural level or regional sector in the society, whose members wield the greatest degree of political, economic, and social power. By way of contrast, the concept of minority, or subordinate social category, refers to the *corresponding* social category (with regard to the same ranking criteria) with subordinate social status *relative to the majority,* and whose members wield a lesser degree of political, economic, and/or social power.

It is important to emphasize that **majority/minority relations,** as conceptualized by social scientists, are intergroup relations predicated on demonstrable disparities in political, economic, and/or social power. They are *not*, necessarily, predicated on disparities in population numbers. This point differentiates the social scientific usage of the concepts of majority and minority (to refer to power disparities) from their political application and from their use in common parlance (to refer to numerical disparities).

The Development of the Minority Concept

Social scientific interest in the study of minorities began and for a long time remained closely connected with the field of race and ethnic relations.

Culture contact among different ethnic populations and the consequent development of multi-ethnic societies has frequently, indeed commonly, given rise to some form of ethnic stratification. Concomitantly, scholars interested in the study of ethnic relations, as well as those whose interests focused on the areas of social stratification and social change, almost inevitably become involved in the study of ethnic minorities (Shibutani and Kwan 1965; Simpson and Yinger 1972; Yetman and Steele 1975). An unfortunate consequence of the long-term association between the concepts of 'ethnicity' and 'minority', until fairly recently, has been a general tendency among scholars and laypersons alike to conceive of all minorities as ethnic groups and to conceive of all ethnic groups as minorities.

The misleading use of the term *ethnics* to set apart ethnic minorities from the dominant population in a society—historically, a common tendency among Canadians—is simply erroneous, for it suggests that members of ethnic majorities, such as Anglo-Canadians, are not 'ethnics' (that is, that they do not stem from or belong to any distinctive ethnic community).

The long-term association of the term *minority* with ethnic differences is similarly misleading, for it suggests that there are no other subordinate and inferiorized populations within the society. Within the current UN framework for human rights, ethnicity is particularly relevant for the question of minority claims based on collective cultural rights; but characteristics other than ethnocultural ones (race, sex, age, sexual orientation, and disability) are as relevant as ethnicity for the question of minority claims based on individual and categorical rights.

The Social Construction of Minority Status

Minorities are not 'natural' entities; they are socially constructed categories of people. No human population is innately or 'naturally' superior or inferior to others. However, some populations have more power than others, and those with superior power (majorities) are able to impose *inferiorizing* labels on those with less power on the basis of their own unsubstantiated assumptions about minority group attributes. Minorities are not 'inferior' by nature, in any of their group attributes, but they become 'inferiorized' by majority definition. The point I want to emphasize here is that it is *not* distinctive minority attributes, in themselves, that are responsible for the social construction of minority status: it is *unsubstantiated majority assumptions* about group attributes. However, once inferiorizing labels are imposed, majority authorities are able to rationalize human rights violations—denial of political, economic, social, or cultural rights—to populations *socially constructed as* inferior.

Human rights violations are represented in acts of discrimination against minorities; acts or practices that deny minority members the political, economic, and social opportunities and rewards accorded majority members. The long-term consequence of human rights violations is that minorities become *collectively disadvantaged*. They come to occupy a subordinate and inferiorized status in society, which we conceptualize as *minority status*.

Definition of the Minority Concept

The minority concept can be defined from an objective and/or a subjective perspective. In order to include all minorities within a comprehensive, *objective* definition, we will define a **minority** as any social category within a society: 1) that is set apart and defined by the majority as incompetent /inferior or abnormal/dangerous on the basis of assumed physical, cultural, and/or behavioural differences from majority norms; 2) whose members are categorically discriminated against by the majority on the basis of arbitrarily imposed, inferiorizing labels; 3) whose members are subject to some degree of oppression (denial of political rights), neglect (denial of economic rights), diminution (denial of social rights/human dignity), and/or deculturation (denial of cultural rights); and 4) that, as a consequence of the self-fulfilling prophecy of systemic discrimination, comes to occupy a socially subordinate, disadvantaged, and inferiorized position within the society.

The foregoing definition of minority differs from the now classic definition of Louis Wirth in three important ways: First, it utilizes only objective criteria, whereas Wirth employed both subjective and objective criteria; second, it is more inclusive than Wirth's definition with regard to the range of minorities that may be subsumed under it, and third, it includes both minority *categories* and minority *groups*.[3]

The comprehensive definition of minority that I have proposed reveals the three stages or steps in the process through which minority status is socially constructed: 1) labelling as inferior; 2) categorical discrimination/human rights violations; and 3) the self-fulfilling prophecy of collective disadvantage that results in minority status.

Majority and Minority: Relative Concepts

Like ethnicity, the minority concept is a relative notion that, even more than ethnicity, is meaningful only in relation to a corresponding out-group. In the case of minorities, the salient out-group with regard to any given human attribute is the corresponding majority or dominant population whose members enjoy a greater degree of political, economic, and social power in the society, and whose particular physical, cultural, and behavioural attributes provide the recognized, legitimate norms for all populations in the society (for example: white/black, male/female, English speaker/Italian speaker, Protestant/Muslim, adult/child, heterosexual/homosexual, Euro-Canadian/Inuit). Note that it is the majority who defines the normative order in society. Thus, for any socially significant human characteristic, the majority attribute provides the *norm* (normative referent) in relation to which minority differences are defined as 'abnormal' and/or 'deviant' (non-normative).

We will define a **majority** as a social category: 1) whose members have the legitimate power (or authority) to define themselves as normal and superior and to define all social categories (minorities) that are presumed to deviate from their physical, cultural, and behavioural norms as abnormal and/or inferior; 2) whose members are able to justify unequal and inferiorizing treatment of minorities through the use of invalidation ideologies or 'ISMS'—like racism, sexism, and ageism—which provide falsified (pseudo) 'evidence' for the inherent abnormality or inferiority of assumed minority attributes; 3) whose members are able to impose their will, norms, and laws on the society at large and to deny or suppress the expression of alternative, minority ideas and lifeways; and 4) whose members exercise the greatest degree of political, economic, and social power in the society and are able to control the life destinies of minorities.

Because minorities are assumed to harbour characteristics that differ from the norms of the dominant population in undesirable or unacceptable ways, minority members tend to be regarded and treated by the dominant population as unworthy or undeserving of equal societal opportunities. It follows from this premise that the more abnormal or inferior the alleged minority attributes are considered, the more pernicious the forms of discrimination against minorities. Put another way, insofar as minorities are branded as *less-than-human* or *substandard* human beings by majority powers, then the stage is set for the rationalization that such populations are not entitled to claim the same rights as *fully human beings*.

Inferiorization versus Stigmatization

As a rule, minorities presumed to be dangerous tend to be treated more inhumanely than those presumed to be inferior, but relatively harmless. *Dangerous* minorities are those perceived by majority authorities as a threat to their entrenched power, that is, minorities perceived to threaten majority political, economic, and social control in the society. Also seen as dangerous are minorities perceived to threaten established majority racial, ethnic, cultural, and moral norms.

Minorities may be labelled as dangerous on the basis of physical attributes (for example, race), cultural attributes (for example, religion), and/or behavioural attributes (for example, lifestyle). The more dangerous the minority is presumed to be, the more likely that discriminatory treatment against its members by dominant powers will involve the use of punitive legal sanctions backed by armed force (police, military, and security guards).

Minorities labelled as dangerous and threatening to society tend to be viewed not just as inferior human beings, but also as subhuman or even anti-human beings. They are not just inferiorized; they are *stigmatized*.

According to Goffman (1963) the term *stigma* in its original Greek meaning referred to forcibly imposed bodily mutilations (for example, cuts or burns) which publicly announced that the bearer was a morally blemished (or ritually polluted) person—a slave, criminal, or traitor—to be shunned by members of society-at-large (and, we would add, to be summarily denied human rights). Today, in social scientific parlance, the term generally refers to any *deeply discrediting* human attribute, rather than to any visible, bodily evidence of it.

Stigmatization serves to dehumanize the minority in the eyes of the majority audience. This can be explained, in part, with reference to the nature of stigma. A central quality of stigma is that of contagion: stigma deriving from one discrediting characteristic tends to spread to other characteristics. This leads to the imputation of a wide range of discrediting attributes on the basis of the original one: blacks are slow-witted and lazy; they hang around in gangs and push drugs; they are the cause of violence and crime in Canada. Indians have only a primitive mentality; they can't hold down a job; they are just a bunch of drunken welfare bums who get into fights and end up in jail. In this way, a highly distorted and wholly discrediting group stereotype of an anti-human or subhuman minority is generated. Once minorities are categorized as less-than-human, majority authorities are able to rationalize flagrant human rights violations with impunity.

During the Second World War, those minorities stigmatized by Nazi authorities in Germany as inherently evil, depraved, subhuman, and polluting creatures (for example, Jews, homosexuals, and gypsies) were singled out for extermination in death camps. Although Canada never adopted such a policy of genocide, during the Second World War when Canada was at war with Japan, Japanese-Canadians—most of whom were Canadian-born citizens and many of whom had never seen Japan—were defined as dangerous enemy aliens, traitors to Canada. Although no evidence of treason had been found by government authorities, collectively stigmatized as dangerous enemy aliens, Japanese-Canadians were incarcerated under armed guard in internment camps for the duration of the war. This case will be elaborated in Chapter 4.

The point of this example is to demonstrate the way in which majority authorities can employ the notion of 'dangerousness' in order to rationalize discriminatory public policies and practices that entail pervasive violations of minority rights. In this connection, it is important to differentiate between 'real' and 'apparent' danger, and to take into account the fact that what is 'real', within the context of majority/minority relations, tends to be what is presumed/alleged to be real by majority authorities.

Master Status and Multiple Minority Status

The preceding discussion has argued that the discriminatory implications of minority status vary with the degree of presumed deviance of minority attributes from majority norms; with the nature of majority-imposed labels (inferior versus dangerous); and with the degree of discreditation of minority attributes (inferiorized or stigmatized). In the pages to follow, we will examine the way in which inferiorization and stigmatization impact upon the personal and social identities of minority members. We will also analyze the discriminatory implications of multiple minority status.

Master Status

Social scientists apply the concept of **master status** to explain the phenomenon that occurs when the inferiorized or stigmatized minority attribute comes to constitute members' overriding, defining characteristic—when it comes to assume precedence over and above all the other human attributes of minority members in the eyes of the majority audience. This conception of master status focuses on the way in which majorities create minorities through singling out particular attributes as the basis for inferiorization and categorical discrimination.

Another conception of master status focuses on the way in which minorities react to inferiorization. When inferiorized or stigmatized minority attributes become perceived by minority members as central to their self-definition; when they come to provide the overriding basis for minority members' self-identification and group identification, then the attribute(s) can be said to have achieved a master status from the subjective point of view of the minority member. When this happens, what it indicates is that minority members have come to *internalize* the inferiorizing labels imposed on them by the majority. Not only have they become acutely conscious of their minority group status and identity, but it has also come to supersede all other statuses and identities.

Quotations from two aboriginal Canadians illustrate this point. The first is taken from an autobiographical essay by Chief Dan George, a First Nations spokesman:

> Do you know what it is like to have your race belittled and to come to learn that you are only a burden to the [white man's] country? . . . We were shoved aside because they thought we were dumb and could never learn. . . . What is it like to be without pride in your race, pride in your family, pride and confidence in yourself? . . . I shall tell you what it is like. It is like not caring about tomorrow for what does tomorrow matter. . . . It is like having a reserve that looks like a junk yard. . . . It is like getting drunk . . . an escape from ugly reality. . . . It is most of all like awaking next morning to the guilt of betrayal. For the alcohol did not fill the emptiness but only dug it deeper (Waubageshig 1970: 186).

The second quotation is taken from a published interview with Shirley Bear, a First Nations spokeswoman:

> The thing I remember the most [was] . . . being called dirty Indian kids, and not understanding. They would say 'dirty brown' or 'dirty black'—'there go the dirty Indian kids.' . . . I remember feeling really embarrassed. . . . I think it is easy for a person of colour to be embarrassed about themselves, to wish they were any colour but. I also remember going home and trying to wash it off (Silman 1987: 55).

Multiple Minority Status

The effect of an overriding master status is to obscure the fact that all human beings have a number of different social statuses and identities based on a variety of human attributes. Some of these statuses may be based on minority attributes, others on majority attributes. Therefore, the same individual may, at the same time, have minority status on the basis of some attributes and majority status, on the basis of others. In the following section, we will examine the social significance of **multiple minority status** and its implications in terms of its impact on personal and social identities and in terms of its discriminatory manifestations.

Insofar as individuals may belong to several minorities at the same time, one question arises:

Which of one's minority attributes will assume master status? Within the context of majority/minority relations, the notion of master status provides a parallel to the notion of primordiality emphasized by some scholars (for example, Isaacs 1977) in connection with ethnicity and ethnic identity. If we adopt the approach of scholars who hold that one's ethnic identity is a person's most basic (primordial) group identity, the argument would follow that, in a case of multiple minority status, one's ethnic attributes would override other minority characteristics and would invariably provide the underpinnings for one's master status, at least from the subjective point of view.

In contrast to this position, I propose that the extent to which it holds true in any given empirical instance must be taken as problematic, since both ethnic and other minority group identities are highly contingent on the nature of the prevailing social environment. I submit that the particular human attribute that will assume master status at any given time will vary with the specific social context and situation.

A number of variables could have bearing here: Which of the minority attributes deviates most markedly from majority norms? Which is most inferiorized or stigmatized? Which minority attribute is at issue in the situation at hand? Which majority group is represented in or relevant to the situation? A black, lesbian woman may be discriminated against in the Canadian context on the basis of race, sexual orientation, and sex, but whether one or more of these human attributes provides the basis for her overarching master status in a given situation is contingent on the relevant variables in that situation.

In cases where an individual has multiple minority status, the various statuses may or may not overlap in their discriminatory implications, under different social conditions. In the case of one black, lesbian woman, blackness may provide the overriding attribute for self-identification and thus may come to assume a master status that remains salient even in situations focusing on either women's or lesbian rights. In another case, this may not hold true. A black, lesbian woman may be involved in the women's movement, the movement for gay/lesbian liberation, and a black women's organization, all of which involve the attribute of sex; but it may only be in the context of the women's movement that the attribute of sex, rendered salient by a focus on gender discrimination, assumes master status. The main point of this example is to show that the way in which multiple minority status impacts on a person's various social identities varies from one individual to another, and from one social context to another. Which, if any, of a given person's minority attributes will assume master status in a given social context is something that must be empirically determined.

In addition to the question of the impact of multiple minority status on one's personal and social identities, a second question that arises is that of its discriminatory impact. Does multiple minority status inevitably beget multiple disadvantage?

Multiple Minority Status/Multiple Jeopardy?

The **multiple jeopardy thesis** has been put forward by social scientific researchers to test the theory that multiple minority status has both objective and subjective disadvantaging effects. The disadvantaging consequences of categorical discrimination on the basis of multiple criteria have thus been measured both in terms of reported fulfillment of life-needs and in terms of reported life-satisfaction.

However, to date, research studies attempting to test the multiple jeopardy thesis with regard to the variables of sex, ethnic status, and/or age have not been able to provide convincing evidence for this thesis with regard to subjective indicators of disadvantage. Although research results clearly support the multiple jeopardy thesis with regard to the inadequacy of fulfillment of the life-needs of multi-disadvantaged minorities, findings do not provide similarly strong support for the thesis with regard to their subjective feelings of life-satisfaction.[4]

How can we explain this seeming inconsistency in research findings? There are a number of factors that can be taken into consideration. First, minority categories—whether based on race, gender, age, ethnicity, or other attributes—are not homogeneous groups, as minority *stereotypes* suggest. Within each category are individual human beings with individual ways of coping with the disadvantages of their minority status. Some members internalize majority-imposed invalidating labels, others come to reject these negative labels. This observation has been documented in the research studies designed to test the multiple jeopardy thesis.

Differences in the strength of an individual's ability to cope with multiple minority status may vary in relation to lines of differentiation within minority communities. Class (socioeconomic status), for example, is important here. Despite the collective disadvantage of minorities at the group level, some members of ethnic and other minorities occupy a superior or elite economic status within their own minority communities. Clearly, such minority members have greater means than do others with which to cope with the disadvantaging ramifications of subordinate status. Another important variable is the availability of minority support systems. Minority members who can rely on minority support networks can find a great deal of help in coping with the invalidating effects of oppression, neglect, and diminution.

There are also interethnic group differences with regard to the extent or pervasiveness of collective disadvantage. Those ethnic minorities whose physical, cultural, and behavioural attributes coincide most closely with mainstream majority norms tend to be the least inferiorized and disadvantaged; those whose group attributes deviate most from majority norms tend to be the most inferiorized and disadvantaged. In Canada, ethnic groups of European ancestry tend to be the least inferiorized and disadvantaged, and aboriginal ethnic groups tend to be the most inferiorized and disadvantaged. Among immigrant ethnic minorities, racial visibility is an important differentiating variable: racially visible minorities tend to be more inferiorized and disadvantaged than do other ethnic minorities.

All of these variables must be considered in order to fully account for the patterns and the pervasiveness of disadvantage resulting from the combined effects of multiple minority status, particularly when multiple jeopardy rests in part on ethnicity.

Multiple Minority Status/ Multiple Jeopardy: Exploitation and Violence against Immigrant Women, Visible Immigrant Women, and Aboriginal Women in Canada

The diversity in the extent and in the patterns of objective disadvantage associated with multiple minority status can be well illustrated by comparing the abusive situations and experiences of immigrant women, visible immigrant women, and aboriginal women in Canada. In these cases, the common subjective indicator of disadvantage is provided in the dehumanizing life-experiences of abuse.

MacLeod and Shin, the authors of the 1990 paper on which Case Study 1 (see Box 3-1) is based, point out that many of the concerns facing immigrant and refugee women who are battered apply as well to racial and cultural minority women who are not immigrants or refugees, according to the working definition employed. This broad definition includes not only recent immigrants, refugees, and refugee claimants, but also those who have temporary status as visitors (tourists, temporary workers, students, or the dependants of students), and 'illegal immigrants'. As well, it includes those Canadian citizens and permanent residents who have been in Canada for many years but who still consider themselves outside the mainstream society in terms of their linguistic, racial, or cultural backgrounds, and who therefore still define themselves as immigrants. The study focus, however, was solely on women who fall into the working definition of immigrant and refugee women who are battered.

BOX 3-1: CASE STUDY 1

Triple Jeopardy: Understanding the Experiences of Immigrant and Refugee Women Who Are Battered

MacLeod and Shin's 1990 study of battered immigrant and refugee women highlighted the added vulnerability and isolation that immigration or refugee experiences impose on women, and showed how these factors complicate the reality of wife abuse. The research study was based on informal interviews, conducted in the summer of 1990, with women and men from governmental and ethnic community-based agencies working with immigrant and refugee women across Canada.

Study findings reveal that many of the women, particularly refugee women, have not had any choice about moving to Canada or about settling in a particular town or city. Others are picture or mail-order brides who have no family or friends in this country, and who may have the added challenge of adjusting to an interracial marriage. Still other women in Canada as visitors (students, temporary workers, or tourists), sponsored by their Canadian resident husbands, are vulnerable because they have no permanent status in Canada while their immigration applications are being processed. These women are particularly susceptible to their husbands' attempts to intimidate them by threatening to or actually withdrawing their sponsorship. For most immigrant or refugee women, the economic difficulties, political upheavals, physical hardships, loss of friends and family, and the racism they experience leave them feeling vulnerable, confused, depressed, and alone. Under these circumstances, women may come to depend strongly on their husbands and find it difficult to contemplate leaving their partners, no matter how brutal the abuse. Added to this is the vulnerability women feel as a result of their fears of the perceived power immigration officers may have over their future. For example, from those people interviewed, the researchers heard that immigration officers have been called on to verify women's status for welfare workers. Women also spoke of their experiences of being asked to discuss the details of their abuse with immigration officers who were not sensitive to their experiences of assault.

In addition, for any woman without landed immigrant status, who is in Canada on a working permit (employment authorization), on a student visa (student authorization), as a tourist (visitor's status), or who is in Canada as an illegal immigrant, access to social assistance and subsidized housing is extremely unlikely. Under these circumstances, the decision to leave an abusive husband and live on her own or with her children is an almost impossible choice for a woman to make.

For all these possible reasons—the fact that her husband may be her only family in this country, the fear shared by many women of the implicit or overt power the immigration system can hold over their futures—most immigrant or refugee women conclude that living with abuse at the hands of their husbands could be preferable to the abuse, uncertainty, and bureaucratic obstacles they would endure if they were to leave.

Given these realities, immigrant and refugee women live with many real and hypothetical fears. One is the fear of deportation, for themselves, for their children, or for their husband. In cultures where a stigma is attached to 'troubled relationships' and to women who do not take responsibility for the happiness and survival of the marriage, women who are abused fear accusations that they have brought shame on the community, and they fear the ostracism from friends and family members that can result. Within this context, women may fear the individualized approach often taken in this country to deal with violence. These women may see efforts to encourage them to take advantage of counselling for themselves as ways to separate them from their families or communities, and as selfish and irresponsible ways of approaching their pain. Many women also fear that they will be unable to survive if they leave their husbands or if their husbands are put in jail. Especially for women with little or no employment history and few or no skills in French or English, this fear is well founded on reality. As well, some women, working as domestic workers, have been abused by their employers. Such women are unlikely to report this abuse because of their temporary status, and therefore are particularly vulnerable to abuse and exploitation by their employers.

Many immigrant and refugee women fear involvement with the justice system, often because of their experiences with police as a repressive force in their country of origin, but often because of their personal experiences of racism from justice system representatives in Canada.

Women who are refugees have often endured great hardship along with their families through political abuse, terrorism, and physical deprivation. Their shared experiences of oppression with their husbands and families often also give them a greater sympathy for the victimization their husbands have experienced, and a desire to seek help for their husbands and their children as well as for themselves.

The experiences and perceptions of violence of many immigrant and refugee women can be very different from those of most non-immigrant women in Canada. The added vulnerability and isolation that immigration or refugee experiences impose on women exacerbate the reality of wife abuse. At the same time, the fears associated with leaving their husbands, dealing with the justice system, possible deportation, and inability to survive alone prevent the vast majority of these women from leaving abusive relationships.

SOURCE: Adapted from MacLeod and Shin 1990.

These women may or may not be members of racial and cultural minorities.

These comments notwithstanding, a perusal of the study findings reveals that many of the women, were, indeed, members of racial and cultural minorities. The findings reveal considerable evidence of double or triple disadvantage, rooted in evident cultural differences and/or racial discrimination, in the reported abusive experiences of many immigrant and refugee women.

BOX 3-2: CASE STUDY 2

Exploitation of Visible Immigrant Women Workers in Canada's Sweatshops

The term *sweatshop*, for most Canadians, conjures up images of dilapidated factories in developing countries where women are paid pennies a day to perform arduous work in tiny, windowless rooms where the hot air is stifling. What most citizens of this 'country of plenty' do not know, or refuse to acknowledge, is that similar sweatshop conditions are found in Canadian cities, like Toronto, right down the street from our homes and places of work.

A 1999 study by OISE/UT professor Roxanna Ng explodes the myth that sweatshop conditions are a Third World phenomenon. In fact, Ng's report suggests garment workers around the world, including those in Canada, face similar situations of exploitation.

Ng's study, released at a press conference at Queen's Park on 18 June 1999, focused attention on the hazardous working conditions and low pay experienced by homeworkers in the Greater Toronto Area. The study findings showed that an overwhelming majority of immigrant women in the garment industry work under substandard conditions, especially those that eke out their living at home. All of the 30 women interviewed by Ng were Chinese immigrants who worked below the standards provided by the Employment Standards Act.

The study findings revealed that there are widespread violations of the Employment Standards Act by employers, demonstrating that existing legislation fails to protect the workers, who are primarily immigrant women from Asia. Garment workers continue to suffer physical and emotional ailments due to their occupation but receive no compensation under the Workplace Safety and Insurance Act.

One-third of the women interviewed in the study make below minimum wage with some being paid as little as $2 per hour. Out of the 30 immigrant women workers interviewed, only 2 receive the 4 per cent vacation pay stipulated by the Employment Standards Act. None of the workers receives overtime pay even though their working week exceeds 44 hours.

Ng's report revealed that the lack of legislative protection for immigrant workers is linked closely to the homeworkers' fear of losing their jobs. This fear makes it very difficult for a worker to come forward and complain.

A garment worker, who chose to remain nameless out of fear of repercussion, was present at the press conference. She described the harsh facts of her employment. Her rate of pay is $3 to $4 an hour and she can only put in about 6 hours per day to support herself and her four-year-old child, while suffering from knee problems resulting from her work.

Ng suggests that one of the key problems is that this is a piecework industry in which the seamstresses get paid according to each piece, that is, a sleeve or a collar that is completed. Theoretically the faster one sews, the more pieces one can accomplish by the hour, and hence, the greater the salary. However, the study findings reveal that the reality is quite different. It is difficult to calculate an hourly rate because salary is determined by each piece that is done and contractors do not agree on the piece rate. Additionally, employers and subcontractors employ a number of strategies to keep wages low. The result is that the conditions applied to all the workers are substandard.

Ng argues that although many of the women know they are in a bad situation, they feel that they have few options. These women know very well that they are being exploited. But the major reason why they work at home is because there is no affordable childcare. If they work outside the home, it most likely will be at a minimum-wage job, and childcare will cost more than their salary. And, if they file a charge against their contractors, they very likely will lose their jobs at home. These visible immigrant women workers are truly in a Catch-22 situation.

Lack of legal protection is one of the main hurdles that these homeworkers face, Ng suggests. She points out that Canada does not have an adequate system in which the Ministry of Labour can inspect and monitor the working conditions of factory and homeworkers. As a result, these workers, mostly visible immigrant women, experience daily violations to their fundamental human rights through exploitation in the garment industry.

SOURCE: Adapted from Ng 1999.

The evidence of economic exploitation and personal abuse of immigrant and refugee women in Canada provided in Case Study 1 and Case Study 2 lends support for the thesis that racial visibility and marked cultural differences from mainstream Canadian norms serve to doubly disadvantage immigrant and refugee women and to make them more highly vulnerable to exploitation and abuse at the hands of husbands, employers, and dominant authorities. Insofar as aboriginality is the ethnic group attribute that deviates most from mainstream dominant Canadian norms, what remains to be tested is the thesis that aboriginal women are the most disadvantaged of all women in Canada, and that they are the category that is most at risk for exploitation and abuse by dominant males, both in their own communities and in society at large.

BOX 3-3: CASE STUDY 3

Wife Abuse and Family Violence in Aboriginal Communities

Although family violence can be found in all cultural, racial, and religious groups, victims of family violence in aboriginal communities face a number of additional concerns when seeking to escape an abusive environment. Often victims who are forced to leave their community experience the distress of having to abandon their support system, kinship network and cultural roots.

Prevalence of Family Violence

A national study by the Aboriginal Nurses Association of Canada indicates that aboriginal women and children under 15 years of age are most frequently physically abused. It is estimated that between 75 per cent and 90 per cent of women in some northern aboriginal communities are abused. The same study found that 40 per cent of children in Northern communities had been physically abused by a family member (Dumont-Smith and Sioui-Labelle 1991). In a similar vein, a study by the Ontario Native Women's Association found that 8 out of 10 aboriginal women in Ontario had personally experienced family violence. Of these women, 87 per cent had experienced physical injury and 57 per cent had been sexually abused (Ontario Native Women's Association, 1989). A Northwest Territories survey found that 80 per cent of aboriginal girls and 50 per cent of aboriginal boys under 8 years old were sexually abused (Canadian Panel on Violence Against Women 1993).

Contextual/Contributing Factors

A broad range of study findings indicate that certain factors can contribute to the prevalence of family violence. Important among these, in the case of aboriginal peoples, are poverty and unemployment, poor education, substandard living conditions, abusive treatment of aboriginal children in the residential school system (which has contributed to intergenerational violence), and alcohol and substance abuse.

Many aboriginal communities exist in conditions of extreme poverty and unemployment. Statistics show that more than 70 per cent of aboriginal households live below the poverty line. Unemployment ranges from 50–90 per cent in some aboriginal communities. Much of the economic crisis facing aboriginal communities originates in their colonization and their removal from mainstream social, economic and political structures (Alberta Advisory Council on Women's Issues 1995). Additionally, aboriginal women have less education and are less likely to be employed than other Canadian women (Statistics

Canada 1995 as reported in Family Violence Prevention Division 1996). Living conditions in most aboriginal communities continue to be substandard. It is estimated that 35 per cent of the aboriginal population living off-reserve is in need of housing. Overcrowded housing, poverty, poor health, chronic unemployment and substandard living conditions can exacerbate tensions within families and perpetuate violence. Similarly, poverty and isolation make it difficult for victims to leave abusive situations (Canadian Panel on Violence Against Women 1993).

Alcohol and substance abuse is prevalent in aboriginal communities. One study found that alcohol abuse was common in 93 per cent of aboriginal communities and drug abuse was common in 81 per cent (Frank 1992).

The effects of the residential school system have contributed to intergenerational violence. Children who were subjected to abusive treatment in schools are more likely to have learned poor parenting skills and to pass that violence on to their families in adulthood (ibid.).

Struggles/Barriers Making It Difficult for Women Victims to Leave Abusive Situations

Access to information (e.g., legal rights) and support services (e.g., transition houses, crisis centres) is often difficult for women who live in geographically isolated communities. Sometimes women must travel long distances from their community to seek help. Leaving an abusive situation also can be difficult for victims of abuse in aboriginal communities because they must often abandon their kinship ties, support network, cultural community and sense of identity. This can also cause feelings of isolation and distress.

Even if services are accessible, aboriginal women often face a number of additional barriers and concerns. These can include: fear of losing one's children; fear of being misunderstood by support staff; lack of resources to obtain treatment or support; a perception that services are not culturally relevant; a misunderstanding and/or fear of the justice system and law enforcement officials; a lack of anonymity in seeking services on reserve, as these are usually very small communities.

Aboriginal women with disabilities often have difficulties in accessing help for abuse, as some community-based services cannot accommodate the specific needs of women with disabilities. Further, services in urban centres may be perceived as culturally inappropriate (Canadian Panel on Violence Against Women 1993).

Aboriginal children who experience family violence and who witness violence against their mothers suffer long-term emotional and behavioural problems. There is an alarming rate of substance abuse among children and youth in aboriginal communities, yet treatment programs often remain inaccessible. This may leave children vulnerable to abuse and places significant barriers on a child/youth's ability to leave an abusive environment. As well, children may grow up normalizing abusive behaviour and replicating this behaviour in their own relationships. The cycle of violence is therefore perpetuated, making it difficult for victims to break free from the violence (ibid.).

Older women in aboriginal communities who experience abuse often do not report their abuse for fear of being sent away to a seniors' residence, or because they have nowhere to go in their own community. Many remain isolated and unable to access support services or inhome care (ibid.).

The Path to Healing: What's Been Done and What Hasn't Been Done

Many aboriginal communities have returned to traditional approaches to healing and recovery from abuse. This includes the use of pipe ceremonies, sweat lodges, talking circles and sentencing circles. Based on a principle of holistic healing, these traditional practices attempt to address the emotional, physical and spiritual needs of victims (ibid.).

However, in this author's view, it is unlikely that the current situation will change appreciably unless the Canadian Government takes giant steps to ensure that the systemic colonialism and racism underlying the disadvantaged life conditions of aboriginal peoples is rooted out. For, without eradicating the disadvantaged life conditions which trigger wife abuse and family violence, the cycle of violence will continue. The prevalence of wife abuse and family violence in Canada's aboriginal communities represents a national disgrace.

SOURCE: Excerpted from *Family Violence in Aboriginal Communities*, Fact Sheet 10, Department of Community Services, Government of Nova Scotia website.

BOX 3-4

Report of the UN Committee Monitoring Implementation by Canada of the UN Covenant on Economic, Social, and Cultural Rights

The 1998 UN Committee Report on Canada's performance in honouring the UN Covenant on Economic, Social and Cultural Rights strongly supports the author's view, stated earlier, that the Canadian Government must take giant steps to ensure that the systemic colonialism and racism underlying the disadvantaged life conditions of aboriginal peoples is rooted out. The Report severely criticizes Canada for neglecting to address the continuing gross disparity between aboriginal and other Canadians with respect to the enjoyment of Covenant rights. The Report levied especially severe criticism at Canada's continuing failure to honour promises made to improve the living conditions of aboriginal peoples. The Committee put forward the following criticisms:

> The Committee is greatly concerned at the gross disparity between Aboriginal people and the majority of Canadians with respect to the enjoyment of Covenant rights. There has been little or no progress in the alleviation of social and economic deprivation among Aboriginal people. In particular, the Committee is deeply concerned at the shortage of adequate housing, the endemic mass unemployment and the high rate of suicide, especially among youth in the Aboriginal communities. Another concern is the failure to provide safe and adequate drinking water to Aboriginal communities on reserves. The delegation of the State Party conceded that almost a quarter of Aboriginal household dwellings require major repairs for lack of basic amenities. The Committee views with concern the direct connection between Aboriginal economic marginalization and the ongoing dispossession of Aboriginal people from their lands, as recognized by the Royal Commission on Aboriginal Peoples (RCAP), and endorses the recommendations of the RCAP that policies which violate Aboriginal treaty obligations and extinguishment, conversion or giving up of Aboriginal rights and title should on no account be pursued by the State Party. The Committee is greatly concerned that the recommendations of the RCAP have not yet been implemented in spite of the urgency of the situation.

Only if the Canadian Government heeds these pointed criticisms, will the deplorable prevalence of wife abuse and family violence in aboriginal communities begin to become attenuated.

SOURCE: Excerpted from *CCPA Monitor*, Canadian Centre for Policy Alternatives, March 1999.

Multiple Minority Status/Multiple Jeopardy: Comparing the Situations and Experiences of Abuse of Immigrant Women, Visible Immigrant Women, and Aboriginal Women

Earlier in this chapter we pointed out that there are significant group-level differences among Canada's racial and ethnic minorities with regard to the nature and extent of their collective disadvantage. In Canada, European ethnic groups are the least disadvantaged, and aboriginal ethnic groups—differing most markedly from mainstream Euro-Canadian racial and cultural norms—are the most disadvantaged. Among immigrant ethnic minorities, racial visibility is an important differentiating variable: racially visible minorities tend to be more disadvantaged than do other ethnic minorities. Moreover, within each of these racial-ethnic minority communities, gender-based differences serve to disadvantage women and to render them a 'minority within a minority'.

The evidence from the three case studies presented suggest that these inter- and intragroup differences in collective disadvantage are reflected in parallel differences in the extent or pervasiveness of abuse of immigrant women, visible immigrant women, and aboriginal women, respectively. In short, the hierarchy of disadvantage is reflected in a parallel hierarchy of abuse. These observations lend support to a variant of the multiple jeopardy thesis: Multiple minority status alone is not sufficient to account for multiple jeopardy; what also must be taken into account is the magnitude of disadvantage associated with each minority status.

An Intersectional Model of Multiple Minority Status

Mullaly (2002: 152) suggests that an intersectional model of multiple minority status highlights the multiplicity of discrimination and its disadvantaging effects. Such a model is presented by Mullaly in graphic form. The model reveals the complexity and intersecting nature of multiple forms of discrimination. Yet, Mullaly argues, no model or theory can account for or explain how individuals will experience dehumanizing forms of discrimination because each person's experience is unique. Nor can a model or theory account for the ways in which different manifestations of discrimination constantly change in relation to each other or how they vary in different contexts. The best we can hope for, Mullaly suggests, is to understand that the different forms, sources, and relations of discrimination are continuous, dynamic, and mutually reinforcing (ibid.). An inherent hazard in analyzing different manifestations of discrimination, Mullaly (2002: 165) points out, is to assume that any particular minority group is united and that every member of the group shares the same experiences and is affected in the same way. Indeed, the opposite is the case. Every minority group is fragmented along multiple lines (as pointed out earlier in this chapter) and these lines of division impact differentially upon the unique experiences of disadvantage of minority members.

Conclusion

This chapter showed how discriminatory barriers imposed by majority authorities, barriers that serve to violate minority rights, have produced group-level inequalities in political, economic, and social power across Canada. Our analysis has demonstrated how institutionalized inequalities in power have led to the development of Canada's system of social stratification, and, at the same time, has played a major role in the social construction of ethnic and other minorities.

Our initial discussion of social stratification pointed out that systems of social stratification can be based on a wide variety of criteria: race, ethnicity, gender, sexual orientation, age, class, and/or other factors. Our later analysis of multiple minority status and multiple jeopardy, however, drew attention to the fact that minority attributes, such as race, ethnicity, sex, age, or class, rather than being discrete phenomena, often share complex links with collective disadvantage and social ranking.

Nevertheless, we can single out ethnic minorities from other types of minorities in Canada whose inferiorized or stigmatized attributes have somewhat different implications for social ranking. Where ethnicity constitutes an important criterion for social ranking, as it does in Canada, the society is ethnically stratified; this system of social stratification can be studied as a system of ethnic stratification. In the next chapter, we will analyze the origin and development of the Canadian system of ethnic stratification, and we will delineate the factors influencing different patterns of majority/minority ethnic relations in Canada.

Key Concepts

- economic power
- majority status
- majority/minority relations
- master status
- minority status
- multiple jeopardy thesis
- multiple minority status
- political power
- social power
- social stratification

Critical Thinking Questions

1. Regardless of the particular criteria on which systems of social stratification may be based, they essentially constitute power-based hierarchies in which intergroup relations are relations of dominance and subordination or majority/minority relations. Discuss.
2. Explain how the development of a system of social stratification leads to the social construction of ethnic and other minorities. Be sure to provide concrete examples to illustrate your points.
3. In any given social context, the concepts of majority and minority are relative concepts: within both conceptual categories, each in-group has meaning only in relation to a corresponding out-group. Illustrate this proposition with specific reference to the criteria of gender, race, national origin, language, and religion, in the Canadian context.
4. It has been said that the effect of an overriding master status is to obscure the fact that all human beings have a number of different social statuses and identities based on a variety of human attributes. Explain the concepts of master status and multiple minority status and provide examples to illustrate the relationship between the two concepts.
5. The multiple jeopardy thesis has been put forward by social scientific researchers to test the theory that multiple minority status has both objective and subjective disadvantaging effects. Does the evidence from research studies provide support for this thesis? Elaborate.

CHAPTER 4

The Vertical Ethnic Mosaic: The Canadian System of Racial-Ethnic Stratification

Introduction

In Chapter 3, we showed how group-level inequalities in political, economic, and social power have led to the development of Canada's system of social stratification. Our analysis also revealed how continuing human rights violations have played a major role in the social construction of *ethnic and other minorities.*

In this chapter, our discussion of social stratification and majority/minority relations in Canada will focus on *ethnic* criteria for social ranking. Accordingly, we will limit our examination of the Canadian structure of social inequality to an analysis of Canada's **ethnic stratification** system.

Racism, Human Rights Violations, and the Social Construction of Ethnic Minorities in Canada

Within the human rights perspective adopted by the International Bill of Human Rights (IBHR), the very existence of ethnic minorities is in violation of their members' fundamental human rights. The Universal Declaration of Human Rights (UDHR) proclaims that all members of every human society should have equal access to political, economic, and social power. Yet, wherever they are found, ethnic minorities are categorically and systemically restricted or excluded from such access on the arbitrary basis of the racist views of the majority, which are used by dominant authorities to rationalize categorical discrimination against ethnic minority target groups. Within the context of majority/minority ethnic relations, racist ideologies are transposed into potent political instruments wielded by dominant ethnic authorities to oppress (deny political rights), neglect (deny economic rights), diminish (deny social rights), and deculturate (deny cultural rights) members of ethnic minorities.

In the Introduction to this book, we pointed out that, in addition to the protection of *individual* human rights and freedoms accorded every human being *qua human being* under the IBHR, members of ethnocultural minorities also are accorded protection for their *collective* cultural, linguistic, and religious rights. Article 27 of the International Covenant on Civil and Political Rights (ICCPR) states that ethnic, religious, and linguistic minorities, wherever they exist within states, should not be denied the right to collectively express and enjoy their own distinctive culture, religion, and language. Current interpretation of this article, as expressed in the Declaration on the Rights of Persons Belonging to National or Ethnic, Religious, and Linguistic Minorities, adopted by the UN General Assembly on 18 December 1992, indicates that it is the *ethnocultural* underpinnings of minority status that provide the basis for collective minority rights.

What distinguishes *sui generis* ethnocultural minorities from other (non-ethnic) minorities is the attribute of 'living' culture, that is, culture (or ethnoculture) in the transgenerational, anthropological sense of the term. It is this attribute that provides the currently recognized basis for the *collective rights* of ethnic minorities, under United Nations Human Rights Codes and Covenants. This distinction is a critical one for our examination of Canada's system of ethnic stratification, for it sets apart *sui generis* ethnocultural minorities from other collectively disadvantaged and inferiorized minorities, as indicated in Tables 5-1 and 5-2 (pages 130 and 132). Under the current system of international human rights protection, only ethnocultural minorities whose collective cultural rights have been violated can, justifiably, put forward collective, cultural rights claims.[1]

The Development of Ethnic Stratification in Canada

The mere existence of ethnic differences between co-existing human populations within a multiethnic society such as Canada's does not mean that ethnic criteria will provide bases for social stratification, and that majority/minority ethnic relations will inevitably follow. It is only when assumed or perceived ethnic differences are utilized by dominant ethnic groups to create and sustain legitimate bases of social stratification that the ethnic 'minority syndrome' (Glaser and Possony 1979: ix) develops.

When one or more ethnic groups, such as the English outside Quebec and the French in Quebec, become powerful enough to define the societal or regional (for example, provincial) situation, to impose their will, their cultural standards, and their laws on all ethnic communities within their sphere of jurisdiction in society, and when less powerful ethnic communities, presumed to differ from majority norms in undesirable ways are thereby denied their political, economic, social, and cultural rights, then the ethnic minority syndrome becomes full blown.

Canada's Vertical Ethnic Mosaic

In his pathbreaking book *The Vertical Mosaic* (1965), John Porter described the nationwide hierarchical structure of the Canadian ethnic stratification system at that time. Based on the findings of a national survey conducted over a period of almost 10 years, Porter reported that members of Canada's various ethnic communities were differentially and unequally represented (in proportion to their numbers in the population) within the Canadian ethnic hierarchy. He suggested that Canada's ethnic hierarchy at the time consisted of three broad social categories:

1. Charter or founding populations (English and French), together with immigrants from the British Isles and those from Northern and Western European countries whose biocultural characteristics were similar to those of the charter populations, were disproportionately represented at the top, within the ranks of the majority or dominant social category.
2. Later immigrant populations, largely from Southern and Eastern European countries, whose biocultural characteristics diverged in varying degrees from those of the dominant populations, were found in the middle ranks among Canada's ethnic minorities.
3. Aboriginal populations (Indians, Inuit, and Métis), whose biocultural characteristics diverged most markedly from those of the dominant ethnic categories, were found at the bottom of Canada's ethnic hierarchy. At the time of Porter's study, Canada's aboriginal peoples constituted a racially stigmatized and structurally dependent ethnoclass having the lowest status of all minorities within the established ethnic hierarchy.

Porter noted that there was a tendency for the vertical structure of the ethnic mosaic to persist, in much the same form, over time. Despite considerable upward and downward status mobility and inconsistency in the middle ranks, Porter pointed out that the ethnic composition of the very top ranks and that of the very bottom tended to remain relatively stable and consistent on the three dimensions of stratification (political, economic, and social power).

Porter's survey indicated that a high degree of status consistency was associated with ethnic rank stability. At the very top, the dominant English elite were characterized by superordinate levels of political, economic, and social power; while the aboriginal minorities at the bottom were characterized by low status and power on all three dimensions. In the middle ranks, however, there tended to be a higher degree of status inconsistency, a factor that may have introduced an element of instability not found to nearly the same degree at the top and bottom levels. Thus, for example, the Jewish ethnic minority was very high in economic power, but somewhat lower in terms of political power, and decidedly lower in prestige. The French, as an ethnic majority, were high in terms of political and social power, but lower than many immigrant populations in economic power. Since the publication of Porter's work, the Franco-Quebecois have come to assume economic and political control in Quebec, but they have not achieved 'founding peoples' equality with the English at the national level. As for the immigrant category, the incoming population is more racially and culturally diverse since the inception of Canada's 'open' immigration policy. Among Canada's new immigrant and refugee populations, *visible minorities*—those whose physical and cultural differences from majority norms are greatest—experience the most formidable barriers to upward mobility.

Porter's observation regarding the stability of the top and bottom levels of Canada's **vertical mosaic** was supported by several later studies (including Clement 1975; Kelner 1969; Lautard and Guppy 1990; Ponting and Gibbins 1980; and Richmond 1972). However, Porter's explanation for the persistence of the vertical mosaic (1979: v) engendered considerable social scientific debate. The debate focused largely on the economic dimension of stratification, specifically the question of the association between ethnicity and socioeconomic class. Porter believed that ethnocultural factors (differences in value priorities) impede economic mobility in a universalistic society. A well-documented critique of this view was provided by Darroch (1979), who argued that it was primarily structural factors (discrimination, job opportunities), rather than ethnocultural ones, that were responsible for the long-term (albeit diminishing) association between ethnicity and economic class in Canada. A later re-assessment of the post-*Vertical Mosaic* literature on the topic provided further support for Darroch's position (see Lautard and Guppy 1990).

Canada's Vertical Mosaic Today

In an analysis based on 1991 Canada census figures, Isajiw (1999: 134) shows that although there is a general correspondence between the economic measures of ethnic stratification based on reported education and income, in specific cases these are not necessarily the same. Filipinos, blacks, and Caribbeans are among the most highly educated groups; yet, they are also those with the lowest income. Italians are overrepresented in the higher income categories, but they are underrepresented in the higher education categories. While the British are overrepresented in the highest income category, the census indicates that their historical educational advantage has waned. The question arises: Does this mean that the British—especially the English—have lost their majority status? Isajiw points out that none of the census measures employed actually directly measure a group's majority status. Since majority status involves having a high degree of political power—indicated by having the final voice in decision-making in the major social institutions—what needs to be assessed is the place of the British in Canada's major economic corporations and political institutions. Several research studies (Herberg 1990; Lautard and Guppy 1990; Ogmundson 1990; Rich 1991) reveal that this elite group has opened up more to other ethnicities, but the British predominance has remained. Isajiw (1999: 134) points out that British and French dominance has also been maintained in the highest political institutions. Over almost one hundred years, the majority of parliamentarians in Canada's House of Commons have been of British origin. Although the House of Commons has opened up to other ethnicities in recent years, it remains predominantly British Canadian and French Canadian.

Porter's observation regarding the stability of the top and bottom levels of Canada's ethnic hierarchy holds true not only for the top level, as shown, but also for the bottom stratum of today's Canadian ethnic hierarchy. The *Report of the Royal Commission on Aboriginal Peoples in Canada* (RCAP) reveals clearly that Canada's aboriginal population remains an economically marginalized and stigmatized underclass, at the very bottom of today's vertical ethnic mosaic (RCAP 2000). According to the RCAP report, as a group, aboriginal people are on the margins of the Canadian economy. Aboriginal people are more likely than other Canadians to be unemployed and, when employed, they are likely to receive lower wages. Because they earn less, they have a substantially lower standard of living than other Canadians. The unemployment rate for aboriginal people soared during the 1980s—far outpacing the increase for Canadians generally—and their average income declined. This happened despite a narrowing of the gap in educational attainment between aboriginal and non-aboriginal Canadians. This trend continued through the nineties as the influx of young people into the labour market and the lack of jobs persisted. This continuing situation brings much suffering to aboriginal people and adds greatly to public indebtedness. More than 150,000 aboriginal adults do not know the satisfaction of earning an adequate income and being economically independent.

In the next section of this chapter, we will focus on the origin and development of the Canadian system of ethnic stratification. Porter's observation regarding the stability of the top and bottom levels of Canada's ethnic hierarchy has significant import for this analysis.

The Development of the Canadian System of Ethnic Stratification

In the initial stages of development, the two founding populations, English and French, wielded their vast power to usurp the territory, which was later to become Canada, from the aboriginal peoples then residing in the area. Moreover, these newcomers established political, economic, and cultural hegemony over the aboriginal populations.

In order to understand how and why this happened, we will first consider the theoretical prerequisites for ethnic stratification; second, we will look at the empirical realities underlying the origin and development of the Canadian ethnic hierarchy.

Prerequisites and Initial Patterns of Ethnic Stratification

Despite ethnic differences between coexisting populations in the same region, majority/minority relations do not develop until one population imposes its will on another. Noel (1968) has argued persuasively that when distinct ethnocultural groups come into continued first-hand contact, a system of ethnic stratification will follow, given three conditions: 1) a sufficient degree of ethnocentrism; 2) competition for scarce, mutually valued resources; and 3) differential power. Noel contends that without a sufficient level of ethnocentrism, social distance between the populations in contact would be minimized, categorical discrimination would not develop, and competition would not be specifically structured along ethnic lines. Without competition for scarce, mutually valued resources there would be no motivation or rationale for establishing the ethnic hierarchy. Without superior power it would be impossible for any one population to become dominant and impose its will and standards (and eventually its laws and institutions) on the other(s).

Once ethnic groups aligned by ethnocultural differences begin to compete against one another, the most important variable in determining which group will emerge as dominant is differential power. Power may derive from the superior size, weapons, property, economic resources, technology, education, skills, or customary or scientific knowledge of a group; but whatever the base, superior power is crucial not only to the establishment of a system of ethnic stratification, but also to its maintenance and development.

Competition among distinct ethnic groups for scarce, mutually valued resources may take place in many contexts: war, territorial expansion, or migration. Over time, competition leads to an unequal distribution and control of resources with the more powerful ethnic group emerging as dominant. Once established, these distributive patterns are maintained through continued control of society's major institutions. The majority ethnic group confers the status of societal-wide norms on its own culture, social institutions, and laws, and requires conformity to these standards by all other ethnic groups. Eventually, prestige becomes associated with control of the society's major resources and social institutions. Thus, the dominant group becomes vested with a relative monopoly of political, economic, and social power (Noel 1968).

Origin of Ethnic Stratification in Canada

The development of the contemporary system of ethnic stratification in Canada began around the mid-fifteenth century with continuing contact between the English and French and the aboriginal peoples in a context of European territorial expansion. Initially, the superior power of the Europeans derived from their possession of firearms, as well as their superior economic and technological skills and resources. Competition between Europeans and (aboriginal) First Nations (then referred to as Indians) resulted in the unequal distribution of land and natural resources, with the potentially most productive areas taken by the more powerful Europeans. Patterson (1972) provides persuasive historical evidence that shows that the French newcomers inaugurated a reserve system whereby Indians from various aboriginal ethnic communities were removed from their aboriginal lands or confined to delimited areas within them, in order to accommodate French settler expansion; the English soon followed suit.[2]

Reserves were typically established in the more isolated, less productive areas of the regions of English and French settler expansion. As English territorial sovereignty expanded, more and more lands traditionally occupied by Indians came under English jurisdictional control, and from 1763 to 1923, land cession treaties with the British Crown formalized the process of Indian Land alienation. Through these initial processes, French and English conquerors and settlers acquired not only the most desirably located and the most resource-plentiful Indian lands, but by far the greatest proportion of this new territory (Patterson 1972).

Initially, contact between Europeans and Inuit populations was sporadic and limited to economic interaction between these aboriginal peoples of the Far North and the whalers or fur traders. The remote Arctic lands of the Inuit were not considered desirable for European habitation, nor valuable in terms of natural resources, fur-bearing animals being the one exception. Traditionally, Inuit peoples moved in small bands within a fixed radius and rarely tied themselves down to definite localities. Their nomadic and semi-nomadic life patterns were predicated on the migratory movements of their animal resources. Today, as a consequence of the domination of European agents in relations with Inuit, Canadian Inuit live in permanent settlements selected, designed, and controlled by the dominant Euro-Canadians.

At the outset, European trading companies interested in exploiting the valuable resources of Arctic fur-bearing animals selected permanent location sites that were readily accessible by sea, possessed safe anchorages, and were located in areas of sufficient population to be profitable to the fur trader (Nichols 1971). At first, European outposts serving the dispersed Inuit bands of the region were administered by a single European agent (for example, the Hudson's Bay Company fur trader). Gradually, however, the areas of European institutional control grew and outposts came to be dominated by the 'Big Three of the North'—the Hudson's Bay Company fur trader, the Anglican and/or Catholic missionary, and the RCMP officer (Hughes 1965).

With the post-Second World War introduction into the North of federal government health and welfare services, the institutional spheres of Euro-Canadian control expanded to include nursing stations, schools, and government administrative centres. Later, with the implementation by the federal government of a large-scale rental-housing scheme for the Inuit (after 1965), the outposts became (from the Euro-Canadian point of view) the natural choice for the location of permanent Inuit settlements. Frequently, however, the animal resources of the permanent settlement locality were not sufficient to provide enough food to support the Inuit population for more than a short time. Thus, the Inuit have come to rely increasingly on European food and later on scarce jobs and government welfare cheques to purchase food (Frideres 1993; Paine 1977; Vanstone 1971). Inuit, like Indians, have become more and more dependent on the Euro-Canadians for their survival. The important point here is that the original decision as to allocation of land for both residence and economic exploitation lay with the most powerful ethnic groups, and these initial distributive patterns, once established, were perpetuated through the continuing exercise of institutional control by the Euro-Canadian majority.

Differential Patterns of Majority/ Minority Relations: Dominant/Aboriginal versus Dominant/ Immigrant Models

Dominant/Aboriginal Relations

Lieberson (1961) contends that in the initial period of Contact between two ethnic populations with dissimilar social orders the critical problem for each population becomes that of maintaining a social order compatible with pre-Contact lifeways. Whether or not particular ethnic communities will be able to successfully resolve this problem will depend largely on the nature and form of dominant/subordinate ethnic relations that develop—on the **patterns of ethnic majority/minority relations.**

Like Noel, Lieberson posits the existence of a significant power differential—particularly with regard to superiority in technology (weapons) and tightness of social organization—as a major factor in the origin and development of ethnic stratification. Further, Lieberson makes a critical distinction between the nature and form of ethnic stratification that emerges from contact between aboriginal peoples and early migrants (migrant superordination) on the one hand, and between established migrants and later immigrants (indigenous superordination) on the other hand.[3]

In the case of the pattern of **migrant superordination,** Lieberson argues that maintenance of the subordinated, aboriginal social order becomes threatened by a number of ensuing social conditions: the numerical decline of aboriginal peoples through warfare and disease; the disruption of aboriginal social institutions by the imposition of a dissimilar (migrant) social order; and the alteration of aboriginal ethnopolitical boundaries within a newly created and larger geopolitical society. Because aboriginal peoples have been subordinated at home (that is, while living in their aboriginal territories or homelands), Lieberson contends that relations between dominant migrants and aboriginal peoples leads to ethnic conflict; aboriginal peoples resist incorporation into the new economy developed by dominant agents and attempt to carry on their traditional, economic pursuits. With the advent of settlers from the migrants' homeland, conflict becomes exacerbated in the competition between settlers and aboriginal peoples for the most resource plentiful land in a given region. In this struggle, the intraethnic priorities of superordinate migrants operate to favour settler interests over the claims of aboriginal peoples, with the consequence that the aboriginal populations become geographically displaced, socially and politically disrupted, and economically impoverished. In short, aboriginal peoples become relegated to the lowest rungs of the developing ethnic hierarchy where their potential for participation in the developing society is marginal, at best.

Dominant/Aboriginal Relations in Canada: The Pattern of Migrant Superordination

Lieberson's outline of the social conditions that threaten maintenance of aboriginal cultures in the early stages of migrant superordination can be amply documented with reference to Canada. Surtees (1971) demonstrates that a marked decline in Indian populations followed directly from Indian involvement in English/French warfare. Entire Indian (First Nation) communities—the Huronia and Nipissings, for example—were annihilated through attacks and starvation ensuing from European-generated wars. Disease, however, was the greatest killer, because First Nation peoples had never been exposed to European diseases and had no immunity to them.

Heagerty (1928: 56) graphically documents the decimating effects of the smallpox epidemic: '[I]it played no mean part in the reduction to a mere handful of the once numerous tribes that roamed the plains.' Among the Inuit, epidemics of diphtheria and tuberculosis similarly extracted a heavy toll, sometimes destroying entire camp communities (Jenness 1964). The Canadian evidence also supports Lieberson's contention that aboriginal peoples inevitably 'lose out' in the competition with technologically superior migrants for control over land and resources, and that they come to represent economically marginal populations, incorporated only peripherally into the public life of the new society. In the Canadian case, the alteration of aboriginal geopolitical boundaries through the establishment of Indian reserves and Inuit settlements, together with their political incorporation into the Canadian state has had disastrous economic and sociocultural consequences for aboriginal peoples. The long-term effect of geosocial isolation and economic depression among aboriginal peoples has been to create structurally dependent welfare populations subsisting on the largess of government handouts. Thus, Canada's aboriginal peoples have come to constitute a stigmatized ethnoclass at the very bottom of the vertical ethnic mosaic (Carstens 1981; Frideres 1993; Paine 1977; RCAP 2000).

Dominant/Aboriginal Relations: The Pattern of Ethnic Segmentation

Breton (1978) points out that the pattern of migrant superordination outlined by Lieberson bears striking resemblance to the pattern of ethnic relations that emerges through amalgamation of contiguous territories following shifts in political boundaries through other means, such as dynastic alliances, wars of conquest, and colonial administration. An essential characteristic of all of these processes, says Breton, is that they bring together populations that already exist as societies, each having a full-fledged, or total institutional structure. Under these conditions, majority/minority ethnic relations between (superordinate) migrants and (subordinate) aboriginal peoples tend to take the form of **ethnic segmentation.** In this pattern, each ethnic community tends to maintain both a high degree of ethnic closure and a high degree of ethnic compartmentalization.

As employed by Breton, the concept of *ethnic closure* refers to the enclosure of social networks along ethnic lines, and the concept of *ethnic compartmentalization* refers to ethnic institutional or structural pluralism. Under relations of ethnic segmentation, these two sets of boundary-maintaining devices function as mutually reinforcing social processes. Each ethnic segment encapsulates separate inclusive networks of social affiliations, separate total institutional structures, and separate total ethnic identities within its ethnic boundaries. Interethnic relations are mutually regulated to preserve the boundaries and to maintain the dichotomous structure of ethnic interaction between the segments. Breton's model of ethnic segmentation may be applied to interethnic relations between segments with different and/or unequal ethnic status (for example, French or English majority and aboriginal minority), as well as to relations between segments with similar and/or equal ethnic status (for example, French and English as charter groups in Canada). In both sets of cases, Breton argues, members of each segment relate to members of other segments *categorically,* in ethnic terms.

The pattern of ethnic segmentation, as outlined by Breton, rests on two fundamental assumptions: first, that each ethnic segment is demographically and institutionally capable of maintaining ethnic closure and compartmentalization; and second, that all or most members of each ethnic segment want to preserve ethnic boundaries. Here, it is suggested that another feature of the pattern of ethnic segmentation is critical to its maintenance, that is, territorial integrity; and it is the strong association between ethnicity and territory in the pattern of ethnic segmentation that gives rise to nationalism.

Breton distinguishes between *territorial* and *ethnic* forms of nationalism: in the former, ethnic segment and national territory are coterminous phenomena; in the latter, the ethnic segment constitutes a legally autonomous, self-governing unit within a larger geopolitical territorial unit. The argument here is that both forms of nationalism are predicated on the territorial integrity of the ethnic segment. In the Canadian context, all of the major nationalistic movements among minority ethnic segments, like the Franco-Quebecois and the Nunavut, are predicated on an assumption of ethnic territorial integrity.

Dominant/Aboriginal Relations in Canada: Colonizers versus Colonized

Lieberson and Breton both adopt an essentially structural approach that downplays the significance of racial and cultural differences in the pattern of migrant superordination. This approach also neglects the very important role played by dominant cultural policies in the early stages of ethnic stratification. Alternatively, Blauner (1972: 11) contends that aboriginal racial visibility and migrant cultural policy are critical variables in the origin of ethnic stratification. Aborigines are 'people of colour' and as such, says Blauner, they have been subjected to a special pattern of migrant superordination, namely, colonization. Unlike other populations, colonized peoples are subject to three conditions: First, they become part of a new larger society through coercion. As the case of Canada's First Nations well demonstrates, colonized peoples are conquered, enslaved, or pressured into movement. Second, colonized peoples are subject to various forms of unfree labour that restrict their mobility and power (for example, Panis [Indian slaves] in early French Canada). Third, the cultural policy of the colonizer disrupts and ultimately destroys the aboriginal way of life (cultural genocide).

The Canadian Indian leader Harold Cardinal was one of the earliest aboriginal spokespersons to charge that the Indian Act has long served as a powerful legal instrument of colonization locking Status Indians into the position of a colonized people (1969). Earlier, Harper (1945) argued that the primacy of the long-term federal government policy of Indian assimilation (the covert agenda behind the Indian Act) gives credence to First Nations' claims that cultural genocide has been an implicit goal in Indian administration throughout the years. The **colonizer versus colonized** pattern of ethnic relations will be discussed further in Chapter 6, in connection with our discussion of the paternalistic/colonial model of ethnic integration in Canada. At this point, we want to address a fourth condition of colonization that Blauner (1972) briefly mentions, viz. the experience of the colonized in being managed and manipulated by outsiders in terms of ethnic status.

The experience of Canada's aboriginal peoples as members of colonized minorities currently provides the subject matter of a growing literature by Canadian Indian, Inuit, and Métis authors. The following excerpts provide only a glimpse of this experience; nevertheless, they illustrate the profound psychic ramifications of inferiorization, indeed, in the case of aboriginal peoples, *stigmatization* on members of colonized minorities:

> As an Indian, it has been very difficult for me to begin thinking about my place in society. It is very difficult because I have been told from early childhood by white teachers and clergymen and community officers that my background is one where people are stupid (Pelletier 1974: 101).

> The white man saw that it was a more powerful weapon than anything else with which to beat the Halfbreeds, and he used it and still does today. . . . They try to make you hate your people (Campbell 1973: 47).

> The thing I remember the most was being called dirty Indian kids. . . . I also remember going home and trying to wash it off. . . . I was one of the darkest ones at school . . . there was definite favoritism shown for the lighter ones. . . . Even the Indian people would, and still do, make jokes about those who are darker . . . [Why?] . . . Maybe they've had good training from the nuns and the white people from close by communities or television (Bear 1987: 55–6).

Dominant/Immigrant Relations (Established Migrant Superordination)

Lieberson (1961) maintains that in the initial stages of ethnic stratification, relations between established migrant populations and newer immigrants are characterized by considerably less conflict than are relations between dominant migrants and aboriginal populations. Unlike aboriginal peoples, immigrants cannot 'opt out' of the dominant economy since none of the aboriginal economic options are open to them. On the other hand, should immigrants become dissatisfied with their subordinate status and/or other life conditions in their new country, they may elect to leave, either to return to their home country or to migrate elsewhere.[4] By way of contrast, aboriginal peoples are not likely to leave their aboriginal territories voluntarily, and their continued presence, together with their refusal to enter the dominant economy, provides a continuing source of conflict.

A second difference between **dominant/aboriginal** and **dominant/immigrant relations** posited by Lieberson is that immigrants are under much greater pressure to assimilate to dominant norms and do so much more rapidly and extensively than do aboriginal peoples. Although Lieberson makes no attempt to account for this difference, it seems obvious that the explanation lies, in large part, in the far greater degree of ethnocultural compatibility between dominant and immigrant populations than is found between dominant and aboriginal populations.

A third difference between the two patterns of interethnic relations relates to the control of immigration that ensures the ethnic hegemony of the established dominant migrants over the newer immigrants. Immigrants perceived as posing a biological, cultural, or numerical threat to dominant superiority can be collectively restricted or excluded from entering the country. This strategy cannot be applied to aboriginal populations, however, since these populations were resident in the area long before the arrival of the now dominant migrants.

Dominant/Immigrant Relations in Canada

The development of early English-Canadian immigration policy illustrates Lieberson's model of **dominant/immigrant relations.** Following Confederation, the English became the dominant ethnic group at the national level. Although Confederation gave English and French Canadians equal status as the two 'founding races', English Canadians increasingly assumed institutional control—culturally, linguistically, and economically—outside the province of Quebec. As the dominant national group, English Canadians, from the beginning, exercised control of federal immigration policies responsible for determining which ethnic groups would be allowed into Canada, where they would settle, what jobs they could assume, and what ranking and social position would be accorded them within the existing system of ethnic stratification. In order to ensure the dominance of the English majority culture and social institutions, and thus to maintain their dominant position, the English Canadians accorded 'preferred status' to linguistically, culturally, and socially similar immigrants from the British Isles and northern and western Europe. Less preferred ethnic groups assumed an 'entrance status' that implied lower-level occupational roles and social position (Porter 1965: 63–4). Changes in immigration policies are indicative of the disposition of the dominant group, under changing social conditions, toward admittance of ethnic groups highly dissimilar to themselves in their physical, cultural, and/or behavioural characteristics. Many scholars, including Richmond (1972: 86) have demonstrated the fact that, until 1962, the Canadian Immigration Act was clearly administered to discriminate against non-European and especially non-white immigration. Immigrants from Britain, northern and western Europe, and white immigrants from the Commonwealth countries had preferred status; those from eastern, central, and southern Europe were in a secondary position; and those from Third World countries—potential migrants whose racial and cultural traits diverged more markedly from the characteristics of the established dominant population(s)—were accorded lowest priority. The long-term consequences of the differential treatment, by the dominant English and French, of various ethnic categories within the immigrant population sector, together with the differential treatment accorded immigrants as a whole, in contrast to aboriginal peoples, produced the vertical mosaic described by Porter.

The Pattern of Ethnic Heterogeneity

Breton (1978) points out that patterns of immigrant adaptation to the new society can be highly varied. He distinguishes between two main categories of migrants: those who are able and willing to establish a full-fledged institutional structure (like the English and French in Canada); and those who cannot or do not wish to do so. (This includes most Canadian immigrants, except for the established dominant populations and some sectarian minorities like the Hutterites.) Most immigrants lack a full-fledged institutional structure, therefore, they are unable to maintain the high degree of ethnic closure and compartmentalization that characterizes the pattern of ethnic segmentation. Breton refers to their typical pattern as one of **ethnic heterogeneity.** This pattern is characterized by the fragmentation or partialization of immigrant ethnicity and ethnic identity. Some areas of the immigrant's life may involve his or her ethnicity, while other areas may not. Typically, in the pattern of ethnic heterogeneity, ethnic ties are principally maintained in private relations of kinship and friendship. In the public sphere (work, politics, and so forth) the immigrant's relationships become de-ethnicized. Even within the boundaries of the immigrant ethnic community, personal networks and institutional affiliations are selectively chosen, and the various sets of ties and relationships activated by different members tend to become dissociated from one another. At the macro-level of the ethnic community, ethnic organizational structures may serve only limited aspects of social life (for example, recreational and religious).

Breton argues that the pattern of ethnic heterogeneity, as opposed to ethnic segmentation, is possible only to the extent that society is functionally differentiated so that some roles are performed in one organizational context, and others are performed in another. In other words, Breton argues that the pattern of ethnic heterogeneity is only possible in a large-scale *Gesellschaft* society, where people relate to each other in terms of specific segmented roles, rather than as whole persons. For only in a large-scale society can people establish fundamental role relationships independent of their ethnic identities. In contrast, Breton argues, a society based on non-segmented, overlapping relationships between whole persons (that is, a small-scale or *Gemeinschaft* society) could not integrate members of different ethnic groups without assimilating them completely or allowing them only peripheral, marginal status as strangers. This observation is clearly supported in the anthropological literature which indicates that in ethnically homogeneous, small-scale societies, ethnic outsiders, such as women and children captured in war or marital partners brought into the society through strategic political alliances, were frequently 'adopted' by a particular kin group as full-fledged members of the ethnic community.

Breton's distinction between the patterns of ethnic segmentation and ethnic heterogeneity seems to be predicated largely on the degree to which the members of ethnic communities are able and/or willing to maintain holistic, *Gemeinschaft*-like ethnic relationships, institutions, and identities within the greater social environmental context of a *Gesellschaft*-like society such as Canada's. Clearly, the dominant ethnic groups—French in Quebec and English in the rest of Canada—are in the most advantageous position to maintain a holistic pattern of ethnic segmentation, for it is their ethnocultural ideas, values, and patterns that are represented in the public institutional structures of Canadian society, within and outside of Quebec, respectively. For ethnic minorities, cultural discrimination denies the institutional expression of their ethnicities in the public sphere, and the degree to which their ethnicity becomes partialized will depend on their ability to maintain group viability in their private lives.

Variations in the Patterns of Ethnic Segmentation and Heterogeneity in Canada

In the early period, Canada's immigration practices reflected not only the dominant English population's desire to maintain their cultural hegemony over British North America, but also their strong desire to spur the economic development of the new nation. This latter aspect led to marked regional differences in the ethnic composition of Canadian society, as immigration priorities responded to both changing social conditions and to continuing marked regional variations in Canada's resources and economic needs. Over time, the differential regional distribution of Canada's ethnic communities has created what Driedger (1978: 10–12) has termed a *regional mosaic,* characterized by different patterns of ethnic segmentation and heterogeneity within each region.

Intraregional Differences: The Case of Toronto

The regional mosaic elaborated by Driedger (1978) is only one level of the Canadian ethnic mosaic. Another important dimension of ethnic diversity is found at the local level. Within each region of Canada there are significant local variations in the patterns of relations among different ethnic communities. For example, while the region identified by Driedger as Upper Canada may be characterized by a pattern of ethnic heterogeneity that is close to that of ethnic segmentation, at the local level of the city of Toronto, ethnic communities differ markedly in the degree to which they represent ethnic 'segments' or ethnic 'fragments' (to paraphrase Breton's terminology). In part, these differences derive from the institutional completeness or incompleteness of the immigrant ethnic community in the early period following arrival in the new country. Over time, however, other factors (for example, population numbers and sex ratio, wave of immigration, duration of residence, degree of acculturation, and experience of discrimination) influence the pattern of dominant-immigrant relations. Thus, at any given time and in any given locality, each observed pattern of dominant-immigrant relations will be a function of multiple variables.

Within the increasingly multiethnic and multiracial context of Metropolitan Toronto, studies published in the seventies revealed striking variations in patterns of dominant-immigrant relations.

Among the older European immigrant populations, the Jewish ethnic community (Glickman 1976; Kallen 1977b; Richmond 1972) and the Italian ethnic community (Jansen 1978; Zeigler 1972) were characterized by a pattern closely approximating ethnic segmentation, while the Polish ethnic community (Matejko 1979; Radecki and Heydenkorn 1976) was characterized by a far less enclaved pattern of ethnic heterogeneity. The Toronto francophone population appeared to be among the least cohesive of the older European immigrants and, accordingly, was characterized as 'invisible' (Maxwell 1979). Among the more recent European immigrants, the tendency toward ethnic enclavement remained strong. Spanish- and Portuguese-speaking populations, for example, closely resembled ethnic segments within the city (Anderson 1979). Striking differences were also found among the various visible minorities—racially defined immigrant ethnic communities, whose numbers had increased substantially following the implementation of Canada's open door policy on immigration. In the case of the Chinese ethnic community, the arrival of new immigrants served to strengthen the historical pattern of ethnic segmentation (Lai 1971). On the other hand, the Japanese ethnic community had changed over the generations from a pattern of ethnic segmentation to a pattern of ethnic heterogeneity (Makabe 1976).

Herberg (1989: 275–9, 306), utilizing 1971 and 1981 census data, described the shifting patterns of ethnic cohesion among Canadian ethnoracial communities. The findings of his analysis, which applied seven central cohesion variables (two language retention factors, residential proximity, religion, two media indices, and endogamy), revealed significant differences in ethnic-cohesion rates among various ethnoracial communities across Canada. Asian (East Indian, Indochinese, and Chinese), Jewish, Italian, French, Greek, and Portuguese exhibited high cohesion for most factors. Conspicuously absent from this category were three visible minorities: Japanese, aboriginal peoples, and blacks. Herberg maintains that racial visibility *per se* clearly does not lead to ethnic cohesiveness. On the basis of the data in his book, as well as external information on institutional development within ethnoracial communities, Herberg suggested that continuing evidence of ethnic cohesion and enclavement among many Canadian minorities does not indicate retention of traditional or immigrant values. Rather, he argues, present forms and methods of group cohesion represent values adapted to the dominant, urban Canadian societal context. Moreover, Herberg argued, ethnic communities are developing group enclosure and compartmentalization mechanisms not to maintain their separation from other Canadians, but to enable integration.

Although it would be difficult to argue against the evidence for value adaptation among virtually all ethnoracial minorities, Herberg's assimilationist stance is inconsistent with the continuing demands of many immigrant ethnic minorities (not to mention aboriginal peoples) for increased constitutional recognition of their collective religious, linguistic, and (broader) cultural rights (see Chapters 8 and 9).

Probably the most intensive Toronto study was a survey of nine ethnic groups carried out in 1979 (Breton et al. 1990). The groups studied included the Chinese, Portugese, West Indian, German, Italian, Jewish, English, and British (English, Scottish, Irish, and Welsh), categorized as 'Majority Canadians'. In part, the study focused on ethnic identity retention over two or three generations, measured in terms of both objective (external) and subjective (internal) indicators. A summary of the results of the study can be found in Isajiw (Breton et al. 1990: 83–5). The study revealed that retention of ethnic identity tended to be highly selective. At least five foci of ethnic identity retention were distinguished: ethnic language, symbolic objects (for example, ethnic food and art), intraethnic friendships and endogamy, community participation and practice of ethnic customs, and support of ethnic group members and causes. Substantial variation was found among the groups as to the selective focus of ethnic identity retention. For example, language was found to be central for Ukrainians, while endogamy was found to be central for Jews. Study findings also showed that there was a substantial variation in degree of ethnic identity retention among the different groups. The highest overall retainers were the Jewish groups, followed by the Ukrainians, Italians, English, 'Majority Canadians', and Germans. Using Breton's conceptualization of ethnic segmentation and heterogeneity, those ethnic communities with the highest rates of ethnic identity retention (Jewish and Ukrainian) more closely resemble ethnic 'segments', whereas those with the lowest rates of ethnic identity retention (German) more closely resemble ethnic 'fragments'.

Dominant/Aboriginal versus Dominant/Immigrant Relations: Implications for Collective Minority Rights Claims

Mede (quoted in Leavy 1979: 3–4) draws a distinction between two kinds of ethnic minorities:

1. *voluntary minorities:* those who, individually or in families, left their country of origin and moved to another country where they live as a community. They preserve certain parts of their own culture and transmit them to their descendants, while integrating to a certain degree with the majority culture of the new country.
2. *involuntary minorities:* those groups that for reasons of war, territorial conquest, or frontier adjustments find themselves in a state where their culture is in a minority situation.

Involuntary minorities (for example, Canada's aboriginal peoples), Mede argues, are justified in making more collective human rights claims than are voluntary minorities (for example, Canada's immigrant ethnic groups). Voluntary minorities would be justified in claiming the right to institutional autonomy, for example, ethnic schools or social services; but only involuntary minorities would be justified in claiming the right to a measure of jurisdictional cultural autonomy, for example, the right to establish standards applicable to their ethnically distinctive school system. The rationale for this distinction, Mede argues, is that there can be no cultural autonomy without territorial autonomy.

Mede's argument supports our conceptual distinction—outlined in the typology of rights in the Introduction to this book (see Table I-1)—between collective rights claims based solely on cultural group rights (immigrants) and those based on national group rights (aboriginal peoples and charter groups). At the theoretical level, this distinction between the range and types of potential human rights claims which may, justifiably, be made by immigrants versus aboriginal peoples is clearly weighted in favour of aboriginal peoples. However, at the level of societal reality, we must take into account the differences in patterns of dominant/immigrant versus dominant/aboriginal relations that may significantly affect the viability of minority ethnic claims. Here, if we accept the thrust of the arguments put forward by Lieberson and Blauner, the pendulum clearly swings in favour of immigrants over aboriginal peoples, certainly in the early stages of ethnic stratification. The salient point of distinction is that aboriginal peoples, racially stigmatized as subhuman 'savages' with 'primitive' cultures, would never have been welcomed as immigrants.

In the next section, we look at the way early patterns of dominant/immigrant and dominant/aboriginal relations become institutionalized within the structure of ethnic inequality, and we assess the differential human rights implications of **institutionalized racism** for Canadian immigrants and aboriginal peoples.

The Persistence of Systems of Ethnic Stratification

The long-term persistence of a system of ethnic stratification depends not only on the will of its majority group(s), but also on the tacit compliance of its ethnic minorities. In order to ensure that members of various ethnic minorities 'know their place' and 'stay in their place', dominant authorities must be able to 'justify' the existing structure of ethnic inequality; they must be able to imbue the system with recognized social legitimacy so that minorities come to accept the stratified order as a moral order. Unless the system of ethnic stratification is based on a high degree of consensus regarding 'place'—the position of various ethnic communities within the established hierarchy—the built-in potential for minority ethnic protest can only be contained through coercion.

The case of South Africa under apartheid well illustrates the latter point. For close to 30 years, the dominant white population was able to rationalize and maintain a relatively stable system of ethnic stratification, and to maintain their superordinate status at the pinnacle of the system, by institutionalizing 'place' for each of the socially and legally defined racial categories in the society, through the racist ideology and policies of apartheid. But when consensus began to break down and black minority protest intensified, coercive measures were increasingly adopted, culminating in the declaration of a state of emergency giving police authorities virtually unlimited powers to suppress minority activism.

Isaacs (1977: 4–5) contends that the global picture of escalating ethnic tension and violence is the result of the worldwide collapse of dominant power systems whose survival was contingent on competition with external rivals and on the compliance of their dominated populations. The established power systems, says Isaacs, managed to hold together their structures of ethnic inequality under the control of a single dominant population or coalition by incorporating the 'rules of the game' into mystiques and mythologies (invalidation ideologies) based on assumptions of cultural and racial superiority/inferiority. Racist myths legitimating place were internalized and accepted by all—rulers and ruled, majority and minority, colonizers and colonized. And racist ideologies legitimating the whole structure of inequality were built into the system's institutions to keep it working. Put another way, Isaacs is arguing that in all of the worldwide systems of ethnic stratification—including such diverse forms as the Hindu caste system in India, apartheid in South Africa, black slavery in the Americas, and all the systems of ethnic inequality predicated on colonial rule—the persistence of the structure of inequality was predicated on the institutionalization of racism, by building into the system laws, policies, and practices of institutional, systemic, and cultural discrimination.

Institutionalized Racism: Techniques of Domination

Institutionalized forms of discrimination against ethnic minorities provide the majority group(s) with legitimate **techniques of domination** and social control. Of all forms of institutionalized racism, *legal racism* provides the most powerful and pernicious instrument of domination and social control. In the following section, we will delineate the main legal and policy initiatives that have provided Canadian authorities with potent techniques of domination used to keep ethnic and racial minorities 'in their place'.

Denial of Franchise

Denial of franchise is an institutionalized form of oppression that denies ethnic minorities the fundamental political right of access to political participation and decision-making power. In some provinces, and on a federal scale, Chinese, Japanese, Hutterites, and Doukhobors have, at one time or another, been denied the right to vote in Canada. Inuit, as full citizens of Canada, have always had a federal vote, but it was not until 1962 that they were given the right to vote in provincial elections as well. Status Indians were denied the franchise until 1960; then pressure from Indian organizations won them federal voting rights, under the (then) new Canadian Bill of Rights.

Control of Land Ownership and Use

Control of land ownership and use is an institutionalized form of neglect that violates the fundamental economic rights of minority members by restricting their access to economic maintenance and opportunities. The usurpation of the lands of aboriginal peoples and their subsequent confinement on reserves and settlements, frequently without a viable economic base, provides the most flagrant example of economic neglect of ethnic minorities in Canada. Less drastic, but nevertheless highly discriminatory, have been the repeated attempts of dominant populations (neighbouring farmers and provincial governments) to control the purchase and use of lands by Hutterite colonies in the Canadian West (see Chapter 5). In both cases cited, the control of land ownership and use by dominant power groups not only violates the minorities' fundamental economic rights, but also infringes upon their collective cultural rights. For in the cases of both aboriginal peoples and Hutterites, their distinctive ethnocultures and economies are rooted in group norms and practices of communal land use and occupancy.

The Controversy over the BC Government's Proposed 2002 Referendum on Aboriginal Treaties: A Case of Control of Land Ownership and Use and Denial of Franchise

In the spring of 2002, most British Columbians rejected the proposed BC government referendum on aboriginal treaties. When the deadline for the Campbell government's controversial referendum had passed, the majority of British Columbians chose not to participate (*Vancouver Sun*, 16 May 2002). From the very beginning, the overwhelming response of First Nations and their supporters was that the referendum process, and the questions themselves, constituted a shameful act for the BC government and for all the people of British Columbia. They claimed that the referendum would provide an opening for a racist agenda and would create division and contention within the province (*Vote No*). Voters were asked to consider and vote yes or no to each of the eight principles shown in Table 4-1.

First Nations and their supporters vehemently argued that the referendum process and questions constituted an attack on the agreements between the Crown and aboriginal peoples and on decisions of the courts that have established aboriginal rights (*Vote No*). The referendum process itself, they insisted, is disenfranchising, and voting in the referendum legitimizes what we view as illegitimate. They argued that the rights of a minority must not be determined by a vote of the majority. Representatives expressed the belief that should the government go ahead, it will first target aboriginal peoples at the same time that it creates a precedent under which any minority can have its basic rights questioned. Moreover, they insisted, it creates the likelihood of slowing or stalling the treaty process, which in itself needs to be made more effective, leading to uncertainty and instability within the province.

Groups calling for a boycott of the referendum included: BC First Nations Summit, Union of BC Indian Chiefs, Anglican Church, Canadian Jewish Congress (Pacific), United Church, Presbytery of Westminster, BC Federation of Labour, BC Teachers Federation, and the David Suzuki Foundation.

The Anti-Referendum lobby was given a large boost when a White Racist group openly campaigned for a 'yes' vote (CBC Radio News, Web-Posted on British Columbia Online News, 17 April 2002). Residents of Kelowna, BC, were reportedly outraged by a treaty referendum leaflet campaign by a White Supremacist group, BC White Pride, which said the government referendum would help promote unity among white people. The leaflets called for support for the referendum to make BC 'a better place for white families'. BC religious leader Cliff Turner of Kelowna reportedly was furious when the leaflets showed up in his neighbourhood: 'It may not meet the definition under hate legislation, but it is hateful, it's producing hate,' he said, 'and it's certainly taking off on the referendum' (ibid.).

Table 4-1 Referendum Questions

1. Private property should not be expropriated for treaty settlements.
2. The terms and conditions of leases and licences should be respected; fair compensation for unavoidable disruption of commercial interests should be ensured.
3. Hunting, fishing, and recreational opportunities on Crown land should be ensured for all British Columbians.
4. Parks and protected areas should be maintained for the use and benefit of all British Columbians.
5. Provincewide standards of resource management and environmental protection should continue to apply.
6. Aboriginal self-government should have the characteristics of local government, with powers delegated from Canada and British Columbia.
7. Treaties should include mechanisms for harmonizing land use planning between aboriginal governments and neighbouring local governments.
8. The existing tax exemptions for aboriginal people should be phased out.

SOURCE: *Treaty Negotiations Office—Backgrounder*, 2 April 2002.

The head of the Union of BC Indian Chiefs reportedly said that aboriginal leaders had predicted that the referendum would be used by racists: 'This so-called referendum has proven itself a vehicle and a venue for white supremacist groups to express that kind of hate propaganda,' said Chief Stewart Phillip.

The 2002 BC referendum provides a stark example of how governments can use techniques of domination to disenfranchise and to usurp lands and resources from target populations. It is to the credit of the anti-racist, anti-referendum groups in BC that the referendum failed through lack of voter support.

Denial of Educational Opportunities

Denial of educational opportunities is another institutionalized form of neglect of ethnic minorities. Because knowledge and skill acquired through formal education are the keys to upward mobility in our modern, industrialized society, denial of equal educational opportunities sets off a self-perpetuating cycle of economic deprivation—one of the concrete manifestations of the self-fulfilling prophecy of racism. Separate and unequal educational opportunities have been largely responsible for the consistent records of low academic achievement, high rates of failure, and early school dropout among aboriginal children (Frideres 1993; Ponting and Gibbins 1980). Until the 1950s, the government delegated the responsibility for educating aboriginal children largely to religious institutions whose missionaries stressed religious indoctrination of the alleged 'savages' and minimized secular curriculum content to fit what they felt was the inferior level of educability of these students (Cardinal 1969). When local secular schools were set up on Indian reserves, the quality of Indian education did not improve appreciably because of inadequate resources such as buildings, equipment, books, etc., as well as poorly trained and often highly prejudiced teachers. In the case of Inuit and other aboriginal peoples living in the Northwest Territories, Canadian government educational policy, until the end of World War II, was largely one of neglect (Jenness 1964). Inuit were expected to live off the land and their education was left to a small number of missionaries and mission schools that served only a minute fraction of the aboriginal children in the Canadian Arctic. As late as 1944, 93 per cent of Indian and Inuit children in the Western Arctic and Mackenzie Delta Regions were receiving no formal education. It was not until 1947 that the federal government built the first public school for its arctic peoples.

Although there has been a considerable increase in the number of schools and the proportion of school-age children regularly attending these schools over the years, the problems of inadequate school facilities, curriculum, and a continuing high rate of teacher turnover remain acute, particularly in the Arctic. Public schools were designed 'to eradicate the "native problem" by destroying native culture'. Early boarding schools were 'little more than prisons where their cultures were denigrated and they were punished for speaking their own languages' (Canadian Council on Children and Youth 1978: 137). Since the late 1960s, there has been a shift towards the development of aboriginal-controlled schools in aboriginal communities. This has resulted in higher retention rates for students, but, beyond the elementary level, the dropout rate for aboriginal students is markedly higher than that of the general population.

Most aboriginal youth today straddle two worlds; they are truly marginal youth simply struggling to survive (RCAP 2000: vol. 3, ch. 5, ss. 4–4.2). They are caught between the expectations, values, and demands of two worlds, unable to find a point of balance. Their despair is manifested in early school-leaving, substance abuse, suicide attempts, defiance of the law, and teen pregnancies. In 1991, 57 per cent of aboriginal people age 15 and over had less than a grade 9 education or did not graduate from high school. The comparable figure for non-aboriginal people was about 37 per cent. Shocking as these figures may seem, dropping out may be an understandable choice if school feels like jail. Unfortunately, those who leave school have few employment options. The rate of unemployment among aboriginal youth who have not completed high school is notoriously high. If they try to return to school, they face many barriers in an education system that is not geared to mature students.

Denial of economic and cultural rights within the sphere of education has also been the characteristic experience of blacks in Canada until recently (Krauter and Davis 1978: 48–51). Throughout Canada from 1850 to 1965, blacks were customarily excluded from the dominant, Euro-Canadian educational structure and relegated to segregated, all-black schools, typically inadequate in space, facilities, and staff. In Ontario the last segregated black school closed in 1965, but in Nova Scotia, despite the abrogation of educational segregation in 1963, several all-black schools, serving black communities, were in operation until the 1970s. While higher-level public education is now open to blacks throughout Canada, racial stereotyping and prejudice on the part of teachers continues to be revealed in the common 'expectation' that blacks will be 'slow learners', and racial discrimination is evident in the practice of 'streaming' black students disproportionately more than others into non-academic schools and classes (Hill and Schiff 1988: 20) (*Paying for the Past*, cbc.ca 2001; *Unequal Access*, CRRF 2001d). Not surprisingly, Canadian-born blacks, like aboriginal peoples, lag far behind white Euro-Canadians in educational attainment.

Denial of Employment Opportunities and Wages

Denial of employment and wage opportunities probably provides the most blatant, direct indicator of neglect of ethnic minorities. Without jobs and earned income, members of ethnic minorities are without access to economic power. In order to subsist, they become economically dependent on 'benevolent' welfare handouts from the dominant controllers of the welfare state.

The current syndrome of economic dependency among Canada's aboriginal peoples is clearly rooted in the multidimensional cycle of denial of opportunities associated with the self-fulfilling prophecy of white racism. Long-term denial of educational opportunities means that most aboriginal people today lack the knowledge, training, and skills that would qualify them to compete for jobs with other Canadians in the mainstream Canadian context. The long-term consequence of denial of educational and occupational opportunities is that aboriginal peoples are overrepresented at the lowest strata of the occupational and income hierarchy in Canada. Those who are fortunate enough to hold jobs tend to be overrepresented in the unskilled and semi-skilled occupations (for example, services, construction, logging, and fishing) and underrepresented in the higher-level managerial and professional occupations. Moreover, Frideres points out, aboriginal persons usually work at seasonal or part-time jobs without job security. The low income of aboriginal peoples as a category reflects both seasonal work and job discrimination: aboriginal persons are less likely to be hired than Euro-Canadians, and when hired they are likely to be paid lower wages than their Euro-Canadian counterparts. As a result, aboriginal peoples remain at the lowest rungs of Canada's income hierarchy, and the disparity in income between aboriginal peoples and other Canadians appears to be growing larger (Frideres 1993: 162, 170) (RCAP 2001).

Among Canada's immigrant ethnic groups, those peoples categorized by the majority as oriental or black have, historically, been accorded the highest degree of discrimination in employment and wages. In the nineteenth and early twentieth centuries, Chinese and Japanese, lumped together under the misleading label 'oriental', were subject to severe job discrimination, particularly in the province of British Columbia. Denied the franchise, they were excluded from the voting lists and thus from licensed professions. Moreover, they were directly prohibited from other licensed occupations, such as the fishing industry, by the customary manipulation of special regulations. They were also denied other positions such as public school teaching. Forced to accept any job at any wage, Chinese and Japanese immigrants fell victim to the self-fulfilling prophecy of white racism: they became, in fact, as in stereotype, 'cheap labour'. Because they accepted low wages, they were perceived as a threat to prevailing wage standards by Euro-Canadian workers and by organized labour. As a result, they were excluded from membership in labour unions, and at times were victims of open and devastating racist mob attacks and violence. It was not until the end of the Second World War that formal union opposition to Chinese and Japanese immigration in large part disappeared (Krauter and Davis 1978: v).

Prior to 1833, black immigrants to Canada were 'employed' as slaves. Since that time, Canadian-born blacks have tended to occupy the very bottom rungs of the urban occupational ladder. Blacks were, for a long time, accorded stereotyped occupations such as railway porters and household domestics. For most Canadian-born blacks, present occupational prospects remain poor because of lack of education and training as well as continuing high levels of job discrimination. Even where educational qualifications are adequate, however, as in the case of many West Indian immigrants, job discrimination persists (Henry and Ginsberg 1988).

A recent report, *Unequal Access* (CRRF 2001d; see Chapter 2) reveals that, although Canada's labour force is becoming increasingly diverse, racial minorities still face limits in their access to employment. Of all groups, aboriginal peoples are the most disadvantaged in education, employment, and income. Even given the same levels of education, the report shows that 'white' Canadians are more likely than visible minorities and aboriginal peoples to be in the top 20 per cent of the income scale. Specifically, given a university education, white Canadians are three times as likely as aboriginal peoples with the same level of education to find themselves at the top of the income scale. Additionally, the report reveals that the unemployment rate, based on the 1996 census, among visible minorities was higher than 'non-racialized groups' (Canadian or foreignborn), and that the rate for aboriginal peoples were highest. In conclusion, what the study findings clearly demonstrate is that racism is still persistent at the individual and systemic levels in both the educational and occupational sectors of Canadian society.

Denial of Adequate Housing

Economic neglect in the control of land ownership and use, denial of educational opportunities, and denial of employment and wage opportunities go hand in hand with denial of the fundamental economic right to adequate housing. Substandard housing breeds sickness and disease; ill health results in high rates of absenteeism, lowered motivation, and poor performance both for adults at work and children at school; poor performance results in loss of jobs and school dropouts; and the crippling cycle of economic dependency perpetuates itself.

For decades, the housing demands voiced by Canada's aboriginal peoples have been ignored, resulting in wide disparities in housing conditions between aboriginal and other Canadians. Frideres (1993: 196) reports that, while there has been an improvement in household amenities (running water, electricity, sewage disposal), overall, aboriginal peoples have the most unfavourable housing conditions of any ethnic group in Canada. This observation is strongly supported by the more recent 1998 report of the UN Committee monitoring Canada's compliance with the Covenant on Social, Economic and Cultural Rights. The committee severely criticized Canada's failure to take steps to improve the deplorable living conditions persisting in many aboriginal communities.

The problem of housing among the Canadian Inuit is a post-World War II phenomenon. The major movement of Inuit from traditional hunting and trapping camps, where they dwelt in temporary snow-houses or tents, depending on the season, to permanent settlements, where they reside in prefabricated housing, followed the implementation of a large-scale housing program initiated by the federal government in 1965. This housing scheme was predicated on the belief that their traditional housing conditions were responsible for the high incidence of disease, especially tuberculosis and influenza, and premature death among the Inuit population (Hughes 1965). Although the relocation of the Inuit has coincided with a decrease in disease and premature death rates, this improvement may be due to vastly improved medical services, rather than the change in housing. The problem of adequate housing remains acute. The expansion of medical services in the Arctic has resulted in a steady increase in population numbers and family size among the Inuit. Consequently, the demand for more and larger houses far exceeds the present supply. Most Inuit families cannot afford to pay more than a part of the rental cost of even a very small house, but most houses are, therefore, at least partially government subsidized. Although Inuit families have become increasingly dependent on government assistance to meet their housing needs, the tremendous cost of both transportation and maintenance of houses in the Arctic, coupled with the continually increasing need for housing, has created the current situation in which government supply lags far behind Inuit need and demand. This has produced a growing problem of overcrowding, similar to that found on Indian reserves, particularly in the more remote Arctic settlements (Frideres 1993: 195).

A recent report in the *Nunatsiaq News* (9 November 2001) entitled 'Staff housing shortage chokes GN' points out that as of 31 March 2001 the Government of Nunavut (GN) listed 547 jobs that it cannot fill. These vacancies exist because there is a serious housing shortage and the territorial government cannot find housing for people it wants to hire. Private Iqaluit housing developers claim that it is not financially feasible for them to build new houses for GN staff. They claim that they are not prepared to risk their companies' financial viability by building 'on spec', without guaranteed government leases, even though there is an acute demand for new housing. However, what is glaringly apparent is that the GN does not have the financial resources that would allow them to provide such guarantees.

Control of Communications Media

Denial of the fundamental human right to dignity as well as denial of minority cultural rights are effected through control of the communications media, a powerful technique of domination. In earlier chapters, our analysis has highlighted the role of the mass media in promulgating derogatory, racist stereotypes. We saw how negative images of visible minorities, linked in media coverage with ethnic violence, has fed public prejudice and, in its most insidious form, has contributed to 'Keep Canada White' campaigns.

In recent times, technological innovations have increased the salience of the communications media as agents of racial and cultural discrimination. In particular, the Internet has become a powerful instrument of racism, particularly through the international spread of racist propaganda on websites operated by organized hate groups (see Box 4-1). The dissemination of hate propaganda—materials characterized by 'a generally irrational and malicious abuse of certain identifiable target groups' (Canada 1966: 11)—constitutes a violation of the categorical right to dignity of target group members and a violation of their fundamental right to freedom from racial hatred, harassment, and degradation. Hate propaganda represents probably the most malignant expression of racist invalidation ideology, for it not only inferiorizes target populations, but it also stigmatizes them as *threatening and dangerous* to society. Not surprisingly, it follows from this premise that hate propaganda urges its readers to take steps to eliminate the purported threat. When the promotion of hate targets racial and ethnic minorities, what begins as racial prejudice is translated into racial discrimination through hate messages that incite action against the targets of hate (Kallen 1992, 1997; Kallen and Lam 1993).

Control of Immigration

Control of immigration, viewed from a human rights perspective, is an area where various principles may come into conflict. Under the normative imperatives of the present United Nations human rights codes and covenants, the principle of non-intervention in the domestic affairs of states is honoured. Thus, the territorial integrity and political independence of all states is recognized and protected. Further, as Richmond (1975: 121) points out, the economies and social systems of Western societies are based not only upon the assumption of national sovereignty but also upon the desire to maintain existing standards of living (that is, levels of wealth, health, and welfare). The modern idea of a 'welfare state', Richmond argues, necessarily implies a certain degree of control over population and labour force growth in order to maintain economic and social stability. These societal ideals are directly opposed to an uncontrolled flow of immigration. Yet, when a state adopts a racist immigration policy that excludes or restricts the immigration of certain categories of people on racially or ethnically defined grounds, it clearly contravenes the anti-discriminatory intent of the International Convention on the Elimination of All Forms of Racial Discrimination. Under the latter convention, any exclusion, restriction, or preference based on ethnic criteria constitutes a violation of fundamental human rights. Taking these different considerations into account, we will argue that a state has the right to screen potential immigrants with regard to their economic contributions, but that it has no right to exclude immigrants on the arbitrary basis of ethnic criteria.

A racist immigration policy is one of the most invidious techniques utilized by those in power to guarantee their ethnic ascendancy in any society. Historically, in Canada, immigration restrictions have most sharply discriminated against non-white immigrants categorized as orientals and blacks. Prior to 1953, the inclusion of the notion of 'climatic unsuitability' in the Immigration Act furnished the legal justification for barring non-white people from non-Western countries (presumably with hot climates). During the nineteenth and early twentieth centuries, the Canadian Immigration Act contained a number of regulations specifically designed to restrict Chinese and Japanese immigration (Krauter and Davis 1978: 63). In 1886, a federal head tax was imposed on Chinese immigrants entering Canada. From 1898 to 1903, the head tax increased from $50 to $500 per head. In 1907,

BOX 4-1: CASE STUDY 1

Contesting Racism on the Internet (*Canadian Human Rights Tribunal v. Zundel*)

The human rights case against notorious Holocaust denier Ernst Zundel could set a legal precedent about whether hateful information is permitted on the Internet in Canada (*Kitchener-Waterloo Record*, 26 February 2001). The Canadian Human Rights Tribunal was expected to rule, in the spring of 2002, on a case launched in 1997 against Zundel over the contents of a website (the ZundelSite), which opponents say exposes Jews to hate and contempt. However, at the time of writing (October 2002), the ruling has not yet been forthcoming.

In response to two complaints, the Canadian Human Rights Commission requested in November of 1996 that a human rights tribunal be appointed to look into allegations that an Internet website operated by Ernst Zundel 'could expose Jews to hatred or contempt on the basis of their race, religion and ethnic origin'. Section 13 of the Canadian Human Rights Act (CHRA) forbids the communication of hate messages 'by means of a telecommunication undertaking within the legislative authority of Parliament'. This is the first time that the tribunal was to consider a complaint alleging hate messages on the Internet (*CHRC Annual Report 1996*, 'Hate Messages').

The ZundelSite contains a stylized logo that resembles a swastika and posts information that the Human Rights Commission says depicts Jews as liars who are corrupt and control governments.

Zundel has refused to attend the hearings. Stripped of his Canadian citizenship a few months ago, Zundel fled to the United States. He's believed to be living in Tennessee with his second wife, Ingrid Rimland. Irene Zundel has testified in the past against her former husband, saying he's the author of the ZundelSite despite a disclaimer on the website that Rimland is the Web master and editor. Zundel's lawyer, Doug Christie, failed to attend closing arguments in his client's case, saying the tribunal has no control over messages emanating from the California-based website. However, commission lawyer Mark Freiman said the tribunal does indeed have jurisdiction because the website can be accessed in Canada through telephone lines. The tribunal possesses no power to influence Internet content in the United States, which supports a strong protection of constitutional rights to free speech. However, Freiman pointed out, France, Germany, and Australia have laws about Internet content. Edward Earle, a lawyer with the city of Toronto, which originally filed a complaint to the tribunal, commented that a ruling against Zundel could lead to his arrest and imprisonment for contempt of a court order should he return to Canada.

The case against Zundel poses wide-ranging implications for content on the Web. The Canadian Human Rights Commission has argued that a section of the Human Rights Act that refers to telephonic devices should apply to the Internet as well. Lawyers representing intervenors for the CHRT argued that if such a broadened definition is accepted, it will form an important precedent for future cases. But Barbara Kulaszka, a lawyer representing Zundel, cautioned the tribunal against making a decision based upon a case she argued is moot because the messages emanate from the US. Tribunal adjudicator Reva Devins acknowledged during the hearing that the potential impact of a decision on the Internet is 'quite staggering'. 'It clearly will have very significant implications for future proceedings,' she said.

International Community Declares War on CyberHatred

At a two-day international meeting on 'Hate on the Internet' held in Berlin in June 2000, the international community has made its first move in the war against cyberhatred declaring that what is illegal offline should remain so online (Y. Sharma, *RIGHTS: International Community Declares War on CyberHatred*). Delegates noted that although freedom of speech must be protected on and off the Internet, incitement to hate and violence should be banned in conventional media and in cyberspace. The conference, which was attended by companies, police officials, and a number of justice ministers, issued a final declaration that called for an international minimum standard which would form the basis for the war against racial hatred, and a code of conduct for the Internet community.

Delegates reported that the Dutch authorities have registered 350 German-language right-wing sites. There are also some 1400 sites in other languages in over 30 countries, particularly from Scandinavia and the United States, containing rightist propaganda, incitement to violence and even instructions for making explosives and calls for violent attacks on political opponents.

According to Rabbi Abraham Cooper of the Los Angeles-based Simon Wiesenthal Center, in 1995, there was only one racist site known to the centre, but by April 1999 this had risen to 1400. Last year alone, 600 new sites were identified. Neo-Nazi groups increasingly use the Web to recruit sympathizers to right-wing demonstrations. Rabbi Cooper contends that the Internet has become an important networking system. 'It is not just the websites, but the links that worry us. The links can lead a youngster to go from the Ku Klux Klan to skinheads,' Rabbi Cooper says.

In its latest report on neo-Nazi Internet activity released at the conference, the OPC said 'in some cases an extremist career could find its beginning in this way.' Anonymous homepages contain black lists of political opponents, including members of rights groups, NGOs, judicial personnel, and police, with clear incitement to violence against them. Neo-Nazi hit lists on the Internet represent a significant threat that is being taken seriously, an OPC spokesman told the conference. For example, in the middle of last year two concrete calls to murder appeared on the Internet with a reward of DM 10,000 offered.

Groups representing targets for the promotion of hate and violence have begun to bring pressure to bear to prevent the dissemination of racist propaganda on the Internet. Jewish groups last year pressured Internet booksellers Barnes and Noble and Amazon to remove Hitler's autobiography *Mein Kampf*, which is banned in Germany, from its stock list. Amazon has said it will no longer mail the book to addresses in Germany. In response to a request from the International League Against Racism and Anti-Semitism in France, a French court recently ordered the US Net company Yahoo to prevent French Internet users from using its servers to obtain Nazi material. The court justified the decision on the grounds that exposition for sale of Nazi materials is against French law. Yahoo complied, removing the Nazi website from Yahoo France, but sees no reason to respect the provision in the United States.

As a result of these actions, many hate groups are migrating to the United States where the supremacy of the First Amendment to that country's Constitution protects the right of free speech and makes it harder for the state to crack down on hate crimes.

The latter point is of significant import in the Canadian context where criminal legislation prohibits the incitement of hatred and violence against racial and ethnic target groups. As indicated earlier, this has led Canada's most infamous anti-Semitic hate promoter—Ernst Zundel—to move his base of operations from Ontario to California, where he now freely operates the ZundelSite on the Internet (ZundelSite).

Canada entered into a 'gentleman's agreement' with the government of Japan restricting Japanese entry to an initial maximum of 400 families per year, later reduced to 150 families. No such pact was possible with China and because of the continuing high level of anti-oriental prejudice, especially in British Columbia, Chinese immigration was perceived as a major problem. By 1903, it was clear to the Canadian government that increases in the Chinese head tax were not discouraging the flow of Chinese immigrants. Accordingly, the Canadian Parliament passed a new law requiring every Asian (except those covered by a special treaty or international agreement) to have $200 in his or her possession upon arrival in Canada. When this deterrent proved to be no more successful than the head tax, the government took more drastic measures. One important tactic, designed to limit population growth, was to prohibit immigration of wives or families of Chinese men. Between 1906 and 1923, only seven Chinese wives were admitted. Finally, in 1923, the Chinese Immigration Act (colloquially referred to as the 'Chinese Exclusion Act') was passed; this Act, which prohibited all Chinese immigration, was not rescinded until after the Second World War. Li (1980) argues that institutional racism as manifested in the immigration system produced far-reaching consequences through the subsequent disruption of Chinese family life, long after the obstacles were removed. The patterns of 'separated families' (spouse in China) and 'married bachelor' society persisted until well after World War II, when changes in immigration policy allowed the reuniting of marital partners and families.

The year 1967 was a major turning point for Canadian immigration policy. At that time specific ethnic and national criteria for the selection of immigrants were abolished in favour of a points system based largely on educational, professional, and occupational qualifications. In addition to immigrants, a new category of 'displaced persons', to be admitted on humanitarian grounds, was introduced. This category was later changed to 'refugees', and was incorporated under the immigrant policy rubric. Over the decades, the implementation of this 'racism-free' immigration policy resulted in a marked increase in the number of visible ethnic immigrants in Canada's population (Isajiw 1999).

The white majority backlash to the increasing numbers of non-white immigrants in Canada was noted previously in our discussion of 'subtle racism' in media portrayal of visible minorities. Here, we note also the parallel backlash to the increasing intake of refugees and to the attendant problems of refugee determination and backlog, highlighted by the media (*Toronto Star*, 8 February 1989). A more recent report in the *Toronto Star* (28 December 1993) highlighted the position of the Reform Party, that high immigration is putting a strain on the system, especially in terms of funding for social programs. While deep-seated public concern with potential cuts in funding for social programs may be raising 'genuine fears' regarding immigration levels, more suggestive of the 'new racism' is the finding of a national survey (reported earlier), which revealed that a majority of respondents agreed with the view that current immigration policy allows too many people of different races and cultures in Canada (CCCJ 1995).

2003—Canada's Immigration Policies: Contradictions and Shortcomings

According to a report in the CRRF newsletter (2001a), in the wake of the tragic and horrific 11 September 2001 terrorist attacks on the United States, Canada's immigration and refugee policies were subject to allegedly racist attacks by closed-door policy enthusiasts. The refugee claim system became one of the direct focuses of attention for the critics. But, according to the CRRF report, there has been an additional fear that 'knee-jerk reactions' could push Canada's immigration laws back to a time when race was a more explicit matter. The report argues that some of today's immigration policies, while neutral on their face, have particular negative effects on people of colour. An example of a policy that is neutral on its face but discriminatory in effect is the requirement that refugees have identity documents to obtain permanent residence. This rule was imposed in 1993. Since it is refugees' identity that puts them at risk of persecution, many flee without any papers and may not be able to get documents later, or at least not without putting family members in danger. But, beyond this general difficulty, the report suggests, a particular problem arose for people from countries with no functioning government in place to issue its citizens documents. This was the situation through the 1990s for Somalis and Afghanis, many of whom found themselves in long-term limbo. In response to this crisis, the Somali community organized itself and challenged the discriminatory nature of this policy in the courts. A settlement involving the use of statutory documents to satisfy the identity document requirement was reached in December 2000. It remains to be seen how effective it will prove to be.

According to the report, an associated problem concerns evaluation of proof of relationship. Prospective immigrants applying to come to Canada on the basis of their relationship to a family member need to satisfy an immigration officer of this relationship. In Canada, and in the West generally, birth and marriage certificates are obvious and accessible proofs of relationship. Such paper evidence is increasingly sought after in the mail-in forms of processing favoured by the immigration authorities. But in many parts of the world, notably the least-developed countries, relationships are not generally and reliably established by paper. As a result, families face significant obstacles in being reunited and many have had to undertake DNA testing, involving both expense and delays (CRRF 2001a).

Additionally, the report argues, a number of provisions in the immigration law leave a wide margin of discretion to immigration officials. This tendency, heightened in the new immigration legislation, Bill C-11, opens the door to decision-making based not on individual facts but supposed group characteristics, or the individual prejudices of the decision-maker. This is evident, for example, in the area of detention. Many people can be detained under the current law. Even more will be liable under the new law and in the heightened security climate after September 11th. But only a portion of those who could be detained actually end up in detention and it seems to turn out that those who do are often racialized groups. In some cases, it becomes clear that there is racial profiling involved. Individuals are detained as flight risks on the basis of their ethnicity or nationality. Because of the wide discretion given to immigration officials to detain or not, it is extremely difficult to challenge this kind of discriminatory practice.

A similar problem, the report alleges, concerns determinations of inadmissibility on the basis of security risk. The law casts a very wide net for security inadmissibility, catching people who were or are members of a terrorist group, without ever defining membership or terrorist. The provisions are used, with extremely painful consequences, against members of certain ethnic groups, notably Kurds, Palestinians, Sikhs, and Algerians. The vaguest association with an organization classified in the immigration officer's mind as terrorist can mean years of delays and uncertainty, and perhaps perpetual inadmissibility to Canada. Again, given the reactions to September 11th, this continues to be a source of concern.

Other areas of concern highlighted in the report are the barriers such as visa requirements set up by Western countries, allegedly forcing people fleeing persecution or grinding poverty to turn to smugglers or traffickers to help them cross borders, often at great peril to their lives. Bill C-11, the report points out, contains a whole panoply of measures which increase penalties for those involved in helping illegal border crossings, even if they are motivated purely by humanitarian concern. The report alleges that, while the Bill sacrifices all kinds of principles of justice in its enthusiasm for punishing the smugglers (mostly people of colour), it offers nothing in the way of protection for the traffickers' victims. They are the vulnerable ones who are exploited and enslaved, often women and children, and usually also people of colour.

The above, the report alleges, are only some of the policy areas in which differential impacts can be felt. The government has recognized the need to improve the quality of its client service. But without a commitment to addressing the broader issues raised by the context of racism, there may be some skepticism about how much is about to change for the better.

An escalating concern is the high cost of settlement funds required for permanent residence applicants. Under the present immigration regulations, the report declares, refugees in Canada as well as immigrants pay $500 per adult and $100 per child for a permanent residence application. Since 1995 immigrants also have to pay $975 for a Right of Landing Fee, which refugees had to pay as well until they were exempted in 2000 (CRRF 2001a).

These funds will be increased under the proposed new legislation (*Building a Nation*). Under section 7, Settlement Funds Required for Permanent Residence Applicants, subsections 64(1)(b) and 126 of the proposed regulations require that applicants demonstrate that they have sufficient funds to establish in Canada. The measure to be used is the low-income cut-off (LICO) figures set by Statistics Canada. The committee heard that the amount currently required is $10,000 for the principal applicant, plus $2000 for each dependant, and that use of the LICO will approximately double the required settlement funds for a family of four. Witnesses argued that the amount required under the proposed system is much too high and will adversely affect many desired applicants, particularly those from developing countries.

Persecution, Extermination, and Expulsion

The ultimate denial of human rights lies in the denial of the right to life. At the level of the ethnic group, violation of this right constitutes the act of *genocide*, a crime against humanity under International Law. The UN Convention on Punishment of Crime of Genocide describes the crime of genocide as measures taken against national, religious, racial, or ethnic groups with a view to exterminating the entire population against whom the measures are directed. This Convention was adopted by the United Nations following the Second World War in response to the atrocities of the Holocaust and to ensure that state policies of genocide, like those adopted in Germany under Hitler's Nazi regime, would never again be enacted. The death of millions of Jews in concentration camps probably provides the single most insidious act of deliberate genocide in modern history, but it is by no means the only such act in modern times. Policies and practices of 'ethnic cleansing', in former Yugoslavia, provide a more recent case in point.

While deliberate acts of persecution, extermination, and expulsion are not characteristic of the treatment of ethnic minorities in this country, Canada, like many other countries, has at times singled out particular minorities for cruel and inhumane treatment. In the case of Canada's aboriginal peoples, the extermination of the Beothuk Indians provides a stark example.[5]

Historically, a major reason for immigration to Canada of Hutterites, and other ethnic minorities, was to escape persecution in the country of emigration. Canada was viewed as a land of opportunity, where people could live without fear of discrimination on religious and/or racially defined grounds. Although Canada has not fully achieved this ideal, the techniques of domination employed by Canadian majority group(s) have tended to be covert, rather than overt, and customary rather than legal. An outstanding exception to this general principle was the deliberate persecution of Japanese-Canadians, during the Second World War, which involved wholesale violations of the political, economic, social, and cultural rights of members of this stigmatized minority (see Box 4-2). In this particular instance, the combined forces of government policy and public opinion, strongly

BOX 4-2: CASE STUDY 2

The Japanese-Canadian Experience

At the turn of the twentieth century, anti-Asian sentiment was rampant. Successive waves of Asian immigration gave rise to a virulently racist public paranoia over the 'Yellow Peril'. It reached a fevered pitch in 1907 when a crowd at an anti-Asian rally suddenly turned into a mob and marched through Vancouver's Chinatown and Japanesetown breaking store windows. The riot was stirred by the consolidation of anti-Asian agitation by industrialist workers and exploitation of the public anxiety by the media and politicians. The government reacted by restricting immigration of Japanese nationals to Canada from 400 in 1908 to 150 in 1923.

Despite the racism, the Japanese Canadian community continued to develop and prosper. During the years of limited immigration, women arrived and families were raised. Japanese Canadians, still without the franchise, volunteered for service in the Second World War. By 1919, Japanese Canadians owned nearly half the fishing licenses in BC, but by 1925, 1000 fishing licences were stripped from them. In 1941, war with Japan was imminent, and Japanese Canadians were finger-printed and photographed and were required to carry registration cards.

On 7 December 1941, Japan bombed Pearl Harbor in a surprise attack. With that event began one of the most shameful chapters in the history of democracy and human rights in North America. Japanese Canadians were declared 'enemy aliens' and were virtually stripped of all their human rights. Immediately after the bombing of Pearl Harbor, 1800 Japanese Canadian fishing boats were seized and impounded. Japanese-language newspapers were closed down. The government enacted the War Measures Act and vested power from the representative Parliament to the prime minister's cabinet. Within three months, federal cabinet Orders-in-Council forced the removal of Japanese-Canadian male nationals to camps, and then authorized the removal of all persons of Japanese origin. The RCMP was given expanded powers to search without warrant, impose a curfew, and confiscate property. A Custodian of Enemy Property was authorized to hold all land and property in trust.

During the evacuation, many people were given only 24 hours' notice to vacate their homes, before being sent to 'clearing sites' where they were detained until internment camps were prepared. A civilian body, the BC Security Commission was in charge of the expulsion orders. By November 1942, after eight months of operation, the Commission managed to break up and uproot families and sent nearly 22,000 individuals to road camps, internment camps, and prisoner-of-war camps.

Forcibly uprooted, Japanese-Canadian internees faced further injustices. All of their property and belongings held by the Custodian of Enemy Property 'in trust', were sold without owners' consent. Land, businesses, cars, houses, and personal effects were liquidated at a fraction of their value. The government justified this action: Proceeds from the sale of goods and property would be used to pay for the living expenses of the interned. Towards the end of the war, the Japanese internees were threatened with further expulsion. They were given the option for 'dispersal' to places and towns east of the Rocky Mountains, or outright 'repatriation' to Japan.

The war ended in 1945 after the United States dropped atomic bombs on Hiroshima and Nagasaki. Japan surrendered. While Japanese Americans pieced their lives together and returned to the West Coast, Japanese Canadians did not have this option. Their choice was to be exiled to Japan, a defeated country unknown to many Japanese Canadians, or to resettle in foreign parts of Canada. Initially, 10,000 Japanese Canadians signed for repatriation. Many signed out of fear, or misguided loyalty to Canada.

In March 1949, four years after the war was over, the last of the wartime restrictions and the War Measures Act were lifted. Japanese Canadians were allowed to travel freely and return to the West Coast. Prior to this date, in 1948, Japanese Canadians received the right to vote. Public sentiment was beginning to lean in the community's favour. Japanese Canadians were gaining strength and resolve to mobilize politically and to seek justice for their inhumane treatment.

Led by the Japanese Canadian Committee for Democracy (JCCD), which later became the National Association of Japanese Canadians, the Movement for Redress and Compensation was waged throughout the 1980s. A full account of this struggle is detailed in the report upon which this excerpt is based.

Finally, after a long and bitter battle, on September 22, 1988, the Japanese Canadian Redress Agreement was signed. In the House of Commons, then Prime Minister Brian Mulroney acknowledged the government's wrongful actions; pledged to ensure that the events would never recur and recognized the loyalty of the Japanese Canadians to Canada. As a symbolic redress for those injustices the government offered individual and community compensation to the Japanese Canadians. To the Canadian people, and on behalf of Japanese Canadians, the government committed to create a national organization that would foster racial harmony and help to eliminate racism. The Canadian Race Relation Foundation opened its doors in 1997.

SOURCE: Adapted from *From Racism to Redress: The Japanese Canadian Experience,* Canadian Race Relations Foundation 2002.

influenced by the traumatic political climate of the times, vented the fear of the nation upon one ethnic minority.

In contrast to the persecution of the Japanese (see Case Study 2 in Box 4-2), little was done to Canadians of German origin, although almost all of Canada's armed forces were engaged against Germany in the war. It seems clear that the racist colour bias that was directed against the Japanese did not apply to 'white' Germans. During the war period, repressive steps were enacted against other Canadian groups, especially Communist, Fascist, and pacifist organizations, but discriminatory measures against the Japanese minority were far harsher than those accorded any other group.[6]

Conclusion

Analysis of the origin and persistence of the Canadian system of ethnic stratification has shown that, from the very beginning, discriminatory treatment towards aboriginal peoples, as compared with immigrants, has been rooted in more insidious racist assumptions, and its disadvantaging consequences in terms of access to political, economic, and social power, have been far more devastating. Among immigrants, visible (racially defined) immigrants from non-Western countries—that is, those ethnic minorities whose racial and cultural attributes have been presumed to deviate most markedly from majority norms—have been most restricted in their access to political, economic, and social power. Institutionalized forms of ethnic discrimination, elaborated as 'techniques of domination' in the last part of this chapter, have served to maintain a vertical ethnic mosaic in which, despite some mobility in the middle ranks, the superordinate status of those at the top (founding partners and immigrants most like them), and the marginalized status of those at the bottom (aboriginal peoples) has remained relatively stable over time.

Throughout our discussion of ethnic stratification in Chapters 3 and 4, we have emphasized the way in which racist restrictions imposed by majority authorities have produced group-level social inequalities and have led to the social construction of invalidated and disadvantaged racial and ethnic minorities. By way of contrast, in Chapter 5, we will first highlight the concept of ethnicity and show how members of both majority and minority ethnic communities, in order to protect and maintain their distinctive ethnocultures and group identities, can manipulate ethnicity. The result is boundary-maintaining mechanisms that entrench restrictive barriers among ethnic communities. Notwithstanding this, our analysis will then demonstrate that it is the racist barriers created by majority boundaries that violate minority rights and lead to collective claims for redress.

Key Concepts

- colonizer versus colonized
- dominant/aboriginal relations
- dominant/immigrant relations
- ethnic heterogeneity
- ethnic segmentation
- ethnic stratification
- institutionalized racism
- migrant superordination
- patterns of ethnic majority/minority relations
- techniques of domination
- vertical mosaic

Critical Thinking Questions

1. Is 'the vertical mosaic', as described by John Porter in 1965, an appropriate characterization of Canada's current system of ethnic stratification? Why or why not? Discuss.
2. Lieberson (1961) has proposed two different models of majority/minority relations: a model of relations between dominant and aboriginal populations, and a model of relations between dominant and immigrant populations. Compare and contrast these models and provide examples to illustrate how they can be applied in the Canadian context.
3. Breton (1978) points out that patterns of immigrant adaptation to the new society can be highly varied. He contrasts two main patterns of immigrant adaptation: the pattern of ethnic heterogeneity, and the pattern of ethnic segmentation. Illustrate the difference between these two patterns as documented in studies of different ethnic minorities in Canada.
4. It has been argued that institutionalized forms of discrimination against ethnic minorities (institutionalized racism) provide the majority group(s) with legitimate techniques of domination and social control. Techniques of domination enable dominant powers to maintain and perpetuate the existing system of ethnic stratification and to secure their established position at its apex. Discuss.
5. Select one technique of domination and develop a case study to demonstrate how it serves/has served to perpetuate the minority status of one racial-ethnic population in Canada.

CHAPTER 5

Ethnicity, Ethnocultural Distinctiveness, and Collective Rights Claims

Introduction

In the last chapter, our analysis emphasized the way in which racist restrictions *imposed by majority boundaries* have served to disadvantage racial and ethnic minorities and have been instrumental in creating and maintaining Canada's system of ethnic stratification—the Canadian vertical mosaic.

In this chapter, we will highlight the concept of ethnicity and show how members of *both majority and minority ethnic communities* can manipulate ethnicity to create *boundary-maintaining mechanisms*. These mechanisms entrench restrictive boundaries between ethnic communities, enabling them to maintain their ethnocultural distinctiveness and separateness. Our analysis will also demonstrate, however, that it is the racist barriers created by *majority* boundaries that violate minority rights and lead to collective claims for redress. These claims will provide the focus in the second part of the next chapter. First, we will examine how alleged violations of the various *components* of ethnicity—language, cultural integrity, religion, territory—are drawn upon to shape the nature of minority rights claims put forward in Canada by representatives of three categories—Franco-Quebecois, immigrants, and aboriginal peoples.

Maintaining Ethnocultural Distinctiveness and Separateness: Ethnicity and Boundary-maintaining Mechanisms

Scientific evidence demonstrates that *racial* boundaries do not, in themselves, present barriers to human intercourse. Members of all human populations belong to the same species, *Homo sapiens*; males and females from different racial groups are thus capable of mating to propagate the human species. Moreover, many of the commonly held racist assumptions as to the natural, innate differences among human so-called 'races' in intelligence, morality, capacity for cultural development, and so forth have never been scientifically proven. Why, then, in an age of scientific enlightenment, do members of humankind continue to place so much emphasis on perceived or assumed *differences* among racial and ethnic populations? More importantly, why do they continue to make invidious comparisons between one human population and another? The answer to this question is anything but simple: a full explanation would necessitate drawing from the pooled resources of theologians, philosophers, historians, and many other scholars, as well as social scientists. Nevertheless, an examination of the multifaceted concept of ethnicity and of the ways in which ethnic communities manipulate ethnicity so as to maintain their ethnocultural distinctiveness and separateness may serve to shed some light on this enigmatic phenomenon.

Race, Culture, and Ethnicity

As indicated in earlier chapters, scholars and laypersons alike have long used the terms *racial* and *ethnic* interchangeably with reference to biological and cultural differences between various human populations. For early anthropologists (late nineteenth and early twentieth centuries) whose evolutionary interests focused on the study of prehistoric and aboriginal human populations, the original meaning of the term *ethnic* pertained to the so-called 'primitive' races and cultures of humankind. Bennett (1975: 5) points out that the concept, ethnic, connoted the 'exotic, less than civilized, and probably less than human creatures out there for the taking, and for the ethnologist, [social and cultural anthropologist] there for studying and preserving like wild species.' Anthropologists, despite their understanding and empathy, were outsiders. Accordingly, as Bennett suggests, concepts employed by early anthropologists reflected their ethnocentric, Euro-Western, cultural assumptions.

The **old ethnicity,** variously defined, equated race, culture, geography, and human identity. Ethnic groups were conceived as 'natural' populations born, living, and dying in a known geographical range. This perspective associated the long-term geographical and social isolation of involuntary human groups with their distinctive biological and cultural attributes. Conceptualized in this way, ethnic groups were seen as corporate entities, highly adapted to particular geographical environments, and uniquely capable of maintaining group membership and cultural continuity through time.

To recapitulate, as typically employed by anthropologists and, later, sociologists (Isajiw 1970), ethnicity was conceived as an attribute of an organized and cohesive ethnic group whose members shared distinctive biocultural attributes that they transmitted from generation to generation through the processes of inbreeding (intraethnic mating) and enculturation (distinctive ethnic socialization). Based on these assumptions, ethnicity could be measured, objectively, in terms of the distinctive features—physiognomy, language, religion, art and artifacts, technology, and modes of social organization—characteristic of members of a given ethnic group.

The New Ethnicity

The contemporary social scientific usage of the concept of ethnicity reflects a shift in theoretical perspective among anthropologists, sociologists, and others, to a more subjective frame of reference (Bennett 1975; Glazer and Moynihan 1975). In part, this shift in orientation reflects radical changes in world conditions that have markedly altered the old ethnic/geographical balance and have brought formerly isolated human populations into face-to-face contact and confrontation. As a consequence of human breakthroughs in science and technology, particularly in the areas of transportation and telecommunications, geographical boundaries and distances no longer present barriers to human intercourse.

In the decades following the Second World War, massive cross-national migrations of human populations, together with the development of instant satellite communications, have led to, indeed necessitated, the growth of an international technological culture and concomitantly, have greatly increased the potential for the creation of a global village of humankind. Yet, paradoxically, while these developments have increasingly muted or eroded former cultural differences between human populations and have generated a certain degree of cultural uniformity at the international level, at the same time they appear to have heightened the salience of ethnic differentiation both within and among modern states.

At the level of the ethnic community, exposure to compelling, new options in ideas, values, and lifeways has led to the fragmentation of former ethnocultures and communities, as well as to the creation of new ones. Consequently, today's ethnic communities do not represent cultural wholes. One of the most typical and most salient lines of internal division within contemporary ethnic communities is found between traditionalists, those members most committed to preservation of the ethnic heritage, ethos, and lifeways, and transitionalists, those most eager to learn and adopt new ways of viewing and doing things. Members not strongly bound by tradition may seek marital partners from outside the ethnic community. When this happens on a relatively large scale, it leads to the creation of a new ethnic strain, whose members may, over time, come to constitute a new ethnic group (the Cape Colored in South Africa, the Métis in Canada, and the Eurasians in Southeast Asia are examples).

Shifts in political boundaries, resulting from wars and treaties between states, as well as from the creation of new geopolitical units by colonial powers, have led to the fracturing of former ethnocultural communities, and to the creation of new ethnic minorities within state boundaries. With the demise of the colonial era, the withdrawal of colonial administrations from former territories, and the subsequent rise of newly created nation-states, many of the old ethnic antagonisms, forcibly contained under colonial rule, have re-emerged in politicized form. Ethnic minorities throughout the post-colonial world are demanding a reassessment of their other-imposed minority status and some are asserting demands for self-determination within existing state boundaries (for example, Canada's aboriginal peoples, Israeli-dominated Palestinians, Iraq's Kurds). Where minority demands for self-determination within the state have been pushed aside or blocked by formidable governmental opposition, more radical demands for political secession have been voiced by some sectors within ethnic minorities (Quebec Separatists, Baltic and other minorities in the former USSR).

Other political shifts—in ideologies, power bases, national boundaries, and cross-national alliances—have also split peoples apart. New ethnic categories are emerging, for example, among political refugees—Palestinians in Israel, Cubans in Florida, and many others.

The shift from the old to **the new ethnicity** owes much to the seminal work of the anthropologist Fredrik Barth (1969), who argued that the old biocultural/territorial-isolate frame of reference could not account for the persistence of viable ethnic communities, despite continuing contact across ethnic boundaries. According to Barth, in order to explain ethnic group persistence in the face of the loss of territorial distinctiveness through migration, loss of cultural distinctiveness through culture contact, and loss of physical distinctiveness through changes in ethnic strain, we must shift our attention from the morphological characteristics of the internal cultures of ethnic groups to the dynamics of interethnic relations and of ethnic boundary maintenance. For Barth, the critical feature of ethnicity is the **ethnic boundary**, rather than the cultural gestalt (content) within it. Barth does not imply that cultural differences are irrelevant; the point he emphasizes is that we cannot assume a simple, one-to-one correspondence between ethnic communities and cultural similarities. Alternatively, we must focus our attention only on those physical and cultural diacritica (bodily mutilations and decorations, names, songs, religious icons, military medallions, and the like) singled out by in-group members as paramount symbols of ethnicity. Barth also stressed the crucial importance, for boundary maintenance, of behavioural norms (such as endogamy) that restrict interaction with outsiders and serve to maintain a high level of *social distance* between insiders and outsiders. These behavioural norms can be conceptualized as **boundary-maintaining mechanisms.**

At this juncture, in order to facilitate our understanding of ethnic boundaries and boundary maintenance, it may be useful to explain the concept of *social distance,* as employed by Barth, and as generally employed by social scientists. **Social distance** refers to the quantity and quality of social interaction among individuals or groups. The degree of social distance between members of different ethnic communities can be ascertained in terms of the number and variety of social relationships, as well as the degree of intimacy and personal involvement that characterizes the social relationships between insiders and outsiders. Since people tend to act in terms of their ethnocentric evaluations of themselves and others, social distance in relationships between insiders (intraethnic relations) tends to be minimized; whereas social distance in relationships between insiders and outsiders (interethnic relations) tends to be maximized. When social distance is high, social relationships among members of different ethnic communities tend to be of a categorical or impersonal nature, based on mutual utility. In this context, insiders relate to outsiders in terms of ethnic stereotypes rather than as individual personalities, because most people do not get close enough to outsiders to test the accuracy of their preconceived, unsubstantiated ethnic prejudices. On the other hand, when social distance is reduced and members of different ethnic communities interact more frequently and more informally, social relationships tend to become more intimate and more individualized. In this context, people become increasingly aware of the similarities, rather than the differences, between insiders and outsiders, while at the same time they become more conscious of individual differences among people categorized as outsiders. When this happens, members of different ethnic groups may come to relate to each other on a close, personal level without reference to ethnic stereotypes, but as social equals and as individual human personalities.

Insofar as ethnic boundaries are designed to keep insiders in and outsiders out, they serve to restrict interaction between ethnic communities and thus to maintain a high degree of social distance in interethnic relations. At the same time, ethnic boundaries serve to intensify interaction within ethnic communities; they thus serve to maintain a low degree of social distance in intraethnic relations.

For Barth and many of his followers, the most critical features of ethnic boundary maintenance are the characteristics of self-ascription and ascription by others. Thus, while selective objective criteria (key symbolic and behavioural attributes) are important, the critical variables underlying processes of boundary maintenance are subjective in nature. Put another way: Ethnicity can be socially constructed by both ethnic insiders and outsiders, and the two social constructs may or may not correspond.

Isajiw (1999: 19–20) takes the position that both subjective (social psychological) and objective (structural) aspects of internal and external boundaries must be taken into critical account in order to understand the processes of boundary maintenance and interethnic relations. Subjective aspects of internal boundaries, Isajiw suggests, are rooted in members' feelings of self-inclusion in one's own ethnic group, feelings of empathy and loyalty towards other members of one's ethnic group and feelings of self-exclusion from membership in other ethnic groups. Objective aspects of internal boundaries are manifested in the way positive feelings towards one's ethnic group are reflected in the propensity to participate in informal relations with persons of the same ethnicity and in the support given to the establishment and maintenance of ethnic institutions.

The subjective aspects of the external boundary, Isajiw contends, refers to the feelings among members of another ethnic group, outside of any specific ethnic group, that members of that group are not 'one of us' and should be excluded from membership in the group. The objective aspects of the external boundary include the institutions and organizational structures that exclude other ethnic groups from one's own.

Following Barth (1969), Isajiw maintains that identification by others—whether or not it corresponds to self-identification—reinforces self-identification. Hence, ethnicity is a matter of a double boundary, a boundary from within, established by the ethnic socialization (enculturation) process and maintained by ethnic institutions, and a boundary from without, established by external barriers of exclusion and maintained in the process of interethnic relations. The **double boundary** that every ethnic group possesses, Isajiw (1999: 20) argues, indicates that no ethnic group can be completely understood without its relationship to other ethnic groups. Interethnic relations are the relationships between the two boundaries. Adopting this perspective, we can explain ethnic continuity by examining the way in which interacting ethnic communities define and maintain their dichotomous relationship, despite their increasing cultural similarities in response to the shared societal and global environmental contexts in which they find themselves.

As a result of these macro-level phenomena, the populations studied by anthropologists and other social scientists can no longer be conceptualized in terms of their old racial or ethnic group labels; nor can they be meaningfully analyzed holistically, in the manner of traditional structural/functional analysis. Ethnicity is no longer coterminous with national and geopolitical boundaries. Indeed, the multiethnic state, as in the case of Canada, has become the global norm. Moreover, ethnic categories now crosscut state boundaries. This phenomenon is very evident in the Canadian context. Consider the ties between immigrants and their homelands; the ties between members of aboriginal ethnic communities artificially split by the Canadian/American border; and the ties between members of widely dispersed ethnic minorities such as Jews resident outside of Israel; all of these vital interstate bonds between members of cross-national ethnic communities demonstrate, unequivocally, that the age of ethnic isolation is over, thereby rendering static concepts of ethnicity obsolete.

Ethnicity as a Symbolic System: The Situational Manipulation of Ethnicity

In arguing that ethnicity needs to be defined with reference to some outside group, Barth highlighted the idea that the new ethnicity is contingent upon the prevailing social environment. Building upon this notion, social scientists have increasingly come to conceptualize ethnicity as a symbolic system that can be manipulated situationally by members. In this view, ethnicity is seen as an organizational strategy, whereby members seek to satisfy their expressive and symbolic needs for ethnic group continuity and belongingness in those social environmental contexts where such emotive needs come to the fore, and/or to satisfy their instrumental needs for economic, political, and social empowerment in those social environmental contexts where such individual and corporate group interests come to the fore.

In some societal contexts ethnicity may be unimportant or irrelevant, while in others it may be in the forefront of individual/group consciousness. In those situations where ethnicity is not highly salient, where other group affiliations and interests take precedence over ethnic ones, members may choose to maintain a low ethnic profile to remain ethnically invisible. Thus, for example, within political pressure groups mobilized around minority issues like women's liberation, gay and lesbian rights, promotion of the rights of persons with physical or mental disabilities—ethnic differences between members may become muted in the pursuit of other common interests and corporate goals. Alternatively, in those situations where members believe that the very existence of the ethnic communities is threatened (for example, the Métis in Canada prior to the Riel Rebellion; the Canadian Jews during the Arab-Israeli wars; and the Franco-Quebecois, following the failure of the Meech Lake Accord) the salience of ethnicity becomes heightened, and the group is perceived both as a refuge and as a vehicle for concerted action in pursuit of corporate interests and goals.

The foregoing lends credence to the position of those who argue (against the neo-Marxists) that ethnicity has become more salient than economic class in advancing corporate interests because it involves more than interests; it can combine interests with affective ties. Taking this argument a step further, we can view the new ethnicity as an ethnic organizational strategy uniquely designed to resolve an inherent human conflict of modern times; a conflict between the expressive need for a sense of rootedness and group belongingness that can best be satisfied within an involuntary *Gemeinschaft* community and the instrumental desire for material gratification and political power that can best be satisfied by participation in the *Gesellschaft* institutions of post-technological society.

BOX 5-1: CASE STUDY

The Hutterites: Ethnoreligious Group Persistence through Double Boundary Maintenance

The Hutterites in Canada are a religiously defined ethnic group whose distinctive ethnoculture developed within the environmental context of sectarian, agricultural communes in Europe, United States, and Canada over a period of some 400 years. During this time, the Hutterites were persecuted, even burned at the stake, for their religious doctrines. Consequently, they fled from one European country to another, and then from the United States to Canada, where they now live in agricultural communes in the Western Prairies.

The case study presented here represents a generalized picture of Hutterian communities, which does not take into account differences among the various Hutterite colonies. In particular, the degree of adherence to traditional religious norms and the degree of acculturation to contemporary Canadian norms varies, sometimes markedly, from one colony to another.

The Hutterite sect originated as part of the Anabaptist Reformation movement in sixteenth-century Europe, which also included the Mennonites, Doukhobors, and Old Order Amish. With the possible exception of the latter sect, the Hutterites have been the most successful of all Anabaptists in maintaining a viable, and highly distinctive religious ethnoculture over time. The Hutterites represent an unusual case of successful ethnic group persistence achieved by a unique pattern of internal, religious boundary maintenance and reinforced by external boundaries of prejudice and discrimination.

The Hutterian Worldview

Like the disciples of Christ who had 'all things common' (*Acts* 2:44), and in contradistinction to the individualistic ethos of mainstream society, the Hutterites choose to reside in voluntary, egalitarian 'communities of love' based on communal ownership of property and possessions, and dedicated to peace, social harmony, and a life of simplicity and austerity. Because the Hutterites are dedicated pacifists whose religious ethos precludes acts of violence, they refuse to actively participate in military service. Because they insist that membership in their communities be voluntary, they have rejected infant baptism in favour of adult baptism, a rite that signifies a voluntary choice by mature persons.

From their beginning as a distinct Anabaptist sect in 1528, Hutterian doctrines directly challenged the values and authority of established Christian Church States in Europe. Consequently, the Hutterites were persecuted for their religious beliefs, first in Germany, and later in the other countries of Europe to which they fled. Historically, the nature of their relations with host nations was one of broken promises, persecution, and flight. Various countries offered them religious freedom and exemption from military service, but inevitably these privileges were withdrawn (Bennett 1969).

In Canada, today, the Hutterites constitute a religious sect in the sociological sense of the term. The sect, in contrast to the church form of religious organization, requires separation from the greater society, which it sees as sinful, evil, and contaminating (Yinger 1970). Viewed from the Hutterian perspective, people were created to worship God, and the true believer's prime orientation is toward everlasting life after death rather than enjoyment of the present, temporal life on earth. The outside world of the non-believer, with its competitive individualistic, materialistic norms and its emphasis on self-gratification is considered sinful, and all true believers must withdraw and isolate themselves from its corrupting influences. Prejudice toward non-Hutterites by virtue of their association with the vices of society serves to sustain a high degree of social distance in interethnic relations. It also accords legitimacy and salience to Hutterian ethnic boundaries.

Maintaining Ethnic Distinctiveness

Hutterites' insistence on maintaining an austere, traditional, and frugal way of life is reflected in what neighbours view as their plain, old-fashioned clothing (for example, women typically wear kerchiefs and long skirts; men wear long beards, dark suits, and outmoded hats). This distinctive attire serves as symbolic ethnic diacritica, distinguishing Hutterites from outsiders in virtually all social contexts. Thus, dress provides an important cultural boundary marker, rendering highly visible members of an ethnic community whose physical characteristics are essentially similar to those of their Euro-Canadian neighbours.

Another key boundary-maintaining mechanism employed by the Hutterites is their use of a distinctive language, that is, an archaic form of German. For Hutterites, English is a second language necessary for basic communication with the outside; but within the ethnocultural community, at home, at church, and in religious school archaic German is used as a language of ritual, a language of everyday conversation, and as a language of instruction for children. Within the self-contained Hutterite communities, the use of a distinctive language, intricately interwoven with a distinctive and exclusive way of life, has been strongly reinforced by the practice of endogamy strictly enforced through religious norms prohibiting marriage outside the community. Thus, cultural and biological forces have worked together to create ethnic homogeneity out of cultural diversity. Consequently, from its sixteenth-century origins as a Christian Anabaptist religious sect, whose members stemmed from various ethnic and national groupings, the Hutterites have become a single, full-fledged Canadian ethnic group.

In keeping with their common religious stance of rejecting the outside world, Hutterites share a common (negative) political ideology. They refuse to participate in military service, to hold political office, and to take legal oaths. As a rule, they even refuse to exercise their right to vote, except in the case of local elections where the interests of Hutterite colonies are directly involved (Sanders 1964). Most importantly, because they constitute total *Gemeinschaft* communities, they have the requisite age and sex ratios to ensure perpetuation of the ethnic group through recruitment of members from other colonies within the sectarian community and through Hutterite ethnoreligious endogamy.

Maintaining Ethnic Enclavement

Probably the most important mechanism of boundary maintenance employed by Hutterites to preserve the integrity of the Hutterian way, is the strategy of geographical and social isolation of their colonies. Each colony buys a huge tract of land consisting of thousands of acres in an area as isolated as possible from the more highly populated local or regional centres. Moreover, the typical plan of the colony is to place the buildings—church, residences, and so forth, in the middle of the tract of land, a design that serves to further isolate Hutterites from their neighbours. Residential concentration also maximizes daily contact between Hutterites (intraethnic relations) and facilitates *Gemeinschaft* modes of social control (for example, gossip, scolding, shunning, and so forth), which curb deviance from Hutterian norms. This strategy is becoming more difficult to realize as such tracts of land become less available in Canada's West. Indeed, Peter (1987) suggests that some Hutterites have had to move to agriculturally marginal areas. Nevertheless, studies on Hutterite settlement and dispersion patterns (Thompson 1984 and Evans 1985) reveal that the method is still a viable one.

In direct contrast to the intensive and extensive nature of interactions between members within the Hutterite colony, relations between Hutterites and outsiders are sharply limited and carefully controlled by the colony's leaders. In the past, visits to local towns were generally made by only the most clearly committed (hence, least corruptible) leaders of the colony, and were dictated almost entirely by requirements that could not be supplied by the colony, e.g., purchase of farm machinery. Increasing pressure on ministers and elders to allow colony members to go to town or to visit neighbouring non-Hutterite farms has resulted in some relaxation of the stringent prohibitions in this area, but requests are still carefully screened (Murphy 2001).

The emphasis on maximization of intraethnic relations, together with the severe curtailment of all but the necessary minimal amount of formalized contact with outsiders, reinforces the double boundary between insiders and outsiders and dovetails well with the norm of endogamy. While the colony enforces a multitude of rules and sanctions which severely restrict social interaction with outsiders (interethnic relations), among these, the most important is the norm of endogamy (intraethnic marriage): the penalty for its violation is excommunication. For a Hutterite, this is the most severe punishment that can be imposed, for it not only means banishment from the Hutterian fold and the good life in this world, but also, and more importantly, it implies banishment from the fold of the elect and exclusion from their extraterrestrial paradise in the everlasting life to come (Hostetler and Huntington 1967). Given these stringent religious boundary-maintaining mechanisms, for colony members, outsiders remain strangers, removed from everyday reality and stigmatized by their association with the allegedly corrupt ideas and life ways of the outside world. The likelihood that a Hutterite would be able to break through the religiously legitimated barriers of social distance and engage in intimate social relations with non-Hutterites is thereby minimized (Peter 1980a).

Despite these stringent sanctions, religious defections have always occurred, from time to time. Peter (1987) projected an estimate of 300 defections out of a total population of more than 21,800. From the Hutterian view, such defections help to maintain the traditional cohesiveness and continuity of the colonies by eliminating the religiously alienated members.

The technique of controlled acculturation (Eaton 1970) whereby Hutterites selectively accept, adapt, and integrate outside ideas and practices into their own value system, gives the Hutterian way a limited but important degree of flexibility enabling them to 'bend and not break' under the ever-increasing pressures posed by compelling outside alternatives. Hutterites have successfully managed to screen, limit, and control the process of secular education for their young; they have continually adapted to the use of farm machinery; some colonies have allowed the limited introduction of outside leisure activities, for example, holding Halloween parties and reading farm magazines (Flint 1975: 121). In all of these new kinds of activities, Hutterite leaders, under pressure for change, have exerted control by defining the areas in which changes can be introduced without sacrificing core religious principles.

To a large extent, the strategy of ethnic enclavement of Hutterite colonies within the Canadian context has been a voluntary mechanism designed to carry out the moral imperatives of the Hutterian worldview. This is not to suggest, however, that discrimination against the Hutterites has not occurred; indeed, discriminatory laws and/or practices are a continuing part of their everyday social reality. For many years, there were discriminatory land laws in Alberta that impeded the expansion of Hutterite colonies. Hutterite leaders interpreted those laws as Divine warnings of the evil intent of outsiders who hate us (Eaton 1970). Thus, legal discrimination has provided a formidable external boundary, which has functioned to increase in-group solidarity among Hutterites.

Maintaining Self-Sufficiency and Independence

The ability of Hutterian communities to maintain high degrees of ethnic enclavement is made possible by their continuing high levels of economic, political, and social self-sufficiency and independence. Each colony is virtually institutionally complete. It has its own political, economic, religious, and educational institutions and each employs similar, religiously legitimated mechanisms of social control.

Today, colonies market their economic surplus in dairy and meat produce and in grain and vegetable produce in order to purchase the latest and best in modern agricultural machinery and equipment, but, in the main, they attempt to produce, insofar as possible, all the necessities for life in the colony. Most colonies produce their own foods, make their own shoes and clothing, build and repair houses and tools, and painstakingly inculcate in their children all of the essential religious values and practical skills necessary for the perpetuation of their distinctive, peaceful, frugal, and religiously committed lifestyle.

Each colony has its own informal network of kinship and friendship, and its own patterns of leisure activities—reading, singing, sports, visiting, and so forth. Thus, in both the secondary and primary spheres of social life, Hutterites are only minimally dependent on outside institutions: in the main, they confine their participation to the economic sphere. They also use the health services of the outside as required by members, but even here, only when deemed absolutely necessary. Hutterite norms mitigate against outside interference in their internal affairs. Accordingly, most colonies refuse to accept government assistance such as family allowances, old age pensions, tax exemptions and/or government welfare payments; such outside interference is perceived as undermining their norms of self-help, self-sufficiency, and communal responsibility for the welfare of all Hutterites (Peter 1980a).

Within Hutterite colonies, the various institutions are highly coordinated: each is based on the same core Hutterian religious values—co-operation, consensus, love, frugality, simplicity, self-discipline, and most importantly, the value of deference of the will of the individual to the will of the community. Ongoing participation by colony members in the multifaceted life of the community reinforces bonds of social solidarity within the colony, and, at the same time, provides a strong segregating mechanism, distinguishing Hutterites from outsiders, and keeping them a people apart.

For the most part, the leadership of Hutterian elders involves decisions, reached by community consensus, concerning the ongoing, internal life of the colony. When, however, Hutterian religious principles are threatened by outside sentiments and actions (for example, acts of discrimination on the part of neighbouring farmers, anti-German alien sentiment during World Wars I and II, discriminatory land laws, conscription laws, and so forth) leaders act to represent Hutterian interests to the outside.

The most outstanding case in point is provided by Hutterian opposition to Alberta's Communal Property Act. Several times in its long term of office (1935–71) the Social Credit government of the Province of Alberta responded to public pressure against the Hutterites by enacting discriminatory legislation. In 1947, in response to widespread public accusations of Hutterite 'land grabbing', the Communal Property Act was put into force. This Act, which prevented anyone from purchasing or owning land communally in the Province of Alberta without government permission, virtually put an end to the expansion of Hutterite colonies in the province. Hutterite attempts to circumvent the Act by individual purchases of land used for communal farming, led to a general build-up of hostility culminating, in 1964, in a formal complaint lodged by a local of the farmers' union, and the laying of charges against Hutterites by the police. The long-term result of the Act was to encourage Hutterites to set up colonies in the neighbouring Province of Saskatchewan as well as in the American states of Montana and Washington. Today, about one-third of the Hutterites live in

Montana. In response, Hutterite leaders broke with their long-term stance against using the courts, a stance which went beyond fundamental religious dictates, and tested the constitutionality of the Act. They argued that common ownership of land was a basis tenet of Hutterite faith and that the Act violated their human right to religious freedom. Further, they argued that since only the federal government could rule on religious matters, the provincial law in question was void. The case was contested as far as the Supreme Court of Canada, in 1969, but the Hutterites lost on the grounds that relations concerning land ownership were a provincial concern. It was not until 1973, under the Conservative government of then Premier Lougheed, that the Communal Property Act of Alberta was repealed. At that time, the provincial legislature agreed that the Act violated both the Canadian Bill of Rights (1961) and the Provincial Human Rights Act of Alberta (1966, 1971). Unfortunately, for the Hutterites, the repeal of the Act did not engender an increase in public tolerance. The establishment of new colonies sparked continuing public hostility on the part of envious non-Hutterite farmers who felt threatened (Flint 1975: 116–17).

Hutterite success in maintaining the self-sufficiency and independence of its colonies can be attributed to the viability of a unique, planned, branching-out method of colony expansion. The continuing population growth among Hutterites enables the parent colonies to plan new daughter colonies, in advance. This strategy ensures that each colony does not exceed the maximal optimum population size of approximately one hundred and fifty persons. The decision to branch out is based, in part, on economic viability. New colonies must be subsidized initially, but each colony is expected to become self-sufficient. Other considerations include the availability of land (an increasing problem), population pressure, and the politics of colony management. With regard to the latter, the branching-out process is a customary procedure for resolving internal factionalism among leaders by providing new positions of authority to be filled.

Because Hutterites do not have and refuse to make use of outside resources and connections, they must ensure continuing recruitment of membership from within the group. Their steady population growth ensures a continuing supply of potential members and their strictly enforced norm of endogamy mitigates against loss of committed adult members through intermarriage. Yet, Hutterites are aware that the voluntary nature of group membership, predicated on the rite of adult baptism, opens the way for defection of young persons during adolescence when they are not yet fully committed to the Hutterian way and when the attractions of the outside world are most compelling.

In keeping with their 'bend but not break' ethos of controlled acculturation, Hutterian elders accept the fact that the 'foolish years' (Hostetler and Huntington 1967: 79) are a time for 'trying the boundaries'. Thus, parents have come to look at the in-between years—the interval between leaving school and adult baptism—as a temporary, experimental time when young people are allowed to be 'tourists' in the outside world. It is generally accepted that young people will engage in normally unpermitted indulgences such as listening to rock music, taking personal photographs, owning cameras or transistor radios, earning some pocket money, and wearing unorthodox attire. In recent years, teenagers have been allowed to adopt contemporary North American dating patterns. Peter (1987) suggests that this new practice has resulted in an increase in premarital pregnancies. However, there is no evidence to suggest that this has led to social ostracization of the teenage partners. Hutterite adults believe that as the young Hutterite weighs the value of these 'indulgences' against the full life of the Hutterite community, and as participation in the daily round of co-operative activities of the colony grows, the long-term satisfactions of colony life will far outweigh those of immediate self-gratification.

The other side of the coin of Hutterian distinctive enculturation, however, lies in the unpreparedness of Hutterian young people for life on the outside (Peter 1980a). Without more than a rudimentary education, without sophistication in the ways of urban living, and without the economic means to set up a home or business, Hutterites must carefully weigh a decision to leave colony life. For when a Hutterite withdraws or is expelled, the sect is under no legal obligation to offer any kind of recompense for his or her contribution (Flint 1975: 27).

Despite all of their ingenious and time-tested mechanisms for ensuring the continuing commitment of members over the generations and for ensuring the continuing distinctiveness and viability of the colonies, the ethnic status of the few thousand Hutterites within Canadian society is that of a small, isolated, and relatively powerless immigrant minority. Thus, the viability of the ethnic group is highly contingent on public, and especially provincial, tolerance. Because they insist on maintaining an isolated alternative way of life, and because they have grown in numbers and have prospered economically (more so than their neighbours) they tend to be regarded with suspicion. They are perceived as an unknown, mysterious, ethnic community, whose economic success poses a potential threat to neighbouring farmers. Sporadic outbreaks of public hostility towards Hutterites in Canada's Western provinces, have served as palpable, external boundary-maintaining mechanisms reinforcing the Hutterites' view of the evils of the outside world and indirectly increasing their ethnic community solidarity. Discrimination against Hutterites has also served as a constant reminder of their immigrant minority status in Canada. Hence, periodic violation of their minority rights has kept alive the option of leaving Canada and of migrating, once again, in search of a climate of national tolerance that would allow them to pursue their plain and peaceful life of religious commitment with a minimum of outside interference.

Addendum: A Visiting Hutterite's Observations of Eight Canadian Hutterite Communities

The main points of our analysis of the Hutterite community in Canada, presented in this case study, are supported by the observations of a member of a Hutterite community in the United States who visited eight Canadian Hutterite colonies in 1993. Don Murphy, a member of the Hutterite colony at Fan Lake, Washington, wrote a journal article describing his visit to eight Hutterite colonies in British Columbia in September of 1993. In his article, 'Way of the Lord', Murphy observed, 'It seems to me that these people probably are like the Hutterites were at the time of Jacob Hutter and Peter Reidemann—early head elders of the Hutterite church—circa 1535—very strong in faith and close to God' (Murphy 2001).

In this article, Murphy also made the following observations: He reported that the people in all the communities, except one, give 50 per cent of their income to the community. He stated that the people in all the communities have a covenant relationship with one another. They verbally agree to the covenant. They forbid men to wear beards but they allow women to wear jewellery and makeup. People must get permission from the elders of both communities before visiting another community. They also must get permission to go to town (even though they may be driving their own vehicles). Murphy noted that at least one of their leaders is in a remarriage situation (his spouse has been married before to someone who is still alive). This, he remarked, will be very difficult for them to face. There appears to be no central organization over the various communities, Murphy noted, and no name for their association, but they do have certain people in several ministries that they recognize as leaders for all the communities. Each community makes their own financial decisions. There does not seem to be much intercommunity financial activity. However, conventions are held several times a year where people gather together from the various communities to hear their intercommunity ministers preach. In closing, Murphy noted, 'They generally feel that they are part of a great move of God' (Murphy 2001).

Key Components of Ethnicity and their Relevance for Collective Rights Claims

Before we proceed to examine, in some detail, the relationship between ethnicity, ethnocultural distinctiveness, and collective rights claims, we will elaborate on the primary **components of ethnicity** that may be drawn upon in making collective rights claims. As indicated in Chapter 1, the concept of ethnicity refers to any arbitrary classification of human populations utilizing the biogeographical criterion of ancestry in conjunction with such sociocultural criteria as nationality, language, and religion. The most important criterion underlying the concept is that of common ancestry or ancestral origin. Common ancestry, in turn, is a multifaceted concept implying at least three criteria: biological descent from common ancestors; maintenance of a shared ancestral heritage (culture and social institutions); and attachment to an (actual or mythical) ancestral territory or homeland. These criteria provide the foundation for the (actual or assumed) distinctiveness of an ethnic category—a people classified as alike on the basis of ethnicity.

It is important to emphasize that all of the criteria used to identify specific components of ethnicity—whether by ethnic insiders or outsiders—are based on *actual* or *assumed* characteristics. The criterion of biological descent from common ancestors underlies physical distinctiveness. When this criterion of ethnicity is emphasized, we speak of a *racially defined* ethnic category. The criterion of attachment to an ancestral territory or homeland underlies distinctiveness deriving from national origin. When this criterion of ethnicity is emphasized, we speak of a *nationally defined* ethnic category. The criterion of maintenance of an ancestral heritage underlies sociocultural distinctiveness. When this criterion is emphasized, we speak of a *culturally defined* ethnic category. Frequently, the criterion of ancestral heritage emphasizes one sociocultural attribute such as language or religion. Thus, we speak of a *linguistically defined* or a *religiously defined* ethnic category, respectively.

Although these distinctions are useful in analysis, in reality a given ethnic category may be *socially constructed* on the basis of any one or any combination of these criteria in a given societal context. Moreover, because ethnicity is contingent on the prevailing social environment, criteria used for ethnic classification will vary with changing social conditions.

For example, the public preoccupation with race during the early years of Canada's development, when White Supremacy was a salient feature of public life and policy, led to the classification of Canada's so-called charter groups—the English and French—as the 'two founding races'. This scientifically invalid conception was found in government policy statements as recently as the 1960s, when the terms of reference of the Royal Commission on Bilingualism and Biculturalism were publicly announced (P.C. 1963: 1106). Yet, the most palpable feature of ethnicity underscoring the historical boundary between English and French was religion. Indeed, it was the Protestant/Catholic division between English and French, respectively, that became constitutionally recognized in section 93 of the British North America Act protecting minority (Protestant and Catholic) denominational schools.[1]

With the growth of the Franco-Quebecois independence movement, language has become the most prominent ethnic criterion behind French/English relations in Canada. The Official Languages Act (1969) accorded legal recognition to this distinction at the national level and the Charter (1982) constitutionally enshrined it.

Another example of changes in criteria for ethnic classification over time is provided in the case of the Jewish people. From the time of their dispersion from Palestine (circa AD 70) to the late nineteenth century, the bulk of the world's Jews lived within various countries of Europe where the Jewish minority was classified by insiders and outsiders as ethnically distinctive, primarily in terms of religion. It was not until 1873, when the racist ideology of anti-Semitism took root in Germany, that the Jews were classified by outsiders (Germans, and later, other Europeans), primarily in terms of biological criteria, as a distinct and inferior race.

The foregoing illustrations demonstrate that the particular components of ethnicity selected as criteria for the social construction of ethnicity, at the level of public policy and practice, may be highly arbitrary, and thus may vary with changing social conditions. Moreover, it is important to note that the defining ethnic criteria selected by outsiders in any given instance may or may not correspond with the criteria selected by insiders for purposes of ethnic self-identification. And, as Isajiw (1999: 20) has pointed out, many misunderstandings between ethnic groups derive from the fact that perceptions based on these differential criteria do not coincide.

To return briefly to examples previously cited; in the case of the Franco-Quebecois, the negative results of the (1980) Quebec Referendum, together with the results of several public opinion polls conducted prior to and following the Referendum, made it clear that the majority of Canadians, within and outside of the Province of Quebec, did not accept the Franco-Quebecois ethnic self-definition as a nation with the right to political independence. Alternatively, most Canadians continued to emphasize the language criterion of ethnicity and to define the French-identified population within and outside of Quebec as francophones.

A similar example is the case of contemporary Canadian Jews. Since the formation of the State of Israel in 1948, increasing numbers of Jews identify themselves as Jews primarily in terms of ancestral territory—Israeli nationality. The Canadian public, on the other hand, continues to ethnically classify Jews primarily in terms of religion (except for self-professed White Supremacists such as the Ku Klux Klan and the Western Guard that employ pernicious, racial criteria).

Ethnicity and Nationality

The above discussion raises an important point of distinction with regard to the concept of **nationality**. Both ethnicity and citizenship can provide bases for nationally defined sentiments and loyalties. As a criterion of ethnicity, the concept of nationality refers to the national, ancestral, and cultural origins associated with a particular ethnic ancestral territory or homeland. This multidimensional criterion of ethnicity underscores the political concept of nationhood. But ethnically defined nationality may or may not correspond to nationality based on *actual* country of birth or citizenship. Where the two concepts of nationality correspond, that is, where the ancestral homeland is coterminous with the territorial enclave occupied by the ethnic community—as in the case of Quebec for the Franco-Quebecois—the criterion of nationality may provide the ethnic rallying point for political mobilization geared toward national independence. On the other hand, where the two concepts provide separate and distinct national frames of reference—as in the case of Canada and Israel for Canadian Jews—each may serve as an important yet different criterion for self-identification. Torontonian Jews, for example, have been reported to be highly ethnically identified with Israel as their national, ancestral homeland and highly nationally identified with Canada as their country of birth or citizenship (Kallen 1977b; Richmond 1972; Taras and Weinfeld 1993).

Ethnicity and Collective Rights in Canada

The distinction between Canadian ethnocultural communities, with and without territorial bases for ethnic claims to nationhood within the state, has important human rights implications. While all Canadian ethnocultural communities can, justifiably, seek recognition of their collective linguistic, religious, and/or broader cultural group rights, only those communities with territorial bases for their ethnic claims, that is charter groups

Table 5-1 Human Diversity and Human Rights

Classification				**Basis of Human Rights Claims**
Species	Homo sapiens			*Universal/Individual*
Race (category)	Mongoloid	Caucasoid	Negroid	Individual and/or categorical
Ethnic origin group	e.g. Inuit/ Chinese	e.g. German/ Spanish	e.g. Jamaican/ Kenyan	Cultural and/or national group
Subethnic social category	Children Aged	Mentally/ Physically Disabled	Women Homosexuals	Individual and/or categorical

and aboriginal peoples, can, justifiably, seek recognition of their collective national group rights.

Another conceptual distinction Canadian ethnic communities with regard to their potential human rights claims is between **ethnic category** and **ethnic group.** Here, the relevant distinction is between arbitrary, artificial categories of classification, designed for analytic purposes (conceptual constructs) or designed for statistical ends (numerical constructs), on the one hand, and *sui generis* living communities, organized on an ethnic basis, on the other. Ethnic categories may be represented empirically by loosely connected, dispersed social aggregates (such as aboriginal peoples and blacks, in Canada) or by highly cohesive, closely knit ethnic groups such as Hutterites and Sikhs.

The Canadian 'Indian', as a socially constructed racial/ethnic category, did not exist prior to contact with Europeans. Members of various aboriginal peoples, such as Cree, Ojibway, and Iroquois, identified themselves and were categorized by other groups as Cree, Ojibway, and Iroquois, respectively. But to the European, and later the Euro-Canadian, anyone who 'looked Indian' was believed to be of common ancestry. On this basis, the category 'Indian' was socially constructed in racially defined terms, and all peoples lumped together in this category were treated as 'Indians'. Despite this arbitrary categorization as Indian by outsiders, insiders among the Cree, Ojibway, and Iroquois peoples continue to ethnically identify themselves as such.

Nevertheless, in the early days of the aboriginal independence movement, various aboriginal peoples subsumed under the arbitrary category 'Indian' began to rally around the Indian concept to mobilize significant numbers of members for political purposes. More recently, the constitutionalization of aboriginal issues and the burning question of defining aboriginal rights has led to a new, pan-ethnic self-definition of members of the Indian, Inuit, and Métis groupings as aboriginal peoples.

The foregoing lends credence to Barth's (1969:14–15) contention that, for purposes of self-ascription and ascription by others, it makes little or no difference whether ethnic criteria selected as the foci for one's ethnic identity are real or artificial; if one feels and says that one is Dene or Indian or First Nation or aboriginal, in contrast to Euro-Canadian, one is aligning oneself with one category of people, and simultaneously setting oneself apart from others.[2]

Ethnic Group and Ethnic Category: Implications for Group-based Human Rights Claims

The foregoing observations notwithstanding, the empirical distinction between ethnic group and ethnic category has important implications for the kinds of group-based human rights claims that can be made. The reader is referred, here, to the typology of rights outlined in Table I-1 in the Introduction.

Ethnic categories defined arbitrarily on the basis of race (Caucasoid/Negroid/Mongoloid or white/black/yellow) do not represent *sui generis* ethnocultural communities. Thus, members of these racial categories cannot make *collective cultural rights* claims. There is no Caucasoid or white ethnoculture. White culture is an essentially racist concept historically employed to refer to the allegedly superior characteristics of modern, Western, civilized, industrialized societies and cultures in contradistinction to the allegedly inferior characteristics of primitive, non-Western, uncivilized, non-industrialized (or underdeveloped) societies and cultures, racially categorized as Negroid and Mongoloid.

While these arbitrary racial categories should not be confused with *sui generis* ethnocultures, they do have important human rights implications. Members of such categories who have been disadvantaged by racial discrimination can make individual or group-based claims to redress against the adverse impact of systemic discrimination on the category as a whole. We have conceptualized such claims as *categorical* human rights claims.[3] To exemplify: blacks and aboriginal peoples in Canada—victims of the self-fulfilling prophecy of white racism—can make categorical human rights claims for redress against the adverse economic impact on their racial category of systemic discrimination. They cannot, however, use 'blackness' and 'aboriginality' as the basis for collective rights claims based on cultural or national group rights. Here, their claims must be ethnically specific, for example, Inuit of Nunavut claims to nationhood (national group rights) and Black Rastafarian claims to freedom of collective religious expression (cultural group rights).

A final conceptual distinction that has implications for the kinds of human rights claims that can be made by different Canadian ethnocultural communities is the distinction between those ethnic territorial claims based on charter group status and those based on aboriginal group status. Territorial claims based on charter group status, that is, the English outside of Quebec and the French in Quebec, are constitutionally based claims to nationhood within Canada by its founding peoples, because of their national group rights.

Territorial claims to nationhood within Canada based on aboriginal status, that is, the Indians, Inuit, and Métis peoples in Canada, represent (as yet) constitutionally unrecognized claims put forward on the basis of pre-colonial nationhood status and aboriginal rights.

Aboriginal Group Status: Aboriginal Rights and Nationhood Claims

A brief historical sketch of the relationship between aboriginal peoples and Euro-Canadian government agents in Canada will provide a background for understanding the kinds of collective human rights claims currently being put forward by spokespersons for various aboriginal organizations.

At the heart of the conflicting positions of aboriginal spokespersons and government authorities with regard to aboriginal peoples' land claims and demands for self-government are different and seemingly incompatible concepts of land. As currently articulated by aboriginal spokespersons, the integral link between people, land, and culture that informs the aboriginal worldview has provided one of the pivotal points of misunderstanding between Europeans and aboriginal peoples since they first came into contact.

Table 5-2 Categories of Human Rights Claims

Ethnic Classification	*Individual*	*Categorical*	*Cultural*	**Collective** *National*	*Aboriginal*
Racial category	●	●			
Immigrant ethnic group	●	●	●		
Charter ethnic group	●	●	●	●	
Aboriginal ethnic group	●	●	●	●	●
Subethnic social category	●	●			

The land and its resources, in the aboriginal view, are the sustainers of human life: people must, therefore, respect them and they must attempt to live in balance and harmony with their natural surroundings. From this view, one could no more own the land than one could own the rain clouds or the sunshine. Each people, that is each tribe, band, or community, is intimately associated with the land and resources within its own territorial boundaries, each people recognizes and respects the others' right to occupy and use their ancestral lands, and to transfer this right to their descendants. This view does not include the notion of *permanent alienation* of aboriginal lands through market sale or exchange. From the perspective of human rights, this means that as long as members of an aboriginal ethnic community occupy, use, and respect their ancestral lands, the lands their people have been intimately associated with 'from time immemorial', they have an *inalienable* collective, aboriginal right to the lands and their resources.

The aboriginal view of sovereignty is closely linked with their view of land. Advocates of the aboriginal view maintain that sovereignty is a gift of the Creator that has never been and can never be surrendered. As the concept 'First Nations' implies, prior to the arrival of European agents, aboriginal peoples were independent, self-governing nations whose members lived and sought their livelihoods within clearly delineated territories. With colonization, they claim, their right to sovereignty was unjustly abrogated and their institutions of self-government systematically dismantled. But, as nations, they assert their *inherent* right to sovereignty and their right to create and administer their own forms of self-government. From this aboriginal view, treaties made between aboriginal peoples and governments should be regarded as treaties between sovereign nations, in the sense of public international law (Frideres 1993: 416–17).

The European view of land ownership differs markedly from the aboriginal view of land occupancy and use articulated by aboriginal spokespersons today. For Europeans, land is a form of property that can be alienated through the market processes of purchase and sale. An individual or a group can buy, own, and sell land in the same way as one can buy, own, and sell other material goods available in the open market. To the European settler, Indian lands were desirable properties that could be purchased and cultivated. From the European view, the land and its resources were things quite distinct from the people occupying and using them; yet, racist ideas about the primitiveness of aboriginal peoples enabled Europeans to view both land and people as things to be exploited and controlled rather than respected.

The European view of nationhood is consistent with their view of land and their view of aboriginal peoples. There is no question that, prior to the arrival of Europeans, aboriginal peoples occupied and governed the land now called Canada. However, the Government of Canada has taken the position that aboriginal peoples were never nations *in the legal sense,* and have no right to be treated as such (Frideres 1993). In refutation of claims based on court decisions that support the aboriginal view, the government has cited the doctrine of continuity. This racist doctrine holds that, in the case of conquest or cession, the rights of 'civilized' indigenous peoples and their laws remain intact until the colonial government changes them through an Act of Parliament. If, however, the aboriginal inhabitants of the land are deemed 'uncivilized' at the time of European entry, the laws of the colonizers take immediate effect. The racist assumptions behind this doctrine have underscored court decisions used by governments to support their view that while agreements with aboriginal peoples (presumed to be 'uncivilized' at the time of contact) have been called treaties, they are not treaties between sovereign nations, in the sense of international law.

The Historical Background: Alienation of Aboriginal Lands/Extinguishment of Aboriginal Rights

Jackson (1979: 269–71) has suggested that the numerical superiority of the Canadian Indians in the early period of European-Indian Contact encouraged Europeans for practical, rather than for moral reasons, to recognize the right of these aboriginal peoples to their lands. Yet, the fact that aboriginal lands were acquired by negotiation and purchase for European settlement and cultivation clearly indicates European recognition that the lands belonged to the Indian peoples. In 1763, this recognition was legally entrenched in a Royal Proclamation that has since been referred to as the 'Magna Carta' of aboriginal rights.

Under this Proclamation, a large area of lands lying west of the Allegheny Mountains (excluding the Hudson Bay region) was reserved to Indians as their hunting grounds. The Proclamation set out procedures for the acquisition of Indian lands, specifying public negotiation and sale between Indians and representatives of the British Crown; private sales of Indian lands were disallowed.

Since then, a series of court cases involving First Nations claims based on aboriginal rights has led to an elaboration by Euro-Canadian legal authorities of a theory of aboriginal rights. In support of this view, Jackson (1979) asserts that (up to 1979) court decisions have held that the right of political sovereignty and legal ownership of land by the discovering country is subject to the aboriginal right of the aboriginal peoples to use and occupy those lands which have been theirs 'from time immemorial'. Second, these cases have confirmed the validity of the collective basis of aboriginal title by asserting that the interest of the aboriginal peoples is a communal one: it is an interest of the tribe or band and not of the individual member, and that interest can only be alienated to the Crown (that is, Canadian Parliament, today), not to private persons. Finally, the qualifications of aboriginal title have been specified. Aboriginal title can be extinguished by conquest, by purchase, or by Acts of Parliament that are inconsistent with the continuation of aboriginal rights.

Jackson goes on to argue that the Royal Proclamation of 1763 provided the legal foundation for the land cession treaties between Indian ethnic communities and the British Crown, which extinguished Indian interest to the largest and most resource-plentiful parts of Canada in the nineteenth and early twentieth centuries.[4] By means of these treaties, various Indian peoples exchanged their lands for monies, reserves, and other privileges.

Since the enactment of the Constitution Act, 1982, according recognition and protection, under section 35, for the existing aboriginal and treaty rights of the aboriginal peoples of Canada—the Indian, Inuit, and Métis peoples, there has been an increasing rejection by aboriginal spokespersons and their Euro-Canadian supporters of some of the key propositions in the foregoing theory of aboriginal right. In particular, opposition has been expressed to the idea that such rights can be extinguished or limited *without* the consent of aboriginal people. Sanders (1990: 128), in his analysis of the pathbreaking Supreme Court decision in *Sparrow* v. *The Queen* (June 1990), argues that the court adopted essential elements of the aboriginal position on section 35(1) by saying that laws passed by governments do not extinguish aboriginal rights unless the sovereign's intention to do so by way of the legislation has been made clear and plain, or unless the consent of the aboriginal people has been given.

Sanders (1990: 128) points out that there are almost no examples of legislation explicitly extinguishing aboriginal or treaty rights. The Supreme Court, then, has taken a position consistent with the aboriginal view that section 35 is a positive affirmation of aboriginal peoples' rights, not a confirmation of the legal *status quo*. The result, Sanders states, is that section 35 has rendered obsolete previous court decisions that upheld casual and unilateral extinguishment of aboriginal rights.

Current Status and Rights of Aboriginal Peoples

Jackson (1979: 269) points out that the question of who is an Indian is a complicated legal issue in Canada. Under the BNA Act section 91(24), the federal government has jurisdiction over Indians and lands reserved for Indians. However, the Supreme Court of Canada has ruled that the term *Indian*, as used under the BNA Act, includes 'Eskimos' (Inuit). Thus, aboriginal peoples, Inuit and Indians alike, are classified as Indians for the purposes of federal responsibility (see Re: Eskimos, 1939, S.C.R. 104).

Within this jurisdictional frame of reference, Parliament has enacted the Indian Act, which provides the legal basis for administration of Indian affairs. But the Indian Act applies to only one subcategory of aboriginal peoples: Status or Registered Indians is the sole category of aboriginal peoples legally defined as Indians under this Act. The Indian Act (4:1) specifically excludes 'Eskimos' from the broader, racially defined Indian category, and it also excludes those persons of Indian or part Indian ancestry who have lost their legal Indian status, that is, non-Status Indians and Métis.

Under the Indian Act (2:1g) 'Indian means a person who pursuant to this Act is registered as an Indian or is entitled to be registered as an Indian.' What these complex and confusing distinctions imply is that, for legal purposes, the constitutional category of 'Indian', that is, aboriginal peoples, is broken down, first, by so-called 'race', into the two racially distinct categories of Indian and Inuit; secondly, the racial category Indian is divided into two subcategories: Status or Registered Indians with legal Indian Status, and Non-Status Indians (including Métis) without legal Indian Status.

In Canada, there are approximately 1,604,000 constitutionally defined aboriginal persons (Frideres 1993: 31). Some 435,000 of these persons are Status Indians, legally defined as Indians under the Indian Act. Another 1,030,000 persons of Indian Ancestry do not have legal Indian Status, but, since changes were made to the provisions of the Indian Act (to be discussed in the pages to follow), some 10,000 non-registered Indians now have band membership. Some 104,000 persons of mixed (Indian/non-Indian) ancestry are categorized as Métis, and some 35,000 are categorized as Inuit.

Status or Registered Indians

Historically, legal Indian Status was acquired in two ways: through land cession treaty or through voluntary registration. These processes gave rise to a division within the legal category of Status Indians into two subcategories: Treaty and Non-Treaty Indians.

Treaty (Status) Indians are those Indians, and their descendants, who signed land cession treaties with the Crown, thereby surrendering huge tracts of aboriginal lands in return for reserves, gifts, and the promise of services. Non-Treaty (Status) Indians are those Indians, and their descendants, who chose legal Indian Status under the Indian Act, by having their names registered on Indian band lists.

A third means of acquiring legal Indian Status is through marriage. By marrying a Status Indian, a non-Indian female acquires legal Indian Status under the Indian Act; moreover, this legal Status is passed on to all descendants. However, until 1985, when the Indian Act was amended, the marriage provision did not apply equally to female Indians. Indeed, the converse was true: a Status Indian female who married any person other than a Status Indian lost her legal Indian Status and she, as well as her descendants, became Non-Status Indians.

To digress briefly, this aspect of the Indian Act formed the basis for legal contests in which Indian women, who had lost their Status by marrying out, argued that the section of the Indian Act in question discriminated against women. However, the Supreme Court found the Indian Act to be lawful, and ruled against the complainants (see *Attorney General of Canada* v. *Lavelle* and *Isaac* v. *Bedard*. Judgment of 1973 08 22, reported in Dominion Law Report 38 (3d) 1973.) Conversely, a decision in 1981 by the United Nations Human Rights Commission (in the *Lovelace case*) found that the Indian Act negatively discriminated against Indian women who marry out by denying them and their children access to their ethnic community and its culture. This persuaded the federal government to change the Act. In 1985, Bill C-31 (An Act to Amend the Indian Act) was introduced, and as a consequence of the removal of the Act's discriminatory provisions against women, thousands of Indian women have been reinstated as Status Indians. The repercussions of these changes on Indian reserve communities are discussed later in this chapter.

Every Status Indian is a Registered Indian, that is, a legally defined Indian whose name (with some exceptions) is registered on a particular band list and on the 'roll' in Ottawa (Frideres 1993). Until 1985, only these registered Status Indians were entitled to live on the Indian reserve on whose band list their name appeared.

In 1985, Bill C-31 (An Act to Amend the Indian Act) created new legislation that added new complexities to the definition of Indian status.[5] The bill also made changes in the rules regarding transmission of legal Indian status. Sexist provisions of the Indian Act denying Indian status to women who married out, and their children, were struck down and the concept of enfranchisement was abolished. In addition, under the provisions of Bill C-31, some persons who have lost their Indian status through marriage or enfranchisement may now reapply for legal Indian status. However, persons whose ancestors, more than one generation removed, lost their status are not eligible to reapply.

The new Act has introduced four types of Indian: 1) Status with band membership; 2) Status with no band membership; 3) Non-Status with band membership; and 4) Non-Status, Non-band. Applications for Indian Status are reviewed by the Department of Indian and Northern Affairs and government authorities determine whether the applicant has a legal right to claim Indian status. Band membership, on the other hand, is determined by the band council. The one exception to this rule is that the approximately 20,000 women who lost their legal Indian status through intermarriage automatically become band members if they are reinstated as Indians by federal authorities.

By 1989, nearly 67,000 Indians who had lost their legal Indian status had been reinstated

(Frideres 1993: 36). However, because acceptance into a band means that ofttimes scarce resources (such as housing) must be shared, many band councils have refused to accept reinstated Indians into their band membership lists.

Indian Ancestry: Non-Status Indians and Métis

Non-Status Indians are persons of Indian or part-Indian ancestry who do not have and are not entitled to acquire legal Indian status. Métis are persons of mixed ancestry who may ethnically identify as Métis, but who do not have and are not entitled to acquire legal Indian status. The non-Status (Indian Ancestry) and Métis subcategories comprise those Indians and their descendants who have renounced or lost their legal Indian status in one of several ways.

Until 1960, the only way Status Indians could assume the full individual human rights of Canadian citizens was through the process of *enfranchisement*. The particulars of this process were fairly specific in their intent: Indians gave up their special legal Indian Status and acquired the right to vote in federal elections, the right to purchase and consume alcohol, and other benefits accorded individual citizens. As legal Status Indians, they had been denied these privileges because they were not defined as persons before the law. Indeed, as stated in the original version of the Indian Act (1876): 'the term *person* means an individual other than an Indian.'

With the introduction of the Canadian Bill of Rights in 1960, the human rights notion of equality of all persons before the law was invoked by Indian leaders and, under pressure exerted by Indian organizations and sympathetic citizens' groups, the right to vote in federal elections (federal enfranchisement) was extended to Status Indians.

Historically, another way that Indian Status was lost was through the *loss of the right to live on a reserve*. Prior to 1985, under the terms of the Indian Act, a Status Indian was required to live on or maintain a residence on a reserve, to which he or she had to return for a specified period every three years. Legal Indian Status was forfeited if these conditions were not met.

For many Indian women, loss of legal Indian status occurred through *intermarriage*. As indicated earlier, until 1985, a Status Indian woman who married someone other than another Status Indian, lost her own legal Indian status, and that of her progeny.

Historically, *hereditary* loss of legal Indian Status also occurred under the provisions of various Indian Acts. Before 1985, under the provisions of the 1951 Act, persons twenty-one years of age or older, who were the descendants of Non-Status Indian parents, were not entitled to be legally registered as Indians.

Another way in which Indians could lose their legal Indian status was through *formal renunciation*. A Status Indian who renounced his or her legal Indian status received a share of the collective assets of the band to which he or she belonged and gave up the right to maintain a residence on a reserve. In this way, a Status Indian became a Non-Status Indian and an ordinary Canadian citizen before the law. The descendants of these Non-Status Indians were not entitled to claim legal Indian status.

Historically, some of the Métis people lost legal Indian status through 'taking scrip' or 'taking treaty'. This loss of entitlement applied specifically to the then legally defined category of Métis, who were the descendants of European fur traders, mainly French, and Indian women, mainly Cree.

The Métis people developed distinctive ethnocultural communities in Canada's West, and their demands for the recognition of their aboriginal rights, in the face of European expansion, sparked the famous Riel Rebellion of 1869. From 1870 until 1875, following the defeat of Riel, the federal government recognized the treaty and aboriginal rights of the Métis in order to facilitate settler expansion. The Métis were pressured to relinquish their aboriginal rights in one of two ways: they could take scrip, that is, cede their lands to the

Crown in exchange for sums of money or land allocations, together with medical and educational subsidies, in which case they would retain their Métis identity and Status; or they could take treaty and, through much the same process, acquire the legal Status of Treaty Indians. In 1940, the Indian Affairs Bureau of the federal government officially abandoned the concept of the special legal Status of the Métis people, and, since that time, the Métis have been administratively classified as Non-Status Indians. As a consequence of this arbitrary classification, the term *Métis* now refers to a particular category of persons of mixed Indian/European ancestry, rather than to a distinctive people with special legal Status.

However, Frideres (1993: 42–3) points out that some of the Métis currently are re-defining themselves as a distinct aboriginal ethnic group in Canada. (It also should be noted here that the Métis have gained constitutional recognition as a distinct category of aboriginal peoples, under section 35 of the Constitution Act [1982].) Frideres suggests that the term *Métis* has two different meanings today. Written with a small 'm', métis refers to the government-defined category discussed in the preceding paragraph (Pan-Métis). Written with a capital 'M', Métis refers to the self-defined Métis ethnic group, descendants of the historic Métis in Western Canada, whose members share a common cultural identity (Historical Métis). However defined, at present, members of the Métis category share one common denominator: loss of legal Indian Status.

Aboriginal Status, Aboriginal Rights, and Nationhood Claims

From the Indian view, the renunciation of legal Indian Status does not affect any potential claims that can be made on the basis of aboriginal rights. For as long as the aboriginal title of the band or tribe from which an Indian is descended has not been recognized and extinguished, the collective aboriginal rights of the group have not been abrogated.

Within the legal category of Status or Registered Indians, the difference between the subcategories of Treaty and Non-Treaty (Status or Registered) Indians has important implications for the question of claims based on aboriginal rights. In the case of Treaty Indians, the Crown has held that their aboriginal title has been recognized and extinguished through the process of signing land cession treaties. In the case of Non-Treaty Indians, whose ancestors did not sign land cession treaties, their aboriginal title has not been recognized or extinguished.

Those Non-Status Indians, Inuit, and Métis, whose ancestors did not sign land cession treaties or engage in other transactions with the Crown (for example, taking scrip) that would abrogate their aboriginal rights, can, like non-Treaty Indians, make collective land claims based on their aboriginal rights.

With regard to nationhood claims, the human rights perspective that informs this book clearly supports aboriginal claims to sovereignty based on aboriginal peoples' inherent right to government as Canada's 'First Nations'. To date, however, Canadian governments have refused to recognize this position. Although the Government of Canada recently has accepted the principle of an inherent aboriginal right to self-government, policy statements support only controlled forms of self-government and implicitly favour the delegated-municipal model, which ensures that ultimate decision-making remains a federal government prerogative (Frideres 1993: 5). To retain government control over aboriginal affairs, and to safeguard aboriginal acceptance of Euro-Canadian values, aboriginal proposals for alternative forms of government rooted in aboriginal values and embodied in political forms consistent with these values invariably have been rejected.

The Relationship between Ethnicity and Human Rights Claims

The preceding analysis of the relationship between ethnicity and human rights in Canada demonstrates that differences in ethnic status, as well as differences between arbitrary categories of ethnic classification and *sui generis* ethnocultural groups, have important implications for the kinds of human rights that can be claimed by different ethnocultural communities.

Conclusion

The first part of this chapter gave a conceptual scheme to aid in understanding the dynamics of intraethnic and interethnic relations. Adopting this conceptual framework, we saw how ethnic communities manipulate ethnicity so as to maintain their cultural distinctiveness and separateness—how members of ethnic communities create social psychological and structural boundaries designed to keep ethnic insiders in, and ethnic outsiders out. Insofar as stringent boundaries are developed and sustained, our analysis demonstrated that the almost inevitable result is the maintenance of a high level of social distance between ethnic communities, the perpetuation of negative racist prejudices and stereotypes of outsiders and the fostering of ethnic antagonisms. Notwithstanding the importance of boundary maintenance for the preservation of ethnocultural distinctiveness of minority communities, our analysis has demonstrated that it is the racist barriers created by majority boundaries that violate minority rights and lead to collective claims for redress.

In the second part of this chapter, we examined the relationship among ethnicity, ethnocultural distinctiveness, and collective rights claims in Canada. Our analysis demonstrated how alleged violations of the various *components* of ethnicity—language, cultural integrity, religion, territory—are drawn upon to shape the nature of minority rights claims put forward in Canada by representatives of three categories—Franco-Quebecois, immigrants, and aboriginal peoples.

Chapter 6 will demonstrate how majority-imposed, racist barriers not only thwart upward mobility of racial and ethnic minorities, but also impede the processes of *ethnic integration* or incorporation of minorities within mainstream Canadian society. Our analysis will show how racist ideologies—institutionalized through public policy and practice—serve to prevent the realization of the Canadian democratic ideal of ethnic equality and national unity.

Key Concepts

- boundary-maintaining mechanisms
- components of ethnicity
- double boundary (external and internal)
- ethnic boundary
- ethnic category
- ethnic group
- nationality
- the new ethnicity
- the old ethnicity
- social distance

Critical Thinking Questions

1. Distinguish between the concepts of the old ethnicity and the new ethnicity. How does this distinction help us understand ethnic group continuity, despite increasing cultural similarities between ethnic groups in contact?
2. It has been argued that every ethnic group possesses a double boundary—internal and external. Accordingly, no ethnic group can be completely understood without its relationship to other ethnic groups. Discuss.

3. Distinguish among the various components of ethnicity and demonstrate how they give rise to different kinds of collective rights claims.
4. How does the conceptual distinction between ethnic group and ethnic category affect the nature of human rights claims that can be raised?
5. Discuss the relationship between ethnicity and nationality. Under what circumstances does nationality give rise to nationhood claims?

CHAPTER 6

Ethnic Integration and Human Rights: Models and Government Policies of Incorporation of Immigrant and Aboriginal Minorities

Introduction

Chapter 5 discussed how members of both majority and minority ethnic communities create social psychological and structural boundaries designed to keep ethnic insiders in, and ethnic outsiders out. Notwithstanding the importance of ethnic-boundary maintenance by minority communities in preserving ethnocultural distinctiveness, our analysis has clearly demonstrated that it is the racist barriers imposed by *majority* boundaries that violate minority rights and lead to collective claims for redress. Our analysis also revealed how alleged violations of the various *components* of ethnicity—language, cultural integrity, religion, territory—are drawn on to shape the nature of minority rights claims put forward in Canada by representatives of three categories—Franco-Quebecois, immigrants, and aboriginal peoples.

This chapter will demonstrate how violations of minority rights through *institutionalized racism* not only block upward mobility of racial and ethnic minorities, but also hamper the processes of *ethnic integration* or incorporation of minorities within mainstream Canadian society. It will delineate some of the major assumptions behind the Canadian democratic paradigm of ethnic equality and national unity, and it will attempt to account for the empirical gap between the egalitarian myth of Canadian democracy and the reality of Canada's institutionalized structure of ethnic inequality. In particular, our analysis will show how majority techniques of domination—institutionalized forms of racist discrimination—serve to prevent the realization of the egalitarian Canadian democratic ideal.

Processes of Ethnic Integration

The concept of **ethnic integration** in this book, as in its (1982 and 1995) predecessors, refers in a holistic sense to the entire set of social processes whereby continuing interaction among members of different ethnic groups within a society leads to changes in the cultural content, structural form, and ethnic identities of those individuals or groups. As an outcome of this process, some participants may become self-identified, accepted, and socially recognized as full-fledged members of an ethnic group or a society other than the one into which they were born or raised.

In an ethnically diverse, post-technological society such as Canada's, ethnic integration may be conceptualized and analyzed in terms of four interrelated sets of social processes. First, members of different ethnic communities come to learn and absorb a common set of cultural values, skills, and lifeways—mainstream (dominant) societal-wide attributes that constitute the cultural prerequisites for effective participation in the public sphere of society at large. Second, they come to participate in the secondary institutions (economic, political, legal, and educational) of society at large by attaining recognized social positions at various levels or ranks of the societal-wide hierarchy. Third, by continuous interaction in public life with ethnic outsiders, they come to learn and absorb some of the distinctive cultural attributes of mainstream society. Fourth, insofar as they come to participate in the private sphere of primary ethnic institutions (religious, friendship and kinship, familial, and marital) of an ethnic community other than their own, they may eventually shift their membership from their own community to another ethnic community.

The first two sets of processes of ethnic integration involve the *secondary* integration of members of different ethnic communities into the public sphere, that is, into the secondary institutions of society at large. The third and fourth sets of processes involve *primary* integration into the private sphere, that is, into the primary institutions of another ethnic community.

Theoretically speaking, all processes of integration are two-way processes whereby members of different ethnic communities interact, exchange views, learn new values and lifestyles, acquire new skills, participate in new institutions, and acquire new reference and membership groups. As a consequence of this ongoing two-way exchange, changes occur in the culture and social institutions of society at large and in the ethnocultures and institutions of the different, interacting ethnic groups. These changes, in turn, impact upon ethnicity and generate shifts in both ethnocultural and national loyalties and identities among society's members.

In reality, in an established ethnically stratified society like Canada's, processes of secondary ethnic integration tend to be largely unidirectional; access to positions of political, economic, and social power is limited and controlled by established majority ethnic elites. Moreover, the culture and form of public institutions largely represent the historical outgrowths of the ethnocultures and institutions of the dominant ethnic groups. In short, in an ethnically stratified society, the particular patterns of ethnic integration that emerge are fashioned largely by the degree of accessibility of various ethnic communities to societal opportunities and institutions controlled by dominant ethnic elites. It is in this context that barriers posed by *institutionalized racism* can present formidable obstacles to the incorporation of ethnic minorities—especially visible minorities, perceived to differ most markedly from majority norms—into mainstream Canadian society.

Processes of Ethnic Integration: Key Variables

In both public and private spheres of life, ethnic integration involves two kinds of social processes—cultural exchange and institutional participation. These will be referred to as **cultural integration** or **acculturation**, and as **structural integration** or **assimilation**, respectively.

Cultural Integration/Acculturation

The concept of *acculturation* or cultural integration, in its broadest sense, refers to the process whereby selected objects, ideas, customs, skills, behaviour patterns, and values are exchanged among different ethnic communities. In this process, each population acquires from the other new cultural attributes that may eventually be absorbed into its own system. Viewed as part of a general learning process, acculturation refers to the process of learning those cultural ways of an ethnic community to which one does not belong, in much the same way as the concept **enculturation** or distinctive *ethnic socialization* refers to the broad process of learning the cultural patterns of the ethnic community to which one does belong.

Within an established system of ethnic stratification, the prime direction of change in the process of acculturation in the public sphere is toward the norms, values, and patterns of the majority/mainstream society. Most members of ethnic communities seek to learn the dominant language and cultural patterns in order to participate in public institutions and to improve their socioeconomic position and life chances. Thus, for example, immigrants to Quebec prior to the passage of Bill 101, which made French the official public language in the province, tended to learn English in order to gain entrance to public life. Since the passage of Bill 101—and with its later reinforcement by Bill 178, Quebec's French-only sign law—new immigrants were more inclined to learn French.

Acculturation, in the direction of majority societal values, refers not only to the acquisition of the dominant cultural attributes, but also to the attainment of a level of proficiency in utilizing these attributes, necessary for effective participation in the public institutions of the society at large. Hence, the degree of acculturation of a particular individual or ethnic community can be measured in terms of the degree of acquisition of cultural attributes, and the degree of proficiency in utilizing these acquired cultural attributes, commensurate with that of people socialized from birth or early childhood into that ethnoculture or society. To return to the French language example, full linguistic acculturation would necessitate that the speaker lose any trace of a foreign accent and become as fluent in speaking French as her or his francophone counterparts.

Structural Integration/Assimilation

In its broadest sense, the concept *assimilation* or structural integration refers to the social processes whereby relations among members of different ethnic communities result in the participation of these individuals in ethnocultural institutions other than those of the ethnic community to which they belong. For analytical purposes, structural integration can be broken down into three broad subprocesses:

1. *Secondary Structural Integration in Relation to Social Mobility*

The degree of structural integration of individuals and/or ethnic communities can be measured in terms of their degree of participation in the major secondary institutions (that is, economic, political legal, and educational) of the society. Secondary structural integration is commonly confused with the concept of social mobility because, in practice, the two social processes to which they refer are frequently linked. However, the two concepts relate to different social phenomena and should be distinguished for analytic purposes.

Secondary structural integration refers to the overall extent of social participation regardless of the rank of the social position attained in public life. It can therefore be measured horizontally in terms of *proportionate representation*, that is, statistical measures of positional attainment by various social categories and/or members thereof, in relative proportion to their actual population size in the society, in the available range of social positions within the different sectors of public life.

Social mobility, on the other hand, refers to the extent of vertical movement between the ranks in a socially stratified society. It can therefore be measured vertically in terms of proportionate representation of various social categories, and/or members thereof, in the rank order of social positions at various status levels in society.

What this distinction implies is that an ethnic community, or an individual member thereof, can be highly structurally integrated within a stratified society at low levels of the social hierarchy, that is, without achieving marked degrees of upward social mobility. This point is illustrated by the observation that many members of majority ethnic groups in Canada participate in public life at low positional levels, while, at the same time, the ethnic category as a whole is overrepresented at the topmost ranks.

Alternatively, an individual or ethnic community cannot achieve high degrees of upward social mobility (that is, attain top-ranking positions) in a stratified society like Canada's without a high degree of cultural and structural integration. Demonstrated skills in the use of valued societal-wide cultural attributes and social acceptance in high-ranking membership groups are both necessary prerequisites for the attainment of elite status (Clement 1975; Porter 1965).

Phrased in terms of the human rights concepts in the Introduction, we can say that, to the degree that the fundamental right of equality of opportunity is honoured in Canadian society, it opens the door for Canada's citizens to participate in public life. However, it does not guarantee upward mobility through the ranks. To obtain high-level societal positions and the advantages associated with them requires the acquisition of prestige—social power demonstrated by accorded respect—which derives from the possession of valued cultural attributes over and above those basic skills required for entrance into the system.

Moreover, it is here that the empirical reality of the Canadian ethnic hierarchy diverges sharply from the national, egalitarian ethos of equality of opportunity. For as Porter, Clement, and others have shown, it is in the area of prestige evaluation that ascribed characteristics, like race, ethnicity, religion, family, and social-class background become crucial criteria for social acceptance and high positional ranking.

To the degree that ethnic minorities have been denied respect, their fundamental human right to dignity has been violated and they have thereby become invalidated. Inferiorized and stigmatized minority communities, regardless of their economic and/or political attainments tend not to be accorded equivalent prestige recognition in all but the most exceptional, individual cases. The continuing inability of ethnic minorities, especially racially defined minorities, to penetrate the ranks of Canada's uppermost corporate elites despite their increasing upward mobility in the political and economic spheres, speaks to this important point.

2. *Primary Structural Integration*

The degree of *primary structural integration* of individuals and/or ethnic communities can be measured in terms of their degree of participation in the private ethnic institutions (that is, religious, social, and recreational institutions; friendship and kinship networks; family and marital alliances) of an ethnic community other than their own. The ultimate step in the process of primary structural integration—*reproductive integration*—awaits the offspring of interethnic marriage. Reproductive integration occurs when the progeny of the partners of an interethnic marriage become integrated either into one of the parental ethnic communities or into a community of ethnic hybrids, like themselves (for example, Métis in Canada; Eurasian in Asia; Cape Coloured in Africa). The reader should note that although *ethnic hybridization* is the natural, biocultural result of interethnic mating, it does not necessarily lead to primary structural integration. Only when the progeny of ethnic hybrids marry and become integrated into a particular ethnic community can primary structural integration ensue.

3. *Identificational Integration*

Identificational integration is a function of both cultural and structural integration. The concept of **identificational integration** refers to the process whereby an ethnic community other than one's own comes to provide one's primary source of expressive/symbolic ties and roots, and also becomes one's primary reference group.

The social scientific concept of **reference group** refers to that social category whose cultural standards provide the normative guidelines for one's behaviour and whose core values provide the ethical and status criteria used to evaluate and rank oneself and others. The reference group need not be the actual group to which one belongs. For example, an aspiring, would-be member of the English elite may use this social category as a behavioural referent, even though he or she belongs to a working-class Italian family.

Identificational integration is a subjective, experiential phenomenon that can best be assessed by attitudinal indicators. For the individual, it can be measured in terms of the extent to which one thinks, feels, and acts in relation to an outside ethnic referent, and the degree to which one's sense of group identity is transferred from one's own ethnic community to another.

In the public sphere of society at large, *secondary* identificational integration can be measured in terms of the degree to which one's national/citizenship ties and loyalties come to supersede or replace one's ethnic or national/

ancestral alignments. In the private sphere of interacting ethnic communities, *primary* identificational integration can be measured in terms of the degree to which one's primary ties, loyalties, social alignments, and commitments have been transferred from one's original ethnic community to another ethnic community.

Integration, Ethnicity, and Ethnic Identity

Profiles

The following excerpts from *The Immigrants* by Montero are drawn from the experiences of Canadian immigrants. The quotations illustrate the conceptual analysis that follows.

Carmen, an immigrant from Spain:

> I didn't speak any English. . . . I realized that I had to learn English and applied for government-sponsored classes . . . in the classes you are taught to love the country. . . . But the moment . . . you get involved in Canadian life [outside of school] things change. . . . The people you bump into at your workplace or your neighbours . . . very often discriminate against you because of the colour of your skin or because they don't like your accent. . . . You realize this isn't the multicultural Canada you were taught about (Montero 1977: 38–41).

Ida, an Italian married to a Euro-Canadian:

> I was born in Italy. . . . I later went to England where I met my husband, a Canadian, and I came to Canada with him. . . . I love Italy. I like the spirit of the people. But I love Canada, too. It took me a while to get used to it (ibid.: 85)

Glenna, a Chinese high school student:

> My mom brought me up to date Chinese boys . . . if I were to marry another colour, she'd disown me . . . this Chinese girl went by [our house] with a black guy. My grandmother said, 'Look at that, she's out with a black boy. If I ever see you doing anything like that I'll kill you.' If some Hong Kong guy sees a Chinese girl going out with a white guy . . . [they] call us bananas. They say we're yellow on the outside and white on the inside (ibid.: 186–7).

Emmy, an Austrian married to a Ukrainian-Dutch farmer:

> Only 46 years ago I was born and 16 of them now I have been in Canada. . . . I had learnt some English [before coming to Canada] but still it did not exactly prepare me for the strangeness of the accents I heard when I reached Calgary . . . [it] was very difficult for me. . . . [I married a farmer of mixed Ukrainian and Dutch parentage and we have two adopted sons.] . . . We are a family. A Canadian family. This is my country now. There is no doubt of it at all (ibid.: 21–3; excerpts reprinted by permission of James Lorimer and Company).

Conceptual Analysis

Processes of cultural integration and secondary structural integration in the public sphere of society at large do not require a significant shift in ethnic identity or ethnic membership for members of ethnic communities. Although acquisition of new reference groups and entrance into new membership groups are inevitable concomitants of ethnic integration, these new referents and social institutions may be political, legal, economic, occupational, or educational rather than ethnic. As the profile of Ida illustrates, one may acquire a variety of new reference and membership groups without necessarily abandoning old ones and without any significant dislocation in one's ethnic reference or membership group.

Alternatively, primary structural integration is predicated on the occurrence of some degree of shift in one's ethnic reference group. Primary structural integration requires that social distance between the interacting ethnic communities be minimized and that interethnic relationships become more intimate and personalized. When this happens, ethnic group boundaries weaken; subjective indicators of ethnicity lose salience;

identification of ethnic outsiders as potential insiders is facilitated; and a major shift in ethnic reference group orientation may occur. The testimonies of Ida and Emmy demonstrate different degrees of identificational integration—partial, in the case of Ida, and virtually total, with regard to self-definition, for Emmy.

A radical shift in ethnic reference group orientation may result in one being an insider in terms of continued membership in one's original ethnic community, but an outsider in primary reference group orientation. This shift in ethnic reference group requires a shift in ethnic self-definition. However, for a change in ethnic membership group to occur, an alteration in both self- and other-definitions of ethnicity is required; one must identify one's self and be identified by others as a member of the aspired to ethnic community. Glenna's profile provides an excellent illustration. 'Bananas' may identify themselves as white, but they are identified by others as yellow. And it is this other-definition that provides the barrier to ethnic integration.

For *full integration* in the primary sphere to occur, aspiring members must be accorded the status of insiders by members of the aspired-to community. This means that ethnic outsiders aspiring to gain membership in another ethnic community must ultimately be deemed suitable as potential marital partners and as *bona fide* members of the group.

As stated earlier, an interethnic marriage does not necessarily lead to the full primary integration of either partner. Where the marriage takes place within a broader familial or community context of cultural and/or religious conflicts, the outcome, for one or both partners, may be one of sociocultural *marginality*. In this situation, one or both partners may harbour a deep-seated feeling of ambivalence towards, or alienation from, both ethnic communities. On the other hand, the partners may seek a new synthesis, without total disavowal for either ethnic tradition. The histories of Ida and Emmy illustrate this latter pattern. Both women came to Canada as immigrants and both married men of different ethnic backgrounds from their own. While Emmy's self-identity is clearly more fully Canadian than Ida's, neither woman (from the full account of their stories) has totally disavowed her own ethnic tradition.

Is Full Integration Possible?

In diachronic perspective, even the ultimate step in primary integration, that is, reproductive integration, does not categorically ensure loss of their original ethnic identities by the offspring of interethnic marriages. The classic anthropological view that a culture must be transmitted over at least three generations before it becomes a 'genuine' ethnoculture may provide an appropriate analogy here: hypothetically, the progeny of interethnic marriages only cease to identify significantly with the separate ancestral heritages of their forebears after a transitional period of at least three generations.

But what happens when future generations of mixed ancestry are singled out by powerful outsiders as racially blemished because of one strain in their ethnic heritage? The example of fully assimilated Jews in Nazi Germany is instructive here. Among the persons identified by Hitler's SS agents as 'Jewish' were many individuals of Jewish and part-Jewish ancestry, but of Protestant persuasion, whose families for at least three generations had identified themselves and been identified by society at large as German Protestants. Nevertheless, these 'Jewish' individuals were subjected to the same programs of internment, torture, and extermination as were self-professed Jews. And many of these fully assimilated Jews who survived the horrors of Nazi concentration camps have re-affirmed their Jewish identity in the strongest terms.

Assumptions behind the Concept of Total Integration

The foregoing discussion reveals that the rhetoric of total integration is rarely realized at the level of reality. Insofar as societies are socially stratified along *ethnic* lines, barriers to full integration are posed by boundary-maintaining mechanisms employed by both majority and minority ethnic communities.

Total integration in the process of cultural integration (acculturation) requires changes in the cultures, reference groups, and ethnic identities of the members of the interacting ethnic communities. At both the individual and collective levels, full acculturation assumes that members of ethnic communities are willing and able to acquire outsiders' cultural attributes, and that there are no barriers of individual, institutional, structural, or cultural discrimination that prevent them from so doing.

Regarding the process of secondary structural integration (secondary assimilation), total integration requires changes in the secondary institutions, membership groups, and group identities of members of interacting ethnic communities.

The degree of acculturation of members of ethnic communities has an important bearing on the question of their potential for secondary assimilation. For it is through acculturation that members of different ethnic communities acquire the societal-wide language(s), skills, and qualifications required for proportionate representation in the major secondary institutions of the society. But total acculturation is not coterminous with, nor does it ensure, total secondary assimilation. At both the individual and collective levels, total secondary assimilation assumes that members of ethnic communities are willing and able to participate effectively in the secondary institutions of society at large, and that there are no barriers of individual, institutional, structural, or cultural discrimination that prevent them from so doing.

Total integration in the process of primary structural integration (primary assimilation) requires changes in the primary institutions and informal networks, ethnic identities, and ethnic membership groups of the members of interacting ethnic communities. At both the individual and collective levels, total primary assimilation assumes that members of ethnic communities are willing and able to shift their ethnic alignments and allegiances from their ethnic origin group to another ethnic group, and that there are no barriers of individual, institutional, structural, or cultural discrimination that prevent them from so doing.

As indicated throughout this discussion, implicit in the notion of total integration are two assumptions: the willingness and ability of members of ethnic communities to interact with outsiders and to engage in a mutual process of cultural exchange and institutional participation; and the absence of barriers posed by individual, institutional, and systemic forms of discrimination that impede integration. The empirical observation that these two assumptions are not, characteristically, built into the reality of interethnic relations renders the practical application of the theoretical concept of total integration problematic.

With regard to majority/minority ethnic relations, in the context of an ethnically stratified society such as Canada's, minority ethnic boundary-maintaining mechanisms, together with continuing, majority violations of the political, economic, social, and cultural rights of ethnic minorities present formidable barriers to total integration.

Differential Outcomes of a One-Way and a Two-Way Process of Ethnic Integration

Theoretical Propositions

In theory, the social processes involved in ethnic integration are two-way processes of cultural exchange and institutional participation. This observation notwithstanding, the direction of ethnic integration in any given empirical instance is a variable influenced by the relative strength of push-and-pull forces impacting on each of the interacting ethnic communities. Should each of the ethnic communities be relatively equal in expressive and/or instrumental strength, then ethnic integration will be a two-way process.

However, should the ethnic communities be unequal in strength, then the process of ethnic integration will be unidirectional favouring the stronger ethnic community.

Hypothetically, the outcome of a two-way process of ethnic integration could take two forms: 1) the *fusion* of the original ethnic communities and the creation of a new, ethnically homogeneous society (**amalgamation** or **melting pot**); and 2) the retention and *federation* of the original ethnic communities and the creation of an ethnically heterogeneous, multiethnic, multicultural society (**cultural pluralism** or **mosaic**).

Hypothetically, the outcome of a one-way process of ethnic integration could take two forms: 1) the *absorption* of the weaker ethnic community by the stronger one, and the creation of an ethnically homogeneous society modelled on the characteristics of the (original) stronger ethnic community (**dominant conformity** or **absorption**); and 2) the institutionalized and/or coerced *suppression* of the weaker ethnic community by the stronger one, and the creation of a castelike society dominated and controlled by the stronger ethnic community (**paternalism/colonialism**).

The Reality of Minority Ethnic Integration in Canada: Barriers and their Human Rights Implications

In reality, societal-wide processes of integration within Canada's ethnic hierarchy are limited and controlled by the dominant ethnic elite(s) through a broad range of techniques of domination. These institutionalized forms of racism, detailed in Chapter 4, enable dominant elites to restrict and/or exclude minorities from full and equal participation in the major dominant institutions, thereby securing their own superordinate status in the societal hierarchy and ensuring their continuing political, economic, legal, social, and cultural hegemony in the society.

Barriers to secondary structural integration violate the fundamental human rights of ethnic minorities by restricting or denying their access to political, economic, and social power in the society. Alternatively, barriers to primary structural integration do not, directly, violate human rights, as all ethnic groups have the internationally recognized right to maintain their group distinctiveness. Yet, in Canadian society, the primary ethnic networks of the dominant elite overlap public and private institutional spheres (Kelner 1969). Thus, exclusion of ethnic minorities from these primary relationships indirectly restricts their social mobility by denying them access to powerful contacts and connections at high positional levels (Clement 1975; Porter 1965).

Barriers to primary integration are also self-imposed by minority ethnic communities; but minority ethnic closure devices lack both the power and the scope to impact upon societal-wide opportunities. Membership in elite social clubs within the minority ethnic community, for example, does not generally provide the kinds of social contacts and connections necessary for entry into the elite positions of public life.

To summarize: Processes of ethnic integration within an ethnically stratified society are limited and controlled by various boundary-maintaining mechanisms—restrictive ideologies, policies, and practices—imposed by both majority and minority ethnic groups. However, it is the barriers arbitrarily imposed by majority powers that restrict minority opportunities in public life. Accordingly, these are the barriers that violate the fundamental human right of all citizens to equality of opportunity for participation in public life. And it is these majority barriers that present formidable obstacles to upward social mobility for ethnic minorities, thus impeding their attainment of the prestige and advantages associated with the top-ranking social positions.

Models of Ethnic Integration: The Accommodation of Ethnic Diversity within Society

To account for this gap between the rhetoric and the reality of ethnic integration, we must give serious attention to the dominant ideologies and models of ethnic integration that have been employed to underscore and legitimate public policy, legislation, and practice.

In North America, scholarly attention has focused on four models of integration.[1] These models, referred to earlier as outcomes of ethnic integration processes, include: melting pot (amalgamation), cultural pluralism (mosaic), dominant conformity (absorption), and paternalism/colonialism. Each of these models contains somewhat different assumptions about the nature of ethnic integration processes, and about the kind of society predicated upon them or resulting from them. It is important to remember that these conceptual constructs do not exactly correspond with the empirical picture of ethnic integration within any society, at any given time; nor do they exhaust the range of conceptual possibilities. Moreover, the model emphasized in public policies and government legislation in a given society may be discarded, under changing social conditions, for another. In addition, the model implicit in majority policy and practice as well as the response of minorities to it may vary from one ethnic community to another, from one region to another, and/or from one time period to another.

'Models of' and 'Models for' Reality

The term *model* has two senses—an 'of' sense and a 'for' sense. In the first (inductive) sense a model is a schematic representation of reality, based on empirical observation. It purports to explain how the reality it represents really works. In this sense, a model of ethnic integration is a conceptual scheme derived from repeated observations of many societal realities and elaborating on the basic principles behind these realities. In the second (deductive) sense, a model is a prescriptive plan or blueprint for reality, based on valued ideals. It purports to represent the ideal version of reality and to show how it can be attained. In this sense, a model of ethnic integration is a social doctrine that provides guidelines for the attainment of an ideal mode of accommodation of ethnic diversity within society. The four models of ethnic integration to be presented in this chapter have been considered both 'models of' and 'models for' social reality in the Canadian context.

Melting Pot and Mosaic: Twentieth-Century North American Myths

The Level of Reality

In contemporary parlance, the melting pot and mosaic models of ethnic integration have come to assume the status of national myths in the United States and Canada, respectively. But on neither side of the Canadian/American border have these essentially egalitarian ideals ever closely represented societal reality. That is to say, neither in Canada nor in the United States have all citizens been accorded full equality of opportunity with full human dignity regardless of ethnic classification.

In the United States, for example, blacks, originally racially defined as Negroes, were never expected to 'melt'. Under the racist laws governing slavery, they were defined and treated as subhuman 'chattels'—things to be bought and sold in the marketplace. It follows that a society need not accord full human rights to populations defined as less than human. Similarly, in both Canada and the United States, aboriginal peoples were not included under the *ethnic* (a term erroneously reserved for immigrants) rubric because they were not deemed fully 'educable' and 'assimilable'.

In reality, the concept of ethnic integration was, from the beginning, a racially and culturally exclusive notion: it was restricted in application to those immigrants whose physical, linguistic, cultural, and behavioural characteristics were considered congruent, or similar enough, to deem them meltable or compatible. Accordingly, when immigration laws were relaxed so as to admit racially visible minorities, both countries were faced with severe problems of ethnic integration.

Table 6-1 Assumptions behind Models of Ethnic Integration in North American Meritocracies

Variables	Melting Pot (Amalgamation)	Mosaic (Cultural Pluralism)	Dominant Conformity (Absorption)	Paternalism (Colonialism)
1. Societal goal: (ethnicity and nationality)	one nation/ one people/ one culture	one nation/ many peoples/ many cultures	one nation/ one people/ one culture (dominant)	one dominant nation/ people/culture subordinated minorities
2. Symmetry/asymmetry of political, economic, and social power	symmetric (all populations relatively equal)	symmetric	asymmetric (dominant population is superordinate)	asymmetric (dominant population monopolizes power)
3. Ethnocentrism (and) willingness/ability to maintain/shed ethnocultural distinctiveness	low ethnocentrism, willing and able to shed distinctiveness (*all* populations)	high ethnocentrism, willing and able to maintain distinctiveness (*all* populations)	*dominant*— high ethnocentrism, willing and able to maintain distinctiveness *minority*— low ethnocentrism, willing and able to shed distinctiveness	*dominant*— high ethnocentrism, willing and able to maintain distinctiveness *minority*— low ethnocentrism, but unable to shed distinctiveness (racial/ascribed)
4. Levels of prejudice and discrimination	non-discriminatory; low or absent prejudice	prejudice and discrimination not institutionalized; moderate or low (tolerance possible)	institutional and cultural discrimination; level of prejudice and discrimination: *dominant*—high (intolerant); *minority*—low (willing to conform to majority norms)	institutional, cultural, and structural discrimination; level of prejudice and discrimination: *dominant*—high (intolerant); *minority*— stigmatized permanently

Table 6-1 (continued)

Variables	Melting Pot (Amalgamation)	Mosaic (Cultural Pluralism)	Dominant Conformity (Absorption)	Paternalism (Colonialism)
5. Critical for social mobility	achieved	achieved	achieved and ascribed	*dominant*— achieved *within* dominant stratum *minority*—ascribed status is permanent: no mobility possible
6. Spheres of ethnocultural distinctiveness	none	—variable; *public* (political, economic, and/or linguistic pluralism) *private* (multiculturalism) *territorial* (nationalism)	*dominant*— public and private: *minority*— acculturation required	*dominant*— public and private *minority*— deculturation promoted/partial acculturation required
7. Collective identity	national identity (de-ethnicized)	hyphenated-identity (ethnic-national)	national identity = dominant ethnic identity	*dominant* – national entity = dominant ethnic identity *minority*—negative valence of marginal identity
8. Human rights	individual human rights	individual and collective rights (collective, cultural and collective, national)	individual rights of minorities predicated on dominant conformity; collective rights of dominant group entrenched at societal-wide level	*dominant*—individual and collective rights *minority*—no human rights, systemic violation of rights

Democracy and Human Rights: Canadian and American 'Models For' Reality

Both the melting pot and the mosaic ideologies are rooted in some common, liberal, North American assumptions about democracy. Canada and the United States share the same democratic ideal of an open class society in which all citizens are accorded equal, individual human rights and equal opportunities for the acquisition of cultural skills, for societal participation, and for social mobility within the public sector. The North American ideal of democracy is predicated on the competitive, economic notion of free enterprise, which emphasizes the value of individual achievement. This means that, in public life, each person should be evaluated and rewarded *as an individual* for his or her *demonstrated qualifications and skills,* and without reference to ethnic or other group membership. Another assumption built into the democratic ideal is that of a **meritocracy,** that is, a stratified social order in which the various social positions are unequally ranked and rewarded on the basis of their socially recognized value to society at a given time.

At the level of societal reality, should the meritocracy truly be based only on individual achievement, given the ubiquitous range in skills, abilities, motivations, and interests among members of every human population, it would follow that members of the country's various ethnic communities should be proportionately represented, according to their numbers in the society, at *all* status levels throughout the ranks of the social hierarchy. Put another way, should the fundamental political, economic, and social rights of all citizens be fully and equally respected, some members of every ethnic community will merit greater social rewards and gain greater advantages than others, in recognition of their superior achievements. Accordingly, individuals, rather than social groups, will acquire greater or lesser access to political, economic, and social power as the rewards of achieved higher social position.

In short, the North American democratic ideal is egalitarian with regard to the distribution of *opportunity* but it is elitist in terms of the distribution of social rewards. This distinction is an important one, because such a meritocracy can only be democratic in practice if all citizens are given equal opportunity to acquire the values, skills, and qualifications that would enable them to compete for valued social positions in all spheres of public life and to achieve upward social mobility within the ranks of the meritocracy.

While Canada and the United States share this common democratic ideal, prevailing ideologies of ethnic integration north and south of the border have diverged markedly at times. Canadians, for at least the first half of the twentieth century, tended to picture Canada as a mosaic in contrast to the alleged American melting pot. Ideally, as 'models for' reality, both the melting pot and mosaic are egalitarian blueprints designed to create national unity and ethnic equality in a multiethnic, democratic society. Where they differ is in their *cultural* goals: the melting pot is designed to create 'unity in homogeneity' while the mosaic is designed to create 'unity in heterogeneity'.

The Melting Pot: Assumptions behind the Amalgamation Model

The melting pot concept achieved public approbation in the United States with the instantaneous success of Israel Zangwill's Broadway play *The Melting Pot*, first performed in 1908. The play focused on the total integration of a Jewish immigrant, who happily abandoned the yoke of persecution historically associated with his minority ethnic status in Europe in the hopes of becoming a one-hundred-per-cent (de-ethnicized) American citizen. In conceptual terms, the goal of this American melting pot dream was a society comprised of one people/one nation/one culture—a society in which national unity was predicated on a goal of ethnic homogeneity.

As a *model for reality* the melting pot ideology assumes first and foremost that members of all ethnocultural communities are able and willing to abandon their ethnically distinctive characteristics. Therefore, the distinctive characteristics must be similar enough or at least congruent enough to be 'meltable'. Moreover, the degree of ethnocentrism must be fairly low as all cultural contributions to the 'pot' must be equally valued. Second, the melting pot model assumes at least a rough equivalence in degrees of power between ethnic communities, so that no one group can easily become dominant. Third, it assumes a virtual absence of prejudice and discrimination; members of all ethnic communities are expected to interact freely and equally, without social barriers of any kind, in both the public and private sectors of their lives. Given these assumptions, the ongoing processes of social participation, the formation of friendships across ethnic lines, and the eventual mating and marriage between members of the various ethnic communities should lead to a total merging and blending of peoples and cultures. Over time, a new ethnic entity should be created—a new, biologically and culturally homogeneous society in which all traces of former ethnic cultures, institutions, and identities have disappeared. In this new society, members' national and ethnic identities would be coterminous. Citizenship and social mobility in the new society would be based solely on individual qualities and achievements. This ideal is predicated on equal recognition of the fundamental political, economic, and social rights of all individual citizens in the society. It leaves no place, however, for the recognition of the collective (cultural or national) rights of the various ethnic communities contributing to the societal melting pot.

The Level of Reality

In the United States, the melting pot ideology has been a popular myth that has never corresponded to or even approximated social reality. Scholars generally agree, however, that at the level of interaction between specific ethnocultural groups, it has been more typical of interethnic relations between European groups in the United States, than in Canada.

In the nineteenth century, a unique, historical melting pot outcome was the development of distinctive ethnic communities of Métis on what is now Canada's Western prairies (Sawchuck 1978; Sealey and Lussier 1975). Then, Métis were legally defined as a people of mixed ethnicity, the descendants of European fur traders, mainly French, and Indian women, mainly Cree. At this time in the Red River area of what is now Manitoba, the Métis constituted a distinct ethnocultural and political community—a 'new nation' that, for a short-lived period, could successfully assert political and legal rights against the national government (Daniels 1979b: 7). The political autonomy of the Red River Métis was shattered with their defeat in the Riel-led rebellion of 1869. From 1870 to 1930, government authorities tried to eradicate Métis claims to aboriginal rights; in 1940, erroneously convinced that they had succeeded, federal officials abolished the special legal status of the Métis people. However, over the past decade or so, Métis organizations have been attempting to reclaim a distinct status for descendants of the Métis people as 'First Nations', under Canada's Constitution.

The Mosaic: Assumptions behind the Cultural Pluralism Model

Despite popular belief, the concept of cultural pluralism is not a uniquely Canadian phenomenon; nor does it clearly differentiate Canadian from American thinking about models of ethnic integration. Indeed, the first spokesperson for cultural pluralism was the American philosopher, Horace Kallen. Writing in 1915, Kallen pictured the ideal American civilization as a multiplicity in a unity—an orchestration of mankind based on the cooperative harmonies of European civilization, without the elements of poverty and persecution.[2] However, this approach, which favoured retention of ethnic distinctiveness, met with widespread criticism. Early in the twentieth century, the melting pot ideology, while never enshrined as policy, was clearly favoured as the most appropriate image for an America bent on shedding its multiethnicity.

In contrast, the concept of cultural pluralism in Canada represents a fairly recent outgrowth of the historical ideal of cultural dualism—the original paradigm legitimating the constitutional separation and guarantees underlying English/Protestant hegemony outside Quebec and French/Catholic hegemony within the Province of Quebec. Early in the twentieth century, with the arrival of large numbers of non-English and non-French immigrants, the myth of cultural dualism began to lose popularity, and, by the third and fourth decades the mosaic myth was increasingly lauded in the speeches of politicians and other dignitaries (Burnet 1981: 29).

However, while the mosaic and melting pot myths flourished in the rhetoric of public life in Canada and the United States, respectively, public policy continued to be governed by the concept of dominant (Anglo) conformity. In Canada, the assumption was that immigrants would assimilate to the British institutional and cultural model, which included the English language and the Protestant religion. It was not until the early decades following World War II that the mosaic rhetoric took on serious multicultural policy implications.

The blooming of the mosaic myth eventuated with the negative reaction of immigrant ethnic minorities to the reports of the Royal Commission on Bilingualism and Biculturalism, in the late 1960s. However, the abridged version of the mosaic myth legitimated through the federal government policy of multiculturalism in 1971, deviated markedly from the original ideal. The multicultural policy and the Act (1988) that put the policy into a statutory framework will be discussed later in this chapter. At this juncture, we will examine the theoretical assumptions behind the mosaic/cultural pluralism ideal.

As a model for reality, the mosaic ideology is predicated on a national goal of one nation/many peoples/many cultures, assuming that members of all ethnic communities are able and willing to maintain their ethnocultural distinctiveness. The implications of this assumption are manifold. First, it implies that all ethnic groups are willing to adopt a laissez-faire stance toward other ethnic groups, whose values and lifeways differ markedly from their own. The second implication is that levels of prejudice and discrimination between ethnic communities are low enough to allow mutual tolerance. Third, it assumes a rough equivalence in the distribution of power, so that no one ethnic community can assume dominance and control. Finally, it implies mutual agreement among members of various ethnic communities to limit and control the extent, spheres, and nature of their interaction. Thus, processes of acculturation and assimilation will be mutually restricted by operation of boundary-maintaining mechanisms sustained by each of the interacting ethnic units.

Given these assumptions, interethnic relations within the mosaic society would take the form of ethnic segmentation (Breton 1978). Each ethnic community would be institutionally complete, and ethnocultural distinctiveness would be maintained through separate ethnic institutions. As an outcome of this cultural and structural pluralism, every citizen's identity would become hyphenated, that is, ethnic-national, with equal weights on both sides of the hyphen. With regard to human rights, the society would recognize both the individual human rights of all its citizens and the collective cultural rights of all its ethnic communities. Given the basic assumption of equality of opportunity built into the notion of a meritocracy, the social position attained by individuals within a mosaic (as within a melting pot) society would be based on individual talents, capabilities, and skills on the one hand, and their assigned societal value on the other. Ethnicity would not be a criterion for personal evaluation or for positional attainment in public life. It would, however, provide the recognized basis for collective rights, in that all ethnic communities would be guaranteed the freedom to express their religious, linguistic, and cultural distinctiveness.

The most important variable in the operation of this model is the relative weights assigned to unity and diversity. The importance of ethnic diversity is reflected in the spheres in which collective rights may be guaranteed. Should the mosaic take the form of pluralism in the public sector, then ethnocultural rights could be guaranteed through political representation, economic control in specified area(s), recognition of linguistic rights, and, in its most extreme form, territorial autonomy. This latter form of pluralism supports nationhood based on geographical separation of ethnic communities sharing language, culture, and territory. If viable for all ethnic groups, it could lead to multi-nationhood—a multinational society within a common political administrative framework—in which the national group rights of all ethnic communities would be recognized.

While variants of the multi-nationhood model have been adopted in several European countries, it was not seriously considered in North America, until very recently. Currently, some scholars have re-conceptualized this model to apply in the analysis of new nationalist movements in North America. Walzer (Kymlicka 1995) and Glazer (ibid.), for example, have re-conceptualized this extreme form of pluralism as the *corporatist model* and the *group rights model*, respectively.

Historically in Canada, however, cultural pluralism was never conceptualized by dominant authorities in *nationhood* terms for populations other than the English and French charter groups. Rather, the mosaic model relegated cultural and structural pluralism for ethnic minorities to the private sphere of life: within the public sector, all *individuals* would be accorded equal opportunities *without* reference to ethnic classification. Glazer (Kymlicka 1995) and Walzer (ibid.) have conceptualized this modification of the cultural pluralism paradigm as the *non-discrimination model*. In Canada, this privatization of minority cultural rights has meant that in the public sector, only the collective rights of the majority groups are recognized. The public sphere was envisaged, from the outset, as an Anglo- or Franco-Canadian cultural monolith; thus, attainment of social positions within secondary institutions would be predicated on acculturation of all minorities to prevailing Anglo or Franco norms and practices. It is this abridged version of the mosaic model that has informed Canada's multicultural policy over the years, and which is still reflected in Canada's Multiculturalism Act (1988).

In order to understand how Canada's particular version of the mosaic ideology came into being, in the following pages we will present a brief historical overview of the development of multiculturalism in Canada.

From Cultural Dualism to Multiculturalism: The Historical Background of the Canadian Mosaic Ideology

As a national ideology of ethnic integration, multiculturalism represents a fairly recent outgrowth of the constitutionally entrenched ideal of cultural dualism.[3] The ideal of Canada as a bilingual and bicultural society has its roots in the confederation pact between Canada's two 'founding partners'—English Protestants and French Catholics. It was not until the late 1960s that the ideal of multiculturalism took on serious policy implications. Until this time, government policy was predicated on the ideal of dominant conformity or absorption. It was assumed that all ethnic minorities would willingly abandon their 'inferior' cultural baggage—their traditional language, religion, and customs—in favour of the 'superior', dominant-Canadian model. Most immigrants to Canada were expected to conform to the dominant English-Protestant model, because historically, immigration was a primary concern only of English Canada. (French Canada's population growth was ensured by a continuing high rate of natural increase). Few immigrants chose to reside in Quebec, and those who did tended to assimilate to the English-Protestant rather than to the French-Catholic cultural milieu within the province.

Over the decades, from the period of massive early twentieth-century immigration through the post–World War II period, public support for multiculturalism among immigrant ethnic groups grew. In response, a new 'Canadian mosaic' ideal was increasingly lauded in speeches by politicians and other dignitaries. But, as conceptualized by these dominant authorities, the mosaic version of multiculturalism digressed radically from the egalitarian, cultural pluralism ideal, because it totally *privatized* the cultural claims of minority ethnic groups. The right of non-English and non-French ethnic groups to freely express their cultural distinctiveness was relegated to the private sphere only. Public institutions, it was assumed, would continue to be predicated on the established model of cultural dualism. For ethnic minorities, then, opportunities for advancement in public life would continue to be predicated on dominant conformity—required linguistic and cultural assimilation to entrenched, Anglo, or Franco majority norms.

My argument here is that *even as an ideal* multiculturalism in Canada did not replace dominant conformity as a blueprint for ethnic integration. It was just an addendum to the principal national agenda that continued to endorse the entrenchment only of the linguistic and (broader) cultural rights of Canada's founding partners throughout public life.

During the 1960s 'Quiet Revolution' in Quebec, French Quebecers began to collectively express their discontent with their subordinate status as 'founding peoples', relative to the English, within Canada *and* within Quebec. They began to voice strong demands for equality of political and economic power with the English, under threat of separation from the Canadian federal state. The federal government's response to French-Quebec's demands was the creation of a Royal Commission with a mandate to inquire into and report on the state of bilingualism and biculturalism in Canada.

The impetus for Canada's multicultural policy lay in the negative response of non-English and non-French immigrant ethnic minorities to the mandate and the recommendations of the Royal Commission on Bilingualism and Biculturalism (the Bi and Bi Commission). The reports of the Bi and Bi Commission supported policy changes designed to entrench a Canada-wide policy based on an ideal of cultural dualism, that is, institutionalized English/French bilingualism and biculturalism across Canada. Spokespersons for a Third Force of immigrant ethnic minorities (a growing population sector already representing more than a quarter of Canada's total population at the time) adamantly rejected the bi and bi model. They argued that it was an elitist model that reinforced the established dominant ethnic status of English- and French-speaking Canadians and relegated non-English and non-French Canadians to the status of second-class citizens in Canada. Immigrant demands for cultural equality and for an equitable distribution of power across all ethnic groups escalated. In response, the government extended the mandate of the Royal Commission and, in 1969, it produced Book 4 of its reports, focusing on the 'other' ethnic groups.[4] This report contained 16 recommendations, which, if implemented, would have necessitated a federal government policy of multilingualism and multiculturalism. However, the federal government rejected the argument behind the report's recommendations, namely, that language and culture are indivisible. The federal government dismissed the notion that multiculturalism necessitates multilingualism and proposed that the multicultural policy be implemented within a bilingual framework.

Multiculturalism as Public Policy in Canada

Prime Minister Trudeau emphasized the fact that, under the terms of the new multicultural policy, the preservation of cultural distinctiveness and of ethnic ties and identities, by individuals or by groups, was to be a *voluntary* and *private* matter. In public life, all individuals were to be free to participate as Canadians without regard to ethnic or other group classification.[5]

The government's policy statement on multiculturalism set forth four objectives: 1) to provide resources for the cultural development of those groups that demonstrate a desire to maintain a distinctive culture and a need for assistance in doing so; 2) to assist all Canadians to overcome cultural barriers to full participation in Canadian society; 3) to promote creative intercultural exchange among groups in order to foster national unity; and 4) to assist immigrants to acquire at least one official language (English or French) in order to become full participants in Canadian society.

The cultural priorities of the federal government are clearly revealed in this fourfold package of multicultural policy objectives. Only one of the stated objectives (1) affords any basis of support for minority cultural diversity. Two objectives (2 and 3) are clearly designed to foster national unity. The final objective (4) supports the central cultural aim of the policy, namely, the preservation of majority (English and French) linguistic/cultural dualism in public life.

Trudeau's announcement of the multicultural policy sparked vociferous debate among scholars and concerned citizens alike. The disagreement among the policy's supporters and its opponents sustained heated public controversy about multiculturalism for more than a decade. In the following analysis, we will offer only a gist of the lines of contention in the early multicultural policy debate.

With regard to the first policy objective (support for cultural diversity), there was a clear line of division in both academic and public opinion. Those who expressed support for this objective tended to support Trudeau's argument that ethnicity serves to meet an individual's expressive needs for emotional security and support. Maintenance of ties to distinctive ethnic communities and cultures, it was argued, provides an important sense of group belongingness and identity necessary in order to counteract the impersonal and alienating environmental influences of a post-technological workaday world. Notwithstanding this symbolic dimension of ethnicity, opponents contended that maintenance of distinctive cultural values impedes upward mobility in a society predicated on dominant conformity in public life. Moreover, they argued, preservation of cultural differences impedes the development of national unity (Brotz 1980; Porter 1979b).

The first policy objective also was attacked by opponents who rejected the government's shallow interpretation of the concept of 'culture', as reflected in the nature of early programs of implementation. Critics argued that multicultural programs fostered the conception of Canada as a kind of 'ethnic zoo' (Brotz 1980) where the function of the zookeeper was to accumulate ethnic exotica and to exhibit them publicly once a year. For example, critics pointed to government-funded ethnic festivals, where the audience could sample ethnic tidbits such as wonton soup, pizza, Madras curry, kosher pastrami, and the like. In a similar vein, critics pointed to government-funded programs focusing on traditional, artistic expressions of ethnicity (what Alan Anderson [personal communication] called the 'just keep dancing' version of multiculturalism). The focus of criticism, here, was on the backward view of ethnoculture as museum culture. Critics argued that this view of multiculturalism nourished stereotypes of minority ethnic groups as strange upholders of quaint customs. At the same time, it denied them support for language, religion, and other institutions essential to their living ethnocultures.

In Michael Hudson's view (1987: 64), the multicultural policy's failure to address the linkage between culture and language and its favouring of bilingualism 'created a major lacuna in the government's response to the "Third Force"'. By neglecting non-official languages, he argued, early multicultural programs 'denied an essential element of self-identification for many ethnic groups'.

In response to expressed minority ethnic dissatisfaction with the linguistic focus of early multicultural programs on French/English bilingualism, and the cultural focus on folk art and museum culture, multicultural programs were expanded to offer limited support for private, non-official language schools as key institutions of 'living' ethnocultures. Since 1973, the policy has supported heritage language teaching in private schools through the Cultural Enrichment Program, but the funding for this endeavour has been minuscule in comparison to that afforded French- and English-language education (Hudson 1987: 68). Moreover, ethnic minority representatives continued to argue that failure to provide support for maintenance of language and culture in public institutions—in primary and secondary schools, community colleges and universities, and in public broadcasting and other media—perpetuates the minority status of non-English/non-French immigrant ethnic groups (Burnet 1981: 31). For the most part, even today, provincially supported heritage language programs are offered outside of the public school system. However, in several Canadian provinces, especially Alberta, Manitoba, and Saskatchewan, acceptance of the principle of multiculturalism has led to the inclusion of a number of ethnic languages into public secondary school teaching programs. In addition, directly or indirectly, the federal multicultural policy also has stimulated the development of other programs and the establishment of agencies and institutions, for example, a multicultural television channel (MTV) in Toronto, ethnic programs on Public Access Network across Canada, and the production of ethnic books and films (Isajiw 1999).

The most biting criticism of the first multicultural policy objective was raised by opponents who argued that the emphasis on culture deflected attention from inequalities in political and economic power across ethnic groups, and did nothing to improve opportunities for empowerment of immigrant ethnic minorities. Taking this line of argument a step further, a number of social scientists suggested that the multiculturalism/bilingualism policy represented the government's attempt to 'appease and contain' the conflicting empowerment demands of immigrant minorities on the one hand, and of French Quebecers on the other. To contain the political and economic demands of both, the government made some concessions to their cultural demands. To appease the immigrants, the government offered some support for the maintenance of minority ethnocultures, in the private sphere. To appease the French Quebecers, it offered nationwide bilingualism. Through this strategy of appeasement and containment, the policy was designed to ensure the continuation of English dominance and control in Canada at the national level (Peter 1981).

It should be noted here that this entire argument took place outside the realm of aboriginal peoples' concerns, for aboriginal peoples' demands focused on their special status and rights that were not addressed in the multicultural policy. Indeed, aboriginal peoples did not want to be 'lumped together' with immigrants as ethnic minorities under the multicultural policy, because they feared that this would jeopardize their claims for special status and their aboriginal and treaty rights.

To return to the debate over the objectives of the multicultural policy, the second and third policy objectives, designed to reduce cultural discrimination and to foster national unity, were accorded virtually unanimous scholarly and public support. In keeping with these objectives, the government provided support for scholarly research through limited funding given—for example, to the Canadian Ethnic Studies Association and the Canadian Heritage Languages Institute. Also, by 1996, to promote the study of Canadian diversity, 30 ethnic chairs had been established at various universities throughout the country (Isajiw 1999). However, critics have continued to point out that these policy objectives have not been adequately funded or implemented.

Another source of criticism relating to these objectives emerged early on from representatives of Canada's growing population of visible minorities. Spokespersons for groups such as Chinese, West Indians, and South Asians argued that early multicultural programs did not place enough emphasis on eliminating *racial* discrimination. In this connection it is important to note that it was not until 1981—10 years after the policy of multiculturalism was established—that the government finally responded to the escalating demands of visible minorities for anti-racism (rather than cultural retention) programs. In this year, a race relations unit was instituted within the Multiculturalism Directorate, and a national program to combat racism was inaugurated. Over the ensuing decades, critics have asserted that the anti-racism initiatives increasingly emphasized under the policy have failed to halt the escalation of anti-white prejudice and discrimination across Canada. Moreover, some critics have argued that the state, through its funding of multicultural and anti-racism activities, is able to officially define program priorities, and thus to exercise fiscal control over ethnic organizations (Li 1990: 14–15). In response to these varied criticisms, in 1996, by a special Act of the federal Parliament, a new government agency, the Canadian Race Relations Foundation (CRRF), was established to deal more directly with issues of racial discrimination and inequalities (Isajiw 1999).

The fourth and last multiculturalism objective (bilingualism) proved to be the most contentious aspect of the entire policy. Multiculturalism within a bilingual framework simply did not seem to make sense to anyone. In the view of critics, even today, the only viable options are bi and bi or multi and multi. Supporters of the egalitarian multiculturalism ideal argue for multilingualism and multiculturalism (Lupul 1982). Supporters of the elitist ideal of English/French cultural dualism argue for bilingualism and biculturalism (Rocher 1976). It is important to note, however, that supporters of multilingualism and multiculturalism are not making demands for minority language guarantees equal to those afforded the English and French majorities. Spokespersons for immigrant ethnic groups are asking for *non-official language* rights. Thus, the privileged position of Canada's two official languages is not challenged by minority demands.

Summary: The Canadian Mosaic and Multiculturalism Policy

From its inception, the federal government policy of multiculturalism did not gain the unqualified approval of Canadian scholars or Canadian ethnic communities. Assessed in terms of the prerequisites of the egalitarian multicultural model, the policy continues to fall far short of the ideal. Although it affords symbolic endorsement for immigrant ethnocultures, it provides no *concrete guarantees of support* for ethnic institutions such as language and religion vital to the maintenance of distinctive, living ethnocultures. With regard to immigrant group demands for political, economic, and social equality within Canada, the policy is silent. Accordingly, by both commission and omission, Canada's multicultural policy perpetuates the 'vertical Canadian mosaic'. It reconfirms the superordinate ethnic status of Canada's two 'founding' partners and it relegates later immigrant groups to the inferior status of ethnic minorities. This observation has been clearly substantiated by the marked priority in government funding accorded 'official languages' over multicultural programs.

On the positive side, critics have pointed out that, despite its serious shortcomings, the multicultural policy has given immigrant ethnic minorities a legitimate basis for making claims on public policy and public funds. Indeed, it was in response to the vigorous, organized lobbying efforts of immigrant ethnic minorities that the Government established the Cultural Enrichment Program, giving support for heritage language teaching (Hudson 1987: 68). More recently, in response to continued ethnic lobbying, in 1988,

Canada became the first country in the world to adopt a national Multiculturalism Act.

Legislated Multiculturalism: The Canadian Multiculturalism Act (1988)

By the mid-1980s, it was obvious to all concerned that the 1971 multicultural policy was dated. In response, the Canadian government appointed commissions to assess the policy in light of submissions from ethnic minorities and to provide recommendations for improvement. The recommendations submitted to the government addressed the major criticisms of the multicultural policy over the years and provided a substantive blueprint for a new, egalitarian Canadian mosaic (Canada 1984a). Unfortunately, but certainly not surprisingly, the response of the federal government was to protect established ethnic priorities. The government legislated a Multiculturalism Act (Canada 1987a; enacted 12 July 1988) that perpetuated the old government strategy of giving in to unthreatening cultural demands to appease and contain the more threatening demands of immigrant groups for equal economic, political, and social opportunities within Canada.

Notwithstanding these critical comments, there are some positive features of Canada's Multiculturalism Act. First, the Act recognizes multiculturalism as a *fundamental characteristic* of the Canadian heritage. Also, unlike the original multiculturalism policy, the Act includes reference to *racial* as well as cultural equality and includes reference to *non*-official as well as official languages. It also includes mention of aboriginal peoples. In a word, the rhetoric of the Act, unlike that of the original policy, suggests that it applies to all Canada's ethnic groups. Again, unlike the original policy, the Act supports measures designed to achieve the *equality* of all Canadians in the economic, social, cultural, and political life of Canada. Thus, the Act can be seen to reflect Charter-endorsed equality rights (under section 15), as well as multicultural rights (under section 27). Most importantly, the Multiculturalism Act provides a *legal* basis for minority ethnic claims at the federal level, and, like other federal legislation, it has served as a model for parallel legislation and/or policies by particular provinces (Alberta, Saskatchewan, Manitoba, Quebec, and Ontario).

During the late eighties and into the nineties, a new critique of Canada's federal and provincial multicultural policies surfaced, now coming from the majority ethnic groups in Canada (Isajiw 1999). Kymlicka (1997) suggests that these policies are now under attack, perhaps more so today than at any time since 1971. The debate has heated up lately, in part because of two recent critiques of the multiculturalism policy: Neil Bissoondath's *Selling Illusions: The Cult of Multiculturalism in Canada* and Richard Gwyn's *Nationalism Without Walls: The Unbearable Lightness of Being Canadian*. Both make very similar claims about the results of the policy. In particular, both argue that multiculturalism has promoted a form of ethnic separatism amongst immigrants. Kymlicka points out that neither of these authors provide any empirical evidence to support their claims.[6] Nevertheless, for a majority audience predisposed to endorse their views, this matters little.

The vociferous attack on multicultural policies voiced by majority critics both in English Canada and in Quebec, indicate that the original policy objectives—and particularly, the retention of diverse ethnicities which it encourages—presents a symbolic threat to the majority's cultural hegemony in Canada. This, Isajiw suggests, can explain the pressures coming from the majority mainstream to discontinue the policy or to revise its priorities so that serves only the goal of facilitating immigrant adaptation to mainstream Canadian society (1999: 251).

In the early 1980s, the annual budget for administration of the multicultural policy was about $30 million. By 1996, it had been reduced to about $17 million. Pressure was exerted on the administrators of the policy by majority ethnic groups to undertake a re-evaluation of its goals, and, in particular, to curtail all grants to ethnic community organizations—grants that had been the backbone of the policy in the past. In response, in the spring of 1997, Multiculturalism Canada issued its new statement of priorities. The statement and the program guidelines (Canadian Heritage 1997) focused on three main goals: identity, civic participation, and social justice. As will be seen, none of the goals offers support for the maintenance of distinctive, living ethnocultural communities. The goal of identity supports recognition of ethnic diversity, but does so with the idea of developing a 'sense of belonging and attachment to Canada'. The goal of civic participation places a stronger emphasis than did the original policy on the development of common community, involving diverse ethnic groups in joint, cooperative ventures. The goal of social justice emphasizes equity among all groups, with the elimination of racism as a necessary prerequisite. However, the program excludes from support the regular annual meetings of an ethnic organization or association, festivals, camps, religious activities, celebrations of foreign national days, regular vehicles of ethnic communication (newspapers, radio, and TV programs, etc.) and several other activities (Canadian Heritage 1997; quoted in Isajiw 1999: 248). Once again, it appears, *dominant conformity*, now poorly camouflaged in the guise of multiculturalism, has been endorsed by Canada's ethnic majority groups.

At this juncture, it is perhaps appropriate that we shift the focus of our analysis to an examination of the dominant conformity model of ethnic integration.

Dominant Conformity: Assumptions behind the Absorption Model

When we contrast the dominant conformity model with the model of cultural diversity (multiculturalism), we find that the two models reflect alternative cultural visions of Canada and Canadian identities: an elitist vision of one nation/two cultures (English- and French-Canadian) as opposed to an egalitarian vision of one nation/many cultures (ethnic-Canadian). Although multiculturalism is predicated on the achievement of national unity through the fostering of respect for cultural diversity, dominant conformity is predicated on the achievement of national unity through the cultural absorption of all ethnic groups to one of the two dominant groups (Anglo- or Franco-conformity).

The dominant conformity model of ethnic integration provides the underlying rhetoric that, historically, has legitimated both Canada's immigration policies and its policies directed toward the integration of immigrants in Canada. The concept of dominant conformity assumes an existing system of ethnic stratification predicated on a highly ethnocentric stance of the established dominant ethnic elites. Majority/minority relations are structured on the assumption of the inherent superiority of established dominant peoples, ethnocultures, and institutions over all others. Given this premise, dominant conformity as a model of ethnic integration posits a total one-way process of acculturation and assimilation whereby all newcomers abandon their (alleged inferior) original ethnocultures, institutions, and identities in favour of the (alleged superior) societal and ethnic model posited by the established dominant group.[7]

Like the melting pot model, the dominant conformity model is built on a societal goal of unity in homogeneity, that is, one nation/one people/one culture. But, unlike the egalitarian melting pot that envisages a 'new nation' created from the equal contributions of all its original ethnic components (a two-way process of acculturation and assimilation), the dominant conformity model is asymmetric and unidirectional: it envisages the absorption of all newcomers through one-way processes of integration to the dominant blueprint.

Early in this century, the dominant conformity model was rationalized, at least in part, through direct reference to the alleged failure of the American melting pot. R.B. Bennett, for example, used this tactic to support his argument that Canadians must endeavour

> to maintain our civilization at that high standard which has made the British civilization the test by which all other civilized nations in modern times are measured. . . . We desire to assimilate those whom we bring to this country to that civilization . . . rather than assimilate our civilization to theirs (Canada 1928: 3925–7).

In a similar vein, but in even stronger words, J.W. Sparling warned that the massive waves of immigrants to Canada from the (alleged backward) non-Protestant countries of southern and eastern Europe posed a national danger. Thus, he cautioned:

> Either we must educate and elevate the incoming multitudes or they will drag us and our children down to a lower level. We must see to it that the civilization and ideals of Southeastern Europe are not transplanted to and perpetuated in our virgin soil (Woodsworth 1972).

As a model for reality, the dominant conformity ideology assumes, firstly, that the established dominant ethnoculture and institutional framework is inherently superior to that of newcomers; and secondly, that all newcomers will realize and appreciate the superiority of established dominant ways and will be both willing and able to shed their inferior ethnocultures, institutions, and identities in favour of the dominant model. These assumptions, in turn, are predicated on the existence of a significant political, economic, and social power differential that enables the dominant group to require conformity to its language, religion, laws, ethical standards, rules of etiquette, and customs. In conceptual terms, this means that the model of dominant conformity is predicated on highly institutionalized forms of cultural discrimination: social participation and mobility are conditional on required acculturation to dominant norms. The dominant conformity model also assumes a high degree of ethnocentrism among the dominant ethnic groups and a low degree among immigrant ethnic minorities. Most important, it assumes that immigrants are not only willing, but also able to become absorbed into the dominant ethnic community and society. Put another way, the model assumes that all immigrants are both *educable* and *assimilable*.

Given this absorptionist premise, potential immigrants whose ascribed characteristics (race, physical, or mental disability) deem them incapable of adapting to dominant norms are denied entry. Dominant conformity also sanctions highly exclusive institutional forms of discrimination (such as expulsion, extermination, or incarceration) against non-conformist minorities whose unwillingness to embrace dominant norms marks them as culturally and/or behaviourally deviant. In short, the degree to which ethnic (and other) minorities are accorded fundamental human rights and societal opportunities is predicated on the degree to which they are both able and willing to shed their distinctive/deviant attributes and to conform to the dominant ethnic/societal model.

On the question of collective rights, the dominant conformity model is clear: Ethnic minority rights are not recognized; the collective cultural and national group rights of the dominant powers are permanently entrenched. Given these assumptions, ethnic integration would result in a society in which all citizens would be absorbed through one-way processes of acculturation and assimilation to the dominant ethnic group(s). The society would be characterized by national unity in dominant homogeneity and each citizen's ethnic identity would be coterminous with that of one of the original dominant population(s).

The Dominant Conformity Model at the Level of Public Policy: Canada's Policies of Immigration and Ethnic Absorption

In the early part of the twentieth century, Anglo Canadians wished to dissociate themselves from the alleged failure of the American melting pot and to legitimate the separate existence of Canada as a British preserve. The Anglo Canadians' sense of nationalism linked pride in their new country with continuing pride in their alleged Anglo-Saxon ethnic heritage, both of which were strongly associated with ties and loyalties to the British Crown. Thus, from the beginning, many Anglo Canadians were supportive of the view that Canada should develop as a British preserve and an Anglo-Saxon nation. This view strongly influenced Canada's immigration policies and related policies of ethnic absorption for decades to come.

Racial extremists of the day argued that *Nordics* were superior to all others (Woodsworth 1972: 164). The racially intensive label *Nordics* referred exclusively to Anglo-Saxon Protestants from the British Isles and countries of northern and western Europe. *Non-Nordics*, it was argued, were racially inferior, and could not be incorporated to the Anglo-Saxon model: they should therefore be barred from immigration to Canada. Their admission, racial extremists warned, might lead to 'miscegenation' and its alleged inevitable consequences—the corruption of the 'pure' Anglo-Saxon stock, the destruction of the 'higher' Anglo-Saxon civilization, and the decay and ruination of the new Canadian nation.

Most Anglo Canadians, however, were more optimistic about immigration. They assumed that the superior initiative and strength of the Anglo-Saxon 'race' would acculturate the lower characteristics of the European 'races' to its higher ideals and standards. This position was less overtly racist than that of the extremists, implying cultural, rather than the biological, Anglo-Saxon superiority, and thus allowing for possible acculturation of *educable* and *assimilable* newcomers.

The immigration policy predicated on this view welcomed only those immigrants able and willing to conform to the distinctive and superior, white, Anglo-Saxon, Protestant values, cultural standards, and lifeways. Non-Anglo-Saxon, non-Protestant immigration was not considered a real danger as long as it was believed that new immigrants could be acculturated to the ways of the majority through the concerted efforts of dominant group agents, especially educators and Protestant missionaries. However, not all were believed capable of acculturating. Distinctions were clearly drawn between the supposedly lower ethnic groups (peoples from southern and eastern Europe) believed capable of acculturation and the alleged inferior races (peoples from less civilized regions) marked and isolated by a skin colour barrier considered incapable of so doing. This racist ideology—one version of the White Supremacy theory—was used to justify exclusion of many peoples racially defined as Negroes and orientals.

The Development of a Racism-free Canadian Immigration Policy: Paving the Way to Multiculturalism

In the post-World War II era, with the horrors of genocide still fresh in people's minds, there was increasing international pressure on nations to take steps to ensure that their laws and public policies reflected the new global climate of racial and ethnic tolerance. In the fifties and sixties, a movement emerged within Canada to develop a racism-free immigration policy. With the post-war economic boom, Canada adjusted its immigration policy to meet economic needs and began to relax restrictions based (overtly or covertly) on race and ethnicity. In addition, bowing to international pressure, Canada began to allow resettlement of 'Displaced Persons', later to be considered as 'refugees'. By the end of the period, Canada had developed a new approach to immigrant admission, a merit point system that emphasized education, training, and skills designed to meet the country's economic needs, and that removed formal racism from the immigration procedures (Isajiw 1999: 83).

The Immigration Regulations of 1967 introduced the new merit point system of Canadian immigration. As a consequence of the new merit point system, there was a significant change in the ethnic composition of Canada's population.

This was the period in which the proportion of white to non-white immigrants was reversed. In the periods that followed, modifications in the numbers of points accorded for various qualifications were made, but, more important, legislation was introduced that designated new types of classes of immigrants. The Immigration Act of 1976 gave statutory status to refugees as designated classes of immigrants. Refugees were previously admitted on an *ad hoc* basis in conformity with Canada's obligation (as a signatory to the UN Convention Relating to the Status of Refugees) to admit a certain number of refugees annually (Isajiw 1999: 85).

In the 1980s, in order to encourage migrants to work in jobs for which there was high demand, the government introduced an employment authorization program. In practice, this program applied largely to domestic work and was aimed at women migrants who were employed as temporary workers. Another special program, introduced in 1985, was designed to attract 'business immigrants' who would invest substantial sums of money in Canada. Immigrants who promised to invest at least half a million dollars in Canada could enter Canada without assessment on the merit point system (Isajiw 1999: 88). Both programs were to become targets of sharp criticism, particularly because of the abuses of the system that ensued. Female temporary workers were often ruthlessly exploited by employers and business entrepreneurs frequently failed to fulfill their obligations to invest in Canada.

Toward the end of the eighties and into the nineties, new criticisms of immigration arose, at first centred on refugees. During the 1980s, increasing numbers of persons claiming refugee status made their way to Canada. By the end of the decade, refugee determination boards, charged with assessing these claims, were severely backlogged and unable to handle their caseloads. In addition, many refugee claimants who had been refused entry went 'underground' and became illegal immigrants. More than 1100 arrest warrants were issued. The criminalization of illegal refugees was compounded by reported cases of smuggling of refugees to Canada, including some with criminal records. These events tainted Canada's refugee program and led to demands for changes. In light of the economic recession of the early 1990s, public voices demanded cutbacks to the numbers of refugees and other immigrants to be admitted (Isajiw 1999).

In 1993, a new amendment to the 1976 Immigration Act went into effect. This amendment (Bill C-86) gave the government the authority to set limits on the number of immigrants to be admitted in each specific category. It also allowed the government to set and announce an annual limit to the total number of immigrants that it could absorb. Additionally, other revisions linked immigration more closely to population and labour market needs. By the mid-1990s, the merit point system challenged prospective immigrants far more than it had done previously. The 1993 amended Act identified three classes of immigrants: family class, refugees, and independent (CIC 2000).

The *family class* category stipulated that Canadian citizens and permanent residents, age 19 and over and living in Canada, have the right to sponsor the applications of certain categories of close relatives who wish to migrate to Canada. Family class applicants were not assessed under the point system, but were required to meet Canadian standards of good health and character. Their sponsors had to make a commitment to support and house them for up to 10 years (Isajiw 1999: 89).

Refugees, called convention refugees, were those persons displaced by emergency situations in any country that the government of Canada recognized under the UN Convention and Protocol Relating to the Status of Refugees, as a special class, for humanitarian reasons. Canadian citizens and permanent residents, age 19 and over and living in Canada, and legally incorporated organizations could sponsor refugees and their

Table 6-2 Immigrant Population by Place of Birth and Period of Immigration, 1996 Census, Canada

	Total Immigrant Population	Period of Immigration				
		Before 1961	*1961–70*	*1971–80*	*1981–90*	*1991–96*
	4,971,070	**1,054,930**	**788, 580**	**996,160**	**1,092,440**	**1,038,990**
United States	**244,695**	45,050	50,200	74,015	46,405	29,025
Central and South America	**273,820**	6,370	17,410	67,470	106,230	76,335
Caribbean and Bermuda	**279,405**	8,390	45,270	96,025	72,405	57,315
United Kingdom	**655,540**	265,580	168,140	132,950	63,445	25,420
Other Northern and Western Europe	**514,310**	284, 205	90,465	59,850	48,095	31,705
Eastern Europe	**447,830**	175,430	40,855	32,280	111,370	87,900
Southern Europe	**714,380**	228,145	244,380	131,620	57,785	52,455
Africa	**229,300**	4,945	25,685	58,150	64,265	76,260
West-Central Asia and the Middle East	**210,850**	4,975	15,165	30,980	77,685	82,050
Eastern Asia	**589,420**	20,555	38,865	104,940	172,715	252,340
Southeast Asia	**408,985**	2,485	14,040	111,700	162,490	118,265
Southern Asia	**353,515**	4,565	28,875	80,755	99,270	140,055
Oceania and Other	**49,025**	4,250	9,240	15,420	10,240	9,875

families, provided that they made a commitment to provide settlement assistance for them for a period of one year (Isajiw 1999).

Independent immigrants were defined as either *business immigrants, skilled workers,* or *assisted relatives.* Business immigrants were admitted on the basis of promised economic investment in Canada; skilled workers were admitted on the basis of the merit point system; and assisted relatives were admitted as independent immigrants with a relative in Canada who was able and willing to help them become established (Isajiw 1999: 90).

By the second half of the 1990s, the composition of immigration to Canada with regard to *national origin* had changed substantially from that of the 1960s. Before 1961, over 90 per cent of all immigrants to Canada came from Europe, and over half of these were from northwestern European countries and the UK. Only 3.1 per cent of immigrants came from Asia. In the 1990s the largest number of immigrants, close to 60 per cent, came from Asia. Only 20 per cent of immigrants came from European countries, and, of these, the largest proportion came from Eastern Europe. The remaining 20 per cent came from Central and South America, the Caribbean, Bermuda, and the United States (Isajiw 1999: 91).

The increasingly multiethnic and multiracial character of Canada's population has had a significant impact on government policies of ethnic integration. Canada has had to seriously rethink its ideological approach to public policy. The result has been the shift from dominant conformity to multiculturalism and anti-racism.

Although changes in immigration policy over the past decades, have markedly reduced the racist bias in the present Act, the treatment of culturally and racially distinctive immigrants after their arrival in Canada indicates that racist barriers continue to impede ethnic integration. As argued earlier, recent changes to Canada's multicultural policy strongly indicate that *dominant conformity*, now poorly camouflaged in the guise of multiculturalism, has been re-embraced by Canada's ethnic majority groups. However, the goal of immigrant absorption through dominant conformity is clearly incompatible with the fact of Canada's increasingly racially and ethnically diverse population. Not surprisingly, the absorption of racial and ethnic minorities in Canada continues to be impeded by individual, institutional, and systemic forms of racial discrimination.

Paternalism in the Context of Colonialism: Assumptions behind the Model

In the discussion of the origins of ethnic stratification (see Chapter 3), we suggested that Blauner's (1972) model of colonizer/colonized relations could be applied to the origins and early development of dominant/aboriginal relations in the Canadian context. Further, in keeping with the stance increasingly documented by spokespersons representing various organizations of Canada's First Nations, we argued that the cultural policy of the colonizers—that of cultural genocide—was most starkly epitomized in Canada by the paternalistic conditions for the treatment of Status Indians set forth under the Indian Act. The paternalistic model of ethnic relations to be outlined as follows will be based on the rhetoric of the colonial underpinnings of dominant/aboriginal relations in Canada, especially underlying the legal conditions of the Indian Act.

The paternalistic model of ethnic integration is highly asymmetric, assuming vast disparities in political, economic, and social power between interacting ethnic groups. In a paternalistic relationship the more powerful (dominant) population is highly ethnocentric: it perceives itself as a superior category of human beings and the less powerful, minority population as subhuman or less than human beings. Van den Berghe (1967: 27–9) suggests that the paternalistic model of ethnic relations is based upon the master-servant relationship. From the master's point of view, the minority population is stereotyped as 'childish, immature, irresponsible, exuberant, improvident, fun-loving, good-humoured, and happy go-lucky; in short as inferior but lovable as long as they stay in their place'.

The concept of *paternalism* stems from the Latin root patterns: *of or belonging to a father*. In practice, a paternalistic system of ethnic relations is one in which the dominant population takes on the role of an authoritarian father toward his children—the childish minorities. The dominant population creates policies, rules, and laws based on a paternalistic ideology of *benevolent despotism* (van den Berghe 1967): the ruling powers of the father are absolute; the children are denied the fundamental right of self-determination and are required to give unquestioned obedience to the dominant authority. As long as they comply with the dominant 'rules of the game', they will be cared for and protected by the dominant authority.

In the colonial era, paternalism was rationalized through racist ideologies of White Supremacy based on the equation: White = Might = Right. Paternalistic relations were predicated on two further assumptions held by dominant European powers: the *white man's burden* and *noblesse oblige*. The white man's burden was to civilize the savages; noblesse oblige meant that privilege, the white man's prerogative, entailed responsibility for the care and protection of the childlike savages. In short, based on the primary assumption that aboriginal peoples were not quite human, the dominant Europeans assumed the obligation of humanizing them. This pattern of paternalistic relations is analogous to the way an authoritative father, operating on the assumption that children are born bad and wild, attempts to morally indoctrinate and control his children.

The Canadian historian John Maclean (1896), reacting against the overtly paternalistic treatment of aboriginal peoples by early Euro-Canadians, attempted to focus public attention on their way of life. In the preface to his book *Canadian Savage Folk* he argues:

> Close contact with our native tribes shows the mistake we have been making in deciding that ignorance, superstition and cruelty belong to these people. . . . A faithful study of the languages and customs compels us to acknowledge that . . . *under the blanket and coat of skin there beats a human heart* . . .[8]

As late as the 1950s, overtly racist views such as those expressed by the French-Canadian writer Yves Thériault were typical. In *Agaguk* he says of the Inuit:

> Now, Eskimos are unpredictable beings, capable of uncontrolled rage, particularly when they are together in a group. Just like animals who are normally easily frightened or inoffensive but become dangerous when surprised (1971 [translation]: 186).

Given these racist assumptions, it is not difficult to understand the zeal with which Christian missionaries undertook the civilizing mission behind their white man's burden. Katherine Hughes, in her book *Father Lacombe: The Black-Robe Voyageur,* recounts:

> With all the ardors of his warm nature, Father Lacombe burned to reach every tribe on the plains—group after group, to gather these poor nomads in fresh colonies . . . while he pushed again into the wilds with his Red Cross flag and his plough to bring into Christian submission still other bands of savages (1920: 106).

Clearly, the civilizing goal of Christian missionaries extended far beyond their efforts at religious conversion. Bringing the 'savages' into submission entailed a high degree of institutional control over the relocated aboriginal peoples—a concerted effort to eradicate aboriginal customs and an attempt to induce dominant conformity in all life spheres.

The paternalistic model of ethnic integration resembles the dominant conformity model in terms of: asymmetric power relations; high degree of ethnocentrism among dominant populations; devaluation of minority ethnoculture(s); and required acculturation to dominant norms. In other respects, it is based on significantly different assumptions.

The paternalistic model assumes, first and foremost, that 'subhuman' aboriginal minorities have permanently limited human capabilities. They are not expected to reach maturity; they are regarded as *permanent children,* inherently unable to fully acculturate and assimilate to dominant ways. Operating on these racist assumptions, dominant agents and agencies promote total deculturation, but only partial acculturation. The civilizing mission is thus characterized by a high degree of cultural, institutional, and systemic discrimination against aboriginal minorities. Strictures on the educational process ensure that minorities do not acquire sufficient knowledge and skills to enable them more than minimal participation in dominant institutions. Thus, access to political, social, and economic power is virtually denied and the self-fulfilling prophecy of white racism is guaranteed. Aboriginal minorities are relegated to the lowest rungs of the ethnic hierarchy, where they are tolerated as long as they 'stay in their place' and are 'seen but not heard'.

Under the paternalistic model of ethnic integration, aboriginal minorities come to occupy a permanently invalidated and stigmatized status, marginal to the dominant society. Their collective stigma is rooted in racial and cultural characteristics assumed by dominant powers to be associated with their 'savage' origin, and which serve to define them as *less than human*. Because this dehumanizing stigma is a permanent one, dominant authorities are able to rationalize and eventually to legitimate wholesale violations of the individual and collective human rights of aboriginal minorities. In consequence, aboriginal minorities become *marginalized*—suppressed populations, in but not of mainstream society.

Marginalization

Mullaly (2002: 43–4) argues that **marginalization** (a long-term consequence of systemic discrimination) affects primarily a growing underclass consisting of members of various, severely disadvantaged minorities, including people of colour, persons with disabilities, and aboriginal peoples. These groups, he asserts, are permanently confined to the margins of society because the labour force cannot or will not accommodate them. Marginalization thus excludes whole groups of people from useful and meaningful participation in the society. Despite the fact that liberal, democratic societies (such as Canada) have put in place modern welfare systems to deal with material deprivation, welfare redistribution has not eliminated the dehumanizing experience of degradation that continues as a consequence of the punitive, demeaning, patronizing treatment of marginalized populations that rely on the support and services of welfare bureaucracies. This dehumanizing treatment, Mullaly points out, is directly associated with arbitrary welfare policies and regulations that interfere with the fundamental rights to privacy, respect, and autonomy of members of marginalized minorities.

By marginalizing aboriginal peoples, the paternalistic model thus ensures that the control wielded by dominant elites is not threatened by minority subordinates and that only the individual and collective rights of the dominant population are recognized and respected in society at large.

The outcome of the paternalistic model for ethnic and national identities is very different, in the case of majority, as opposed to aboriginal minority populations. For the dominant ethnic group(s)—recognized as human beings—it parallels that of the dominant conformity model, that is, unity in dominant homogeneity—one dominant nation/culture/people.

For minorities, whose aboriginal identities have been stigmatized and dehumanized, whose cultures and institutions have been denigrated and destroyed, and whose identification with the oppressor has been repudiated, the outcome is one of cultural marginality and economic/political marginalization (Fanon 1967).

Paternalism/Colonialism: Canadian Public Policy and Societal Reality

In Canada, the paternalism model has historically provided the rhetoric behind virtually all varieties of aboriginal policy. In the various Indian Acts (1896–1950), federal policies specifically designed for so-called 'Native Peoples' have given racist, paternalistic assumptions their clearest institutional expression. Waubageshig argues persuasively that the Indian Act is the 'principal variable of colonialism in Canada'. Further, he contends that the cultural and geographical fragmentation of Canadian aboriginal peoples that has ensued from colonial 'divide and rule' policies has eased the way for the long-term continuance of colonial relations between administrative authorities and aboriginal peoples in Canada (1970: 97). Ponting and Gibbins (1980) have provided a sociopolitical profile of Indian affairs in Canada, which affords clear documentation for Waubageshig's view from a non-Indian perspective. And Weaver (1981) has published an excellent analysis of the 'hidden agenda' behind the making of Canadian Indian policy.

Weaver's book was based on several years of intensive research into the politics of the

BOX 6-1: CASE STUDY

Residential Schools: Aboriginal Child Abuse and Cultural Marginality

The first residential schools for aboriginal children in Canada were run by Christian missionaries bent on 'civilizing' and 'Christianizing' their 'heathen' pupils (Kallen 1972). Mission schools typically were staffed by European (and, later, Euro-Canadian) missionaries imbued with the racist ideologies of colonialism. As religious agents working in conjunction with the colonial government, they emphasized their 'Christianizing' mission and limited their introduction of secular skills to the basic rudiments (the 3 Rs). The racist assumption behind this strategy was that 'savages' could not be expected to absorb the full force of Western civilization, thus, education had to be watered down, reduced to the presumed low level of intelligence, the 'permanently limited capabilities' of the aboriginal students. Mission schools thus adopted a kindergarten-level approach that virtually guaranteed that their students would not acquire the skills necessary for full participation in Euro-Canadian society.

Mission education was designed to eradicate aboriginal cultures (cultural genocide), but it was not designed to provide aboriginal students with sufficient knowledge of Euro-Canadian culture or sufficient training in Euro-Canadian skills to enable them to fully participate and integrate in Euro-Canadian society. For aboriginal pupils, the outcome of mission education was the creation of a category of marginal aboriginal youth unequipped for life in either the Euro-Canadian or the aboriginal cultural milieu (Kallen 1972).

Missionaries believed that the sooner they could separate children from their parents, the sooner they could prepare aboriginal people to live a civilized (that is, Euro-Christian) lifestyle. Residential schools were established for two reasons: to separate children from their families and communities, and to eradicate 'primitive' aboriginal culture so that aboriginal children would learn and adopt the superior ways of the 'advanced' European civilization.

Early residential schools were similar to religious missions. Later, the mission-run schools were administered jointly by Canadian churches and the federal government, and for a number of years, residential schools became official Canadian policy for the education of aboriginal children. Aboriginal children as young as six left the world of their families and were separated from their families and sent into the unfamiliar world of the 'white man'. Children were usually rounded up in August and transported by train, plane, or bus to the residential schools. They were issued 'proper' clothes and assigned a bed number. Even though many of the children could not speak any English, the supervisors spoke only English to them. The children were, in fact, punished for speaking their native languages. Examples of other punishments given to aboriginal children at residential schools include the following:

- For failing a test—no food for a day;
- For not working hard enough—4 hours of extra work (in school or garden);
- For disobedience, and rude or disorderly conduct—no food or water for a day, a beating (with a stick on the back), extra garden work;
- For speaking native language—(first offence) no supper—(second offence) no supper and

beating—(third offence) considered disobedience and punished as such;
- For going off by yourself (without another student present)—several hours of kneeling alone on a rock floor where all can see.

There are many similarities between these punishments and the treatment received by prisoners of war. Research on some prisoner-of-war camp experiences compares them to those of Indian children in residential schools. Beyond these routine forms of punishment, what has come to light in graphic detail over the last decade or so is the shocking documentation of emotional, physical, and sexual abuse of aboriginal children at the hands of residential school authorities.

In cultural terms, the Euro-Canadian-dominated residential school contradicted everything these aboriginal children had learned at home. Thus, when some children were able to return home for two short summer months, parents found that they had changed. They had lost respect for their people, and they often refused to 'listen' to elders. Instead they 'talked back'. Even more difficult for parents was the children's loss of ability to speak their own language. This led to an inability of children and elders to communicate meaningfully across the generational and cultural divide created by the residential school system. The most damaging part of residential schools, from an aboriginal perspective, was that children were taught that their culture was not worth preserving. Students learned that aboriginal traditional values were wrong and primitive, and that white Canadians came from a more 'advanced' form of social organization. Students came to see their homes as 'dirty' and 'cold,' their parents as dressing 'funny' and as smelling 'bad.' Students began to believe that the ceremonies and rituals which harmonized the spiritual and social life of the community and gave its members a sense of personal significance and group identity, were 'heathen' and 'the work of the Devil.' The organization of the schools and the content of the curriculum conveyed to aboriginal children that the human values, the political institutions, the spiritual practices, and the economic strategies of other Canadians were infinitely superior to the 'primitive' ways of their traditional lifestyles.

It was disorienting for aboriginal children to spend the first (formative) years of life living in a traditional aboriginal way, and then to be thrust into a foreign, concentration-camp-style school. Residential schools disrupted the smooth transmission of beliefs, skills, and knowledge from one generation to the next, and deliberately divorced aboriginal children from their background by discrediting their culture, punishing them for speaking their language, and preaching the superiority of European attitudes. The experience often caused severe, and in many cases, unalterable damage to the children and to the family and to the community to which they would eventually return.

By the 1950s, the Canadian government began to realize the residential school policy was a failure. The last residential school in Canada was closed some 30 years later. Today, aboriginal people want recognition of what was done to their communities as a result of the residential schools. Aboriginal people have demanded, and received, official apologies from the Anglican, United, and Roman Catholic churches that operated residential schools. As more and more former students of residential schools come forth with stories about the emotional, sexual, and physical abuse they experienced, several religious authorities who administered the schools are being charged criminally.

The residential school experience continues to plague First Nations' education. Aboriginal children continue to have difficulties fitting in to the existing schools, which are still designed around a culture alien to their own. Today, the cross-Canada average of the percentage of aboriginal children who complete grade 12 is about 20 per cent, and even lower in northern regions. In response, many First Nations are taking over the running of their schools from the government. By designing their own curriculums and running their own schools, aboriginal people intend to reclaim the education of their children and put the residential school experience in the past.

Long-Term Effects of Residential Schools on Aboriginal Students: The Experience of Marginality

Consider the following quotation, from Brian Maracle's book *Crazywater* in which the subject is explaining why native alcoholism is connected to the residential schools:

> Figure it this way, over sixty thousand natives were processed through those schools since they started, and you got generation on generation just piled on top and now we're trying to figure out, 'What is love?' How in the hell are you supposed to know how to f—in' love when you're not given love for ten months out of every year? It's obvious they don't know how to love. They ran away because they knew there was something missing. They didn't have it. Same thing with me . . .
>
> The question is not, 'Why do we drink?' Ask first the question, 'Do you know how to love?' And you'll find a very thin line between them because they come from each other. You booze because you can't love and you booze under the guise of pretending that you can.' Why do you think that a residential school experience would lead an individual to alcohol abuse?' (quoted in *Residential Schools* 2001).

SOURCE: Adapted from *Residential Schools*, Contemporary Aboriginal Issues website.

formulation of the 1969 White Paper on Indian Policy. This draft policy statement, designed to terminate special Indian Status in Canada and to incorporate all aboriginal persons *as individuals* to the dominant cultural and institutional blueprint, was proposed by the federal government in 1970. But negative, indeed hostile, reaction from nascent Indian organizations and (later) other aboriginal groups, together with widespread public sympathy in favour of aboriginal peoples' expressed desire to preserve their distinctive communities and cultures, led to its eventual withdrawal.

Although the policy outlined in the 1969 White Paper was never formally implemented, Ponting and Gibbins agree with Weaver's contention that it has had a lasting influence on federal Indian policy, favouring incorporation ('assimilation' in government political parlance) of aboriginal peoples, *as individuals*, into the Canadian mainstream. And, as an indirect consequence, it engendered increasingly stronger, organized aboriginal protest. The relationship between the federal government/majority and aboriginal minorities in the context of the aboriginal protest movement is discussed at length in Chapter 7.

At this juncture, however, it may be appropriate to note, in advance, that attempts by aboriginal political leaders, as well as by a growing cadre of aboriginal cultural elites, to articulate the distinctive cultural value premises behind aboriginal demands for self-determination have had little success in persuading federal authorities that aboriginal peoples should be constitutionally recognized as self-determining *nations* within Canada.

The Status Indian Reserve: A Total Institution[9]

The Indian Act has been the legal instrument responsible for the encapsulation, oppression, neglect, and diminution of Status Indians within the total institution of the reserve. Under this Act, the federal minister of Indian affairs, until recently, has had the ultimate authority over all decisions affecting the lives and destinies of Indians residing on reserves. Throughout the years, the minister and his agents have dominated and controlled all of the bands' resources—land, housing, capital and income, livestock and equipment—and have wielded decision-making authority over medical services, employment, education, wills, and virtually all aspects of Indian life. Even the decision of a Status Indian to give up legal Indian Status has had to be approved. While their special legal Status gives reserve Indians some economic benefits, such as certain tax exemptions, it systemically violates their fundamental human rights by heavily restricting their freedom and by keeping them in a perpetual state of dependency. Under increasing pressure from Indian leaders, Indian affairs' ministers have turned over more and more of the responsibility for the everyday administration of reserves to their elected band councils. Yet, ultimate decision-making authority remains in the hands of federal authorities. In response to increasingly vociferous demands for Indian self-government, the federal government has agreed to turn Indian reserves into self-governing units. But their model (based on delegated authority) still leaves ultimate control in the hands of the state, thus it has been rejected by those Indian leaders who seek independent 'First Nation' status and self-government on the basis of national group rights.

The long-term, unintended, yet disastrous consequence of policies, laws, and practices toward Indians—epitomized by the reserve—is the ugly reality of the self-fulfilling prophecy of White Racism, under the model of paternalism. Treated as irresponsible children, Indians living on reserves have suffered oppression: they have been denied their human right to make the critical decisions affecting their own lives. Assumed to be naturally racially inferior in intelligence to Euro-Canadians, they have been denied equal educational and economic opportunities, and reserves have become riddled with neglect. Substandard housing breeding disease and death, closed schools due to lack of teachers, heat, and/or running water are only two examples of continuing, dehumanizing life conditions on many reserves.

Status Indians' human right to dignity and respect as persons has been violated at every turn: it has been violated every time an adult Indian has had to ask permission to go about the ordinary business of life. It is not surprising, given these long-term paternalistic conditions, that many reserves have become centres of Indian cultural alienation, characterized by all of the symptoms of the self-fulfilling prophecy of paternalism—poverty, crime, alcohol and drug addiction, apathy, and anomie.

Although this paternalistic picture of dominant-Indian relations is slowly changing, the long-term outcome of paternalism was to create a stigmatized, dependent, welfare population, whose very existence at the margins of Canadian society demonstrated unequivocally the dehumanizing consequences of denial of human rights and the utter failure of policies predicated on the paternalistic ideology of the white man's burden.

Models of Ethnic Integration: Comparative Implications for Human Rights

The four models of ethnic integration outlined in this chapter have very different implications for relationships among ethnic groups, as well as for the kinds of human rights recognized in the society. All of these models have, in varying degrees, underscored relations between ethnic groups in Canadian society. At the level of societal reality, the melting pot and mosaic models have remained largely mythical, while the dominant conformity model has underscored dominant /immigrant relations, and the paternalism model has underscored dominant/aboriginal relations.

At the level of rhetoric, the melting pot and mosaic models are essentially egalitarian with regard to individual human rights and individual opportunities for social mobility, both of which are accorded all citizens regardless of ethnic classification. Ethnicity does not provide a recognized criterion in either model for social stratification. In their North American, democratic versions, both models are rooted in (assumed) meritocracies in which differential rewards are accorded on the basis of positional attainment of individuals on criteria of specified qualifications and demonstrated performance. Social stratification in both models thus derives from unequally rewarded social positions based on achieved criteria.

The essential difference between the melting pot and mosaic ideals lies in their evaluation of ethnocultural distinctiveness and in their assumptions about processes of acculturation and assimilation of ethnic groups. The melting pot devalues ethnic distinctiveness and posits total two-way acculturation and assimilation; the mosaic values ethnic distinctiveness and posits partial (mutually controlled and restricted) acculturation and assimilation. Accordingly, in the former model, there is no place for collective rights of distinctive ethnic communities, while in the latter, the collective rights of all ethnic communities are recognized and protected.

In contrast, the dominant conformity and paternalism models of ethnic integration are essentially inegalitarian or asymmetric in their ethnic orientation. Both models are predicated on racist assumptions that serve to underscore and legitimate a system of ethnic stratification based on ascribed and achieved criteria.

The essential difference between these two models lies in their evaluation and accommodation of ethnic distinctiveness. In the dominant conformity model, non-violation of the political, economic, and social rights of members of various ethnic minorities is conditional upon their willingness and ability to acculturate to dominant norms and lifeways. This implies that various ethnocultural minorities are unequally evaluated in terms of their members' presumed *educability* and *assimilability*; presumed non-educable and non-assimilable ethnic groups are excluded from the society. In this model, the collective rights of the dominant ethnic group(s) are permanently guaranteed and protected. Alternatively, the collective rights of ethnic minorities are not recognized, and institutionalized forms of cultural discrimination ensure denial of minority cultural rights within the society. While the dominant conformity model makes human rights conditional on acculturation to dominant norms, the paternalistic model goes much further in violating the human rights of minorities. Under paternalism, aboriginal minorities are defined as subhuman and are, accordingly, denied all of the human rights accorded human beings. Racism provides the ideological underpinnings for a comprehensive system of institutional, systemic, and cultural discrimination against subhuman minorities; and institutionalized racism, in turn, ensures that aboriginal minorities become permanently locked into a stigmatized, marginal status in society. By way of contrast, the individual and collective rights of the dominant ethnic group(s) are permanently entrenched and strongly enforced throughout the society.

The paternalism model has special implications with regard to the collective cultural, aboriginal, and national group rights of aboriginal peoples. Because it denies the essential humanity of aboriginal peoples, it denies the validity of aboriginal cultures and it fails to recognize the vital link between aboriginal peoples, their distinctive ethnocultures and institutions of self-government, and their aboriginal territories. Paternalistic relationships thus give rise to aboriginal claims to nationhood.

Although the melting pot and mosaic models are clearly far less discriminatory in their ideological intent than are the dominant conformity and paternalism models, they nevertheless can be seen to violate the individual and/or collective human rights of members of some social categories. The melting pot model clearly denies the collective rights of its constituent ethnocultural communities, thus it discriminates against minority members who are unwilling to abandon their distinctive ethnocultures and lifeways. In both melting pot and mosaic models, equality of opportunity is conceptualized in terms of standard (same) rather than equivalent (special) treatment. Thus, they both discriminate against those individuals whose authentic disabilities disadvantage them by impeding their access to the opportunities accorded others. At the level of rhetoric, these models do not address the *categorical rights* claims of disabled minorities for whom actual (as opposed to rhetorical) equality of opportunity necessitates *equivalent* (as opposed to standard) treatment, including the provision of specialized, affirmative measures designed to compensate for and overcome the handicapping effect of their disabilities.

Conclusion

This chapter examines the four major models of ethnic integration that have provided the ideological rhetoric for public policy controlling the incorporation of racial and ethnic minorities into the mainstream society and culture in North America. It also reviews critically the public policies predicated on these models, at the level of social reality in Canada. For both aboriginal and immigrant racial-ethnic minorities, racist assumptions that have been institutionalized through these public policies have served to perpetuate barriers to both upward mobility and incorporation into the mainstream of Canadian society. In particular, majority techniques of domination—institutionalized forms of racist discrimination—serve to prevent the realization of the egalitarian Canadian democratic ideal of ethnic equality and national unity.

In Chapter 7, our focus will shift to highlight *minority responses* to institutionalized racism. It will analyze the social conditions that give rise to minority ethnic protest movements and examine the factors responsible for their ultimate success or failure. Minority rights movements, as a particular form of ethnic protest, will be analyzed with specific reference to aboriginal peoples, immigrant ethnic minorities, and the Franco-Quebecois in Canada.

Key Concepts

- acculturation (cultural integration)
- assimilation (structural integration)
- enculturation
- ethnic integration
- identificational integration
- marginalization
- meritocracy
- models of ethnic integration: melting pot (amalgamation); mosaic (cultural pluralism); dominant conformity (absorption); paternalism/colonialism
- reference group
- total integration

Critical Thinking Questions

1. Taking into consideration the key factors affecting processes of ethnic integration, consider the question: Is total integration possible? Refer specifically to aboriginal peoples and visible immigrants in Canada.
2. From a human rights perspective, compare and contrast the melting pot and mosaic models of ethnic integration.
3. Is the paternalism/colonialism model simply a variant of the dominant conformity model of ethnic integration, or are there marked differences between the two models? Adopt a human rights perspective in your discussion of this question.

4. In what ways does Canada's multicultural policy diverge from the cultural pluralism/mosaic model? Explain the significance of this difference for the human rights of racial and ethnic minorities in Canada.
5. Put into practice, could any of the four models of ethnic integration delineated in this chapter serve to provide equity and justice for all individuals and groups in a North American meritocracy?

CHAPTER 7

Minority Protest Movements: The Mobilization of Ethnicity in Pursuit of Protection for Minority Rights

Introduction

The preceding chapters have illustrated the ways in which institutionalized forms of racism within Canadian society have impeded the processes of ethnic integration and social mobility for members of various ethnic minorities. Institutionalized racism has provided majority authorities with powerful techniques of domination and control over ethnic minorities, and these instruments of human rights violation have enabled ethnic majorities to maintain the established ethnic hierarchy and their superordinate status at its apex.

How, then, can changes in the established ethnic hierarchy come about? What can invalidated members of ethnic minorities do to improve their group status and opportunities and to regain their sense of human dignity? In this chapter I employ both established social movement theory (Clark et al. 1975) and new social movement theory (Kreisi et al. 1995; Melucci 1980, 1996) in order to provide a sociological framework for my analysis of three major, human rights-oriented minority ethnic protest movements in Canada: the Franco-Quebecois, aboriginal and multicultural movements.

The Development of Minority Protest

As long as ethnic minorities accept the existing ethnic hierarchy as legitimate or as long as they are prevented from acquiring competitive advantages that bring them into direct power struggles with the dominant populations, the established structure of ethnic inequality remains unchallenged as a moral order. Within a highly institutionalized system of ethnic stratification, ethnicity may serve the expressive needs of members of ethnic minorities by providing them with a source of roots and a sense of primary group belongingness. For most members, however, it is unlikely to fully meet their instrumental needs, for the corporate ethnic interests of the minority are denied expression in the society.

Earlier, it was suggested that the new ethnicity is highly contingent upon the prevailing social environment. Hence, it is not until social conditions change markedly, throwing the very legitimacy of the structure of ethnic inequality into question, that the mobilization of ethnicity into organized minority protest can be initiated.

Sources of Minority Ethnic Protest

Minority ethnic protest develops when social conditions change so suddenly or radically that new alternatives, hopes, and competitive advantages become available for minorities. Such major changes may be a result of forces emanating from outside a community or society. Natural disasters such as floods, famine, or disease can wipe out entire communities or populations. Similarly, human atrocities such as war and conquest can upset the demographic balance, as well as the relative balance of power among the ethnic groups in contact. The influx of new ethnic groups and the exodus of others, urban migration, and shifts due to transient or migrant labour can result in important demographic changes that result in positional changes of different ethnic groups within the overall hierarchy.

Today, with increasing modernization, urbanization, and industrialization of societies throughout the world, scientific, economic, and technological developments have emerged as major forces of interethnic conflict and change. In a modern nation such as Canada, there is an ever-increasing demand for skilled workers while the demand for the traditional artisan is on the wane. Education assumes a heightened role as the demand for specialists increases. When members of ethnic minorities acquire new skills crucial to the economy, they become vitally important to the labour force. Similarly, when ethnic minorities gain purchasing or bargaining power they acquire new competitive advantages. All of these changes can increase the instrumental strength of ethnic minorities and can further the process of politicization of ethnicity.

One of the major modern developments affecting interethnic relations on a global scale is the tremendous advance in the fields of transportation and communication. Whether through travel or telecommunication members of ethnic minorities are today exposed to a plethora of new values, ideas, and standards that challenge established ways and entrenched authorities. With the 1972 launch of the Canadian satellite Anik, even the most remote Inuit community in the high Arctic had access to radio, television, telephone, and even Internet communication. Exposure to new ideas and values, and comparisons with other ethnic minorities that have improved their status, raises expectations. As a result, many aboriginal and immigrant ethnic minorities are critical of the existing hierarchy and discontented with their lowly position in it.

In today's global village, ethnic tensions in other countries and voiced minority discontent within Canada impact on Canadians. The media focus on violence and sensationalism makes events depicting ethnic conflict prime targets for daily news coverage, editorials, television documentaries, and so forth. In turn, this constant exposure renders the instrumental aspect of ethnicity highly salient. Most important for this discussion are the political strategy models provided minority ethnic leaders for the pursuit of instrumental, corporate ethnic goals. Guerrilla tactics, hijackings, and myriad other acts of sabotage are globally communicated in vivid media imagery on an almost continuous basis.

Provision of successful role models for minorities throughout the world to emulate is becoming a crucial aspect of modern communication. The post–World War II achievement of independence and nationhood by formerly colonized peoples throughout Africa had a marked influence on the global development of black nationalism. Black power movements in the West Indies, the United States, and Canada have, in turn, influenced protest movements among other ethnic minorities. In Quebec, members of the ill-fated FLQ (*Front de Libération du Québec*) initially identified themselves as the alleged 'White Niggers of America' (Vallières 1971) and early nationalist movements among Canada's Indians emphasized 'Red Power' (Stewart 1970).

The spread of the minority coalition idea—as exemplified in the concepts of Third World (developing countries, previously subject to overseas colonialism) and Fourth World (aboriginal nations, subject to internal colonialism) can be largely attributed to developments in transportation and communication. Identification with the plight of similarly disadvantaged and inferiorized minorities throughout the world has sparked efforts of leaders of ethnic minorities to expand their power bases by forming coalitions to pursue common ethnopolitical goals.

Protest Movements among Ethnic Minorities: The Quest for Roots, Rights, and Empowerment

A **minority ethnic protest movement** represents a particular kind of social movement, one that arises in response to long-term, collective disadvantage and inferiorization of minorities, resulting from *racist-motivated* forms of discrimination.

Clark, Grayson, and Grayson (1975) define a **social movement** as a social process through which substantial numbers of participants attempt to bring about or to resist social change. It is a conscious effort to create new social and cultural frameworks or designs for living, or to restore old ones. Following the approach of the Chicago School, these scholars argue that minority discontent is rooted in profound dissatisfaction with prevailing life conditions arising out of perceived value inconsistencies. Discontent may arise from a perceived conflict between values, from a perceived discrepancy between values and their implementation, from a perceived gap between expectations and achievements, from status inconsistency and from a host of similar variables. Whatever the perceived source, discontent is expressed in a rejection of societal values, norms, and/or leaders and an attempt to find meaningful alternatives.

The process of organization of the minority in order to achieve better life conditions involves the formulation of guidelines for new lifestyles (group ideologies) and the gaining of the commitment of the discontented to the new designs for living. Minority discontent is initially unfocused. Before demands for change can be made, it must be mobilized and directed toward clearly defined goals. Central to this initial phase of minority organization is the rejection by minorities of majority-imposed, *inferiorizing* labels and their replacement with positive minority self-definitions. This change in nomenclature—from Nigger to black, from Indian to First Nation, from Jap/enemy alien to Japanese-Canadian—symbolizes a shift from negative to positive minority identities, a shift that is essential in order to mobilize minority discontent around human rights and empowerment goals.

When the existing system of ethnic stratification is regarded by more and more members of an ethnic minority as unjust and corrupt, **contrast conceptions** develop that stereotype the majority as evil perpetrators of human rights violations and the minority as virtuous victims of majority discrimination. Such contrast conceptions heighten *consciousness of kind* among members of the minority ethnic collectivity and strengthen the salience of ethnic group boundaries. They also reinforce positive minority identities and, at the same time, provide moral justification for concerted, aggressive action against the alleged enemy. In this way, contrast conceptions facilitate the mobilization, focus, and direction of minority discontent toward the alleged majority persecutors.

Contrast conceptions abound in the protest literature. The following illustration is fairly typical. Here the contrast is between the Euro-Canadian majority (the paleface) and the aboriginal minority (the Red People) depicted in Caibaiosai's 'The Politics of Patience':

> YOU RED PEOPLE ARE STRONG . . . much stronger than PALEFACE. . . .
>
> We have survived over four hundred and seventy years of the worst treatment possible, and we still are STRONG. All the paleface has to show for these years is his loot, but . . . his putty hands grow more and more spastic, his lies more and more obvious (Waubageshig: 146, 151–2).

Minority ethnic protest movements often gain impetus from marginal members, highly assimilationist in orientation, who realistically assess their own chances for status improvement in terms of the collective advancement of their ethnic community. Frustrated ethnic marginals, prevented from attaining majority ethnic status, may seek to assume leadership of their own ethnic group in order to mobilize members around collective empowerment goals. Early leaders tend to stem from the ranks of the well educated and politically sophisticated ethnic elites capable of manipulating their ethnicity to further their own political and economic interests. Yet, in order to win and hold the collective support of members of their communities they must establish personal credibility. This involves convincing ethnic compatriots that their personal goals are coincident with the ultimate goals of the movement and that both are legitimate.

A second and critical task of leaders of minority protest movements is the mobilization of members to participate in activities designed to effect social change. Clark, Grayson, and Grayson (1975) posit four key variables affecting the potential for success of a social movement in the mobilization of members: the development of a unifying ideology; the recruitment of willing, able, and representative leadership; the availability of channels for communication and the existence/cultivation of networks of cooperative relationships; and the development of an autonomous organizational base.

In the case of minority ethnic protest movements, we posit three additional variables: formulation of a *legitimating* (as well as unifying) ideology to justify protest; formalization of corporate ethnic strategies and goals; and organization of the ethnic collectivity as a pressure group.

Another important factor in the effective organization of minority protest movements is the extent of social segmentation (cleavages between groups) in the society at large. Minority discontent is more likely to give rise to protest movements in stratified societies marked by great disparities in cultural values and in political, economic, and social power among groups. Further, in stratified societies, minorities will be more likely to have a heightened sense of collective consciousness, agreed-on group values and goals, existing channels of communication, and networks of cooperative relationships to organize protest movements.

The conceptual distinction between 'communal' and 'associational' forms of minority organization (the *Gemeinschaft/Gesellschaft* typology) has important implications for mobilization and retention of members of protest movements (Clark, Grayson, and Grayson 1975). Communal groups are based on traditional cultural and kinship linkages among people (ethnicity). Associational groups are based on special interests (political, economic, religious, civic). Communal groups are more likely than associational groups to have value consensus beyond one set of issues, and are more likely to have developed an organizational base for a protest movement.

These observations relate importantly to the conceptual distinction between (ethnic) *group* and *category* emphasized earlier in this book. Members of minority *groups* with the requisite institutional infrastructure for maintenance and transmission of a distinctive subculture or ethnoculture are more likely to have and/or to develop the collective consciousness and the organizational basis for a successful protest movement than are members of minority *categories*. A minority category represents a conceptual or statistical classification of a population based on one or more criteria (race, age, gender), which may or may not give rise to a sense of collective consciousness or to minority organization. Minority categories (for example, aboriginal people) are more likely than minority groups (for example, Inuit of Nunavut) to be represented empirically by dispersed, fragmented population aggregates whose members' only common attribute is the inferiorizing label imposed on them by majority authorities. The propensity for factionalism to impede organization for minority protest is, therefore, much greater within minority categories than within minority groups.

The course and potential success of a minority protest movement is determined by the continual interaction of internal (minority) and external (majority) forces as well as by changes in the broader environment. A crucial task for minority leadership is to create and maintain ingroup solidarity. Lines of fragmentation based on differences in values, interests, priorities, and sources of discontent among minority members must be contained through the development of a strong, collective commitment to the ideology and goals of the movement. Rivalries among minority leaders must be resolved so that leadership is perceived by both insiders and outsiders to represent the membership.

Lobbying efforts by minority representatives must convince majority authorities that minority demands are valid and must be dealt with. When minority ethnic leaders begin to lobby influential majority bodies and governmental officials in pursuit of corporate ethnic goals, the relative success of their early efforts will depend on a number of key factors. Two of the most important will be: 1) the credibility of ethnic leaders and the legitimacy of their cause, as perceived by the majority bodies being lobbied; and 2) the demonstrable strength of minority ethnic political, economic, and social power, and the degree to which minority protest is regarded by majority bodies as a palpable threat to their entrenched societal dominance and control.

Dominant bodies may perceive ethnic minority demands as both legitimate and threatening but they may, nevertheless, be unwilling and/or more realistically unable to accede to these demands, at least in the short term. In response, they may attempt to appease and contain minority ethnic demands through strategies designed to maintain majority hegemony. They may, for example, accede to limited, expressive (cultural) demands of ethnic minorities in order to contain more threatening instrumental (political) demands.

As pointed out in the discussion of the federal policy of multiculturalism in Chapter 6, some scholarly critics have suggested that the policy of multiculturalism within a bilingual framework essentially represents a strategy of appeasement and containment. It is designed to contain the conflicting empowerment demands of the Third Force and the French nationalists, through limited appeasement of the cultural demands of the Third Force, and through major concessions to the linguistic demands of French supporters of bilingualism and biculturalism.

Another common strategy employed by dominant bodies is to decapitate the minority by coopting their most effective leaders and incorporating them into positions of power within the dominant establishment. This strategy maintains dominant hegemony by simultaneously depriving the minority of leadership skills and power and buttressing the dominant society with additional talent (Shibutani and Kwan 1965: 334–6). In Canada this strategy may have been utilized to diffuse and contain at least three minority ethnic protests over the past several decades. Three powerful and potentially threatening minority ethnic leaders have been given important governmental posts: Pierre Vallières (Franco-Quebecois Independence), Harold Cardinal (Red Power), and Stanley Haidasz (Third Force).

A third technique of dominant management of ethnic minority demands is through government funding of minority ethnic organizations, legitimated under a special policy rubric. Funding bodies are controlling agencies. The dominant fund-giving agency sets the terms under which funds are allotted, selects the recipients, and regulates distribution and expenditure. Hence, government funding allows subtle dominant intervention in minority affairs. Thus, the ethnic minority is kept in a dependent position and minority ethnic protest is diffused.

We discussed this phenomenon earlier in connection with a critique of multicultural policy. Ponting and Gibbins (1980: 124–5) provide incontrovertible evidence of the foregoing principles in their description of the nature of 'sociofiscal control' exercised by the federal government over Indians. To cite but one example, here: Sociofiscal control may be exercised in a blatant fashion to curb political deviance as in the case when the Department of Indian Affairs and Northern Development (DIAND) withheld funds from the Dene and Métis organizations in the Mackenzie Valley until they ended their political squabbling and agreed on a joint position in land claim negotiations with DIAND.

Currently in Canada, minority organizations within the three major ethnic status categories—charter, immigrant, and aboriginal populations—are funded by the government of Canada under special policy rubrics. Many minority ethnic organizations (for example, aboriginal organizations) were virtually created by government funding and remain almost totally dependent on government handouts for their survival. Few Canadian ethnic minorities have sufficient economic power to refuse government funding and the intrusion in their affairs that it entails.[1]

Clark, Grayson, and Grayson (1975) suggest that the response of majority authorities (in most instances, governments) to minority protest may take the form of indifference, accommodation and/or obstruction. If management techniques—like modes of federal sociofiscal control—fail to diffuse and contain minority discontent and protest, dominant bodies may resort to more coercive measures, that is, they may employ various techniques of domination, as outlined in Chapter 4.

A response of indifference is most likely when the movement is not perceived as a threat of any kind by governments (for example, Jesus Freaks). Accommodation implies a willingness of governments to negotiate, based upon the recognition of some minority demands as valid and based also upon the perception of the minority movement as non-threatening, provided that its demands are addressed (for example, multicultural movements). A response of obstruction is most likely if the success of the movement is perceived by governments to threaten the social order (for example, FLQ). While these conceptual distinctions are important for analytic purposes, in reality, a combination of responses may occur. A government may accommodate a minority protest movement (or be indifferent) but it may obstruct particular tactics. For example, the government of Canada has accepted the demands of the aboriginal movement for settlement of aboriginal land claims and has accepted the *principle* of aboriginal self-government, but the armed protest of Mohawk Indians against encroachment on their alleged lands during the Oka confrontation was forcibly curtailed by police and armed forces.

Routinization of Charisma: Prerequisite for Institutionalization of the Minority Movement

When their demands for reform are continually and effectively blocked, the ethnic minority may adopt various strategies of adaptation (Wallace 1956). Original leaders, drawn from the ranks of marginal or assimilationist minority elites, may be replaced by new, charismatic leaders, bent on cultural transformation. The authority of the charismatic leader does not rest primarily on the individual's social status. Initially, the leader's authority derives from a special quality of personality, a personal power of extraordinary magnetism that attracts followers.

A major problem deriving from the nature of charismatic leadership is what Max Weber termed routinization of charisma. Initially, followers are drawn to the movement more through emotional commitment to the leader, than through ideological commitment to the cause. It is, therefore, of the utmost importance that the initial, personal power of the leader be converted into the authority of office within a stable institutional framework.

Routinization of charisma, the process by which this is accomplished, is a critical issue in movement organization; for if it does not occur, leadership authority cannot be delegated and distributed to other personnel, and the movement itself may die with the death or failure of its original leader.

While examples of failure abound, two cases of successful routinization of charisma are provided by the Hutterites (founded by Jacob Hutter) and the Parti Québécois (founded by René Lévesque). The former provides an example of a successful, introverted/expressive, religious revitalization movement; the latter is an example of a successful, extroverted/instrumental, political movement.

Minority protest movements frequently fail to achieve their original ideals, but some succeed at least in part by compromising ofttimes unrealistic goals and by adapting group ideologies and strategies in order to gain acceptance by insiders and outsiders. When movements succeed, they become 'routinized' (in Weber's classic term): they become institutionalized in a stable organizational form. They may become absorbed through legislation as part of the majority society; they may develop organizational bases independent of the majority society; they may overthrow the majority order and establish their own organizational base as dominant. Whatever happens, minority protest movements leave their mark on society. They identify an area of perceived human rights violation needing redress, and even if they fail to achieve such redress, they provide the inspiration for future movements that may arise to revitalize the quest.

Types of Minority Ethnic Protest Movements: Contention and Revitalization

In broad terms, the goals of minority ethnic protest movements are twofold: 1) to eradicate the cultural and structural bases of minority oppression, diminution, and neglect in the society; and 2) to attain ethnocultural legitimacy, self-determination, and empowerment for the minority ethnic community.

Minority protest in pursuit of corporate ethnic goals may take the form of contention, leading to movements for social and political reform, or of revitalization, leading to more radical, secessionist, or revolutionary movements.

In **contention,** the ethnic minority protests against its subordinate status and disadvantaged life conditions and demands ethnic group equality within the existing societal order. Contention may be predicated on either a melting pot or a mosaic model of ethnic integration, depending on the degree of importance attached to ethnocultural distinctiveness by the minority. In the former case, the minority will demand recognition of their fundamental individual human rights; in the latter, demands will be based on recognition of both individual and collective rights.

The evolution of black protest in the United States is instructive here. The early civil rights movement, led by the Reverend Martin Luther King Jr, sought social reforms through legislation aimed at guaranteeing the individual rights of black Americans—the melting pot model. Later forms, under the rubric of Black Power, focused on collective economic and political rights—the mosaic model. Full blown, the black power movement became Black Nationalism (Carmichael and Hamilton 1967; Malcolm X 1966) and the minority response of contention gave way to revitalization. Nationalistic revitalization movements among American blacks have assumed a wide range of forms: separatist, secessionist, religious, and revolutionary (Killiam 1968; Kilson 1975). The Black Muslims (Lincoln 1961) provide an outstanding example of a religious revitalization response, while the now legendary Black Panthers provide a well-known example of a revolutionary formation among black Americans.

In **revitalization,** the ethnic minority seeks to establish a viable new ethnocultural form designed to meet the present and future needs of its members within a new societal order or, failing this, outside the existing social order. Revitalization is predicated on holistic ethnocultural transformation: it presents a design for a new ethnic world order. Revitalization thus necessitates a pluralistic model of ethnic integration or a model of ethnic separation. The ideological orientation is on collective rights, sometimes emphasized at the expense of individual rights. The latter is most likely to be the case in religious revitalization movements, such as the Black Muslims (Lincoln 1961).

A revitalization movement represents a long-term, collective response not only to oppression, neglect, and diminution, but also to severe ethnocultural deprivation or alienation. It offers hope to those who had long given up hope for human dignity, cultural legitimacy, and/or status improvement. The theme of revitalization, whether couched in religious or secular terms, is to build a better world. Its premises, strategies, and goals, articulated in a clearly defined ideology, tend to be framed in terms of contrast conceptions, that is, it conveys a portrait of conflict between the minority ethnic group and its opponents, as a historical struggle between the good ethnic insiders and the evil outsiders. The ideology of revitalization not only denies the majority claim to superior status, but also affirms the alleged moral and ethical superiority of the minority. The majority is depicted as the evil oppressor and is blamed for the disabilities and sufferings of the allegedly innocent minority victims. Revitalization of the good life of the minority, it is argued, necessitates the expulsion of evil, that is, the elimination of the majority persecutors and the creation or recreation of the 'just society' by members of the ethnic minority. Revitalization thus involves a deliberate, organized effort by members of ethnic minorities to create a totally new social and cultural world in accordance with their own values, goals, and standards (Wallace 1956).

Revitalization may involve a politically revolutionary response, in which members of ethnic minorities attempt to overthrow the established social order or politically secede to build their own version of the truly just society. These responses are exemplified in the goals of some black nationalist movements in the United States, as well as some Franco-Quebecois nationalists in Canada, as noted earlier. It may, on the other hand, lead to a reactionary or counterrevolutionary movement, or to a response of near total withdrawal from the existing social order through ethnocultural secession. The latter response is typical of religious revitalization movements, particularly in their early stages of development. In the Canadian context, the Hutterites provide a good case in point.

Although it is important to distinguish between the models of contention and revitalization for purposes of analysis, the reader should note that at the level of empirical reality the boundaries between the two analytic constructs may overlap, particularly with reference to the priority accorded the cultural dimension of protest.

Later in this chapter, I conceptualize the multicultural movement in Canada as an example of contention. However, within this overall movement, some ethnic minorities have, from time to time, revitalized particular aspects of their cultural traditions (religion, language, and nationality, for example) in ways that have markedly altered the lifestyles of ethnic members. Among Jews, for example, religious differentiation, commitment to Israel, and the shift from Yiddish to Hebrew as the 'ethnic' language, have led to marked alterations in ethnocultural lifestyles and have increased their diversity (Kallen 1977b). Elsewhere (Kallen 1988), I have conceptualized the current gay and lesbian liberation movement (in contrast to the gay and lesbian rights movement) as a revitalization movement, on the ground that, in large urban areas of North America, it has led to the creation of new and distinct communities and subcultures (without roots in a historical tradition). Moreover, these gay and lesbian communities, like many of their ethnic counterparts, through time have developed the necessary institutional infrastructures to transmit their distinctive subcultural lifestyles.

From Contention to Revitalization: The Evolution of Minority Protest

We suggested earlier that movements for social reform generated by ethnic minorities often gain impetus from marginal or assimilationist members, who realistically assess their own chances for status improvement in terms of the collective advancement of their ethnic community. Thus, contention often develops when frustrated ethnic elites, denied access to valued social positions and prevented from attaining majority ethnic status, re-identify strongly with their own ethnic group, assume leadership, and mobilize discontent.

Reformer leaders support the ideals of the established order and thus can often rally support from both dominant and minority ethnic groups through mass appeals to public opinion. An outstanding illustration is provided in the case of Martin Luther King, leader of the American civil rights movement.

Attempts to overthrow the existing order or secede from it do not usually occur until leaders of ethnic minorities have failed or given up hope of achieving desired reforms. More radical leaders may then attempt to organize subversive, revolutionary movements utilizing illegal, violent tactics such as terrorism and guerrilla warfare. Militant black nationalist movements in the United States and the FLQ (*Front de Libération du Québec*) and the NARP (National Alliance for Red Power) in Canada provide striking examples.

Minority Ethnic Protest Movements as New Social Movements

Melucci's Conceptualization of New Social Movements

In 1980, Melucci (1980, 1996) introduced the concept of the **new social movement** into the sociological literature. This concept was applied to increasingly emerging forms of collective action giving precedence to culture, meaning, and identity, which Melucci associated with feminism, ecological radicalism, ethnic separatism, and other variants of 'identity politics' (identity and solidarity-seeking movements). Melucci's approach emphasizes the importance of the psychology of collective emotional experiences in the active construction of collective identity, and—especially in his 1996 work—highlights the significance of global communication and information, especially the Internet, in this process.

A brief exposition of Melucci's central thesis reveals that his theory can contribute significantly to our understanding of the three minority ethnic protest movements highlighted in this chapter. Melucci (1980) proposes that changes in the structure of advanced, postindustrial societies have given rise to a singular category of social movements, which he calls the new social movements. In today's advanced societies, he argues, the dominant class has assumed control, and a capacity for intervention, in spheres of society well beyond that of the production structure. Their reach now extends into the areas of consumption, information, services, and interpersonal relations. The control and manipulation of the centres of technocratic domination are increasingly penetrating everyday life, encroaching in the individual's possibility of controlling his or her time, space, and relationships.

This expansion of the societal arenas of dominant control, says Melucci, has changed the form of expropriation of social resources. The movement for reappropriation of society's resources is therefore carrying its fight into new territory. Increasingly, what is deemed to be at stake in conflict between the agencies of social manipulation and the forces pressing for reappropriation is the personal and social identity of individuals. Defence of the identity, continuity, and predictability of personal existence is beginning to constitute the substance of the new conflicts. In the new social movements, individuals are collectively claiming the right to realize their own identity and to control their personal creativity, their affective life, and their biological and interpersonal existence.

Melucci points out several characteristics shared by the various new social movements to confirm his hypothesis that sees in the appropriation of identity the key to understanding them. First, these movements reject the traditional separation between public and private spheres. Those areas traditionally confined to the private sphere—sexual relations, interpersonal relations, biological identity—have become stakes in conflict situations and now are foci of collective action. At the same time, individual needs and demands have penetrated the sphere of the public and political. Birth and death, illness and aging have all become foci of collective action.

Melucci's contention that the new social movements reject the traditional separation between public and private spheres is borne out by our analysis, in Chapter 3, of the testimony detailing the dehumanizing experiences of abused immigrant, refugee, visible minority, and aboriginal women in Canada. The fact that these issues are now in the public spotlight lends clear support for Melucci's thesis.

A second characteristic found in some of the new movements is what Melucci calls the superposition of deviance and social movements. In response to dominant control and manipulation of daily life—on the rules of existence and ways of life—opposition takes the form of marginality and deviance. Public intervention tends to reduce conflicts to the status of pathology, by subjecting non-conformists to preventative therapies or to 'rehabilitation'. Because the power structure's control over dissemination of information enables it to stigmatize all conflict-based behaviour as 'deviant', social revolts against this kind of domination are often the work of minorities, and frequently lead to violence.

In Canada, a critical case in point is provided by media coverage of the continuing confrontation between aboriginal groups and the police, epitomized in the example of the Oka crisis. As detailed in Chapter 1, sensational media coverage has led to insidious stereotyping of aboriginal peoples as 'violent and deviant'.

Another characteristic suggested by Melucci is that the new social movements are not primarily focused on empowerment. Essentially, they are not oriented toward the conquest of political power or of the state apparatus. Rather, these movements are oriented toward the control of a particular social space where they have autonomy or independence vis-à-vis the system.

Solidarity as an objective, Melucci suggests, is another characteristic of the new social movements. The struggle centres on the issue of group identity, based on ascriptive criteria such as sex, age, race, and territory. The movements, Melucci points out, also have instrumental objectives, and seek political advantages, but this dimension is secondary to the expressive nature of the relations sought in the search for solidarity, the primary thrust of the movements.

The Franco-Quebecois, aboriginal, and multicultural movements in Canada, discussed later in this chapter, bear out Melucci's contention that the new social movements are not primarily bent on usurption of power from dominant authorities; they are not aiming to overthrow the state apparatus. Rather, these movements are oriented toward the control of a particular social space where they have autonomy or independence vis-à-vis the system. Similarly, our analysis of the three minority ethnic protest movements later in this chapter supports Melucci's emphasis on *solidarity as an objective* as a characteristic of the new social movements. In all three Canadian movements, the struggle centres on the particularistic issue of ethnic group identity, based on ascriptive criteria such as ethnicity, race, and territory. As Melucci suggests, these movements also have instrumental objectives and seek political advantages, but this dimension is secondary to the expressive nature of the relations sought in the search for solidarity, the primary thrust of the movements. Our upcoming analysis of Canadian ethnic protest movements will lend partial support for this thesis, but will reveal a quite different balance between expressive and instrumental objectives in the three movements discussed.

Finally, Melucci mentions the characteristic of direct participation and rejection of mediation. Since what is at stake is the reappropriation of individual and group identity, Melucci argues that all mediation is rejected as suspect, because it is seen as likely to reproduce the very mechanisms of control and manipulation against which the struggle is directed. The emphasis on direct action and direct participation galvanizes the spontaneous, anti-authoritarian, anti-hierarchical nature of the protests originating in these movements. Melucci suggests, however, the emphasis on direct participation and the concomitant nature of the protests contribute to the risks of discontinuity and fragmentation that constantly threaten these new movements.

Clearly, all these characteristics are not found in every new social movement: Melucci presents them basically as common themes. As will be shown, the extreme emphasis on direct participation and total rejection of mediation characteristic of some of the new social movements is not found to be characteristic of the three minority ethnic protest movements highlighted in this chapter.

Kriesi and Colleagues' Conceptualization of New Social Movements

Kriesi and colleagues (1995) posit a hierarchy of political issues that affect the degree to which a new social movement is perceived by dominant authorities as a threat to their superordinate status and power. These authors argue that the more material resources are involved, and the more political power is at stake, the more threatening a social movement may be for political authorities. The non-aboriginal, subcultural, and ethnocultural movements, such as Canada's multicultural movement, Kriesi and colleagues suggest can be categorized as 'low-profile', posing no real threat to the high priority policy domains of the dominant powers. In the case of the aboriginal movement, however, their overarching emphasis on control of land and land-based resources and their demands for political autonomy, places them in a more 'high profile' category than the other movements. Kriesi and associates suggest that aboriginal movements are perceived as posing a palpable threat to the high-priority policy domains of the dominant powers. However, the new aboriginal movements are far less threatening to state powers than are nationhood movements seeking independence from the state (such as the Franco-Quebecois). The new aboriginal movements do not pose the threat of secession because their nationhood demands centre on self-determination within the (Canadian) state.

Minority Rights Movements

A **minority rights movement** represents a particular form and direction of collective minority protest. This type of social movement is most likely to emerge when minority discontent focuses on the inconsistency between declared societal ideals endorsing human rights principles and the non-implementation of these ideals in public institutions and in public practice.

Ironically, as pointed out more than a century ago by Alexis de Toqueville: 'generally speaking, the most perilous moment for a bad government is one when it seeks to mend its ways' (quoted in Clark, Grayson, and Grayson 1975: 11). When governments begin to replace discriminatory social policies and laws with anti-discriminatory, human rights instruments, the expectations of minorities, the targets of discrimination, begin to rise. When minority expectations rise at a faster rate than actual achievements, the gap between expectations and achievements widens, and minority discontent escalates.

When human rights principles become legally entrenched, it follows that minority expectations will reach new heights. Minority expectations for explicit statutory and constitutional recognition of minority rights and for actual equality of societal opportunities may then come to outstrip the manifest increase in achievements. When this happens, minority discontent rises palpably.

The emergence and proliferation of minority rights movements in Canada over the past two decades provides evidence for this theoretical position. Minority protest on the part of both ethnic and non-ethnic groups initially focused on policy changes. In the 1970s (the 'human rights decade') protest came increasingly to incorporate demands for legal changes such as enumeration of the minority status criterion under the non-discriminatory grounds of statutory human rights instruments. Since the advent of the Charter in 1982, minority rights issues have become constitutionalized, and minority protest has focused on constitutional changes designed to guarantee minority rights. However, actual achievements have lagged behind soaring minority expectations. Accordingly, expressed minority discontent, in the form of continued lobbying for change, and in the form of legal claims for redress against violations of minority rights put forward at both the statutory and constitutional levels, has increased. Chapters 8 and 9 will look at the legal framework of human rights protection in Canada.

Minority Rights Movements and Human Rights Claims

The conceptual distinction between *contention* and *revitalization* as forms of minority rights movements has important implications for the nature of human rights claims that will be put forward by minority organizations. Drawing on the typology of human rights claims in Table I-1 of the Introduction, we will argue that *contention* focuses on individual, categorical, and/or collective rights claims, while *revitalization* tends to prioritize collective rights claims, including nationhood claims, over and above individual and categorical rights claims.

Individual rights claims represent demands for recognition and protection of the individual human rights of minority members. Such claims may seek specified changes in constitutional and/or statutory law. *Categorical rights claims* represent demands for collective redress against the collective adverse impact of systemic discrimination upon the minority as a whole. Such claims may seek the implementation of affirmative action measures designed to remedy group inequities. Like individual rights claims, categorical claims do not rest on assumptions about cultural distinctiveness or alternative lifestyles, thus, they can justifiably be put forward by representatives of minorities with and without a viable cultural base. Accordingly, members of non-ethnic as well as ethnic minorities may put forward categorical rights claims. Alternatively, *collective rights claims* contain the underlying assumption of the right of an ethnic minority *as a community* to express and perpetuate a distinctive ethnoculture. Accordingly, collective rights claims may only be justifiably put forward by representatives of minorities with a viable ethnocultural base. *National rights (nationhood) claims*, as a distinct form of collective rights claim, are predicated on a demonstrable and integral link between a particular ethnic group, its ancestral territory and its distinctive ethnoculture. Such claims can only justifiably be put forward by those ethnic groups with an ancestral territorial base (homeland) within the state.

Differential Minority Ethnic Status and Collective Rights Claims: Charter, Immigrant, and Aboriginal Ethnic Communities

In the current Canadian context, differential ethnic status—charter, immigrant, or aboriginal status—has important implications for the kinds of minority protests that arise, and for the kinds of categorical and collective human rights claims proposed by ethnic minority organizations. In the following section of this chapter, three minority ethnic protest movements will be examined in light of these considerations. The human rights framework for our analysis is shown in Table 7-1. This discussion will focus on the collective and categorical human rights claims made by representatives of three minority ethnic protest movements. Individual claims put forward by particular minority members on the basis of perceived human rights violations are not included in the discussion; cases based on such claims are detailed in Chapter 8.

Three Minority Ethnic Protest Movements and Their Human Rights Implications

Breton (1978: 65) has identified three broad movements of minority ethnic protest operative in Canada: the Québécois Independentist movement, the multiculturalism movement, and the Red Power movement.[2] These three social movements represent the differential responses of charter, immigrant, and aboriginal minorities to their subordinate status within Canadian society. As Breton points out, each of these movements is heterogeneous—each rubric covers a variety of different ethnic organizations, platforms, and proposals. Moreover, none of the movements can be taken to represent all of the diverse communities and organizations within the ethnic category as a whole.

Table 7-1 Minority Ethnic Protest Movements and Human Rights*

Minority Ethnic Status	Categorical	Cultural (Linguistic Religious)	Territorial	
			National	*Aboriginal*
Charter: Quebecois Independence	●	●	●	–
Immigrant: Multiculturalism	●	●	–	–
Aborigines: Aboriginal Rights and New Nationhood	●	●	●	●

● Kinds of Rights Claimed

* The discussion of the three minority ethnic protest movements will highlight those aspects most relevant to our focus on human rights. For those readers who wish to pursue the topics in greater depth, selected references are provided throughout the text.

For the present analysis, which focuses on the human rights implications of the movements, it is the differentiation *between*, rather than *within* these movements that is salient.

Franco-Quebecois Independence Movement

The Franco-Quebecois Independence movement may be conceptualized as a revitalization movement bent on politicoeconomic sovereignty and cultural transformation. As such, it represents a politically revolutionary response to long-term ethnic inequality. Franco-Quebecois's demands for a sovereign Quebec are rooted in claims based on the constitutionally recognized charter group status of the French as one of Canada's two founding peoples.

The Franco-Quebecois Independence movement germinated in the Quiet Revolution following the election of the Quebec Liberal Party in 1962. The electoral slogan of the Liberal Party, *Maîtres chez nous* (Masters in our own home) symbolized a radical shift in the political, economic, and cultural components of the nationalism of French Quebecers away from passive maintenance of the provincial *status quo*—symbolized by the slogan *la survivance*—to active control of the development of the state (Lee 1979). A variety of less radical options to Quebecois independence emerged in this period, but widespread disillusionment with their failure led more and more Quebecers to favour the route of independence (Morris and Lanphier 1977).[3]

Lee (1979) provides an insightful analysis of the evolution of nationalism in Quebec that clearly shows the way in which the Franco-Quebecois Independence movement represents a revitalization response to the suppression of long-term yearnings for new nationhood among French Quebecers.[4]

Traditional Nationalism: La survivance

Politically, traditional nationalism also emphasized ethnic isolation as a means of preserving French/English 'unity in duality' within Canada. The mission of Quebec was to guard French-Canadian culture, and to protect and defend provincial rights from federal intervention. Cultural nationalism implied the maintenance of the religious, linguistic, and cultural *status quo* through the continuing battle against assimilation to Anglo influences.

Modern Nationalism: *Maîtres chez nous*

Lee (1979) argues persuasively that the increasing impact of industrialization, urbanization, and political modernization upon Quebec from without, and later from within, the boundaries of the province, virtually destroyed the bases of traditional nationalism, as its conservative bias proved both inappropriate and ineffective in a modernizing Quebec fraught with radical changes in all spheres of life.[5] Together with *maîtres chez nous*, the Liberal slogan of the 1960s was *Il faut que ça change* (Things must change). As the relative isolation of the Quebec French community was penetrated, the goal of self-sufficiency became dissociated from the need to maintain the *status quo* and nationalism was redefined as the need to control both internal institutions and relations with the outside. Expanding Anglo-American capitalism had created an increasingly economically dependent French urban ethno-class, as the 'habitant' population without available land to farm and without modern occupational skills, surged to the city. In the face of the subordinate economic status of the French 'in their own country', the modernizing elite took steps to increase the control of the state in economic matters (for example, nationalization of Hydro Québec).

Lee contends that new responsibilities in the areas of taxation, health and welfare, and education necessitated a marked expansion of Quebec bureaucracy. Thus, political nationalism included the administration of new spheres of activity associated with expanding industrialization as well as social and welfare services previously managed by the Catholic Church. In turn, cultural nationalism meant the assumption of control over cultural matters, and the concomitant breaking of the church's monopolistic front.

With the decline in power and ideological salience of the Catholic Church, the focus of French cultural control shifted to issues of language and immigration. In this process, the *maîtres chez nous* nationalism moved from a goal of bilingualism and biculturalism for French Canadians throughout Canada, to one of unilingualism and uniculturalism for the Franco-Quebecois in the Quebec state. As the Province of Quebec assumed a more active role in decisions concerning its economic, educational, and health and welfare institutions, it provided a new territorial basis for French ethnic alignment and identification. Ethnic territoriality for the French thus became disassociated from Canada and redefined in terms of the 'state' of Quebec, since, by definition, a state has jurisdiction over a given territory. In this process, the boundaries of the national French-Canadian ethnic community disappeared and new, narrower, group boundaries emerged around a new Franco-Quebecois ethnic identity.

According to Lee, the political implications of this shift in ethnic group boundaries are manifold, and all signs point towards the movement for Franco-Quebecois independence and nationhood. At the time of writing, Lee asserted that all scenarios concerned the self-sufficiency and self-determination of Quebec, not Canada, and not French Canada. While the modern nationalist options ranged from the *status quo* to separatism, Lee contended that the options of decentralization, special status, or sovereignty-association were probably among the more viable scenarios in the immediate future. More than a decade later, the scenarios outlined by Lee were in the forefront of the protracted debate on Canadian unity.[6]

The Revitalization Option: Conceptualizing Franco-Quebecois Independence in Human Rights Terms

The Franco-Quebecois Independence movement is predicated on both instrumental and expressive corporate ethnic goals. Demands for political autonomy and control over economic resources rest, in part, on claims for categorical rights as redress for long-term political and economic discrimination. However, an important aspect of alleged past discrimination has been its linguistic basis (Joy 1972); thus, demands for linguistic rights are closely associated with politicoeconomic demands. Language is also importantly linked with expressive goals: the ethnocultural identity of the Franco-Quebecois has a strong linguistic character. Finally, and most importantly, because of their ethnic status as a charter group, the Franco-Quebecois can make nationhood claims based on collective, national group rights. In this connection, the self-definition of the Franco-Quebecois as a distinctive ethnocultural group whose ancestral homeland is the Province of Quebec, is critical.

René Lévesque, the prime catalyst and charismatic leader of the Franco-Quebecois Independence Movement, clearly identified his people's ethnocultural destiny with their right to their ancestral homeland. In his seminal book *An Option For Quebec* he asked:

> Of all the rights that are recognized—or at least proclaimed—by twentieth-century man, is there a more fundamental one than the right to a genuine homeland, the right to live (and hence to work) in one's own language, the right to have a daily environment in harmony with one's culture and mentality, the right to take part in the concert of nations, freely and directly (1968: 116)?

His own answer, succinct and to the point, provided the charter for the Franco-Quebecois Independence movement:

> If we want to remain French, if we want to conduct our lives in French, like a normal nation, there is no path to take other than that which leads to the political sovereignty of Quebec, along with an economic union with the rest of Canada. This means independence without total separation. This means freedom from our perpetual minority status to associate ourselves in true liberty and equality' [with English Canada] (1968: 118).

With the 1976 electoral victory of the Parti Québécois under Lévesque's leadership, the politicization of the Franco-Quebecois Independence movement as a revitalization movement became full blown. While not all Quebecois independentists supported the Parti Québécois as a political party, it managed to bring together most of the small, independentist groups under a social democratic program with a strong emphasis on cultural nationalism (Morris and Lanphier 1977: 249). This cultural nationalism was clearly expressed in Bill 101, which made French the single official language in Quebec.

Notwithstanding internal differences regarding the precise blueprint for Quebec's future, Lévesque's sovereignty-association model for Quebecois independence was proposed in the historical 1980 Referendum question:

> The Government of Quebec has made public its proposal to negotiate a new agreement with the rest of Canada, based on the equality of nations; this agreement would enable Quebec to acquire the exclusive power to make its laws, administer its taxes and establish relations abroad—in other words, sovereignty—and at the same time, to maintain with Canada an economic association including a common currency; any change in political status resulting from these negotiations will be submitted to the people through a referendum; on these terms, do you agree to give the Government of Quebec the mandate to negotiate the proposed agreement between Quebec and Canada?

Despite the (59.5 per cent) rejection of this option in favour of federalism by the people of Quebec, Lévesque refused to abandon his dream for a revitalized Franco-Quebecois nation.[7] To his campaign supporters he offered these words of hope: 'Let us accept, but not let go, never lose view of such legitimate, universal objectives as equality. It will come' (*Globe and Mail*, 21 May 1980).

The Aftermath: The Quebecois Quest for Nationhood Continues

In the wake of the Quebec Referendum in May 1980, the federal government made a commitment to renew Canadian federalism through greater recognition of the needs and aspirations of Quebec. But, in November 1981, Premier Lévesque refused to endorse the constitutional agreement (enacted on 17 April 1982 as the Canada Act) because it was deemed to abrogate the government of Canada's commitment of 1980 and to counter the particular interests and historic rights of Quebec society, the only society in Canada with a French-speaking majority (Remillard 1989: 29). Premier Lévesque's refusal to sign the constitutional Accord reached on 5 November 1981 clearly demonstrated his fervent commitment to the principles of Quebecois nationhood. At that time, he proclaimed that Quebec, as an equal partner in Confederation, had the right to veto a constitutional package that did not recognize and protect the special status and character of the Quebec nation (*Globe and Mail*, 25 November 1981).

The death of René Lévesque and the election of a Liberal government under Robert Bourassa in 1985 put Lévesque's dream of sovereignty-association for Quebec on hold. Nevertheless, since that time, the Franco Quebecois quest for equality with English Canada and survival as a distinct society within (or in some form of association with) the Canadian state continued. The 'Quebec Question' was the central issue in the context of three national debates: the controversy surrounding Bill 101, Quebec's French Language Charter; the constitutional debates over the provisions of the proposed 1987 Meech Lake Accord and the 1992 Charlottetown Accord; and the question of Quebec sovereignty.[8]

While the Franco-Quebecois succeeded in their struggle to make French the 'national' language in Quebec, they failed to achieve constitutional changes that would put them on an equal footing with English Canada and, most significantly, they failed to achieve the goal of sovereignty-association with English Canada. Nevertheless, the leaders of the movement for Franco-Quebecois independence took their failures, particularly the rejection of the Charlottetown Accord, as a clear expression of the extreme dissatisfaction of their Quebec compatriots with the constitutional *status quo*, and an irrepressible desire for change in the direction of sovereignty. This gave the movement renewed vigour for their pursuit of independence, and before long, a new, sovereignist federal party—the Bloc Québécois—an offshoot of the Parti Québécois, burst onto the political scene. In the federal election held on 25 October 1993, the Bloc Québécois under the leadership of Lucien Bouchard captured 54 of the province's 75 seats (most of the province's predominantly French-speaking ridings) and emerged as the federal party with the second largest number of seats. This put the Bloc in position for the role of official Opposition party to the new Liberal government under Prime Minister Jean Chrétien.

A few days before the federal election, Parti Québécois leader Jacques Parizeau predicted that Quebec would be sovereign by 1995. Parizeau said that the PQ's support of the Bloc is part of a three-stage plan to achieve this goal: 1) strong representation of the Bloc in the federal parliament; 2) victory of the PQ in the next provincial election in Quebec; and 3) a provincial referendum 'to achieve sovereignty' (*Toronto Star*, 22 December 1993). At the time, many commentators appeared to believe that this would be the most likely political scenario in Quebec's future. But it has not come to pass.

Into the Millennium: Parizeau, Liberal Nationalism, and the Failure of Independence

On 12 September 1994, Quebec once again elected a PQ government committed to a referendum on independence. The singular issue and challenge ahead was the road to political independence. It was clear that the language of nationalism had to be adapted to fit the new realities of Quebec. This articulation came in the form of liberal nationalism (Chevrier 1996; Freire 1996).

Liberal nationalism rejects appeals to ethnicity, race, or language. Yet, it is an identity-focused new social movement as conceptualized by Melucci (1980, 1996). Lucien Bouchard, leader of the Bloc Québécois, said that '[O]urs is not an ethnic nationalism, for it recognizes that the "nation Québécoise" is constituted by the people as a whole who inhabit Quebec' (*New York Times*, 2 November 1995). Gone were the racial and ethnic appeals of Lévesque, the evoking of a unique and separate history and destiny. The new inclusive nationalism emphasized universal values of democracy, religious and ethnic tolerance, and equality. The Quebec of the 1990s possessed a modern economy, a multicultural and multilingual society and a long history of self-government and democratic institutions. These were the qualities to which Parizeau referred during the referendum debate.

The Declaration of Sovereignty issued with the independence bill did use language reminiscent of traditional nationalism. References to a French history and culture as well as Anglo domination are made. 'Ancestors' are evoked as well as the principle of Canada originating with 'two founding peoples'. The French language is again used to identify a 'distinct society'. But liberal nationalism took over. Parizeau emphasized the varied contributions of all linguistic and ethnic communities in all regions of the new 'country' of Quebec and acknowledged the moral duties of all Quebecers of respect, of tolerance, of solidarity towards one another.[9] Parizeau evoked the more traditional element of nationalism in several of his speeches, but again, the unmistakable emphasis was upon the new liberal variety.

Léveque's ethnic-national distinct society was one rooted in a distinctive Quebecois language and culture. Liberal nationalism's distinct society applies to all Quebecers. The distinction lies not in ethnicity but a commitment to economic and political values and rights that are basically universal in nature, along with a conviction that the 'country' of Quebec warrants independence in order to pursue these values more effectively (Chevrier 1996; Freire 1996). Parizeau's campaign for sovereignty was a broad-based appeal to all Quebecers to join in a movement originating in the ethnocentrism of Quebecois nationalism but presently advocating a future prosperity for all. Thus the stage for the Referendum was set: Parizeau and the advocates for independence articulated a vision of a future Quebec characterized by a modern economy, liberal society, and democratic politics.

The Referendum was held on 31 October 1995. As with its 1980 predecessor, the separatists lost. This time, however, the margin was razor thin. Only 50.6 per cent of the Quebec electorate voted to remain within confederation. On receiving the results, Parizeau resigned as leader of the PQ, but not before uttering a revealing statement. He blamed the defeat on the 'ethnic vote'. Parizeau's comment suggested that, in his view, liberal nationalism may have yet to replace many of the older sentiments of ethnic and racial divisions within Quebec society. Regardless, the 49.4 per cent who voted for political independence points to the effectiveness of the Liberal nationalist argument (Freire 1996).

There can be no doubt that nationalism has been, and remains a force within Quebec. What is unclear is how and in what form this nationalism will articulate itself and shape the future of Quebec.

The Multicultural Movement: Conceptualizing the Rights of Non-English and Non-French Immigrant Groups

As a movement of minority ethnic protest, the multicultural movement represents a response of contention designed to achieve the goal of an egalitarian Canadian mosaic. Immigrant ethnic groups' demands for cultural and structural reform within Canadian society involve claims based on both categorical and collective cultural rights. Unlike the Franco-Quebecois Independence movement that addresses its design for the future to a single ethnic audience, the multicultural movement encompasses the diverse and sometimes conflicting claims of a wide range of immigrant ethnic communities.

As indicated in Chapter 6, the multicultural movement emerged in response to the expressed discontent of immigrant ethnic minorities with their relegation to second-class status under the terms of the Royal Commission on Bilingualism and Biculturalism. The Bi and Bi Commission was instructed to recommend steps for the development of Canadian Confederation on the basis of an equal partnership between the 'two founding races'—a term that confuses race and culture—in reference to the English and French charter groups in Canada (P.C. 1963: 1106). This bicultural goal, protestors argued, relegated all other peoples and cultures to minority status within Canada. Similarly, objections were raised against the goal of bilingualism that supported only the English and French languages, later enshrined in the Official Languages Act (1969).

The earliest and most powerful spokesperson for the multicultural movement was Senator Paul Yuzyk, who, in his maiden speech to the Canadian Senate (3 May 1964), introduced the idea of a Third Force—a coalition of all non-English and non-French ethnic communities in Canada. Yuzyk clearly articulated the instrumental goal of the movement when he pointed out that the Third Force (then) represented almost one-third of the Canadian population, and as a united organizational force could hold the balance of power between the English and French. The expressive goal of the multicultural movement soon became evident in demands for the implementation of the Canadian mosaic ideal through a federal policy of multiculturalism and multilingualism. Spearheaded largely by Ukrainian spokesmen, such as Yuzyk, the movement was supported even in its early stages by representatives of other long-resident immigrant ethnic communities, such as Jews, and later by a variety of newer immigrants, including Italians, Armenians, Portuguese, Greeks, and others.

The majority response to the conflicting demands of the Third Force, on the one hand, and of the French nationalists who supported a model of English/French bilingualism and biculturalism, on the other hand, was represented in the compromise policy of multiculturalism within a bilingual framework. Minority ethnic protest against the terms of the policy, since its inception, has indicated clearly that it has not satisfied the demands of either of the constituencies whose claims it sought to address. Just as proponents of bilingualism and biculturalism continue to argue that the latter necessitates the former, proponents of the multicultural movement continue to argue that language and culture are indivisible; therefore multiculturalism is meaningless without multilingualism. While the early proponents of the multicultural movement focused on fundamental human rights, especially the right of equal access of all ethnic groups to political, economic, and social power, spokespersons for a variety of ethnic organizations over the years have increasingly made demands for collective minority (cultural, religious, and linguistic) rights.

Concessions to ethnic minority linguistic demands, in the form of provincial heritage language programs, have not adequately addressed minority concerns. From the viewpoint of the multicultural movement, unless multicultural policy (at both federal and provincial levels) affords equitable support for minority, as for majority cultural maintenance in public institutions, it continues to violate the collective rights of non-English and non-French immigrant ethnic communities.

This position was strongly endorsed in minority ethnic representations before the Special Joint Committee of the Senate and the House of Commons on the Constitution. Witnesses were virtually unanimous in their insistence that multiculturalism be formally acknowledged in the Constitution, and the many witnesses who spoke in favour of non-official language rights indicated clearly that the Third Force was seeking positive, constitutional protection of non-official languages, particularly in education (Hudson 1987: 78). However, the outcome of their efforts was not an amendment to the Charter's provisions for official languages that would provide parallel protection for non-official languages, but a separate, vaguely worded provision on multiculturalism (section 27) which makes no mention of language.

Hudson and Magnet agree that there are no clear clues as to how the phrase 'multicultural heritage' in section 27 of the Charter is to be interpreted. Hudson (1987: 78) has argued that the constitutional background sheds no light on the meaning of the phrase, and Magnet (1989:745) has suggested that the broad range of opinion as to the meaning of section 27 revealed by ethnic lobbying prior to the constitutional entrenchment of the provision allows the courts to interpret the phrase 'multicultural heritage' in a wide variety of ways. In any event, in the view of the Third Force, section 27 of the Charter *should* be interpreted so as to afford positive protection for collective, linguistic, religious, and broader cultural, minority rights (see Chapter 9 for an analysis of the constitutional debates and the provisions of the Charter). With regard to government support for minority religious education, the tiny amount of funding for instruction in private minority religious schools afforded under multicultural programs indicates beyond doubt that this is not a priority item on the government's multicultural agenda.[10]

For members of visible minorities, the multicultural movement represents a forum for protest against racism and an instrument through which to combat racial discrimination. The empowerment goals articulated by representatives of visible minorities are based on three institutional imperatives: *access* (openness to visible minorities), *representation* (proportionate to numbers in the population), and *equity* (equality of opportunity and removal of systemic barriers) (Elliot and Fleras 1990: 69). Despite the shift in multicultural program emphasis—from cultural retention to anti-racism—over the decades, visible minority spokespersons have asserted that the anti-racism initiatives—anti-racist educational programs, employment equity measures for visible minorities, sensitivity training for police forces—have failed to halt the escalation of anti-white prejudice and discrimination across Canada.

In response to these varied criticisms, in 1996, by a special Act of the federal Parliament, a new government agency, the Canadian Race Relations Foundation (CRRF), was established to deal more directly with issues of racial discrimination and inequalities. Although the CRRF is staffed mainly by visible minorities and provides a valuable ally and resource base for visible minority activists, it is, nevertheless, a federal government agency. As such, CRRF is controlled by dominant ethnic-group authorities who can continue to wield their power by defining program priorities.

The competing *collective rights* claims of ethnocultural minorities, on the one hand, and *categorical rights* claims of visible minorities, on the other hand, have resulted in a deepening rift between racial and cultural minorities within the multicultural movement. Moreover, the difference in priorities between the two factions within the movement is compounded by the fact that they must compete with each other for the very limited government funding available under the multicultural rubric. The implications of this split for the future of the movement are manifold: it has seriously weakened the potential of the multicultural movement as a Third Force coalition comprised of all immigrant ethnic groups.

Not only internal but also external forces have placed the future of the multicultural movement into serious question. The critical national issue of Canadian unity, in the face of Quebec's persistent threat of sovereignty, has made Canadians increasingly wary of the divisive potential of cultural demands. Accordingly, the ideological premises of multiculturalism have come under intensified criticism by dominant Canadians as minority cultural claims have escalated. The rising numbers of non-white immigrants has created a parallel backlash: increasingly, established white Euro-Canadians feel racially and culturally threatened.

As pointed out in Chapter 6, during the late 1980s and into the 1990s, the majority backlash against multiculturalism became increasingly expressed in vocal majority opposition to the terms of the federal multicultural policy. In both English Canada and Quebec, hostile majority opposition clearly reflected the symbolic threat posed by the flourishing of distinct minority ethnocultures to the majority's cultural hegemony in Canada. Pressures exerted by majority spokespersons to discontinue the policy or to revise its priorities to favour and facilitate only the goal of immigrant absorption escalated.

In response to increasing majority opposition to the multicultural policy, the Department of Multiculturalism and Citizenship was abolished, and multiculturalism was demoted. It was housed in a new Canadian Heritage Ministry, together with parks, culture, sports, official languages, and the status of women, a ministry headed by low-profile, junior administrators. Not surprisingly, this demotion was accompanied by sharp budget cuts. In the early 1980s, the annual budget for administration of the multicultural policy was about $30 million. By 1996, it had been reduced to about $17 million. Pressure was continually exerted on the administrators of the policy by majority ethnic groups to undertake a re-evaluation of its goals, and, in particular, to curtail all grants to ethnic community organizations—grants that had been the backbone of the policy in the past.

In response to continuing, vociferous majority opposition to the federal policy, in the spring of 1997 Multiculturalism Canada issued its new statement of priorities. The statement and the program guidelines focused on three main goals: identity, civic participation, and social justice. These goals provide a clear blueprint for immigrant ethnic absorption. None of the goals offers support for the maintenance of distinctive, living ethnocultural communities. The program excludes all ethnic community organizations, activities, celebrations, and ethnic communication media, previously supported under the original multicultural policy. This giant step backward clearly reveals that the *dominant conformity* blueprint for integration of Canada's immigrant ethnic minorities, now ineptly camouflaged in the guise of multiculturalism, has been resurrected and endorsed by Canada's ethnic majority groups. Taking into account recent news reports and survey findings that reveal increasing public disenchantment with what is perceived as a disturbing trend toward separation from the Canadian mainstream by racial-ethnic minorities, the survival of the multiculturalism movement is highly problematic.

The Aboriginal Nationhood Movement: Conceptualizing Aboriginal Rights and Nationhood Rights

Like the Quebecois Independence movement, and in contrast to the multicultural movement, the aboriginal movement can be conceptualized as a revitalization movement bent on politicoeconomic sovereignty and cultural transformation. In one of its early, radical expressions, articulated by the Native Alliance for Red Power (NARP), it represented a politically revolutionary response to long-term, colonial suppression. The goal was separation from Canada, to be achieved through violence, if necessary (Jack 1970). For the most part, however, demands for economic equality and for political and cultural sovereignty voiced by various organizations under the general rubric of the Aboriginal movement represent claims for First Nations status within Canada.

The Aboriginal Nationhood Movement as a Human Rights Movement

As Canada's original occupants, who were self-governing nations before European encroachment into their territories, aboriginal peoples are making national rights claims. The intimate association between aboriginal peoples, their land-based cultures, self-governing institutions and their aboriginal territories, provides the basis for aboriginal claims to nationhood based on collective, national group rights. Aboriginal peoples also are making aboriginal (land) rights claims, based on their continuing occupancy and use of their aboriginal lands 'from time immemorial'.[11] Lastly, on the basis of massive, incontrovertible evidence of their collective disadvantage and marginalized social status, consequent upon long-term institutional and systemic forms of racial discrimination against all categories of aboriginal peoples, leaders of the aboriginal movement advance strongly documented claims based on categorical rights.

Aboriginal Protest Movements as New Social Movements

From the perspective of new social movement theory, particularly as expounded by Melucci (1980, 1996) and Kriesi et al. (1995), current aboriginal liberation movements manifest many of the characteristics of non-aboriginal subcultural and ethnocultural movements within modern societies; yet they differ in important respects. Like the other movements of this type, they place a strong emphasis on group solidarity and collective identity. Where they differ is in their territorial emphasis and their demands for political, economic, and cultural sovereignty within the territories claimed as their ancestral homelands. Kriesi and associates posit a hierarchy of political issues: they argue that the more material resources are involved, and the more power is at stake, the more threatening a social movement may be for political authorities.

The non-aboriginal subcultural and ethnocultural movements, Kriesi et al. suggest, can be categorized as 'low-profile', posing no real threat to the high priority policy domains of the dominant powers. In the case of the aboriginal movement, however, their overarching emphasis on control of land and land-based resources as an integral aspect of their aboriginal ethnocultures, and their determination to re-gain their status as independent and self-governing nations, within their ancestral homeland territories, places them in a more 'high profile' category than the other movements. Kriesi et al. (1995) suggest that aboriginal movements are perceived as more threatening to dominant interests than are other subcultural and ethnocultural movements: they are perceived as posing a palpable threat to the high priority policy domains of the dominant powers. However, whereas aboriginal movements are in a real sense 'nationalist' movements, as new social movements they depart radically from the traditional conception of post-colonial nationalist movements, such as those that have arisen among externally colonized peoples in Africa, India, and other non-Western countries. These post-colonialist nationalist movements are highly instrumental and political in thrust: they aim to overthrow the colonial structure imposed on them, to overtake the state apparatus, and to usurp power for themselves (Connor 1993). Unlike these post-colonial nationalist movements, the new nationhood movements generated by internally colonized aboriginal peoples are limited in their instrumental goals to attaining self-determination as internal nations on aboriginal territories within existing post-colonial, Euro-Western-dominated societies. Thus, while the new aboriginal movements are seen to pose a threat to dominant interests, particularly as their demands relate to what Kriesi et al. call 'high-profile' policy issues, they do not pose the threat of secession (as does the Franco-Quebecois Nationhood Movement), nor do they pose the threat of usurption of power from existing authorities, who will continue to rule the country as a whole, according to Euro-Western cultural standards of governance, law, and justice.

History of the Aboriginal Nationhood Movement in Canada

The inception of the aboriginal movement was as a highly negative response to proposals for change in Indian affairs outlined in the federal government's White Paper of 1969 (Weaver

1981). This document, purportedly intended to accord Status Indians and other aboriginal peoples full ethnic equality within Canadian society, proposed: the abolition of the special constitutional and legislative status of aboriginal peoples; the repeal of the Indian Act; the phasing out of the reserve system; and the transfer of responsibility for services from the federal to provincial governments (Jackson 1979: 284).

Ponting and Gibbins (1980: 25–9) argued that the White Paper clearly reflected the liberal ideology of the Liberal government of the time led by then Prime Minister Trudeau. This ideology strongly endorsed the protection of individual rights but was antagonistic to the notion of collective rights. Thus, the White Paper emphasized the equality of aboriginal and non-aboriginal Canadians, as individuals, at the expense of the collective survival of aboriginal ethnic groups, as culturally distinctive peoples.

With specific reference to Status Indians, the policy paper gave some recognition to treaty rights, but it interpreted the wording of treaties historically negotiated between Indian bands and the Crown as revealing only 'limited and minimal promises' (Canada 1969: 11). Further, it virtually ignored the gigantic liabilities that Indians had accumulated as a long-term result of the self-fulfilling prophecy of racism. It did not attempt to compensate for the economic, political, and social disadvantages that would continue to impede the integration of Indians as 'ordinary citizens' within Canadian society. In a word, it failed to recognize the validity of potential Indian claims based on categorical rights.

In explanation of the negative response of Status Indians to the abolition of the Indian Act, Weaver (1981: 19) argues that while they clearly resent its paternalistic constraints, they embrace the special rights it provides, particularly with regard to the protection of their lands. Their overriding concern—shared by Canada's other aboriginal peoples—is to protect their historical relationship with aboriginal lands, which they view as critical for the survival of their distinct cultures. The White Paper was perceived to pose a direct threat to this valued relationship.

Aboriginal protest to the White Paper surfaced in a number of documents written by angry Indian leaders. In his pathbreaking book *The Unjust Society*, Harold Cardinal charged that the program suggested by the White Paper represented 'nothing better than cultural genocide'. For the Indian to survive, Cardinal contended, he must become 'a good little brown white man'. In effect, the policy implied 'The only good Indian is a non-Indian' (1969: 1). Another document, *Citizens Plus* (Red Paper 1970), authored by the Indian chiefs of Alberta, strongly reinforced Cardinal's position by arguing that Indians should be recognized as 'Citizens Plus', that is, citizens who possess additional rights as 'charter' members of Canadian society.

The White Paper proposals had their most immediate impact on Registered Treaty Indians because the recommendations to abolish the special legal status of Indians under the Indian Act threatened their treaty rights. But other aboriginal peoples—Registered Non-Treaty Indians, Non-Status Indians, and (later) Métis and Inuit—were soon swept up in the aboriginal tide of protest, since the White Paper proposals also threatened any potential claims that might be based on aboriginal rights. These aboriginal fears were intensified by a speech given by then Prime Minister Trudeau, in which he said that his government would not recognize aboriginal rights. However, under mounting pressure from aboriginal organizations, and after many months of public debate, the government finally retracted the White Paper proposals in 1971.

Since then, the various associations within the aboriginal movement have, with one voice, demanded recognition of their special status as the *original peoples* (First Nations) within Canada. They have argued that they have the fundamental right to political and cultural sovereignty, and that they have the right to retain ownership of sufficient aboriginal lands to ensure their independence and their economic and cultural survival. While there is considerable diversity among the kinds of claims put forward by representatives of particular aboriginal organizations, the principles of collective aboriginal and nationhood rights underscore them all.

As pointed out in Chapter 5, spokespersons for aboriginal organizations maintain that sovereignty is a gift of the Creator that has never been and can never be surrendered. Prior to the arrival of European agents, aboriginal peoples were independent, self-governing nations whose members lived and sought their livelihoods within clearly delineated territories. With colonization, they claim, their right to sovereignty was unjustly abrogated and their institutions of self-government systematically dismantled. But, as nations, they assert their sovereignty and their right to create and administer their own forms of self-government. From this aboriginal view, treaties made between aboriginal peoples and governments should be regarded as treaties between sovereign nations, in the sense of public international law.

This ideological thrust of the aboriginal movement was most clearly articulated in the initial proposals for settlement of land claims and for self-government put forward by representatives of the Dene Nation (1976) and the Inuit of Nunavut (1979). Both of these proposals have undergone considerable alteration, over the years, in the attempt of the aboriginal nations to achieve negotiated settlements with the federal government. And, in both cases, original nationhood claims have been compromised in the process.

For purposes of illustration, we will focus on the Nunavut proposal. In the author's view, the *Nunavut claim* represents the strongest single case for nationhood based on the demonstrably continuing links between the Inuit ethnic group, its distinctive ethnoculture, and its aboriginal territory/homeland (see Box 7-1).

Government Response to the Aboriginal Movement

To date, government response to proposals put forward by representatives of the aboriginal movement have favoured assimilationist settlements like the precedent-setting James Bay Agreement (1975) and have opposed proposals like the original versions of the Dene and Nunavut claims that seek political self-determination as nations. While the goal of aboriginal nationhood remains elusive, the aboriginal movement has come a long way in its attempt to persuade federal government authorities of the legitimacy of its position. 'Special status' for aboriginal peoples, rejected out of hand in the 1969 White Paper, now has become accepted in principle by government. The federal government also has endorsed the principle of limited forms of aboriginal self-government through public policy (Canada 1984b), and a number of reserve Indian communities already have established limited forms of self-government. Nonetheless, the federal government's restrictive interpretation of the concept of aboriginal self-government, based on the delegated/municipal model that keeps ultimate decision-making power over aboriginal affairs firmly in government hands, differs radically from the nationhood model endorsed by the aboriginal movement.

Most recently, during the 1992 round of constitutional negotiations, the *principle* of an inherent aboriginal right to self-government was accepted by Canada's federal and provincial premiers (*Toronto Star*, 12 May 1992). The final constitutional proposal (the Charlottetown Accord) agreed on by all Canada's premiers on 28 August 1992, proposed that the Constitution would recognize the inherent right to self-government of all aboriginal peoples, and aboriginal governments would also be recognized as one of three orders of government, the others being federal and provincial. Additionally, under the newly proposed Canada clause, the right of aboriginal peoples to promote their languages, cultures, and traditions and to ensure the integrity of their societies would be guaranteed. The Accord also guaranteed that there would be a political accord that recognized the right of aboriginal peoples to a significant say over future constitutional amendments that affect them.

BOX 7-1: CASE STUDY

The Inuit of Nunavut: An Aboriginal Success Story?

New Nationhood: The Nunavut Proposals (1979–92)

In order for the Inuit to regain aboriginal nationhood status, the national Inuit organization, Inuit Tapirisat of Canada (ITC), deemed it essential that the Inuit people regain political, economic, and cultural sovereignty within their aboriginal territory. Thus, it was necessary to validate their claim to national self-determination. What this involved at the outset, was to document their claim that their aboriginal right to their territory had never been surrendered by war or by treaty, and that the Inuit had continued to occupy and use their lands in their traditional ways, 'from time immemorial'. To fully document their nationhood claim, Inuit representatives had to provide evidence for the continuing integral links between the Inuit people, their aboriginal territory, and their land-based, aboriginal ethnoculture. In other words, the Inuit nationhood claims rested on the premise that the collective cultural, aboriginal, and national group rights of the Inuit people had never been abrogated in any 'official' way.

As put forward by the Inuit Committee on National Issues, the Inuit claim was based on a holistic conception of aboriginal and nationhood rights. This position holds that aboriginal title to land, water, and sea ice flows from aboriginal people's rights to practice their customs and traditions, to retain and develop their languages and cultures, and the right to self-government. In the Inuit view, aboriginal rights are fundamental human rights, because these are the things that the Inuit need to continue to survive as a distinct people in Canada.

This position was clearly articulated in the original ITC land claims proposal which was supported by extensive research studies documenting (among other things) actual Inuit land use and occupancy over the centuries. One study, directed by Dr Milton Freeman, an anthropologist at McMaster University, showed that, from prehistoric times, the Inuit have used and occupied virtually all of an estimated 750,000 square miles of land claimed as their aboriginal territory, as well as an estimated 800,000 square miles of northern ocean. This documentation was essential in order for the Inuit to validate their collective land claim, based on aboriginal rights.

With regard to Inuit nationhood claims, a number of proposals were circulated among the many, dispersed Inuit communities before a widely agreed-on position paper was drafted. The first agreed-on proposal was put forward by the ITC in 1979, as a position paper entitled 'Political Development in Nunavut'. In this paper, the ITC outlined Inuit demands for a newly defined territory that would assume provincial status over a period of about 15 years. The proposal made several important claims, among them, the right to self-determination of the Inuit people, the right of the Inuit to conduct their affairs in their own language (Inuktitut), the right of the Inuit to their traditional lands, waters and resources therein, their right to preserve and use their traditional hunting, trapping, and fishing resources, their right to define who is an Inuk (Inuk = singular of Inuit), and their right to economic compensation for past, present, and future use by non-Inuit of Inuit lands, waters, and resources.

From the beginning, the federal government rejected the conception of Nunavut as an 'ethnic' province, to be administered by the Inuit in ways that differed from that of other provinces. Throughout the 20 years of negotiations, the federal government invariably divided the political and economic package proposed by the Inuit, and focused on providing economic compensation for non-Inuit use of Inuit lands and resources. The Inuit proposals, on the other hand, focused on the sharing of Inuit lands and resources with the federal government and the people of Canada, on the understanding that the Inuit would have a prominent voice on all matters within their territorial jurisdiction.

The first step toward Inuit self-government was the proposed creation of a new territory, Nunavut, on Inuit aboriginal lands in the NT. This proposal envisaged the division of the NT into two separate jurisdictions, with Nunavut comprising the Eastern Arctic jurisdiction, north of the treeline. The Inuit proposed an elected system of government, for Nunavut, similar to that of the existing NT government. Since the vast majority of people within the jurisdiction would be Inuit, the Inuit would assume a substantial degree of control over their economic and cultural destinies.

In 1982, what seemed at the time to be a major breakthrough for the Inuit was the result of a NT plebiscite that approved division of the NT into two territories. The split received federal government approval in principle, subject to agreement on a boundary between the two new jurisdictions, and settlement of outstanding aboriginal land claims in the NT. Soon after, the Nunavut Constitutional Forum was established to work out the details of a Nunavut Constitution. In 1987, a proposal for a Nunavut Constitution was completed and a proposal for a Boundary and Constitutional Agreement between Western and Nunavut Constitutional Forums was put forward. However, the boundary dispute continued until October of 1990, when Inuit and territorial government leaders finally reached agreement on how to divide the Northwest Territories and create Canada's third territory—the territory of Nunavut.

In December of 1989, agreement in principle was reached between the Tungavik Federation of Nunavut, representing the Inuit in the central and Eastern Arctic regions, and the federal government on the long-standing land claim of the Inuit. The terms of the agreement would give the Inuit possession of over 260,000 square kilometres of land, with surface rights to approx. 225,000 square kilometres of the land, and with subsurface rights to about 36,000 square kilometres of the land. Additionally, the Inuit would receive $580 million in financial compensation, over 14 years. With indexation for interest rates, the total would be about $1.15 billion. In exchange, the Inuit would surrender aboriginal rights and title to the land. The agreement did not address the question of Inuit self-government.

At this point, the entire package still had to clear three outstanding hurdles: 1) a plebiscite on the proposed new borders by voters in the existing NT; 2) ratification of the agreement by a majority of Inuit voters age 16 and over, not just by a majority of those who do vote; and 3) ratification of the details of the agreement by a vote in Parliament and the passage of legislation to create the territory of Nunavut.

On 4 May 1992, voters in the NT narrowly supported a controversial boundary to split the NT into two territories, Nunavut in the east and the Western Arctic (or Denendeh, as the Dene prefer) in the west.

The plebiscite saw the eastern NT, where 80 per cent of the population is Inuit, vote overwhelmingly in support of the boundary, while Western Arctic residents voted strongly against it. Only a low voter turnout in the west, where just 47 per cent of voters cast ballots, allowed for a victory for boundary supporters. Rejection of the boundary highlighted several long-term concerns of opponents: 1) complaints by the Dene in Saskatchewan, Manitoba, and the NT that the boundary placed traditional lands used by Dene Indians under Inuit jurisdiction; 2) complaints by aboriginal (Indian) leaders such as Ovide Mercredi, then national chief of the Assembly of First Nations, that the Inuit should have reserved their inherent right to self-government, as part of the package, instead of setting a precedent of abandonment of self-government that could be harmful to other aboriginal nations seeking self-government as part of their land claim negotiations; and 3) fears of Western Arctic residents of the demise of a central government and the fragmentation of the territory into diverse, regional governments, together with the dire economic consequences of such an occurrence.

In November 1992, Inuit residents in the Eastern Arctic voted 69 per cent in favour of the final Nunavut land claim package. The package gave the Inuit clear title to 350,000 square kilometres (140,000 square miles) of land, as well as $1.15 billion dollars in compensation for land ceded over a period of 14 years. The Inuit also have the right to hunt, fish, and trap in all of Nunavut, a region that is 2.2 million square kilometres (880,000 square miles). An Accord signed prior to the vote between federal government and Inuit negotiators called for the legal establishment of Nunavut by 1999. In the summer of 1993, legislation was introduced to ratify the agreement and to establish the Nunavut territory.

Nunavut Today

The territory known as Nunavut was established under the Statutes of Canada 1993, Bill C-132—the Nunavut Act. It received royal assent on 10 June 1993. Inuit had made the creation of the territory through this act a prerequisite to signing their land claim. The Nunavut Land Claims Agreement Act came into law at the same time as the Nunavut Act. The Nunavut Land Claims Agreement (NLCA) and the Nunavut Act—the Act that created the new territory and government—work together in several ways. First, the NLCA guarantees that Inuit participation in the civil service (85 per cent, ultimately) will reflect the ethnic makeup of the territory. The ethnic breakdown of Nunavut's population (1996 census) is: Inuit: 20,480; non-aboriginal: 3,975. Also, under the NLCA, both Inuit and the territorial and federal governments have guaranteed representation on institutions of public government responsible for issues that are left to the federal government alone in Canada's territories—these include agencies such as the Nunavut Water Board and Nunavut Wildlife management Board, which make decisions affecting Crown (federal) lands and offshore areas. It is hoped that provisions in the NLCA intended to kick-start Nunavut's wage economy will eventually make Nunavut less dependent on federal government transfers.

The government of Nunavut today—similar to the territorial administration in Yellowknife NT—is run on the dominant (Euro-Canadian) model, not on the model of traditional Inuit self-government. In other words, this model of government is not based on the right of the Inuit to self-determination as a distinctive people, culture, and nation. It represents a compromise position. Nevertheless, given the fact that the Inuit make up some 85 per cent of the population in the new territory of Nunavut, their voting power can now be used to ensure that the individual and collective, cultural rights of the Inuit people are recognized and protected. Inuit nationhood, however, remains a dream deferred.

However, in the national Referendum held on 26 October 1992, a significant majority of Canadians voted to reject the Charlottetown Accord. A mixed response from Canada's aboriginal communities revealed that there were sharp lines of division over the aboriginal package. The Inuit of the Eastern Arctic, with the vote on their Nunavut proposal only weeks away after some 20 years of negotiation, voted to support the Accord. On the other hand, most Indians on reserves voted 'no'. Ovide Mercredi, then national chief of the Assembly of First Nations (representing Status Indians), suggested that Status Indians rejected the Accord for two reasons: first, distrust of the government and disbelief in good-faith negotiations with governments, and second, dissatisfaction with alleged inadequacies of the proposed aboriginal package, and additional (unmet) demands (*Toronto Star*, 28 October 1992).

Prior to the vote, it had been made clear that aboriginal women were divided in support for the aboriginal package. Indeed, the Native Women's Association of Canada had sought an injunction to block the referendum on the grounds that women's equality rights, under the Charter, would be secondary under the agreement because, under the proposed Canada clause, it would give priority to the upholding of traditional aboriginal values. These could encompass systems of aboriginal government presided over by hereditary male chiefs, in which women historically have been excluded from voting or holding office (*Toronto Star*, 9 October 1992). While not all aboriginal women supported this interpretation of the proposed package, a substantial number were suspicious enough of the possibility of such an interpretation that they put themselves clearly on the 'no' side.

Notwithstanding the failure of the Charlottetown Accord, aboriginal peoples have not abandoned their fight for national self-determination. Indeed, a number of Indian (band) communities across Canada have already stated that they intend to proceed to establish their own nation-like governments, unilaterally. Aboriginal leaders have pointed out that the federal government has the power to reach self-government agreements with aboriginal groups, outside of the constitutional process. The question is: Does the government have the will to do so? If not, leaders say, aboriginal peoples may use civil disobedience to attain their goals (*Toronto Star*, 31 October 1992).

Despite internal differences in the positions of representatives of various aboriginal organizations, there is general agreement that self-government means the right of aboriginal peoples to determine their own destinies. Aboriginal representatives are united in their commitment to the position that aboriginal peoples have an *inherent* right to self-government, meaning, *that it has always existed and was never surrendered*. Whether or not this definition will be accepted by governments is a question for the future. At present, like the constitutionally recognized aboriginal and treaty rights of Canada's aboriginal peoples, their newly accepted inherent right to self-government has not, as yet, been defined.

The hiatus between aboriginal and government positions on definitions of aboriginal rights and aboriginal self-government created a formidable obstacle to progress in the earlier constitutional negotiations of 1980–2, and in the four constitutional conferences (1983, 1984, 1985, and 1987) convened in order to define aboriginal peoples' rights. However, while the First Ministers' conferences failed to culminate in an agreement on the definition of aboriginal rights, they did reveal a new pattern of interaction between government and aboriginal representatives, one in which the voice of aboriginal peoples is taken into serious account. This new pattern also is evident in the involvement of aboriginal peoples in the formulation and implementation of federal government policy, and most recently, in their involvement in the latest (1992) round of constitutional negotiations. The paternalistic pattern of unilateral policy-making without the participation of aboriginal representatives has given way, under continuing pressure from aboriginal organizations, to a new pattern in which aboriginal input (however circumscribed) is deemed essential (Canada 1984b).

Despite the increased input of aboriginal representatives in government policy-making, the deplorable life conditions of aboriginal peoples have shown little evidence of improvement. In an attempt to address the continuing and escalating discontent of aboriginal peoples with their disadvantaged life conditions and minority status in Canada, in August of 1991 the federal government established the Royal Commission on Aboriginal Peoples (RCAP). The commission was tasked with a broad range of issues, many of which deal with long-standing concerns in the relationship between aboriginal and non-aboriginal peoples in Canada. The RCAP final report, released in November 1996, represents extensive consultations with aboriginal and non-aboriginal peoples in Canada on various subjects and contains 440 recommendations. A brief digest of the report and critical responses to it are presented in Box 7-2.

Addendum: First Nations Governance Act

At the time of writing, Ottawa has just unveiled a controversial legislative package that introduces changes to the Indian Act that would force First Nations leaders to open up their finances and, potentially, face disciplinary action by band members (*First Nations Governance Act*; Canadian Press, 15 June 2002). However, the bill was barely tabled in the House of Commons (14 June 2002) before First Nations leaders said they would challenge it in the courts because it infringes on their right to self-government. Earlier in the day, Grand Chief Matthew Coon Come of the Assembly of First Nations ripped up the bill in full view of hundreds of aboriginal protesters who came to Parliament Hill to demonstrate against it. Thus, the tug of war between First Nations peoples and the federal government over the inherent right of First Nations to self-government continues.

Summary: Comparative Analysis of the Franco-Quebecois, Multicultural, and Aboriginal Movements

What are the prospects for the future of these three minority ethnic protest movements?

As suggested earlier, our analysis of the Franco-Quebecois, aboriginal, and multicultural movements in Canada, highlighted in this chapter, bear out Melucci's contention that the new social movements are not primarily bent on usurption of power from dominant authorities, that is, they are not oriented toward the overthrow of the state apparatus. Rather, these movements look to control a particular social space where they have autonomy or independence vis-à-vis the system. Similarly, our analysis of these three minority ethnic protest movements lends support for Melucci's emphasis on *solidarity as an objective* as a characteristic of the new social movements. In all three Canadian movements, the struggle centres on the particularistic issue of ethnic group identity, based on ascriptive criteria such as ethnicity, race, and territory. As Melucci points out, these movements also have instrumental objectives, and seek political advantages, but this dimension is secondary to the expressive nature of the relations sought in the search for solidarity, the primary thrust of the movements. With specific regard to this point, our analysis bears out Melucci's thesis to some extent, but also reveals marked differences among the three Canadian movements in the extent of their emphasis on instrumental objectives: the multicultural movement comes closest to Melucci's model in its primary focus on cultural solidarity; the aboriginal movement, as a nationhood movement, is, necessarily, more instrumentally oriented, while the Franco-Quebecois nationhood movement, which incorporates secession from Canada as an option, appears to be equally weighted between expressive and instrumental objectives.

These differences among Canada's three new social movements lend support for the thesis put forward by Kriesi et al. (1995) that a there is a hierarchy of political issues that affect the degree to which a new social movement is perceived by dominant authorities in a society as a threat to their superordinate status and power. As indicated earlier, these authors argue that the more material resources are involved, and the more political power is at stake, the more threatening a social movement may be for political authorities. In light of this proposition, Canada's multicultural movement can be categorized as 'low-profile', posing no real threat to the high priority policy domains of the dominant powers.

BOX 7-2

The Royal Commission on Aboriginal Peoples: The RCAP Report, Government Response, and Critical Commentary

The report centred on a vision of a new relationship, founded on the recognition of aboriginal peoples as self-governing nations with a unique status in Canada. It set out a 20-year agenda for change, recommending new legislation and institutions, additional resources, a redistribution of land and the revitalizing of aboriginal nations, governments, and communities. The report acknowledged that aboriginal community autonomy is not feasible without significant community development, accordingly, the RCAP called for early action in four areas; healing, economic development, human resources development, and the revitalization of aboriginal institutions. The commission's implementation strategy proposed that governments increase spending to reach $1.5 billion by Year 5 of the strategy, and $2 billion in the subsequent 15 years. (The report argued that the additional investment over 20 years would save money in the long term.) The report highlighted several realities of importance to legislators and policy-makers. For example, today a significant percentage of aboriginal people in Canada live in urban areas. Questions of urban self-government and disputes over government responsibility for the provision of services are therefore becoming increasingly prominent. A second demographic fact is that the aboriginal population is currently growing at about twice the rate of the Canadian population; over half the aboriginal population is under the age of 25. This has accentuated the need to address issues of education, job creation, justice, health, and recreation for aboriginal youth.

The RCAP report was generally welcomed by aboriginal groups, although not without some disagreement, and generated expectations for an early government response. It received significant media attention on its release, but faded from the public agenda in the ensuing months. In typical fashion, the federal government employed politically motivated delay tactics: in December 1996, the prime minister said that the government needed time to study the recommendations and would not issue a response *prior to a general election*. The then minister of Indian affairs stated that it would be difficult to increase spending to the level proposed by the commission.

In April 1997, the Assembly of First Nations held a national day of protest to express its anger over perceived government inaction and the refusal of the prime minister to meet with First Nations leaders to discuss the report. In January 1998, the government finally responded to the RCAP report. In a policy paper entitled *Gathering Strength: Canada's Aboriginal Action Plan,* the government set out a policy framework for future government action based on four objectives, each addressing a number of aboriginal concerns and outlining general initiatives designed to meet these concerns. In July 2000, the government issued a follow-up report which asserts that a process of change 'has begun to address key dimensions of the relationship between the Crown and Aboriginal people' and that 'though *Gathering Strength* is a long-term plan, in just two short years it has produced impressive results'.

In sharp contrast, in April 2000, then national chief of the Assembly of First Nations Phil Fontaine stated that 'the promises made by the Government of Canada represented the *potential* for a major step', but that these commitments arising out of the RCAP report 'have not fully been implemented or honoured in the way in which we had anticipated'. He nevertheless expressed hope that they would 'one day, with proper management, and implementation in good faith . . . bear fruit.' Others have viewed *Gathering Strength* measures less optimistically, and have questioned their adequacy as a response to the RCAP report. The government's general approach to the RCAP report has been the subject of critical observations by national and international human rights bodies. In December 1998, the United Nations Committee on Economic, Social and Cultural Rights '[viewed] with concern the direct connection between Aboriginal economic marginalization and the ongoing dispossession of Aboriginal people from their lands, as recognized by RCAP', and expressed its '[great] concern that the recommendations of RCAP have not yet been implemented, in spite of the urgency of the situation.' In April 1999, the United Nations Human Rights Committee also expressed concern that Canada had 'not yet implemented the recommendations of the [RCAP]', and recommended 'that decisive and urgent action be taken towards the full implementation of the RCAP recommendations on land and resource allocation.' In its 1999 *Annual Report*, the Canadian Human Rights Commission reiterated the view expressed in previous annual reports that the government's response to the 1996 report of the [RCAP] has been slow. The commission's 1999 report emphasized the need for decisive and urgent action to be taken by the government to promptly and adequately deal with pressing issues.

Hurley and Wherrett, the researchers who prepared the foregoing report for the Library of Parliament, suggested in their closing comments that 'at this time, it remains difficult to predict whether or to what degree *Gathering Strength* programs may produce outcomes equivalent to those advocated by the RCAP's principal recommendations'. In the view of this author, taking into account the serious criticisms already levied at the government response to the RCAP Report, and taking into account the long history of federal government's broken promises to aboriginal peoples, a more realistic prediction would be that promised federal government programs will not be implemented in ways that come anywhere near meeting the recommendations of the RCAP. And, if this is indeed the case, the struggle of Canada's aboriginal communities to regain their autonomy, their cultural vitality, their health, and their human dignity will continue for a long time to come.

SOURCE: Adapted from the *Report of the Royal Commission on Aboriginal Peoples*, Hurley and Wherrett 2000.

In the case of the aboriginal movement, however, their overarching emphasis on control of land and land-based resources and their demands for political autonomy, places them in a more 'high-profile' category than the multicultural movement. However, although Canada's aboriginal movement is a nationalist movement, a new social movement that has arisen among *internally colonized* peoples, it departs radically from the traditional conception of post-colonial nationalist movements, such as those which have arisen among *externally colonized* peoples in Africa, India, and other non-Western countries. As Kriesi and associates suggest, these post-colonialist nationalist movements are highly instrumental and political in thrust: they aim to overthrow the colonial structure imposed on them, to overtake the state apparatus, and to usurp power for themselves (Connor 1993). In contrast, Canada's aboriginal nationhood movement is limited in its instrumental goals to attaining self-determination of aboriginal communities as *internal nations* within Canada. Thus, while Canada's aboriginal nationhood movement is seen to pose a threat to dominant interests, particularly as its demands relate to what Kriesi et al. (1995) call 'high-profile' policy issues, it does not pose the threat of usurpation of power from existing authorities, nor does it pose the threat of secession. On the other hand, the Franco-Quebecois nationhood movement poses a palpable threat to Anglo-Canadian dominance and control in Canada. Although the movement does not aim to *overthrow* the existing state apparatus, it does pose both an economic and a political threat to Anglo-Canadian dominance, through its demands for sovereignty-association, and even more so, in its threat of secession from Canada.

What are the prospects for the future of the Franco-Quebecois, aboriginal, and multicultural movements?

To some degree, the futures of all three movements are interdependent. A most important factor lies in the question of Franco-Quebecois independence. Should the Franco-Quebecois achieve their goal of a sovereign Quebec, the futures of aboriginal and multicultural minorities within and outside Quebec could be quite different. In the case of the multicultural movement outside Quebec, it could benefit, indirectly, from the achievement of Franco-Quebecois Independence, for the bilingual framework of multiculturalism would then lose salience. Within Quebec, the multicultural movement could give rise to an increasing alliance of ethnic minorities with the English Rights bloc. For the aboriginal movement, Quebec sovereignty could give new impetus to nationhood claims of aboriginal peoples within the state of Quebec.

Prospects for the Future: A Guarded Prognosis

All things considered, we can conclude at the present time that none of the movements is likely to make substantial gains in achieving stated goals in the near future. The Franco-Quebecois movement is still reeling from the defeat of the 1995 Quebec Referendum. The aboriginal movement, despite the positive rhetoric of the recent federal policy mandate, remains bogged down by government delays in implementation of policy initiatives, and, in any case, is unlikely to ever realize the dream of nationhood. The multicultural movement has been severely thwarted by recent changes to the federal multicultural policy that have withdrawn support for the distinctive cultures and institutions of Canada's minority ethnic communities.

Moreover, the climate of public opinion in Canada, while sympathetic to the plight of aboriginal peoples, and supportive of measures to combat racism, is not supportive of the primary goals of cultural distinctiveness and solidarity common to all three movements. Numerous research surveys (reported earlier in this book) reveal that majority ethnic Canadians, both inside and outside Quebec, perceive minority demands for recognition of collective cultural rights as a threat to their cultural hegemony, in Quebec and in Canada, respectively. Seen as most dangerous, however, is the threat posed by Quebec's separation from Canada.

A national Angus Reid/Southam news poll designed to gauge the reactions to the 1995 Quebec Referendum among Canadians in English Canada and in Quebec was conducted by telephone on 1 and 2 November 1995. The survey interviewed a representative crosssection of 1805 Canadian adults. For purposes of our analysis in this closing section of the chapter, our presentation of the results of the poll will focus on the reactions of Canadians living in English Canada only.

The poll found that English-speaking Canadians' overall perspectives on the state of national unity did not differ markedly from the public opinion landscape back in 1991. One-half of all Canadians (46 per cent) said that they believe 'Canada is in serious trouble' as far as national unity is concerned. However, the poll also found that many Canadians in English Canada—42 per cent—said that they have become 'more hardline' toward Quebec over the past year or so compared to 16 per cent who indicated they have become 'more sympathetic' (41 per cent report no change). Most important, the survey findings reveal that most English-speaking Canadians are 'prepared to see some concessions made to keep Quebec in Canada'—61 per cent chose this perspective compared to 32 per cent who said they would 'rather see Quebec leave than make any concessions'. The previous time the Angus Reid Group asked this question in May 1994, there was an even split in the responses. This finding may suggest that in English Canada, the perceived threat posed by Quebec's separation has intensified since the 1995 Referendum.

Conclusion

In this chapter we have focused our analysis on three minority ethnic protest movements in Canada. These new social movements represent the differential collective responses of members of Canada's charter, immigrant, and aboriginal minorities to their subordinate group status in society. Our analysis has demonstrated that ethnic status differences among the three movements are reflected not only in the kinds of collective rights that each can claim, but also in the differential potential for success of the movements.

Both the Franco-Quebecois Independence movement and the aboriginal movement can make collective claims based on national group rights on the evidence of the inextricable link between the ethnic group, its language and culture, and its ancestral territory within Canada. But the enormous difference in power between the two movements indicates that, at least in theory, the chances for eventual success are far greater for the Franco-Quebecois than for the aboriginal nations—who have modelled their demands for special status as 'distinct societies' on those of the Franco-Quebecois.

The multicultural movement, unlike the others, cannot make territorial claims based on any link with an ancestral homeland in Canada. Thus, proponents of multilingualism and multiculturalism can make collective claims based on minority religious, linguistic, and cultural rights, but not on national group rights. Visible (racial) minorities, proponents of anti-racism initiatives, cannot make cultural claims, on the basis of race: their claims are based on categorical rights. Further, the competing and, increasingly conflicting interests and claims of visible minorities and ethnocultural minorities within the multicultural movement weaken its political clout and impede its chances of success.

Unfortunately, for all three movements, our analysis suggests that their prospects for success have diminished since the time of writing the 1995 edition of this book. Assessed in terms of changes in government policy and public attitudes, the aboriginal movement appears to have gained government and public support, the Franco-Quebecois movement appears to have stagnated, and the multicultural movement has taken a giant step backwards. For the aboriginal nationhood movement, policy gains remain largely at the level of rhetoric—government promises, many of which are vague and unlikely to be implemented in practice, and the goal of nationhood remains a 'dream deferred'.

Throughout the foregoing analysis of the protest movements that have emerged among Franco-Quebecois, multicultural, and aboriginal minorities in Canada, we have alluded, from time to time, to the attempts by minority representatives to use *legal* (statutory and constitutional) protection for human rights as levers for their particular claims. In Chapters 8 and 9 we will examine and evaluate the legal framework of human rights protection across Canada, in light of the standard provided by the provisions of international human rights instruments. We will pay particular attention to protection for ethnic minority rights and to the ways in which minorities have responded to legal endorsement of human rights by putting forward individual, categorical, and collective rights claims under the provisions of statutory human rights legislation and under the constitutional Charter.

Key Concepts

- contention
- contrast conceptions
- minority ethnic protest movement
- minority rights movement
- new social movement
- revitalization
- routinization of charisma
- social movement

Critical Thinking Questions

1. Outline the factors leading to the development of ethnic minority protest and discuss the factors affecting the success or failure of two minority ethnic protest movements.
2. Minority rights movements can be expressed in the form of contention or revitalization movements. Distinguish between these two forms of minority rights movements with specific reference to minority ethnic protest movements in Canada.
3. The three minority rights movements focused on in this chapter have been conceptualized as new social movements. To what extent is this paradigm appropriate in all three cases? Elaborate.
4. It has been argued that the Franco-Quebecois, multiculturalism, and aboriginal movements in Canada represent the differential responses of charter, immigrant, and aboriginal minorities to their subordinate status within Canadian society. Discuss.
5. In what ways do the kinds of human rights goals sought affect the chances of success or failure of minority rights movements? Discuss, with specific reference to Canada.

CHAPTER 8

The Legal Framework for Protection of Minority Rights in Canada: Human Rights Statutes

Introduction

In preceding chapters of this book, our analysis has demonstrated the ways in which institutionalized forms of racism within Canadian society have impeded the processes of ethnic integration and social mobility for members of various ethnic minorities. We have shown how institutionalized racism has provided majority authorities with powerful techniques of domination that serve to perpetuate Canada's established ethnic hierarchy and the superordinate status of its ethnic majorities at its apex.

Chapter 7 elucidated the processes involved in the organization of collective protest among racial and ethnic minorities against their disadvantaged, subordinate status within Canada's ethnic stratification system. From a human rights perspective it provided an analysis of three major, human rights-oriented minority ethnic protest movements in Canada: the Franco-Quebecois, aboriginal, and multicultural movements. From time to time, our analysis has referred to the attempts by minority representatives to use *legal* (statutory and constitutional) protection for human rights as levers for their particular human rights claims. In this chapter and in Chapter 9 we will examine and evaluate the *legal framework* of statutory and constitutional human rights protection across Canada, in light of the global standard provided by the provisions of international human rights instruments. We will pay particular attention to protection for ethnic minority rights and to the ways in which minorities have responded to legal endorsement of human rights by putting forward individual, categorical and collective rights claims under the provisions of statutory human rights legislation and under the constitutional Charter.

Human Rights Statutes: Human Rights Legislation and the Control of Ethnic Discrimination in Canada

In this section, we will examine the historical forces underlying attempts to control ethnic discrimination through the development and implementation of *statutory* human rights legislation in Canada.

Critics of human rights legislation have long argued that 'You can't legislate morality' (Hill 1977: 23). In fact, as Hill has suggested, human rights legislation is not intended to turn self-professed racists into loving ethnic neighbours. Rather, it is intended to *reduce discrimination* and to ensure fair and equitable treatment of all Canada's diverse ethnic communities *despite the existence of prejudices*. Nevertheless, while legislation may not change attitudes, it can introduce a climate that maximizes the possibility of attitudinal change (Case 1977: 52). The relationship between prejudice and discrimination, discussed in Chapter 2, is instructive here in terms of the differential implications of these two phenomena for programs of social action. In any attempt to combat racism, it is important to recognize that an individual or group may harbour strong ethnic prejudices and yet be prevented from acting out these prejudices through overt discriminatory policies and practices (Hill 1977: 2). It is precisely this function—*prevention of discriminatory acts*—that is the prime objective behind **human rights statutes** in Canada.

Originally developed by sociologist Robert Merton (1949), the table in Box 8-1 helps to explain the relationship between prejudice and discrimination. This chapter will show how that relationship can be influenced by changes in the social context—in law, social policy, and practice—and especially by human rights legislation.

Background of Human Rights in Canada

The British North America Act (the Constitution Act, 1867) makes no explicit reference to human rights. Further, aside from the provisions protecting English and French languages in section 133, and others protecting the rights of Protestants and Catholics to their denominational schools in section 93, the BNA Act does not address the kinds of collective human rights associated with ethnic group membership.

For almost a century after the British Emancipation Act of 1833, which marked the official demise of slavery in Canada, the trend at the federal, provincial, and municipal levels of Canadian government was to enact discriminatory legislation. As demonstrated in earlier chapters, among the most pernicious pieces of legislation was the Indian Act whereby Canada's Status Indians were denied virtually all their fundamental human rights; many other discriminatory laws also impeded the rightful participation of Asians, blacks, and other racial and ethnic minorities from anything like full participation in Canadian society.

Although there were isolated legislative attempts to overcome ethnic discrimination in Canada as far back as the 1930s, Tarnopolsky (1979: xv) contends that it was not until the end of World War II that a real interest in anti-discrimination legislation developed. As part of the aftermath of the war, knowledge of racist atrocities committed under Nazi policies of genocide began to penetrate the Canadian consciousness forcing at least some Canadians to reflect on racism within their own borders.

Hill (1977: 18) argues that it was during the World War II period that Canadians bore witness to some of the most flagrant examples of racism in this country's history. In 1939, humanitarian petitions for Canadian acceptance of a fair quota of Jewish refugees fleeing the threat of extermination were ignored. In 1942, a policy of forceful evacuation of Japanese-Canadians from West Coast areas led to the confiscation of their property and their internment as 'enemy aliens' in Canadian-style concentration camps.

Following the war, Canadian public opinion became more sensitive to incidents of ethnic discrimination. As various pressure groups began to lobby for anti-discrimination legislation and for more adequate means of implementation and enforcement of the laws, governments ventured slowly and carefully into the area of human rights legislation.

In the 1940s, the provinces of Ontario (Racial Discrimination Act, 1944) and Saskatchewan (Bill of Rights, 1947) enacted quasi-criminal statutes that declared certain practices illegal and imposed sanctions on them. The Ontario Act was very limited in scope: it prohibited only the public display of signs, symbols, or other racially or religiously discriminatory representations. The Saskatchewan bill was much broader: the anti-discrimination provisions applied to accommodation, employment, occupation, land transactions, business enterprises, and included the government. Tarnopolsky (1979: 296) argues that a major weakness with both pieces of legislation lay in their quasi-criminal status, which made many people reluctant to use them. To overcome this impasse, Fair Accommodations and Fair Employment Practices Acts were

BOX 8-1

Human Rights Legislation and the Relationship between Prejudice and Discrimination

	Prejudice + high	Prejudice – low
Discrimination + high	+ +	– +
Discrimination – low	+ –	– –

Key
+ + prejudiced discriminator
– + unprejudiced discriminator
+ – prejudiced non-discriminator
– – unprejudiced non-discriminator

The situations represented by the (+ +) and (– –) boxes are self-explanatory: (+ +) a person acts on a particular prejudice s/he holds to discriminate against the members of the population that is the target of the prejudice; (– –) a person holding no prejudice against a particular population does not discriminate against members of that population.

The more relevant situations regarding the development of law, public policy, and practice are the situations represented in boxes (– +) and (+ –). Under what social conditions would an unprejudiced person be likely to discriminate? Under what social conditions would a prejudiced person be unlikely to discriminate? To answer these questions, think about the way prevailing public policies and laws in a society can influence the relationship between prejudice and discrimination.

What this table can illustrate, in relation to law, public policy, and practice, is that a prejudiced person can be prevented from discriminating by human rights legislation that imposes moral pressure and legal penalties against acts of discrimination. In contrast, an unprejudiced person can be forced into discriminating by discriminatory legislation that legitimizes acts of discrimination and imposes legal penalties for not discriminating. Finally, a prejudiced person can be allowed to discriminate by the absence of anti-discriminatory laws (institutional discrimination by omission).

To illustrate these points, let us consider the impact of changes in laws and social policies towards racial and ethnic minorities in Canada. Until the 1960s, Canada's racist immigration laws and regulations, supported by the climate of public opinion at the time, were designed to exclude people of colour, and to prevent them from immigrating to Canada. This social context virtually ensured that an immigration officer who was *not prejudiced* against visible racial-ethnic groups, nevertheless, would be constrained to discriminate against them by enforcing the law. Not to do so, would mean that the officer would not only lose his/her job, but also would likely be exposed to public censure.

Although not entrenched in law, other discriminatory barriers routinely violated the human rights of racial-ethnic minorities already in Canada. Aboriginal persons, Canadian-born blacks (descendants of slaves), Jews, and other minority members were highly stigmatized and were frequently denied employment opportunities, housing, and access to public services. Insofar as no anti-discriminatory legislation existed to protect the rights of members of racial and ethnic minorities, employers, landlords, restaurant owners, and others who were prejudiced against these minorities were allowed to discriminate against them *(discrimination by omission)*.

By way of contrast, when anti-discriminatory, human rights legislation was introduced within a particular jurisdiction, prohibiting discrimination on the grounds of race, ethnic and national origin, and religion, the social context and the climate of public opinion shifted perceptibly. The critical change was from *institutionalized discrimination* to *institutionalized non-discrimination*. Moral pressure and legal penalties imposed by the law against racist acts of discrimination, in this social context, became increasingly effective as deterrents, acting to prevent a *prejudiced* employer, landlord, restaurant owner, or other service provider from discriminating against members of racial and ethnic minorities.

What also should be re-emphasized, with specific regard to our discussion of legal protections for human rights, is that human rights legislation is designed to prevent discrimination, not to eradicate prejudice. As mentioned earlier, human rights laws cannot force you to love your neighbour, but they can prevent you from violating your neighbour's human rights. And that is precisely what they are intended to do. Over the long term, human rights legislation may indirectly serve to reduce prevailing prejudices by helping to create a social environment that strongly disapproves of and discourages the invalidation of persons and groups in the society. However, the primary purpose of human rights laws is to protect individuals and groups against harmful acts of discrimination—ideally, to prevent violations of the fundamental human rights of all persons and groups in the society.

enacted, first in Ontario in 1954, and within one decade, in most of the other provinces. Although these acts clearly represented a step forward, they still contained a major weakness in that the victims of discrimination were responsible for lodging the complaint. Racism apparently was held to be their problem and their responsibility.

A giant step was taken in 1962, when the Province of Ontario consolidated its legislation into the Ontario Human Rights Code, to be established by the year-old Ontario Human Rights Commission. By 1975, all Canadian provinces had established human rights commissions to administer anti-discriminatory legislation and, two years later, the Canadian Human Rights Act established a federal commission.

The Role of the Ombudsman

The role of the ombudsman as protector of citizens' rights against abuse by government bodies is a relatively recent development in Canada. As a consequence of the increasingly enormous powers of the modern, administrative state over the lives of ordinary citizens, the potential for friction between the individual citizen and the administrative bureaucracy has grown and intensified. A variety of solutions to this problem have been suggested and tried in many of the world's countries and, of these, two have been proposed as potentially most effective: 1) a system of administrative courts; and 2) the ombudsman (Friedmann 1979: 340–3).

The first system, developed by the Roman-law countries of continental Europe, has a decided advantage for the individual in that the onus of proof is on the government administration. However, this system also has some serious shortcomings, such as its enormous costs to all concerned and the complexity of its judicial procedure.

The second system, that of the ombudsman, has been preferred in common-law countries such as Canada. One of the primary advantages of this system is that its costs to society as compared with those of a system of administrative courts are extremely low, and there are no costs to the complainant. Further, as Friedmann argues, a one-person institution promises much easier access and inspires far more confidence in the individual citizen than does a vast, impersonal bureaucracy.

Nevertheless, there are two major disadvantages of the ombudsman system: 1) the onus of proof is on the individual complainant; and 2) the ombudsman has the power only to *recommend* corrective action and to report publicly the findings and recommendations of the investigation; the office does not have the authority to change administrative decisions (Hill 1974: 1077). The role of the ombudsman is to facilitate the lodging of complaints against public administration (Friedmann 1979: 345). The office of the ombudsman is legally established, functionally autonomous, and external to the government administration. The ombudsman, in short, is an independent and non-partisan intermediary between citizens and their governments, who acts as an impartial investigator of citizen complaints against government administration. The institution of the ombudsman may be introduced at any or all levels of government. A number of the world's countries currently have ombudsmen at the central government level. Canada, like many other federal states, has instituted the office at both the national and the subnational (provincial) levels.

At the federal level, Canada has established ombudsmen for four highly sensitive areas of public concern: a linguistic ombudsman—the Commissioner of Official Languages; a prison ombudsman—the Correctional Investigator; a media CBC (Canadian Broadcasting Corporation) ombudsman; and a military DND (Department of National Defence) ombudsman.

The Commissioner of Official Languages

For purposes of this book, with its focus on the collective rights of Canada's ethnic minorities, the most relevant Canadian ombudsman at the federal level of government is the Commissioner of Official Languages. This office was developed in response to the 1967 recommendation of Book 1 of the Reports of the Royal Commission on Bilingualism and Biculturalism. Specifically, the commission recommended that Parliament adopt an Official Languages Act and appoint a commissioner of official languages to ensure respect for the equal status of English and French in all federal institutions (Yalden 1979). The Act, passed in 1969, affirms the principle that French and English enjoy equal status, rights, and privileges in their use as federal languages of work and as languages of service to the public. The commissioner is the legal watchdog of the Official Languages Act for Parliament and has the authority to intervene in linguistic matters in all areas under federal jurisdiction, including Crown corporations. The commissioner is entitled to investigate any complaint involving either lack of recognition of the status of an official language or non-compliance with the spirit and intent of the Act by governmental bodies.

Yalden (1979: 379) points out that the Official Languages Act (and, we would add, the role of the commissioner) continues to be widely misunderstood by the Canadian public. For many Anglo-Canadians, Yalden's assertion that the federal government is still accused of trying to 'force French . . . down the throats' of unwilling citizens of this country, still holds true. Yalden, a strong supporter of the Trudeau government position on bilingualism and biculturalism, contends that investing in the future of Canada necessitates more than an Official Languages Act and Commissioner. It means firmer commitments from federal and provincial governments and from educational systems at all levels to producing truly bilingual citizens.

While this position clearly aims to protect the linguistic rights of English and French Canadian citizens, many non-English and non-French Canadians vehemently oppose it. Proponents of multilingualism and multiculturalism support the alternative position based on the recommendation of Book 4 of the Reports of the Royal Commission on Bilingualism and Biculturalism, namely that, where numbers warrant, the linguistic rights of all of Canada's ethnic groups must be recognized and respected. It follows from this latter position that the Office of Commissioner of Official Languages should be changed to the

Office of Official and Non-Official Languages, and that the mandate of the linguistic commissioner/ombudsman should be expanded, accordingly, so as to protect the linguistic rights of members of all of Canada's ethnic communities.

The larger debate concerning non-official minority language rights, to which the foregoing discussion alludes, will be addressed in Chapter 9 within the broader context of the Canadian constitutional debate preceding the adoption of the Charter of Rights and Freedoms in 1982.

Canadian Legislation Prohibiting Ethnic Discrimination

There are significant differences in detail among current human rights statutes—in their **enumerated grounds of discrimination**, areas of application, and so forth. However, statutes at the provincial and federal levels share fundamental similarities in content and administration (Canadian Human Rights Law Centre). All the human rights statutes in Canada prohibit discrimination on the grounds of race, religion, colour, nationality or national origin, and sex. Discrimination on ethnic grounds is thereby prohibited in the broad sense of the term *racial* as outlined in the International Convention on the Elimination of All Forms of Racial Discrimination. All the statutes refer to both 'race' and 'colour' as well as to other terms relating to ancestral origin such as 'national extraction (or) origin', 'place of birth (or) origin', 'ancestry', 'ethnic origin', and 'nationality'. All the statutes are designed to ensure equality of access to places, activities, and opportunities. Accordingly, they all prohibit discrimination in hiring, terms, and conditions of employment, job advertisements, job referrals by employment agencies, and membership in unions. Most also prohibit discrimination in professional, business, and trade associations.

Both federal and provincial statutes prohibit discrimination in the provision of accommodation, services, and facilities to which the public has access. The provinces and territories prohibit discrimination in residential property rentals and sales; many also cover commercial properties.

Enforcement of Human Rights Codes

Tarnopolsky (1979: 297) has argued that the importance of consolidation of human rights legislation into codes to be enforced by administrative commissions lies in the fact that this structure ensures community vindication of the victim of discrimination. Human rights legislation recognizes that it is not only bigots but also 'nice guys' who discriminate: most Canadians discriminate not so much because of racist convictions as from fear of loss of comfort, convenience, or monetary revenues.

The philosophy underlying the contemporary human rights approach blends educational and legal techniques in the pursuit of social justice. All jurisdictions have both administrative staff and citizen commissioners responsible to ministers of government, whose task is to administer the legislation and to act in an advisory and policy-making capacity. In accordance with the legislation, the staff and commissions are required to enforce the acts, carry out research on human rights, and conduct public education programs (Hill and Schiff 1988).

The enforcement process in all jurisdictions typically begins with the submission of a complaint of discrimination to the commission by the alleged victim of discrimination or by interested private groups, third parties, or (in some cases) officers of the administering agency. Following the receipt of a complaint, the commission is required to conduct an investigation and conciliate the matter or affect a settlement, should sufficient grounds be established to justify the complaint. Terms of settlement vary, depending on the nature of the complaint, but these may require provision for accommodation, employment, and/or services previously denied. Other forms of redress commonly include recompense for the victim's financial loss and/or injury to dignity. In some cases, respondents also are required to undertake special (affirmative action or pay equity) programs to improve minority opportunity in their establishments (Hill and Schiff 1988).

Initially, those who are found to discriminate are given the opportunity to redress their ways by being confronted with the severity of the injury to the human dignity and economic well-being of the victim as compared with their own (real or anticipated) loss of comfort or convenience. However, if persuasion, conciliation, and efforts to effect a settlement fail, a board of public inquiry or tribunal may be ordered. The public aspect of the inquiry, especially where the events capture media attention, is considered to be an important component of the public education mandate of commissions. Ultimately, a discrimination complaint, if not settled to the satisfaction of both parties, and/or the commission, may reach the courts. Some statutes empower commissions to bypass public inquiry and take cases directly to court. In any case, on summary conviction, the discriminator may be subject to fines that, depending on the jurisdiction, may be in as high as $25,000, or even higher.

Effectiveness of the Current Human Rights System in Canada

Anti-discrimination legislation has clearly served to raise the level of public consciousness of racism in Canada. But how successful has it been in achieving its ultimate goal, that of reducing the societal level of ethnic discrimination? The evidence presented throughout this book demonstrates that while discrimination has lost its public respectability, it has definitely not disappeared in Canada. What has happened is that blatant racism has gone 'into the closet', where it has become transformed into its more subtle, 'polite' counterpart—the 'new racism'. Human rights advocates have long argued that in order for anti-racist legislation to be effective in practice, it must have teeth in it. The vigorous and intelligent enforcement of human rights legislation, with forceful sanctions against those who discriminate on the grounds of race, ethnicity, or any other prohibited grounds, advocates argue, is the most convincing form of public education.

Limitations of the Current Human Rights System

Since the coming into effect of the equality rights provisions of the Charter in 1985, the statutory human rights model has come under increasing criticism. Section 15(2) of the Charter allows for the provision of affirmative measures to remedy group-based disadvantage resulting from systemic discrimination. In conformity with this Charter standard, most human rights statutes now allow for the provision of affirmative measures to redress group-based inequalities.

Critics of the current human rights system claim that the **individual complaint-based procedure** at the centre of the system has failed to adequately address and remedy systemic group-based inequalities. For example, Day has argued that systemic discrimination cannot be addressed effectively by a procedure that is designed for individuals, and that is *passive*, coming into play only when a victim of discrimination puts forward a complaint. Nevertheless, she points out, commissions do have the capacity to accept and investigate systemic complaints; they can even initiate such complaints. The failure of commissions to fully and effectively tackle widespread systemic discrimination and group-based inequality stems from the inappropriateness of the procedures, designed for processing individual complaints, as well as the current overload of unresolved individual complaints. Because of inadequate funding resources, Day asserts, there are long delays in the resolution of individual complaints and few resources for anything else. Additionally, Day contends, there is a lack of will on the part of commissioners, and more importantly, on the part of governments, to 'shift direction' in order to see systemic discrimination effectively addressed. In short, Day argues, it is difficult to make the human rights processes match the Charter-endorsed promise of group-level as well as individual equality in the law when procedures are designed for a narrow, individual complaint system, when resources are scarce, and when governments do not provide support for tackling larger, systemic problems (1990: 22–3, 25).

Day's critique of the human rights system was vividly demonstrated in a scathing 1991 report on the practices of the Ontario Human Rights Commission, based on an investigation headed by Ontario Ombudsman Roberta Jamieson. Jamieson stated that the backlog, at that time, of over 2800 complaints was so overwhelming that the agency could no longer enforce the law. The investigation of the commission found that complaints had not been adequately handled. Because the commission was underfunded, there were virtually no resources for staff training, and because the commission was understaffed, the workload precluded the adoption of speed-up procedures to deal with the backlog of cases (*Toronto Star*, 20 July 1991). Clearly, under these onerous conditions, it was all but impossible to tackle larger problems of systemic discrimination and group-based inequality.

An editorial in the *National Post* (1 November 1998) offered an even more acerbic critique of Canada's human rights system, in this case targeting the federal system—the Canadian Human Rights Commission (CHRC) and the Canadian Human Rights Tribunal. The editorial reported that in October 1998, Michelle Falardeau-Ramsey, chief commissioner of the CHRC, was called to task for a litany of problems unveiled by the federal auditor general earlier in the year at both the CHRC and the Canadian Human Rights Tribunal. The alleged problems included delays in handling complaints, potential conflicts of interest, and repeated errors in interpreting the law. The editorial suggested that at least part of the problem at the CHRC was insufficient funding because the commission was continually expanding its mandate by adding new enumerated grounds of discrimination, thus increasing the number of minority complaints. Moreover, the editorial contended, there were other issues raised by the auditor general that were especially disturbing. In particular, the Federal Court had repeatedly found that the federal human rights tribunal had an impoverished grasp of the law. Of 19 appeals since 1996, the court had overturned the tribunal 11 times owing to errors of law. Both the Federal Court and the auditor general had pointed to the interdependence between the commission and the tribunal as a potential problem. Also, within the CHRC, there were a multitude of potential conflicts of interest. For example, commission staff could both mediate the rights disputes before it and assist a complainant to take his/her case before the courts. In fact, the commission could solicit a complaint about discrimination, help draft the complaint, investigate it, and then appear before the human rights tribunal to argue it. The editorial strongly suggested that one agency wearing so many hats leads to one-sidedness (*National Post,* 1 November 1998).

The CHRC was set up in 1977 to offer an alternative to the lengthy and often costly process of adjudicating discrimination cases through the Federal Court system. It was meant to focus on mediation and conciliation, and to raise awareness of discrimination in society. However, the *Post* editorial pointed out that the current, indeed escalating, situation of problems implied that the CHRC and the human rights tribunal, instead of constituting a less expensive and less contentious way of mediating disputes to the satisfaction of both parties, may simply duplicate the court system. In closing, the editorial proposed that while the court system may be just as cumbersome, expensive, and timeconsuming as the CHRC, at least Canadians can be confident in its impartiality and respect for the rule of law—and these are important human rights (*National Post,* 1 November 1998).

The foregoing critiques of Canada's human rights system focus on problems in the *implementation* of the human rights model. Although the current system was designed to operate on a case-by-case basis, in light of changes that have taken place in the legal interpretation of discrimination, it may be argued that the current human rights system, *given adequate resources,* is able to deal both with *individual* rights complaints (based on alleged individual and institutional discrimination) and *categorical* rights complaints (based on alleged systemic discrimination).

The following section of this chapter will show how the human rights system works, in practice, by examining the process of resolution of complaints of alleged human rights violations put forward by minority claimants under the provisions of statutory human rights legislation in Canada.

The Process of Legal Resolution of Minority Claims: Cases Filed under Provincial and Federal Human Rights Statutes

Ontario Human Rights Commission and Theresa O'Malley v. Simpsons Sears Ltd.
[1985] 2 SCR
Ground: Religion
Area: Employment

Accommodating the needs of employees who observe religious days of obligation other than traditional Christian holy days has been the subject of several cases. In 1979, Theresa O'Malley, a newly converted Seventh-Day Adventist, complained to the Ontario Human Rights Commission that she had been discriminated against because of her religious beliefs. Since becoming a Seventh-Day Adventist, she is bound to observe the day of Sabbath (no work) from sundown Friday to sundown Saturday. Because of this religious rule, she could no longer work the required weekend shifts at the Simpsons Sears store where she was employed. Because she could not work the weekend shifts, she lost her full-time position and had to become a part-time employee. In her complaint, as a remedy, she asked to receive the difference between her full-time salary and her part-time pay until 6 July 1979, the date she had planned to marry and leave her job.

Her demands would be met. The case took seven years to complete and attracted some serious interest as the Supreme Court of Canada recognized what it called **adverse affect discrimination.** On 17 December 1985, seven Supreme Court judges agreed that an employment rule—even one made honestly and for sensible business reasons—can still be discriminatory, with regard to results. In other words, the Supreme Court decreed that indirect, unintentional discrimination (adverse affect discrimination) is as serious a human rights violation as is direct, intentional discrimination.

The Court argued that since Theresa O'Malley is a Seventh-Day Adventist and wishes to keep her Sabbath, the rule that requires her to work on Saturdays has an unintentional 'adverse affect' on her. The necessity or intention of the rule doesn't prevent it from being discriminatory. In keeping with its decision, the court established the following rules:

1. When adverse affect discrimination exists, an employer has a duty to take reasonable steps to accommodate an employee who has been affected short of undue hardship in the operation of the business.
2. If these reasonable steps don't solve the problem, then the employer can't be expected to do anything more. The person affected has to choose between either his or her religious principles or his or her employment.
3. The person complaining must show that he or she is experiencing discrimination because of a rule. If he or she does, then the employer must show that it has taken reasonable steps to accommodate the employee without suffering undue hardship.

In this case, the Supreme Court decided that Simpsons Sears had not taken reasonable steps to try to accommodate Theresa O'Malley. It could have shuffled her work schedule without causing a problem, but it had not done so. The company had simply offered Theresa part-time work. The court decided that this was 'adverse effect discrimination' in action, and Theresa O'Malley was awarded her full-time paycheque.

Richmond* v. *Canada (A.G.)
(*Canadian Human Rights Commission Legal Report 1997*. CHRC 1997b)
Ground: Religion
Area: Employment
The most recent authority on the question of accommodating the needs of employees who observe religious days of obligation other than traditional Christian holy days is the decision reached in *Richmond* v. *Canada (A.G.)*. The issue before the Federal Court of Appeal was whether the federal government must provide Jewish and other non-Christian employees with paid leave to observe their religious holidays. In 1992, Sheldon Richmond was refused three days' leave with pay for the Jewish high holidays, Rosh Hashanah and Yom Kippur. Mr Richmond was told that while the government would not grant him 'special leave' with pay for religious observance, he could take unpaid leave with several options to make up the loss of pay, including using annual or compensatory leave or by working extra hours. Richmond and 15 other employees who had been refused similar requests, filed grievances claiming religious discrimination, contrary to the 'non-discrimination' clause of their collective agreement. Both the Public Service Commission adjudicator and the Federal Court rejected their cases, finding that the employer had met its duty to accommodate. Richmond and the other grievers appealed. In a split decision, the Federal Court of Appeal held that while the policy of providing paid leave for Christian holidays and not for other religious holidays was discriminatory, the options to make up the loss of pay constituted reasonable accommodation. The court cited the Supreme Court decision in *Chambly* v. *Bergevin*, which held that providing all employees with paid leave only for Christian holidays, though neutral on its face, had the effect of discriminating against religious minorities. The Federal Court of Appeal unanimously agreed that the employer's 'Designated Paid Holidays' calendar, which included Christmas and Easter, amounted to adverse effect discrimination. The justices, however, differed on the issue of whether the employer had reasonably accommodated its employees. Madam Justice Desjardins, for the majority, held that 'the employer in order to establish reasonable accommodation, had to demonstrate that "real efforts" had been made, short of "undue hardship" so as to eliminate the adverse effect discrimination suffered by its employees.' In Madam Justice Desjardins' opinion, compelling the government to use discretionary special leave provisions of the collective agreement for the observance of religious holidays would constitute undue hardship. Serious disruption of the collective agreement would result if Jewish employees were entitled to three more days of mandatory leave with pay for religious holidays than Christian employees. The judge dismissed the argument that non-Christian employees might work during Christmas and Easter and then take paid leave during their own religious holidays. She held that it would be a breach of the collective agreement and the Canada Labour Code to expect the employer to open its offices on Christmas and Good Friday, since all employees are entitled to these holidays. While the holiday schedule is discriminatory, the government is under no obligation to provide paid leave for non-Christian holidays where it offers affected employees the opportunity to make up the absences without loss of pay. The Supreme Court denied an application by the employees for leave to appeal, and so this decision stands as the most recent authority on this question.

Like the court decision in the *Theresa O'Malley case*, the decision in the *Richmond case* upheld the principle of reasonable accommodation (of diversity) as a means of redressing and preventing (future) adverse impact (systemic) discrimination.

National Capital Alliance on Race Relations* v. *Health Canada
Canadian Human Rights Commission Legal Report 1997 (CHRC 1997a)
Grounds: Race, colour, national, or ethnic origin
Area: Employment

Most complaints of racial discrimination involve isolated instances of discrimination against a single individual. However, in an important decision released in March 1997, a federal human rights tribunal found discrimination within an entire government department. After reviewing a discrimination complaint filed by the National Capital Alliance on Race Relations, an Ottawa-based community group, a tribunal concluded that visible minority employees at Health Canada had been subjected to systemic discrimination that hindered their opportunities for career advancement. The alliance offered as evidence statistics showing that a disproportionally low number of visible minority employees had progressed into senior management positions. Statistical evidence is helpful in cases of this type because systemic discrimination is not motivated by a conscious act, it is more subtle to detect, and it is necessary to look at the consequences of, or the results of, a particular employment system. Here, the tribunal found that visible minority groups were significantly underrepresented in both senior management and the administrative and foreign service categories, and were 'bottlenecked' in scientific and professional jobs. Specific discriminatory staffing and promotion practices were also noted. Surveys of Health Canada employees indicated that white employees were twice as likely to be asked to serve on selection boards as non-white employees for reasons that have little to do with the level of education, experience, or responsibility. Visible minorities were also given fewer opportunities to acquire the experience necessary for management positions. Minority employees had less chance of being appointed to acting positions with supervisory responsibilities. Acting appointments were often made without competition and on an informal basis. When the positions were filled on a permanent basis, the person acting in the job was usually appointed to the position. White employees were informed about training opportunities and acting appointments by their supervisors, whereas visible minorities were required to be 'more self-reliant' in seeking these opportunities. The tribunal was also presented with an internal departmental memorandum detailing racist attitudes held by some senior managers. In a unanimous decision, a three-member panel of the human rights tribunal concluded that staffing practices of Health Canada had a disproportionately negative effect on visible minorities, which the tribunal found discriminatory. Since Health Canada called no evidence to explain the reasons for the underrepresentation in senior management, the complaint was upheld. Health Canada argued that the tribunal did not have the jurisdiction to order an 'employment equity' remedy, and that it only had the power to make a 'cease and desist' order. The tribunal rejected the department's argument, stating that 'an employment equity order was necessary in this case to prevent future systemic discrimination and to eliminate past barriers arising out of the discriminatory practices identified'. The tribunal ordered Health Canada to implement a wide range of corrective measures, including setting numerical targets over the next five years. During that period, 18 per cent of senior management promotions and 16 per cent of administrative and foreign service promotions were targeted for members of visible minorities. Similar targets exist for the appointments of minorities to acting positions in senior management. Health Canada must also implement mandatory diversity and employment equity training for all senior managers and human resource specialists, and develop recruitment sources for members of visible minorities, including advertising in ethnic newspapers.

Jacobs and Jacobs and the Canadian Human Rights Commission v. Mohawk Council of Kahnawake

Decision rendered on March 11, 1998
Canadian Human Rights Act, R.S.C. 1985, c. H 6 (as amended)
Grounds: National or ethnic origin, race, colour, and family status
Area: Service

This case is of particular significance because it involves a conflict between individual and collective rights—specifically, a conflict between the individual right of an aboriginal person to non-discrimination, under section 5 of the Canadian Human Rights Act (CHRA), and the collective right of an aboriginal community (Status Indian band) to determine its own membership, under section 10 of the Indian Act.

This case was heard before the Canadian Human Rights Tribunal for 18 days, extending over a period from August 1995 to November 1997. It began with the written Complaint of Peter Jacobs (Peter) on his behalf and on behalf of his family against the Mohawk Council of Kahnawake (MCK) dated 22 October 1991, alleging that the council was engaging in or had engaged in a discriminatory practice since 1986 and ongoing on the grounds of national or ethnic origin, race, colour, and family status. The particulars contained in the Complaint are as follows:

> The Mohawk Council of Kahnawake is discriminating against me (Peter Jacobs) and my family in the provision of services by refusing us benefits and privileges including residency, land allotment and land rights, housing, medication and dental privileges because of my race, colour, national or ethnic origin and family status in violation of section 5 of the Canadian Human Rights Act.
>
> I was legally adopted by two Indians from Kahnawake when I was a baby. My biological parents were of black and Jewish descents. At my 2lst anniversary, I lost my membership status as an Indian of Kahnawake because of my biological origins. I recovered my Indian status only in 1988. In April 1988, the Mohawk council of Kahnawake informed me that even though I was entitled to be registered as an Indian with the Department of Indian Affairs, I did not meet the criteria for becoming a registered Indian with the Mohawk of Kahnawake under the Mohawk Law of Kahnawake. Furthermore, my wife Trudy Jacobs, who is originally a Mohawk from Kahnawake and to whom I am legally married since 1986, lost her Kahnawake's membership status because of our relationship. Thus, in July 1990, my wife Trudy Jacobs received a letter from the Council of Kahnawake stating that our family could not be registered on the Kahnawake Mohawk [Band] List. Therefore, because we are not registered on the Kahnawake Mohawk list based on my biological origins and on my wife family status, the Band Council deprived us of many services and benefits. Among other things, the Mohawk Council of Kahnawake continue to deny our requests for the housing assistance program, even though I own a piece of land given by my foster-mother.

The tribunal pointed out that what might appear to be a rather straightforward matter is anything but that. What lies at the heart of this complaint, particularly from the MCK's perspective, is the entire question of aboriginal rights to self-determination within the Canadian framework. Particularly at issue is the right of an aboriginal community to determine its own membership and the resulting entitlement to certain services, benefits, and privileges. The question is complex as it rests within a web of legal, political, and social considerations that are continually evolving. The matter is further complicated, the tribunal asserted, by the checkered history of the long-term relationship that has existed between the Government of Canada and its aboriginal peoples.

It was pointed out, at this juncture in the hearing, that the complainant had nowhere to turn except to the courts or to the human rights commission. As a result of certain funding arrangements made between DIAND and the MCK, the Jacobs family found itself in the following Catch-22 situation: Because Peter, for example, was not on the Mohawk List, he was refused certain benefits by the MCK, but when he turned to DIAND for relief, he was advised that because of these funding arrangements, he must seek those benefits from the MCK.

The case involved a central conflict of rights between the individual equality rights of the complainant (non-discrimination) and the collective rights of the Mohawk community (self-determination). Expert witnesses testified that, beginning in the 1970s and continuing in the early 1980s, the community had come to a point where it was prepared to take concrete measures to reassert control over its own affairs and particularly, over its own membership. This was seen to be absolutely essential in order to promote sovereignty and to prevent further cultural erosion. The thrust toward sovereignty was prompted in part by pressures that were being exerted on the federal government to amend the Indian Act by granting status to Status Indian women who married non-Indian men. At that time, such women lost their status on marriage and this was greatly resented especially because non-Indian women who married Status Indian men had status under the Act.

As a major step to reassert control over community matters, the MCK enacted a Moratorium effective 22 May 1981. The content of the Moratorium itself provides some explanation of its purpose. It appears that the greatest problem that was addressed in the Moratorium related to mixed marriages although it dealt with the adoption of non-Indian children as well. Following the enactment of the Moratorium in 1981, the Mohawks of Kahnawake maintained a Mohawk List that had been created in consultation with the elder women of the community. This consultation was in keeping with the matriarchal structure of the traditional Mohawk community. The Mohawk List contained the names of those persons who met the criteria set out in the Moratorium. All the while, however, DIAND maintained its own Band List that now differed in content from the Mohawk List.

The Moratorium sought to permit the community of Kahnawake to regain control of its own affairs, a most important element of which was the assertion of control over membership. The criteria of membership based on blood content and quantum appeared to be objective and relatively easy to apply. The *status quo* regarding marriages between Status Indian men and nonIndian women was not disturbed partly because of the large numbers involved but also as a result of the desire not to be overly disruptive. The Moratorium was also seen as accommodating the basic Mohawk principle that the overall good of the community was more important than the rights of the individual.

As the prospect of the amendments to the Indian Act loomed larger, the Moratorium was replaced by the Kahnawake Mohawk Law on 11 December 1984. The tribunal pointed out that the Moratorium and Mohawk Law were not submitted to DIAND for approval under section 10 of the Indian Act. This, it was asserted, was done deliberately and in defiance of the federal authority in this respect but very much in keeping with the overall political initiatives that were being undertaken by the community to acquire rights to self-government and self-determination. The community considers it to be of fundamental importance that only it can determine issues relating to the definition of who was to be considered a member of its community. Control of membership is seen to be the core power necessary to recreate a community based on traditional Mohawk values.

In his evidence, Grand Chief Norton made it clear that subsequent to the enactment of the Mohawk Law of 1984, the Mohawks of Kahnawake had continued the policy of pressing the federal and Quebec governments for greater control over their own affairs. This was evident in the areas of elections to Band Council, control over funds earmarked for education, welfare, housing, and other social benefits, the acquisition of land for the Territory or compensation for land taken, an aboriginal justice system and self-policing. These efforts were accelerated by the events of 1990 commonly referred to as the Oka Crisis and the blockading by the Mohawks of Kahnawake of the Mercier Bridge leading from their Territory to the Island of Montreal. Since then, the politics surrounding the relations between the federal government in particular and the Mohawks of Kahnawake had escalated to the point where they have clearly impacted on the lives of ordinary people such as the complainants in this case to an unprecedented but not unpredictable extent.

The Indian Act was amended in 1985 by the now legendary Bill C-31. This bill had the effect, among other things, of granting status to Indian women such as Trudy Jacobs who married non-Indian men. The community of Kahnawake advised the federal government that it would not accept these provisions as they were in conflict with the Mohawk Law of 1984. DIAND replied that the Mohawk Law was in conflict with the Indian Act and so a 'stand-off' existed.

It is within the context of the foregoing happenings that the tribunal returned to the complaints of Peter and Trudy Jacobs. The respondent had asserted that Peter and Trudy are not on the Mohawk List of Kahnawake and are not considered members of the Kahnawake community since they do not satisfy the membership criteria set out in the Moratorium and Mohawk Law. Peter was excluded because he was a non-Indian with no Mohawk blood content. According to Mohawk Law, he was not entitled to any of the rights, privileges, and benefits available to a Mohawk. Trudy was excluded because she married a non-Indian after the Mohawk Law was enacted. According to the Mohawk Law, she was deprived of residency, land allotment, and land rights and voting privileges and any other benefits and privileges that fell under the jurisdiction of the Mohawk people of Kahnawake. The Jacobs children were also excluded from membership.

After a consideration of all the evidence presented, the tribunal decided that a *prima facie* case of discrimination had been established. The onus now shifted to the respondent to establish on a balance of probabilities the defence of *bona fide* justification, viz. that there is a *bona fide* justification for the impugned practices.

The respondent submitted, that in this case, the impugned practices were justified because it was necessary for the community of Kahnawake to define and control its own membership by adopting the Moratorium of 1981 and enacting the Mohawk Law of 1984 in order to first insure the survival of Kahnawake as a culturally distinct Mohawk community and second, to protect the limited land base within the community. The MCK submitted that the justification for both the Moratorium and the Law are found within the documents themselves.

There was no dispute between the parties as to the appropriate test that should be applied in resolving this issue. While the test agreed on was developed in the context of employment cases, it was pointed out that courts have consistently held that the terms *bona fide* occupational requirement and a *bona fide* justification convey the same meaning: the former is used in the context of employment situations while the latter relates to other situations.

To be a *bona fide* occupational qualification and requirement a limitation must be imposed honestly, in good faith, and in the sincerely held belief and not for ulterior or extraneous reasons aimed at objectives that could defeat the purpose of the Human Rights Code. In addition, it must be related in an objective sense to the performance of the employment concerned, in that it is reasonably necessary.

On the basis of the evidence heard, the tribunal stated that it was entirely satisfied that the subjective part of the test for determining *bona fide* justification had been met. Indeed, the commission and the complainants seemed to concede that this was the case. In the tribunal's view, in applying the membership criteria set out in the Moratorium of 1981 and the Mohawk Law of 1984, the respondent was acting honestly, in good faith and in the sincere belief that these criteria were necessary in order to insure the survival of Kahnawake as a culturally distinct Mohawk community and in order to protect its limited land base. However, it was pointed out that satisfying the objective part of the test is far more problematic. In order to establish *prima facie* direct discrimination, it must be demonstrated not only that it was done in good faith, but also that it was 'reasonably necessary' to do so, which is both a subjective and an objective test.

The question was raised: Can it be said that enacting the Moratorium and Mohawk Law that denies Peter and Trudy (or persons in the same circumstances) the services and benefits that they applied for or may apply for in the future is reasonably necessary and required in order to insure the survival of Kahnawake as a culturally distinct Mohawk community and in order to protect its limited land base?

The tribunal decided that this was not the case. Peter and Trudy, it was pointed out, were raised as Mohawks. They adhere to Mohawk traditions and values. Peter speaks the Mohawk language although not fluently. Trudy is a Mohawk woman. Their children are being raised as Mohawks. They attend a Mohawk immersion school. Peter already owns land in the Territory and has built a family home. And by persevering with this complaint for the past seven years, Peter has demonstrated a firm and resolute will to be part of the community of Kahnawake and contribute to it like all other Mohawk men. That Peter or Trudy could reasonably be considered a threat to the distinct Mohawk culture of this community or its land or resource base is simply unsupportable. Furthermore, it was argued, in order for the MCK to satisfy the objective part of the test relating to *bona fide* justification, it must demonstrate that the alleged discriminatory practice is based on 'sound and accepted . . . practice and there is no practical alternative'. But, it was asserted, the MCK has not satisfied us that no practical alternatives exist.

In summary, the tribunal stated that the evidence indicates that the MCK has engaged and is engaging in acts of direct discrimination against Peter, Trudy, and their children by denying them services and access to services that are ordinarily available to members of the public. The tribunal stated that the defence of *bona fide* justification fails and that the discriminatory practices are not immune from scrutiny pursuant to section 67 of the CHR Act except for the right to vote and hold office in MCK elections.

With regard to remedies to be awarded, the tribunal stated that it was quite clear that neither Trudy nor Peter were seeking financial relief in this case. Rather they sought a remedy that would recognize that they are Mohawks and are part of the community of Kahnawake. They expressed the wish to be included on the Mohawk List and treated like all other Mohawks in the community with entitlement to all of the rights, benefits, and privileges afforded to other Mohawks.

The Canadian Human Rights Commission was specific in the remedy that it sought. It asked for a number of specified privileges and benefits to be accorded the Jacobs family with regard to residency, welfare, education, voting, and so forth.

In response, the tribunal asserted that it is not possible for anyone, certainly not a statutory tribunal, to make effective an Order that someone be accepted as part of a community if the community is unwilling to have them. Acceptability within a community, it pointed out, is a matter for the mind, the soul, and the spirit and is not the subject matter of Orders. No matter what we might do, we cannot 'make' Peter and Trudy members of this community—only the community can do that. The MCK had submitted that only the Kahnawake community can determine issues of membership and in doing so a line must be drawn somewhere resulting in some being included and some being excluded. The Tribunal asserted that while this may be so and while it may be that only the community can draw that line, it must be drawn in a manner that avoids prohibited acts of discrimination contrary to the Canadian Human Rights Act.

With regard to the remedy proposed by the complainants, the tribunal stated that it was not prepared to grant a remedy in these specific terms. Rather, the tribunal declared that the remedy would take the form of a declaration and mandatory Order as follows:

1. WE DECLARE that when Peter Jacobs was denied a grant for water and sewage facilities in 1992, the MCK committed a discriminatory practice contrary to the provisions of Section 5 of the CHR Act on the basis of race, national and ethnic origin;

2. WE DECLARE that when Trudy Jacobs was denied the right to vote in the Mohawk Council of Kahnawake election of 1990, and when she was denied an application for a low interest loan in 1991, the MCK committed discriminatory practices contrary to the provisions of Section 5 of the CHR Act on the basis of her family status;
3. WE DECLARE that by excluding Peter and Trudy Jacobs and their children from the Mohawk List and thereby denying them the opportunity to apply for rights, benefits, privileges and services (other than the right to vote and hold office) that are available to others on the List, the MCK is engaging in a direct discriminatory practice contrary to the provisions of Section 5 as aforesaid;
4. WE ORDER that the MCK should cease and desist from committing acts of discrimination against Peter and Trudy Jacobs and their children by refusing them access to the rights, benefits, privileges and services available to other members of the Mohawk community of Kahnawake and under its jurisdiction (except for the right to vote or hold office in MCK elections) as follows: band number; residency; land allotment and land rights; housing assistance—loan, repair, servicing or related services; welfare; education; burial; medicines; and, tax privileges.
5. By 'access', we mean the right to be considered for those rights, benefits and privileges in accordance with the terms and conditions of the programs in place in the community.

This case highlights several important points regarding the application of human rights legislation in Canada. First, it highlights the fact that human rights legislation is primarily designed to prevent discrimination, not to change prejudiced attitudes. In this case, the tribunal asserted that it is not possible for anyone, certainly not a statutory tribunal, to make effective an Order that someone be accepted as part of a community if the community is unwilling to have them. What this means in this case is that only the members of the Mohawk community can grant acceptance to the complainants. The second point concerns the question of collective cultural rights, specifically, the right of self-determination of ethnic communities in Canada. Although ethnic communities may govern themselves in culturally distinct ways—ways that differ from those of the Euro-Canadian mainstream—they cannot create and enforce laws that are contrary to the laws of the Canadian state in which they reside. In this case, the MCK created a law that contravened the provisions of the federal Indian Act. Additionally, with specific reference to the complaint, the tribunal decided that the MCK committed a discriminatory practice contrary to the provisions of section 5 of the CHR Act on the basis of race, national origin, and ethnic origin, and it ordered the council to cease and desist this practice.

Ontario Human Rights Commission (OHRC)

(*Abouchar* v. *Metropolitan Toronto School Board et al.* OHRC. 1999 Case Summaries)

Grounds: Race, ethnic origin, place of origin

Area: Employment

On 27 March 1998, a board of inquiry found that the complainant, a francophone of Lebanese origin who emigrated to Canada from Egypt, had been subject to discrimination in two competitions for the position of assistant superintendent of programs for the new French-language public school board, Le conseil des écoles françaises de la communauté urbaine de Toronto (CEFCUT). The board of inquiry found that the first competition, held by Metropolitan Toronto School Board (Metro Board) was tainted by the consideration of the complainant's prior human rights complaint, and that the second competition, held by CEFCUT, was tainted by consideration of the complainant's non–Franco-Ontarian heritage. In the first competition, the board found that the complainant should have been appointed to the position, whereas in the second competition, the board found that the selection of another candidate was appropriate, notwithstanding the failure to treat the complainant's application in a nondiscriminatory manner. The hearing reconvened to decide remedy issues and a further decision was released on 23 April 1999. The board ordered Metro Board to reimburse the complainant for the differential in wages between the position he had competed for, and what he earned for one year after the competition, at which time the complainant accepted a position of superintendent with the Ottawa-Carleton school board. The complainant was also awarded reasonable relocation expenses, as it was foreseeable that the complainant would seek comparable employment in Ottawa. The board declined to order damages for the cost of maintaining two residences, since it was a personal decision for the complainant not to relocate his family to Ottawa. Each respondent was ordered to pay the complainant $6000 in general damages. In addition, damages for mental anguish of $8000 were ordered against Metro Board and damages of $10,000 were ordered to be paid by CEFCUT. Interest was awarded on the damages. CEFCUT was ordered to provide a written statement to the complainant acknowledging that it had infringed his rights and undertaking to comply with the orders of the board of inquiry and to publish a notice to that effect in its internal newsletter for senior staff. Both respondents were ordered to provide notice to the complainant of all vacancies for management positions above the level of principal, for a period of one year.

The respondents were also ordered to post the board of inquiry decision in their administrative offices, to post a summary of the decision in the staff room of all schools in the Toronto area, and to publish a summary of the decision in their newsletter for senior staff. CEFCUT was also ordered to develop and file with the commission recruitment policies to ensure that the profile of its senior staff reflected the diversity of its school communities and to develop and implement a policy acknowledging reprisal protection under the Ontario Human Rights Code. On 11 May 1999 the board of inquiry released a further decision denying costs to the respondent CEFCUT. Metro Board did not seek costs against the commission. Although CEFCUT spent almost $1,000,000 in legal costs, the board found it did not suffer undue hardship and that in any event, some of the costs claimed were unrecoverable. Although only the allegation of discrimination on the basis of place of origin was upheld, the board of inquiry found that none of the allegations that were dismissed (race, ethnic origin) were trivial, frivolous, or vexatious.

This case, and many others like it, highlight the importance that human rights statutes place on violations of the human right to dignity. Whenever relevant, as in this case, damages are awarded for mental anguish and for injury to dignity and selfrespect. Additionally, this case (like *National Capital Alliance on Race Relations v. Health Canada*) shows how an individual complaint can result in a *categorical* remedy in the form of affirmative measures designed to redress and prevent further systemic (adverse impact) discrimination. In this case, the respondent was ordered to develop and file with the commission recruitment policies to ensure that the profile of its senior staff reflected the diversity of its school communities and to develop and implement a policy acknowledging reprisal protection under the Ontario Human Rights Code.

Redressing Adverse Impact Discrimination: Affirmative Action Programs

The preceding analysis of legal cases brought forward under human rights statutes in Canada has drawn attention to the need for special programs and techniques of positive compensatory discrimination to redress the long-term, disadvantaging effects of systemic discrimination on racial and ethnic minorities.

The fact that a great many historical traditions and public practices embedded in the everyday operations of Canadian public institutions have had and continue to have a collective adverse impact on Canada's minorities clearly demonstrates the need for *intervention*, if these minorities are to enjoy, in fact, the equality of opportunity and treatment promised by human rights legislation and guaranteed under section 15 of the Charter. Even if all minorities were to be afforded explicit protection under the enumerated grounds of all non-discriminatory legislation, this would assure non-discrimination only in the *future*, it would not provide remedies for the adverse impact of *past* human rights violations. The strategy of intervention that has been developed both to counteract and to provide immediate redress for the disadvantaging effects of systemic discrimination is that of **affirmative action**.

One of the earliest definitions of affirmative action was provided in 1979 by Glaser and Possony, two American political scientists. These scholars defined affirmative action in general terms as a system of positive discrimination in favour of groups hitherto discriminated against—compensatory discrimination in favour of disadvantaged populations in the society (Glaser and Possony 1979: 57). In Canada, Hill and Schiff (1988: 35) have defined affirmative action in more specific terms as 'a program of temporary measures designed to eliminate systemic factors that prevent members of minority or other groups from competing equally with members of the majority for opportunities, usually in employment or education.' This is the definition we will use.

Constitutional Endorsement for Affirmative Action in Canada

Section 15 of the Charter of Rights and Freedoms in the Canadian Constitution (1982) not only prohibits individual discrimination, but also recognizes the validity of laws, programs, or activities designed to ameliorate the disadvantaged conditions of individuals or groups. Section 15(2) thus guarantees that affirmative action programs, designed by government agencies to provide forms of collective redress against the adverse impact of systemic discrimination on disadvantaged (minority) groups, will be allowed. This guarantee provided by section 15(2) of the Charter was deemed to be imperative in order to ensure that special measures of affirmative action would not constitute 'reverse discrimination' under the non-discriminatory provisions of Charter section 15(1). More specifically, the inclusion of section 15(2), in part, represented an attempt to prevent a repetition, in Canada, of the negative backlash to affirmative action that occurred in the United States. Let us, then, consider what happened south of the border before going on to discuss the process of implementation of affirmative action in Canada.

Affirmative Action in the United States

In the United States, the concept of affirmative action began to gain public approbation (at least in liberal sectors) by the 1960s. This development represented a public response to a concerted effort on the part of the government to reduce and eventually to eliminate racial, ethnic, and gender discrimination. In 1964, Congress enacted Title VII of the Civil Rights Act that made it unlawful for employers to discriminate on the basis of race, colour, religion, sex, or national origin. Initially, the Act applied only to the private sector, but in 1972, public sector employers and agencies were included.

There are two major programs enforced under the Civil Rights Act. The Equal Employment Opportunity Commission is responsible for enforcement of the (1964) legislation and also for information gathering. Under this program, every company with more than 100 employees must file an annual form listing the numbers of women and of four major racial and ethnic minorities (blacks, Spanish-surnamed, orientals, and American Indians) in their employ. The other major federal program is administered by the Office of Federal Contract Compliance (OFCC). This program requires that government contractors commit themselves to non-discrimination in business practice and to incorporating programs of affirmative action in their companies. Since 1970, each contractor and subcontractor must file an affirmative action plan with OFCC (Pie n.d.).

During the 1970s, public support for affirmative action fell off sharply, and programs began to be legally contested by majority members. Three key court cases challenging the constitutionality of affirmative action programs resulted in decisions specific to the particular case at hand that provided no clear guidance on how far employers could go in giving preferential treatment to minorities. This lack of clarity as to the *limits* of affirmative action was one factor feeding the backlash against such programs, but in the United States, at least two other factors were important. First, unlike the earlier Johnson administration, the Reagan and Bush administrations were not supportive of affirmative action, and, second, the economic climate, during recessionary years when promotional opportunities were limited and layoffs frequent, did not favour preferential treatment for protected classes of minorities.

Affirmative Action in Canada

Unlike the case of the United States, in Canada, affirmative action programs for the most part are voluntary, and a set of voluntary affirmative action guidelines have been developed at the federal level. Weinfeld (1981) locates the origin of affirmative action in Canada in the efforts of the Royal Commission on Bilingualism and Biculturalism, in the 1960s, to increase francophone participation in the federal government service. At that time, not only were there disproportionately few francophones employed overall, but those who were employed were also concentrated at the lower salary levels. Among senior decision-makers, francophone representation was minuscule.

At the time, underrepresentation of francophones in the federal public service was acknowledged to be a manifestation of systemic discrimination in federal employment systems. Thus, it was deemed necessary by government authorities to introduce affirmative action programs designed to recruit, place, and promote francophones. Such programs were put in place, and, by 1977, as a mark of their effectiveness, overall francophone representation in government employment had almost reached the proportion of francophones in the general population (Hill and Schiff 1988: 39).

At the federal government level, the legal foundation for affirmative action policies was provided in 1977 with the passage of the Canadian Human Rights Act (CHRA). With regard to employment, section 15 of the CHRA states that it is not a discriminatory practice to carry out a special program, plan, or arrangement designed to prevent, eliminate, or reduce disadvantages suffered by individuals or groups because of race, national or ethnic origin, colour, religion, age, sex, marital status, or physical handicap, by improving their opportunities respecting goods, services, facilities, accommodations, or employment. In short, section 15 of the CHRA insures that programs of affirmative action toward historically disadvantaged populations will not constitute 'reverse discrimination'. Further, under the terms of reference of the Canadian Human Rights Commission, the body that administers the Act, an affirmative action program may be required as part of the settlement of a discrimination complaint, as a measure designed to prevent the future recurrence of discriminatory practices. At the federal level, then, mandatory affirmative action plans may be deemed appropriate as preventative measures when a case of discrimination against an individual is found to be indicative of categorical discrimination against the minority s/he represents. Beyond this, the CHRA allows for, but does not require affirmative action remedies. In Canada, following the mandate of section 15(2) of the Charter, human rights statutes, from the 1980s, have increasingly incorporated provisions allowing for programs of affirmative action.

Although affirmative action programs and legislation operate in both Canada and the United States, there continues to be a major difference between the two countries with regard to the directive of the regulatory agencies. In the United States, affirmative action is *compulsory;* in Canada, for the most part, it is *voluntary*.

Identification of Practices of Systemic Discrimination

In the area of employment, a number of systemic practices have been identified as barriers to equality of opportunity for aboriginal peoples, women, and visible minorities. For example, 'old-boys' networks' among white males have been found to provide convenient channels for word-of-mouth job recruitment in some employment sectors, ensuring that knowledge of job vacancies is confined to the white male in-group. Women and non-whites are thereby excluded. Additionally, inflated or non-job related requirements have been found to pose systemic barriers for some minorities. Inflated educational requirements serve to bar competent (but poorly educated) aboriginal peoples and certain non-essential height and weight standards have been found to discriminate against women, some ethnic minorities, and aboriginal peoples (Abella 1984).

Affirmative Action Special Measures: Active Recruitment and Training Programs

The objective of special affirmative action programs is to create a more equitable distribution of opportunities and benefits across diverse social and cultural groups in Canada. Toward this end, measures such as active recruitment and hiring strategies are undertaken by various governments and private bodies to move qualified aboriginal peoples and visible minorities into labour force positions that they have previously been prevented from attaining. Another special measure undertaken at various levels of government is training programs, designed to equip members of long-disadvantaged minorities with skills and qualifications previously unavailable to them.

Planning for Affirmative Action

In employment and education, two key areas in which affirmative action programs have been developed, the planning of special programs involves, at the outset, the establishment of a measuring structure to set and meet specified goals. The measuring structure is designed to ascertain, on a statistical basis, the distribution of opportunities and associated benefits across the various population groups in the relevant locale (society, region, organization, etc.). Once identification of group disadvantage has been established, corrective action is undertaken through programs designed to redress the identified disadvantaged condition of the target population(s). The following examples illustrate how this process operates.

In the early 1980s, the Saskatchewan Human Rights Commission approved several multifaceted affirmative action projects whose chief beneficiaries were aboriginal peoples (Hill and Schiff 1988). One project was implemented by the Key Lake Mining Corporation in connection with the construction of a uranium mine in a sector of the province where aboriginal persons comprised 70 per cent of the population and where unemployment among them was over 80 per cent. In this program, recruitment officers were sent out to aboriginal communities to contact potential workers and the work schedules of aboriginal employees were adapted to accommodate the commuting distance between the worksite and the aboriginal community. As well, traditional academic requirements that were not essential to the job were waived and advisors were employed to help aboriginal workers adjust to conditions on the site and to protect their rights under the collective agreement.

In 1986, the federal government, through the Treasury Board, initiated a number of affirmative action measures for visible minorities in the Public Service of Canada (Jain 1989: 174). These included a special employment program, a visible minority employment office at the Public Service Commission in Ottawa, regional visible minority coordinators, special training for public service managers, a monitoring program for the recruitment, referral, and appointment of visible minorities in the public service, and the granting of Canadian educational equivalences of certain foreign university degrees. Further, in August 1987, the Treasury Board established numerical targets for visible minorities. These targets were to be set by occupational category and instituted by departments for a three-year period beginning 1 April 1988.

Contract Compliance: An Alternative to Voluntary Programs

One of the alternatives to voluntary affirmative action already in use by the federal and some provincial governments is **contract compliance**. Although there is no comprehensive contract compliance legislation in Canada, the principle of contract compliance has become embedded in some Canadian statutes and embodied in regulations governing dealings of some governments with the private sector. Under contract compliance, any firm to which a government pays public funds for the purchase of goods or services must, as a condition of its contract, comply with the government's human rights requirements (Hill and Schiff 1988: 48–9). In some cases, the requirement may simply be one of non-discrimination in employment and services. In other cases, however, the firm may be required to undertake a program of affirmative action. Companies with which governments do business may, for example, be required to take positive steps to redress any existing imbalance in what could be reasonably expected to be an equitable distribution of minority members throughout the ranks of their employees. Specific affirmative action programs constitute part of the contract with the government; thus, programs are carefully monitored by officers of human rights commissions. Failure to comply with the affirmative action provisions can result in penalties, which include, at least minimally, cancellation of the contract and exclusion of the firm from future government business.

A current example of contract compliance measures is provided in the case of the agreement between Union Local 13173 Cameco Corporation and the Province of Saskatchewan. Article 24 of the agreement—Affirmative Action/Employment Equity—reads as follows:

- 24.01 The Union acknowledges the Company has entered into a Surface Lease Agreement with the Province of Saskatchewan which has as one of its objectives, the maximizing of employment of residents of Saskatchewan's north. The Union further acknowledges the company has as one of its objectives, the maximizing of employment of northern residents of aboriginal ancestry.
- 24.02 The Company will hire northern residents of aboriginal ancestry who are qualified to perform the work required, when it is necessary for the Company to hire replacement or additional workers.
- 24.03 The Company will utilize, amongst other sources of employment, available northern hiring programs to assist in the hiring of northern residents of aboriginal ancestry.
- 24.04 Subject to Article 24.05, it is agreed that preference will be given to northern residents of aboriginal ancestry in matters of hiring and recall. In the case of a reduction in the work force, preference will be given to retaining northern residents of aboriginal ancestry.
- 24.05 Notwithstanding Article 24.04 hereof, it is understood and agreed that no employee who was hired prior to November 16, 1993 shall have his seniority rights affected in matters relating to a reduction in the work force or recall, as a result of preference being given to northern residents of aboriginal ancestry.
- 24.06 The Union and the Company agree to the establishment of a Joint Affirmative Action/ Employment Equity Committee comprised of up to four (4) representatives from the Union and up to four (4) representatives from the Company. The development, implementation and maintenance of the Affirmative Action/ Employment Equity program will be mutually agreed upon.

Contract compliance, under the regulations of human rights legislation, clearly provides more forceful leverage for affirmative action than does permissive legislation simply *allowing* voluntary programs. One example of human rights compliance regulations is provided by section 19 of the Canadian Human Rights Act. Section 19 of the Act gives the Government of Canada the power to make regulations providing for the placing of terms and conditions relating to anti-discrimination in contracts, grants, or licences from the federal government. Under such regulations, organizations are required to comply with the affirmative action provisions of the Canadian Human Rights Act (section 9(15)).

Hill and Schiff have shown that the principle of contract compliance has broad support throughout Canada. They point out that both the Commons Committee on Visible Minorities (1984) and the Abella Royal Commission (1984) recommended the adoption of such policies. Further, policies of contract compliance are advocated by the Public Service Alliance of Canada, the Canadian Civil Liberties Association, and virtually all visible minority organizations. Moreover, Hill and Schiff insist, most advocates of the principle believe that a legislative base for contract compliance is necessary in order to ensure continuance of effective policies over successive governments (1988: 49–50).

Mandatory Affirmative Action: Pros and Cons

Before we undertake a consideration of the policy option of mandatory affirmative action in Canada, it is important to address the basic issues that have plagued the controversy surrounding the policies and programs of mandatory affirmative action south of the border, since their inception in the US over a quarter of a century ago. The issues in the debate involve discussion at two levels: the level of ideology and the level of public practice.

The ideological debate focuses on the meritocracy principle and on the contradictions to this principle posed by programs of affirmative action. The first issue to be addressed in relation to the meritocracy principle is that of the legitimacy of collective redress against the adverse impact of systemic discrimination (categorical rights claims). Opponents argue that when compensation is offered to groups (rather than to individual complainants) it is because of some collective characteristic (disadvantage) members (assumedly) share, not because of demonstrable evidence that, *as individuals,* they were victims of discrimination. Affirmative action programs accordingly are open to criticism on the ground that evidence has not been provided to show that all minority members have been (equally) subject to systemic discrimination. The possibility exists, therefore, that some minority members without need of affirmative action programs may be unjustly advantaged by them.

Opponents of affirmative action have argued that American-style affirmative action, with its imposition of quotas for minorities, represents a retreat from the dogmas of universalism, the protection of individual rights, and the merit principle, which represent the fundamental democratic principles behind North American society. It has been suggested further that, at the level of public practice, affirmative action may have an effect that is opposite to its intention, namely, to force individual minority members to identify, perhaps unwillingly, with their minority community, thus crystallizing the subordinate status of the group and reducing its members prospects for upward mobility.

A related set of issues, arising from the American experience with mandatory affirmative action programs, concerns their unintended, harmful, psychosocial consequences. Special opportunity programs have been perceived to have negative effects on the self-image of the minority participants and on the quality of inter-group relations. Minority members given 'special treatment', critics argue, may come to see themselves as less worthy, less meritorious, than those who have made it on their own. Further, both minority and majority members excluded from or by affirmative action programs may harbour resentment towards minority participants and may feel that they have been discriminated against. Finally, in the cases where unqualified or less-qualified minority participants are selected for an affirmative action program (in the American experience, in order to fill arbitrary quotas) the outcome, in many cases, has been the failure of the participant to fulfill the objectives of the program. The negative consequences of failure have been psychologically devastating for the participant, in many instances. In these particular cases, which represent an abuse of the goals of affirmative action, hostile majority backlash has been all but inevitable. The failure of minority members has rendered these programs counterproductive: they have served to reinforce and 'justify' stereotypes of minority inferiority. Glaser and Possony (1979: 325) have argued that the mounting injustice not only to victims of 'reverse discrimination' but even to the beneficiaries of positive programs under policies of mandatory affirmative action renders them inappropriate as a means of achieving equality of opportunity for minorities.

A recent critique of affirmative action in the United States by the distinguished sociologist Nathan Glazer (1998) again raises serious questions as to the appropriateness of programs instituted. Glazer points out that affirmative action has in part been a 'hand up' to 'people who have had a hard time', but, he contends that its original design was so faulty that it soon became counterproductive. Glazer argues that the minority groups placed under the special terms of affirmative action—African-Americans, Hispanics, Asians, and American Indians (Native Americans), and women—are so widely various in their histories, in the discrimination they have faced, in the obstacles they meet today, and in their claims to special treatment, that inevitably a great number of the policy's beneficiaries have not had a hard time, and have not needed a hand up.

On the cost side of affirmative action, Glazer asserts, perhaps the greatest cost has been exacted by the requirements for affirmative action plans, with their elaborate record-keeping of recruitment, employment, and promotion, and the openings thus made possible for litigation. Affirmative action, he argues, has undoubtedly burdened every employer, public and private. Some of the costs of this burden have been tallied, and, Glazer argues, they appear to exceed the benefit, however it is calculated.

As for the question of 'mending' or 'ending' affirmative action, Glazer argues that certain initiatives seem to be necessary. He contends that America does need black members of police departments if black areas are to be policed effectively. Similarly, the country does need black teachers and administrators in its public schools. Glazer contends that the degree of racial self-consciousness among African-Americans is so strong that, except under special circumstances, an educational system that does not take account of race and ethnicity will not succeed.

Glazer argues, in closing, for a change from mandatory to voluntary affirmative action initiatives. Where maintaining some form of preferential treatment of minorities, especially blacks, is deemed genuinely necessary, colleges and universities, public contractors, and employers should be free to do what they feel impelled to do. That, Glazer asserts would be much better than either a universal standard that says there must be preferences or a universal standard that says there must not be preferences.

Glazer's argument clearly reveals the underlying tension between the ideological and practical dimensions of the affirmative action debate. Ideologically speaking, Glazer clearly favours the meritocracy principle and is harshly critical of affirmative action initiatives that have, in his view, unfairly advantaged minority members who did not need preferential treatment. On the other hand, in the case of American blacks in particular, Glazer deems it necessary, from a practical point of view, to maintain some forms of preferential treatment in order to 'level the playing field'.

Mandatory Affirmative Action: A Summary of the Issues in the Debate

Opponents of mandatory affirmative action have argued against this policy option on both ideological and practical grounds. Ideologically speaking, critics have argued that special measures of 'collective redress' against the adverse impact of systemic discrimination on minorities as wholes offends one of the most fundamental principles of North American democratic society, the individualistic principle of meritocracy.

In Canada, this point of view was recently put forward forcefully in the context of parliamentary debates (*Parliamentary Debates* [online]). Vehement opposition to affirmative action was expressed in the following remarks:

Hiring quotas based on race or gender imply that members of target groups are somehow inferior and therefore incapable of competing on a level playing field. Such programs foster suspicion and resentment, and rob us all of dignity. . . . Affirmative action programs breed resentment and suspicion among co-workers, and these hiring quotas foment inequality and bitterness in society at large. That is because of an inescapable universal truth which is that it is not possible to discriminate in favour of someone because of their race or gender without discriminating against someone else. Affirmative action and employment equity programs are inherently unfair, they violate the principles of equality and merit based hiring, and they must therefore be stopped.

From a practical view, two routine arguments have been raised against legislating mandatory affirmative action in Canada: first, the financial cost and difficulties of implementation of programs and second, the alleged, negative results of such legislation in the US. Proponents of mandatory affirmative action counter that the financial cost of such programs must be weighed against the tremendous social costs of maintaining the *status quo*: the cost of systemic discrimination, they argue, is demonstrably greater than the expense of redressing historic wrongs. In financial terms alone, Canadians pay very high welfare costs when employers categorically exclude various minorities from employment, not to mention the concomitant costs of poor human resources planning and utilization. Accordingly, the Canadian economy suffers when aboriginal peoples, women, visible and other minorities are categorically excluded from various sectors of the workforce. As regards the second point, proponents of mandatory affirmative action argue that Canadians have been able to learn from the cumulative American experience. The negative results of early, affirmative action programs with imposed quotas led to marked policy changes in the US, favouring the setting of 'reasonable goals'. Canada's voluntary affirmative action programs have followed this later course, rather than the earlier, quota system and also have adopted monitored recruitment, hiring, and promotion strategies in order to reach projected goals. Most important, Canada's emphasis has been on education and training programs designed to assist target minority populations in the attainment of trade skills and professional certification that will provide them with legitimate qualifications for jobs. In this way, some of the major problems encountered south of the border, specifically, the filling of educational and occupational 'quotas' with unqualified or underqualified minority members have been circumvented.

Affirmative Action and Human Rights in Canada Today

Despite some variation in the scope of human rights legislation and in the powers of different commissions, human rights legislation in Canada is largely permissive, rather than prescriptive. Section 15(2) of the Charter and parallel, statutory legislation throughout the country, *permit* affirmative action by stating that it is not a discriminatory practice to implement special programs for (minority) groups disadvantaged through the effects of systemic discrimination. Although legislation is essentially permissive, federal and provincial governments increasingly have gone on record in favour of affirmative action. The constitutional sanction for affirmative action, given by its incorporation under section 15 of the Charter makes Canada one of the few countries in the world where programs of affirmative action, including special measures, have gained status recognition under the provisions of the supreme law of the land. These positive accomplishments notwithstanding, when it comes to assessing the concrete results of voluntary affirmative action programs, their inherent weakness comes to the fore. For several decades, the federal government has been actively promoting voluntary affirmative action programs, yet, only a small number of employers have actually instituted such programs.

A recent, comparative analysis of provincial **employment equity** policy across Canada (Bakan and Kobayashi 2000) revealed marked variations in conceptualization, structure, and implementation of policy initiatives. Seven provinces in Canada today (British Columbia, Manitoba, Saskatchewan, Quebec, Nova Scotia, New Brunswick, and Prince Edward Island) have employment equity policy. Only British Columbia has employment equity legislation. Only Quebec extends its mandate beyond the public service. Have these policies achieved substantial results? For those provinces where data were available, the results showed limited progress, except in the case of women, where substantial progress was indicated.

In general, the study revealed that the climate of debate on the underlying principles behind employment equity in Canadian provinces today stands along a spectrum from extreme commitment to extreme opposition. Moreover, within each province, further debates concern implementation, accountability, policy results, and future directions. Across the 10 provinces, Bakan and Kobayashi (2000) report, there is widespread interest among employment equity advocates and among its opponents, in the unique experience of Ontario. Case Study 1 in Box 8-2 should shed light on the importance of the Ontario experience.

Mandatory Programs of Employment Equity in Canada

In 1984, the Royal Commission on Equality in Employment, chaired by Judge Rosalie Abella, reported on the findings of their national investigation of systemic discrimination in employment. The commission recommended that the federal government put into place mandatory 'employment equity' programs in all crown and government corporations where underrepresentation of designated target groups—women, aboriginal peoples, disabled and visible minorities—was identified.

In response to the Abella Report, the federal government instituted two mandatory programs of employment equity. In 1986, the government passed the Employment Equity Act (Bill C-62). This Act applied to Crown corporations and federally regulated employers with 100 or more employees. The second mandatory federal program was the Federal Contractors Program (FCP) (Jain 1989: 173). This program was restricted to contractors with 100 or more employees who bid on contracts for goods and services worth $200,000 or more. Under this program, contractors were required to sign an agreement to design and carry out an employment equity program that will identify and remove discriminatory barriers to the selection, hiring, promotion and training of women, aboriginal peoples, persons with disabilities, and visible minorities. Unlike the Employment Equity Act, the FCP did not require employers to file an employment equity plan, only to make a commitment to develop a plan.

Critics of the federal government's two employment equity programs argued that these programs, though garbed in mandatory trappings, were *de facto* voluntary because they lacked mandatory implementation of plans with specific goals and timetables, systematic monitoring mechanisms, and effective sanctions for non-compliance (Jain 1989: 175; Stasiulis 1990). Critics also pointed out that the federal programs did not apply to all agencies under federal jurisdiction. The employment equity legislation applied only to employers under federal jurisdiction, while the federal government's affirmative action program applied only to the federal public service. Neither of these affirmative policies applied to the RCMP or the Armed Forces. Critics insisted that the federal government should

BOX 8-2: CASE STUDY 1

The Rise and Fall of Employment Equity Legislation in Ontario

Throughout the 1990s, the Ontario Legislature witnessed a dramatic shift in its ideological orientation to employment equity. The shift was dramatic, from one end of the spectrum—unwavering government support—to the other—vociferous opposition. The swing of the pendulum coincided with a political shift in the parties in power—from the New Democratic Party under Premier Bob Rae, elected in 1990, to the Progressive Conservative Party, under Premier Mike Harris, elected in 1995. Under the NDP, in 1994, the Ontario government passed into law the Act to Provide for Employment Equity for Aboriginal People, People with Disabilities, Members of Racial Minorities and Women. The legislation and accompanying regulations were designed to ensure that barriers to equal access for the four designated groups, in every workplace in the broader public sector, were challenged. The legislation covered most employers in the province and required them to prepare an employment equity plan in accordance with the regulations. The plan was required to provide for the elimination of systemic barriers, and for the implementation of positive measures and supportive measures for each of the four designated groups in all areas of employment from recruitment through promotion, with consequences for non-compliance.

In sharp contrast to the lengthy process of consultation, assessment, review, and amendment that had characterized the development of Ontario's Employment Equity Act, its repeal was a speedy process. In the first sitting of the new PC government, Bill 8, which became An Act to Repeal Job Quotas and to Restore Merit-based Employment Practices in Ontario, was tabled, moved through three readings in the legislature, and enacted into law. Commonly referred to simply as the Job Quotas Repeal Act, the title of the bill (incorrect in its implication that the previous Employment Equity Act had required job quotas) reflected a profound ideological rejection not only of employment equity policy, but also of its underlying premise of systemic discrimination. The repeal was explicit in its renunciation of any notion of systemic discrimination. Not only did it withdraw the law, but also it reversed, retroactively, all policy directives of the Employment Equity Commission and the Employment Equity Tribunal and it required the repeal of all previous amendments to laws, including the Ontario Human Rights Code, which had been intended to ensure employment equity.

In place of the former Employment Equity Act, the Ontario Government established a policy program committed to advancing 'equal opportunity' in the private sector. With regard to the public sector, the Management Board Secretariat was ordered to design an equal opportunity initiatives program emphasizing the merit principle, removal of barriers, and zero tolerance of workplace harassment and discrimination. In the EO plan, there is no notion of systemic discrimination against designated groups in society. The operative notion in the EO plan is the individual, not the group. Moreover, there has been an ideological shift from equity, advanced as a principle of democratic fairness, to equal opportunity, advocated for its contribution to profit maximization.

Although other channels for the redress of workplace discrimination continue to be in place, particularly through the Ontario Human Rights Commission and the Ontario Pay Equity Commission, both organizations have been subject to severe budgetary restrictions and limited support at the ministerial level. The

Job Quotas Repeal Act has contributed significantly to the atmosphere of sharply polarized debate on employment equity that continues, unabated. Most importantly, it sparked a Charter Challenge, under Canada's Constitution, alleging that it violated the Canadian Charter of Rights and Freedoms.

The Charter Challenge

Early in 1996, the Alliance for Employment Equity—a coalition of community, legal and labour organizations—prepared a challenge to the Job Quotas Repeal Act by seeking a legal injunction to block the new law from taking effect. However, this initial effort failed. The Job Quotas Repeal Act was then challenged by four individuals, each representing one of the four designated groups under the previous Employment Equity Act, on the basis that it violated the Canadian Charter of Rights and Freedoms. The case was supported by a number of respected authorities prepared to testify to the importance of employment equity laws in redressing systemic discrimination.

Under the umbrella coalition of the Alliance for Employment Equity, the Charter challenge was heard in Ontario Court, General Division by Judge Dilks on 26–9 November 1996. Among the key arguments put forward in support of employment equity laws, and supported by an extensive array of research studies, was the argument that human rights legislation such as the Ontario Human Rights Code, operating on the individual complaints-based system, had provided ineffective protection against systemic discrimination and had not, to date, made any significant progress towards the elimination of systemic discrimination. Nevertheless, the Ontario Court rejected the appeal on 8 December 1998. The Alliance for Employment Equity then announced its intention to appeal before the Supreme Court of Canada. But, on 10 December 1999 the Supreme Court of Canada denied leave to appeal.

The Ontario Supreme Court's rejection of this appeal did not deny the existence of systemic discrimination in employment. The court avowed, however, that it could not stop governments from repealing laws, even if it is shown that such a repeal reverses or challenges positive steps in human rights protection.

The Ontario story of the rise and fall of employment equity remains an open-ended one. Even in the face of a legislative backlash, the struggle of its advocates to achieve employment equity appears to have gained in strength, and proponents remain determined to challenge systemic discrimination and to secure full and public government accountability.

SOURCE: Adapted from Bakan and Kobayashi 2000.

extend its affirmative action mandate to include the RCMP and the Armed Forces. Furthermore, Jain pointed out that there were few employment equity programs or contract compliance programs at the provincial level, where affirmative action plans remain voluntary. To remedy this situation, he recommended that provincial and territorial governments introduce mandatory employment equity and contract compliance programs. A succession of key reports documenting racism in Canada, including the reports of the Commons Committee on Visible Minorities (Canada 1984a) and the Abella (1984) commission pressed the case for mandatory affirmative action. For advocates of mandatory affirmative action, the admonition of the Abella commission embodied the last word on the subject: 'A government genuinely committed to equality in the workplace will use law to accomplish it and thereby give the concept credibility and integrity. . . . Equality in employment will not happen unless we make it happen.'

Some 10 years later, in partial response to continuing, vociferous criticism, in 1996, the

BOX 8-3: CASE STUDY 2

Employment Equity for Visible Minorities: Embracing Change in the Federal Public Service

On 23 April 1999, the president of the Treasury Board established the Task Force on the Participation of Visible Minorities in the federal Public Service. The Task Force was mandated to develop a government-wide action plan, with benchmarks, to address the persistent underrepresentation of persons in visible minority groups within the federal Public Service.

It was acknowledged that persons in visible minority groups are the most underrepresented of the four designated groups within the federal Public Service. While the other designated groups (aboriginal people, persons with disabilities, and women) have made progress in recent years, the gap still persists for persons in visible minority groups between their representation in the public service (5.9 per cent) and their labour market availability (8.7 per cent). It was therefore deemed necessary to take special measures to address this gap.

The Task Force presented its Action Plan, entitled Embracing Change in the Federal Public Service, to the president of the Treasury Board in April 2000. It was endorsed by the government in June 2000. Although focused on persons in visible minority groups, the measures included in the Action Plan are designed to contribute to a workplace that is welcoming to all four designated groups.

On 12 June 2000, the president of the Treasury Board of Canada released the government response, endorsing the Task Force's report with a commitment to integrate the recommendations into the broader human resources strategies being pursued by the federal Public Service. These include a focus on recruitment, retention, and workplace well-being. A new fund, the Employment Equity-Embracing Change Support Fund (EE-ECSF) was established to provide financial support to departments and agencies for the implementation of the Task Force's Action Plan. The government's stated goal is to have a Public Service that reflects the diversity of Canadian society.

The Task Force outlined its recommendations in the following six broad categories; an overview of the government's actions is given for each.

I. Benchmarks

The Task Force proposed the use of benchmarks, which they described as tools to assist the federal Public Service in improving performance in the representation of visible minorities. The purpose of benchmarks is to seize the opportunity to make progress over a reasonable period. In proposing this approach, the Task Force indicated that it was not seeking quotas for visible minorities. The Task Force also emphasized that the merit principle would not be undermined by the program. It stated: 'The driving principle must be that what an individual can do on the job must matter more than his or her race or colour.'

a) *External recruitment set at 1 in 5 by 2003*

The Task Force proposes that a benchmark of 1 in 5 is achievable for recruitment into the Public Service as a whole. The Government responded that the federal Public Service is developing a concerted approach to recruitment and retention as part of its overall human resources strategy to replenish and renew the Public Service workforce. The benchmark of 1 in 5 for external recruitment will be incorporated within the Public Service's overall recruitment efforts.

b) *Acting appointments and entry into Executive feeder groups and Executive levels by 2005*
The Task Force proposes that a benchmark of 1 in 5 acting appointments at the levels of Executive feeder groups is achievable as well as at the entry level into Executive feeder groups and Executive levels by 2005. The Government responded that while acting appointments provide an excellent vehicle for development, there are many other vehicles that will be considered to assist in broadening the skills and experiences of employees so that they can assume roles at higher levels. Increasing the appointment share of visible minorities into the Executive feeder groups and Executive category will require a combination of strategies, which could include external recruitment, Interchange Canada assignments, and coaching and developmental opportunities such as the Career Assignment Program and the Management Trainee Program. Other strategies will be developed and considered in the context of corporate opportunities that emerge through the development of individual departmental action plans.

II. Help Departments and Managers Achieve the Benchmarks

The Task Force recognized that departments and managers would require assistance in implementing the benchmarks and therefore made recommendations with respect to sharing of best practices, education, widening of areas of selection, use of inventories, and selection criteria. The Government responded that the Treasury Board Secretariat, the Public Service Commission and the Canadian Centre for Management Development will continue to work with departments in consultation with the bargaining agents to elaborate appropriate recruitment and development strategies to ensure the availability of the widest possible pool of qualified candidates for appointment and promotion. Communications tools will be put in place to enable departments to share best practices and successes. The Public Service Commission and departments are committed to continue the assessment of their employment systems to ensure that they are barrier-free.

III. Change the Corporate Culture

The Task Force underscored the need for cultural change. It recommended activities such as the integration of diversity in human resources policy and training, the development of career and leadership programs, and a new youth internship program and renewed efforts to attract and recruit visible minority youth.

The federal Public Service recognized that recommendations like those offered by the Task Force are essential for changing the corporate culture to ensure an inclusive workplace and becoming an 'Employer of Choice'. In recognition of the fact that a representative Public Service is closely linked to the concept of inclusiveness, the Task Force on an Inclusive Public Service was given the mandate to further explore ways and means of creating a new culture in the Public Service. Several initiatives have been developed, such as the Agent of Change Workshops and the Diversity Diagnostic Tool, to help take stock of the current cultural climate and to assist in sensitizing and training Public Service employees on the benefits of a diverse workforce. This initiative has created a momentum for change and 2000 employees have signed on as agents of change committed to an inclusive Public Service. The Canadian Centre for Management Development has also developed a variety of tools, one of which is the 'Diversity: Vision and Action' course, which guides Executives and managers to see diversity as a way to enrich the workforce and strengthen the leadership capacity and effectiveness of their organizations.

IV. Provide for Implementation and Accountability

The Action Plan of the Task Force on the Participation of Visible Minorities in the federal Public Service envisages heightened roles for the Clerk of the Privy Council, the Secretary of the Treasury Board and the President of the Public Service Commission to identify where strategic progress can be made, encourage and monitor progress, and where progress is not achieved, guide departments accordingly.

The Head of the Public Service has made diversity a key theme in the Corporate Priorities under the Performance Management Program for Deputy Heads. A corporate Diversity and Employment Equity Awards Program will be announced to focus on best practices and to celebrate successes. In accordance with the requirements of the Employment Equity Act, the President of Treasury Board will report the progress achieved in the representation for visible minorities in the Annual Employment Equity Report to Parliament.

V. External Advice and Independent Review

The Task Force held that external advice is essential to sustain momentum for change and therefore recommended the appointment of an external advisory group to the Secretary of the Treasury Board and an independent review of progress at the end of three years.

In response, an External Advisory Group [three of the five members of the advisory group are representatives of visible minorities] has been established, whose role will be to provide advice and guidance to the Secretary and the President of the Public Service Commission, concerning ways in which the federal Public Service can sustain the momentum for change. The members of the Advisory Group will be asked to review and comment on the overall progress made in fostering an inclusive workplace and to provide recommendations on the effectiveness of strategies to increase the federal Public Service recruitment share of members of visible minority groups. At the end of three years, the President of the Treasury Board will assess progress achieved to date and based on the results, decide on the necessity of an independent review.

VI. Provide for Incremental Financial Resources

The Task Force believed that additional financial resources would be needed to fund startup activities under their Action Plan and recommended that the Treasury Board Secretariat manage a reserve to assist in implementation by departments and agencies. The Government responded that financial resources up to $10M in the current year and each of the next two years will be made available based on submission of a business case, to ensure successful implementation of the Action Plan.

SOURCE: Treasury Board of Canada website.

federal government drew up a new Employment Equity Act. The new Employment Equity Act and related Regulations came into effect in 1996, creating a new legislative framework for employment equity that governs both private and public sector employers under federal jurisdiction. The purpose of the Act is to ensure that members of four general groups achieve representation and participation in the workforce. These four groups are women, aboriginal peoples, persons with disabilities, and members of visible minorities. The Canadian Human Rights Commission has been given an audit and enforcement mandate under the new Act.

Bakan and Kobayashi assert that the federal government's current employment equity policies and programs rank among the most advanced in the world. In contrast to those of most provinces, the federal program is well established, supported by a substantial bureaucracy, and entrenched in legislation that covers the federal public service, federally regulated employers, Crown corporations, and firms that bid on federal contracts. Additionally, these authors state, the current policies are both comprehensive and integrated (2000: 13). At issue, is whether having invested so heavily in a comprehensive employment equity system, the federal public service will, in the foreseeable future, show significant results in increasing the representation of designated minorities. Bakan and Kobayashi point out that, over the last decade, progress in achieving the aims of employment equity policies and programs has been very modest, especially in the case of visible minorities, whose current representation is less than 60 per cent of their workforce availability. Needless to say, this seemingly sluggish rate of progress, given the high cost of maintaining the employment equity system, feeds the sharp edge of criticism levied by opponents of employment equity.

The new millennium, however, appears to be bringing fresh hope to Canada's dream of equity for members of all racial and ethnic groups in the country. Specifically, with regard to underrepresentation of visible minorities in the federal public service, the government has responded to criticisms with a new plan for Employment Equity for Visible Minorities. The history behind the new plan and its key equity measures are presented in Case Study 2 (see Box 8-3).

Conclusion

This chapter has focused on legal mechanisms designed to prevent and/or eradicate ethnic discrimination in Canada. It has analyzed the legal structure of human rights protection at the statutory level, and has attempted to point out its limitations, particularly with regard to its inadequacy in resolving group-level complaints based on systemic discrimination. In the latter regard, it examines the continuing debate as to the appropriateness of the remedy of voluntary and/or mandatory affirmative action, as a measure of collective redress against systemic discrimination.

In Chapter 9, we will focus on the legal structure of human rights protection at the constitutional level in Canada. We will examine the differences between statutory and constitutional protection for human rights, and we will critically analyze the provisions of the Charter as an instrument designed to ensure equal protection for the human rights of all Canadians. We will then analyze a number of Charter challenge cases of alleged racial and ethnic discrimination in existing statutory law, in order to demonstrate the way Canada's legal Constitution protects citizens across the country against legal discrimination. Finally, we will move beyond the Canadian court context and examine cases in which claims based on alleged legal discrimination in Canada have been put forward directly to the United Nations Human Rights Committee, under the Optional Protocol to the International Covenant on Civil and Political Rights.

Key Concepts

- adverse affect discrimination
- affirmative action
- contract compliance
- employment equity
- enumerated grounds of discrimination
- human rights statutes
- individual complaint-based procedure

Critical Thinking Questions

1. Explain how human rights legislation can influence the relationship between prejudice and discrimination. Using concrete examples to back up your points, illustrate both what human rights laws can do and what they can't do to better interethnic relations.

2. From the point of view of an aboriginal claimant, provide a critique of the current human rights system. Outline the kinds of changes that could be made to accommodate the demands of aboriginal claimants.
3. Using specific legal cases to illustrate your arguments show how an individual complaint can result in a categorical remedy in the form of affirmative measures designed to redress and prevent further systemic (adverse impact) discrimination.
4. A central aim of the current human rights system is to recognize and protect the fundamental human right to dignity of person. Provide examples from legal cases to demonstrate the way the system attempts to carry out this mission.
5. Should affirmative action programs be mandatory? Outline the pros and cons in the debate raised by this question.

CHAPTER 9

The Legal Framework for Protection of Minority Rights in Canada: The Canadian Constitution and Its Charter of Rights and Freedoms

Introduction

Chapter 8 focused on statutory protections for human rights in Canada. It presented a brief history of the development of human rights statutes and, through an examination of cases brought before federal and provincial human rights commissions, we saw how human rights statutes serve, in practice, to provide minority claimants with appropriate forms of redress against demonstrable, past violations to their fundamental human rights.

In this chapter, the focus of analysis will be on Canada's constitutional Charter of Rights and Freedoms (CRF) and on the process through which claimants put forward Charter challenges to alleged discriminatory *laws* in Canada. Before undertaking a critical analysis of the provisions of Canada's Charter of Rights and Freedoms and of the current model of interpretation and implementation of the Charter's provisions, it is important to distinguish clearly between the nature and scope of human rights protection afforded under constitutional Charter and statutory legislation.

Statutory versus Charter Protection for Minority Rights

A summary of **statutory versus Charter protection for minority rights** follows:

1. Statutory human rights laws deal with claims of discrimination by and against private individuals or groups; the Charter deals with discrimination by governments (for example, discriminatory government laws and/or policies).
2. Statutory human rights legislation applies primarily to discrimination in employment, accommodation, and public services; the Charter applies to all areas under government jurisdiction.
3. Federal and provincial human rights commissions provide investigative services at no cost to the complainant, but individuals or organizations bringing complaints under the Charter must pay for the costs involved (for example, hiring a lawyer to defend the case in court). Because this is beyond the means of many persons, particularly members of disadvantaged minorities, the federal government provides some funding for selected Charter challenge cases, under the Court Challenges Program.

The current Court Challenges Program of Canada is a national non-profit organization that was set up in 1994 to provide financial assistance for important court cases that advance language and equality rights guaranteed under Canada's Constitution. The program has a volunteer board of directors responsible for administering it. In addition, there are specialized, independent panels of experts to make decisions as to which cases or projects will be funded and in what amounts. The Court Challenges Program is an important instrument for minorities because the cost of Charter challenges prohibits most minority members and organizations from pursuing this option on their own.

A Critique of Constitutional Provisions Protecting Minority Rights in Canada: Do Constitutional Guarantees Ensure Ethnic-Group Equality or Inequality?

Insofar as constitutional provisions are in accordance with fundamental human rights principles, they should afford equal/equivalent protection not only for the individual rights of all persons but also for the collective rights of all ethnic groups within the state.[1] Yet, Canada, from Confederation, has been constitutionally predicated on the inegalitarian notion of special group status. Under the Confederation pact and the subsequent Constitution Act of 1867, Canada's 'founding peoples'—English/Protestant and French/Catholic ethnic groups—acquired a special and superordinate status as the majority or dominant ethnic groups, each with a claim for nationhood within clearly delineated, territorial boundaries (Upper Canada/Ontario; Lower Canada/Quebec). Moreover, under the terms of sections 93 and 133 of the 1867 Constitution, the collective, religious/educational, and language rights of the two 'charter groups' were protected even outside of their respective territorial jurisdictions, in localities where their members constituted *numerical* minorities.

By way of contrast, under the terms of section 94(24) of the 1867 Constitution, aboriginal nations, lumped together under the racist rubric of 'Indians', became Canada's first ethnic minorities. The provisions of section 94(24) gave the Parliament of Canada constitutional jurisdiction to enact laws concerning Indians and lands reserved for Indians. Under ensuing legislation, notably the various Indian Acts, once proud and independent aboriginal nations, living and governing themselves within the territorial bounds of their indigenous homelands, acquired a special and inferior status as virtual wards of the state.

Later immigrant ethnic groups, *without* constitutional provisions for special status—superior or inferior—have come to constitute a third (multicultural) category of ethnic groups, whose collective claims rest on a goal of *equal* ethnic status and equal ethnocultural rights.

For purposes of this book, the significance of constitutionally rooted status differences among founding, aboriginal, and multicultural ethnic groups is that they afford differential bases for collective claims: claims based on special (founding or aboriginal) status and claims based on equal (multicultural) status. Moreover, a direct consequence of this tripartite division is that minority rights claims put forward by representatives of each of the three categories are in competition, if not in direct conflict with each other.

The crucial question at this point is: To what extent were each of the three sets of claims recognized during the 1980–2 constitutional debates and to what degree have the collective rights of minority claimants been specified and protected through ensuing (1982) amendments? The analysis to follow may serve to shed light not only on the ethnic priorities underscoring the amending process but also on the concomitant version of Canadian 'unity in diversity'—on both ethnic and non-ethnic grounds—entrenched through constitutional amendments.

Constitutionalizing a Canadian Charter of Rights and Freedoms

Throughout the 1980–2 constitutional debate, legal scholars who voiced support for constitutional entrenchment of a Charter of Rights and Freedoms argued that an entrenched Charter would override existing legislation and would thus render all discriminatory laws throughout the country inoperative. Moreover, it was argued, an entrenched Charter would serve to eliminate existing disparities in the provisions of federal and provincial human rights legislation as it would provide the standard to which all legislation should conform (Kallen 1982).

It follows from this line of argument that a constitutionally entrenched Charter should provide all Canadian minorities with an equal/equivalent basis for making claims for redress against perceived human rights violations. But, is this in fact the case? Is the Charter truly an egalitarian human rights instrument or is it informed by established ethnic and non-ethnic group priorities that serve to render some categories of Canadians *more equal* than others?

In order to answer this question at least three variables relating to the nature of the provisions of the Charter must first be taken into account:

1. *Negative versus Positive Protections*
Negative protections guarantee only non-interference by the state in the exercise of human rights by individuals or groups. **Positive protections,** on the other hand, obligate the state to take appropriate measures, including the provision of resources out of public funds, in order to guarantee the full exercise of rights.

2. *Specified versus Unspecified Protections*
Unspecified protections apply generally; they do not specify particular target populations. **Specified protections,** on the other hand, apply specifically to particular, *enumerated* target populations.

3. *Undefined versus Defined Rights*
Undefined rights are not spelled out with regard to meaning and content. Accordingly, the nature of the state obligations and of the protections to be afforded are neither clarified nor elaborated. **Defined rights,** on the other hand, are spelled out with regard to meaning and content, and the protections to be afforded by the state are delineated.

When the foregoing variables are taken into account in assessing the provisions of the Charter, it becomes evident that the Charter is not a truly egalitarian human rights instrument. Rather, the Charter, together with related (1982) constitutional provisions, can be seen to perpetuate and to further legitimate long-institutionalized status inequalities between and among different ethnic and non-ethnic populations in Canada.

Ethnic Inequalities

The special and superordinate status of Canada's two founding peoples is reconfirmed and bolstered through Charter provisions protecting their collective rights. Under Charter sections 16–21 and section 23, *positive, specified* protections are afforded for *clearly defined* English- and French-language and educational rights. Under Charter section 29, the constitutionally entrenched, *positive, specified* protections for the *clearly defined* religious denominational education rights of Protestant and Catholic religious groups throughout Canada are reconfirmed.

Conversely, there are no parallel protections for the collective linguistic and religious rights of multicultural or aboriginal minorities. Charter section 27 mentions the 'multicultural heritage' of Canadians, but the vagueness of this provision leaves its interpretation entirely in the hands of the courts. Certainly, section 27 affords no *positive* protections for minority rights as this provision neither *specifies* nor *defines* the nature of the rights alluded to. Similarly, Charter section 22 provides only a vague, *negative* protection for non-official language minorities by allowing, but neither *specifying* nor *defining,* their linguistic rights.

Constitutional amendments (section 35 and Charter section 25) represent a positive move to improve the constitutionally entrenched, special, and inferior status of Canada's aboriginal peoples by recognizing their collective, aboriginal rights. Yet, these provisions afford only *negative* protections for the aboriginal and treaty rights of Indian, Inuit, and Métis minorities. The nature and content of collective, aboriginal rights is not elaborated, and, after four constitutional conferences convened for the singular purpose of defining aboriginal rights, these remain *undefined.*

The unwavering priority given the collective rights of Canada's founding peoples over the parallel rights of multicultural and aboriginal minorities was evident throughout the amending process. In the original (1980) version of the Charter, there was no mention of the notion of 'multicultural heritage'. In response to unflagging lobbying by representatives of ethnic minorities, section 27 eventually was added—in the view of many scholars, as a tokenism, a 'motherhood' statement (Kallen 1987).

Amendments pertaining to aboriginal peoples' rights proved to be highly vulnerable to the ongoing moves of the intergovernmental political chess game, and sections were inserted, deleted, and altered, before the (undefined) rights of aboriginal peoples were finally recognized in section 25 of the Charter and section 35 of the Constitution Act. The end result of the constitutional amendment process was the enactment of a Charter that both reflects and entrenches the ethnic and non-ethnic priorities informing the entire debate.

My earlier analysis of the Charter revealed an apparent hierarchy of ethnic groups constitutionalized through its protections for collective rights. In the following section, my analysis will reveal a parallel hierarchy when we compare the Charter's protections for the equality rights of members of ethnic and non-ethnic minorities.

Equality Rights: Constitutionalizing Ethnic and Non-Ethnic Inequalities

Section 15(1) and (2) of the Charter, under **'Equality Rights'**, provides the key constitutional basis for individual and categorical rights claims for equal status and equal/equivalent treatment. While there is general agreement among scholars that the non-discriminatory grounds of section 15 are 'open', that is, that claims can be put forward by minorities not enumerated in its provisions, enumerated minorities are afforded *specified* protection for their human rights, while non-enumerated minorities have only *unspecified* protection. Enumerated minorities, specified on the grounds of race, national or ethnic origin, colour, religion, sex, age, or mental or physical disability, thereby have a firmer basis for claims than have non-specified minorities. Even among the different enumerated minorities, a covert status hierarchy can be found. Ethnic (aboriginal and multicultural) minorities and women have *specified* human rights protections under other Charter provisions (section 25, section 27, and section 28, respectively), whereas other enumerated minorities do not. In light of the fact that the provisions of section 15 of the Charter are subject to the possibility of provincial government override under section 33, while section 25, section 27, and section 28 are not vulnerable in this respect, it becomes apparent that aboriginal and multicultural minorities and women enjoy greater Charter protections than do other minorities enumerated under section 15.

The foregoing analysis suggests that the provisions of section 15 of the Charter can be seen to underscore a status hierarchy in which enumerated minorities with other constitutional protections (namely, aboriginal and multicultural minorities and women) rank highest; other enumerated minorities (namely, those specified on the basis of race, age, or physical or mental disability) rank second, and non-enumerated minorities (namely, unspecified populations whose minority status is based on sexual orientation, political belief, criminal record, or other grounds) rank lowest. Acknowledging this underlying inequity in equality rights provisions, taken in the context of other Charter provisions, Judge Walter Tarnopolsky (1982) suggested that it would not be surprising if some version of the American approach to equality rights were to be adopted by the courts in their assessment of equality rights claims. The American model involves three levels of judicial scrutiny: strict, intermediate, and minimal. This model, he said, could be applied to claims put forward by non-enumerated minorities, enumerated minorities without other constitutional protections, and enumerated minorities with other protections, respectively. Should this happen, Tarnopolsky advised, the discriminatory implications for minorities of the inegalitarian nature of the Charter's provisions could be profound. For it would follow that the lower the status of the minority the greater would be the burden of proof upon the victim of discrimination.

Tarnopolsky's admonition was borne out to some extent by judicial interpretation made in connection with the ruling of the Supreme Court of Canada in the *Andrews and Kinersly case* (*Andrews* v. *Law Society of British Columbia* [1989] 1 S.C.R. 143, (1989), 56 D.L.R., (4th) 1, [1989] 2 W.W.R. 289). In releasing its first judgment under section 15 of the Charter, the court ruled that a British Columbia statute (the Barristers and Solicitors Act), which stipulated that only Canadian citizens could practice law in that province, violated section 15 on the basis of citizenship. Citizenship is not enumerated in the non-discriminatory grounds of section 15, but the court ruled that it is akin to the kinds of characteristics listed.

The court adopted Justice McIntyre's broad definition of discrimination as a distinction, intentional or not, based on grounds relating to the personal characteristics of an individual or group which has the effect of imposing disadvantages not imposed on others or of limiting advantages available to others. This definition was not intended to eliminate all distinctions; rather, the court sanctioned an approach tied to the grounds of distinction covered by section 15, by limiting distinctions to those found in the enumerated grounds and in grounds *analogous* to them.

In assessing the facts in the *Andrews case*, McIntyre J. maintained that non-citizens are a minority group analogous to those enumerated under the grounds of section 15 and that they come within the protection of section 15. He held further that the citizenship requirement imposed a burden in the form of a delay on permanent residents who had acquired some or all of their legal training abroad and was, therefore discriminatory. He concluded, therefore, that the law requiring citizenship was in violation of section 15.

In the early days of Charter interpretation, legal observers had been looking to the court for guidance on whether the prohibited grounds of discrimination extended beyond those *enumerated* in section 15. Judge McIntyre's decision clearly supported the inclusion of analogous grounds of discrimination, but the Judge also cautioned that, for the foreseeable future, non-enumerated grounds would be judged on a *case-by-case* basis. What this suggests is, as Tarnopolsky had predicted, that claims brought forward on non-enumerated grounds could be more strictly scrutinized than claims brought forward on enumerated grounds. Hence, section 15 of the Charter would continue to afford clearer protection for the rights of enumerated versus non-enumerated minorities.

At the time of writing (2002), Supreme Court decisions in a number of pivotal Charter challenge cases reveal that the distinction between claims based on enumerated versus non-enumerated grounds of Equality Rights (under Charter section 15) continues to disadvantage the latter.

Egan v. Canada: The Disadvantage of Claims made on Analogous Grounds

Egale Submission to the Supreme Court of Canada in *Egan v. Canada* (1993), 103 D.L.R. (4th) 336 (F.C.A.)

Background

The *Egan case* was a Charter challenge to the spouse's allowance provision of the Old Age Security Act. The appellants Jim Egan and Jack Nesbit were in a long-term same-sex relationship. On meeting the statutory requirements (other than the requirement that his spouse be of 'the opposite sex'), Mr Egan applied for a spouse's allowance for his partner. His application was denied on the basis that his partner was of the same sex.

The spouse's allowance is available to the spouse of a pensioner under the Old Age Security Act if their joint income falls below a fixed level and the spouse is between the ages of 60 and 64.

'Spouse', as defined in the legislation, includes persons who are married as well as 'a person of the opposite sex who is living with that person, having lived with that person for at least one year, if the two persons publicly represented themselves as husband and wife'. The appellants challenged the constitutionality of the definition of common-law spouse, claiming that it was discriminatory under section 15(1) of the Charter on the basis of sexual orientation. Both levels of the Federal Court dismissed the application, finding that the denial did not amount to discrimination under section 15. The case was then placed on appeal to the Supreme Court of Canada.

On 25 May 1995, the Supreme Court released its decision in the *Egan case*. The appellants' claim for the spouse's allowance benefit was rejected by the court. Although a majority of the court held that the exclusion of same-sex couples from the spouse's allowance program violated the section 15 equality guarantees of the Charter of Rights, a majority of five judges also concluded that this violation was saved under section 1 of the Charter—the 'reasonable limits' clause. It is significant to point out, however, that the Supreme Court decision was reached despite the fact that all nine judges agreed that sexual orientation is an **analogous ground** of discrimination under section 15 of the Charter. This pivotal decision—and several others, preceding and following it—based on the same ground (sexual orientation) reveal the fundamental weakness of claims based on analogous grounds.

Despite the limitations of the Charter's protection for minority rights elaborated in the preceding pages, it has proven to be a valuable instrument, embraced by Canada's racial and ethnic minorities in their continuing attempts to fight racism institutionalized in discriminatory laws. When constitutional amendments designed to bring Quebec into the constitutional consensus were proposed—first in the 1987 Meech Lake Accord and then in the 1992 Charlottetown Accord—minorities were quick to perceive that several key amendments posed a threat to their Charter-endorsed rights. Racial and ethnic minorities were united in their vociferous opposition to both proposals. Their voiced opposition was not an insignificant factor in helping to defeat both proposed constitutional amendments.[2]

Until such time as future constitutional amendments are enacted, Canada's Charter of Rights and Freedoms, in its present form, will provide the standard for the legal protection of minority rights in Canada. It may therefore be appropriate, at this juncture, to undertake a brief consideration of the strengths and weaknesses of the Charter.

The Charter's Protection for Minority Rights: Strengths and Weaknesses

Strengths

1. The Charter primarily applies to actions of governments. As part of Canada's (1982) constitution, the supreme law of the land, its provisions override those of statutory law. Accordingly, federal and provincial governments must ensure that their laws conform to Charter standards. The Charter has an enforcement provision that authorizes courts to strike down laws that do not conform to its standards (section 52) and to order appropriate and just remedies to complainants (section 24).
2. The Charter also provides private, non-governmental bodies and individuals with a constitutional basis for challenging their federal and provincial governments when their laws or policies do not conform to Charter standards. Prior to the enactment of the Charter, private individuals and organizations could bring forward complaints alleging human rights violations against other private individuals or organizations only under the provisions of statutory human rights legislation at the federal and provincial levels. However, claimants could not challenge any alleged discrimination in the laws themselves,

or in government policies and practices under these laws.

3. Because the Charter provides a nationwide standard for all legislation, this means that once all laws have been brought into conformity with Charter provisions, Canadians should be afforded the same protection for their human rights throughout the country, rather than differential protection from one jurisdiction to another.

Weaknesses

1. Section 1 of the Charter (the 'reasonable limits' clause) limits Charter rights in a number of ways. We know that, even as universal moral principles, human rights are never absolute rights: the justification for imposing limits on rights at the most fundamental level, is non-violation of the rights of others. Under section 1 of the Charter, limits must be 'reasonable, prescribed by law, demonstrably justified, and in keeping with the standards of a free and democratic society'. The problem with this articulation of limits on human rights is that it is subject to questionable, *subjective* interpretation by the courts. Three of the four criteria are open to judicial bias in interpretation because of their subjective nature: only the criterion 'prescribed by law' is objective.
2. Section 33 of the Charter (the 'opting out' clause) allows governments to exclude their laws from the requirements of the Charter with regard to section 2 (fundamental freedoms) and sections 7–15 (legal and equality rights) for a period of five years at a time.

Interpretation of the Provisions of the Charter of Rights and Freedoms: The Purposive Approach

Because the Charter represents a fairly recent amendment to Canada's Constitution, there is little pre-Charter precedent to guide judicial interpretation of its provisions. To facilitate Charter interpretation, the Supreme Court has sanctioned a 'purposive' approach that involves a two-stage process of analysis for the application of the Charter in a specific case (Pentney 1989: 23). At the first stage, the right or freedom involved in the case must be defined and a determination must be made as to whether it has been infringed or abrogated. At the second stage, it must be determined whether the 'limit' on the right or freedom meets the 'reasonable limit' standard set out in section 1 of the Charter.

The model for the purposive approach derives from the view expressed by Dickson, J. in *R. v. Big M Drug Mart*:

> In my view, this analysis is to be undertaken, and the purpose of the right or freedom in question is to be sought by reference to the character and the larger objects of the Charter itself, to the language chosen to articulate the specific right or freedom, to the historical origins of the concepts enshrined, and where applicable, to the meaning and purpose of the other specific rights and freedoms with which it is associated within the text of the Charter (quoted in Pentney 1989: 24).

With reference to the 'character and larger objects of the Charter', Dickson, J. (quoted in Pentney 1989: 22–3) has pointed out that one of the critical features of the Charter as a constitutional, rather than a statutory, legal instrument is that once enacted, its provisions cannot be easily repealed or amended. Accordingly, it is drafted with an eye to the future, for it must be capable of application to new social, political, and historical realities unimagined by its framers. In interpreting its provisions, then, the judiciary must adopt a broad approach that will facilitate its application under new and unforeseen social conditions (ibid.).

Pentney (1989: 24) argues, with reference to the 'language chosen to articulate the specific right or freedom', that, as a general rule, the exact words of the provision should be adhered to, for these have not been arbitrarily chosen by the drafters. Only if a literal reading of the provision defeats the purpose of the section and detracts from its underlying values, should a departure from a literal interpretation be undertaken.

The purposive approach also requires an examination of the 'historical origins of the concepts enshrined' in order to glean the values underlying the right or freedom and thus to provide an understanding of the concept embodied in it. In some cases, the content of a particular right or freedom may be determined with reference to the 'meaning and purpose of the other specific rights and freedoms with which it is associated within the text of the Charter'. The purposive approach thus requires that the Charter be viewed *as a whole* so that the meaning and scope of a particular right or freedom is consistent with and in part gleaned from, similar guarantees, usually found under the same heading in the Charter (Pentney 1989: 25–6).

In summary, the **purposive approach** requires the derivation of the underlying values that a specific right or freedom is intended to protect and an analysis of principles drawn from legal and broader, historical traditions that reflect these values in order to ensure that the interpretation of a particular right or freedom furthers its purpose. Moreover, the purposive approach requires that the interpretation adopted incorporate the forward-looking view appropriate for constitutional judgments and is sensitive to the future political, economic, and social implications of the decision (Pentney 1989: 27–8).

The way in which the Charter is being used as a standard in statutory human rights cases is highlighted in the following two Supreme Court cases, Charter challenges, alleging discrimination on the ground of religion.

Regina v. Big M Drug Mart Ltd.

(1985), 18 C.C.C. (3d) 385, 18 D.L.R. (4th) 321, [1985] 1 S.C.R. 295

In their decision on this landmark case, the Supreme Court of Canada struck down the Lord's Day Act, a federal, Sunday closing statute, as unconstitutional by reason of its violation of the guarantee of freedom of conscience and religion under section 2a of the Charter. In reaching their decision, the court reasoned that the Act discriminated against non-Christians by taking Christian religious values, and, using the force of the state, translating them into a positive law binding on believers and non-believers alike. The court also pointed out that to accept that Parliament retains the right to compel universal observance of the day of rest preferred by one religion is not consistent with the values underlying section 27 of the Charter which sanction the preservation and enhancement of the multicultural heritage of Canadians. The protection of the dominant religious culture and the concomitant non-protection of minority religions was held to be inimical to the spirit of section 2a of the Charter and to the dignity of non-Christians. In the words of Justice Dickson: 'A free society is one which aims at equality with respect to the enjoyment of the fundamental freedoms'. For persons of a non-Christian religion, the practice of that religion, it was argued, at least implies the right to work on Sunday if the person wishes to do so. Any law, purely religious in purpose, that denies the person that right infringes on that person's religious freedom.

Moreover, the court ruled that the Act could not be justified as a reasonable limit under section 1 of the Charter. While the government sought to support the Act on the basis that it had a secular purpose, namely to provide a uniform day of rest, the Supreme Court held that the Act had never been held by the courts to have this objective. Accordingly, the court declared the Lord's Day Act to be of no force and effect.

As suggested earlier, this case is a landmark case with regard to minority cultural rights claims. This was the first Supreme Court decision interpreting the right to freedom of religion in the Charter, and the Supreme court interpretation represented a sharp break with pre-Charter decisions that had interpreted that freedom very narrowly (*Canadian Human Rights Advocate*, May 1985). What is most interesting about the interpretation is that it took into account equality rights, even though section 15 of the Charter was not yet in effect, and it also took into account section 27 of the Charter, the multicultural provision. By so doing, the interpretation of freedom of religion was broadened from its customary interpretation as an individual right (freedom of choice) to an interpretation reflecting the principle of ethnocultural equality that includes collective (religious) rights, that is, the right of minorities to express their difference from the dominant religious culture.

In connection with this particular case, it is important to point out that it has not been precedent-setting for parallel provincial legislation, insofar as the Supreme Court has indicated that statutes requiring businesses to remain closed on Sunday may be valid if it can be demonstrated that they are designed to ensure workers a day off (a common pause day) rather than to enforce religious beliefs. In September of 1984, the Ontario Court of Appeal, in considering the Ontario Retail Business Holiday Act that requires many businesses to remain closed on Sunday, found that the purpose of this law was not to protect the Christian Sabbath, but to ensure a day off. For that reason, the Court held that the law was not invalidated by the Charter, for most purposes. However, the Court recognized that the unintended effect of the law was to discriminate against religious minorities whose Sabbath day of rest fell on another day of the week. Therefore, the Court held that those who closed on another day due to religious beliefs were exempted from the law and could remain open on Sunday (*Canadian Human Rights Advocate,* May 1985). The Act is still in effect, but the Ontario government has amended it so as to shift the onus of decision-making on the question of Sunday closing to the municipalities (*Toronto Star,* 8 February 1989).

Re McTavish et al. and Director, Child Welfare Act et al.

(1986), 32 D.L.R. (4th) 394 (Alta. Q.B.)

There have been a number of cases testing the Charter's protection against religious discrimination that have been brought forward in the context of legislation authorizing compulsory medical treatment or other care or custody for children found to be in need of protection. The earliest of these cases all involved challenges to such laws or challenges to steps taken under them by Jehovah's Witness parents who were religiously opposed to the administering of blood transfusions to their children. Almost all these challenges have been unsuccessful (Gibson 1990: 198).

In the abovementioned case, the Alberta Court of Queen's Bench rejected a Charter challenge that alleged that the province's Child Welfare Act violated the equality rights provisions of section 15 by discriminating against a religious minority, Jehovah's Witnesses. The Court reasoned that the Act was not discriminatory, first, because it treated all children in need of protection alike, regardless of religion, and second, because, in any event, it represented a reasonable limit on equality rights, justified under section 1 of the Charter. The Court recognized that the effect of the Act, conferring jurisdiction on the Court to authorize medical treatment of a child notwithstanding the refusal of consent by the child's guardian, is to impinge on the parents' right to direct the medical treatment of their child in accordance with their religious beliefs. Nevertheless, it held that where the Court is satisfied that the treatment is in the best interests of the child, the need to protect the health of the child justifies this infringement on freedom of religion.

Charter Protection for Religion: Discussion

The reasoning behind the judicial decisions in the first case (*Regina v. Big M Drug Mart*) provides a clear demonstration of the application of the purposive approach to Charter interpretation. The principal Charter right invoked in the challenge was freedom of conscience and religion under section 2a. However, the court also took into account the 'character and larger objects of the Charter itself' and made reference to values of equality and multiculturalism, protected under other Charter provisions (section 15 and section 27, respectively). As a result, in this case, the ruling of the court, reflecting the spirit of the Charter as a whole, afforded protection not only for the individual right of freedom of conscience and religion, but also for the collective rights of non-Christian and non-religious minorities.

In the second case (*Re McTavish et al. and Director, Child Welfare Act et al.*), the reasoning behind the judicial decisions revealed how section 1 of the Charter is used to justify the imposition of reasonable limits on Charter rights in order to serve the best interests of a person or a society. In the *McTavish case*, a restriction was imposed on the guarantee of religious equality under section 15 of the Charter in order to serve a child's 'best interests' through the protection of his/her health.

The next two Supreme Court cases to be presented are based on allegations of discrimination on the grounds of race, colour, ethnicity, and/or nationality. The arguments put forward by counsel in these cases serve to confirm that the Charter prohibits unintentional, systemic discrimination as well as deliberate discrimination.

R. v. Kent, Sinclair and Gode

(1986), 21 C.R.R. 372 (Man. C.A.)

In this case, the Manitoba Court of Appeal rejected a Charter challenge that alleged that accused persons of aboriginal [native] origin had been discriminated against, in violation of the equality rights provisions of section 15, by reason of underrepresentation on their jury of persons with aboriginal backgrounds. The accused were convicted of murdering two prison guards. Counsel for one of the accused (a Status Indian) unsuccessfully challenged the selection of jurors at the beginning of the trial and again, on appeal, on the ground that the jury panel did not adequately represent the accused's 'peers'. The population of Status Indians in the province, at the time, represented approximately 5 per cent of the total population. The panel from which the jury was chosen was drawn from a provincial Health Services Commission list of 150 eligible, adult, health care recipients, only two of whom were Status Indians. One of the latter served on the accused's jury.

The Manitoba Court of Appeal rejected the allegation that the accused had been discriminated against because he had not been accorded a jury of his 'peers'. The Court found no evidence of deliberate exclusion from the jury of persons of a particular race or origin, a finding that clearly would have violated the Charter. The court held, further, that the equality rights provisions of section 15 of the Charter do not require a jury to be composed entirely or proportionately of persons belonging to the same race as the accused. It was held that to interpret the Charter in this way would run counter to Canada's multicultural and multiracial heritage and to the right of every person to serve as a juror (unless otherwise disqualified). The court held that the jurors' list in the case was racially neutral and that it must be assumed to provide a fair cross-section of the country and to be reasonably representative.

In his discussion of the court's ruling in this case, Gibson (1990: 180–1) points out that, in view of the fact that both the jury panel and the jury itself contained roughly the same proportion of Status Indians as were represented in the provincial population, it would be difficult to challenge the court's decision on the question of representativeness. He submits, nevertheless, that there are grounds for challenging the court's suggestion that only deliberate exclusion of persons of a particular race or origin from the jury would violate the Charter. Citing the Supreme Court decision in the *Andrews case*, Gibson points out that it has now been confirmed that the Charter prohibits unintentional, systemic discrimination as well as deliberate discrimination. He contends, therefore, that if procedures for jury selection had the systemic effect of excluding or underrepresenting particular racial or ethnic groups from jury service, a Charter challenge could be put forward.

Perera, Bloch, Boahene v. The Queen in Right of Canada

(Memorandum of Fact and Law of the Intervenor, Public Service Alliance of Canada. Court File No. A14697; dated at Ottawa, 26 January 1998)

In the Federal Court of Appeal
Public Service Alliance of Canada, Intervenor

Part I: Statement of Facts
The Public Service Alliance of Canada (Alliance) stated that the appellants maintain that they have been subject to discrimination by the respondent and various departments or agencies acting on behalf of the respondent on the basis of their race, national or ethnic origin, and colour, contrary to section 15 of the Canadian Charter of Rights and Freedoms. Included among the remedies claimed are specific orders that would require the Canadian International Development Agency (CIDA) to take positive measures to correct the derogatory effects of these discriminatory actions including the adoption of a special program or plan which will rectify the adverse effect of discriminatory practices on visible minorities employed by CIDA.

In reviewing the case, the Alliance reported that, following a motion to strike portions of the Appellants' Amended Statement of Claim, the trial division judge struck those paragraphs that seek these affirmative action/employment equity remedies on the basis that the court has no jurisdiction to grant them. Pursuant to an Order of the Court, the Public Service Alliance of Canada (PSAC or Alliance) was granted leave to intervene in support of the appellants' appeal on this issue only.

Part II: Statement by the Intervenor (Public Service Alliance of Canada) of Its Position Concerning the Points at Issue [The following is a summary version of the main points in the submissions of the Alliance on this issue.]
In the submission of the Alliance, as these remedies were claimed in the course of an action alleging a Charter violation and seeking relief pursuant to section 24 of the Charter, the court has a broad jurisdiction to grant appropriate remedial orders to correct the effects of the Charter violation. The Alliance submitted, therefore, that the learned trial division judge erred when he concluded that the court had no jurisdiction to grant these remedies.

Part III: Argument
The Alliance contended that the protection against discrimination that is provided by section 15 of the Charter is a fundamental component of our Constitution and of the application of the rule of law in a free and democratic society. The intervenor stressed that the importance of anti-discrimination initiatives has been underlined repeatedly in those cases that deal with human rights legislation in general and discriminatory practices in the workplace in particular. Indeed, in *Chambly*, the Supreme Court of Canada has confirmed that the achievement of a workplace free from discrimination is a fundamentally important goal.

As acknowledged by the Trial Division Judge, the Alliance asserted, section 24 of the Charter affords to courts of competent jurisdiction 'broad remedial power' to rectify violations of the Charter. The Alliance pointed out that, given the broad language that was employed in section 24 of the Charter, the Supreme Court of Canada has emphasized that, where there is a demonstrable violation of a Charter right, access to a court of competent jurisdiction to seek a remedy is essential to ensure that the Charter is meaningful for those who seek its protection. Citing several key cases as evidence, the Alliance asserted that providing a remedy to the corresponding right has been characterized as an obligation of a court in light of the constitutional imperatives of the Charter.

In assessing the jurisdiction of the court to issue a particular remedy under section 24 of the Charter, the Alliance submitted that it is relevant to consider the manner in which courts have addressed claims in the past for various types of remedies.

Citing a broad range of key cases as evidence, the Alliance argued that Canadian courts have often accepted, in principle, the jurisdiction to grant positive remedies in the face of a demonstrated Charter violation. The need for such remedies, the Alliance insisted is particularly the case when one considers the nature of relief required to remedy violations of section 15 of the Charter. Section 15 is purposively broad in its scope and prohibits direct, indirect, and systemic discrimination. A remedy requiring mandatory action is often necessary in order to address the damages that result from the discriminatory actions. Moreover, in the case of a finding of systemic discrimination, the circumstances may require that the remedy also be systemic in nature. Indeed, the Supreme Court of Canada has stated that, in some cases, affirmative action or employment equity-type remedies may be the only means to appropriately and justly address indirect or systemic discrimination. In support of its position the Alliance quoted a statement made by Kent Roach in his text on the Charter remedies:

> One of the remedies that may be appropriate to enforce equality rights is ordering affirmative action or employment equity measures as a means of combating systemic discrimination in a governmental institution. As is the case with structural injunctions, courts will likely be concerned with balancing the interests affected by remedies for the violation of equality rights and not exceeding their institutional role. Nevertheless, section 15(2) suggests that court-ordered programs or activities designed to improve the conditions of disadvantaged groups will not in themselves violate section 15, and may in some circumstances be an appropriate and purposive remedy.

For these reasons, the Alliance submitted that, *prima facie*, a court must have jurisdiction under section 24 to issue the remedies requested by the appellants.

Partial Settlement

Following the court hearings in the case, extensive negotiations were carried out through an external mediator. These negotiations revealed new facts and they resulted in what was deemed to be a fair and equitable settlement for all parties. Agreement on a final settlement was reached out of court by Frank Boahene and Fred Bloch and the Government of Canada. Among other things, the agreement stipulates that Frank Boahene and Fred Bloch be appointed to positions at level 4 in the Program Administration Group at the Canadian International Development Agency. The order confirms that Frank Boahene and Fred Bloch meet the Standards for Selection and Assessment established by the Public Service Commission of Canada, and they are fully qualified for the positions to which they will be appointed. It also stipulates that they give full and final release to the Queen in right of Canada. The settlement was deemed to be in the public interest in that it puts an end to long and expensive judicial proceedings and it provides stability in the work environment.

This case not only demonstrates the fact that the Charter offers protection for both deliberate and unintentional (systemic) discrimination, but also that courts may order an affirmative action remedy in Charter challenge cases where systemic discrimination has been documented.

Beyond the Canadian Courts

This chapter has focused on the role of the constitutional Charter of Rights and Freedoms in minority rights cases alleging legal violations of human rights at the statutory level of government. It has shown how successful charter challenge cases have served to redress human rights violations by mandating courts to strike down discriminatory laws and policies. But what avenue of appeal is there for appellants who have lost charter challenge cases? Within the Canadian legal framework, the Supreme Court is the last avenue of appeal. However, insofar as Canada is a signatory to the Optional Protocol to the International Covenant on Civil and Political Rights (ICCPR), an individual citizen who has exhausted all domestic legal avenues may seek to have the case heard by the United Nations Human Rights Committee.

Claims Put Forward to the United Nations Human Rights Committee under the Optional Protocol to the ICCPR

As shown in the Introduction, The International Covenant on Civil and Political Rights adopts an individual perspective, which places the onus on nations and judiciaries to protect all citizens against cruel, inhuman, and degrading treatment. This Covenant recognizes the fundamental human rights of every person, including protection against discrimination on any ground such as race, colour, sex, language, religion, political or other opinion, national or social origin, property, birth, or other status.

These rights and freedoms that guarantee protection to the individual, include protection from abuses by governments. The burden of responsibility to uphold individual freedoms, therefore, lies not with governments but with the judicial system.

Nations that ratify this Covenant are expected to introduce laws that will reflect its provisions. Canada has taken measures to fulfill its commitment by enacting human rights legislation at both provincial and federal levels of jurisdiction and by entrenching a Charter of Rights and Freedoms in the Canadian Constitution (1982).

The **Optional Protocol to the ICCPR** provides individual citizens with direct recourse to the United Nations (UN). Persons who believe that their rights as specified in the Covenant have been violated can state their case before the UN Human Rights Committee. Such persons must first have exhausted all legal avenues within their own country. To date, Canada is one of only a small number of the nations signing the Covenant that has ratified the Optional Protocol.

Cases brought forward under the Optional Protocol to the ICCPR show how the protection for human rights afforded under international human rights covenants provide avenues of redress against human rights violations for Canadian citizens, beyond the Canadian legal system. Most important, these cases demonstrate how international pressure can be brought to bear on governments of signatory nations to amend or eliminate discriminatory laws that violate international human rights covenants.

Over the years, a significant number of complaints have been filed by Canadian citizens versus Canada, under the Protocol. Among the most significant of these, in terms of its eventual impact, was the very first case, that of *Lovelace v. Canada*.

The *Lovelace Case*

The Sandra Lovelace case concerned an Indian woman from the Tobique Reserve in New Brunswick, Sandra Lovelace, who had lost her Indian status upon marrying a non-Indian as a result of Section 12(10)(b) of the Indian Act, which declared that 'the following persons are not entitled to be registered, namely . . . a woman who married a person who is not an Indian'. Her case was accepted by the UN Human Rights Committee, notwithstanding the fact that she had not exhausted all domestic remedies, that is, by going to the Supreme Court of Canada. The committee accepted the fact that in the 1973 Lavell case another native woman had already gone on a similar issue before the Supreme Court and had lost. Thus, Sandra Lovelace stated in 1977 that Canada had infringed a number of rights contained in the International Covenant on Civil and Political Rights, including the right to protection from discrimination as provided under Articles 2(1) and 26; equality of men and women under Article 3; protection of the family under Article 23(1); equality of rights and responsibilities in terms of marriage under Article 23(4); and, the right to enjoy her own culture under Article 27.

In its 1981 decision, the Human Rights Committee declared that Sandra Lovelace (*Lovelace v. Canada* 1984) had lost her rights prior to the entering into force of the Covenant on Civil and Political Rights and that her right to enjoy her

BOX 9-1: CASE STUDY 1

The Battle for Equality in the Funding of Religious Schools in Ontario

The analysis presented in this case study is based on the main gist of the recorded views of the United Nations Human Rights Committee, elaborated at the Committee's meeting on 3 November 1999 with specific regard to the communication submitted on 29 February 1996 by Arieh Hollis Waldman (alleged victim) in complaint against Canada (State party).

On 29 February 1996, Mr Arieh Hollis Waldman, a Canadian citizen residing in the province of Ontario, submitted a communication to the United Nations Human Rights Committee, under article 5, paragraph 4, of the Optional Protocol to the International Covenant on Civil and Political Rights, in the form of a complaint against the Canadian State alleging discrimination on the basis of religion.

The case was brought under consideration by the United Nations Human Rights Committee (UNHCR) under the provisions of the Optional Protocol to the International Covenant on Civil and Political Rights (ICCPR), in claim of violations of specific provisions of the ICCPR. Under the provisions of the Optional Protocol to the ICCPR, individuals a) who are citizens of countries in which a State Party to the Covenant (ICCPR) has become a Party to the Optional Protocol, b) who claim that any of their rights enumerated in the Covenant have been violated, and c) who have exhausted all available domestic remedies, may submit a written communication to the United Nations Human Rights Committee for consideration by the Committee. Article 5, para. 4 of the Optional Protocol states that, once the complaint has been fully considered by the Committee, '[t]he Committee shall forward its views to the State Party concerned and to the individual.'

Relevant Provisions of the International Covenant on Civil and Political Rights Invoked in the *Waldman Case*

Article 2

1. Each State Party to the present Covenant undertakes to respect and to ensure to all individuals within its territory and subject to its jurisdiction the rights recognized in the present Covenant, without distinction of any kind, such as race, colour, sex, language, religion, political or other opinion, national or social origin, property, birth or other status.

Article 18

1. Everyone shall have the right to freedom of thought, conscience and religion. This right shall include freedom to have or to adopt a religion or belief of his choice, and freedom, either individually or in community with others and in public or private, to manifest his religion or belief in worship, observance, practice, and teaching.
4. The States Parties to the present covenant undertake to have respect for the liberty of parents and, when applicable, legal guardians to ensure the religious and moral education of their children in conformity with their own convictions.

Article 26

All persons are equal before the law and are entitled without any discrimination to the equal protection of the law. In this respect, the law shall prohibit any discrimination and guarantee to all persons equal and effective protection against discrimination on any ground such as race, colour, sex, language, religion, political or other opinion, national or social origin, property, birth or other status.

Article 27
In those States in which ethnic, religious or linguistic minorities exist, persons belonging to such minorities shall not be denied the right, in community with the other members of their group, to enjoy their own culture, to profess and practice their own religion, or to use their own language.

Having concluded its consideration of communication No.694/1996 submitted on behalf of Arieh Hollis Waldman, under the Optional Protocol to the International Covenant on Civil and Political Rights, and, having taken into account all written information made available to it by the author of the communication, his counsel and the State party, the Human Rights Committee espoused the following views, under article 5, paragraph 4, of the Optional Protocol:

History of the Case

1.1 The author of the communication is Mr Arieh Hollis Waldman, a Canadian citizen residing in the province of Ontario. He claims to be a victim of a violation of ICCPR articles 26, and articles 18(1), 18(4) and 27 taken in conjunction with article 2(1).

1.2 The author is a father of two school-age children and a member of the Jewish faith who enrols his children in a private Jewish day school. In the province of Ontario Roman Catholic schools are the only nonsecular schools receiving full and direct public funding. Other religious schools must fund through private sources, including the charging of tuition fees.

1.3 In 1994 Mr Waldman paid $14,050 in tuition fees for his children to attend Bialik Hebrew Day School in Toronto, Ontario. This amount was reduced by a federal tax credit system to $10,810.89. These tuition fees were paid out of a net household income of $73,367.26. In addition, the author is required to pay local property taxes to fund a public school system he does not use.

The Facts

2.1 The Ontario public school system offers free education to all Ontario residents without discrimination on the basis of religion or on any other ground. Public schools may not engage in any religious indoctrination. Individuals enjoy the freedom to establish private schools and to send their children to these schools instead of the public schools. The only statutory requirement for opening a private school in Ontario is the submission of a 'notice of intention to operate a private school'. Ontario private schools are neither licensed nor do they require any prior Government approval. As of 30 September 1989, there were 64,699 students attending 494 private schools in Ontario. Enrolment in private schools represents 3.3 per cent of the total day school enrolment in Ontario.

2.2 The province of Ontario's system of separate school funding originates with provisions in Canada's 1867 constitution. In 1867 Catholics represented 17 per cent of the population of Ontario, while Protestants represented 82 per cent. All other religions combined represented 2 per cent of the population. At the time of Confederation it was a matter of concern that the new province of Ontario would be controlled by a Protestant majority that might exercise its power over education to take away the rights of its Roman Catholic minority. The solution was to guarantee their rights to denominational education, and to define those rights by referring to the state of the law at the time of Confederation.

2.3 As a consequence, the 1867 Canadian constitution contains explicit guarantees of denominational school rights in section 93. Section 93 of the Constitution Act 1867 grants each province in Canada exclusive jurisdiction to enact laws regarding education, limited only by the denominational school rights granted in 1867. In Ontario, the section 93 power is exercised through the Education Act. Under the Education Act every separate school is entitled to full public funding. Separate schools are defined as Roman Catholic schools. The Education Act states: '1. (1) 'separate school board' means a board that operates a school board for Roman Catholics; . . . 122. (1) Every separate school shall share in the legislative grants in like manner as a public school'. As a result, Roman Catholic schools are the only religious schools entitled to the same public funding as the public secular schools.

2.4 The Roman Catholic separate school system is not a private school system. Like the public school system it is funded through a publicly accountable, democratically elected board of education. Separate School Boards are elected by Roman Catholic ratepayers, and these school boards have the right to manage the denominational aspects of the separate schools. Unlike private schools, Roman Catholic separate schools are subject to all Ministry guidelines and regulations. Neither section 93 of the Constitution Act 1867 nor the Education Act provide for public funding to Roman Catholic private/independent schools. Ten private/independent Roman Catholic schools operate in Ontario and these schools receive no direct public financial support.

2.5 Private religious schools in Ontario receive financial aid in the form of (1) exemption from property taxes on non-profit private schools; (2) income tax deductions for tuition attributable to religious instruction; and (3) income tax deductions for charitable purposes. A 1985 report concluded that the level of public aid to Ontario private schools amounted to about one-sixth of the average total in cost per pupil enrolled in a private school. There is no province in Canada in which private schools receive funding on an equal basis to public schools. Direct funding of private schools ranges from 0 per cent (Newfoundland, New Brunswick, Ontario) to 75 per cent (Alberta).

2.6 The issue of public funding for non-Catholic religious schools in Ontario has been the subject of domestic litigation since 1978. The first case, brought 8 February 1978, sought to make religious instruction mandatory in specific schools, thereby integrating existing Hebrew schools into public schools. On 3 April 1978, affirmed 9 April 1979, Ontario courts found that mandatory religious instruction in public schools was not permitted.

2.7 In 1982 Canada's constitution was amended to include a Charter of Rights and Freedoms which contained an equality rights provision. In 1985 the Ontario government decided to amend the Education Act to extend public funding of Roman Catholic schools to include grades 11 to 13. Roman Catholic schools had been fully funded from kindergarten to grade 10 since the mid-1800s. The issue of the constitutionality of this law (Bill 30) in view of the Canadian Charter of Rights and Freedoms, was referred by the Ontario government to the Ontario Court of Appeal in 1985.

2.8 On 25 June 1987 in the Bill 30 case the Supreme Court of Canada upheld the constitutionality of the legislation which extended full funding to Roman Catholic schools. The majority opinion reasoned that section 93 of the Constitution Act 1867 and all the rights and privileges it afforded were immune from Charter scrutiny. Madam Justice Wilson, writing the majority opinion stated: 'It was never intended... that the Charter could be used to invalidate other provisions of the constitution, particularly a provision such as section 93 which represented a fundamental part of the Confederation compromise.'

2.9 At the same time the Supreme Court of Canada, in the majority opinion of Wilson, J. affirmed: 'These educational rights, granted specifically to... Roman Catholics in Ontario, make it impossible to treat all Canadians equally. The country was founded upon the recognition of special or unequal educational rights for specific religious groups in Ontario...' In a concurring opinion in the Supreme Court, Estey J. conceded: 'It is axiomatic (and many counsel before this court conceded the point) that if the Charter has any application to Bill 30, this Bill would be found discriminatory and in violation of sections 2(a) and 15 of the Charter of Rights.'

2.10 In a further case, *Adler v. Ontario*, individuals from the Calvinistic or Reformed Christian tradition, and members of the Sikh, Hindu, Muslim, and Jewish faiths challenged the constitutionality of Ontario's Education Act, claiming a violation of the Charter's provisions on freedom of religion and equality. They argued that the Education Act, by requiring attendance at school, discriminated against those whose conscience or beliefs prevented them from sending their children to either the publicly funded secular or publicly funded Roman Catholic schools, because of the high costs associated with their children's religious education. A declaration was also sought stating that the applicants were entitled to funding equivalent to that of public and Roman Catholic schools. The Ontario Court of Appeal determined that the crux of Adler was an attempt to revisit the issue which the Supreme Court of Canada had already disposed of in the Bill 30 case. Chief Justice Dubin stated that the Bill 30 case was 'really quite decisive of the discrimination issue in these appeals.' They also rejected the argument based on freedom of religion.

2.11 On appeal, the Supreme Court of Canada by judgement of 21 November 1996, confirmed that its decision in the Bill 30 case was determinative in the Adler litigation, and found that the funding of Roman Catholic separate schools could not give rise to an infringement of the Charter because the province of Ontario was constitutionally obligated to provide such funding.

The Complaint

3.1 The author contends that the legislative grant of power to fund Roman Catholic schools authorized by section 93 of the Constitution Act of Canada 1867, and carried out under sections 122 and 128 of the Education Act (Ontario) violates article 26 of the ICCPR. The author states that these provisions create a distinction or preference which is based on religion and which has the effect of impairing the enjoyment or exercise by all persons, on an equal footing, of their religious rights and freedoms. He argues that the conferral of a benefit on a single religious group cannot be sustained. When a right to publicly financed religious education is recognized by a State party, no differentiation should be made among individuals on the basis of the nature of their particular beliefs. The author maintains that the provision of full funding exclusively to Roman Catholic schools cannot be considered reasonable. The historical rationale for the Ontario government's discriminatory funding practice, that of protection of Roman Catholic minority rights from the Protestant majority, has now disappeared, and if anything has been transferred to other minority religious communities in Ontario. A 1991 census is quoted as indicating that 44 per cent of the population is Protestant, 36 per cent is Catholic, and 8 per cent have other religious affiliations. It is also unreasonable in view of the fact that other Canadian provinces and territories do not discriminate on the basis of religion in allocating education funding.

3.2 The author also claims that Ontario's school funding practices violate article 18(1) taken in conjunction with article 2. The author states that he experiences financial hardship in order to provide his children with a Jewish education, a hardship which is not experienced by a Roman Catholic parent seeking to provide his children with a Roman Catholic education. The author claims that such hardship significantly impairs, in a discriminatory fashion, the enjoyment of the right to manifest one's religion, including the freedom to provide a religious education for one's children, or to establish religious schools.

3.3 The author further points out that this violation is not sustainable under the limitation provisions of article 18(3), which only permits those limitations which are prescribed by law and are necessary to protect public safety, order, health or morals, or the fundamental rights and freedom of others. According to the author, a limitation established to protect morals may not be based on a single tradition.

3.4 The author further asserts that when a right to publicly financed religious education is recognized by a State party, no differentiation should be made on the basis of religion. The full and direct public funding of Roman Catholic schools in Ontario does not equally respect the liberty of non-Roman Catholics to choose an education in conformity with a parent's religious convictions, contrary to article 18(4) taken together with article 2.

3.5 The author states that Article 27 recognizes that separate school systems are crucial to the practice of religion, that these schools form an essential link in preserving community identity and the survival of minority religious groups and that positive action may be required to ensure that the rights of religious minorities are protected. Since Roman Catholics are the only religious minority to receive full and direct funding for religious education from the government of Ontario, Article 27 has not been applied, as required by Article 2, without distinction on the basis of religion.

State Party's Position

4.2 In its submission of February 1998, the State party denies that the facts of the case disclose violations of articles 2, 18, 26, and 17 of the Covenant (ICCPR). The main points of the State Party's defence of its position, are countered by the author (complainant) in the following commentary put forward by his counsel.

Author's Comments

5.1 Counsel submits that the State party has admitted the discriminatory nature of the educational funding, and based this on a constitutional obligation. Counsel argues that article 26 of the Covenant does not allow exceptions for discriminatory constitutional laws and that historical anomalies cannot thwart the application of the equality provisions of the Covenant. Counsel rejects as circular the State party's argument that the difference between the funding of Roman Catholic schools and other religious schools is one between public and private schools. Counsel notes that the public quality of Roman Catholic schools is a bureaucratic construct assigned to one group of ratepayers based on their religious affiliation to the discriminatory exclusion of all other ratepayers.

5.2 Counsel rejects the State party's argument that the extension of non-discriminatory public funding to other religious schools would harm the goals of a tolerant, multicultural, non-discriminatory society, and argues that on the contrary, the current circumstance of discriminatory and selective funding of only one religious denomination in the establishment and operation of religious schools is highly detrimental to fostering a tolerant, non-discriminatory society in the province and encourages the divided society along religious lines that it claims to defeat.

5.3 According to counsel, the State party's argument that the claim under article 18 is inadmissible *ratione materiae* because article 18 does not include a right to require the State to fund public schools, is a misrepresentation of the author's submissions. Counsel argues that article 18(1) includes the right to teach religion and the right to educate one's children in a religious school. If this is possible for some and not for others on discriminatory grounds, then article 18 is violated in conjunction with article 2. According to counsel, in order to give article 2 its full and proper meaning, it must have the effect of requiring nondiscrimination on the listed grounds with respect to the rights and freedoms in the Covenant, even if in the absence of discrimination, no violation of the Covenant existed. If a violation of the Covenant was always required without the application or consideration of article 2, article 2 would be superfluous, in counsel's opinion. Counsel clarifies that he does not claim a violation of article 18 on its own, but only in conjunction with article 2, because the funding of only Roman Catholic schools results in discriminatory support for Roman Catholic education.

5.4 According to counsel, the State party makes the same error in replying to his claims under article 27 in conjunction with article 2. He argues that, since Roman Catholic schools are the only religious minority to receive full and direct funding for religious education from the Government of Ontario, article 27 has not been applied, as required by article 2, without distinction on the basis of religion.

5.5 Counsel agrees with the State party that the fact alone that it does not provide the same level of funding for private as for public schools cannot be deemed to be discriminatory. He acknowledges that the public school system in Ontario would have greater resources if the Government would cease funding any religious schools. In the absence of discrimination, the withdrawal of such funding is a policy decision which is for the Government to take. Counsel notes that the amendment of the provision of the Canadian Constitution Act 1867 [in this regard] requires only the agreement of the Government of the province affected and the federal Government. Such amendments have been recently passed in Quebec and Newfoundland to reduce historical commitments to publicly funded education for selective religious denominations.

5.6 Counsel maintains that when a right to publicly financed religious education is recognized by State parties, no differentiation shall be made among individuals on the basis of the nature of their particular beliefs. The practice of exclusively funding Roman Catholic religious education in Ontario therefore violates the Covenant. Counsel therefore seeks funding for all religious schools which meet provincial standards in Ontario at a level equivalent to the funding, if any, received by Roman Catholic schools in Ontario.

After a further set of arguments, in which the complainant and the State party each attempted to reinforce their original positions, the Human Rights Committee undertook a consideration of the issues in the case and rendered its view on the matter.

Issues before the Committee

10.1 The Human Rights Committee has considered the present communication in the light of all the information made available to it by the parties, as provided in article 5, paragraph 1, of the Optional Protocol.

10.2 The issue before the Committee is whether public funding for Roman Catholic schools, but not for schools of the author's religion, which results in him having to meet the full cost of education in a religious school, constitutes a violation of the author's rights under the Covenant.

10.3 The State party has argued that no discrimination has occurred, since the distinction is based on objective and reasonable criteria: the privileged treatment of Roman Catholic schools is enshrined in the Constitution; as Roman Catholic schools are incorporated as a distinct part of the public school system, the differentiation is between private and public schools, not between private Roman Catholic schools and private schools of other denominations; and the aims of the public secular education system are compatible with the Covenant.

10.4 The Committee begins by noting that the fact that a distinction is enshrined in the Constitution does not render it reasonable and objective. In the instant case, the distinction was made in 1867 to protect the Roman Catholics in Ontario. The material before the Committee does not show that members of the Roman Catholic community or any identifiable section of that community are now in a disadvantaged position compared to those members of the Jewish community that wish to secure the education of their children in religious schools. Accordingly, the Committee rejects the State party's argument that the preferential treatment of Roman Catholic schools is non-discriminatory because of its Constitutional obligation.

10.5 With regard to the State party's argument that it is reasonable to differentiate in the allocation of public funds between private and public schools, the Committee notes that it is not possible for members of religious denominations other than Roman Catholic to have their religious schools incorporated within the public school system. In the instant case, the author has sent his children to a private religious school, not because he wishes a private non-Government dependent education for his children, but because the publicly funded school system makes no provision for his religious denomination, whereas publicly funded religious schools are available to members of the Roman Catholic faith. On the basis of the facts before it, the Committee considers that the differences in treatment between Roman Catholic religious schools, which are publicly funded as a distinct part of the public education system, and schools of the author's religion, which are private by necessity, cannot be considered reasonable and objective.

10.6 The Committee has noted the State party's argument that the aims of the State party's secular public education system are compatible with the principle of non-discrimination laid down in the Covenant. The Committee does not take issue with this argument but notes, however, that the proclaimed aims of the system do not justify the exclusive funding of Roman Catholic religious schools. It has also noted the author's submission that the public school system in Ontario would have greater resources if the Government would cease funding any religious schools. In this context, the Committee observes that the Covenant does not oblige State parties to fund schools which are established on a religious basis. However, if a State party chooses to provide public funding to religious schools, it should make this funding available without discrimination. This means that providing funding for the schools of one religious group and not for another must be based on reasonable and objective criteria. In the instant case, the Committee concludes that the material before it does not show that the differential treatment between the Roman Catholic faith and the author's religious denomination is based on such criteria. Consequently, there has been a violation of the author's rights under article 26 of the Covenant to equal and effective protection against discrimination.

10.7 The Committee has noted the author's arguments that the same facts also constitute a violation of articles 18 and 27, read in conjunction with article 2(1) of the Covenant. The Committee is of the opinion that in view of its conclusions in regard to article 26, no additional issue arises for its consideration under articles 18, 27 and 2(1) of the Covenant.

11. The Human Rights Committee, acting under article 5, paragraph 4, of the Optional Protocol to the International Covenant on Civil and Political Rights, is of the view that the facts before it disclose a violation of article 26 of the Covenant.

12. Under article 2, paragraph 3(a), of the Covenant, the State party is under the obligation to provide an effective remedy, that will eliminate this discrimination.

13. Bearing in mind that, by becoming a State party to the Optional Protocol, the State party has recognized the competence of the Committee to determine whether there has been a violation of the Covenant or not and that, pursuant to article 2 of the Covenant, the State party has undertaken to ensure to all individuals within its territory and

subject to its jurisdiction the rights recognized in the Covenant and to provide an effective and enforceable remedy in case a violation has been established, the Committee wishes to receive from the State party, within ninety days, information about the measures taken to give effect to the Committee's Views. The State party is also requested to publish the Committee's Views.

Canada's Response

(The Permanent Mission of Canada to the United Nations, Note No. 0164, Geneva, 3 February 2000)

In its response to Communication number 694/1996, in which the UN Committee presented its views to Canada on the Waldman case, the federal government reported that it had sought the co-operation of the Province of Ontario in seeking a satisfactory solution to the matter. The Government emphasized, however, that within Canada, decisions regarding education are ultimately for the provinces to resolve in accordance with their constitutional authority. The Government of Canada then conveyed the position of the Government of Ontario, as communicated to it in a letter of 1 February 2000:

> The position remains that Ontario has no plans to extend funding to private religious schools or to parents of children that attend such schools, and intends to adhere fully to its constitutional obligation to fund Roman Catholic Schools. We affirm that our commitment is to providing an excellent public education system that is open to all students regardless of religious or cultural background.

SOURCE: *Waldman v. Canada*, Communication No. 694/1996 [05/11/99], UN Doc. CCPR/C.

family was only indirectly at stake. However, the Committee concluded in her favour by ruling that the effects of her loss of rights continued after the Covenant had come into force and that the particular right being denied was the right to enjoy her culture in her community. Following the release of the statement of the Human Rights Committee, the Canadian government agreed to modify the Indian Act to bring it in harmony with the Covenant. It took four years for Sandra Lovelace's case to be decided at the UN and another four years for the Indian Act to be amended. The Government of Canada first introduced legislation in June 1984 to amend the Indian Act in order to remove the discriminatory clause. The amendment was re-introduced in the new parliamentary session in 1985 and became law in June 1985, thereby putting an end to sexual discrimination in the Indian Act.

To further illustrate the way in which individual citizens can seek redress against discrimination under the ICCPR Protocol, in the following section of this chapter we will present a case study, based on a recent, and highly controversial complaint.

The Aftermath: 'Passing the Buck' Gives Rise to Parental Protest

On 2 November 2000, a multifaith parents' coalition marched between the federal and provincial government offices in Toronto to mark the first anniversary of the UN Human Rights Committee ruling that held that religious discrimination in Ontario education funding violates international law. Christians, Sikhs, Jews, and Muslims marched peacefully together to protest continuing federal-provincial buckpassing and refusal to eliminate discrimination (Canada NewsWire, 2 November 2000).

Representatives called on the federal government to provide federal tax credits and equal provincial funding for non-Catholic denominational schools. Law professor Anne Bayefsky, who successfully argued the *Waldman v. Canada* case at the United Nations Human Rights Committee, stated that the federal government deliberately chose to ignore international law and to maintain the violation of one of the most fundamental human rights of Canadians—freedom from discrimination on the basis of religion. Professor Bayefsky insisted that Canada has a clear legal obligation to provide a remedy for Protestants, Jews, Sikhs, Muslims, and other religious minorities in Ontario. Instead, she said, the government has tarnished Canada's international reputation by pretending that it is not their responsibility and by shifting the responsibility entirely to the Government of Ontario.

Ontario's Undisclosed Response

Although not openly admitting that its action represented a response to the UN Committee Decision in the *Waldman case,* during the year 2001, the Government of Ontario drafted new legislation that led to the introduction of the Equity in Education Tax Credit.

On 17 December 2001, Ontario's Deputy Premier and Finance Minister Jim Flaherty announced regulations to establish eligibility for Ontario's new Equity in Education Tax Credit [communication from the Ministry of Finance, Queen's Park Toronto]. The Equity in Education Tax Credit supports parents who want more choice in their children's education, particularly those who want their children educated in their own culture and religion. The credit was announced in the 2001 Ontario Budget and was passed into law in June 2001.

Flaherty commented that the Ontario Government had listened to the advice of many representatives from independent schools, and had developed regulations that best meet their needs and priorities. The regulations came into effect on 1 January 2002, and the Equity in Education Tax Credit can be claimed by parents for the first time when they file their 2002 tax returns in 2003. Parents will be eligible to receive up to 50 per cent of the eligible tuition costs paid to an independent school.

Other provinces supporting independent schools include British Columbia, Alberta, Saskatchewan, Manitoba, and Quebec, which provide grants directly to independent schools. Ontario has taken a different approach by providing support to parents so that they can make the decisions that they believe are right for their children [communication from the Ministry of Finance, Queen's Park Toronto, 17 December 2001].

The new provincial tax credit, together with federal tax exemptions for religious donations should bring the level of government funding for independent, non-Catholic religious schools up to about 75 per cent of the full funding currently provided to Catholic schools. While this does not represent *equal* funding of Catholic and non-Catholic religious schools, supporters of the equal funding lobby agree that it represents a positive step forward toward equal funding [Arieh Waldman, personal communication].

Comments on Case Study 1

Case Study 1 highlights a number of very important points that have been reviewed throughout this book. The first point, raised in the Introduction, is that the reason for the drafting of the two UN covenants elaborating on the provisions of the UDHR—the ICCPR and the ICESCR—was that, while the UDHR was *morally* binding on nations ratifying it, it was not *legally* binding. Therefore new, stronger covenants were drafted which would have more force and effect because they would be legally binding on signatories.

In 1976, Canada ratified the ICCPR with the written approval of Ontario and all the other provinces. Canada and the provinces also ratified the Optional Protocol. This allows for individual complaints to be brought before an impartial tribunal, the UN Human Rights Committee, and *requires* the state to implement the rulings of the Committee. The outcome of the *Waldman case,* like that of the *Lovelace case* that preceded it, demonstrates the importance of the ICCPR and its Optional Protocol, in providing individuals with an avenue of appeal beyond state borders in order to gain redress against discrimination by state governments.

The second point, raised in the beginning of this chapter, is that not only statutory law, but also constitutional law can be discriminatory. In our analysis of Canada's Charter of Rights and Freedoms, we showed how the Charter, influenced by historical constitutional provisions going back to Confederation, endorses a hierarchy of rights, with the two founding groups English/Protestant and French/Catholic at the pinnacle. The arguments in the *Waldman case* highlight the glaring inequalities built in to Canada's Constitution from its inception. Specifically, the UN Committee rejected the Government of Canada's argument that the preferential treatment of Roman Catholic schools is non-discriminatory because of its constitutional obligation. In its arguments, the committee implied that Canada's Constitution, given the current religious diversity of the Canadian population, clearly discriminates against non-Catholic religious denominations.

A third important point, raised throughout this book, but emphasized in the legal cases considered in Chapter 8 and in this chapter, is that a complaint of discrimination brought forward by an individual, but which in essence involves a violation of categorical or collective rights, can lead to a settlement that benefits the entire group to which the individual belongs. In several cases detailed in Chapter 8, I showed how individual complaints of discrimination in the areas of employment and service, resulted in mandates for affirmation action programs. In this chapter, I have presented Charter challenge cases that resulted in the striking down of laws that discriminated on the basis of religion. The decision in the *Waldman case* highlights the way in which an individual complaint alleging violation of collective religious rights has resulted in the introduction of legislation that benefits all religious minorities in the province of Ontario and, hopefully, paves the way for equality in the funding of all independent religious schools in Ontario, and throughout the country.

Toward the Full Recognition and Protection for Ethnic Minority Rights in Canada: Strategies for Change

The Introduction pointed out that international human rights instruments are continually being amended and expanded, in response to input from minority representatives, in order to provide stronger and more explicit protection for the individual, categorical, and collective rights of ethnic minorities. Nevertheless, throughout this book, I have shown that the current provisions of international instruments do not fully endorse minority claims for explicit recognition and positive protection of their collective cultural rights and/or nationhood rights within states. At the international level, then, one important strategy for change is to bolster the lobbying efforts and consultative roles of NGOs, at the United Nations, whose platforms support positive protections for collective minority rights.

Similarly, within Canada, support for the lobbying efforts of minority rights organizations seeking strong and explicit legal protections for collective minority rights at both the statutory and constitutional levels is of the utmost importance. Insofar as the constitutional Charter provides the national standard for all human rights statutes, it should follow that human rights statutes should be amended so as to reflect Charter-endorsed protections for the collective rights of Canada's ethnocultural minorities. To achieve this goal, it is essential that minority rights groups and coalitions work together with human rights commissions to ensure that the Charter standard is reflected in the legal protection for ethnic minority rights at the statutory level.

In addition to legal human rights protection, it is important that social policy measures designed to ameliorate group-level disadvantage among racial and ethnic minorities be expanded and implemented at all levels of government. Minority rights organizations and coalitions can play an important role here by lobbying for improved policy measures directed toward equitable treatment of ethnic minorities.

Alternative Minority Services and Organizations

Majority members and organizations can help minorities empower themselves and enhance their cultural identities by supporting alternative minority services and organizations that are operated by and serve members of particular minority communities (Mullaly 2002: 194). These alternative services and organizations are usually established because their traditional, mainstream counterparts tend to be culturally specific, that is to say, they are set up by majority members and operate in accordance with majority norms, values, and expectations. Alternative minority services and organizations, Mullaly points out, are countersystems to mainstream agencies because they are founded on different cultural principles, values, and ideals. They represent attempts by minority communities to gain control over their own destinies.

A prime example of this strategy is provided by the Aboriginal Justice Learning Network.

Aboriginal Justice Learning Network

The Aboriginal Justice Learning Network (AJLN) is a broad-based voluntary network of representatives of the conventional justice system and aboriginal communities across Canada. Together, members of the AJLN work for change in the administration and provision of justice services by and for aboriginal peoples. The AJLN was set up in 1996 and given the mandate to:

- act as a vehicle of communication between the current justice system and aboriginal communities;
- help ensure that aboriginal women participate as full partners during both the negotiation and implementation of community justice programs;
- train enforcement officers, prosecutors, judges, and members of aboriginal communities in the objectives, values, and mechanics of the approaches to justice in the agreements; and
- help participating communities and the current justice system implement community-based justice programs, with a focus on ensuring that the new approaches are fully integrated into the day-to-day operation of the principal justice system.

While the Network includes groups from across the country, it is managed through the National Coordinator's Office in the Department of Justice in Ottawa. The Coordinator's Office works closely with the AJLN Advisory Committee, which advises the deputy minister of justice and the Learning Network as a whole regarding proposed activities and makes recommendations about the communications strategy and the use of financial and human resources. It meets three or four times a year.

The AJLN serves as a vehicle for development, evaluation, communication, education, and information-sharing on alternative, restorative justice processes that are consistent with aboriginal values and traditions. The network promotes understanding of the implications of culture differences and of the dynamics of racism, especially in relation to the justice system.

To accomplish these aims, the AJLN has three basic roles. First, the network acts as a link that enables groups from across Canada to share ideas and information and to stay informed about developments in the field. These might include local or regional programs, conferences, new publications, court decisions, or new legislation. The AJLN newsletter *LINK*, with a circulation of 3000, is the main tool for this activity. Second, the network website offers free resources, publications, and videos on aspects of aboriginal justice, community programs, and similar initiatives. The third role of the network is to provide funding and other support for projects that offer creative solutions to the various issues related to aboriginal community justice. The AJLN has supported conferences, workshops, and training programs across the country dealing with such subjects as sentencing circles, dispute resolution, victim services, and legal issues.

New Social Movements and Coalition Building among Minorities

Mullaly (2002: 197) maintains that a major obstacle to coalition building among members of new social movements is that these movements tend to have a single-stranded focus on the identity, community and culture of a particular minority group. Thus, a political challenge is posed in the formation of multiple identity groups and movements by the problem of forming alliances and building solidarity that transcends, rather than subjugates, their differences. The tendency of minority groups and movements to focus solely on their respective singular issues obscures their awareness of and identification with the potentially shared political interests of other minorities.

Another obstacle to coalition building is externally imposed. Mullaly cites Wineman (1984: 159), who contends that the biggest obstacle to coalition building among different minorities is the 'divide and rule' strategy of dominant political and economic authorities, imbedded in social policies that serve to create and sustain deep divisions among different minorities. This dominant strategy engenders a competition among minority groups for resources and attention, a point well documented in the earlier discussion of the aboriginal, multicultural/anti-racism and Franco-Quebecois movements in Canada.

Mullaly (2002: 198–200) suggests four strategies (originally developed by Wineman) designed to overcome internal and external obstacles to coalition building among different minority groups. The first, and essential element of coalition building, is the mutual identification of different minorities as groups (albeit for different reasons) disadvantaged and subordinated by dominant agencies in the society. The second element is for members of different minority groups to recognize that they share a common goal: that of transforming the structure of society from one based on group inequality to one based on group equality. A third element, directly related to the second, is for members of different minority groups to understand that it is the same, mainstream political and economic elites who are responsible for the inferiorization and disadvantaged status common to all minority groups. A fourth element, critical for coalition building, is the recognition that most minority group members experience minority status on multiple grounds (multiple minority status). This fact enables the development of caucuses of internal minorities (minorities within minority communities) that facilitate the development of links with other minority groups. For example, an aboriginal women's caucus within an anti-poverty group becomes a link between First Nations, women's, and anti-poverty organizations. These internal caucuses not only manifest overlapping minority statuses and identities, but also become the points of contact between various minority organizations, and can spearhead coalition building through the development of common goals and joint actions.

Human Rights Education

Throughout this book, I have argued that human rights legislation is needed to combat and eradicate acts of ethnic discrimination. As a parallel strategy for change, I will argue that education is needed to counteract and eradicate the ethnic prejudices and stereotypes that serve as catalysts for discrimination.

Within the educational system, systemic barriers can discriminate against particular minorities by practices of omission or commission. For example, a number of early research studies (Barrie et al. 1982) identified sex-stereotyping of occupational roles in standard course curricula (commission), while others (McDiarmid and Pratt 1974) revealed the absence of materials dealing with aboriginal peoples' languages, cultures, and histories (omission).

Racism continues to operate in Canadian schools today to disadvantage students from racial minorities. A Canadian Race Relations Foundation (CRRF) report entitled *Racism in Our Schools* (2001b) indicates that racism remains a serious *systemic* barrier to the equal access of visible minority and aboriginal children to educational achievement. Evidence drawn from various studies reveals that continuing barriers to equal educational achievement for visible minority children, particularly black children, include: negative differential treatment, racial stereotyping, bias in testing and evaluation, streaming, a monocultural curriculum, unfair and unusual discipline, and the self-fulfilling prophecy of low expectations. This evidence has highlighted the pressing need for the forceful *implementation* of anti-racism initiatives 'collecting dust on policymakers' desks'.

Eradicating Prejudice and Teaching Human Rights: The Role of Public Education

To truly reflect the multiethnic character of Canada, it is essential that all forms of public education, from the schools to the media, not only integrate multicultural and anti-racist mandates within their policy directives, but also that they ensure that such mandates are forcefully implemented. Equally important, in order to provide a balanced curriculum, it is essential that public education include teaching which emphasizes the *similarities* and *affinities* among all Canadians, as members of the same human family—the family of humankind.

In order to ensure that public education presents a balanced picture of human unity and diversity, it must be informed by a strong human rights mandate. The human rights directive of public education should include teaching not only about international human rights principles, but also about the structure of legal protection for human rights in Canada. With regard to the latter point, I would argue that unless Canadians are informed about human rights principles, legislation, and investigative and conciliation procedures, they may well be unaware of the help available to them in an instance of ethnic or other forms of discrimination. Thus, there is a need for much greater publicization of human rights materials, including codes, cases, decisions, etc., as well as the findings of research studies on human rights issues.

Probably the most glaring case of omission in this area lies in the neglect of formal instruction about human rights in the curricula of public education institutions in this country. The latter point draws attention to the deplorable lack of available resources and the lack of teacher training in the area of human rights.

UDHR Mandate for the Teaching of Human Rights

As part of the preamble to the UDHR, the following declaration sets out the mandate for human rights education:

> Now therefore, the General Assembly proclaims this Universal Declaration of Human Rights as a common standard of achievement for all peoples and all nations to the end that *every individual and every organ of society, keeping this Declaration constantly in mind, shall strive by teaching and education to promote respect for these rights and freedoms and by progressive measures, national and international, to secure their universal and effective recognition and observance*, both among the peoples of Member States themselves and among the peoples of territories under their jurisdiction.

This mandate is reinforced in section 2 of Article 26 of the UDHR as follows:

> Article 26
> (2) *Education shall be directed* to the full development of the human personality and *to the strengthening of respect for human rights and fundamental freedoms*. It shall promote understanding, tolerance and friendship among all nations, racial or religious groups, and shall further the activities of the United Nations for the maintenance of peace.

Case Study 2 (see Box 9-2) illustrates how teachers can serve as human rights role models while engaging students in activities that enable them to experience, at first hand, how human rights principles can be put into practice.

Table 9-1 Protection for Ethnic Minority Rights in Canada

LAW
Constitution/Charter
Human rights statutes
Specified and defined protection for the individual, categorical, and collective rights of ethnic minorities including the right to self-determination of aboriginal First Nations
PUBLIC POLICY
Implementation of multiculturalism and anti-racism mandates
Affirmative action programs designed to ameliorate group-level disadvantage in economic, political, social, and cultural spheres
Public education about human rights principles and legislation
Equitable distribution of public resources across minorities
PUBLIC PRACTICE
Support for NGOs at the international UN level
Support for alternative minority rights organizations within Canada
Encouragement for the formation of minority rights coalitions
Liaison between minority rights advocacy groups and human rights Commissions
Encouragement for the practice of human rights principles by Canadian citizens in everyday life

BOX 9-2: CASE STUDY 2

ABC: Teaching Human Rights

At the International Conference on Human Rights, held in Tehran in 1968 to review the progress made since the adoption of the Universal Declaration of Human Rights and to formulate a program for the future, it was resolved to call upon all States to ensure that 'all means of education' be used to provide youth with the opportunity to grow up in a spirit of respect for human dignity and equal rights. It saw the basis of such education as 'objective information and free discussion', and urged the use of 'all appropriate measures' to stimulate interest in the problems of the changing world, and to prepare young people for social life.

The United Nations General Assembly resolved the same year to request its members to take steps as appropriate, and according to the scholastic system of each State, to introduce or encourage the principles proclaimed in the Universal Declaration of Human Rights and in other declarations. It called for progressive instruction of this sort in the curricula of both primary and secondary schools, and invited teachers to seize every opportunity to draw the attention of their students to the growing role the United Nations system plays in fostering peaceful international relations and cooperative efforts to promote social justice and economic and social progress in the world.

Similar requests have been reiterated since then. In 1978 in particular, UNESCO organized an international congress in Vienna on the teaching of human rights—a landmark event that gathered together for the first time a wide range of both governmental and non-governmental education specialists. A similar congress was held in Malta in 1987. Within the framework of the 40th anniversary of the Universal Declaration of Human Rights, the United Nations Centre for Human Rights held an international seminar on the teaching of human rights in Geneva (late in 1988), with the participation of representatives of more than 40 countries, governmental and nongovernmental organizations, and the concerned media.

Despite general agreement *in principle* of the desirability of education of this sort, there remains a marked paucity of practical materials for the purpose. To help meet this need for educational materials, the Office of the High Commissioner for Human Rights (United Nations) produced a booklet entitled *ABC, Teaching Human Rights: Practical Activities for Primary and Secondary Schools*. This booklet provides basic information for teachers in primary and secondary schools who want to foster awareness and knowledge of human rights and the sense of reciprocity and universality upon which it is based. It also offers practical activities for students. It is a starting point that, it is hoped, will be supplemented by further research and study on the subject and/or by national manuals and audiovisual materials already available. It will hopefully be used to initiate an ongoing process of adaptation and development at all teaching levels within the world's many and varied cultural regions.

The ABC Booklet

This booklet covers a number of basic human rights issue areas (such as inequality, poverty, political oppression, racism, genocide). Each issue area has been defined in terms of particular questions, and specific activities are keyed to these questions. In performing the activities, the relevant questions are raised, answers are discussed, and this leads to the fostering of an understanding of the particular issue area involved. Ideally, the booklet points out, a human rights culture should be built into the whole school curriculum, yet in practice, particularly at the secondary school level, it tends to be introduced in a narrower context, as part of the established disciplines within the social and economic sciences and the humanities. Yet, the booklet emphasizes, a genuine effort at teaching human rights, even in a limited context, is much better than not at all.

The booklet begins with suggestions for nurturing the sense students have of their own worth and that of others. This section is meant mainly for preschool and lower primary school teachers. The suggested activities are designed to evoke the humane values that make specific human rights principles meaningful. The exercises for upper primary and secondary school students are of a more sophisticated nature and deal with current human rights issues. The exercises are intended to give students a more profound awareness and understanding of those issues, upon which later analysis and study can be built.

The booklet points out that it has been found that upper primary and secondary school students sometimes suffer from a lack of confidence, and that they find it hard to socialize with others as a result. It is difficult to care about someone else's rights when you do not expect to have any yourself. Where this is the case, teaching for human rights could require going back to the beginning, and teaching confidence and tolerance first. To this end, the booklet offers trust exercises. These exercises can be used with any group and help establish a human rights-oriented classroom climate. They also can be used to encourage students to engage in activities that require group participation. They are designed to foster the human capacity for empathy by stressing the fact that no person is more of a human being than another and no person is less. We are human beings first. We are boys and girls, state citizens or refugees, or members of a specific race or social group only secondly.

Teaching For and Teaching About

Already implicit above is the idea—central to this booklet—that teaching *about* human rights is not enough. The teacher will want to begin, and never to finish, teaching *for* human rights. Students will want not only to learn of human rights, but learn to exercise them, for what they *do* will be of the most practical benefit to them. That is why the main part of the text consists of activities. For example, a history of human rights legislation (including information on complaints procedures), unless taught with the greatest skill and care, can be very difficult to bring alive in the classroom. The same applies to teaching human rights principles. If the UDHR, for example, is to have more than intellectual significance, it is important to have students exercise their own sense of justice, freedom, and equity. The activities enable students to do this.

Role-play is considered a most effective way of transmitting the meaning of the human rights message. Briefly, a role-play is similar to a brief drama played out before the class. It is largely improvised. Having set the scene with the basic ideas (for example, the rights elaborated in the various articles of the UDHR), the teacher will want to allow time for those chosen to take part to think about what they will say (individually or in groups), or the teacher can proceed at once to enact it. This can be done as a story (with a narrator, and key characters) or as a situation (where the key characters interact, making up dialogue on the spot—perhaps with the help of the teacher and the rest of the class). Close reference is made to the United Nations Declaration of Human Rights, so that what is done can be assessed in the light of the principles and ideas it lists. The booklet points out that is important for teachers to stress that these human rights have received universal recognition.

Teaching and Preaching: Actions Speak Louder Than Words

The fact that the Universal Declaration of Human Rights is of virtual global validity and applicability is very important for teachers. By working with precepts that have been so widely endorsed for so many years now, the teacher can honestly say that he or she is not preaching. However, wherever teaching *for* human rights is undertaken, teachers have a second obligation: that is, to teach in such a way as to respect human rights in the classroom and the school environment itself. This means avoiding any hypocrisy. At its simplest, hypocrisy refers to situations where what a teacher is teaching is clearly at odds with how he or she is teaching it. For example: 'Today we are going to talk about freedom of expression—shut up in the back row!' Students will learn mostly about power this way, and considerably less about human rights. Consistent teaching practice that is compatible with basic human rights, will be a model: this would also enable a mathematics teacher, for example, to teach *for* human rights even though the subject-matter may have little to do with human rights issues.

Negotiating a set of classroom rules and responsibilities is a long-tested and most effective way to begin teaching human rights. Since the activity of working out some classroom rules has a direct effect on classroom climate, it can be a very significant one. It is a clear demonstration of a teacher's willingness to involve students in how the classroom is run, and her or his own trust in its members. It also makes students think about what rules are desirable and what are possible in class, how they might be observed, and the teacher's own role in having the primary responsibility for ensuring that everyone in the class observes the agreed-upon rules.

Aiming at Full Respect for Human Rights and Fundamental Freedoms

This booklet views the human rights culture as an ongoing attempt to define human dignity and worth. The history of human rights tells a detailed story of the attempts made to define basic dignity and worth of the human being and his or her most fundamental entitlements. These efforts continue to this day. The teacher will want to include an account of this history as an essential part of human rights teaching, and it can be made progressively more sophisticated as students become older and more able to understand it. The fight for civil and political rights, the campaign for the abolition of slavery, the fight for economic and social rights led to a Universal Declaration of Human Rights plus two subsequent Covenants, and all the Conventions and Declarations that followed this lead—all provide an international legislative-normative, human rights framework. This booklet provides teachers with an appropriate instrument with which to introduce fundamental human rights principles to students and with which to generate in them a basic understanding of the legislative-normative, human rights framework of today's international human rights culture.

SOURCE: *ABC, Teaching Human Rights: Practical Activities for Primary and Secondary Schools*, United Nations, Office of the High Commissioner for Human Rights (OHCHR) website.

Prospectus for the Future

In the foregoing discussion of strategies for change we have attempted to demonstrate that no single strategy or measure—legal, political, economic, educational—will be sufficient in order to make real progress in working towards a goal of equity and justice for all racial and ethnic groups across Canada. Table 9-1 schematizes the general areas in which the strategies for change outlined can be implemented: strengthening of legal protections for minority rights across Canada, affirmative action programs, redistribution of resources, political lobbying efforts and human rights education.

Conclusion

In the last analysis, the problem of discrimination must be solved by people, rather than by governments. It is the people, in any society, who must work toward achieving the human rights goal of respect for the dignity of all human persons, and, it is the people who must develop the ability to accept racial and ethnic group differences. It is the people, in any society, who must work toward achieving the human rights goals of equity and justice for all.

In support of this view, the sentiments quoted in the predecessor to all editions of this book are reaffirmed here.

If our struggle towards full observance of human rights and fundamental freedoms throughout Canada is to be given more than lip service, we, as Canadian citizens, must insist upon and work for consistent enforcement of anti-racist legislation; and we must take upon ourselves the crucial responsibility for educating our children towards the spirit of human rights: we must demonstrate in our own public and private lives, that 'race' does not define 'place' in the truly just society (Hughes and Kallen 1974: 214).

Key Concepts

- equality rights: enumerated versus analogous grounds
- Optional Protocol to the ICCPR
- purposive approach
- statutory versus Charter protection for minority rights

Critical Thinking Questions

1. With the use of examples, compare and contrast the scope of Charter versus statutory protections for human rights.
2. Is there a Charter-endorsed hierarchy of minority rights? Take the position of a member of particular racial or ethnic minority on this question.
3. Explain the relationship between international human rights principles and legal protections for human rights. Use Charter challenge cases and cases brought forward under the Optional Protocol to the ICCPR to illustrate your main points.
4. Outline the part which education can play in promoting human rights. Highlight the roles of both teachers and students in this process.
5. Prospectus for the future. Using a human rights perspective, outline ways in which informed citizens can help to ensure that that 'race' does not define 'place' in the truly just society.

FURTHER READING

Introduction

Borovoy, A.A. 1988. *When Freedoms Collide: The Case for Our Civil Liberties*. Toronto: Lester Orpen & Dennys. In this book, Borovoy presents the case for a civil libertarian view of human rights as fundamental, individual rights and freedoms. As the title of the book suggests, the underlying theme of the book addresses the critical question of the appropriate resolution of rights in conflict. Key areas of human rights focused on include: the freedom of each versus the welfare of all; racial inequity and legal redress and the constitutional entrenchment of our fundamental freedoms.

Human Rights Research and Education Centre, University of Ottawa. Website: www.uottawa.ca/hrrec/. This site provides a valuable source for human rights information, including library and research resources and links to both Canadian and international human rights websites.

Kymlicka, W., ed. 1995. *The Rights of Minority Cultures*. Oxford: Oxford University Press. This volume comprises some of the most important contemporary articles on the rights of minority cultures. While drawing on particular case studies, the articles focus on the more general theoretical and normative issues raised by the accommodation of cultural differences. The authors represented in this volume come from a variety of countries and disciplines, and reflect a wide range of opinion. The book explores the nature and value of cultural membership, models of cultural pluralism, individual and group rights, minority representation, immigration, and secession.

Murumba, S.K. 1998. 'Cross-Cultural Dimensions of Human Rights in the Twenty-First Century'. In *Legal Visions of the 21st Century: Essays in Honour of Judge Christopher Weeramantry*. Anghie, A., and Sturgess, G., eds. The Hague/London/Boston: Kluwer Law International: 201–40. This insightful article presents a comprehensive overview of the ongoing debate concerning the universality of human rights.

Office of the United Nations High Commissioner for Human Rights. Website: www.unhchr.ch/html/intlinst.htm. All United Nations human rights documents are available for download from this website. The site also includes links to a wide variety of UN and related websites providing information on human rights issues, human rights bodies, human rights education, news, conferences, and so forth.

UDHR 50 History of the Declaration. Website: www.udhr.org/history/default.htm. Honouring the 50th anniversary of the UDHR, this website provides a comprehensive background to the formulation of the Declaration.

Chapter 1

Anti-Defamation League. Website: www.adl.org/. For more than 88 years, ADL has been combating anti-Semitism and racism of all kinds. The ADL website provides a wide range of information on racism and anti-racist activities in North America, and internationally.

Barrett, S.R. 1987. *Is God a Racist? The Right Wing in Canada*. Toronto: University of Toronto Press. In this book, Barrett analyzes the rise of right-wing, racist, and fascist organizations in Canada. Based on first-hand, fieldwork methodology, his analysis reveals a disturbing portrait of institutionalized racism in Canada.

Canadian Race Relations Foundation. Website: www.crr.ca/. The CRRF was established by the government of Canada to develop and implement Initiatives Against Racism. The CRRF website provides valuable sources of information on racism and racial discrimination in Canada, and highlights the contributions of groups affected by racism and racial discrimination, notably aboriginal peoples and racial minorities.

Montagu, A., ed. 1999. *Race and I.Q.* London: Oxford University Press. This compendium of articles, edited by the renowned anthropologist Ashley Montagu debunks the mythology attributing differences in IQ scores to racial differences. What emerges in chapter after chapter is a deep skepticism about the scientific validity of intelligence tests, especially as applied to evaluating innate intelligence, if only because scientists still cannot distinguish between genetic and environmental contributions to the development of the human mind.

Satzewich, V., ed. 1998. *Racism and Social Inequality in Canada: Concepts, Controversies and Strategies of Resistance*. Toronto: Thompson Educational Publishing. This collection of essays provides a variety of scholarly insights into the understanding of the nature and extent of racism in Canada, and how best to combat it. The authors analyze, in different ways, the conditions that give rise to racism in various forms, the extent to which racism permeates the way various social institutions operate, how groups of people have organized against racism, and the ways that racism is linked to class, gender, and ethnicity. They also try to provide readers with some conceptual tools and empirical evidence as a basis for discussion and debate about the meaning of race, racism, racialization, and social inequality in contemporary Canada.

Urban Alliance for Race Relations. Website: www.interlog.com/~uarr/. The UARR is a Toronto-based anti-racist organization undertaking educational, research, and advocative activities that seek to promote racial and ethnic harmony. The UARR website provides information on all of these undertakings.

Chapter 2

Abella, Judge R. 1984. *Equality in Employment: A Royal Commission Report*. Ottawa: Supply and Services Canada. This report presents the findings of the national investigation carried out by the Abella Commission of systemic discrimination in employment against four designated minority groups: women, [aboriginal] native peoples, disabled persons and visible minorities.

Canadian Ethnic Studies. Website: www.ss.ucalgary.ca/ces/. *Canadian Ethnic Studies* is Canada's foremost academic journal focusing on issues of race, ethnicity, ethnic and racial prejudice and discrimination, racism and systemic inequality. The CESA website, while not yet fully developed, provides references to abstracts, articles, and book reviews published in the journal.

Mosher, J.C., and Hagan, J. 1998. *Discrimination and Denial: Systemic Racism in Ontario's Legal and Criminal Justice Systems, 1892–1961*. Toronto: University of Toronto Press. This book examines the antecedents of systemic racism in Canada's legal and criminal justice systems. Focusing on the experiences of Asians and blacks in Ontario, the authors' analysis reveals the pivotal roles of prejudice, discrimination, and stereotypes behind systemic racism.

Racism in Our Schools. Report of the CRRF. Available from CRRF website: www.crr.ca/. This report reveals how negative prejudice, stereotypes, and discrimination impose racist barriers to educational achievement for visible minority and aboriginal students in Canadian schools.

Report on Systemic Racism and Discrimination in Canadian Refugee and Immigration Policies, 2000. Available from Canadian Council for Refugees website: www.web.net/~ccr/antiracrep.htm. This report looks at two distinct but interrelated problems: 1) the discriminatory manner in which some groups of newcomers, particularly racialized groups, are affected by Canadian refugee and immigration policies; and 2) the way in which refugees and immigrants collectively are treated with prejudice and discriminated against in the enjoyment of their rights.

Stangor, C., ed. 2000. *Stereotypes and Prejudice: Essential Readings*. University of Maryland at College Park. This book offers a collection of classic and contemporary readings contributing to the understanding of stereotyping and prejudice from a social-psychological perspective.

Chapter 3

Canadian Council on Social Development website: www.ccsd.ca. The Canadian Council on Social Development (CCSD) is one of Canada's most authoritative voices promoting better social and economic security for all Canadians. A national, self-supporting, non-profit organization, the CCSD's main goal is to provide information through ongoing research on social and economic inequalities in Canada.

Canadian Social Research Links. Website: www.canadiansocialresearch.net/research.htm. This website provides links to key Canadian social research organizations and offers summaries of reports and activities of these research centres. The website affords access to key research studies documenting social and economic inequalities in Canada.

Centre for the Study of Living Standards website: www.csls.ca. The CSLS focuses on research in the area of living standards. The two main objectives of CSLS are to contribute to a better understanding of trends in living standards and factors determining trends through research, and to contribute to public debate on living standards by developing and advocating specific policies through expert consensus.

Curtis, J., Grabb, E., and Guppy, N. 1999. *Social Inequality in Canada: Canada: Patterns, Problems and Policies*. 3rd edn. Scarborough, ON: Prentice-Hall. Designed for use in courses on social inequality or social stratification, this collection of 31 articles introduces students to all the major aspects of social inequality in Canada. The readings are divided into four sections: Power and Class, Socio-Economic Bases of Social Inequality, Ascription and Social Inequality, and Some Consequences of Social Inequality. This compendium includes separate sections on gender, race, and ethnicity, as well as significant coverage of each of these issues in other sections, such as Education, Income, and Occupation.

Das Gupta, T. 'Political Economy of Gender, Race and Class: Looking at South Asian Immigrant Women in Canada'. In *Canadian Ethnic Studies* 26, 1: 59–73. This article analyzes the intersecting dimensions of gender, race, and class on the status of South Asian immigrant women in Canada.

Garcia, J., and Keough, K. 1999. *Social Psychology of Gender, Race and Ethnicity*. Toronto: McGraw-Hill Higher Education. This book offers a range of useful readings dealing with issues of race, gender, and ethnicity, drawing on intersections among the three concepts, instead of treating them independently.

Chapter 4

Backhouse, C. 1999. *Colour Coded: A Legal History of Racism in Canada, 1900–1950*. Toronto: University of Toronto Press. This book is a groundbreaking text that illustrates the undeniable assertion of deeply imbedded racism within Canada's legal system. From thousands of cases, legal scholar Constance Backhouse selected six court cases that focus on Aboriginal, Inuit, Chinese-Canadian, and African-Canadian individuals. In each case study the author provides extensive documentation about the people, context, and the legal question with clarity and precision.

Helmes-Hayes, R., and Curtis, J., eds. 1998. *The Vertical Mosaic Revisited*. Toronto: University of Toronto Press. This collection of papers by five of Canada's top sociologists subjects John Porter's landmark study to renewed scrutiny and traces the dramatic changes since Porter's time—both in Canadian society and in the agenda of Canadian sociology. Based on papers written for a conference held in commemoration of the 30th anniversary of *The Vertical Mosaic*'s publication, the five essays revisit the central themes of the original work: including gender and race inequality; citizenship and social justice; and class, power, and ethnicity from the viewpoint of political economy. An introduction by the editors provides a historical biography of Porter and discusses his influence on Canadian sociology.

Kallen, E. 1997. 'Hate on the Net'. In *Electronic Journal of Sociology (EJS)* 3, 2 (December 1997). Available from the EJS website: www.sociology.org/. In this article the author argues that cyberhate messages promoted on the Internet by organized political and religious hate groups incite hatred and promote harmful action against racial, ethnocultural, religious, and same-sex–oriented minorities. The author's analysis of cyberhate messages directed against these target groups provides empirical evidence to support the thesis that, by manipulating deeply held invalidation myths to provide 'evidence' for their arguments, high-tech hatemongers incite virulent hatred of and harmful action toward targeted minorities. By so doing, high-tech hatemongering violates minority members' human rights to dignity and equality by denying their fundamental freedom from group defamation and harassment.

Paying for the Past. Documentary available from *The National* CBC News Online. Website: www.c.c.ca/national/news/reparations/index/html. This documentary, aired on the CBC on 5 September 2001, reveals a growing movement calling for reparations for black communities in Nova Scotia. At the time, the issue of reparations was already sparking debate in Canada, especially in Nova Scotia where members of the black community were raising their voices, arguing that it's high time they were compensated for what their ancestors suffered and for what they say they are still suffering as part of this country's shameful legacy of slavery, broken promises and racism. What they are demanding is not a cheque for each member of the black community, but for an opportunity to have economic and political benefits that accrue to future generations of African descendant Canadians. This documentary details the appalling legacy of slavery, segregation, economic exploitation, inferior education, and inhumane treatment of Nova Scotia's black population.

Porter, J. 1965. *The Vertical Mosaic*. Toronto: University of Toronto Press. When *The Vertical Mosaic* first appeared in 1965, it became an instant classic. Its key message was that Canada was not the classless democracy, the egalitarian mosaic of ethnic communities it fancied itself to be. In fact, Canada was a highly inegalitarian society comprising a 'vertical mosaic' of hierarchically ranked ethnic groups. Porter's initial interest was in the relationship between ethnicity and social class. As the study proceeded, however, the hierarchical relationship between Canada's many ethnocultural groups became a recurring theme in terms of both class and power.

Report of the Royal Commission on Aboriginal Peoples. Highlights. Updated 21 June 2000. Indian and Northern Affairs Canada. Available from www.aincinac.gc.ca/ch/rcap/ [14 November 2001]. This report documents the devastating impact upon the life conditions of Canada's aboriginal peoples of a century of racist techniques of domination employed by federal government authorities.

Chapter 5

Barth, F. 1969. *Ethnic Groups and Boundaries*. Boston: Little Brown. Barth's seminal work, *Ethnic Groups and Boundaries*, marked the conceptual transition from the old to the new ethnicity. In this book, Barth argues that the focus of social scientific concern should shift from cultural differences to ethnic group boundaries. He argues that ethnic groups are not groups formed on the basis of a shared culture, but rather the formation of groups rests on the basis of cultural differences. Accordingly, it is the boundaries between ethnic groups that provide the essential underpinnings for self and other-definition.

Bill's Aboriginal Links. Website: www.yorku.ca/research/ionline/nateth.htm. This extensive site provides links to a wide variety of aboriginal websites, both national and international. The site has been compiled by a Canadian attorney who often represents aboriginal peoples on legal issues. This site was one of the first on the Net.

Harmony Movement. Website: citd.scar.utoronto.ca/harmony/index.html. Founded in 1994, the Harmony Movement encourages Canadians of all racial, cultural, and religious origins to embrace and promote harmony and diversity, as well as equality. Members of the Harmony Movement hope to dispel myths and eliminate the barriers to mutual understanding that perpetuate prejudice and discrimination in our society. The movement seeks to enable Canadians to experience and appreciate the many faces, the many voices, and the visions that make up the human landscape of Canada.

Levin, M.D., ed. 1993. *Ethnicity and Aboriginality: Case Studies in Ethnonationalism*. Toronto: University of Toronto Press. This compendium includes articles by seven anthropologists and one legal scholar who examine the legal, historical, and cultural aspects of issues surrounding claims to nationhood made by various ethnic groups on the basis of their ethnicity, among them French Canadians, Australian Aborigines, Malays, and peoples of Kenya and Nigeria.

Race, Ethnicity and National Identity Resources. Website: www.yorku.ca/research/ionline/nateth.htm. This online resources site offers a wide range of links to national and international websites focusing on issues of race, ethnicity, national identity, and human rights.

Shapiro, I., and Kymlicka, W., eds. 1997. *Ethnicity and Group Rights*. New York: New York University Press. This book examines questions that lie at the heart of ethnocultural conflict: Can the system of individual citizenship rights within liberal democracies sufficiently accommodate the legitimate interests of ethnic communities? How important is ethnicity to personal identity and self-respect? Perhaps most important, what forms of ethnocultural accommodations are consistent with democratic equality, individual freedom, and political stability? In order to answer these questions, the articles in this book address the issue of ethnicity from a range of perspectives, and the authors invoke numerous case studies to support their arguments.

Chapter 6

Citizenship and Immigration Canada. Website: www.cic.gc.ca/english/index.html. This Government of Canada website provides documentation on immigration and refugee policy and issues, immigrants, refugees, online services, news, and publications.

Ethnic Diversity in a Multicultural Society. 1996. Special Issue of the *Canadian Journal of Behavioural Science* 28. The articles in this special issue of CJBS cover a wide range of topics relating to ethnic diversity and multiculturalism in Canada. Articles include discussion of the changing ethnic composition of Canada; analysis of Canada's policy of multiculturalism, and an assessment of the current state of ethnic identity and ethnic attitudes in Canada.

Frideres, J.S. 1993. *Native Peoples in Canada: Contemporary Conflicts*, 4th edn. Scarborough, ON: Prentice-Hall. This book contains a wealth of information on aboriginal peoples of Canada. Topics covered include colonialism and aboriginal history, Indian Affairs and government policy, demographic and socioeconomic profiles of aboriginal life conditions, aboriginal women, and aboriginal self-government.

Gordon, M. 1964. *Assimilation in American Life*. New York: Oxford University Press. This classic volume represents the first full-scale sociological survey of the assimilation [integration] of minorities in America. This classic work questioned the appropriateness of the prevailing 'melting pot' and 'mosaic' models, and suggested, instead, that while many American minorities experienced high degrees of acculturation, minority communities tended to retain significant degrees of structural separation. Prejudice and discrimination were identified as major barriers to integration of minorities.

Indian and Northern Affairs Canada. Website: www.aincinac.gc.ca/index_e.html. This Government of Canada website provides documentation on Canada's aboriginal peoples. The site provides information on aboriginal claims, self-government, lands, economic development, housing, education, and other issues. The site also provides up-to-date news as well as publications and links to related sites.

Multiculturalism—Canadian Heritage. Website: www.pch.gc.ca/multi/intro_e.shtml. This Government of Canada website provides documentation on multicultural initiatives, policy, programs, and legislation. The site also provides up-to-date news as well as publications and links to related sites.

Chapter 7

Canadian Ethnocultural Council. Website: www.ethnocultural.ca/about_cec.html. This website provides information about CEC, including news releases, publications, and links to related sites. Founded in 1980, the Canadian Ethnocultural Council (CEC) is a non-profit, non-partisan coalition of national ethnocultural umbrella organizations that, in turn, represent a cross-section of ethnocultural groups across Canada. The CEC's objectives are to ensure the preservation, enhancement, and sharing of the cultural heritage of Canadians, the removal of barriers that prevent some Canadians from participating fully and equally in society, the elimination of racism and the preservation of a united Canada.

Carroll, W.K., ed. 1997. *Organizing Dissent: Contemporary Social Movements in Theory and Practice*, 2nd rev. edn. Aurora, ON: Garamond Press. This compendium of articles includes key theoretical arguments and empirical case studies addressing a wide variety of contemporary social movements in Canada and elsewhere. William Carroll, one of Canada's foremost social scientists, has assembled several new contributions in this edition of his book, including theoretical discussions of the new social movements and on language, power, and politics.

Connor, W. 1993. *Ethnonationalism*. Princeton, NJ: Princeton University Press. In these essays, which have appeared over the course of the past three decades, the author argues that Western scholars and policy-makers have almost invariably underrated the influence of ethnonationalism and misinterpreted its passionate and non-rational qualities. Several of the essays have become classics: together they represent a rigorous and stimulating attempt to establish a secure methodological foundation for the study of a complicated phenomenon increasingly, if belatedly, recognized as the major cause of global political instability.

Melucci, A. 1980. 'The New Social Movements: A Theoretical Approach', *Social Science Information* 19, 2: 199–226. In this seminal article, Melucci introduced the term *new social movement* into the sociological lexicon. His distinctive approach gives analytical priority to the active construction of collective identity, emphasizing the importance of the psychology of collective emotional experiences. By giving precedence to culture, meaning, and identity, Melucci highlights the significance of communication and information, and argues that their globalization has created new spaces for collective action.

National Aboriginal Organizations in Canada. Website: www.aincinac.gc.ca/pr/info/info112_e.html. There are many national aboriginal organizations dedicated to advancing the political, social, economic, and cultural well-being of aboriginal peoples in Canada. This information sheet briefly describes the aims of some of the principal national aboriginal organizations. Further details about these organizations are provided through links to specific organizations.

National Council of Visible Minorities. Website: www.hcsc.gc.ca/ncvm/. The National Council of Visible Minorities (NCVM) in the federal public service was inaugurated on 27 October 1999 to further the following objectives: to maximize the potential of visible minorities to achieve equality in employment and employment opportunities that lead to career progression; and to encourage a climate in the public service that ensures that visible minorities reach their full potential and participate in all levels of decision-making.

Chapter 8

Access to Justice Network Canada. Website: www.acjnet.org/home.cfm. This informative website provides links to a variety of sites dealing with issues of law and social justice. Key linked sites include access to legislative materials by jurisdiction, Canadian Legal FAQs, CanLII—Canadian Legal Information Institute, Department of Justice Canada, and news releases about law and justice.

Berger, T.R. 1982. *Fragile Freedoms: Human Rights and Dissent in Canada*. Toronto: Irwin Publishing. In this collection of essays, Berger documents key events of Canadian history in which the voices of minority dissent have given impetus to constitutional debates eventuating in the Charter of Rights and Freedoms. In Berger's words, this is a book about minorities and dissenters, about their struggles, their victories, and their defeats. The book includes, among other key events, chapters on the Riel Rebellion, the expulsion of the Acadians, the internment of Japanese Canadians, the FLQ crisis, and the Nishga Indians and aboriginal rights.

Canadian Human Rights Law Centre. Website: www.wwlia.org/cahr.htm. This website provides links to federal and provincial human rights commissions and legislation, as well as to human rights tribunals and agencies. Most of these sites provide information on how to file a complaint. Links are also provided to human rights articles of general or specific interest and to some of the earliest human rights documents.

Canadian Legal Resources. Website: www.gahtan.com/cdnlaw/. This website provides links to a wide variety of Canadian legal sources including legislation, courts, and tribunals, cases, administration of justice, publications, and discussion groups.

Howe, R.B., and Johnson, D. 2000. *Restraining Equality: Human Rights Commissions in Canada*. Toronto: University of Toronto Press. *Restraining Equality* addresses the contemporary financial, social, legal, and policy pressures currently experienced by human rights commissions across Canada. Through a combination of public policy analysis, historical research, and legal analysis, the authors trace the evolution of human rights policy within this country and explore the stresses placed on human rights commissions resulting from greater fiscal restraints and society's rising expectations for equality rights over the past two decades.

Pentney, W. 1990. *Discrimination and the Law.* Toronto: Carswell. The original edition of this book was authored by the late M. Justice Walter Tarnopolsky; this second edition has been revised by William Pentney. This valuable reference tool provides a comprehensive review of human rights issues. The book includes a legal history of discrimination in Canada; definitions of discrimination and affirmative action; an exhaustive analysis of case law—from every board of inquiry, tribunal, or court, including illuminating comparisons to British and American practice and affording practical insights into the administration and enforcement of human rights legislation.

Chapter 9

Beaudoin, G.A., and Mendes, E., eds. 1995. *The Canadian Charter of Rights and Freedoms*, 3rd edn. Toronto: Carswell. Revised and expanded commentaries by Canada's foremost constitutional experts provide invaluable insight into application of the Charter by Canadian courts, and on its pervasive impact on the civil and criminal law. The third edition of this seminal work distills, analyzes, and interprets the many Charter decisions that have shaped the face of the legal system and provides guidance as to the likely developments in the future.

Cholewinski, R.I., ed. 1990. *Human Rights in Canada: Into the 1990's and Beyond.* Ottawa: Human Rights Research and Education Centre, University of Ottawa. This interdisciplinary collection of articles by Canadian scholars provides a useful source of materials dealing with a variety of human rights issues including equality rights, human rights, and the criminal justice system, language rights, multiculturalism, and overcoming racism and sexism.

Court Challenges Program of Canada. Website: www.ccppcj.ca/. The Court Challenges Program website provides information on all aspects of the program including its mission statement (About the Court Challenges Program) and links to the various sections including: Our Equality Rights in the Charter; Your Right to Equality; Equality Rights Panel Members; Constitutional Language Rights; Funding for Language Rights Cases; Funding for Equality Rights Cases and Key Sections of the Charter. Links also are provided to the key domains related to the program, including: Colour, Race, National Origin, Ethnicity; Aboriginal; Human Rights; Immigration; Judiciary; Laws and Legal Organizations.

Human Rights Program (Government of Canada). Website: www.pch.gc.ca/ddphrd/main_e.shtml. The mission of the Human Rights Program is to promote the development, understanding, respect for, and enjoyment of human rights in Canada. To accomplish this, the program undertakes educational and promotional activities involving the public, educators, non-governmental organizations, government departments, and others. This includes providing a selected number of grants and contributions to eligible organizations. The program is also responsible for coordinating, with provincial and territorial governments, the domestic implementation of international human rights instruments and the preparation of Canada's reports to the United Nations.

The website also provides links to other sites with valuable information on human rights, including: Human Rights in Canada; International Human Rights; Official Documents; Tribute to John Humphrey and other links.

Schabas, W.A. 1996. *International Human Rights Law and the Canadian Charter*, 2nd edn. Toronto: Carswell. This text discusses the use of international human rights treaties and declarations as well as decisions from international human rights tribunals in interpreting the scope of the Charter. It reviews the origins of international human rights law and discusses the theoretical justifications for the use of international human rights law before the Canadian courts. The applications of international rights law by Canadian courts are reviewed in a section-by-section analysis of the Charter. The text also includes a list of cases in which international authorities were cited.

Supreme Court of Canada. Website: www.scccsc.gc.ca/home/index_e.html. This website provides a wealth of information about the Supreme Court of Canada. The site provides access to Supreme court cases, judgments, news releases, and frequently asked questions.

GLOSSARY

aboriginal rights: refers to the collective right and title to aboriginal lands by aboriginal ethnic group based on collective use and occupancy 'from time immemorial'.

acculturation (cultural integration): refers to the process whereby selected objects, ideas, customs, skills, behaviour patterns, and values are exchanged among different ethnic communities. In this process, each population acquires from the other new cultural attributes that may eventually be absorbed into its own system. Viewed as part of a general learning process, acculturation refers to the process of learning those cultural ways of an ethnic community to which one does not belong, in much the same way as the concept *enculturation* or distinctive *ethnic socialization* refers to the broad process of learning the cultural patterns of the ethnic community to which one does belong.

adverse affect discrimination: refers to indirect, unintentional discrimination that has discriminatory results. For example, an employment rule made honestly and for sensible business can still be discriminatory, with regard to results. In Canada, the Supreme Court has decreed that adverse affect discrimination is as serious a human rights violation as is direct, intentional discrimination.

affirmative action: refers, in general terms, to a system of temporary measures of positive discrimination in favour of groups hitherto discriminated against; compensatory discrimination in favour of disadvantaged populations in the society. In Canada, affirmative action refers, in more specific terms, to programs consisting of temporary measures designed to eliminate systemic factors that prevent members of minority or other groups from competing equally with members of the majority for opportunities, usually in employment or education. The ultimate goal of such programs is to equalize opportunities for members of all populations in the society. In Canada, for the most part, programs of affirmative action are voluntary; in the United States, they are mandatory.

assimilation (structural integration): refers to the social processes whereby relations among members of different ethnic communities result in the participation of these individuals in ethnocultural institutions other than those of the ethnic community to which they belong. *Secondary structural integration* refers to the extent of participation by individuals and/or ethnic communities in the public institutions (that is, political, economic, educational) of the mainstream society, institutions predicated on the cultural norms of an ethnic group/s other than their own. *Primary structural integration* refers to the extent of participation by individuals and/or ethnic communities in the private ethnic institutions (that is, religious, social, and recreational institutions; friendship and kinship networks; family and marital alliances) of an ethnic community other than their own.

boundary-maintaining mechanisms: refers to the distinctive ethnocultural identities, loyalties, symbols, norms and practices that restrict interaction with ethnic outsiders and serve to maintain a high level of *social distance* between insiders and outsiders, thereby maintaining both a social psychological and structural boundary between ethnic communities.

categorical rights: are group-level claims predicated on perceived violations of fundamental individual rights (freedom, equality, dignity), rather than violations of collective cultural rights. Accordingly, they may be put forward by members of both ethnic and non-ethnic groups. Categorical rights claims may represent claims for redress against past, categorical discrimination on the basis of ethnicity, nationality, race, religion, age, sex, sexual orientation, mental or physical disability, or other grounds. Any representative of a specified social group or category who perceives that his/her group as a whole has experienced violations of the right/s to freedom, equal opportunity, or dignity on the arbitrary basis of (assumed) membership in the group, and has as a result suffered unfair disadvantage can make categorical rights claims.

collective cultural rights: are rooted in the diversity of the ethnocultures developed by different ethnic groups within humankind. Collective cultural rights are predicated on the fact that every human being is born not only into the human species, but also into a particular human population and ethnocultural community. Like human unity, cultural diversity is recognized under international human rights covenants as a characteristic feature of humankind. Collective human rights represent the principle of cultural diversity, the right of each of the various ethnic populations of humankind, ethnic community to develop and express the differentness of their unique cultures or blueprints for living. Taken together, individual and collective human rights represent the twin global principles of human unity and cultural diversity.

colonizer versus colonized: refers to the typical pattern of majority/minority relations that develops under colonialism between dominant/colonizers and dominated aboriginal peoples. A foreign, colonial power controls and exploits aboriginal populations by appropriating their lands and resources, and by violating their human rights and limiting their opportunities to such an extent that they become a marginalized segment of the developing society. Colonizers typically legitimize racist policies towards aboriginal minorities through the use of racist invalidation ideologies that stigmatize and dehumanize aboriginal minorities. Blauner (1972) contends that aborigines, unlike immigrants, are indigenous peoples, and 'people of colour' who have been subjected to a special pattern of internal colonization. First, they become part of a new larger society through coercion. As the case of Canada's First Nations well demonstrates, colonized peoples are conquered, enslaved, or pressured into movement. Second, colonized peoples are subject to various forms of unfree labour that restrict their mobility and power. Third, the cultural policy of the colonizer disrupts and ultimately destroys the aboriginal way of life (cultural genocide).

components of ethnicity (see **ethnicity**): include the biogeographical component of ancestry in conjunction with such sociocultural components as nationality, language, and religion. Common ancestry, in turn, is a multifaceted concept implying at least three components: biological descent from common ancestors; maintenance of a shared ancestral heritage (culture and social institutions); and attachment to an (actual or mythical) ancestral territory or homeland. These components provide the foundation for the (actual or assumed) distinctiveness of an ethnic category—a people classified as alike on the basis of ethnicity.

It is important to emphasize that all of the criteria used to identify specific components of ethnicity—whether by ethnic insiders or outsiders—are based on *actual* or *assumed* characteristics. The criterion of biological descent from common ancestors underlies physical distinctiveness. When this component of ethnicity is emphasized, we speak of a *racially defined* ethnic category. The criterion of attachment to an ancestral territory or homeland underlies distinctiveness deriving from national origin. When this component of ethnicity is emphasized, we speak of a *nationally defined* ethnic category. The criterion of maintenance of an ancestral heritage underlies sociocultural distinctiveness. When this component is emphasized, we speak of a *culturally defined* ethnic category. Frequently, the criterion of ancestral heritage emphasizes one sociocultural component such as language or religion. Thus, we speak of a *linguistically defined* or a *religiously defined* ethnic category, respectively.

Although these distinctions are useful in analysis, in reality a given ethnic category may be *socially constructed* on the basis of any one or any combination of these components in a given societal context. Moreover, because ethnicity is contingent on the prevailing social environment, criteria used for ethnic classification will vary with changing social conditions.

contention: minority protest in pursuit of corporate ethnic goals may take the form of contention, leading to movements for social and political reform, or of revitalization, leading to more radical, secessionist, or revolutionary movements.

contract compliance: refers to one of the alternatives to voluntary affirmative action already in use by the federal and some provincial governments in Canada. Although there is no comprehensive contract compliance legislation in Canada, the principle of contract compliance has become embedded in some Canadian statutes and embodied in regulations governing dealings of some governments with the private sector. Under contract compliance, any firm to which a government pays public funds for the purchase of goods or services must, as a condition of its contract, comply with the government's human rights requirements. In some cases, the requirement may simply be one of non-discrimination in employment and services. In other cases, however, the firm may be required to undertake a program of affirmative action. Companies with which governments do business may, for example, be required to take positive steps to redress any existing imbalance in what could be reasonably expected to be an equitable distribution of minority members throughout the ranks of their employees. Specific affirmative action programs constitute part of the contract with the government; thus, programs are carefully monitored by officers of human rights commissions. Failure to comply with the affirmative action provisions can result in penalties, which include, at least minimally, cancellation of the contract and exclusion of the firm from future government business.

contrast conceptions: refers to the characterization by a long-oppressed minority of the majority as evil perpetrators of human rights violations and the minority as virtuous victims of majority discrimination.

cultural discrimination: is a function of ethnic diversity in a socially stratified society. In a hierarchical, multiethnic society, only representatives of ethnic majority group(s) have the power to transform their ethnocentrism into cultural discrimination by imposing their cultural attributes, values, standards, and definitions of reality on all peoples in the society. For it is the normative imperatives of the dominant or majority ethnic group(s) that become sanctioned in law and incorporated into public institutional policies, thereby providing the moral and cultural guidelines for the whole society.

Cultural discrimination occurs when alternative ethnocultural moral imperatives are denied expression in public life. Cultural discrimination is thus built into the majority group(s)' requirement of minority acculturation, since this automatically denies the validity of minority ethnocultural alternatives.

discrimination: refers to biased acts or practices towards members of particular human groups that afford categorical advantage or disadvantage on the basis of unsubstantiated assumptions about their shared physical, cultural and/or behavioural characteristics.

discrimination of silence: refers to discrimination *by omission*. This occurs when laws, policies, and public practices fail to recognize and to afford protection against discrimination against particular social categories.

dominant/aboriginal relations (see **colonizers versus colonized**)

dominant/immigrant relations: refers to the patterns of majority/minority relations that develop between dominant ethnic groups in a society and newer immigrant ethnic groups. Although these patterns vary with changes in the character of ethnic immigrant groups and changing government policies towards them, Lieberson (1961) maintains that in the initial stages of ethnic stratification, relations between established dominant populations and newer immigrants are characterized by considerably less conflict than are relations between dominant and aboriginal populations. Unlike aboriginal peoples, immigrants cannot 'opt out' of the dominant economy since none of the aboriginal economic options are open to them. On the other hand, should immigrants become dissatisfied with their subordinate status and/or other life conditions in their new country, they may elect to leave, either to return to their home country or to migrate elsewhere. By way of contrast, aboriginal peoples are not likely to leave their aboriginal territories voluntarily, and their continued presence, together with their refusal to enter the dominant economy, provides a continuing source of conflict.

A second difference between dominant/aboriginal and dominant/ immigrant relations, posited by Lieberson, is that immigrants are under greater pressure to assimilate to dominant norms and do so more rapidly and extensively than do aboriginal peoples. The explanation lies, in large part, in the far greater degree of ethnocultural compatibility between dominant and immigrant populations than is found between dominant and aboriginal populations.

A third difference between the two patterns of interethnic relations relates to the control of immigration that ensures the ethnic hegemony of the established dominant groups over the newer immigrants. Immigrants perceived as posing a biological, cultural, or numerical threat to dominant superiority can be collectively restricted or excluded from entering the country. This strategy cannot be applied to aboriginal populations, however, since these populations were resident in the area long before the arrival of the now dominant groups.

double boundary (external and internal): refers to the interface between the internally and externally imposed, subjective and objective boundaries separating ethnic communities that restrict interaction with outsiders and serve to maintain a high level of *social distance* between insiders and outsiders. A critical subjective feature of the double boundary is that *identification by others*—whether or not it corresponds to *self-identification*—reinforces self-identification. Hence, ethnicity is a matter of a double boundary, a boundary from within, established by the ethnic socialization (enculturation) process and maintained by ethnic institutions, and a boundary from without, established by external barriers of exclusion and maintained in the process of interethnic relations. The *double boundary* that every ethnic group possesses indicates that no ethnic group can be completely understood without its relationship to other ethnic groups. Interethnic relations are the relationships between the two boundaries.

economic power: refers to the accumulation and means for accumulation of the valued material and technological goods or resources of society. Social indicators of economic power in Canadian society include wealth, property, income, education, and occupation. Non-Marxian sociologists often refer to this dimension of a stratified system as 'socio-economic class'. Scholars who favour a Marxian or quasi-Marxian approach to social scientific analysis emphasize economic control. The latter dimension of economic power is seen largely as a function of the ownership of the means of production in a society.

employment equity: refers to fairness in employment. The purpose of an employment equity program is to ensure that all equally qualified individuals have equal access to positions and that their qualifications are assessed in relation to the requirements of the position. The program seeks to eliminate any recruitment, selection, promotion, or training practices that have the effect of being discriminatory and to provide a workplace where individuals are treated with respect.

enculturation: or distinctive *ethnic socialization* refers to the broad process of learning the cultural patterns of the ethnic community to which one belongs.

enlightened and pernicious ethnocentrism: enlightened ethnocentrism seeks the self-interest of the in-group, but does so with due regard for the rights and interests of the out-group; pernicious ethnocentrism seeks the self-interest of the in-group at the expense of the rights and interests of outsiders.

enumerated grounds of discrimination: refers to the specified grounds of race, national or ethnic origin, colour, religion, sex, age, or mental or physical disability.

equality rights: enumerated versus analogous grounds: refers to the provisions of section 15 of Canada's Charter of Rights and Freedoms. The provisions are as follows:

15. (1) Every individual is equal before and under the law and has the right to the equal protection and equal benefit of the law without discrimination and, in particular, without discrimination based on race, national or ethnic origin, colour, religion, sex, age, or mental or physical disability.

(2) Subsection (1) does not preclude any law, program or activity that has as its object the amelioration of conditions of disadvantaged individuals or groups including those that are disadvantaged because of race, national or ethnic origin, colour, religion, sex, age, or mental or physical disability. [This provision allows for programs of affirmative action.]

Although there is general agreement among scholars that the non-discriminatory grounds of section 15 are 'open', that is, that claims can be put forward on **analogous grounds** by minorities not enumerated in its provisions, **enumerated** minorities are afforded *specified* protection for their human rights, while non-enumerated minorities have only *unspecified* protection.

ethnic boundary: refers to the ideological and structural barriers created by ethnic communities to keep insiders in and outsiders out.

ethnic category and **ethnic group:** the distinction between the concepts of ethnic category and ethnic group is between arbitrary, artificial categories of classification, designed for analytic purposes (conceptual constructs) or designed for statistical ends (numerical constructs)—ethnic category, and *sui generis* living communities, organized on an ethnic basis—ethnic group.

ethnic heterogeneity: refers to a pattern of majority/minority relations between dominant and immigrant groups characterized by the fragmentation or partialization of immigrant ethnicity and ethnic identity. Some areas of the immigrant's life may involve his or her ethnicity, while other areas may not. Typically, in the pattern of ethnic heterogeneity, ethnic ties are principally maintained in private relations of kinship and friendship. In the public sphere (work, politics, and so forth) the immigrant's relationships become de-ethnicized. Even within the boundaries of the immigrant ethnic community, personal networks and institutional affiliations are selectively chosen, and the various sets of ties and relationships activated by different members tend to become dissociated from one another. At the macro-level of the ethnic community, ethnic organizational structures may serve only limited aspects of social life (for example, recreational and religious).

ethnic integration: refers to the entire set of social processes whereby continuing interaction between members of different ethnic groups within a society leads to changes in the cultural content, structural form, and ethnic identities of the interacting individuals or groups.

ethnic segmentation: refers to a pattern of majority/minority relations in which each ethnic community tends to maintain both a high degree of ethnic closure and a high degree of ethnic compartmentalization. As employed by Breton, the concept of *ethnic closure* refers to the enclosure of social networks along ethnic lines, and the concept of *ethnic compartmentalization* refers to ethnic institutional or structural pluralism.

ethnic stratification: refers to a system of social stratification and majority/ minority relations based on *ethnic* criteria for social ranking.

ethnicity: refers to any arbitrary classification of human populations based on the biological factor of common ancestry in conjunction with cultural factors such as language or religion. Ethnicity, then, has both biological and cultural dimensions. It refers to one's biological ancestors, their ancestral territory or homeland, and their ancestral culture or ethnoculture. For members of existing ethnic communities, in addition to common ancestry that links members through time, there are the bonds of common kinship and ethnoculture that link living members of these communities.

ethnocentrism: refers to the ubiquitous tendency to view all the peoples and cultures of the world from the central vantage point of one's own particular ethnic group and, consequently, to evaluate and rank all outsiders in terms of one's own particular cultural standards and values.

ethnoculture: refers to the culture developed and maintained by a particular people or ethnic group. Ethnoculture refers to the distinctive ways of viewing and doing things—eating, dressing, speaking, worshiping, loving—shared by members of a particular ethnic community and transmitted by them from one generation to the next; it is the unique design for living of a particular ethnic group.

formal equality and substantive equality: formal equality prescribes identical treatment of all individuals regardless of their actual circumstances; substantive equality requires that differences among social groups be acknowledged and accommodated in laws, policies, and practices to avoid adverse impacts on individual members of the group. A substantive approach to equality evaluates the fairness of apparently neutral laws, policies, and programs in light of the larger social context of inequality, and emphasizes the importance of equal outcomes that sometimes require equal, standard treatment and sometimes different but equivalent treatment.

freedom, dignity, and equality: freedom to decide/political rights—the fundamental right of every human being to participate in the shaping of decisions affecting one's own life and that of one's society; dignity of person/social rights—the fundamental right of every human being to respect and dignity of person regardless of individual qualities and/or group membership; equality of opportunity/economic rights—the fundamental right of every human being to reasonable access to the economic resources that make meaningful decision-making and societal participation possible.

human rights principles: universal moral guidelines for human relations; the internationally sanctioned, universal human rights ideals and standards, to which all systems of justice should conform.

human rights statutes: refers to anti-discriminatory legislation enacted at both the federal and provincial levels in Canada. All Canadian jurisdictions have established Human Rights Commissions to administer anti-discriminatory legislation. In accordance with the legislation, the staff and commissions are required to enforce the acts, carry out research on human rights, and conduct public education programs. There are, however, significant differences in detail among current human rights statutes—in their enumerated grounds of discrimination, areas of application, and so forth. Nevertheless, statutes at the provincial and federal levels share fundamental similarities in content and administration. All the human rights statutes in Canada prohibit discrimination on the grounds of race, religion, colour, nationality or national origin, and sex. Discrimination on ethnic grounds is thereby prohibited in the broad sense of the term *racial* as outlined in the International Convention on the Elimination of All Forms of Racial Discrimination. All the statutes refer to both 'race' and 'colour' as well as to other terms relating to ancestral origin such as 'national extraction (or) origin', 'place of birth (or) origin', 'ancestry', 'ethnic origin', and 'nationality'. All of the statutes are designed to ensure equality of access to places, activities, and opportunities. Accordingly, they all prohibit discrimination in hiring, terms, and conditions of employment, job advertisements, job referrals by employment agencies, and membership in unions. Most also prohibit discrimination in professional, business, and trade associations. Both federal and provincial statutes prohibit discrimination in the provision of accommodation, services, and facilities to which the public has access. The provinces and territories prohibit discrimination in residential property rentals and sales; many also cover commercial properties.

human unity and human cultural diversity: refers to respectively the roots of **individual and collective human rights**

identificational integration: refers to the process whereby an ethnic community other than one's own comes to provide one's primary source of expressive/symbolic ties and roots, and also becomes one's primary reference group.

individual complaint-based procedure: refers to the current system of enforcement of human rights statutes in Canada. In all jurisdictions, the enforcement process typically begins with the submission of a complaint of discrimination to the commission by the alleged victim of discrimination or by interested private groups, third parties, or (in some cases) officers of the administering agency. Following the receipt of a complaint, the commission is required to conduct an investigation and conciliate the matter or affect a settlement, should sufficient grounds be established to justify the complaint. Terms of settlement vary, depending on the nature of the complaint, but these may require provision for accommodation, employment, and/or services previously denied. Other forms of redress commonly include recompense for the victim's financial loss and/or injury to dignity. In some cases, respondents also are required to undertake special (affirmative action or pay equity) programs to improve minority opportunity in their establishments.

Initially, those who are found to discriminate are given the opportunity to redress their ways by being confronted with the severity of the injury to the human dignity and economic well-being of the victim as compared with their own (real or anticipated) loss of comfort or convenience. However, if persuasion, conciliation, and efforts to effect a settlement fail, a board of public inquiry or tribunal may be ordered. The public aspect of the inquiry, especially where the events capture media attention, is considered to be an important component of the public education mandate of commissions. Ultimately, a discrimination complaint, if not settled to the satisfaction of both parties and/or the commission, may reach the courts. Some statutes empower commissions to bypass public inquiry and take cases directly to court. In any case, upon summary conviction, the discriminator may be subject to fines that, depending on the jurisdiction, may be as high as $25,000, or even higher.

individual discrimination: at the level of the individual, an act of discrimination may stem from conscious, personal prejudice.

individual human rights: fundamental individual

human rights are predicated on the inalienable right of each and every human being to freedom, equality, and dignity of person.

institutionalized discrimination: when an act of discrimination does not derive from the personal prejudice of the actor, but from the carrying out by the actor of the dictates of others who are prejudiced or of a prejudiced social institution, this form of discrimination is institutional discrimination.

institutionalized racism: refers to institutionalized forms of discrimination against ethnic minorities which provide the majority group(s) with legitimate *techniques of domination and social control*. Of all forms of institutionalized racism, *legal racism* provides the most powerful and pernicious instrument of domination and social control. The main legal and policy initiatives that have provided Canadian authorities with potent techniques of domination used to keep ethnic and racial minorities 'in their place' are the following: Denial of franchise, Control of Land Ownership and Use, Denial of Educational Opportunities, Denial of Employment Opportunities and Wages, Denial of Adequate Housing, Control of Communications Media, Control of Immigration and Persecution, Extermination, and Expulsion.

invalidation myths: falsified statements that allege that identified human populations are innately inferior or invalid (defective) with regard to particular human attributes; **invalidation ideologies:** unsubstantiated theories that are designed to give credibility to invalidation myths by providing *pseudo-scientific* or *pseudo-religious* 'evidence' for them. In general, invalidation ideologies—like ideologies of racism, sexism, and ageism—can be conceptualized as a set of beliefs, policies, and/or practices designed to justify and legitimate invalidation myths by fabricating theories that offer *pseudo-scientific* or *pseudo-religious* evidence for them.

legal rights: refers to rights based on the incorporation of human rights principles into law. Legal rights can be invoked by persons or groups who perceive that their human rights have been violated in order to seek redress for the alleged violation.

majority status: (or dominant social category) within any system of social stratification refers to the social category with superordinate social status at a given structural level or regional sector in the society, whose members wield the greatest degree of political, economic, and social power.

majority/minority relations: refers to inter-group relations based on group-level inequalities in political, economic, and social power within a society. As conceptualized by social scientists, these are inter-group relations predicated on demonstrable disparities in political, economic, and/or social power. They are *not* necessarily predicated on disparities in population numbers. This point differentiates the social scientific usage of the concepts of majority and minority (to refer to power disparities) from their political application and from their use in common parlance (to refer to numerical disparities).

marginalization: refers to a long-term consequence of systemic discrimination that creates a growing underclass consisting of members of various, severely disadvantaged minorities, including people of colour, persons with disabilities, and aboriginal peoples. These groups become permanently confined to the margins of society because the labour force cannot or will not accommodate them. Marginalization thus excludes whole groups of people from useful and meaningful participation in the society.

master status: refers to the phenomenon that occurs when one particular human attribute—race, ethnicity, gender, sexual orientation—comes to constitute a person's defining characteristic; when it comes to assume precedence over and above all one's other human attributes. In the context of majority/minority relations, social scientists ordinarily apply the concept of master status to explain the phenomenon that occurs when the inferiorized or stigmatized minority attribute comes to constitute members' overriding, defining characteristic; when it comes to assume precedence over and above all the other human attributes of minority members in the eyes of the majority audience. This conception of master status focuses on the way in which majorities create minorities through singling out particular attributes as the basis for inferiorization and categorical discrimination.

Another conception of master status focuses on how minorities react to inferiorization. When inferiorized or stigmatized minority attributes become perceived by minority members as central to their self-definition, when they come to provide the overriding basis for minority members' self-identification and group identification, then they have achieved a master status from the subjective point of view of the minority member. When this happens, minority members have come to *internalize* the inferiorizing labels imposed on them by the majority. They not only have become acutely conscious of their minority group status and identity, but also, they have superseded all other statuses and identities.

meritocracy: refers to a democratic society in which differential rewards are accorded on the basis of positional attainment of individuals on criteria of specified qualifications and demonstrated performance. Social stratification in a meritocracy derives from unequally rewarded social positions based on achieved criteria.

migrant superordination: refers to a pattern of majority/minority relations that emerges from contact between aboriginal peoples and early migrants.

minority ethnic protest movement: refers to a particular kind of social movement, one that arises in response to long-term, collective disadvantage and inferiorization of minorities, resulting from *racist-motivated* forms of discrimination. In broad terms, the goals of minority ethnic protest movements are twofold: 1) to eradicate the cultural and structural bases of minority oppression, diminution, and neglect in the society; and 2) to attain ethnocultural legitimacy, self-determination, and empowerment for the minority ethnic community. Minority protest in pursuit of corporate ethnic goals may take the form of contention, leading to movements for social and political reform, or of revitalization, leading to more radical, secessionist, or revolutionary movements.

minority rights movement: refers to a particular form and direction of collective minority protest. This type of social movement is most likely to emerge when minority discontent focuses on the inconsistency between declared societal ideals endorsing human rights principles and the non-implementation of these ideals in public institutions and in public practice. For example, as the case of Canada well illustrates, when governments begin to replace discriminatory social policies and laws with anti-discriminatory, human rights instruments, the expectations of minorities, the targets of discrimination, begin to rise. When minority expectations rise at a faster rate than actual achievements, the gap between expectations and achievements widens, and minority discontent escalates. These movements focus on demands that governments *implement, in policy and practice*, human rights guaranteed in legislation.

minority status: (or subordinate social category) refers to the *corresponding* social category (with regard to the same ranking criteria) with subordinate social status *relative to the majority*, and whose members wield a lesser degree of political, economic and/or social power.

models of ethnic integration: refers to the hypothetical outcomes of processes of ethnic integration for the constituent ethnic communities in the society. A two-way process of ethnic integration could take two forms: 1) the *fusion* of the original ethnic communities and the creation of a new, ethnically homogeneous society (amalgamation or melting pot); and 2) the retention and *federation* of the original ethnic communities and the creation of an ethnically heterogeneous, multiethnic, multicultural society (cultural pluralism or mosaic).

A one-way process of ethnic integration could take two forms: 1) the *absorption* of the weaker ethnic community by the stronger one, and the creation of an ethnically homogeneous society modelled upon the characteristics of the (original) stronger ethnic community (dominant conformity or absorption); and 2) the institutionalized and/or coerced *suppression* of the weaker ethnic community by the stronger one, and the creation of a caste-like society dominated and controlled by the stronger ethnic community (paternalism/colonialism).

multiple jeopardy thesis: refers to the thesis put forward by social scientific researchers to test the proposition that multiple minority status has both objective and subjective disadvantaging effects. The disadvantaging consequences of categorical discrimination on the basis of multiple criteria have thus been measured both in terms of reported fulfillment of life-needs and in terms of reported life-satisfaction.

multiple minority status: refers to the fact that a given individual may have minority status on the basis of more than one inferiorized or stigmatized human attribute.

nationality, national rights, and nationhood claims: both ethnicity and citizenship can provide bases for nationally defined sentiments and loyalties. As a criterion of ethnicity, the concept of nationality refers to the national, ancestral, and cultural origins associated with a particular ethnic ancestral territory or homeland. This multidimensional criterion of ethnicity underscores the political concept of nationhood. But ethnically defined nationality may or may not correspond to nationality based on *actual* country of birth or citizenship.

Where the two concepts of nationality correspond, that is, where the ancestral homeland is coterminous with the territorial enclave occupied by the ethnic community within the society, the criterion of nationality may give rise to nationhood claims based on national rights (in Canada, Franco-Quebecois and aboriginal nationhood claims).

the new ethnicity: refers to the shift of social scientific focus from the morphological characteristics of the internal cultures of ethnic groups to the dynamics of interethnic relations and of ethnic boundary maintenance. This new focus on ethnic group boundaries and boundary-maintaining mechanisms owes much to the seminal work of the anthropologist Fredrik Barth (1969), who argued that the old biocultural/territorial-isolate frame of reference could not account for the persistence of viable ethnic communities, despite continuing contact across ethnic boundaries. According to Barth, in order to explain ethnic group persistence in the face of the loss of territorial distinctiveness through migration, loss of cultural distinctiveness through culture contact, and loss of physical distinctiveness through changes in ethnic strain, we must shift our attention from the morphological characteristics of the internal cultures of ethnic groups to the dynamics of interethnic relations and of ethnic boundary maintenance. For Barth, the critical feature of ethnicity is the ethnic boundary, rather than the cultural *Gestalt* (content) within it. Barth does not imply that cultural differences are irrelevant; the point he emphasizes is that we cannot assume a simple, one-to-one correspondence between ethnic communities and cultural similarities. Alternatively, we must focus our attention only on those physical and cultural diacritica (bodily mutilations and decorations, names, songs, religious icons, military medallions, and the like) singled out by in-group members as paramount symbols of ethnicity. Barth also stressed the crucial importance, for boundary maintenance, of behavioural norms (such as endogamy) that restrict interaction with outsiders and serve to maintain a high level of *social distance* between insiders and outsiders.

the new racism: is a concept adopted by theorists who argue that, in order to maintain the status quo of racial-ethnic inequality in face of an anti-racist/egalitarian national ideology, majority authorities have shifted their ideological stance from a focus on inherent (biological) racial inferiority to a focus on 'natural' cultural difference. This shift, however, does not alter the fundamental premise of 'white racism', that of blaming the victim for social and economic problems perceived as a 'natural' consequence of group differences. Theorists such as Baker (1981) argue that the new racism is expressed in a language of innocence that disguises its insidious intent by framing its messages in a way that endorses 'folk' values of egalitarianism, social justice, and common sense.

new social movement: refers to increasingly emerging forms of collective action, giving precedence to culture, meaning, and identity. Melucci, who introduced the term *new social movement* in 1980, associated the concept with feminism, ecological radicalism, ethnic separatism, and other variants of 'identity politics' (identity and solidarity-seeking movements). Melucci's approach emphasizes the importance of the psychology of collective emotional experiences in the active construction of collective identity, and—especially in his 1996 work—highlights the significance of global communication and information, especially the Internet, in this process.

the old ethnicity: refers to the classic conception of ethnicity which, variously defined, equated race, culture, geography, and human identity. Ethnic groups were conceived as 'natural' populations born, living, and dying in a known geographical range. This perspective associated the long-term geographical and social isolation of involuntary human groups with their distinctive biological and cultural attributes. Conceptualized in this way, ethnic groups were seen as corporate entities, highly adapted to particular geographical environments, and uniquely capable of maintaining group membership and cultural continuity through time. In sum, ethnicity was conceived as an attribute of an organized and cohesive ethnic group whose members shared distinctive biocultural attributes that they transmitted from generation to generation through the processes of inbreeding (intraethnic mating) and enculturation (distinctive ethnic socialization). Based on these assumptions, ethnicity could be measured, objectively, in terms of the distinctive features—physiognomy, language, religion, art and artifacts, technology, and modes of social organization—characteristic of members of a given ethnic group.

ombudsman: refers to the official whose role is to facilitate the lodging of complaints by citizens against public administration and to make recommendations to governments. The office of the ombudsman is legally established, functionally autonomous, and external to the government administration. The ombudsman, in short, is an independent and non-partisan intermediary between citizens and their governments, who acts as an impartial investigator of citizen complaints against government administration. The institution of the ombudsman may be introduced at any or all levels of government.

Optional Protocol to the ICCPR: provides individual citizens with direct recourse to the United Nations. Persons who believe that their rights as specified in the Covenant have been violated can state their case before the UN Human Rights Committee. Such persons must first have exhausted all legal avenues within their own country. To date, Canada is one of only a small number of the nations signing the Covenant that has ratified the Optional Protocol. Cases brought forward under the Optional Protocol to the ICCPR show how the protection for human rights afforded under international human rights covenants provide avenues of redress against human rights violations for Canadian citizens beyond the Canadian legal system. These cases demonstrate how international pressure can be brought to bear on governments of signatory nations to amend or eliminate discriminatory laws that violate international human rights covenants.

patterns of ethnic majority/minority relations (see **colonizers versus colonized** and **dominant/immigrant relations)**

political power: refers to the ability of some people to control the life chances of others. The prime social indicator of political power, in a modern industrialized society such as Canada, is the attainment of strategic decision-making positions within major societal institutions. Through the attainment of these high-ranking positions, members of some social categories are able to make the crucial decisions that affect the life chances (opportunities and rewards) of others.

prejudice: refers to biased beliefs about and attitudes toward members of particular human groups, based on unsubstantiated assumptions about their shared physical, cultural, and/or behavioural characteristics.

purposive approach: refers to an holistic, historically-based, yet forward-looking approach to Charter interpretation. As currently adopted, the purposive approach requires that the Charter be viewed *as a whole* so that the meaning and scope of a particular right or freedom is consistent with and in part gleaned from, similar guarantees, usually found under the same heading in the Charter. This approach also requires the derivation of the underlying values that a specific right or freedom is intended to protect and an analysis of principles drawn from legal and broader, historical traditions which reflect these values in order to ensure that the interpretation of a particular right or freedom furthers its purpose. Moreover, the purposive approach requires that the interpretation adopted incorporate the forward-looking view appropriate for constitutional judgments and is sensitive to the future political, economic, and social implications of the decision.

race: refers to any arbitrary classification of human populations using biological measures such as observable physical traits and/or genetic indicators (gene frequencies for particular traits). It is very important to point out that this scientific definition of race is based solely on biological differences between human populations, and not on cultural or behavioural differences.

racialization: refers to the process of identification of a population, whether externally imposed or self-defined, by reference to physical and/or genetic criteria or by reference to the term *race*.

racism: a set of beliefs, policies, and/or practices predicated on the erroneous assumption that some human populations are inherently superior to others and that human groups can be ranked in terms of their members' innate (biological) superiority/ inferiority. A second erroneous assumption behind racism is that biology determines culture, temperament, and morality. Following from these premises, the diverse *socially constructed* populations of humankind are ranked in accordance with the presumed superiority/inferiority of their member's physical, cultural, and behavioural characteristics.

reference group: refers to that social category whose cultural standards provide the normative guidelines for one's behaviour and whose core values provide the ethical and status criteria used to evaluate and rank oneself and others. The reference group need not be the actual group to which one belongs.

revitalization: minority protest in pursuit of corporate ethnic goals may take the form of contention, leading to movements for social and political reform, or of revitalization, leading to more radical, secessionist, or revolutionary movements.

routinization of charisma: as coined by Max Weber, refers to the process through which the initial, personal power of a charismatic leader, drawing followers to a minority protest movement, is converted into the authority of office within a stable institutional framework.

Routinization of charisma is a critical issue in movement organization; for if it does not occur, leadership authority cannot be delegated and distributed to other personnel, and the movement itself may die with the death or failure of its original leader.

social construction of race and ethnicity: reflects the ideological, political, economic, and cultural biases of the ruling authorities of the society. Populations defined in terms of the social constructs of race and ethnicity are not merely categorized or classified in a statistical sense; they also are evaluated in terms of the values and standards established by majority authorities as the norms for all members of the society. It follows, then, that the social constructs of race and ethnicity are not in any way neutral or scientific classifications. Their social relevance, however, lies not in themselves, but in the use to which they can be put in the hands of majority authorities. When social constructs of race and/or ethnicity are used by majority authorities to rationalize differential treatment of populations so-classified, socially created 'race' becomes translated into the social reality of racism.

social distance: refers to the quantity and quality of social interaction among individuals or groups. The degree of social distance between members of different ethnic communities can be ascertained in terms of the number and variety of social relationships, as well as the degree of intimacy and personal involvement that characterizes the social relationships between insiders and outsiders. Since people tend to act in terms of their ethnocentric evaluations of themselves and others, social distance in relationships between insiders (intra-ethnic relations) tends to be minimized; whereas social distance in relationships between insiders and outsiders (interethnic relations) tends to be maximized. When social distance is high, social relationships among members of different ethnic communities tend to be of a categorical or impersonal nature, based on mutual utility. In this context, insiders relate to outsiders in terms of ethnic stereotypes rather than as individual personalities, because most people do not get close enough to outsiders to test the accuracy of their preconceived, unsubstantiated ethnic prejudices. On the other hand, when social distance is reduced and members of different ethnic communities interact more frequently and more informally, social relationships tend to become more intimate and more individualized. In this context, people become increasingly aware of the similarities, rather than the differences, between insiders and outsiders, while at the same time they become more conscious of individual differences among people categorized as outsiders. When this happens, members of different ethnic groups may come to relate to each other on a close, personal level without reference to ethnic stereotypes, but as social equals and as individual human personalities.

Insofar as ethnic boundaries are designed to keep insiders in and outsiders out, they serve to restrict interaction between ethnic communities and thus to maintain a high degree of social distance in interethnic relations. At the same time, ethnic boundaries serve to intensify interaction within ethnic communities, they thus serve to maintain a low degree of social distance in intraethnic relations.

social movement: refers to a social process through which substantial numbers of participants, expressing deep discontent with their life conditions in the prevailing society, attempt to bring about or to resist social change. It is a conscious effort to create new social and cultural frameworks or designs for living, or to restore old ones. Whatever its perceived source, discontent is expressed in a rejection of societal values, norms, and/or leaders and an attempt to find meaningful alternatives.

social power: refers to the social recognition of honour (dignity) accorded members of society by others on the basis of their particular status, that is, their culturally defined position in society.

social stratification: refers to the hierarchical structuring of society that ensues from the differential ranking of various social categories with regard to their members' degree of political, economic, and social power.

statutory versus Charter protection for minority rights:

1. Statutory human rights laws deal with claims of discrimination by and against private individuals or groups; the Charter deals with discrimination by governments (for example, discriminatory government laws and/or policies).
2. Statutory human rights legislation applies primarily to discrimination in employment, accommodation, and public services; the Charter applies to all areas under government jurisdiction.
3. Federal and provincial human rights commissions provide investigative services at no cost to the complainant, but individuals or organizations bringing complaints under the Charter must pay for the costs involved (for example, hiring a lawyer to defend the case in court). Because this is beyond the means of many persons, particularly members of disadvantaged minorities, the federal government provides some funding for selected Charter challenge cases, under the Court Challenges Program.

stereotype: refers to an overgeneralized, standardized image of a particular human group that amplifies selected physical, cultural, and/or behavioural characteristics and disregards others. A stereotype is, in essence, a distorted group image or 'picture in one's head', akin to the cognitive or ideological component of prejudice.

structural or systemic discrimination: refers to group-level inequalities that have become rooted in the system-wide operation of society as a long-term consequence of institutional discrimination against particular minorities. Unlike individual and institutional forms of discrimination, the structural or systemic form of discrimination cannot be attributed to prevailing prejudices (except, perhaps, with reference to their historical origins). Established, system-wide policies and practices in a society can have *unintended* yet pervasive discriminatory effects on disadvantaged minorities, by sustaining long-term, group-level inequalities.

techniques of domination: refers to institutionalized racism, *legal racism* being the most powerful and pernicious instrument of domination and social control. The main legal and policy initiatives that have provided Canadian authorities with potent techniques of domination used to keep ethnic and racial minorities 'in their place' are: denial of franchise, control of land ownership and use, denial of educational opportunities, denial of employment opportunities and wages, denial of adequate housing, control of communications media, control of immigration and persecution, extermination, and expulsion.

total integration: in the process of cultural integration (acculturation), total integration requires changes in the cultures, reference groups, and ethnic identities of the members of the interacting ethnic communities. At both the individual and collective levels, full acculturation assumes that members of ethnic communities are willing and able to acquire outsiders' cultural attributes, and that there are no barriers of individual, institutional, structural, or cultural discrimination that prevent them from so doing. In the process of secondary structural integration (secondary assimilation), total integration requires changes in the secondary institutions, membership groups, and group identities of members of interacting ethnic communities.

universality of human rights: in a world of widely varying cultures, this has been a controversial theme in international politics and law since the Universal Declaration of Human Rights was adopted in 1948. It has spawned a vigorous scholarly debate over the question of the normative and conceptual universality of human rights.

vertical mosaic: refers to Canada's system of ethnic stratification. The term comes from the title of John Porter's groundbreaking book, *The Vertical Mosaic* (1965), in which he described the nationwide hierarchical structure of the Canadian ethnic stratification system at that time. Based on the findings of a national survey conducted over a period of almost 10 years, Porter reported that members of Canada's various ethnic communities were differentially and unequally represented (in proportion to their numbers in the population) within the Canadian ethnic hierarchy. He suggested that Canada's ethnic hierarchy at the time consisted of three broad social categories: 1) Charter or founding populations (English and French), together with immigrants from the British Isles and those from Northern and Western European countries whose biocultural characteristics were similar to those of the charter populations, were disproportionately represented at the top, within the ranks of the majority or dominant social category. 2) Later immigrant populations, largely from Southern and Eastern European countries, whose biocultural characteristics diverged in varying degrees from those of the dominant populations, were found in the middle ranks among Canada's ethnic minorities. 3) Aboriginal populations (Indians, Inuit, and Métis), whose biocultural characteristics diverged most markedly from those of the dominant ethnic categories, were found at the bottom of Canada's ethnic hierarchy. At the time of Porter's study, Canada's aboriginal peoples constituted a racially stigmatized and structurally dependent ethnoclass having the lowest status of all minorities within the established ethnic hierarchy.

Porter noted that the vertical structure of the ethnic mosaic persisted, in much the same form, over time. Despite considerable upward and downward status mobility and inconsistency in the middle ranks, Porter pointed out that the ethnic composition of the very top ranks and that of the very bottom tended to remain relatively stable and consistent on the three dimensions of stratification (political, economic, and social power).

NOTES

Introduction

1. All current UN international human rights instruments are available from the website of the Office of the United Nations High Commissioner for Human Rights.
2. In 1989, the United Nations adopted the Second Optional Protocol to the International Covenant on Civil and Political Rights, aiming at the abolition of the death penalty.
3. The position on nationhood rights currently put forward by various aboriginal leaders throughout Canada holds that, before contact with European colonizers, aboriginal peoples were independent, self-governing nations with distinctive cultures. With colonization, their right to sovereignty was unjustly abrogated, their political institutions dismantled, and their cultures systematically decimated. Aboriginal representatives argue that Canada's 'First Nations' have an inherent right to self-government: It is a gift from their creator that has never been and can never be surrendered. As in the past, they assert their right to sovereignty and the right to create and administer their own, culturally distinctive political, economic, and social institutions (Frideres 1993: 416).

Chapter 1

1. This point will be elaborated in Chapter 3 in connection with our analysis of the differences between *sui generis* ethnocultural minorities and other kinds of minorities within human societies.
2. In fact, some scholars attribute this phrase to the earlier writings of H. Spencer (Banton 1967: 37).
3. Modern racism refers to the political use of racist ideologies to justify group discrimination through exclusion, subordination, exploitation, and genocide.
4. Fuelling the current fire of condemnation of Rushton as an out and out racist is the fact that he has promoted his theories—most recently, in his article *Race as a Biological Concept*—on well-known racist websites such as the David Duke WebPage (www.duke.org/) and the FreedomSite (www.freedomsite.org/). It should also be noted that Rushton reportedly received $240,000 in funding for his research from the Pioneer Group, an openly racist organization dedicated to 'racial betterment' through such techniques as selective genetic breeding (eugenics). He thanks this group for their support in the preface to the 1999 special abridged edition of his 1995 book.

   With regard to the latter, I wish to add a personal note. I received a complimentary copy of the 1999 edition from Professor Rushton. To my dismay, I discovered that this edition is unsourced. Yet it was sent to a fellow academic . . .

Chapter 3

1. For a thorough and intellectually incisive overview and analysis of the debates, see D.K. Stasiulis, 'Theorizing Connections: Gender, Race, Ethnicity and Class', in P.S. Li, ed., *Race and Ethnic Relations in Canada* (Toronto: Oxford University Press, 1990).
2. In a later section of this chapter, I will address the issues of multiple minority status and the multiple jeopardy thesis in some detail.
3. Wirth's definition of a minority reads as follows: 'We may define a minority as a group of people who, because of their physical or cultural characteristics, are singled out from the others in the society in which they live for differential and unequal treatment and who therefore regard themselves as objects of collective discrimination' (1945: 347).
4. See, especially, *Canadian Ethnic Studies*: special issues on *Ethnicity and Femininity* 13, 1 (1981) and *Ethnicity and Aging* 15, 3 (1983); Gee and Kimball 1987; and Driedger and Chappell 1987.

Chapter 4

1. Elsewhere, I have attempted to demonstrate that the concept of collective minority rights can (and should) be extended to include non-ethnic minorities whose members have developed and sustained viable and distinctive subcultures and communities (e.g., gays and lesbians in large urban centres of Canada); see Kallen 1989: 171–6.
2. Early French/English differences in patterns of majority/minority relations with aboriginal peoples notwithstanding, Patterson (1972) and Wade (1970), among others, have argued that the French were far more assimilationist than the English, seeking to absorb, rather than to subordinate (or exterminate) the aboriginal population. One outcome of this policy was the creation of the Métis population.
3. Lieberson's use of the term *indigenous* to refer first to aboriginal populations and second to established, dominant migrants (in the common sense of 'native' inhabitants) is confusing. Our analysis will substitute the term *established migrant* for *indigenous* in the

second sense of the term; *aboriginal* will be used in place of *indigenous*, in the first sense of the term.

4. Lieberson's model does not address the special status of refugees. According to the 1951 UN Convention on Refugees, refugees are defined as persons with a well-founded fear of persecution by reason of race, religion, nationality, membership in a social group or political opinion, who are outside their country of nationality or habitual residence and who are unable or unwilling to return.
5. Although the Beothuk example is regarded as the classic case of genocide in the Canadian context, historical evidence now indicates that European-introduced diseases played an important part in the demise of this population (see Marshall 1981).
6. For readers who wish to pursue this subject in greater detail, there are a number of key works available. Recommended are: Adachi 1976; Broadfoot 1977; La Violette 1948; Sunahara 1979; and Sunahara 1981; see also *From Racism to Redress: The Japanese Canadian Experience*, CRRF 2002.

Chapter 5

1. This observation notwithstanding, it should be noted, that even in the early period, the Protestant/Catholic division subsumed different ethnicities under each religious rubric.
2. The difficulty in finding a multipurpose term that is both succinct and precise in its reference to the ethnically dominant, white, English-speaking, Christian Canadian of British or Northwest European origin, has led scholars to employ such inaccurate terms as WASP (White Anglo Saxon Protestant); WACP (White Anglo Celtic Protestant) and the like. For the sake of simplicity, in this connection, we will employ the term *Anglo-Canadian* in those contexts where English/French differences are relevant; the broader term *Euro-Canadian* will be used otherwise.
3. While the focus of this book is on *ethnic* minorities, it is important to note that non-ethnic minorities, like persons with disabilities, women, aged, gays and lesbians, and others, can make similar claims on the basis of categorical human rights.
4. There were also a number of peace and friendship treaties negotiated between Crown representatives and aboriginal leaders, but only the land cession treaties abrogated aboriginal title to the land.
5. Bill C-31 redefined Indian status and created new categories of Indian. Some of the key changes introduced by Bill C-31 will be discussed in the following section of this chapter. However, we will not attempt to address all the complexities of reinstatement and of transmitting one's status, which vary for different categories of claimants. For a detailed discussion of these issues, the reader is referred to Frideres (1993: 34–8).

Chapter 6

1. In the North American context, the classic statement concerning these models is provided by Gordon (1964). Palmer (1976) provides a critical review of the scheme with particular relevance for Canada.
2. In Canada, Sir Wilfrid Laurier made a strikingly similar analogy, albeit in British cultural terms. He pictured the Canadian mosaic in terms of the Gothic architecture of England—as a cathedral of marble, oak, and granite with each element distinct, yet molded into a harmonious whole (Yusyk 1967: 7).
3. The arguments in the section to follow represent a distillation of the author's published commentary on multiculturalism. For further elaboration, see Kallen 1982, 1987, and 1990.
4. *Report of the Royal Commission on Bilingualism and Biculturalism. Book IV: The Cultural Contribution of the Other Ethnic Groups* (Ottawa: Information Canada, 1970).
5. Statement of Prime Minister Trudeau, 8 Oct. 1971, House of Commons, *Debates*.
6. Kymlicka presents a documented counter-argument in support of multiculturalism in 'Immigrants, Multiculturalism and Canadian Citizenship,' paper presented at the symposium on Social Cohesion Through Social Justice, Canadian Jewish Congress, Ottawa, 2 Nov. 1997.
7. Because the model was originally conceived within the North American societal context in which the dominant population was ethnically categorized as Anglo-Saxon, the particularized concept Anglo-conformity was employed to refer to the broader notion of dominant conformity.
8. Emphasis in italics is that of the author. While Maclean's view indicates that he considered the aboriginal peoples to be human beings as such, the tone of the book suggests they were still somewhat childlike and inferior in nature.
9. The concept *total institution* refers to a physical and social environmental context in which the lives and destinies of insiders are completely controlled and regulated by more powerful outsiders. The concept had its origins in the literature on physically confined populations, in jails, mental institutions and the like, which documents the paternalistic model of treatment and its self-fulfilling outcome—a syndrome of social and psychological dependency; see Gove (1976).

Chapter 7

1. A notable exception is provided in the case of a small number of religious sectarian communities, such as the Hutterites, who refuse outside funding which they perceive as unwanted interference of outsiders in their internal affairs. This point is elaborated further in connection with our discussion of minority religious rights in Chapter 5.
2. For purposes of our analysis, we will refer to these three movements as: 1) Franco-Québécois Independence; 2) multiculturalism; and 3) Aboriginal Nationhood.
3. Morris and Lanphier (1977) provide a comprehensive account of the various options to Quebecois independence. Their conceptual analysis is framed in terms of a threefold classification of rights (individual, collective, and cultural), which in several ways parallels the author's distinction between individual, categorical, and collective (cultural) rights, respectively. However the territorial basis of aboriginal and national rights of aboriginal peoples and charter groups is not differentiated or included in their conceptual design.
4. A brief recapitulation of her argument is given here; however, the entire selection is recommended reading.
5. The literature on the evolution of Quebecois nationalism in Canada abounds. The following selections are particularly recommended: Rioux 1971; Milner and Milner 1973; McRoberts and Posgate 1976; and Dion 1976. For readers who wish to pursue this topic further, excellent coverage of the 'National Question' can be found in a special issue on Quebec of the *Canadian Review of Sociology and Anthropology* 15, 2 (1978). This issue also contains a well-selected bibliography.
6. Bernier (1981) takes a somewhat different view, but arrives at the same conclusion with regard to contemporary Quebecois nationalism. He argues that capitalistic developments since the Duplessis era eroded the power base of the reactionary petty bourgeoisie class that Duplessis purportedly represented. Contemporary Quebecois nationalism, consequent on modern, capitalistic developments, focuses on the necessity to create a new nation-state within Quebecois national territory—the state of Quebec. Unlike its reactionary predecessor, contemporary nationalism is a forward-looking activist movement whose ideology is promoted by a new political-oriented, national bourgeoisie and whose main instrument is the Quebec state bureaucracy.
7. Lévesque took comfort in the fact that, despite considerable support for federalism in some ridings, overall it was clearly the non-French Quebecers who won the day for the federalists.
8. For the interested reader, these debates are discussed in detail in the 1995 edition of this book; see Kallen (1995: 204–10).
9. As employed here, the term *Quebecois* refers to French-speaking residents of the province. *Quebecer* is used to describe all residents: French-speaking, English-speaking, and those who have a different language as a native tongue.
10. A recent (1999) decision by the UN Committee on the International Covenant on Civil and Political Rights (ICCPR), upheld the complaint of religious discrimination brought forward under the Optional Protocol by a private citizen of Canada, resident in Ontario. Mr A.H. Waldman, a person of the minority Jewish faith, claimed that he was a victim of a violation of several articles under the ICCPR because he does not receive funding for his children's private (Jewish) religious education equitable to that which is provided for those of the minority Roman Catholic faith. This case, and its implications for minority religious education in Canada, will be discussed more fully in Chapter 9.
11. For a comprehensive overview of the historical foundation for aboriginal peoples collective rights claims based on aboriginal, treaty and national group rights, see Frideres (1993: chs. 3, 4, 11, and 12).

Chapter 9

1. The analysis of the Charter's protection for minority rights in the section to follow has been adapted from my 1988 article 'The Meech Lake Accord: Entrenching a Pecking Order of Minority Rights', *Canadian Public Policy: The Meech Lake Accord*, Supplement, Sept. 1988. For a broader analysis of the constitutional issues relating to both ethnic and non-ethnic minorities, together with a full listing of sources drawn on, the reader is referred to my original work.
2. A detailed analysis of the debates over the provisions of both proposed Accords is provided in the 1995 edition of this book. The interested reader is referred to Kallen (1995: 255–9).

REFERENCES

Abella, Judge R. 1984. *Equality in Employment: A Royal Commission Report*. Ottawa: Supply and Services Canada.

Aboriginal Justice Learning Network (AJLN). [Cited 13 June 2002.] canada.justice.gc.ca/en/ps/ajln/about.html

Abouchar v. Metropolitan Toronto School Board et al. OHRC. 1999 Case Summaries. [Cited 25 January 2002.] www.ohrc.on.ca/english/cases/index.shtml

Adachi, K. 1976. *The Enemy That Never Was*. Toronto: McClelland & Stewart.

Alberta Advisory Council on Women's Issues. 1995. In *Family Violence Prevention Division: Breaking the Links between Poverty and Violence against Women*. Ottawa: Health Canada, 1996.

Albrecht, G.L., ed. 1976. *The Sociology of Physical Disability and Rehabilitation*. Pittsburgh: University of Pittsburgh Press.

Anderson, A.B. 1967. 'Anti-Semitism and Jewish Identity in Montreal'. MA thesis (New School for Social Research).

Anderson, A.B., and Driedger, L. 1980. 'The Mennonite Family: Culture and Kin in Rural Saskatchewan'. In Ishwaran, ed. (1980): 161–80.

Anderson, A.B., and Frideres, J.S. 1981. *Ethnicity in Canada: Theoretical Perspectives*. Toronto: Butterworths.

Anderson, G.M. 1979. 'Spanish and Portuguese-speaking Immigrants in Canada'. In Elliott, ed. (1979): 206–19.

Anderson, W.H., and Williams, B.M. 1983. 'TV and the Black Child: What Black Children Say About the Shows They Watch', *The Journal of Black Psychology* 9, 2: 27–42.

Andrews v. Law Society of British Columbia [1989] 1 S.C.R. 143, (1989), 56 D.L.R., (4th) 1, [1989] 2 W.W.R. 289.

Anti-Defamation League (ADL) website. [Cited 28 October 2001.] www.adl.org

Anti-Semitic Incidents Rise in Canada in 2000 [press release]. B'nai Brith. 20 February 2001. [Cited 28 October 2001.] www.bnaibrith.ca/press4/pr01022008.htm

Aryan Nations [press release]. ADL. 2 March 1998. [Cited 24 October 2001.] www.adl.org/presrele/neosk_82/aryan_nations_82.asp

Asch, M. 1984. *Home and Native Land: Aboriginal Rights and the Canadian Constitution*. Toronto: Methuen.

Ashworth, M. 1979. *The Forces Which Shaped Them*. Vancouver: New Star Books.

Baker, Martin. 1981. *The New Racism: Conservatives and the Ideology of the Tribe*. London: Junction Books.

Bagehot, W. 1873. *Physics and Politics, or Thoughts on the Application of Principles of 'Natural Selection' and 'Inheritance' to Political Society.*

Bakan, A., and Kobayashi, A. 2000. *Employment Equity Policy in Canada: An Interprovincial Comparison*. Ottawa: Status of Women Canada.

Bandura, A. 1973. *Aggression: A Social Learning Analysis*. Englewood Cliffs, NJ: Prentice-Hall.

Banton, M. 1967. *Race Relations*. London: Tavistock.

Barcus, F.E. 1983. *Images of Life on Children's TV*. Westport, CT: Praeger.

Barker, M. 1981. *The New Racism*. London: Junction Books.

Barrie, M., et al. 1982. *Images of Women: Report of the Task Force on Sex-Role Stereotyping in the Broadcast Media*. Hull, QC: Supply and Services Canada.

Barrett, S.R. 1987. *Is God a Racist? The Right Wing in Canada*. Toronto: University of Toronto Press.

Barth, F. 1969. *Ethnic Groups and Boundaries*. Boston: Little Brown.

Bear, S. 1987. *Enough Is Enough: Aboriginal Women Speak Out*. Toronto: The Women's Press.

Beaudoin, G., and Ratushny, F., eds. 1989. *The Canadian Charter of Rights and Freedoms*. Toronto: Carswell.

Beckton, C.F. 1987. 'Section 27 and Section 15 of the Charter'. In Canadian Human Rights Foundation (CHRF) (1987): 1–14.

Behiels, M.D., ed. 1989. *The Meech Lake Primer: Conflicting Views of the 1987 Constitutional Accord*. Ottawa: University of Ottawa.

Bendix, R., and Lipset, S.N., eds. 1953. *Class, Status and Power*. Glencoe, IL: Free Press.

Bennett, J.W. 1969. *Plains People: Adaptive Strategy and Agrarian Life on the Great Plains*. Glencoe, IL: Adline.

———, ed. 1975. *The New Ethnicity: Perspectives From Ethnology*. New York: West.

Berger, Mr Justice T.R. 1977. *Northern Frontier, Northern Homeland: A Report of the Mackenzie Valley Pipeline Inquiry.* Vol. 1. Ottawa: Supply and Services Canada.

Berkeley, H., Gaffield, C., and West, W.G., eds. 1978. *Children's Rights: Legal and Educational Issues*. Symposium Series 9. Toronto: Ontario Institute for Studies in Education.

Bernier, B. 1981. 'Construction d'un espace national et identité ethnique: le cas du Quebec 1930–1970', *Culture* 1, 1.

Berry, J.W., Kalin, R., and Taylor, D.M. 1977. *Multiculturalism and Ethnic Attitudes in Canada*. Ottawa: Supply and Services Canada.

Betcherman, L.R. 1975. *The Swastika and the Maple Leaf*. Toronto: Fitzhenry & Whiteside.

Binavince, E.S. 1987. 'The Juridical Aspects of Race Relations', paper presented at Canada 2000 Conference, 1 November, Carleton University, Ottawa.

Bissoondath, N. 1994. *Selling Illusions: The Cult of Multiculturalism in Canada*. Toronto: Penguin.

Black, W., and Smith, L. 1989. 'The Equality Rights'. In Beaudoin and Ratushny, eds (1989): ch. 14.

Blauner, R. 1972. *Racial Oppression in America*. New York: Harper & Row.

Block, E., and Walker, M.A., eds. 1981. *Discrimination, Affirmative Action and Equal Opportunity*. Vancouver: The Fraser Institute.

Boldt, M., and Long, J.A., eds. 1985. *The Quest for Justice: Aboriginal Peoples and Aboriginal Rights*. Toronto: University of Toronto Press.

Borovoy, A.A. 1988. *When Freedoms Collide: The Case for Our Civil Liberties*. Toronto: Lester Orpen & Dennys.

Bourassa, R. 1971. 'Objections to Multiculturalism'. Open letter to Prime Minister Trudeau in *Le Devoir*, 17 November.

Bozonelos, P. 'The Strong Smell of Sweat in Our Own Backyards'. *Varsity Feature* [online]. 15 November 1999. [Cited 13 November 2001.] www.varsity.utoronto.ca/archives/120/nov09/feature/thestrong.html

Breton, R. 1964. 'Institutional Completeness of Ethnic Communities and the Personal Relations of Immigrants', *American Journal of Sociology* 70, 2: 193–205.

———. 1978. 'The Structure of Relationships between Ethnic Collectivities'. In Driedger, ed. (1978): 55–73.

Breton, R., Isajiw, W.W., Kalbach, W.W., and Reitz, J.G. 1990. *Ethnic Identity and Equality: Varieties of Experience in a Canadian City*. Toronto: University of Toronto Press.

Broadfoot, B. 1977. *Years of Sorrow, Years of Shame*. Toronto: Doubleday.

Brody, H. 1975. *The People's Land: Eskimos and Whites in the Eastern Arctic*. Middlesex, UK: Penguin.

Brotz, H. 1980. 'Multiculturalism in Canada: A Muddle', *Canadian Public Policy* 6, 1: 41–6.

Brym, R.J., Shaffir,W., and Weinfeld, M., eds. 1993. *The Jews in Canada*. Toronto: Oxford University Press.

Bryne, N., and Quarter, J., eds. 1972. *Must Schools Fail?* Toronto: McClelland & Stewart.

Buchignani, N.L. 1977. 'A Review of the Historical and Sociological Literature on East Indians in Canada', *Canadian Ethnic Studies* 9, 1: 86–108.

Bullivant, B.M. 1979. *Pluralism, Teacher Education and Ideology: Report Presented to the Education Research and Development Committee*. Canberra (June).

Burnet, J. 1975. 'Multiculturalism, Immigration and Racism', *Canadian Ethnic Studies* 7: 35–9.

———. 1976. 'Ethnicity: Canadian Experience and Policy', *Sociological Focus* 9, 2: 199–207.

———. 1978. 'The Policy of Multiculturalism within a Bilingual Framework: A Stock-taking', *Canadian Ethnic Studies* 10, 2: 107–13.

———. 1981. 'The Social and Historical Context of Ethnic Relations'. In Gardner and Kalin, ed. (1981): 17–35.

Caibaiosai, L.R. 1970. 'The Politics of Patience.' In Waubageshig, ed. (1970).

Cairns, A., and Williams, C., eds. 1986. *The Politics of Gender, Ethnicity and Language in Canada*. Toronto: University of Toronto Press.

Campbell, M. 1973. *Halfbreed*. Toronto: McClelland & Stewart.

Canada. 1928. Parliament. House of Commons. *Debates*. Ottawa: Queen's Printer. Statement made by R.B. Bennett on 7 June.

———. 1966. *Report to the Minister of Justice of the Special Committee on Hate Propaganda in Canada*. Committee chair was M. Cohen. Ottawa: Queen's Printer.

———, Government of. 1969. *[The White Paper] Statement of the Government of Canada on Policy*. Ottawa: Queen's Printer.

———. 1970. *Report of the Royal Commission on Bilingualism and Biculturalism. Book IV: The Cultural Contribution of the Other Ethnic Groups*. Ottawa: Information Canada.

———. 1971. Parliament. House of Commons. *Debates*. Ottawa: Supply and Services Canada. Statement made by Prime Minister P.E. Trudeau on 8 October.

———. 1984a. Parliament. House of Commons. *Equality Now! Report of the Special Committee on Visible Minorities in Canadian Society*. [Ottawa]. Committee chair was B. Daudlin.

———. 1984b. *INAC Response of the Government to the Report of the Special Committee on Indian Self-Government* (5 March). Ottawa: Indian affairs and Northern Development.

———. 1984c. *Multiculturalism: Building the Canadian Mosaic, Report of the Standing Committee on Multiculturalism* (June). [Ottawa]. Committee chair was G. Mitges.

———. 1985. Parliament. House of Commons. Bill C-31: An Act to Amend the Indian Act.

———. 1987a. Parliament. House of Commons. Bill C-93: An Act for the preservation and enhancement of multiculturalism in Canada. The Secretary of State of Canada, 22427-27-11-87 [enacted 1988].

———. 1987b. Meech Lake Accord. Constitutional Amendment, 1987 [defeated 23 June 1990].

———. 1992. Charlottetown Accord. Consensus Report on the Constitution [defeated 26 October 1992].
———. Department of Justice, 2000. [Cited 24 May 2002.] canada.justice.gc.ca/en/dept/pub/guide/appendix_C.htm
———. 2002. Parliament. House of Commons. *Building a Nation: Report of the Standing Committee on Citizenship and Immigration* (March). Committee chair was Joe Fontana, MP. [Cited 4 June 2002.] www.parl.gc.ca/InfoComDoc/37/1/CIMM/Studies/Reports/cimmrp04e.htm
Canadian Bar Association. 1988. *Aboriginal Rights in Canada: An Agenda For Action*. Committee Report [Ottawa].
Canadian Bill of Rights. 1960. An Act passed by the Parliament of Canada and assented to on 10 August.
Canadian Centre for Policy Alternatives. *CCPA Monitor* (March 1999).
Canadian Council on Children and Youth. 1978. *Admittance Restricted: The Child as Citizen in Canada*.
Canadian Council of Christians and Jews (CCCJ). *Survey on Public Attitudes Toward Ethnic Diversity*. 1995. [Cited 5 November 2001.] www.interlog.com/~cccj/survey/1995/Default.htm
Canadian Ethnocultural Council. 1989. 'A Dream Deferred: Collective Equality For Canada's Ethnocultural Communities'. In Behiels, ed. (1989): 335–48.
Canadian Heritage. 1997. *Multiculturalism: Respect, Equality, Diversity; Program Guidelines*. Ottawa: Multiculturalism Canada.
Canadian Human Rights Commission (CHRC). 1979. *Discrimination in Canada* (September) [Ottawa].
———. 1996. 'Hate Messages'. *Annual Report 1996*. [Cited 9 February 2002.] www.chrcccdp.ca/arra/ar1996/casee.html
———. 1997a. *Canadian Human Rights Commission Legal Report: National Capital Alliance on Race Relations v. Health Canada*. [Cited 13 January 2002.] www.chrcccdp.ca/arra/ar1997/ l_97toc_e.html
———. 1997b. *Canadian Human Rights Commission Legal Report: Richmond v. Canada (A.G.)*. [Cited 9 January 2002.] www.chrcccdp.ca/arra/ar1997/l_97toc_e.html
Canadian Human Rights Foundation (CHRF). 1987. *Multiculturalism and the Charter: A Legal Perspective*. Toronto: Carswell.
Canadian Human Rights Law Centre. [Cited 13 June 2002.] www.wwlia.org/ca-hr.htm
Canadian Panel on Violence against Women. 1993. *Changing the Landscape: Ending Violence—Achieving Equality*. Ottawa: Minister of Supply and Services.
Canadian Race Relations Foundation (CRRF). 2001a. 'Canada's Immigration Policies: Contradictions and Shortcomings', *CRRF Perspectives: Focus on Immigration and Refugee Issues* (autumn/winter). [Cited 3 June 2002.] www.crr.ca/en/Publications/ePubHome.htm
———. 2001b. *Racism in Our Schools. Report of the CRRF*. [Cited 2 November 2001.] www.crr.ca/en/
———. 2001c. *Racism in Policing. Report of the CRRF*. [Cited 28 October 2001.] www.crr.ca/en/Publications/ePubHome.htm
———. 2001d. *Unequal Access: A Canadian Profile of Racial Differences in Education, Employment and Income*. [Cited 24 October 2001.] www.crr.ca/EN/MediaCentre/NewsReleases/eMedCen_NewsRe20010110.htm
———. 2002. *From Racism to Redress: The Japanese Canadian Experience*. [Cited 5 January 2002.] www.crr.ca/en/Publications/ePubHome.htm
Canadian Review of Sociology and Anthropology. 1978. 15, 2 (Special Issue).
Cardinal, H. 1969. *The Unjust Society*. Edmonton: Hurtig.
———. 1977. *The Rebirth of Canada's Indians*. Edmonton: Hurtig.
Carmichael, S., and Hamilton, C. 1967. *Black Power: The Politics of Liberation in America*. New York: Random House.
Carstens, P. 1981. 'Coercion and Change.' In Ossenberg, R., ed. (1971).
Case, F.I. 1977. *Racism and National Consciousness*. Toronto: Plowshare Press.
Cerna, C.M. 1994. 'Universality of Human Rights and Cultural Diversity: Implementation of Human Rights in Different Socio-Cultural Contexts', *Human Rights Quarterly* 16: 740–52.
Chamberlain, H.S. 1899. *Foundations of the Nineteenth Century*.
Chenier, N.M. 1995. *Suicide Among Aboriginal People: Royal Commission Report*.
Chevrier, M. 1996. *Canadian Federalism and the Autonomy of Quebec: A Historical Viewpoint*. [Cited 20 December 2001.] www.mri.gouv.qc.ca
Cholewinski, R.I., ed. 1990. *Human Rights in Canada: Into the 1990s and Beyond*. Ottawa: Human Rights Research and Education Centre, University of Ottawa.
CIC (Citizenship and Immigration Canada). 2000. *Canada's Immigration Law* [online]. [Cited 2 February 2002.] cicnet.ci.gc.ca/english/pub/immlaw.html
Clark, S.D., Grayson, J.P., and Grayson, L.M. 1975. *Prophecy and Protest: Social Movements in Twentieth-Century Canada*. Toronto: Gage.
Clement, W. 1975. 'Access to the Canadian Corporate Elite', *Canadian Review of Sociology and Anthropology* 12, 1: 33–52.

Collins, D. 1979. *Immigration: The Destruction of English Canada*. Richmond Hill, ON: BMG Publishing.
Condon, R.G. 1987. *Inuit Youth: Growth and Change in the Canadian Arctic*. London: Rutgers University Press.
Connor, W. 1978. 'A Nation Is a Nation, Is a State, Is an Ethnic Group, Is a . . .', *Ethnic and Racial Studies* 1, 4.
———. 1993. *Ethnonationalism*. Princeton NJ: Princeton University Press.
Coon, C.S. 1962. *The Origin of Races*. New York: Knopf.
———. 1965. *The Living Races of Man*. New York: Knopf.
Corpus. 1979. *The Canadian Family Tree: Canada's Peoples*. Ottawa: Supply and Services Canada.
Costa, E., and Di Santo, E. 1972. 'The Italian-Canadian Child, His Family, and the Canadian School System'. In Bryne and Quarter, eds (1972).
Curtis, J.E., and Scott, W.G., eds. 1979. *Social Stratification: Canada*, 2nd edn. Scarborough, ON: Prentice-Hall.
Curtis, J., Grabb, E., Guppy, N., and Gilbert, S., eds. 1988. *Social Inequality in Canada: Patterns, Problems, Policies*. Scarborough, ON: Prentice-Hall.
Dahlie, J., and Fernando, T., eds. 1981. *Ethnicity, Power and Politics in Canada*. Toronto: Methuen.
Dailey, R.C., and Dailey, L.A. 1961. *The Eskimo of Rankin Inlet: A Preliminary Report*. Ottawa: Northern Coordination and Research Centre, Department of Northern Affairs and Research Resources.
Daniels, H.W. 1979a. *The Forgotten People: Metis and Non-Status Indian Land Claims*. Ottawa: Native Council of Canada.
———. 1979b. *We Are the New Nation: The Metis and National Native Policy*. Ottawa: Native Council of Canada.
Darroch, A.G. 1979. 'Another Look at Ethnicity, Stratification and Social Mobility in Canada', *Canadian Journal of Sociology* 4, 1: 1–25.
Darwin, C. 1859. *On the Origin of Species by Means of Natural Selection or the Preservation of Favoured Races in the Struggle for Life*.
Das Gupta, Tania. 1986. *Learning from Our History: Community Development by Immigrant Women in Ontario 1958–1986—A Tool for Action*. Toronto: Cross-Cultural Communication Centre.
David Duke website. [Cited 3 November 2001.] www.duke.org/
Day, S. 1990. 'The Process of Achieving Equality'. In Cholewinski, ed. (1990): 17–30.
Despres, L.A. 1975. 'Ethnicity and Ethnic Group Relations in Guyana'. In Bennett, ed. (1975): 127–47.
DIAND (Department of Indian Affairs and Northern Development). 1980. *Indian Conditions: A Survey*. Ottawa: Indian and Northern Affairs.
Dion, L. 1976. *Quebec: The Unfinished Revolution*. Montreal: McGill-Queen's University Press.
D'Oyley, V.R., ed. 1978a. *Black Presence in Multi-Ethnic Canada*. Toronto: Ontario Institute for Studies in Education.
———. 1978b. 'Schooling and Ethnic Rights'. In Berkeley, Gaffield, and West, eds (1978): 137–44.
Draft Declaration on the Rights of Indigenous Peoples. 1994. E/CN.4/SUB.2/1994/2/Add.1.
Driedger, L., ed. 1978. *The Canadian Ethnic Mosaic*. Toronto: McClelland & Stewart.
———. 1989. *The Ethnic Factor: Identity in Diversity*. Toronto: McGraw-Hill Ryerson.
Driedger, L., and Chappell, N. 1987. *Aging and Ethnicity: Toward an Interface*. Toronto: Butterworths.
Dumont-Smith, C., and Sioui-Labelle, P. 1991. *National Family Violence Survey: Phase One*. Ottawa: Aboriginal Nurses of Canada.
Dworkin, R. 1977. *Taking Rights Seriously*. London: Duckworth & Co.
Dwivedi, O.P., D'Costa, R.D., Stanford, C.L., and Tepper, E., eds. 1989. *Canada 2000: Race Relations and Public Policy*. Guelph, ON: Department of Political Studies, University of Guelph.
Dyck, N. 1981. 'The Politics of Special Status: Indian Associations and the Administration of Indian Affairs'. In Dahlie and Fernando, eds (1981): 279–91.
Eaton, J. 1970. 'Controlled Acculturation: A Survival Technique of the Hutterites'. In Kurokawa, ed. (1970).
Egan v. Canada (1993), 103 D.L.R. (4th) 336 (F.C.A.).
Elliott, J.L., ed. 1971a. *Minority Canadians*. Vol. 1, *Native Peoples*. Scarborough, ON: Prentice-Hall.
———. 1971b. *Minority Canadians*. Vol. 2, *Immigrant Groups*. Scarborough, ON: Prentice-Hall.
———. 1979. *Two Nations, Many Cultures*. Scarborough, ON: Prentice-Hall.
Elliott, J.L., and Fleras, A. 1990. 'Immigration and the Canadian Ethnic Mosaic'. In Li, ed. (1990): 51–76.
Enloe, C.H. 1973. *Ethnic Conflict and Political Development*. Boston: Little Brown.
Epp, F.H. 1974. *Mennonites in Canada 1786–1920: The History of a Separate People*. Toronto: Macmillan.
Espiell, H.G. 1998. 'Universality of Human Rights and Cultural Diversity', *International Social Science Journal*, UNESCO (December).
Evans, S. 1985. 'Some Developments in the Diffusion Patterns of Hutterite Colonies', *Canadian Geographer* 29, 4.
Family Violence in Aboriginal Communities. Fact Sheet 10. Department of Community Services, Government of Nova Scotia. [Cited 10 November 2001.] www.gov.ns.ca/coms/files/facts10.asp

Fanon, F. 1967. *Black Skins, White Masks*. New York: Grove.

First Nations Governance Act. [Cited 16 June 2002.] www.fnggpn.gc.ca/fnga_e.asp

Fleras, A. 1995. ' "Please Adjust Your Set": Media and Minorities in a Multicultural Society'. In B. Singer, *Communications in Canadian Society*, 4th edn. Toronto: Nelson Canada.

Fleras, A., and Elliot, J. 1995. *Unequal Relations: An Introduction to Race, Ethnic and Aboriginal Dynamics in Canada.* Scarborough, ON: Prentice-Hall.

Flint, D. 1975. *The Hutterites: A Study in Prejudice*. Toronto: Oxford University Press.

Foucher, P. 1990. 'Language Rights in the 1990s'. In Cholewinski, ed. (1990): 117–38.

Frank, S. 1992. *Family Violence in Aboriginal Communities: A First Nations Report*. British Columbia: Minister of Women's Equality.

FreedomSite. [Cited 19 January 2002.] www.freedomsite.org/

Freire, S.A. 1996. *Evolutions in Quebec Nationalism* [Cited 19 November 2001.] www.trincoll.edu/zines/papers/1996/quebec.html

Frideres, J.S. 1993. *Native Peoples in Canada: Contemporary Conflicts*, 3rd edn. Scarborough, ON: Prentice-Hall.

Friedmann, K.A. 1979. 'The Ombudsman'. In Macdonald and Humphrey, eds (1979): 337–58.

Gardner, R.C., and Kalin, R., eds. 1981. *A Canadian Social Psychology of Ethnic Relations*. Toronto: Methuen.

Gee, E.M., and Kimball, M.M. 1987. *Women and Aging*. Toronto: Butterworths.

Gibbins, R., and Ponting, J.R. 1986. 'An Assessment of the Probable Impact of Aboriginal Self-Government in Canada.' In Cairns and Williams, eds. (1986): 171–239.

Gibbon, J.M. 1938. *The Canadian Mosaic*. Toronto: McClelland & Stewart.

Gibson, D. 1990. *The Law of the Charter: Equality Rights*. Toronto: Carswell.

Gilroy, Paul. 1991. *'There Ain't No Black in the Union Jack: The Cultural Politics of Race and Nation*. Chicago: University of Chicago Press.

Glaser, K., and Possony, S.T. 1979. *Victims of Politics: The State of Human Rights*. New York: Columbia University Press.

Glazer, N. 1995. 'Individual Rights and Group Rights'. In Kymlicka, ed. (1995): 123–38.

———. 1998. 'Is Affirmative Action on the Way Out? Should It Be? A Symposium', *Commentary Magazine* (March).

Glazer, N., and Moynihan, D., eds. 1975. *Ethnicity: Theory and Experience*. Cambridge, MA: Harvard University Press.

Glickman, Y. 1976. 'Organizational Indicators and Social Correlates of Collective Jewish Identity.' Ph.D. dissertation (University of Toronto).

Gobineau, J.A. de. 1854. *Essai Sur L'Inegalite des Races Humaines*. Paris.

Goffman, E. 1963. *Stigma: Notes on the Management of Spoiled Identity*. Englewood Cliffs, NJ: Spectrum Books.

Gordon, M. 1964. *Assimilation in American Life*. New York: Oxford University Press.

Gove, W.R. 1976. 'Societal Reaction Theory and Disability'. In Albrecht, ed. (1976).

Graburn, N.H. 1969. *Eskimos Without Igloos: Social and Economic Development in Sugluk*. Boston: Little Brown.

———. 1981. '1, 2, 3, 4 . . . Anthropology and the Fourth World', *Culture* 1, 1: 66–70.

Gwyn, R. 1995. *Nationalism Without Walls: The Unbearable Lightness of Being Canadian*. Toronto: McClelland & Stewart.

Harper, A.G. 1945. 'Canada's Indian Administration: Basic Concepts and Objectives', *America Indigena* 4, 2: 119–32.

Hawthorn, H., ed. 1955. *The Doukhobors of British Columbia*. Vancouver: Dent and University of British Columbia Press.

———. 1967. *A Survey of the Contemporary Indians of Canada*. Vol. 2. Ottawa: Queen's Printer.

Head, W.A. 1975. *The Black Presence in the Canadian Mosaic. A Study of the Perception and the Practice of Discrimination Against Blacks in Metropolitan Toronto.* Report submitted to the Ontario Human Rights Commission (September).

Heagerty, J.L. 1928. *Four Centuries of Medical History in Canada*. Vol. 1. Toronto: Macmillan.

Hendrickson, Robert. 1987. *The Facts On File Encyclopedia of Word and Phrase Origins*. New York: Facts on File Publications.

Henry, F. 1977. *The Dynamics of Racism in Toronto: A Preliminary Report*. Toronto: York University.

———. 1993. 'Democratic Racism and the Perpetuation of Inequality in Canada', plenary address for the Twelfth Biennial Conference of the Canadian Ethnic Studies Association, 27–30 November, Vancouver.

Henry, F., and Ginsberg, E. 1988. 'Racial Discrimination in Employment'. In Curtis et al. (1988): 214–20.

Henry, F., Tator, C., Mattis, W., and Rees, T. 1995. *The Colour of Democracy: Racism in Canadian Society*. Toronto: Harcourt Brace.

Herberg, E.N. 1989. *Ethnic Groups in Canada: Adaptations and Transitions*. Scarborough, ON: Nelson Canada.

———. 1990. 'The Ethno-Racial Socioeconomic Hierarchy in Canada: Theory and Analysis of the New

Vertical Mosaic', *International Journal of Comparative Sociology* 31: 3–4, 206–21.

Herman, S.N. 1977. *Jewish Identity: A Social Psychological Perspective*. London: Sage.

Hidden Discrimination and Polite Racism Prevents Aboriginal Peoples and Visible Minorities from Gaining Equal Access to Jobs, Study Finds [press release]. CRRF. 10 January 2001. [Cited 2 November 2001.] www.crr.ca/EN/MediaCentre/NewsReleases/eMedCen_NewsRe20010110.htm

Hill, D.G. 1977. *Human Rights in Canada: A Focus on Racism*. Ottawa: Canadian Labour Congress.

Hill, D.G., and Schiff, M. 1988. *Human Rights in Canada: A Focus on Racism*, 3rd edn. Ottawa: Human Rights Research and Education Centre, University of Ottawa.

Hill, L.B. 1974. 'Institutionalization, the Ombudsman and Bureaucracy', *American Political Science Review* 68: 1075–85.

Hill, M. 'Staff Housing Shortage Chokes GN', *Nunatsiaq News* [online]. 9 November 2001. [Cited 11 December 2001.] www.nunatsiaq.com/news/nunavut/11109_2.html

Hostetler, J.A., and Huntington, G.E. 1967. *The Hutterites in North America*. New York: Holt, Rinehart and Winston.

Hudson, M.R. 1987. 'Multiculturalism, Government Policy and Constitutional Enshrinement—A Comparative Study'. In Canadian Human Rights Foundation (1987): 59–122.

Hughes, C.C. 1965. 'Under Four Flags: Recent Culture Change Among the Eskimos', *Current Anthropology* 6, 1: 3–73.

Hughes, D.R., and Kallen, E. 1974. *The Anatomy of Racism: Canadian Dimensions*. Montreal: Harvest House.

Hughes, K. 1920. *Father Lacombe: The Black-Robe Voyageur*. Toronto: McClelland & Stewart.

Hurley, M.C., and Wherrett, J. 1999. *The Report of the Royal Commission on Aboriginal Peoples* (PRB 9924E) [revised 2 August 2000]. [Cited 20 November 2001.] www.parl.gc.ca/information/library/PRBpubs/prb9924e.htm

Hussain, A. 1981. 'Have Power, Have Rights?' paper presented at the International Peace Research Association, Ninth General Conference, 21–6 June, Geneva Park, Ontario.

Isaacs, H.R. 1977. *Idols of the Tribe: Group Identity and Political Change*. New York: Harper & Row.

Isajiw, W.W. 1970. 'Definitions of Ethnicity', *Ethnicity* 1: 1.

———, ed. 1977a. *Identities: The Impact of Ethnicity on Canadian Society*. Toronto: Peter Martin Associates.

———. 1977b. 'Olga in Wonderland: Ethnicity in a Technological Society', *Canadian Ethnic Studies* 9, 1: 77–85.

———. 1999. *Understanding Diversity: Ethnicity and Race in the Canadian Context*. Toronto: Thompson Educational Publishing.

Ishwaran, K., ed. 1980. *Canadian Families: Ethnic Variations*. Toronto: McGraw-Hill Ryerson.

Jack, H. 1970. 'Native Alliance for Red Power'. In Waubageshig, ed. (1970).

Jackson, M. 1979. 'The Rights of the Native People'. In Macdonald and Humphrey, eds (1979): 267–88.

Jacob, A. 1993. Le Service de police de la communauté de Montréal et la gestion de la diversité en milieu pluriethnique. Rapport de rechereche. Ottawa: Ministére du Soliciteur-General du Canada.

Jacobs and Jacobs v. Mohawk Council of Kahnawake T.D. 3/98. Decision rendered on 11 March 1998, The Canadian Human Rights Act R.S.C., 1985, c. H6 (as amended).

Jaenen, C.J. 1972. 'Cultural Diversity and Education'. In Bryne and Quarter, eds (1972).

Jain, H.C. 1989. 'Affirmative Action/Employment Equity Programs and Visible Minorities in Canada'. In Dwivedi et al., eds (1989).

Jansen, C.J. 1978. 'Community Organization of Italians in Toronto'. In Driedger, ed. (1978).

Jenness, D. 1964. *Eskimo Administration 11*. Technical Paper No. 14 (May). Canada: Arctic Institute of North America.

John Humphrey and the Universal Declaration of Human Rights [online]. Copyright 1998–99 New Brunswick Human Rights Commission. [Cited 30 December 2001.] www.gov.nb.ca/hrc

———. Documentary aired on CBC Radio's *This Morning*, 10 December 1998. [Cited 3 January 2002.] radio.cbc.ca/insite/THIS_MORNING_TORONTO/1998/12/10.html

Joy, R. J. 1972. *Languages in Conflict*. Toronto: McClelland & Stewart.

Kallen, E. 1972. 'Eskimo Youth: The New Marginals'. In *International Biological Program: Human Adaptability Project*. Annual Report 4, Anthropological Series 11. Toronto: University of Toronto.

———. 1977a. 'Legacy of Tutelage: Divided Inuit.' In Paine, ed. (1977): 129–43.

———. 1977b. *Spanning the Generations: A Study in Jewish Identity*. Toronto: Longman Canada /Academic Press.

———. 1982a. *Ethnicity and Human Rights in Canada*. Agincourt, ON: Gage.

———. 1982b. 'Multiculturalism: Ideology, Policy and Reality', *Journal of Canadian Studies* 17, 1: 58–63.

———. 1987. 'Multiculturalism, Minorities and Motherhood: A Social Scientific Critique of Section 27'.

In Canadian Human Rights Foundation (1987): 123–38.

———. 1988. 'The Meech Lake Accord: Entrenching a Pecking Order of Minority Rights', *Canadian Public Policy*, 14 (Special Issue: *The Meech Lake Accord*, suppl. to vol. 14): 107–20.

———. 1990. 'Multiculturalism: The Not-So-Impossible Dream'. In Cholewinski, ed. (1990): 165–82.

———. 1992. 'Never Again: Target Group Responses to the Debate Concerning Anti-Hate Propaganda Legislation'. In *Windsor Yearbook of Access to Justice*. Vol. 11. Windsor, ON: Faculty of Law, University of Windsor.

———. 1995. *Ethnicity and Human Rights in Canada*, 2nd edn. Toronto: Oxford University Press.

———. 1997. 'Hate on the Net'. *Electronic Journal of Sociology* [online] 3, 2 (December): www.sociology.org/

Kallen, E., and Lam, L. 1993. 'Target for Hate: The Impact of the Zundel and Keegstra Trials on a Jewish-Canadian Audience', *Canadian Ethnic Studies* 25, 1.

Kallen, H. 1915. 'Democracy Versus the Melting Pot', *The Nation* (February).

Kamateros, M. 1998. 'The Isolated Immigrant Family', *Transition Magazine* 28, 3 (September).

Kelner, M. 1969. 'The Elite Structure of Toronto: Ethnic Composition and Patterns of Recruitment'. Ph.D. dissertation (University of Toronto).

Kelner, M., and Kallen, E. 1974. 'The Multicultural Policy: Canada's Response to Ethnic Diversity', *Journal of Comparative Sociology* 2: 21–4.

Kemar-D'Souza, C. 1981. 'Political Economy and Human Rights', paper presented at the International Peace Research Association, Ninth General Conference, 21–6 June, Geneva Park, Ontario.

Kennedy, J.R. 1944. 'Single or Triple Melting Pot? Intermarriage Trends in New Haven, 1870–1940', *American Journal of Sociology* 49: 331–9.

Kidd, B. 1894. *Social Evolution*.

Killiam, L.M. 1968. *The Impossible Revolution?* New York: Random House.

Kilson, M. 1975. 'Blacks and Neo-Ethnicity in American Political Life'. In Glazer and Moynihan, eds (1975): 236–66.

Knox, R. 1850. *The Races of Man: A Fragment*. London: Renshaw.

Krauter, J.F., and Davis, M. 1978. *Minority Canadians: Ethnic Groups*. Toronto: Methuen.

Kriesi, H., Koopmans, R., Dyvendak, J.W., and Guigni, M.G. 1995. *New Social Movements in Western Europe: A Comparative Analysis*. Minneapolis: University of Minnesota Press.

Kunz, J.L., Milan, A., and Schetagne, S. 2001. *Unequal Access: A Canadian Profile of Racial Differences in Education, Employment and Income*. Canadian Race Relations Foundation (CRRF). [Cited 10 December 2001.] www.crr.ca/en/Publications/ePubHome.htm

Kurokawa, M., ed. 1970. *Minority Responses*. New York: Random House.

Kymlicka, W., ed. 1995. *The Rights of Minority Cultures*. Oxford: Oxford University Press.

———. 1997. 'Immigrants, Multiculturalism and Canadian Citizenship', paper presented at Social Cohesion Through Social Justice, Canadian Jewish Congress symposium, 2 November, Ottawa.

———. 1999. '"Liberal Complacencies": Response to Susan Okin's "Is Multiculturalism Bad for Women?"' In Okin et al., eds (1999): 31–4.

Lautard, H., and Guppy, N. 1990. 'The Vertical Mosaic Revisited: Occupational Differentials Among Canadian Ethnic Groups'. In Li, ed. (1990): 189–208.

La Violette, F. 1948. *The Canadian Japanese and World War II*. Toronto: University of Toronto Press.

Lai, V. 1971. 'The New Chinese Immigrants in Toronto'. In Elliott, ed. (1971b): 120–40.

Lam, L., and Richmond, A.H. 1987. 'A Decade in Canada: Immigration, Human Rights and Racism, 1978–1987' *New Community* 14, 1–2 (fall).

Leavy, J. 1979. Working Paper for a series of regional conferences on minority rights, sponsored by the Canadian Human Rights Foundation (October).

Lee, D.J. 1979. 'The Evolution of Nationalism in Quebec'. In Elliott, ed. (1979): 60–74.

Lévesque, R. 1968. *An Option for Quebec*. Toronto: McClelland & Stewart.

Lewin, K. 1948. *Resolving Social Conflicts*. New York: Harper Bros.

Li, P.S. 1980. 'Immigration Laws and Family Patterns: Some Demographic Changes Among Chinese Families in Canada 1885-1971', *Canadian Ethnic Studies* 12, 1: 58–73.

———, ed. 1990. *Race and Ethnic Relations in Canada*. Toronto: Oxford University Press.

Lieberson, S. 1961. 'A Societal Theory of Race and Ethnic Relations', *American Sociological Review* 26: 902–10.

Lincoln, C.E. 1961. *The Black Muslims in America*. Boston: Beacon.

Loehlin, J.C., Lindzey, G., and Spuhler, J.N. 1975. *Race Differences in Intelligence*. San Francisco: W.H. Freeman.

Lovelace v. *Canada*. 1984. Communication No. 24/1977 (31/07/80), UN Doc. CCPR/C/OP/1: 37.

Lupul, M. 1982. 'Political Implementation of Multiculturalism', *Journal of Canadian Studies* 17, 1 (spring).

McDiarmid, G., and Pratt, D. 1971. *Teaching Prejudice: A Content Analysis of Social Studies Textbooks Authorized for Use in Ontario*. Toronto: Ontario Institute for Studies in Education.

Macdonald, R. St. J., and Humphrey, J.P. 1979. *The Practice of Freedom*. Toronto: Butterworths.

Mckie, C., and Thompson, K., eds. 1990. *Canadian Social Trends*. Toronto: Thompson Educational Publishing.

Maclean, J. 1896. *Canadian Savage Folk: The Native Tribes of Canada*. Toronto: Briggs.

MacLeod, L., and Shin, M. 1990. 'Isolated, Afraid and Forgotten: The Service Delivery Needs and Realities of Immigrant and Refugee Women Who Are Battered'. Ottawa: National Clearinghouse on Family Violence, Health and Welfare Canada.

McRoberts, K.H., and Posgate, D. 1976. *Quebec: Social Change and Political Crisis*. Toronto: McClelland & Stewart.

Magnet, J.E. 1987. 'Interpreting Multiculturalism'. In Canadian Human Rights Foundation (1987): 145–54.

———. 1989. 'Multiculturalism and Collective Rights'. In Beaudoin and Ratushny, eds. (1989): 740–80.

Magsino, R.M. 1978. 'Student Rights in Canada: Nonsense Upon Stilts?' In Berkeley, Gaffield, and West, eds. (1978): 89–107.

Makabe, T. 1976. 'Ethnic Group Identity: Canadian-born Japanese in Metropolitan Toronto'. Ph.D. dissertation (University of Toronto).

Malcolm X. 1966. *The Autobiography of Malcolm X*. New York: Grove.

Manitoba Public Inquiry into the Administration of Justice and Aboriginal People. 1991. *Report*. Vol. 1, *The Justice System and Aboriginal People*. Winnipeg: Queen's Printer.

Manuel, G., and Posluns, M. 1974. *The Fourth World: An Indian Reality*. New York: Free Press.

Marshall, I. 1981. 'Disease as a Factor in the Demise of the Beothuck Indians', *Culture* 1, 1: 71–8.

Matejko, A. 1979. 'Multiculturalism: The Polish-Canadian Case.' In Elliott, ed. (1979): 237–49.

Maxwell, T.R. 1979. 'The Invisible French: The French in Metropolitan Toronto.' In Elliott, ed. (1979): 114–22.

Mede, M.P. 1979. In Leavy (1979): 3–4.

Melucci, A. 1980. 'The New Social Movements: A Theoretical Approach', *Social Science Information* 19, 2: 199–226.

———. 1996. *Challenging Codes: Collective Action in the Information Age*. Cambridge: Cambridge University Press.

Merton, R.K. 1949. *Social Theory and Social Structure*. Glencoe, Ill.: Free Press.

Miles, R. 1989. *Racism*. London: Tavistock.

Milner, H., and Milner, S.H. 1973. *The Decolonization of Quebec: An Analysis of Left-Wing Nationalism*. Toronto: McClelland & Stewart.

Montagu, A., ed. 1999. *Race and I.Q.* London: Oxford University Press.

Montero, G. 1977. *The Immigrants*. Toronto: James Lorimer.

Morris, R.N., and Lanphier, C.M. 1977. *Three Scales of Inequality: Perspectives on French-English Relations*. Toronto: Longman.

Mullaly, B. 2002. *Challenging Oppression: A Critical Social Work Approach*. Don Mills, ON: Oxford University Press.

Murphy, D. *Way of the Lord*. CANADA JOURNAL. [Cited 8 November 2001.] www.anabaptistchurch.org/canada_journal.htm

Murumba, S.K. 1998. 'Cross-Cultural Dimensions of Human Rights in the Twenty-First Century'. In A. Anghie and G. Sturgess, *Legal Visions of the 21st Century: Essays in Honour of Judge Christopher Weeramantry*. The Hague: Kluwer Law International: 201–40.

Ng, R. 1999. *Homeworking: Home Office or Home Sweatshop? Report on Current Conditions of Homeworkers in Toronto's Garment Industry*. Toronto: NALL, OISE.

Nichols, P. 1971. 'Since the Days of Barter'. In *People of Light and Dark*, ed. M. van Steensel. Ottawa: Information Canada.

Noel, D.L. 1968. 'A Theory of the Origin of Ethnic Stratification', *Social Problems* 16: 157–72.

Nozick, R. 1974. *Anarchy, State and Utopia*. New York: Basic Books.

Ogmundson, R. 1990. 'Perspectives on the Class and Ethnic Origins of Canadian Elites: A Methodological Critique of the Porter/Clement/Olsen Tradition', *Canadian Journal of Sociology* 15: 165–77.

Okin, S.M. 1999. 'Is Multiculturalism Bad for Women?' In Okin et al., eds. (1999): 7–26.

Okin, S.M., Cohen, J., Howard, M., and Nussbaum, M.C., eds. 1999. *Is Multiculturalism Bad for Women?* Princeton, NJ: Princeton University Press.

Onalik, J. *The Next Generation*. Nunavut website. [Cited 15 November 2001.] www.nunavut.com/nunavut99/english/next.html

Ontario Human Rights Commission and Theresa O'Malley v. Simpsons Sears Ltd. [1985] 2 S.C.R.

Ontario Native Women's Association. 1989. *Breaking Free: A Proposal for Change to Aboriginal Family Violence*. Thunder Bay: Ontario Native Women's Association.

Ossenberg, R., ed. 1971. *Canadian Society: Pluralism, Change and Conflict*. Scarborough, ON: Prentice-Hall.

Paine, R., ed. 1977. *The White Arctic: Anthropological Essays on Tutelage and Ethnicity*. St. John's: Memorial University of Newfoundland.

Palmer, H. 1976. 'Mosaic vs Melting Pot? Immigration and Ethnicity in Canada and the United States', *International Journal* 31: 3.

Parekh, B. 1999. '"A Varied Moral World": Response to Susan Okin's "Is Multiculturalism Bad for Women?"' In Okin et al., eds (1999): 69–75.

Parliamentary Debates [online]. *Remarks in Opposition to Affirmative Action.* [Cited 4 December 2001.] www.parl.gc.ca/36/2/parlbus/chambus/house/debates/047_20000211/han047_1115e.htm

Parsons, T. 1953. 'A Revised Analytic Approach to the Theory of Social Stratification'. In Bendix and Lipset, eds (1953): 92–128.

Patterson, E.P. 1972. *The Canadian Indian: A History Since 1500*. Toronto: Collier-Macmillan.

Paying for the Past. The National CBC News [online]. 5 September 2001. [Cited 24 October 2001.] www.cbc.ca/national/news/reparations/index.html

Pelletier, W. 1974. 'For Every North American Indian That Begins to Disappear I Also Begin to Disappear'. In Frideres, ed.(1993): 101–9.

Pentney, W.F. 1989. 'Interpreting the Charter: General Principles'. In Beaudoin and Ratushny, eds (1989): ch 2.

Perera, Bloch, Boahene v. The Queen in Right of Canada (Memorandum of Fact and Law of the Intervenor, Public Service Alliance of Canada. Court File No.: A 14697).

Peter, K. 1978. 'Multi-cultural Politics, Money and the Conduct of Canadian Ethnic Studies', *Canadian Ethnic Studies Association Bulletin* 5: 2–3.

———. 1980a. 'Problems in the Family, Community and Culture of Hutterites'. In Ishwaran, ed. (1980): 221–35.

———. 1980b. 'The Decline of Hutterite Population Growth', *Canadian Ethnic Studies* 12, 3: 97–110.

———. 1981. 'The Myth of Multiculturalism and Other Political Fables'. In Dahlie and Fernando, eds (1981): 56–67.

———. 1987. *The Dynamics of Hutterite Society: An Analytic Approach*. Edmonton: University of Alberta Press.

Pie, B. n.d. 'Affirmative Action: Can the Voluntary Approach Work?' In *Viewpoint*. Toronto: Women's Bureau, Ontario Ministry of Labour.

Poisoning the Web: Internet as a Hate Tool. [Cited 4 February 2002.] www.adl.org/poisoning_web/net_hate_tool.html

Ponting, J.R. 1990. 'Public Opinion on Aboriginal Peoples' Issues'. In Mckie and Thompson, eds (1990): 19–27.

Ponting, J.R., and Gibbins, R. 1980. *Out of Irrelevance: A Socio-Political Introduction to Indian Affairs in Canada*. Toronto: Butterworths.

Porter, J. 1965. *The Vertical Mosaic*. Toronto: University of Toronto Press.

———. 1975. 'Ethnic Pluralism in Canadian Perspective'. In Glazer and Moynihan, eds (1975): 267–304.

———, ed. 1979a. *The Measure of Canadian Society: Education, Equality and Opportunity*. Agincourt, ON: Gage.

———. 1979b. 'Melting Pot or Mosaic: Revolution or Reversion?' In Porter, ed. (1979a): 139–62.

Price, A.G. 1950. *White Settlers and Native People*. Melbourne: Georgian House.

Putnam, C. 1961. *Race and Reason*. Washington, DC: Public Affairs Press.

QHRC. 1988. Comité d'enquête sur les relations entre les police forces et les minorités visibles. *Rapport de recerche*. Montréal: Commission des droits de la personne du Québec.

R. v. Kent, Sinclair and Gode (1986), 21 C.R.R. 372 (Man. C.A.).

Racial Stereotypes in Children's Programs. [Cited 29 October 2001.] www.richmond.edu/~psych/tvgenethracial.html

Radecki, H., and Heydenkorn, B. 1976. *A Member of a Distinguished Family: The Polish Group in Canada*. Toronto: McClelland & Stewart.

Ramcharan, S. 1976. 'The Economic Adaptation of West Indians in Toronto, Canada', *Canadian Review of Sociology and Anthropology* 13, 3.

Rawls, J. 1993. *Political Liberalism*. New York: Columbia University Press.

Re McTavish et al. and Director, Child Welfare Act et al. (1986), 32 D.L.R. (4th) 394 (Alta. Q.B.).

Red Paper. 1970. *Citizens Plus*. Response of the Indian Chiefs of Alberta to the White Paper (1969), presented to Prime Minister Trudeau (June).

Redi, H., and Young, C. 1939. *The Japanese Canadians*. Toronto: University of Toronto Press.

Reference re: An Act To Amend The Education Act. 25 D.L.R. (4th) 1, 53 O.R. (2nd) 513, 13 O.A.C. 241 (Ont. C.A.).

Regina v. Big M Drug Mart Ltd. (1985), 18 C.C.C. (3d) 385, 18 D.L.R. (4th) 321, [1985] 1 S.C.R. 295.

Remillard, G. 1989. 'Quebec's Quest for Survival and Equality via the Meech Lake Accord'. In Behiels, ed. (1989): 28–42.

Repo, M. 1971. 'The Fallacy of Community Control', *Transformation: Theory and Practice of Social Change* 1, 1.

Report of the Royal Commission on Aboriginal Peoples. Highlights (RCAP). Indian and Northern Affairs Canada [updated 21 June 2000]. [Cited 14 November 2001.] www.aincinac.gc.ca/ch/rcap/

Report of the UN Committee Monitoring Implementation by Canada of the UN Covenant on Economic, Social and Cultural Rights. 1999. CCPA Monitor (March).

Residential Schools. Contemporary Aboriginal Issues website. [Cited 21 June 2001.] www.school.net.ca/aboriginal/issues/schools-e.hml

Rex, J. 1983. *Race Relations in Sociological Theory*. London: Routledge & Kegan Paul.

Rich, H. 1991. 'Observations on Class and Ethnic Origins of Canadian Elites by Richard Ogmundson', *Canadian Journal of Sociology* 16: 419–23.

Richard, M. 1991. *Ethnic Groups and Marital Choices: Ethnic History and Marital Assimilation, Canada 1871 and 1971*. Vancouver: University of British Columbia Press.

Richmond, A.H. 1972. *Ethnic Segregation in Metropolitan Toronto*. Toronto: Institute for Behavioural Research, York University.

———. 1974. 'Language, Ethnicity and the Problem of Identity in a Canadian Metropolis', *Ethnicity* 1: 175–206.

———. 1975. 'The Green Paper: Reflections on the Canadian Immigration and Population Study', *Canadian Ethnic Studies* 7, 1: 5–21.

Rioux, M. 1971. *Quebec in Question*. Toronto: James Lewis & Samuel.

Rocher, G. 1976. 'Multiculturalism: Doubts of a Francophone'. In *Report of the Second Canadian Conference on Multiculturalism*. Ottawa: Canadian Consultative Council on Multiculturalism.

Rose, P.I. 1968. *The Subject Is Race*. London: Oxford University Press.

Rosenstock, J., and Adair, D. 1976. *Multiracialism in the Classroom: A Survey of Interracial Attitudes in Ontario Schools*. Report prepared for the Multicultural Directorate, Department of Secretary of State, Ottawa.

Rushton, J.P. 1995. *Race, Evolution and Behavior*. New Brunswick, NJ: Transaction.

———. 1996. *Race as a Biological Concept* (4 November) [Cited 26 October 2001.] www.duke.org/library

Russell, B. 1972. *A History of Western Civilization*. New York: Simon & Schuster.

Sandel, M. 1992. *Liberalism and the Limits of Justice*. London: Cambridge University Press.

Sanders, D. 1964. 'The Hutterites: A Case Study in Minority Rights', *Canadian Bar Review* 42: 225–42.

———. 1987. 'Article 27 and the Aboriginal Peoples of Canada'. In Canadian Human Rights Foundation (1987): 155–66.

———. 1990. 'The Supreme Court of Canada and the "Legal and Political Struggle" Over Indigenous Rights'. In *Canadian Ethnic Studies* 22, 3: 122–9.

Saskatchewan Human Rights Commission. 1974. *Prejudice in Social Studies Textbooks: A Content Analysis of Social Studies Textbooks Used in Saskatchewan Schools*. Saskatoon.

Satzewich, V. 1998a. 'Race, Racism and Racialization: Contested Concepts'. In Satzewich, ed. (1988b): 25–45.

———, ed. 1998b. *Racism and Social Inequality in Canada*. Toronto: Thompson Educational Publishing.

Sawchuck, J. 1978. *The Metis of Manitoba*. Toronto: Peter Martin Associates.

Schermerhorn, R.A. 1970. *Comparative Ethnic Relations: A Framework For Theory and Research*. New York: Random House.

Sealey, D.B., and Lussier, A.S. 1975. *The Metis: Canada's Forgotten People*. Winnipeg: Manitoba Métis Federation.

Sharma, Y. *RIGHTS: International Community Declares War on CyberHatred*. [Cited 21 December 2001.] www.oneworld.org/ips2/june00/00_41_003.html

Shibutani, T., and Kwan, K.M. 1965. *Ethnic Stratification: A Comparative Approach*. New York: Macmillan.

Silman, J. 1987. *Enough Is Enough: Aboriginal Women Speak Out*. Toronto: The Women's Press.

Simpson, G.E., and Yinger, J.M. 1972. *Racial and Cultural Minorities: An Analysis of Prejudice and Discrimination*, 4th edn. New York: Harper & Row.

Skinheads of the Holy Racial War website. [Cited 20 November 2001.] www.rahowa.com/skinheads

Slobodin, R. 1971. 'Métis of the Far North'. In Elliott, ed. (1971a): 150–68.

Stasiulis, D.K. 1990 'Theorizing Connections: Gender, Race Ethnicity and Class'. In Li, ed. (1990): 269–305.

Statistics Canada. 1995. In *Family Violence Prevention Division: Breaking the Links between Poverty and Violence against Women*. Ottawa: Health Canada, 1996.

———. 'Immigrant Population by Place of Birth and Period of Immigration'. *1996 Census, Canada. Nation Tables*. [Cited 6 January 2002.] www.statcan.ca/english/Pgdb/People/popula.htm#imm

Stenning, P.C. 1994. *Police Use of Force and Violence against Members of Visible Minority Groups in Canada*. Ottawa: Solicitor General of Canada and Canadian Centre for Police-Race Relations.

Stewart, W. 1970. 'Red Power'. In Kurokawa, ed. (1970): 364–72.

Stonequist, E.V. 1937. *The Marginal Man*. New York: Scribner's.

Sunahara, A.G. 1981. *The Politics of Racism*. Toronto: James Lorimer.

Sunahara, M.A. 1979. 'Federal Policy and the Japanese Canadians: The Decision to Evacuate, 1942'. In Ujimoto and Hirabayashi, eds (1979): 93–120.

Surtees, R.J. 1971. *The Original People*. Toronto: Holt, Rinehart and Winston.

Taras, D., and Weinfeld, M. 1993. 'Continuity and Criticism: North American Jews and Israel'. In Brym, Shaffir, and Weinfeld, eds (1993): 293–310.

Tarnopolsky, W.S. 1975. *The Canadian Bill of Rights*, 2nd edn. Toronto: McClelland & Stewart.

———. 1979. 'The Control of Racial Discrimination'. In Macdonald and Humphrey, eds (1979): 289–307.

———. 1982. 'The Equality Rights'. In Tarnopolsky and Beaudoin, eds (1982).

Tarnopolsky, W.S., and Beaudoin, G.A., eds. 1982. *The Canadian Charter of Rights and Freedoms: Commentary*. Toronto: Carswell.

Taylor, C. 1995. 'Cross-Purposes: The Liberal-Communitarian Debate', *Philosophical Arguments*. Cambridge, MA: Harvard University Press.

Tepper, E. 1993. 'Multiculturalism in Canada: Twenty Years On—And Under?' paper presented at the Twelfth Biennial Conference of the Canadian Ethnic Studies Association, 27–30 November, Vancouver.

Thériault, Y. 1971. *Agaguk*. Montreal: l'Actuelle.

Thompson, N. 2001. *Anti-Discriminatory Practice*, 3rd edn. Basingstoke, UK: Palgrave.

Thompson, W.P. 1984. 'Hutterite Community: Its Reflex in Architectural and Settlement Patterns'. *Canadian Ethnic Studies* 16, 3: 53–72.

Treasury Board of Canada website. *Employment Equity for Visible Minorities: Embracing Change in the Federal Public Service*. [Cited 13 November 2001.] publiservice.tbssct.gc.ca

Troper, Harold. 1993. 'As Canadian as Multiculturalism: An Historian's Perspective on Multicultural Policy', plenary address at the Twelfth Biennial Conference of the Canadian Ethnic Studies Association, 27–30 November, Vancouver.

Ujimoto, K.V., and Hirabayashi, G. eds. 1979. *Visible Minorities and Multiculturalism: Asians in Canada*. Toronto: Butterworths.

Ungerleider, C.S. 1993. *A Program Review of the Ottawa and Vancouver Police Race Relations Initiatives: Final Report*. Ottawa: Ministry of the Solicitor General of Canada.

United Nations. 1948. Convention on the Prevention and Punishment of the Crime of Genocide. A/RES/260 A (111) (9 December).

———. 1965. International Convention on the Elimination of All Forms of Racial Discrimination. A/RES/2106 (XX) (21 December).

———. 1978, 1988. International Bill of Human Rights (IBHR). New York [includes i–v below]:

i) Universal Declaration of Human Rights. 1948. A/RES/217 A (111) (10 December).

ii) International Covenant on Civil and Political Rights. 1966. A/RES/2200 (XXI) (16 December).

iii) International Covenant on Economic, Social and Cultural Rights. 1966.A/RES/2200 (XXI) (16 December).

iv) Optional Protocol to the International Covenant on Civil and Political Rights. 1966.A/RES/2200 (XXI) (16 December).

v) Second Optional Protocol to the International Covenant on Civil and Political Rights, aiming at the abolition of the death penalty. 1989. A/RES/44/128 (15 December).

———. 1992. Declaration on the Rights of Persons Belonging to National, Ethnic, Religious and Linguistic Minorities. Adopted by United Nations General Assembly on 18 December.

———. 1994. Draft Declaration on the Rights of Indigenous Peoples. E/CN.4/SUB.2/1994/2/Add. 1.

———. 2001. Office of the High Commissioner for Human Rights. *ABC, Teaching Human Rights: Practical Activities for Primary and Secondary Schools*. [Cited 1 December 2001.] www.unhchr.ch/html/menu6/2/abc.htm

———. 2002. Office of the High Commissioner for Human Rights. [Cited 6 February 2002.] www.unhchr.ch/html/intlinst.htm

United Nations Economic Social and Cultural Organization (UNESCO). 1978. Declaration on Race and Racial Prejudice. Adopted by the General Conference (twentieth session) at Paris in November.

Urban Alliance for Race Relations. 1977. 'Affirmative Action: What Is It?' *Newsletter* (4 October).

Vallières, P. 1971. *White Niggers of America*. Toronto: McClelland & Stewart.

van den Berghe, P.L. 1967. *Race and Racism: A Comparative Approach*. New York: Wiley and Sons.

———. 1978. 'Race and Ethnicity: A Sociobiological Perspective', *Ethnic and Racial Studies* 1, 4.

van Steensel, M., ed. 1966. *People of Light and Dark*. Ottawa: Information Canada.

Vanstone, J.W. 1971. 'Influence of European Man on the Eskimos.' In van Steensel, ed. (1966): 10–13.

Vote No. [Cited 1 June 2002.] www.sqwalk.com/voteno.htm

Wade, M. 1970. *The French-Canadian Outlook*. Toronto: McClelland & Stewart.

Waldman v. Canada. 1996. Communication No. 694/1996 (05/11/99). UN Doc. CCPR/C/67/D/694/1996.

Wallace, A.F.C. 1956. 'Revitalization Movements', *American Anthropologist* 58 (April).

Walzer, M. 1995. 'Pluralism: A Political Perspective'. In Kymlicka, ed. (1995): 139–54.

Waubageshig, ed. 1970. *The Only Good Indian*. Toronto: New Press.

WCAR (World Conference Against Racism, Racial Discrimination, Xenophobia and Related Intolerance)

Declaration. [Cited 6 June 2002.] www.unhchr.ch/html/racism/Durban.htm

Weaver, S.M. 1977. 'Segregation and the Indian Act: The Dialogue of Equality vs. Special Status.' In Isajiw, ed. (1977b): 154–61.

———. 1981. *Making Canadian Indian Policy: The Hidden Agenda 1968–70*. Toronto: University of Toronto Press.

Weinfeld, M. 1981. 'The Development of Affirmative Action in Canada', *Canadian Ethnic Studies* 13, 2: 23–39.

Weizmann, F., Wiener, N.I., Wiesenthal, D.L., and Ziegler, M. 1990. *Eggs, Eggplants and Eggheads: A Rejoinder to Rushton*. Report 40: The LaMarsh Research Programme Reports (October). North York, ON: York University.

Wiberg, H. 1981. 'Self-Determination as an International Issue', paper presented at the Ninth Conference of the International Peace Research Association, Orillia, Ontario, 21–6 June.

Williams, J.E., and Morland, J.K. 1976. *Race, Color and the Young Child*. Chapel Hill: University of North Carolina Press.

Wilson, W.J. 1978. *The Declining Significance of Race*, 2nd edn. Chicago: University of Chicago Press.

Wineman, S. 1984. *Justice and the Politics of Difference*. Princeton, NJ: Princeton University Press.

Winks, R.W. 1971. *The Blacks in Canada: A History*. Montreal: McGill-Queen's University Press.

Wirth, L. 1945. 'The Proble of Minority Groups'. In Linton, R., ed. *The Science of Man in the World Crisis*. New York: Columbia University Press: 347.

Woodsworth, J.S. 1972. *Strangers within Our Gates*. Toronto: University of Toronto Press.

Wuttanee, W.I.C. 1971. *Ruffled Feathers*. Calgary: Bell Books.

Yalden, M.F. 1979. 'The Office of Commissioner of Official Languages'. In Macdonald and Humphrey, eds (1979): 375–82.

Yetman, N.R., and Steele, C.H. 1975. *Majority and Minority*, 2nd edn. Boston: Allyn and Bacon.

Yinger, J.M. 1970. *The Scientific Study of Religion*. New York: Macmillan.

Yusyk, P. 1964. Senatorial Address, 3 May.

———. 1967. *Ukrainian Canadians: Their Place and Role in Canadian Life*. Toronto: Ukrainian Canadian Business/Professional Federation.

Zeilig, K. 'U of T Study Explores Local Sweatshop Conditions'. *Varsity News*. [online] 7 August 1999. [Cited 13 November 2001.] www.varsity.utoronto.ca/archives/120/jul99/news/uoftst.html

Ziegler, S., and Richmond, A.H. 1972. *Characteristics of Italian Householders in Metropolitan Toronto*. Toronto: Institute for Behavioural Research, York University.

ZundelSite. Ernst Zundel's website. [Cited 6 February 2002.] www.zundelsite.org/index.html

INDEX